INFECTIOUS GREED

Frank Partnoy is currently a professor at the University of San Diego School of Law. He has worked as an investment banker, derivatives broker, and corporate securities attorney. He consults on regulation of the markets and white-collar crime. His expert testimony before the Senate committee investigating the Enron collapse has been widely cited in the media. Partnoy is the author of the bestselling *F.I.A.S.C.O.: Blood in the Water on Wall Street*. He lives in San Diego, California.

INFECTIOUS
GREED

■ HOW DECEIT AND RISK
CORRUPTED THE
FINANCIAL MARKETS

FRANK PARTNOY

P
PROFILE BOOKS

This paperback edition published in 2004

First published in Great Britain in 2003 by
PROFILE BOOKS LTD
58A Hatton Garden
London ECIN 8LX
www.profilebooks.co.uk

First printed in the United States in 2003 by
Henry Holt and Company

1 3 5 7 9 10 8 6 4 2

Printed and bound in Great Britain by
Bookmarque Ltd, Croydon, Surrey

A CIP catalogue record for this book is available from the British Library.

ISBN 1 86197 473 6

For Fletch

"An infectious greed seemed to grip much of our business community. . . . It is not that humans have become any more greedy than in generations past. It is that the avenues to express greed have grown so enormously."

—Alan Greenspan, testimony before the
Senate Banking Committee, July 16, 2002

"In principle, the losses will be spread across a broader range of investors than in past debt crunches, suggesting risks have been well diversified and the financial system is secure. In practice, financial market and corporate innovation during the 1990s has meant it is impossible to be sure, a source of concern to financial regulators."

—Stephen Fidler and Vincent Boland,
Financial Times, May 31, 2002

CONTENTS

INFECTIOUS GREED

INTRODUCTION

This book is a financial history, a story of the dramatic changes in markets during the past fifteen years. It brings together the most important characters and events of this period, connects the dots among them, and explains what happened—and why. It shows how the levels of deceit and risk grew so dramatically, so quickly, and offers suggestions about how to avoid another round.

The recent happenings in financial markets are mysterious to many investors. The names alone evoke vague memories of scandal, but few common denominators. Think not only of WorldCom, Global Crossing, and Enron, but back to the dot-com bubble, the panic surrounding the collapse of Long-Term Capital Management, the fall of the venerable Barings Bank, the bankruptcy of Orange County, the financial crises in Mexico and Asia, and so on. Most investors recall some of these events, but few people understand how they interconnect.

The year 2003 is no exception. Freddie Mac, the home mortgage company, falsified billions of dollars of profits. Dan Gordon, a 25-year-old energy trader at Merrill Lynch, persuaded Merrill to wire $43 million to his offshore accounts in what one commentator called the largest employee theft from a financial institution in modern times.[1] Daimler-Chrysler earned half of its profits not from the sale of cars, but from foreign currency trading. And so on.

Each story is remarkable, but the headlines can seem isolated, like

2 | FRANK PARTNOY

distinct cells within different bodies. Even when scandals pique the attention of investors, the details are evanescent, and any links to events of the recent past slip away. Investors periodically become outraged, and the media seize on a few indignities, but over time everyone seems to lose the ability to relate back—especially as markets begin going up again.

This was especially true during the 1990s, a decade of persistently rising markets—ten solid years of economic expansion, with investors pouring record amounts into stocks and pocketing double-digit returns year after year. The recent stock-price boom was the longest-lived bull market since World War II. Some stocks or sectors suffered periodically, but almost anyone who remained invested throughout the decade made money.

During this time, individuals came to believe in financial markets, almost as a matter of religious faith. Stocks became a part of daily conversation, and investors viewed the rapid change and creative destruction among companies as investment opportunities, not reasons for worry. In 1990, the ten largest U.S. firms—including companies such as Exxon and General Motors—were in industrial businesses or natural resources. By 2000, six of the largest ten firms were in technology, and the top two—Cisco and Microsoft—had not existed a generation before. These stocks almost always went up. Microsoft met analysts' expectations in 39 of 40 quarters, and for 51 straight quarters the earnings of General Electric—a leading industrial firm that was also heavily involved in financial markets—were higher than those of the previous year.

The decade was peppered with financial debacles, but these faded quickly from memory even as they increased in size and complexity. The billion-dollar-plus scandals included some colorful characters (Robert Citron of Orange County, Nick Leeson of Barings, and John Meriwether of Long-Term Capital Management), but even as each new scandal outdid the others in previously unimaginable ways, the markets merely hiccoughed and then started going up again. It didn't seem that anything serious was wrong, and their ability to shake off a scandal made markets seem even more under control.

When Enron collapsed in late 2001, it shattered some investors' beliefs and took a few other stocks down with it. But after a few months, many investors began yawning at Enron stories, confident that the markets had survived yet another blow. Few considered whether the problems at Enron were endemic, or whether it was possible that Enron was only the tip of the iceberg. Instead, investors shrugged off the losses, and went back to watching CNBC, checking on their other stocks.

Then, Global Crossing and WorldCom declared bankruptcy, and dozens of corporate scandals materialized as the major stock indices lost a quarter of their value. Congress expressed outrage and mollified some investors with relatively minor accounting reforms. But most investors were perplexed. Should they wait patiently for another upward run, confident that Adam Smith's "invisible hand" would discipline the bad companies and reward the good? Or should they rush for the exits? The conventional wisdom was that markets would remain under control, that the few bad apples would be punished, and that the financial system was not under any serious overall threat. The most recent episodes at Freddie Mac, Merrill Lynch, and others also seem unrelated, both to each other and to prior scandals.

The argument in this book is that the conventional wisdom is wrong. Instead, any appearance of control in today's financial markets is only an illusion, not a grounded reality. Markets have come to the brink of collapse several times during the past decade, with the meltdowns related to Enron and Long-Term Capital Management being prominent examples. Today, the risk of system-wide collapse is greater than ever before. Although a handful of regulators and Wall Street managers have known about some of the systemic problems, individual investors have been largely oblivious to the fact that they have dodged, not a bullet, but a nuclear meltdown. The truth is that the markets have been, and are, spinning out of control.

What is the evidence that markets are out of control? How did they get away? What were the major changes in finance, law, and culture since the late 1980s that drove them to the edge? Why were investors unaware of the potential calamities? What are the threads that bind together the stories of spectacular gains and even more spectacular collapses during the past decade? And what can be done to avoid a crisis? Those are the questions addressed in these pages.

The relatively simple markets that financial economists had praised during the 1980s as efficient and self-correcting had radically changed by 2003. The closing bell of the New York Stock Exchange was barely relevant, as securities traded 24 hours a day, around the world. The largest markets were private, and didn't touch regulated exchanges at all. Financial derivatives were as prevalent as stocks and bonds, and nearly as many assets and liabilities were off balance sheet as on. Companies' reported earnings were a fiction, and financial reports were chock-full of disclosures that would shock the average investor if she ever even glanced at them, not that anyone—including financial journalists and analysts—ever did. Trading volatilities were sky high, with historically unrelated markets moving in lockstep, increasing the risk of systemic collapse.

In just a few years, regulators had lost what limited control they had over market intermediaries, market intermediaries had lost what limited control they had over corporate managers, and corporate managers had lost what limited control they had over employees. This loss-of-control daisy chain had led to exponential risk-taking at many companies, largely hidden from public view. Simply put, the appearance of control in financial markets was a fiction.

If investors believe in the fiction of control, and ignore the facts, the markets can continue to rise, as they did for over a decade. But if investors question their faith, as they have more recently, and head for the exits, the downturn will be long and hard. As investment guru James Grant recently put it, "People are not intrinsically greedy. They are only cyclically greedy."[2] The most recent cycle of greed appears to have ended, but at some point, inevitably, the next one will begin.

This book traces three major changes in financial markets during the past fifteen years. First, financial instruments became increasingly complex and were pushed underground, as more parties used financial engineering to manipulate earnings and to avoid regulation. Second, control and ownership of companies moved greater distances apart, as even sophisticated investors could not monitor senior managers, and even diligent senior managers could not monitor increasingly aggressive employees. Third, markets were deregulated, and prosecutors rarely punished financial malfeasance.

These changes spread through financial markets like a virus through the population. Before 1990, markets were dominated by the trading of relatively simple assets, mostly stocks and bonds. The sine qua non of the 1980s was the junk bond, a simple, fixed-income instrument no riskier than stock. The merger mania of the 1980s—driven by leveraged buyouts, in which an acquirer borrowed heavily to buy a target's stock—involved straightforward transactions in stocks and bonds.

Back then, individual investors shied away even from stocks, and most people kept their savings in the bank or in certificates of deposit, which paid more than 10 percent annual returns during most of the decade.

Mutual funds became popular briefly—with stock-picking legend Peter Lynch of the Fidelity Investments' Magellan Fund attracting several billion dollars—but from 1968 through 1990, individuals sold more stock than they bought and money flowed out of the market. Few stocks traded at prices of more than twenty times their annual earnings, and stocks with no earnings were shunned.

Derivatives—the now-notorious financial instruments whose value is derived from other assets—were virtually unknown. The two basic types of derivatives, options and futures, were traded on regulated exchanges and enabled parties to reduce or refocus their risks in ways that improved the overall efficiency of the economy. Customized over-the-counter derivatives markets—where derivatives were often used for less laudable purposes—were less than one percent of their current size, and most complex financial instruments still had not been invented. It is telling, for example, that in *Barbarians at the Gate,* the classic book about 1980s finance, derivatives are not even listed in the index, and stock options merit only a footnote on page 364.[3]

Some companies used basic forms of derivatives during the 1980s, including so-called "plain vanilla" interest-rate swaps, where one party agrees to pay a fixed rate of interest to another party, who agrees to pay a floating rate. But the forms of structured financing and over-the-counter gizmos that later would bring hundreds of companies to their knees simply did not exist. Moreover, the exchange-traded derivatives some investors bought and sold were not especially risky; they had changed little from financial instruments the ancient Greeks created and used.

Even stock options—the derivatives that became the primary source of executive compensation during the 1990s—were relatively uncommon. A typical 1980s executive received cash salary and bonus, with perhaps a little stock, but few or no options.

The legal environment during this period was harsh. The go-go 1980s led prosecutors to clamp down hard on securities fraud, indicting dozens of financial-market participants, nearly 100 in January 1989 alone. Looking back on the decade, the *Wall Street Journal* noted that "the word 'indictment' became almost as central to Wall Street lexicon as stock or bond."[4] The financial-market watchdogs made investors feel secure—almost smug—about financial fraud.

In several high-profile cases, judges imposed heightened duties on corporate directors, bankers, accountants, and lawyers, who came to understand that they violated the law at their peril. Regulators tightened rules against insider trading and other financial abuses. Joseph Grund-fest, a commissioner of the Securities and Exchange Commission during the 1980s, opened a 1988 speech by saying, "It's a pleasure to appear before so many unindicted participants in the financial markets."[5] The decade closed with Judge Kimba Wood sentencing the infamous finan-cier Michael Milken, of Drexel Burnham Lambert, to ten years in federal prison. By that time, prosecutors certainly had Wall Street's attention.

Top managers of large companies lived with another fear, too. Well-known corporate raiders—including Ivan Boesky, Carl Icahn, Ronald Perelman, and T. Boone Pickens—routinely bought large stakes in com-panies and then ousted ineffective managers to boost the value of shares. Greed was good for these raiders (and, sometimes, for shareholders), but it wasn't good for the managers, who scrambled to create defenses against these takeovers and thus preserve their jobs. To the extent the 1980s involved complex financial dealings, they were focused on these increasingly intricate takeover defenses.

Still, most finance professionals—even highly paid investment bankers—were technologically primitive, without e-mail or the Internet. They used HP12C calculators instead of computer spreadsheets and statis-tical software. Few had formal finance training, and almost no one had a math or finance Ph.D. A 1980s trader would be virtually unemployable today; his HP12C would be about as useful on a trading floor as an abacus.

Individuals were technologically primitive, too. Investors placed orders to buy and sell stock by letter or over the phone, not with the click of a computer mouse. People learned how their stocks were performing at most once a day, from the financial pages of the morning newspaper, not in real time on television. Financial analysis was available through the mail at a price, not on the Internet for free.

In sum, the 1980s were a relatively primitive period on Wall Street. Life was uncomplicated, if aggressive. Participants were labeled barbar-ians, predators, even thieves. At the same time, the financial markets became increasingly competitive and profit margins dwindled. The stock market crash of October 19, 1987, didn't help matters. After the Dow Jones Industrial Average tumbled 508 points, or more than 22 percent, in one day, investors became skittish. As analysts struggled to explain the collapse, the investment bankers' business sputtered. The last years of the decade were likely to be lean, and the future looked grim. It was not a good time to be working on Wall Street.

All of this was about to change.

INFECTION

STAGE ONE

PATIENT ZERO

Andy Krieger was one of those kids who, it seemed, could do everything. He was an excellent high school student, and was admitted to the University of Pennsylvania, where he was elected to Phi Beta Kappa.[1] He was a competitive athlete and briefly played professional tennis on the European circuit.[2] He was an advocate for the poor, and was especially interested in the plight of lepers in India. As a graduate student during the late 1970s, he studied South Asian philosophy, translated obscure Sanskrit texts, and planned for a career in academia.[3] He was a vegetarian.

One day, Krieger's dissertation adviser told him that although his work had been first-rate, he would not be able to land an academic job until one of a handful of people working in his area died. Krieger wanted to help the poor, not become one of them, so he decided to trade careers. After six years of graduate study, he enrolled in business school.

Almost immediately, his life was transformed. Krieger studied finance at the Wharton School of Business, whose graduates included the infamous financiers Michael Milken and Donald Trump, men who had thrived in the relatively simple 1980s world of junk bonds and corporate takeovers. Krieger took a course in international finance, and was captivated by a new, more esoteric phenomenon: trading in foreign-currency options, the rights to buy and sell currencies at specified times and prices.

The curriculum at Wharton—which by 2002 would include more than twenty specialized courses in finance—barely touched currency options when Krieger was there.[4] But J. Orlin Grabbe, a young finance professor at Wharton and a pioneer in the area,[5] became Krieger's mentor and taught him just enough to whet his appetite.[6] Krieger sought to reinvent himself as a currency options specialist; in 1984, he wrote a computer program to assess the value of currency options, and when he learned that Salomon Brothers, the New York investment bank, would be interviewing Wharton students for a position trading currency options, he submitted his résumé.

At Wharton, Krieger had learned how foreign currencies whose value had been linked to gold or to the U.S. dollar were now floating freely. Instead of requiring that their currencies be exchanged for a fixed amount of gold or dollars, various central banks—including the Federal Reserve— were permitting the value of their currencies to fluctuate in the market. Trading in these currencies was increasing exponentially, and companies had moved beyond simply exchanging U.S. dollars for Japanese yen, or German marks for British pounds, to betting on dozens of currencies in all sorts of new and fantastic ways.

During school, Krieger did a stint at O'Connor & Associates, an options trading firm in Chicago. He found that in currency trading, "you're pitted against some of the sharpest minds in the world."[7] The currency markets were intensely competitive, with hundreds of billions of dollars changing hands every day. Firms that traded the more exotic instruments— including currency options—were cleaning up. When Krieger discovered that some of these traders were making millions in bonuses, he quickly found "an inner drive to see how good I could be."[8] So much for Sanskrit.

Krieger gave up his tennis career and put his academic interests to the side. He persuaded the interviewers from Salomon that his brief experience as a trader, plus his detailed understanding of currency options, plus his knowledge of foreign languages and cultures, made him the ideal hire.[9] Salomon agreed, and Krieger began his career there after graduation.

Four years later, during early 1988, Krieger briefly was as well-known as some of the men who had come before him at Wharton. The publicity didn't last long, and few people remember Krieger today. But Krieger's story from that time is an object lesson in the risks associated with financial innovation.

•   •   •

It was 1984, and few bankers knew much about currency options. The Chicago Mercantile Exchange had just introduced them, and they had been trading for less than two years on the Philadelphia Stock Exchange, where Andy Krieger had traded a bit during business school.[10]

Few bankers knew about the theory of options pricing, either. A decade earlier, three economists—Fischer Black, Myron Scholes, and Robert Merton—had published formulas for evaluating options, coincidentally at the same time the Chicago Board Options Exchange opened for business.[11] Within six months, Texas Instruments was advertising that traders could calculate options values by plugging the formulas—known generally as the Black-Scholes model (Merton, unfortunately, lost out on credit)—into a calculator.[12] Within twenty years, virtually every company would use the Black-Scholes model to evaluate options, and the formulas would be taught in introductory finance courses in business school.

But bankers are slow, and it took more than a decade for options theory to migrate from the trading pits of Chicago to the banks of Wall Street. At Citibank in the early 1980s, only one trader on the trading floor even had a computer, a clunky Radio Shack TRS-80, which was primitive even for its time.[13] At J. P. Morgan, one customer persuaded a treasurer named Dennis Weatherstone (who later became the bank's chairman) to do a currency option, but the bank's traders had no idea how to price the option and ended up losing money.[14] Options were a mystery to most bankers, who were wary of these new markets.

In fact, the state of knowledge on Wall Street in 1984 was such that if you read the next five paragraphs, you will know just as much as a typical investment banker knew at the time.

In simple terms, an option is the *right* to buy or sell something in the future. The right to buy is a *call* option; the right to sell is a *put* option. Options on all kinds of commodities were traded on exchanges during the 1980s, mostly in Chicago but also in Philadelphia. These options were straightforward and standardized, and currency options were no exception. They were simply options to buy and sell amounts of various currencies at a specified time and exchange rate.

To understand how currency options work, suppose you are planning to take a vacation in Mexico a month from now. If the Mexican peso weakens during the next month, you can plan to eat some fancier dinners during your trip, because you will be able to buy more of the weakened pesos when you arrive. But if the peso strengthens, you might be eating at taco stands.

To hedge this risk, you might pay someone money today for the right to buy pesos at a set price a month from today. For example, if one dollar is worth ten pesos today, you might want to lock in that rate. You could pay a foreign-exchange broker a fee (called a *premium*) in exchange for the right to buy pesos at the ten-for-one rate in one month. If you did so, you'd be buying a peso call option.

The peso call option would act as an insurance policy. A month from now, if the peso had weakened, so that a dollar bought eleven pesos, you wouldn't exercise your right. As a purchaser of an option, you aren't *required* to buy; it is your option. Instead, you would buy pesos at the eleven-for-one rate in the market, and let your right expire. In other words, you wouldn't need the insurance policy. On the other hand, if the peso had strengthened, so that a dollar bought only nine pesos, you would exercise your right to buy at the more attractive ten-for-one rate. In other words, the insurance would protect your downside.

Options transactions typically are too costly for individuals taking vacations, because foreign-exchange brokers charge very high premiums. Instead, currency options are designed for big banks and corporations, which trade in much higher volumes. The value of these options is based on several variables, but the most important variable is volatility—how much the underlying currency has been moving up and down. The more volatile the currency, the more valuable the option.

Krieger understood options better than a typical banker. He knew the Black-Scholes formula and, more important, its limitations. The computer program Krieger had written at Wharton did a better job of assessing currency options than the models other traders were using, because it didn't rely on the same assumption as Black-Scholes. In particular, Krieger understood that traders should not look to history alone in calculating the volatilities of currencies, which were prone to periods of calm followed by abrupt twists and turns. Krieger easily completed the highly quantitative training program at Salomon, and he entered the new world of currency options trading at the perfect time.

Krieger was at Salomon during its heyday, the period described so memorably by Michael Lewis in his book *Liar's Poker*.[15] Salomon's trading desk was legendary, but small. Krieger sat two seats down from John Meriwether, the top trader at the firm. Next to Meriwether was Tom

Strauss, the firm's vice chairman, and John Gutfreund, the chairman. To Krieger's immediate left was Lawrence Hilibrand, an aggressive trader who would earn a $23 million bonus in 1990. Next to Hilibrand was Eric Rosenfeld, a former Harvard business-school professor and options expert. A few steps away was Victor Haghani, a researcher who worked for Krieger. Across the room was Paul Mozer, a bond trader who was about to become embroiled in a scandal that would nearly sink Salomon (more on that in Chapter 4).

By the late 1990s, Meriwether, Hilibrand, Rosenfeld, and Haghani would become well-known as the key players in the rise and fall of Long-Term Capital Management (more on that in Chapter 8). During the mid-1980s, these men were simply the most profitable group of traders in the world. And Krieger was sitting right in the middle of this group, at the center of the financial universe.

Krieger thrived in the hard-driving, aggressive environment, where—it was said—you needed to begin the day ready to "bite the ass off a bear," and where traders began their mornings with rounds of onion cheese-burgers from the Trinity Deli.[16] Given the gluttony, it seemed silly to have scruples about harming animals. Krieger began eating meat again.

Salomon was the ideal training ground for Krieger, and he was successful from the start. He traded all day long, from the early morning when the London markets opened until the early evening, when the New York markets closed. Then he went home, and traded the Tokyo markets by phone. He made $30 million for Salomon during the year, but the firm paid him a first-year bonus of just $170,000[17]—more than any other beginning trader, but still only a fraction of the commissions he arguably was due.

Given the vicious competition among Wall Street traders, it might seem surprising that Krieger—a relative novice—was able to make as much money trading as he did. The consensus among economists during the 1970s and early 1980s was that financial markets were efficient—that is, market values generally reflected available information. Economists loved to tell the story of the finance professor who refused to pick up a $20 bill lying on the ground, arguing that it couldn't actually be there because if it was, someone would have picked it up already. Picking up "free" $20 bills was a good business, while it lasted. But it never lasted long, especially on Wall Street, where even compassionate traders used the phrase "sell your mother for a nickel."

As Nobel laureate economist Paul Samuelson put it, "It is not easy to get rich in Las Vegas, at Churchill Downs, or at the local Merrill Lynch office."[18] Samuelson had plenty of followers. Economist Eugene Fama presented extensive evidence of market efficiency at the American Finance Association meeting in 1967,[19] and the presumption among economists since then had been that trading strategies based on available information did not outperform the market.

That presumption made sense. It *was* difficult to outperform the market. Even in new markets—such as the market for currency options—Wall Street traders were very quick to exploit any mispricings, and therefore mispricings didn't last long. If a particular stock, bond, or currency were too cheap, traders would buy it, and continue to buy it—just as people buy gasoline from the station with the lowest price—until the asset was fairly valued.

Yet there were some examples of market inefficiencies, and traders—including some of those at Salomon—were very good at finding and milking them. John Meriwether's group—which was shrouded in secrecy, even at Salomon—was especially skilled at exploiting these inefficiencies. Meriwether's ability to make money, year after year, was puzzling to efficient-market believers, and was a sign of cracks in their scholarly foundation. By the mid-1980s, a few financial economists (branded heretics at the time) had begun questioning whether financial markets actually were efficient.[20]

But if any markets could be efficient, surely currency markets would be. Currency markets were the largest in the world; the amount of trading dwarfed that of the stock exchanges. And even though currency options were new, they were based on the currency markets themselves. Most traders agreed that they could not outguess or even affect currency markets in the long run.

Then how did Andy Krieger make so much money? One possible answer was luck: Krieger made one-way directional bets on the values of various currencies, occasionally without much more than a hunch to support his directional position. After studying the historical charts of various currencies, he became a believer in trends, making bets based on where he thought currencies were headed. On a net basis, Krieger always bought options, because of what he described as a "personal abhorrence to selling options."[21] He won many of these bets, although to an outsider he didn't seem to have any particular strategy that would generate sustained trading profits over time. Charts were available to any trader, and any bank could trade based on trends. A 1980s financial economist assessing Krieger's early profits—on their face—might have claimed they were due mostly to dumb luck.

Yet there was more to Krieger's strategy than he let on. Yes, he was using options to bet on currencies, but only when his research and computer models told him volatility was so low—and therefore the options were so cheap—that the bets were good ones. Krieger became a master of volatility, combining the art of assessing patterns in foreign-currency markets with the science of using options models to determine the best way to make currency bets. In Krieger's view, the markets were not efficient, because traders—and their computer models—often underestimated the volatility of a currency, and therefore undervalued the related currency options. When markets did so, Krieger swooped in and bought the options, like a gambler at the racing track who had discovered a way to buy two betting tickets for the price of one.

Moreover, because the cost of an option was only a fraction of the value of the currency it was based on, Krieger could use options to make much larger bets than competing traders who did not use options. A $30 million options position might control a billion dollars worth of currency. Given that Krieger was using more sophisticated models than his competitors, and then using options to place much larger bets, he had an edge. According to Krieger, the other traders were still "using conventional artillery in what had become a nuclear world."

Although Krieger sat next to the members of John Meriwether's group, he was not formally a member of Meriwether's inner circle, known as the Arbitrage Group, which included the highest-paid people at Salomon. Other banks quickly learned of Krieger's prowess and began recruiting him. Although Krieger was successful at Salomon, it soon became apparent that he could make more money elsewhere.

In 1986, Bankers Trust, then the eighth largest commercial bank in the United States, hired Krieger to set up a currency-options trading business to compete with Salomon. Bankers Trust was becoming more sophisticated, but the bank's managers had little expertise in currency options. Krieger accepted the offer, with a guaranteed minimum bonus of $450,000, and an oral promise of a five percent commission on his trading profits. He was 29 years old.

.   .   .

At Bankers Trust, Krieger faced some daunting challenges. By 1986, it already was becoming difficult to make money trading currency options on the various exchanges. Like most exchange-based trading, currency options were a ruthlessly competitive business; within a year the markets were crowded and profit margins were slim. And Bankers Trust was late to the game.

Worse still, there were limits to the amount and types of trading Bankers Trust could do on the exchanges where options were traded. Exchanges in Chicago and Philadelphia offered only a limited menu of standardized options. Traders who wanted to place other bets couldn't do it with the exchanges, and neither could a bank's customers. In particular, the exchanges fixed two of the key variables in currency-options contracts: the exercise price and the expiration date.

The exercise price—sometimes called the strike price—is the price at which the purchaser of an option can buy or sell the relevant currency. For example, the exercise price of the option purchased by the vacationer off to Mexico was 10 pesos per dollar. The exchanges offered options contracts only for a handful of exercise prices (typically round numbers), so a customer wanting an option at 9.43 pesos per dollar could not buy that option from an exchange.

Likewise, the exchanges offered currency options with only a few specified expiration dates, the dates on which the rights of option holders expired. The exchanges offered only one expiration date per month (by convention, the third Friday), and currency options typically did not have expiration dates more than twelve months into the future. That meant a customer who was due to receive Mexican pesos on, say, the first Tuesday in April, and wanted to hedge the currency risk of the payment by purchasing an option to sell pesos on that date, could not do so. Nor could a customer expecting to receive a payment in foreign currency several months into the future use exchange-traded options to insure against those risks; such options simply were not available. Numerous corporations—from automobile manufacturers to banks—had long-term exposure to changes in various currencies, and for them exchange-traded currency options were not flexible enough.

As if this weren't enough, exchanges were regulated by various federal agencies, and were subject to disclosure and margin requirements. The exchanges prohibited manipulation. All of these factors meant that, by 1986, it wasn't easy for a currency-options trader to make an honest living.

Krieger maintained it was possible to make money consistently, even in the more competitive currency-options markets. He said traders continued to make mistakes in assessing volatility, especially during 1986. In particular, Krieger noticed that volatility estimates varied among different maturities: the six-month and twelve-month estimates might be 20 percent, whereas the nine-month estimate was only 10 percent. By closely examining volatility estimates, Krieger was able to find currency options that were cheaper than they should have been. He made $56 million trading such options during 1986. A five-percent commission on $56 million was $2.8 million, a huge bonus during this time period. By comparison, Martin Siegel, the investment banker from Kidder Peabody who was at the center of the massive insider-trading scandal described in the book *Den of Thieves*, received a $2 million bonus in 1986—at the peak of his career.[22]

As 1987 began, Krieger found what he believed was an incredible opportunity to make money trading currency options. The U.S. Federal Reserve and various central banks in Europe had implemented policies to maintain their currencies within a stable zone. The dollar had been falling for several years, but during 1987 it stabilized, and by the fall of 1987 the volatility numbers traders were using to evaluate currency options were very low. As a result, currency options were incredibly cheap.

Krieger thought traders were foolish to assume that the values of currency options should be based on the recent low-volatility levels. Any student of history understood that currencies had been unusually calm. Just a few years earlier, currencies had been much more volatile. Krieger thought the dollar would fall, and he began buying options that represented bets against the dollar.

In addition, Krieger had a trick up his sleeve. At Salomon, Krieger had begun developing techniques to increase the amount of currency other banks would be willing to trade with him, by taking advantage of other traders' greed. For example, if Krieger needed to sell a large amount of a particular currency—say one billion British pounds—when no one in the market was willing to transact in that size, he first would place an order with traders at other banks to *buy* one billion British pounds at a price below the market price. Greedy traders at other banks would then begin buying hundreds of millions of British pounds in an effort to "front run" Krieger, profiting from the increase in the value of British pounds they thought would occur due to Krieger's increased demand. But then Krieger would *sell* British pounds to the banks, as he originally had intended, instead of buying. This whipsaw strategy made it easier and more profitable for Krieger to trade his positions.

Krieger was taking advantage of the fact that, given the limited set of variables driving supply and demand in the short run—including the fact that many foolish central bankers consistently lost money trading even their own currencies—many traders believed they could profit from manipulative strategies within a particular day, just by buying or selling large amounts of currency. If these traders had been buying and selling stocks instead of currencies, such efforts to move short-term prices would have constituted "market manipulation," which was illegal in most stock markets. But the currency markets were an unregulated free-for-all, where manipulative trading tactics were quite common and perfectly legal. By manipulating prices, a trader might be able to generate profits even if the markets were otherwise efficient. This was something the academics studying financial markets hadn't yet considered. And it was something the traders loved to do.

Manipulative practices were especially common in the over-the-counter markets—the wild Wild West of trading. Instead of buying and selling options on a centralized exchange, which acted as the counterparty to all trades, traders could enter into private contracts with buyers and sellers, typically other banks. These trades were called *over-the-counter*, because the options buyer was like a person walking up to the counter in a store and buying something from a storekeeper. The exchange and its regulators wouldn't play a role; they might not even know about the trading. Instead, counterparties to a trade would agree to a private contract "in the wild," specifying the terms of a particular currency option and the rules to govern their contract. The exchanges monitored manipulative practices, but nobody watched the over-the-counter traders.

The difference between the exchanges and over-the-counter markets was dramatic. An exchange is like a Las Vegas–casino sportsbook, where a gambler can place a limited set of bets, perhaps on who will win a sporting event or on how many points teams will score, but not on anything much more specific than that. Casinos, like exchanges, aren't in the business of taking risk, so they only "make book" for bets if they know there will be gamblers on both sides. In other words, casinos and exchanges are simply intermediaries for standardized bets, and they make money by keeping a percentage of the bet, not by taking on risk.

As a result, casinos and exchanges allow bettors to place only a narrow set of prespecified bets. On Super Bowl Sunday, casino gamblers can place more exotic bets—which team will kick the first field goal or which player will have the most rushing yards—but even on that special gambling day no one can bet on whether a kicker will hit one of the goalpost uprights or on whether a player will rush for more than, say, 126 total yards.

Such limitations didn't apply in the over-the-counter markets, where gamblers and traders could design any trade they wanted. Imagine a counter at the casino sportsbook, where gamblers could find several counterparties willing to place any bet at all. With no supervisor or regulator to say what they could or could not do, gamblers would be limited only by their imaginations.

Andy Krieger had a powerful imagination, and during 1987 he was trading a vast array of over-the-counter options not available on the exchanges. These options had customized features based on numerous currencies. For example, many of Krieger's big trades—including a few of what he described as "nasty experiences"—were options on the New Zealand dollar, a currency traders affectionately called the "kiwi." (The dollar coin has a kiwi bird on one side.)

It was much easier to make money in the over-the-counter markets than on the exchanges, especially if a trader could use options to hide his trading strategies from other traders. Krieger placed hundreds of trades each day at Bankers Trust, although he made most of his money on five or six major "plays" every year. Krieger still abhorred the "naked" selling of options; so, for his major plays, he typically bought options—in industry parlance, he was *long*. As he put it, "I am always net long of options. My downside risk is always defined and limited."[23]

It is worth pointing out that these positions were hidden, not only from other traders, but also from investors in Bankers Trust. The bank's shareholders would have been quite surprised to learn that instead of owning a stake in a bank that made loans or perhaps held junk bonds, in reality they were rolling the dice with a bet on the New Zealand kiwi.

Krieger attributed some of his success as a trader to a strategy in which he would indicate to the market that he was taking a particular position, when in reality he was taking the opposite one. In referring to practices such as feigning one way while really going the other, which might be regarded as manipulative in other markets, Krieger noted that "there was nothing illegal about it,"[24] and he was absolutely correct. Krieger's misdirection plays grew over time until they involved billions of dollars.

Krieger masked his strategies by using a combination of options and other trades to make it look to the outside world as if he were placing the opposite bet of his true one. His misdirection strategy was like judo: he tried to beat other traders by making them move in the wrong direction first, then using the directional force of their own trading positions against them. On occasion, Krieger trading positions became so large that they dwarfed Bankers Trust's other businesses.

In one infamous episode, Krieger sold, or *shorted,* roughly the entire money supply of New Zealand.[25] He also held call options—of similar amounts—which would benefit if the kiwi went up, and therefore would offset any losses from his short position. With these two bets, Krieger faced two possibilities: first, if the kiwi rose, he would break even, because the money he lost on his short bet against the kiwi would be offset by money he made on his call-option bet that the kiwi would go up; second, if the kiwi fell, he would make money, because he would profit from his short bet against the kiwi, and would simply let his call option expire worthless (recall that as an option buyer he was not required to buy kiwi). In sum, Krieger paid money upfront for a bet that made money when the kiwi went down. In other words, Krieger had—in a convoluted way—bought a *put* option on the kiwi: the right to sell kiwi at a specified time and price.

Krieger's strategy drew from one of the central insights of modern finance, generally known as *parity* (or *put-call parity*), and it is worth taking a few minutes to contemplate. It is one of the mind-blowing concepts of modern finance, and investors who don't understand it are disadvantaged relative to those who do. Parity has become—and will continue to be—a major theme in financial markets.

Here is the parity notion, simply put: there are many ways of creating a bet, all of which should have the same value. This notion is sometimes called the Law of One Price. For example, suppose I want to bet $100 on New England in the Super Bowl. One way is simply to bet $100 on New England. Another would be to bet $100 on St. Louis and $200 on New England. In the second strategy, some people might think I had bet on St. Louis, even though—on a net basis—my money was on New England. I feigned the favorite, but really bet the underdog. Either way, the value of the betting strategies should be the same, because the two strategies have "parity"—they are both really $100 bets on New England.

The same parity principles work for currency options. One way for Krieger to bet that the New Zealand kiwi would fall was to buy a kiwi put option, which gave him the right to sell kiwi and became more valuable as the kiwi declined. But Krieger also could make *exactly* the same bet by doing two things: first, selling—or shorting—the kiwi outright; second, buying a kiwi call option, which gave him the right to buy kiwi and became more valuable as the kiwi rose.

The second strategy was more complicated, but both strategies performed the same, regardless of how the value of the kiwi changed. If the kiwi went up, Krieger broke even with either strategy (the put option was worthless; the short position and call option cancelled each other). If the kiwi went down, Krieger made money with either strategy (the put option became valuable; the short position also became valuable, and the call option was worthless). With either strategy, Krieger didn't care what happened if the kiwi went up, and if the kiwi went down, he made money. In other words, buying a put option was equivalent to shorting plus buying a call option;[26] because these two strategies had "parity," they should have the same value.

Why might Krieger employ the second, complex strategy instead of the first, simple one? The reason, according to Krieger, was that some traders might not know about both trades, because options were traded in separate markets from the currencies they were based on. In both the options and currency markets, there were a handful of *dealer banks,* and a trader from one of these banks typically would buy and sell from any of several people: the bank's customers, the relevant central bank, and traders' other dealer banks. There was no centralized exchange; instead, it was an over-the-counter market in which traders simply phoned each other all day long and agreed to trade at different prices. Traders made money by buying low and selling high, and thus were pitted against each other. Frequently, a bank employed one person to trade currency options and another person to trade the currencies themselves.

Some traders would see only Krieger's short position, and would think Krieger was betting against the kiwi (and therefore would be hurt by a rising kiwi). Traders in over-the-counter markets frequently tried to profit by manipulating the market in the opposite direction of a bet they knew a trader at another bank had placed. For example, if another trader had bet that the kiwi would fall, they might try to take advantage of him by buying kiwi, trying to push the price upward, until his losses became so painful that he was forced to unwind his bet. Then, the dealers would sell their kiwi at a profit.

However, currency traders dealing with Krieger apparently didn't know that Krieger's short position was only half of the story. Because Krieger also bought a call option in the options market, he wasn't vulnerable to a rise in the value of the kiwi at all—any money he lost on his short position was offset by a gain from his call option. When traders attempted to force the kiwi up by buying kiwi, Krieger didn't lose money—but now he knew they had bet that the kiwi would rise, and he could take advantage of them by selling kiwi. When their losses became so painful that they were forced to unwind their bets, Krieger could unwind his position at a profit.

In the unofficiated world of currency trading, Krieger's ploy worked perfectly. He could dodge his opponents' punches, and then—with a judo move—fling them to the mat.

Krieger was quite proud of this strategy, and bragged about his misdirection play on several occasions. Stunned traders would tell him, "Huh? Uh—you want to *sell* the pounds?" or "You want to sell the kiwi?"[27] According to Krieger,[28]

> [I]t was unusual for my cash positions to correspond to my market views. At Salomon, Bankers, and Soros [where Krieger later worked], banks would often observe my trades or look at my cash positions and believe that they corresponded to my market views. But often that wasn't the case. Usually my cash positions were hedges against my option views. Sometimes I used my cash positions to put on synthetic option positions, or as a hedge to reduce exposure in a position that I thought would continue the opposite way of my cash position. In other words, just because I was short pounds in spot didn't necessarily mean I was bearish on the pound. In fact, I might have been wildly bullish on the pound—and was simply taking some profits by selling some pounds against an otherwise more dominant option portfolio.

That sneaky Andy Krieger! Until other traders figured out the connection between currency and options markets, Krieger could use parity as a sword, profiting from this misdirection play. And remember, these markets were unregulated, so market manipulation was perfectly legal. Indeed, manipulation was precisely what other traders were trying—and failing— to accomplish.

Krieger's strategies were far from foolproof, although he insisted that they were low risk. He claimed he needed to be correct only about 25 to

30 percent of the time to "yield substantial results."[29] He said he limited his downside risk by spending only 10 to 15 percent of his capital to buy options. The result: "So, even if I'm wrong on every play, the downside is quite tolerable."[30]

Nevertheless, Krieger's strategies obviously wouldn't have been appropriate for many investors. The strategies resembled an average investor putting her savings into stock options, or a tourist putting his travel budget into currency options. These strategies worked for Krieger for two reasons: first, he used his superior knowledge of pricing models to buy cheap options during periods of market inefficiency; second, he used his misdirection play to take positions he believed were good bets. A little luck wouldn't hurt his strategies, either.

Krieger was clever, but not *that* clever, and soon other traders would grasp what he was doing. When they did, Krieger would shift to a more dependable, lower-volatility trading strategy, which would prove to be more appropriate for individual investors. But until then, Krieger's misdirection strategy was the $20 bill on the ground. It wouldn't be there for long.

During 1987, Bankers Trust's newly appointed chairman and CEO, Charles S. Sanford Jr., was encouraging his traders to speculate with the bank's capital, and he seemed to believe Krieger had a winning strategy. Sanford reportedly gave Krieger a whopping $700 million of capital to use as a base, much more than he gave other traders.[31] With that much capital, Krieger easily could control billions of dollars of currency positions. Suddenly, the 29-year-old trader had access to more capital than virtually any other trader. He could place bets that rivaled those of many central banks.

Although Krieger's bets during 1987 were quite complex, his strategy essentially was to bet that the dollar would fall. As Krieger settled in at Bankers Trust, his bets got bigger and bigger, and as he made money he "played with his gains," increasing the size of his trades. In June 1987, Krieger sold $1 billion of German marks and mark options, betting that the U.S. dollar would appreciate relative to the mark; he made more than $70 million on that trade. Later, Krieger referred to the risk associated with a $3 billion position in German marks.[32] He also told *Institutional Investor* magazine, "As a straight open-spot position, I wasn't happy going any more than $700 million—so I was comfortable with, say, a 2 percent loss of $10 million to $15 million. But if I wanted to take a really serious view, I would take an option position, which might start as an investment of, say, $4 million or $5 million. The position might end up controlling $1 billion or $2 billion of currency."[33] A billion here and a billion there—and pretty soon Bankers Trust was betting some serious money.

During 1987, Krieger made such huge bets against the New Zealand kiwi that his trading caused a ruckus in Wellington, where—as one trader recalled—the kiwi fell "like a wounded pigeon."[34] As the currency plunged, some of New Zealand's banks lost huge sums, because their assets were denominated in kiwi. At first, banks couldn't identify the source of the downward pressure on their currency. But, eventually, they found their man, through private investigation of the unregulated and anonymous over-the-counter markets. According to public reports, when government officials eventually traced the trading to Bankers Trust, New Zealand's chancellor of the exchequer telephoned Chairman Sanford to complain.[35] But New Zealand officials privately told Bankers Trust they had known about Krieger's bets against their currency and were happy about the decline, which would make exports cheaper and help spur economic growth. In any event, Sanford paid no heed; Krieger had made too much money for Sanford to worry about a miffed central banker.

After the U.S. stock market crashed on October 27, 1987, the dollar briefly increased in value, as foreign investors rushed to put their money into U.S. Treasury bonds, which were regarded as the ultimate safe investment. Oddly, the higher price of the dollar began creating *higher* demand, the opposite of what basic economics suggested (economists generally believed that higher prices led to lower demand). At this point, Krieger thought it was so obvious that the dollar would crash that "it was just a gift—it was almost disgraceful to make money on this trade. It was one of the easiest trades I've ever seen, a special opportunity."

Again, Krieger bet against the dollar; again, the bet paid off. He also made money trading other currencies, including British pounds and German marks, in various complex strategies. Krieger described his sense of the market during this time as "preternatural." He was extremely confident he could make money trading in the panic of the post-crash markets. All totaled, his options trades represented roughly $40 billion of underlying currency positions; these trades were fluctuating in value by as much as $20 million a day. Krieger referred to such changes as "just noise." He felt $50 million was an amount he "easily could make up in trading." In December 1987, Krieger finally stopped trading for the year, and left for the British Virgin Islands. At the time, his positions were so large that he wasn't sure exactly what his profits for the year had been, but he believed he had made perhaps as much as $250 million. By any measure, it had been an incredible year.

By late 1987, Bankers Trust had become a one-man show, and Krieger's profits were carrying thousands of other employees. Without Andy Krieger, the bank was having a terrible year. Many of Bankers Trust's businesses were losing money, and the bank had huge losses on loans to the Third World. The stock-market crash had hurt other parts of Bankers Trust's business, and from the outside it looked as if Bankers Trust might have its first losing year in the bank's fifty-year history. As the year closed, shareholders of Bankers Trust nervously awaited news of the bank's earnings.

On the morning of January 20, 1988, Bankers Trust sent out a press release reporting its preliminary, unaudited earnings for the prior year. Thanks to Andy Krieger, the bank had squeaked out a tiny $1.2 million profit. Shareholders cheered. Miraculously, the bank's losses in several areas were offset by $593 million of income from currency trading, including $338 million during the fourth quarter of 1987.[36] According to Bankers Trust, more than half of the total profits—about $300 million—was from one person: Krieger. In all, Bankers Trust reported more income from currency trading that year than any other bank in the world. It was a remarkable feat, and to many employees Krieger was a hero. Before he had arrived at Bankers Trust, the most any currency trader had made for the bank was $18 million.

Shareholders were relieved, but some employees questioned how a 30-year-old trader could have made so much money in such competitive markets. They wondered how much risk he was taking. Stock analysts were skeptical, too. Was it really possible for one person to make $300 million in markets that most economists argued were efficient? Rumors were swirling that Krieger hadn't really made so much money, and that someone at Bankers Trust had misvalued Krieger's options.[37]

But Bankers Trust's management dismissed the rumors and began working on the most important task of the year: awarding bonuses. In January 1988, the prevailing worry among managers at Bankers Trust was not the riskiness or legitimacy of Krieger's trading; instead, it was how much he should receive as a year-end bonus. Bankers typically spend much of January debating bonus-related issues, and it was difficult to do business with—or even speak to—a trader during this time. The only topic most traders will discuss in January is their "number."

A common trading commission at the time was in the range of five percent, so that a trader who generated $10 million in profits might receive a $500,000 bonus. In fact, five percent was precisely the promise Bankers Trust had made, according to Krieger. But five percent of Krieger's profits would have been $15 million, and no Bankers Trust employee had ever received anything approaching such a huge bonus. Charlie Sanford wanted to reward risk-taking, but not excessive risk-taking. Paying Krieger $15 million might set a dangerous precedent.

Moreover, Krieger's boss, Jay Pomrenze, did not support awarding Krieger $15 million. Pomrenze and Krieger were close friends (Pomrenze even came to Krieger's house for Krieger's daughter's naming), and Pomrenze said he thought Krieger was "the most powerful trader he'd ever seen." But Pomrenze was reportedly "really, really nervous" about Krieger's huge trading positions.[38] There was no guarantee Krieger could repeat his trading profits. If anything, other traders had caught on to his strategies. Krieger's profits might have been due to simple luck, and even if his trading profits were due entirely to skill, the markets would be more competitive next year. Why give Krieger a windfall this year if he wasn't going to repeat his performance?

There also was concern that Krieger was not a "team player." When Krieger placed a billion-dollar trade, he moved the market. Some employees felt that Krieger did not keep them informed about these moves. They claimed they lost money when Krieger's trades caused currencies they were trading to rise or fall. In reality, many of the traders also had been profiting from Krieger's strategies, because they were involved indirectly in the trades. But their profits had been middling compared to Krieger's.

Even if Krieger had made $300 million for the bank, $15 million was simply too much money, given the circumstances. Management decided to pay Krieger $3 million, a very substantial bonus during a very poor year on Wall Street.

The $3 million bonus was seven times the amount Bankers Trust had guaranteed Krieger the previous year, twenty times his bonus at Salomon three years earlier, and 60,000 times his bonus at O'Connor the year before that. It was even double the bonus of the bank's chairman, Charlie Sanford. However you sliced it, Krieger would be paid big money in 1987, more than just about anyone working on Wall Street, and much more than he ever had received before. It was decided that Jay Pomrenze would tell Krieger his "number" in late January. Krieger was told, "You're only 30 years old, you don't need any more than this." Krieger didn't say a word in response.

It is hard to imagine that the son of an accountant—a man who four years before had received a bonus check for $500—would be disappointed by a $3 million paycheck. But Wall Street traders are hard to imagine; besides, Krieger insisted he had been promised more. On February 23, 1998, he resigned, saying the bonus was too small relative to his profits for the year.[39]

Krieger claimed Bankers Trust should have paid him a bonus in the range of $15 million. "I was very, very disappointed with the bonus on principle, rather than the actual amount. It was more money than I ever thought I'd need, but it wasn't fair."[40] Krieger said he was tired of working 120-hour weeks. He had been ignoring his family and badly needed a vacation. He spent a few weeks "pairing off" his trades, so that Bankers Trust would not be exposed to any currency risk associated with his positions, which already were up more than $50 million for 1988. Then he left for the Caribbean.

Currency-options traders were shocked, and trading in currency options nearly halted for a few hours after Krieger resigned. Again, rumors swirled about Krieger's resignation, including word that Bankers Trust had incurred huge losses in currency options, perhaps as much as $100 million. A spokesman denied the rumors, but the denial only fed speculation about what had happened at Bankers Trust.

Krieger experienced his first fifteen minutes of fame, complete with front-page coverage in the *Wall Street Journal*. But the markets quickly settled down, and traders soon forgot about him.

Meanwhile, back at Bankers Trust, the nightmare was just beginning, with the startling revelation that makes Krieger the unwitting "patient zero" of the virus that has spread through the financial markets during the past fifteen years.

Bankers Trust had issued its January 20, 1988, press release, announcing a profit for the year, a little too hastily. Bank managers typically receive end-of-the-year reports on the value of the bank's trading positions, just as individual investors do for their own investments. Like most banks,

Bankers Trust initially relied on its traders to evaluate the profits or losses in their own portfolios. Krieger simply used his own computer spreadsheet to do this, because Bankers Trust did not have any systems for traders to use. Every day, financial-control teams—sometimes called the *back office*—used their own spreadsheets to *mark to market* the value of the trades. At the end of the year, the back office marked to market all of the traders' positions, and these *marks* were the basis for reporting annual results.

Unfortunately, Bankers Trust had announced its profit before the back office control teams had finished checking the values of Krieger's trades. There was no reason to think the values Bankers Trust had assigned to Krieger's trades would be inaccurate. But as the control teams continued their work, it appeared that Krieger had not made as much money as the managers initially had thought.

In order to mark an options trade, the back office personnel typically input an estimate of what a particular trade was worth, based on computer models, publicly available information, and quotes from competing banks. The goal in marking to market these positions was to reflect as accurately as possible the market value of each trade.

The key factor in determining the value of options—as the Black-Scholes model showed—was the volatility of the underlying currency. For example, if the New Zealand kiwi had been fluctuating greatly on a daily basis, kiwi options would be very valuable, because there was a good chance the right to buy or sell kiwis at a specified rate would be valuable. But if the kiwi had been stable, kiwi options wouldn't be worth much.

For options traded on an exchange, the value of the option was set by supply and demand, and was easy to determine. The value of such options was whatever people would pay for them, and those amounts were published every day. But Krieger's options were traded in the over-the-counter markets, where there were no published prices and not as many buyers. Consequently, the value of these options was more open to question.

No one had seriously questioned the values of Krieger's trading positions when Bankers Trust issued its press release. But now the control teams were concluding that the volatility estimates used in marking Krieger's trades were higher than they should have been. According to one report, the volatility measurements for Krieger's portfolio were overstated by as much as 25 percent.[41] That meant that the value of Krieger's positions was overstated by—in aggregate—$80 million.[42] In other words, Krieger had only made $220 million, not $300 million, as everyone at the bank originally had anticipated. Krieger was no longer as much of a hero. And Bankers Trust no longer had a profit for 1987.

By late February, the managers at Bankers Trust were in a serious bind. Their January press release had included the $80 million of phantom profits. It had been inaccurate, and now they knew it. They were approaching the deadline for the bank's 1987 annual report and Form 10-K, the annual filing public companies were required to make with the Securities and Exchange Commission. If they now admitted that the January press release had contained an $80 million mistake, shareholders almost certainly would sue, and the media would vilify them for their recklessness in issuing the press release. Even worse, without the $80 million, the bank's tiny profits from 1987 would be wiped out, and Bankers Trust would record its first loss since the 1930s.

But if they didn't include the mistake in their Form 10-K, they would be knowingly committing securities fraud. In the late 1980s, federal securities prosecutors were aggressively pursuing criminal securities-fraud cases. And every banker knew the scene from Oliver Stone's 1987 film *Wall Street,* in which federal agents lead Bud Fox from the floor in handcuffs. That scene was based on a real case, and no one at Bankers Trust wanted to be in the sequel.

Now the rumors were really swirling, and Bankers Trust's managers continued to deny them, saying they believed any impact on earnings related to Krieger's departure would be "immaterial." They admitted—in a private phone call to a group of stock analysts—that someone at the bank had mispriced several one-year currency-options contracts, based on Japanese yen, West German marks, and New Zealand kiwi.[43] They pleaded with the analysts that such options were extremely difficult to value; it could happen to anyone. Shareholders were not privy to this call, and as far as they knew Bankers Trust was still profitable.

Krieger said he was out of the country when the options were valued.[44] He also said he rarely acted alone at Bankers Trust: "I sat next to the worldwide manager for forex [foreign exchange], Jay Pomrenze, and he was my boss. We had loss limits, and everything was worked out."[45] The most likely explanation for the mistake was that someone at Bankers Trust had tapped into the wrong data source for the volatility numbers used to value Krieger's trades. Other traders at Bankers Trust had experienced similar problems, when the computer system occasionally applied volatility numbers from a simulation, instead of from a live data feed. As Krieger put it, "I don't know exactly what happened, but they certainly didn't have Victor Haghani from Salomon writing their systems." Whatever the truth was, by the time Bankers Trust's managers were trying to decide whether to disclose the fact that $80 million of income had "disappeared," Andy Krieger had resigned and was no longer involved in the decisions, and no one at Bankers Trust was claiming responsibility.

What could Bankers Trust do? The choices were bleak. They consulted their outside accountants, from Arthur Young & Co., now part of Ernst & Young. Arthur Young was conducting its annual audit of Bankers Trust and was preparing to issue its opinion that Bankers Trust's financial statements were "fairly presented." This opinion was a crucial part of the bank's Form 10-K filing.

The question was: how could the bank account for the missing $80 million? Was there a way Bankers Trust nevertheless could claim to have earned a $1.7 million profit, even though it now knew it had $80 million less in trading profits?

Remember, this was 1988, more than a decade before dozens of companies—from Cendant to Enron to WorldCom—were accused of inflating revenues and reducing expenses to meet quarterly earnings targets. Some senior managers were willing to whisper information about the upcoming quarter to the securities analysts covering their companies, but few would consider manipulating their accounting statements to fit expectations. That was fraud, after all, and reputable managers simply didn't do it.

Someone—it remains unclear who—suggested that Bankers Trust could resolve its problems and avoid the need to correct its January press release by simply reducing its compensation expenses by $80 million, to offset the loss exactly. Was it possible? Could the managers really argue that bonuses would be lower because of the losses, that the $80 million of phantom profits was offset by exactly $80 million less in bonus payments? That position would provide cover for Bankers Trust managers, who could argue they were not knowingly making any misstatements. Instead, they were relying on their accountants' advice that it was reasonable to reduce the bank's compensation expense.

And they did it. The accountants at Arthur Young made an entry reducing by $80 million an account that recorded Bankers Trust's obligation to pay employees' future bonuses. The bank issued its Form 10-K, reporting the same profit it had announced in its January press release. Arthur Young issued a signed opinion that this profit was fairly presented. And the bank's shareholders didn't know a thing about any of it. Bankers Trust was gambling that no one would discover the $80 million reduction that exactly matched the $80 million of missing profits.

The bank might have gotten away with this accounting sleight of hand if a few sharp-eyed banking regulators at the Federal Reserve hadn't spotted the $80 million discrepancy in a banking call report Bankers Trust filed privately with the Fed. They forced the bank to file an amended call report. In their view, the accounting entry was dubious at best. Hidden accounts for future reserves were illegal, and the $80 million exact match was too much of a coincidence. Besides, Bankers Trust's bonuses couldn't be cut, because they had already been paid, and one person whose bonus arguably should have been reduced—Andy Krieger—was no longer an employee. An $80 million compensation reduction was absurd.

With the cat out of the bag, Bankers Trust was forced to adjust its Form 10-K filing after all. The Securities and Exchange Commission—and the bank's shareholders—were about to learn the truth.

On July 20, 1988, six months after Krieger's profits were first reported to investors—and five months after Krieger resigned—Bankers Trust announced $80 million of "adjustments" to its income from the previous year. The Bankers Trust press release stated that the company and its auditors believed the adjustments were "not material."[46] The managers put on the best spin they could. Chairman Charlie Sanford said, "What's the big deal? There's nothing sinister here. There's no effect on earnings. The company is worth the same amount. It's just an accounting thing."[47]

Securities analysts appeared to be furious, even though many of them had known about the discrepancy for months. They called the bank's valuation process "loosey-goosey," something "you could drive a truck through," and threatened that the bank "is going to pay for this."[48] One analyst said, "I don't want to invest in a casino."[49] Another summed up the sentiment: "Everybody in the world would like to see Bankers take a hiding."[50]

Other banks distanced themselves from Bankers Trust's risky trades. A spokesman for Chase Manhattan said, "The majority of our business is customer driven. We don't take the same large bets that other banks take."[51]

But, surprisingly, the Securities and Exchange Commission and the

Department of Justice did not take any action. They didn't bring charges against Bankers Trust, Andy Krieger, or any other current or former bank employee. It wasn't an unwillingness to prosecute securities fraud. They were bringing dozens of insider-trading cases, and Michael Milken was about to go on trial. So why didn't the federal prosecutors bring charges in this case?

One reason was that the charges related to options valuation were extraordinarily complex and novel; most prosecutors had never heard of the Black-Scholes model. Another was that it was an election year, and it might not have been such a good idea to bring a high-profile case against a top investment bank and a top accounting firm when those two industries were also top campaign contributors. The federal government took the position that Bankers Trust and Arthur Young had corrected the mistake; that was enough.

In fact, the details of the episode remained a secret for more than three years, until *Fortune* magazine—in an article entitled "How Bankers Trust Lied About $80 Million"—unearthed the discrepancy. The article was ruthless, calling the events "mind-boggling," and asking whether the regulators' decision not to bring a case implied "that it is okay for companies to falsify line items?"[52] Again, there was no response from the government. In 2002, when the memories of most of the participants had faded, one former federal official involved in the decision not to bring a case, who wished to remain anonymous, still clung to the notion that the accounting judgments had been reasonable under the circumstances.

While on vacation in March 1988, Krieger considered leaving trading altogether, perhaps to teach Sanskrit or work with lepers, as he originally had planned. But bankers who have tasted a seven-figure bonus often find it hard to leave the money behind, and Krieger still found currency-option trading to be interesting. By April, Krieger was back trading currency options, this time for billionaire George Soros, whose Quantum Fund held almost $2 billion of assets, about $600 million of which belonged to Soros personally.[53]

Not all of the traders at Quantum appreciated Soros's decision to hire Krieger. Traders never like the new kid, especially the new kid who has been promised a huge bonus. They joked about starting to learn Sanskrit, and said, "We all remember his goal of working with lepers."[54] According to one source, Krieger was the ninth person Soros had hired as a potential successor to come in and "learn how the master does it." According to Krieger, Soros promised him a $2 million base salary, plus 10 percent of any trading profits.

Krieger began trading with a flurry, right where he had left off at Bankers Trust. Soros was having a bad year, and Krieger began placing very large currency bets—and winning. Soros had bet nearly a billion dollars on the British pound, but Krieger thought the pound would decline. Krieger reversed the position, and bet against the pound. A single trade with Chemical Bank was for more than $1.8 billion.

According to public reports, Krieger's trades were so substantial that they alarmed officials at the Bank of England, which contacted Soros, just as the New Zealand officials had contacted Charlie Sanford of Bankers Trust. But according to Krieger, he spoke to officials from the Bank of England every day, and they were delighted that someone in the market was betting against the pound, which they believed was overvalued. (Recall that if a country's currency declines, exports become cheaper, which helps the economy.) The London press began reporting on the size of Krieger's trades, and after a few months both Soros and Krieger had had enough. Krieger said he made $42 million trading for Soros, of which he should have been entitled to 10 percent, but he didn't want to continue working for Soros until the end of the year. Krieger left his $4.2 million on the table, and experienced another fifteen minutes of fame after he resigned again, this time citing "personal interests."[55]

The level of Krieger's 1987 profits was not sustainable, for him or for anyone else. A few currency traders made money betting on the directions of particular currencies during the early 1990s, including George Soros,[56] but these traders eventually ran out of luck. In the end, the efficient markets theorists were at least partially vindicated. Many of the opportunities for huge profits trading currency options had disappeared.

During the 1990s, Krieger raised funds for his own trading firms, Deerhurst Management and Northbridge Capital. He continued to advocate his strategy of buying—but never selling—currency options, on a net basis. He wrote an occasional column for *Forbes* magazine, and told readers of *Pensions and Investments* magazine that currency options were "easy to do."[57]

In 1991, H. Ross Perot took a break from his presidential campaign and approached Krieger with a proposal to trade using computer programs based on "rhythmic movements" in the currency markets. With Perot as a partner, Krieger began changing the focus of his trading, in an attempt to generate returns in the 10-to-15 percent range, with very low risk. Krieger still made some directional currency bets—which suffered in 1994, when the Mexican peso was devalued, but made money in 1997 (more than 40 percent), when various Asian currencies were devalued. During the 1990s, when investors were earning huge returns in the stock market, this trading program's average return was slightly above 10 percent.[58]

Krieger persevered and Perot stuck with him. Krieger hired several computer scientists and claimed they continued to find inefficiencies in the foreign-exchange markets. As of 2002, Krieger was managing about $400 million, and continuing to generate returns in the range of 10 to 15 percent, even in 2001 and 2002, when investors in other markets sustained massive losses. Many investors realized that Krieger's low-risk approach was outperforming the stock markets, and his business boomed. At the end of 2002, Krieger was still running his trading operations, in the relative quiet of Fort Lee, New Jersey, far from the klieg lights of the recent financial scandals.

Andy Krieger is an important first case in understanding the trajectory of financial markets during the past fifteen years. His trading of currency options was an early example of how financial instruments were becoming more complex, and how traders were quick to exploit new trading strategies. Krieger's experience also showed how easily an employer could lose control of its employees dealing in these instruments: Krieger was permitted to take substantial risks with options, and no one at Bankers Trust was able to evaluate his profits from complex trades. In addition, the government, by not prosecuting anyone involved in the Bankers Trust accounting scandal, signaled to the financial community that it would not closely scrutinize the largely unregulated over-the-counter markets.

These three changes—increasing complexity, loss of control, and lack of regulation—would become the most important issues in financial markets during the next decade. Financial instruments would become more complex and, increasingly, would be used to avoid legal rules; control and ownership of companies would move further apart, leaving individual managers unable to monitor increasingly aggressive employees; and markets would become deregulated, as prosecutors continued to avoid complex financial cases, and accounting firms and banks were insulated from private lawsuits. These developments began with Andy Krieger, but soon would spread throughout Bankers Trust, then to CS First Boston and Salomon Brothers, and then to numerous other financial institutions and their clients.

For many bankers, the news about Krieger's trading was a wake-up call. It was time for them to go back to school, to learn to use computers and spreadsheets, and to delve into the details of options pricing and finance theory. Notwithstanding its problems in 1988, Bankers Trust was well positioned in the over-the-counter derivatives markets, which would soon become the largest markets in the world, far surpassing the New York Stock Exchange in overall size.

With these new instruments, a rogue employee could inflate trading profits, or even put much of a company's capital at risk, all in a matter of seconds. Bankers could easily dodge regulators, who were overwhelmed. Lawmakers, if lobbied effectively, were unlikely to subject these markets to much scrutiny. In this new world, shareholders—and even boards of directors—would quickly become lost, struggling to decipher their company's financial statements. If a financial officer's direct supervisors couldn't monitor or accurately evaluate his trades, how could shareholders or directors be expected to do more?

The major financial fiascos of recent years—think Enron—would have been unimaginable during the time Andy Krieger was at Bankers Trust. The financial markets were still relatively simple in 1988. But Bankers Trust's approach to evaluating Krieger's trading was a foreboding precedent, and as the seeds sown in this saga began to take root, the previously inconceivable would soon become commonplace. Bit by bit, the markets were losing control. And several Bankers Trust employees who had followed in Andy Krieger's footsteps were about to take a different and more troubling path.

MONKEYS ON THEIR BACKS

When Andy Krieger left Bankers Trust in early 1988, the markets were in decline. Charles S. Sanford Jr., the newly appointed chairman and CEO of Bankers Trust, had put out the fire surrounding Krieger's currency-options trading. But now, in only his second year at the helm, Sanford confronted a much bigger problem. The future of Bankers Trust—and the future of banking generally—was in question.

The go-go period of the mid-1980s was ending, and Wall Street was hurting. Merger-and-acquisitions work was stagnant, and investors were pulling money out of stocks. Many banks were posting losses. Although Bankers Trust had reported a slim profit for 1987, in truth—without Andy Krieger's $80 million of phantom earnings—the bank had lost money. Sanford couldn't count on another last-minute bonanza from one of his traders, and no one at Bankers Trust wanted to depend on another Krieger. To avoid another losing year, Sanford needed to find a new and reliable source of profits, fast.

Sanford was a Wharton graduate, like Krieger, but he had twenty more years of experience. Sanford was a Savannah, Georgia, native, and had majored in history and philosophy at the University of Georgia, where the football stadium was named after his grandfather, the university's chancellor. After graduation, Sanford tried teaching, but he lasted only a year, deciding—as he put it in his Southern drawl—that "I didn't want to spend my life in a profession where I couldn't be measured."[1] He left

Georgia for Wharton, and joined Bankers Trust—which, at the time, was still hiring history and philosophy majors—right after business school.[2]

From the start, Sanford refused to believe Bankers Trust was merely another commercial bank. He began working as a loan officer in the bank's Southern division in 1961, but he acted more like a trader than a staid commercial banker. He was quickly promoted to head of the bank's bond-trading operations,[3] and he pressed his employees to emulate traders at Wall Street investment banks. He persuaded his bosses to lift a cap on bonuses so top performers could be paid as much as their investment-banking counterparts.

Sanford's greatest strength was his intuition about risk. For example, as an executive vice president of Bankers Trust in 1975, Sanford ignored political pressures and pulled out of an underwriting syndicate for a New York bond deal; he felt that New York was simply too risky (as the city flirted with bankruptcy, he was proved correct).[4] He was the key voice persuading his bosses to sell the bank's eighty New York branches in 1978, thereby moving away from the traditional commercial banking business of taking deposits.

During this time, Sanford—ever the trader—began using much of the bank's capital to place bets on whether interest rates would go up or down; not surprisingly, he won more than he lost.[5] The bank's top management viewed him as a "golden boy," a nitty-gritty, roll-up-the-sleeves guy; he was Bankers Trust's obvious heir-apparent.[6] Employees described Sanford as having a "constitutional inability to be second-best at anything."[7] Sanford's boss, Alfred Brittain III, told him at the time, "Charlie, you'll turn this bank into a Wall Street trading house."[8]

When Sanford was promoted to president of the bank in 1983, he began his quest to do precisely what Brittain had predicted, focusing on three issues: financial technology, incentives for employees, and deregulation. He developed sophisticated risk-measurement systems; applied intense pressure to his traders and salespeople, who increasingly had math and science backgrounds; and took full advantage of existing deregulation (and lobbied for more).

Sanford was named chairman and CEO, as expected, in 1987. As he celebrated his 50th birthday, finally in charge, he shifted into high gear. Bankers Trust was the most technologically sophisticated bank in the world. Within a few years, it would be the most profitable one, too.

· · ·

Sanford hired people other banks wouldn't touch, most notably "quants" and "rocket scientists" who didn't have the pedigree or connections necessary to land a job at, say, Morgan Stanley. Sanford wasn't the first one to realize that new employees didn't really need to know anything about banking; white-shoe investment banks had been hiring employees with family connections and little industry knowledge for decades. But Sanford was the first one to understand that, in the financial markets of the next decade, mathematical smarts would matter more than a low golf-handicap index.

By the late 1980s, it was no longer as easy for history and philosophy majors to get jobs at Bankers Trust. Instead, the bank hired chess masters and physics Ph.D.s with no knowledge of banking, and trained them in finance. Interviewers more frequently asked questions such as, "What do the numbers 1 through 500 add up to?" than "What are a bank's assets and liabilities?" The nerds found banking a breeze compared to chess openings or general relativity theory. The Bankers Trust training program was so complete that, after a few months, new employees had become smooth-talking salesmen, eager to out-pitch their peers elsewhere.

One observer described Bankers Trust during this era as a "techno-loony bin of crazed nerds."[9] According to a former managing director of the bank, "They were really nice kids, basically smart nerds, mostly guys without girlfriends. They would hang out in the office and work all night."[10] Sanford crammed several hundred of these nerds into a noisy room stacked with computer terminals on the 33rd floor of the bank. According to one former employee, "The ceilings were very low, very poor air circulation. You barely had any room."[11] But they all loved it, and Sanford had persuaded them that Bankers Trust would soon become the greatest financial institution of all time.

With his new intellectual horsepower, Sanford could move quickly into new businesses, exiting when the competition arrived and profit margins dwindled. The bank's recent moves had been frenetic. In 1986, Bankers Trust was focused on *plain-vanilla* swaps—contracts between the bank and another party to exchange cash flows, based on various indices, including interest rates. At $30 billion total, Bankers Trust was the second biggest swap dealer at the time, just behind Citicorp.[12] But as the margins for interest-rate swaps began a nearly twenty-fold decline,[13] Bankers Trust looked elsewhere.

During 1987, Bankers Trust had turned to currency trading, and Andy Krieger. But now Krieger was gone, and the currency markets were becoming saturated, with profit margins dwindling.[14]

In 1988, Sanford did another quick pivot, and moved three of his nerds into a new business: long-term stock-index options. These stock options were different from those already traded on the various options exchanges. They had maturities of a year or more, and were based on stock-exchange indices, rather than on individual stocks. In other words, they resembled Andy Krieger's over-the-counter options, except that they were based on stock indices instead of currencies.

Bankers Trust executives expected the long-dated stock-index-options business to generate modest returns of perhaps $5 million during 1988. Instead, the business exploded—particularly in Japan—and became the focus of Bankers Trust's derivatives operations, with dozens of employees. Here is how, and why, these options worked.

A typical stock option gives the buyer the right to buy or sell stock at a specified time and price. For example, a June 100 IBM call is the right to buy IBM stock for $100 in June. In contrast, a stock-index call option is the right to buy *all* of the stocks in a particular stock index. For example, you might purchase the right to buy the stocks that made up the Nikkei 225 index—the major Japanese stock market index of the top 225 stocks—for 10,000 yen during the next year. This right would cost you, say, 500 yen.

If the Nikkei 225 went up to 12,000, you could exercise your right, and buy all the stocks in the index for 10,000. If the Nikkei 225 index were worth 12,000 yen, the stocks also should be worth that much the index is just the sum of the stocks' values—so you could sell the stocks for a 2,000-yen profit. Deduct the cost of the option and you made 1,500 yen. If the Nikkei 225 went down, the most you could lose was 500 yen, your initial investment.

If the individual stocks in the Nikkei 225 weren't worth the same, in aggregate, as the index itself, Wall Street traders—including those at Bankers Trust—would swoop in, buying the undervalued stocks and selling the index, or vice versa. Such trading—buying low and selling high at the same time—was called *arbitrage,* and the traders who engaged in arbitrage were called *arbitrageurs.* Arbitrage was a key force ensuring that markets would be efficient, because if prices did not reflect available information, traders could profit from buying and selling with little or no risk. Not surprisingly, true arbitrage opportunities—like the $20 bill on the ground—were difficult to find. It was easy for traders to "arb" the Nikkei 225 index, buying low and selling high, and profit opportunities from such arbitrage disappeared quickly. Charlie Sanford planned to find some other way to profit from this new business.

Bankers Trust employees knew Japanese investors were bullish about their own stock market. Japanese insurance executives, who especially thought stocks were going up, were frustrated by legal rules that prohibited insurance companies from investing in stocks. As Japanese stocks skyrocketed, and everyone else was making money in the markets, the insurance executives were stuck with their lackluster bond portfolios.

Other banks had concluded there was nothing they could do to satisfy the Japanese insurers. But Bankers Trust came up with an ingenious solution, a kind of cross-continental ménage à trois, which gave the Japanese insurance companies exactly what they wanted, while addressing the needs of two other clients: Canadian banks and European investors.

What did Japanese insurers, Canadian banks, and European investors have in common? And how could Bankers Trust be their yenta? The answer was complicated, and revolutionary.

First, Bankers Trust went to the Canadian banks and pitched a special kind of loan: the Canadians would borrow Japanese yen, instead of Canadian dollars, and instead of agreeing to pay interest, they would give the lender an option on the Nikkei 225 stock index. The desperate Japanese insurance executives jumped at the chance to make these loans. Although they weren't permitted to play in the stock market directly, they were permitted to lend money. If the loan also involved a bet on the Nikkei 225, well . . . the Japanese regulators didn't need to know about that.

Second, to persuade the Canadian banks that their borrowings did not depend on the yen, or on selling bets related to the Japanese stock market—risks they were horrified by—Bankers Trust agreed to exchange the yen for Canadian dollars, and to sell the Canadians an option that exactly mirrored the one the Japanese had bought. If the Nikkei 225 went up, Bankers Trust would pay the Canadians exactly the amount they owed to the Japanese. The Canadians were perfectly hedged. Their incentive to do this deal was that, in exchange for the hedge from Bankers Trust, they would pay Bankers Trust a lower rate than any they could get borrowing elsewhere.

Third, Bankers Trust needed to find someone to take on its bet against Japanese stocks. If the Nikkei 225 went up, Bankers Trust had to pay the

Canadians, who would pay the Japanese. But who would pay Bankers Trust? Now enter the European investors, who were eager to bet against Japanese stocks, especially if Bankers Trust could offer a longer-term bet than those available on the exchanges. The Nikkei 225 options were of the same maturity as the Canadian bank's loan; typically, three or four years. These longer-term options were over-the-counter and unregulated, just like Andy Krieger's. The European investors gobbled them up.

Effectively, a Nikkei 225 gamble was being passed from European investors to Bankers Trust to Canadian banks to Japanese insurance companies. It was one of the first examples of how complex financial techniques, including derivatives, could turn risk into a hot potato. All of the participants in this adventure were happy with the result, especially Bankers Trust, which pocketed substantial fees on the various deals. The Japanese regulators and citizens would not be as happy in a year when the Nikkei 225 crashed, and they learned that—over the course of a decade—their insurance companies had been loading up on stock-market bets they should not have been making. But for now, the Japanese markets were rising, and there was bliss.

Bankers Trust offered several versions of this matchmaking exercise, all collectively under the rubric of *equity derivatives*. A small group that had been expected to make just $5 million in a year could easily make more than that in a week. In 1989 the group made $200 million, one-third of Bankers Trust's profits that year.[15]

As was typical, other bankers quickly learned of Bankers Trust's deals, and they entered this market immediately. In early 1990, four investment banks—Bear Stearns, Goldman Sachs, Salomon Brothers, and Morgan Stanley—sold hundreds of millions of dollars of long-term Nikkei options in various structures.[16] Like Bankers Trust, the other banks set up free-standing new businesses to do these deals, which they also called equity derivatives.

As the outside competition increased, tensions mounted between Charlie Sanford and Allen Wheat, the fiery New Mexican who was in charge of equity derivatives at Bankers Trust. Wheat was smart and enormously popular. He had led the international capital-markets group, and many saw him as the eventual heir to Sanford. Some even thought he was gunning for Sanford's job already. But Charlie Sanford—now in just his fourth year as CEO—was not planning to leave anytime soon. Moreover, Sanford would not say that he would back Wheat as the next CEO, when Sanford eventually stepped down.

Capitalizing on these tensions—and on Allen Wheat's ambitions—another investment bank, First Boston, entered the market for equity derivatives in a big way, hiring Wheat away from Bankers Trust. Wheat brought along eighteen key employees and all of their expertise in over-the-counter derivatives. With them, Bankers Trust's expertise and culture would be spreading to another bank. The defection reportedly sent "shock waves" through Bankers Trust; *The Economist* reported that "Bankers Trust's 40-strong equity-derivatives group is now ruined."[17]

It was time for Sanford to regroup yet again. But this was nothing unusual for him or his employees, most of whom remained. If equity derivatives wouldn't be a huge source of profits anymore, Sanford would find another. Sanford described Bankers Trust as "250 smart guys who all have monkeys on their backs that force them to come in every day and say, 'Never mind what I did yesterday. What's next?'"[18] In 1990, he continued to walk the trading floor, constantly quizzing, "What's next?" and encouraging his 250 smart guys to find new and creative deals.

Sanford deliberately tried to create anxiety among his managers. The head of human resources at Bankers Trust described Sanford as an "obsessive-compulsive neurotic." But in the aftermath of Andy Krieger's losses, Sanford was briefly circumspect. He had learned the importance of a more-stable source of revenue that did not require the bank to put so much capital at risk. Ira Stepanian, the CEO of Bank of Boston—one of Sanford's competitors and friends—had expressed concern about Bankers Trust's aggressive practices: "Any company that makes a lot of money from trading can also lose that much. It all depends on having the right controls in place, and I'm sure that Charlie Sanford has thought a lot about that."[19]

Sanford had thought a lot about controls. He downplayed Bankers Trust's cowboy image, saying "we don't bet the bank."[20] He admitted Bankers Trust had made some bad decisions, as in a $100 million unsecured loan to Donald Trump ("We were brain dead when we made that loan"[21]), but he continued to defend Krieger's trading ("We didn't take too big a position for Bankers Trust, but we may have taken too big a position for that market.")[22] He focused on the bank's risk-management systems, which were state-of-the-art, but obviously needed improving.

Sanford had initiated the idea of measuring the profitability of a particular business by its *Risk-Adjusted Return On Capital* (he used the acronym RAROC, pronounced RAY-rock), rather than simply looking at returns.[23] RAROC was a revolutionary concept, which many large corporations soon adopted.

The idea behind RAROC was that a company should reward employees based not only on how much money they made, but also on how risky their business was. A particular business—currency-options trading, for example—might generate huge returns; but, if it was too risky, the bank might be better off allocating its resources somewhere else. Employees could take on risks, but they needed to be smart about it. Bankers Trust would force employees to be smart by creating incentives for them to generate consistent returns relative to their risks.

RAROC required a kind of thought experiment. Bankers Trust would look at the history of a particular market and hypothetically allocate enough capital to cover expected losses in that market for one year at, say, the 99 percent level.[24] That meant employees in risky businesses needed more of this hypothetical capital, so their returns appeared smaller relative to that capital. In contrast, less risky businesses looked more profitable, because they needed less of this hypothetical capital.

Different divisions within Bankers Trust competed for capital, and were judged—on a risk-adjusted basis—against each other. Andy Krieger, for example, made a lot of money, but the business of currency-options trading was risky, so his RAROC was lower. That was one reason why his bonus had been *only* $3 million, even though his profits were so high. Equity derivatives in Japan had been an attractive business because it didn't put much capital at risk, and those salesmen were very well paid.

In this way, Sanford's RAROC system encouraged employees to focus both on how much money they were making for Bankers Trust, and on how much of the firm's precious capital they were risking. Much more than other banks, Bankers Trust gave its employees a road map for how they could make big bonuses. As a former member of Bankers Trust's management committee put it, Sanford "set the tone in a simple way—compensation."[25]

As the pressures mounted, Bankers Trust personnel at all levels began to push the edges of the law. Since the 1930s, a law called the Glass-Steagall Act had separated investment and commercial banking, in response to public outcry about banks' alleged abuses in the stock-market mania before the Great Crash of 1929. The solution had been to split the two functions of banking. Commercial banks were left with the traditional business of making loans and taking deposits. Investment banks would trade and underwrite securities.

Not surprisingly, the law was unpopular among commercial bankers. As early as 1982, Sanford was saying, "We're hoping to see some break in Glass-Steagall."[26] Although Congress would not repeal Glass-Steagall for more than a decade, Charlie Sanford began running circles around this law, finding loopholes and lobbying regulators to make exceptions for Bankers Trust.

For example, Bankers Trust had lobbied the administration of President Ronald Reagan to deregulate the process of securities offerings so that banks could participate. Regulators began allowing so-called *shelf registrations,* in which companies—instead of processing from scratch all of the documentation necessary to create new securities each time they wanted to raise money from investors—created the documentation upfront and put it "on the shelf," to be used at a later date. That way, companies could issue new stocks or bonds much more quickly and at lower cost. Only securities firms—which Bankers Trust was not—could actually underwrite the securities, putting them on the shelf. But Sanford had argued that, once that was done, anyone, including Bankers Trust, could use the shelf registration to distribute new securities. Officials at the Securities and Exchange Commission winked and nodded, and Bankers Trust got its first foothold in the securities business.

Bankers Trust began distributing securities—mostly bonds—to institutional investors through deals known as *private placements.* In a private placement, the borrower did not need to register under the securities laws, and did not need to comply with generally accepted accounting principles. The bank aggressively pursued these deals, doing about $1 billion of them in 1983, and billions more in later years,[27] even though the Securities and Exchange Commission did not formally allow companies to raise funds in this way. (In April 1990, the SEC approved the now widely used Rule 144A, which allows companies to do private placements with so-called Qualified Institutional Buyers—basically, large companies and very rich people.)

Bankers Trust entered other new businesses, too, arranging hundreds of interest-rate and currency swaps, and dealing in government bonds and short-term corporate debt. It was a lender in many leveraged buyouts—the high-profile merger deals developed in the 1980s—in which corporate raiders purchased stocks with borrowed money.[28] Sanford also began selling and trading billions of dollars of the bank's own loans, a profitable practice that other banks soon followed.[29]

By the mid-1980s, Bankers Trust was starting to look a lot like an investment bank—something Glass-Steagall supposedly had made illegal. Regulators didn't like Sanford's reluctance to hold loans, and one banking regulator reportedly suggested Bankers Trust should give up its bank charter.[30] But the bank insisted that it wasn't *really* an investment bank; it was simply acting as an agent in a few deals, nothing for the regulators to fret about. As one Bankers Trust veteran put it, "We are obviously law-abiding citizens, but we mean to press on all legitimate fronts."[31]

The bank's experience in the market for interest rate and currency swaps was critical to its plans for the early 1990s. (Recall that swaps are contracts where parties agree to exchange payments based on interest rates or currencies.) The competition for swaps in the mid-1980s had been fierce. By 1984, interest-rate swaps were a $70 billion business, considered huge at the time.[32] But profit margins were dwindling, and various regulators—including the Federal Deposit Insurance Corp., the Federal Reserve Board, and the Comptroller of the Currency—were starting to ask questions about the risks of swaps.

There were a few ugly stories about firms using swaps to manipulate their accounting results. One bank contemplated internal swaps—swaps with itself—whereby it would set aside reserves depending on how much profit it wanted to declare in a particular quarter. In 1984, Morgan Stanley began experimenting with delaying the starting dates of swaps, which made them more difficult to evaluate.[33] Japanese banks in particular used swaps to inflate profits and hide losses.

In February 1985, the Financial Accounting Standards Board (FASB)—the private group that established most accounting rules—asked whether banks should begin including swaps on their balance sheets, the financial statements that recorded their assets and liabilities.[34] Banks already accounted for loans as assets, because the right to receive loan payments from borrowers was valuable. Banks also accounted for deposits as liabilities, because the obligation to pay depositors was costly.

However, since the early 1980s, banks had not included swaps as assets or liabilities, arguing that swaps were different from loans and deposits, and belonged off their balance sheets. In a swap, the parties agreed to exchange payments based on some reference amount, say, $100 million, but—unlike borrowers who repaid the principal amount of their loans, and depositors who could withdraw the entire amount of their deposit— the parties to a swap never actually paid each other the underlying reference amount. Instead, parties merely used the reference amount to calculate the amount they owed each other at different times. (For example, a swap contract might require one party to pay 10 percent every year. If the reference amount were $100 million, that party would pay $10 million per year, but would never pay the underlying $100 million reference amount.)

Thus, the argument went, a swap was not really an asset or a liability, even though it carried both the right to receive payments and the obligation to make payments. Moreover, banks argued, it wasn't fair to require them to list swaps as assets and liabilities on their balance sheets, because they often used swaps to reduce their risks, and if banks were forced to record the fluctuation in the value of swaps over time, investors would perceive that the banks were riskier than they really were.

The banks' argument was deeply flawed. The right to receive money on a swap was a valuable asset, and the obligation to pay money on a swap was a costly liability. The fact that swaps, unlike loans and deposits, didn't require repayment of the reference amount meant only that swaps would have different values from loans and deposits, but it didn't justify removing them from the balance sheets altogether. Moreover, if swaps, indeed, were fluctuating in value, as banks claimed, that fact was important to the banks' shareholders. If banks wanted to explain in a footnote of their financial statements why shareholders shouldn't worry about these fluctuations (e.g., because the swap actually was reducing some other risk), nothing prevented the bank from doing so.

But bankers knew that the fluctuations in their swaps would worry their shareholders, and they were determined to keep swaps off their balance sheets. FASB's inquiry about banks' treating swaps as *off-balance sheet*—a term that would become widespread during the 1990s—mobilized and unified the banks, which until that point had been competing aggressively for business, and not cooperating much on regulatory issues. All banks strongly opposed disclosing more information about their swaps, and so they threw down their swords and banded together at several high-level meetings, temporarily suspending their fierce competition. Within weeks after FASB's February 1985 inquiry, the ten largest swaps dealers had formed the International Swap Dealers Association.

Bankers Trust was one of the founding members of ISDA. According to Jonathan Berg, a vice president at Bankers Trust at the time, the banks formed ISDA to "organize before any problems arise."[35] The dealers planned to establish standardized documentation and practices, to lobby against new regulations, and to determine how big the swaps market really was. Estimates were in the $100 billion range, but it was embarrassing that no one knew such a basic fact, especially now that regulators were asking some hard questions.

ISDA's first press release said the group's goal was to "advance general market practices and to discuss issues of relevance to the financial community."[36] But everyone involved understood that the primary role would be to lobby against regulation of swaps, or—as one commentator put it—to "explore the accounting and regulatory implications."[37] ISDA would prove to be the most powerful and effective lobbying force in the recent history of financial markets.

It is striking—given the dramatic changes in financial markets since the mid-1980s—how little the lineup of industry leaders has changed. The ten original dealer members were Bankers Trust, Citicorp, First Boston, Goldman Sachs, Kleinwort Benson, Merrill Lynch, Morgan Guaranty Trust, Morgan Stanley, Salomon Brothers, and Shearson Lehman Brothers; together, they made up 80 percent of the swaps market.[38] With the exception of a few mergers and name changes, the list of top dealers would look essentially the same for nearly two decades.

In 1989, the Federal Reserve permitted some commercial banks—including Bankers Trust—to form investment-banking subsidiaries to engage in the securities business, but only if total revenues from investment banking were less than 10 percent of the bank's total revenues. Bankers Trust formed a securities subsidiary, not too creatively named BT Securities Corporation. Its competitors followed, and Sanford predicted that *universal banking* would soon come to the United States, meaning that banks would offer securities, banking, and insurance services under one roof.[39] The banks, having just tasted the profits from equity derivatives, began circling the securities waters like sharks that had just tasted blood.

The Fed helped banks in another way: by lowering short-term interest rates, which had been above eight percent. Fed Chairman Alan Greenspan wanted to encourage investors and institutions to borrow more to invest in various aspects of the economy, including long-term bonds and stocks. This policy created the perfect environment for investors who wanted to borrow short term, betting interest rates would stay low.

However, the Fed was not all-powerful, and it could not make the economy turn on a dime. The year 1990 was a horrific one on Wall

Street. Every financial asset collapsed: junk bonds, commercial real estate, investments related to savings and loans, even Japanese stocks. On February 13, 1990, Drexel Burnham Lambert—Michael Milken's bank—which had epitomized the 1980s financial culture, filed for bankruptcy. That marked the end of an era, and it seemed unlikely that banks would ever again generate 1980s-like profits. Even traditionally profitable businesses were hurting: stock commissions paid to Wall Street during 1990 were a relatively paltry $8.9 billion.

Wall Street, by becoming so ruthlessly efficient, was destroying itself. New markets became competitive more quickly than ever, with profit margins narrowing, within months, as other financial institutions entered the business. Bankers Trust was in a quandary: every time it discovered a new source of profit, it was victimized by this inevitable competition. Yes, Bankers Trust's employees had quantitative and risk-management skills that were superior to those of any bank. But how could it use them to make a consistent profit?

The answer came from an unlikely source. Merton Miller, a Nobel-laureate economist at the University of Chicago, was an enthusiastic supporter of swaps and other derivatives. He agreed with many dealers that swaps were important financial innovations that enabled parties to allocate risks more efficiently.

But Miller also believed these instruments served a different, perhaps more dubious, purpose. In 1986, Miller argued that a major impulse for financial innovation was a desire to avoid regulation.[40] Financial-market participants faced very different regulatory environments, and they often were governed by rules they would prefer not to follow. By using derivatives, they could avoid rules that seemed senseless to them. Miller was a free-market economist and thought these rules were senseless, too, so he applauded companies' efforts to avoid regulation, efforts that came to be called "regulatory arbitrage."[41]

The accounting rules for swaps were a perfect example. Swaps were simply investment contracts, and they were economically equivalent to many other financial instruments, including exchange-traded futures and options, all of which were regulated. Yet swaps were unregulated and immune from most securities-law disclosure requirements. Merton Miller's insight implied that companies would do swaps not necessarily because swaps allocated risk more efficiently, but rather *because* they were unregulated. They could do swaps in the dark, without the powerful sunlight that securities regulation shined on other financial instruments.

And here was the crucial point: to the extent companies and their financial officers could use custom-tailored swaps to avoid regulation or to hide risks, Bankers Trust's profits from selling swaps to those companies might not disappear so quickly. Corporate treasurers hoping to benefit from such swaps would pay a premium—it wasn't *their* money, after all—if the swaps were structured in a way that created more opportunity for profit, but hid the risks from their bosses. Just as the Japanese insurance executives paid large fees for equity derivatives, even fully informed financial officers would pay a hefty premium if they could avoid disclosing the risks of swaps to shareholders and regulators. Unlike the plain-vanilla instruments from earlier years, these swaps could have all sorts of hidden bells and whistles, and shareholders and regulators might not ever even know about them.

Substantial fees from these complex swaps would persist so long as companies valued the difference in legal treatment between swaps and their regulated brethren. And if other banks were reluctant to sell such swaps to companies in the shadow of the law, there wouldn't be as much competition for Bankers Trust.

Finally, a business that might last for more than a year! Bankers Trust began gearing up to sell custom-tailored swaps.

Gibson Greetings, Inc., was a Cincinnati, Ohio, company that made and sold greeting cards. Gibson had a traditional commercial-banking relationship with Bankers Trust, dating back to 1983.[42] To finance its business, Gibson borrowed money from various sources, including a standard revolving-credit agreement arranged by Bankers Trust.

In May 1991, Gibson borrowed $50 million in a straightforward debt deal arranged by a different bank, at an interest rate of 9.33 percent.[43] As interest rates fell during fall 1991, Jim Johnsen, the company's treasurer, began to explore the idea of using interest-rate swaps to reduce the interest rate on its debt.[44] In an interest-rate swap with a bank, Gibson could agree to receive a fixed rate (offsetting the fixed rate on its debt deal), and pay a much lower floating rate. In other words, Gibson could reduce its effective interest rate in exchange for the risk that rates might rise, just as a homeowner could switch from a fixed-rate mortgage to an adjustable one. Such plain-vanilla swaps were well established by 1991, and margins were low. A basic $50 million interest-rate swap would cost around $50,000.

When Johnsen told various banks Gibson might be interested in a swap, he was besieged by proposals, in the same way a homeowner who indicated an interest in refinancing would be bombarded by mailings and early-evening calls. Banks, having tasted the profits from equity derivatives and other similar transactions, were aggressively seeking new customers. Gibson was a perfect candidate for a new custom-tailored swap. It was big enough to do a deal, but not sophisticated enough to understand how to evaluate it properly.

Gibson had an ongoing relationship with Bankers Trust, run by two senior commercial bankers. But the two salesmen who flew out to see Johnsen in November 1991 were much younger and much more sophisticated than these commercial bankers. Two of Charlie Sanford's nerds—Gary Missner and Mitchell Vazquez—made just the right pitch to Gibson. Jim Johnsen remembered the salesmen as "forthright and honest, not like hard-sell securities salesmen who call you up at home during dinner."[45] On November 12, 1991, Gibson agreed to do two interest-rate swaps with Bankers Trust, each for $30 million.[46]

Although these two swaps initially appeared to be plain vanilla, they actually were a bit more complicated. The first was a "two-year" swap, in which Gibson agreed to pay a low fixed rate of 5.91 percent and receive a floating rate. The second was a "five-year" swap, in which Gibson agreed to do the opposite: pay a floating rate and receive a higher fixed rate of 7.12 percent.[47]

The effect was to create two different payment periods for Gibson. For the first two years, Gibson would pay a low rate (5.91 percent). For the three years after that, it would pay a floating rate. Bankers Trust would hedge its position in the market, so that it pocketed a fee, but did not put its capital at risk.

This trade had what the dealers called attractive *optics*. It looked simply marvelous. Gibson reduced its interest cost by several percent for the next two years. It took on some risks in years three through five, but rates might be low then, too. Who *wouldn't* do this trade?

In fact, this was a fairly common trade at the time,[48] and it turned out to be a winner. Interest rates declined during early 1992 and the swaps moved in Gibson's favor. Seven months later, in July 1992, Johnsen got a call from Bankers Trust with good news: Gibson could close out its positions right away, at a profit of $260,000. What would he like to do?

What would you do, in Johnsen's situation? Could you determine whether $260,000 was a fair payment? One way to do it would be to create a computer model, and input various data and assumptions regarding interest rates, credit risk, and other variables to come up with a valuation. But few corporate treasurers—including Johnsen—were capable of this in 1991. He could have called another bank for a second opinion. But that risked offending Bankers Trust, and he wouldn't necessarily get a better price. Besides, as long-standing advisers to Gibson, Bankers Trust wouldn't fudge the valuation of a couple of simple interest-rate swaps, would they?

Johnsen should have made a few calls, but he apparently didn't think it was necessary. He decided to trust Bankers Trust and closed out the swaps for a $260,000 gain. That decision would cost Gibson dearly. The actual value of the swaps to Gibson at the time has been disputed, but it was at least $550,000 and probably closer to the amount Gibson ultimately claimed in a lawsuit: $750,000.[49] The difference of several hundred thousand dollars was gravy for Bankers Trust.

Gibson's willingness to close out the swaps at such a bad price meant that Gary Missner and Mitchell Vazquez had found a sucker. If Gibson couldn't evaluate a reasonably simple trade, it would have no chance with a complex one, and that meant Bankers Trust could charge an even higher fee for a more complex deal. Missner and Vazquez were doing exactly what Charlie Sanford had indicated he wanted: generating big profits, with little capital at risk.

From November 1991 to March 1994, the nerds of Bankers Trust lobbed salvo after salvo of complex swap proposals at the greeting-card maker. Many of them hit, and before it was all over, Gibson and Bankers Trust would enter into twenty-nine derivatives transactions, in which Gibson placed huge interest-rate bets, and Bankers Trust booked huge profits.

Gibson's second swap, in October 1992, made the first one look like a plain U.S. savings bond. In this deal, also for $30 million, Gibson agreed to receive a fixed rate of 5.5 percent and to pay a floating rate, squared and then divided by 6 percent.[50] That's right: squared, as in "to the second power." The swap payments would be based on the London Interbank Offered Rate, known as LIBOR, multiplied by itself and then divided by 6 percent. Let me repeat: Gibson's payments would be LIBOR multiplied by itself and then divided by 6 percent.

Why on earth would anyone buy a LIBOR-squared swap? One possible reason was that they didn't know it was a LIBOR-squared swap, or that they didn't understand what squared meant. But that hardly seemed plausible. Jim Johnsen knew plenty of math to understand that, and surely he had been able to spot the little "2" in the numerator.

No, the more likely reason was greed: the squared feature was a way to bet big on declining interest rates. If floating rates remained low, as they had been, Johnsen could turn his little treasury operation into a profit center. For example, if floating rates stayed at 3 percent, then Gibson would be obligated to pay just one-and-a-half percent (the math was 3 times 3 divided by 6). But if rates increased, losses would increase, well, exponentially. If rates hit 6 percent, Gibson would owe 6 percent. If they hit 10 percent . . . well, no one wanted to think about that. Moreover, even a small increase in rates in the short run—to, say, 3.5 percent— would create big losses for Gibson, because it would increase the chances that, during the term of the swap, rates would go higher, causing Gibson exponential losses.

The squared feature magnified the bet's risks and potential returns, much as a *trifecta* bet—which names, in order, the top three horses to finish a race—magnifies the risks and potential returns relative to a simple win, place, or show bet. Treasurers bought squared swaps for the same reason gamblers played trifectas. (Gibson wasn't alone in gambling: one former Bankers Trust salesman even claimed that a client had bought a LIBOR-cubed swap—raised to the third power—although he wouldn't say which client it was.)[51]

Thanks to ISDA's lobbying against regulation of swaps, Gibson could make this bet in secret, in an unregulated market. A swap that was being used to hedge debt—as Gibson might argue its loony swap was—did not need to be disclosed to shareholders at all. But even if the swap wasn't obviously a hedge, the disclosure requirements were minimal. In any event, Gibson couldn't possibly tell its shareholders about such a bizarre trade, and it did not.

Unfortunately, rates began rising during the final months of 1992, and even a fractional increase was enough to cause Gibson some serious pain. LIBOR rose from 3.0625 percent to 3.375 percent, and by the end of the year—with that increase squared—Johnsen was facing a loss of $975,000.[52] Or at least that was what the salesmen at Bankers Trust told him.

Gibson wasn't capable of discerning the swap's actual value, but that didn't matter much. Gibson wasn't about to walk away from the gambling tables with a million-dollar loss. During the next fourteen months, Gibson did deals with Bankers Trust that it described as "even more volatile and risky than the 'Libor Squared' transaction."[53] These were the financial markets' version of the *superfecta,* a horse-racing bet like the trifecta, but with all of the top four horses.

In a so-called *Treasury-Linked Swap,* Gibson agreed, among other things, to receive the lesser of $30.6 million or an amount determined by the following formula: $30 million–(103 × 2-year Treasury Yield/4.88%)–(30-year Treasury Price/100). Another trade, called a *knock-out* option, became worthless when rates hit a specified level (it "knocked out" at that point). Financial economists would spend the next several years attempting to create pricing models for knock-out options. Still another Gibson trade, called a Wedding Band, was too complex to describe without a mathematician and a psychotherapist.

Gibson's swap smorgasbord included the most sophisticated derivatives anyone had invented, and they all were hidden from regulators and shareholders. In its 1993 annual report, Gibson disclosed $96 million of swaps outstanding, without any detail as to their risks.

These swaps were incredibly profitable for Bankers Trust. From late 1991 to early 1994, the more Gibson lost the more it traded, and the more Bankers Trust made. In all, Bankers Trust made about $13 million from the swaps with Gibson,[54] all of which supposedly began as an effort to find a low-cost hedge for a simple fixed-rate debt.

How did Charlie Sanford react to all of this aggressive behavior by his salesmen? Substantial bonuses, of course. In late September 1993, Sanford proudly announced in a memorandum that he was promoting Gary Missner—the senior salesman covering Gibson—to the position of managing director.[55]

Gibson Greetings was not alone. Numerous Bankers Trust clients were actively buying and selling similar swaps: Air Products and Chemicals, Equity Group Holdings, Federal Paper Board, Jefferson Smurfit, Sandoz, Sequa, and others, including two Indonesian companies—PT Adimitra Rayapratama and PT Dharmala Sakti Sejahtera—that made some of the biggest trades of all. Bankers Trust was everywhere. As David Urbani, assistant treasurer at Air Products and Chemicals, put it, "If I mention to another company that we were thinking about doing some weird derivative, they'll say you must have been talking to Bankers Trust."[56]

The most publicized losses on swaps with Bankers Trust were on those done by Procter & Gamble. An investor in P&G stock—like an investor in Gibson Greetings—had no clue the firm was gambling on derivatives. Shareholders thought they were buying a soap company. The company's 1993 Form 10-K filing with the Securities and Exchange Commission reinforced this notion, describing its derivatives activity as minimal and low risk.

Kevin Hudson, another smooth-talking Bankers Trust salesman, covered P&G. In the early 1990s, Bankers Trust and P&G had done little business together. Other than an early 1993 deal—linked to the Mexican peso—Bankers Trust had made few inroads with P&G's treasurer, Raymond Mains.[57]

In October 1993, Hudson began talking to Dane Parker, a junior treasury analyst who reported to Mains. P&G had been borrowing money in the short-term *commercial-paper* market to fund its consumer products business. In that market, there is a floating-rate index, like LIBOR, called the Commercial Paper index, or *CP* for short.

A well-respected company such as P&G could borrow at roughly the Commercial Paper index rate. But P&G's goal was to use swaps to borrow at less than the Commercial Paper index, hopefully by as much as 40 hundredths of a percent, or 40 basis points. In the industry parlance, Parker might call Hudson and say, "I want CP minus 40 basis points."

In the commercial-paper world, every basis point was precious. If P&G's treasury could outperform its peers by 40 of them, Mains and Parker would be supermen. To do it, they would need to take on some risk, of course, and Bankers Trust had just the recipe: a complex trade resembling Gibson's Treasury-Linked Swap.

It seemed incredible that a big, sophisticated company like P&G would pay Gibson-like fees to gamble on interest rates. But early on, Parker demonstrated that he was potentially just as much of a sitting duck as Johnsen had been. Soon, Hudson was regaling his colleagues with stories about how "smooth" he had been during his visits with P&G. In one taped conversation, Hudson described the deal he had proposed to Parker to a friend, and bragged, "You're looking at an $8 million trade." In other words, he had estimated that Bankers Trust's profit from this one deal would be $8 million. The friend was impressed and responded, "It's like our greatest fantasy." Hudson couldn't help but agree. "I know. It is. It is. This is a wet dream."[58]

Charlie Sanford's pressures were having their intended effect. His nerds were aggressively pursuing deals, and—because their customers couldn't evaluate complex swaps properly—Bankers Trust was making unheard-of profits. During this time, a fee of one percent, called a "point," was substantial. But Bankers Trust was earning multiple points on deals of unprecedented size. The companies were no longer clients of Bankers Trust; they were pigeons.

As one former managing director put it, "Guys started making jokes on the trading floor about how they were hammering the customers. They were giving each other high fives. A junior person would turn to his senior guy and say, 'I can get [this customer] for all these points.' The senior guys would say, 'Yeah, ream him.'"[59]

During this period, Bankers Trust developed a training video for new employees. In one segment of the video—which Bankers Trust officials have maintained was in jest—a bank employee described a hypothetical derivative transaction among Sony, IBM, and Bankers Trust: "What Bankers Trust can do for Sony and IBM is get in the middle and rip them off—take a little money." The employee then nervously added, "Let me take that back. I just realized that I'm being filmed."[60]

Belita Ong, a former managing director and senior derivatives saleswoman at Bankers Trust, believed that Bankers Trust had developed "an amoral culture." She said, "You saw practices that you knew were not good for clients being encouraged by senior managers because they made a lot of money for the bank."[61] One salesman noted, "Funny business, you know. Lure people into that calm and then just totally fuck 'em."[62]

Ong was the managing director who had called the Bankers Trust nerds "mostly guys without girlfriends." But sweet-talking Kevin Hudson, the salesman covering P&G, had a girlfriend—a fiancée even—another salesperson at Bankers Trust named Alison Bernhard. And he was telling her all of the details about how Bankers Trust was milking P&G, on taped telephone conversations at the bank.

When Hudson finally persuaded P&G to do a swap with Bankers Trust, he immediately called Bernhard to tell her about it. "I just took the biggest trade of the year," he told his fiancée.[63]

In the swap, P&G would pay the CP rate minus 75 basis points on $200 million, giving it a cushion so it could lose a bit and still lock in the goal of "CP minus 40." In addition, P&G would effectively sell some put options to Bankers Trust, giving the bank the right to profit if interest rates increased. If interest rates increased, P&G would pay the following spread:[64]

[98.5 × (5-year Treasury Yield / 5.78%) – 30-year Treasury Price] / 100

Don't stop reading; you don't need to understand precisely how to value this spread to understand what it did. There were two variables in the formula: the 5-year Treasury Yield (the interest rate on 5-year government bonds) and the 30-year Treasury Price (the price of 30-year government bonds). Yields and prices moved in opposite directions: in simple terms, the more cheaply you could buy a Treasury bond, the more yield you would earn over time. The spread formula consisted of a multiple of the 5-year Treasury Yield *minus* the 30-year Treasury Price, but it just as easily could have *added* a multiple of the 30-year Treasury Yield.

Why use the 30-year Treasury Price instead of the 30-year Treasury Yield? And why multiply the 5-year Treasury Yield by 98.5 and then divide—first by 5.78%, and then, at the end, by 100? As in the Gibson Greetings swaps, these terms were there for what traders called optics: they made the spread look more attractive than it really was. For example, 98.5 and 5.78 were roughly the price and yield, respectively, of a 5-year Treasury bond. They focused P&G on the current market values of the bond instead of on the risks of the trade. In reality, these numbers were meaningless: a savvy investor would simply do the math and notice that 98.5 divided by 5.78% divided by 100 was about 17.04, meaning that the spread actually was magnified—or *leveraged*—about 17 times. The same was true of the use of the 30-year Treasury Price instead of the 30-year Treasury Yield. A savvy investor would convert the price to a yield, so as to compare apples to apples within the spread formula. Because the price was much higher than the yield, the 30-year Treasury variable also was leveraged, by a similar amount.

In other words, P&G's $200 million swap with Bankers Trust really was a $3.4 *billion* bet that 5-year and 30-year interest rates would remain low. If 5-year rates stayed at around 5.78 percent and the 30-year price remained at its current level, the spread would be close to zero. But if interest rates increased, watch out.

It is unclear whether anyone at P&G did this math. Former P&G chairman Edwin Artzt called his underlings who bought the swap "farm boys at a country carnival" and derided their inability to seek the advice necessary to understand the deal. In discussing two of these employees, Carol Loomis, a veteran reporter for *Fortune*, concluded that "plainly, neither understood the derivatives they bought from Hudson."[65]

P&G certainly didn't seem sophisticated to anyone at Bankers Trust. When the profits were tallied, Kevin Hudson and Bankers Trust had made $7.6 million from this one trade. When Hudson told his boss, Jack Lavin, about the trade, Lavin reportedly said, "I think my dick just fell off."[66]

His fiancée had a different reaction, in a taped phone call:

> BERNHARD: Oh, my ever-loving God. Do they understand that . . .
> what they did?
> HUDSON: No. They understand what they did, but they don't un-
> derstand the leverage, no.
> BERNHARD: They would never know. They would never be able to
> know how much money was taken out of that.
> HUDSON: Never, no way, no way. That's the beauty of Bankers
> Trust.[67]

In late January 1994, P&G did another swap with Bankers Trust, with a similarly complex formula, this time betting that German interest rates would remain low. This trade was *only* leveraged ten times. In one year, Kevin Hudson had done deals with more than $25 million in fees. His fiancée was beginning to worry.

> BERNHARD: You're headed for trouble. . . . It's gonna blow up
> on you.
> HUDSON: I'm a glutton for punishment, and well, you know, I'm
> rollin', man, I gotta make money here.
> BERNHARD: You're not gonna have a job, you're not gonna have
> customers . . . you're gonna blow them up . . . you're getting greed-
> ier as the days roll by.[68]

The leverage factors in these trades were so large that the size of the bets was a significant percentage of the entire amount of money the U.S. and German governments borrowed. If P&G elected to close out the trade early—as Gibson had—its actions would rock the world's government-bond markets.

As it turned out, Dane Parker at P&G wasn't the only person unable to figure out the value of these complex swaps. Smooth-talking Kevin Hudson couldn't do it either, and he admitted as much to Parker, saying he didn't build the computer models that valued the options in P&G's

trades—a trader had done that.[69] As a result, Hudson was taken to the cleaners, too. Incredibly, a Bankers Trust trader squeezed profits from Hudson on the first P&G swap, just as Hudson had squeezed them from P&G.

Guillaume Henri André Fonkenell began his career as a junior swap trader at Bankers Trust in June 1990.[70] He was very successful, and by November 1993 had been promoted to a senior trader in New York.

During October 1993, Kevin Hudson had been working on the P&G trade with Kassy Kabede, one of Fonkenell's junior traders. When Kabede left the country on November 1—the day before the first P&G trade—Fonkenell took over. After the swap was done, there was the key question: how much money did Bankers Trust make on the trade? Just as Andy Krieger had needed to come up with a valuation of his trades, Fonkenell needed to determine the value of the complicated put options embedded in the P&G swap.

When a salesman booked a trade, he obtained a price from the trader. Commissions went to the salesman; trading profits went to the trader. If the trader valued a trade at $90, gave the salesman a value of $95, and the salesman sold it for $100, Bankers Trust would make $10 and the trader and salesman each would make $5.

But if the trader gave the salesman a higher value (say, $97), then the trader would declare more profit ($7), leaving less for the salesman ($3). Bankers Trust made the same amount of money on the trade either way, but the salesman received less credit for it in the second example. Wall Street is a dog-eat-dog world where, it is said, salesmen wear Milkbone underwear. Traders are the alpha dogs, and they frequently lie to salesmen about trade values, especially on complex deals, when they know the salesmen won't be able to figure out the valuation themselves. One of a bank manager's challenges is to keep the traders honest, and to keep the salesmen from killing the traders.

As with Krieger's trades, the valuation of the first P&G swap depended on volatility. At the time, volatility was not quoted in the markets. Instead, a trader would select an appropriate volatility measure based on historical data or on the range of prices for options similar to those embedded in the swap. By plugging those prices into an options model, such as Black-Scholes, the trader would get a range of numbers called *implied volatilities*. Then, the trader would input those volatility numbers into a spreadsheet or computer program to calculate the swap's value.

To improve controls at Bankers Trust, Charlie Sanford required that the back-office employees mark to market the bank's trades every day. That meant someone in the back office would need to report a daily value for the P&G swap. These values were the basis for a ten-page bank-wide risk assessment Sanford received every day. The Krieger incident had made it especially important that those numbers be accurate, and Bankers Trust supposedly had been improving its control systems during the five-and-a-half years since then.

The value of the first P&G swap depended on two key inputs: the volatility of the 5-year Treasury Yield and the volatility of the 30-year Treasury Price. The swap was so large that a one-percentage-point change in the volatility estimates would change the profit by $3 million.

Kevin Hudson would be compensated based on the *new-deal profit*— the profit recorded at the time of the trade. The more Fonkenell could reduce the new-deal profit, the greater his trading profit—and bonus— would be.

Before the trade, the 5-year volatility was recorded as 18 and the 30-year volatility was 10. Fonkenell then directed the back office to lower each volatility measure by one point, thereby cutting the new-deal profit by about $3 million.

The day after the trade, Fonkenell told the back office to move the 5-year volatility back up to 18. The back-office worker apparently misunderstood the instruction and moved the 3-year rate instead of the 5-year rate. The mistake, which eventually was corrected, was attributed in part to the fact that employees called the 3-year note "Losh" and the 5-year note "Bosh." The comic mixing of "Loshes" and "Boshes" sounded more like a Dr. Seuss children's book than a cutting-edge risk-management operation. In any event, it didn't look like Sanford's controls had improved much. A few days later, Fonkenell instructed the back office to move the 30-year volatility back up to 10. Now the trade was worth $3 million more, and that portion of the profit belonged to the traders.

It is unclear whether Kevin Hudson ever discovered that Fonkenell had jiggered the volatilities. But no one was crying for Hudson, who received a sizeable bonus for 1993, anyway. His total compensation that year was almost $1.5 million.

Charlie Sanford was rewarded for his efforts, too. His total 1990 compensation, including options, was more than $5 million, based on calculations by *Fortune* magazine.[71] *Fortune* compared CEO compensation to stock performance, and found that Sanford was the thirteenth most-overcompensated CEO in the United States in 1990, just behind Kenneth Lay of Enron. Sanford received similar compensation in later years.

Notwithstanding the *Fortune* ranking, by some financial measures Sanford had earned his pay. From 1990 to 1993, Bankers Trust was the most profitable major bank in the United States. During this time, about a third of its profits were from derivatives, including swaps; another third was from trading. The bank's return on shareholders' equity was above 20 percent every year, almost double the return for a typical bank.[72]

However, the bank's stock price was in a rut, which was why many argued Sanford was overpaid. Securities analysts—burned once by the Krieger incident—no longer trusted the bank. To some sophisticated investors, the bank's glowing financial statements only spelled more trouble. As a result, Bankers Trust's *price/earnings ratio*—its stock price divided by its earnings per share—was a measly 8, whereas other banks had ratios almost twice as high.[73] Sanford frequently said that the single most important measure of a CEO was his company's stock price; but, by that measure, he was a failure.

In just a few years, Chairman Sanford had radically transformed Bankers Trust, as he had promised. But the transformation had its price. Shareholders didn't do nearly as well as employees. And within a few months, this short-term, product-oriented focus would nearly destroy the bank.

Bankers Trust had proved that technology and financial innovation could generate substantial profit for banks, just as they enabled companies to take on new risks in fantastic ways. From the equity-derivative deal that went European-investor-to-Canadian-bank-to-Bankers-Trust-to-Japanese-insurer, to Gibson's squared swap, to P&G's complex three-billion-dollar bet, the possibilities using derivatives seemed endless.

Brian Walsh, head of derivatives at Bankers Trust, would later admit that Bankers Trust had inappropriately emphasized complex, high-margin products over the needs of its customers: "What happened that I'm not happy about is that we fell in love with a product instead of trying to understand the client."[74] But this emphasis seemed inevitable, given Charlie Sanford's relentless questioning about "what's next?"

Bankers Trust also learned that a relentless focus on short-term profit can turn employees into rogues. Charlie Sanford couldn't control Gary Missner, Mitchell Vazquez, or Kevin Hudson any better than his clients could keep tabs on Jim Johnsen of Gibson Greetings or Dane Parker of

P&G. Nor was Bankers Trust's back office able to evaluate complex options, even though Sanford supposedly had improved controls years earlier, after the Krieger incident.

Meanwhile, regulators were gone from the scene entirely, lobbied away by the newly powerful International Swap Dealers Assocation. Shareholders, too, were largely unaware of these dealings. The only effective police force was the securities analysts, who at least tried to keep Bankers Trust honest by punishing its stock price.

From 1988 to 1994, the culture of Bankers Trust had changed in ways that benefited employees, but perhaps not shareholders or clients. In 1994, the world would learn about the swaps Bankers Trust sold to Gibson Greetings and Procter & Gamble. But first, the question remained whether these changes—increasing complexity, loss of control, and deregulation— were affecting other institutions. Put another way, if the Bankers Trust culture were set loose in another bank, what would happen?

This question wasn't merely hypothetical. Allen Wheat, Bankers Trust's derivatives guru, had left the bank in 1990 to join First Boston, where he was breeding the aggressive culture of Bankers Trust with First Boston's dying and dysfunctional investment-banking practice. Months after Wheat arrived at First Boston, a group of even more fantastic products was being born.

WHEAT FIRST SECURITIES

Before Allen Wheat joined First Boston, in February 1990, the investment bank was in a death spiral. In 1986, it lost $100 million trading government bonds. In 1987, it lost $60 million trading stocks. In 1988, it lost Bruce Wasserstein and Joseph Perella, the co-heads of its lucrative mergers-and-acquisitions group. In 1989, it lost $1 billion on loans to companies involved in takeovers.[1] In one late 1980s deal, First Boston had foolishly loaned $450 million—40 percent of its equity—to just one firm, Ohio Mattress, in a deal later dubbed "the burning bed."[2]

Finally, in 1990, Credit Suisse, the huge Swiss commercial bank, bailed out First Boston with $300 million of its own capital in exchange for a 45 percent stake[3]—the most it could own under Glass-Steagall, the law that separated investment and commercial banking. Ultimately, First Boston got a new name, too: CS First Boston (the CS stood for Credit Suisse).

Not surprisingly, several awful years had turned First Boston into a nasty place, with low morale and vicious infighting. So many people were leaving that some called the firm "Second Boston." Still, First Boston had potential. From the 1940s through 1985, First Boston and Morgan Stanley had been alone at the top of the investment-banking elite. The Swiss bankers were hoping to resuscitate the once-profitable First Boston of yore.

They would need some new talent, especially in derivatives, where

First Boston had virtually no presence. And the obvious place to look for talent was Bankers Trust, then regarded as the top firm in that area. The swaps Bankers Trust had sold were part of a broader class of derivatives—financial instruments based on the value of some other instrument or index—which was growing at a breakneck pace.

Allen Wheat was not a rocket scientist, although his father—a nuclear physicist—was: "He was always blowing things up. There would be a huge hole and we would have to move. I was always the kid introduced halfway through term."[4] But what he lacked in mathematical training, Wheat made up for with a quick wit and a good nose for profitable business opportunities.

Wheat had attended Wharton—like Andy Krieger and Charlie Sanford—although he received his M.B.A. from New York University. He had worked as an assistant treasurer at Chemical Bank, but left after a few years because "I was underpaid, and oddly at that time industry was paying more than banking." Wheat spent the next eight years in the treasury department at General Foods, where he set up a finance company and dealt extensively with bankers.[5] When banking began paying more than industry, Wheat left General Foods for Bankers Trust.

Wheat focused on one thing: money. As one colleague described him, "He is one of the most openly self-centered individuals that I have ever come into contact with. His only focus in life is making money for here, now, and the hereafter. He only wants to be rich."[6] This was meant as a compliment. On 1980s Wall Street, the money-obsessed were saints, not sinners.

Wheat led Bankers Trust's swaps efforts in the early 1980s, took over options and private placements in 1984, and ran the bank's Asian operations from Tokyo beginning in 1986. Wheat's focus on money worked, and everything he touched was profitable. Wheat was a popular and approachable leader. He told jokes and even played dice with lower-level employees in Singapore when he visited that office. His one weakness was that he neglected client relationships.[7] But who at Bankers Trust *didn't* neglect clients?

Nevertheless, when Charlie Sanford needed to staff his six-man management committee, he excluded Wheat in favor of Eugene Shanks, one of Wheat's contemporaries. *The Economist* conjectured that Wheat was "too much of a quip-tongued outsider."[8] Whatever the reason, Wheat didn't take the snub very well.

On Friday, February 9, 1990, when Wheat left his office in London, he told colleagues at Bankers Trust that he might go skiing for a few days. The next Monday, at two P.M. London time, he called Charlie Sanford and abruptly quit. First Boston sent out press releases within two hours.[9] Wheat had worked at Bankers Trust for nine years. Now he was out to prove Charlie Sanford had been wrong for not backing him.

When Helen Dunne of the *Daily Telegraph* in London asked Wheat about his favorite pastimes, he joked that "I don't do anything that is constructive. I mean I don't do pottery or anything like that."[10] A sardonic 41-year-old, with no hobbies and no interests other than banking, was the perfect hire for First Boston. The 1980s had ended, and the image of the handsome, slicked-back trader in the movie *Wall Street* was fading. It was appropriate, then, that First Boston's diminutive new superstar—with his disarming humor and self-deprecating style—was more like Woody Allen than Gordon Gekko.

Allen Wheat was given two immediate tasks: stop the losses in the Tokyo office and set up a new derivatives business. He would spend the next three years jetting back and forth between London and Tokyo. Fortunately, he had no problem sleeping on planes.

The two tasks were related. Much of Bankers Trust's derivatives profits had been from Asia, including fees from equity derivatives sold to Japanese insurers who weren't supposed to be betting on the stock market. Like Sanford, Wheat understood the benefits of combining commercial banking with investment banking, so he began by creating a new bank—called Credit Suisse Financial Products—a joint venture between the Swiss commercial bank and the U.S. investment bank. CSFP, as it would become known, would handle all the swaps and derivatives activities of both firms, although Credit Suisse would have control.[11]

CSFP was located in London, so it wouldn't have to comply with U.S. banking laws. This would be a huge advantage, because many of First Boston's clients were governed by regulations that made it much cheaper for them to deal with London banks than U.S. securities firms.[12]

Moreover, CSFP would have a AAA credit rating, the same as Credit Suisse, and the highest possible rating—several notches higher than most Wall Street banks, especially investment banks, which typically were rated only single-A. That high rating was important for the same reason as the London location: it would make it easier for CSFP's regulated clients to enter into deals with the bank. Allen Wheat was not trained as a lawyer but, like Charlie Sanford, he knew his way around a legal rule or two.

Wheat persuaded his bosses to give CSFP $150 million of capital, and he hired about 100 employees, many from Bankers Trust.[13] CSFP's risk-taking and pricing functions would be in London, also for regulatory purposes, but the bank would do its marketing in New York, where most of First Boston's salespeople worked. Wheat was obviously excited; he told a reporter, "It should be pretty big. Our objective is to be the best in this market."[14]

On July 16, 1990, the Bank of England sent CSFP its letter of authorization, and Allen Wheat completed his first four transactions that day. It had taken him just five months to build the business from scratch.

That month, CSFP employees learned that Hammersmith & Fulham, a London local government authority, was refusing to pay hundreds of millions of dollars it owed to several banks on seventy-two interest-rate swaps, claiming it had not been authorized to do them.[15] Essentially, the borough claimed that the swaps had been done for a trading purpose that was outside its authority, and that therefore the swaps were null and void. It was a valuable lesson for CSFP to learn at the start; it would be more careful than other dealers—especially those in the United States—to ensure that clients were authorized to do complex derivatives.

A few months later, CSFP obtained the approval of New York State banking regulators, so it could officially do business in New York. CSFP did four deals on its first day in New York, too, all of them clearly authorized.[16]

In the United States, the bank's AAA rating was especially important and was the first item CSFP mentioned in the press release it sent out when it opened in New York.[17] With this top credit rating, Allen Wheat could modify Bankers Trust's clever practices to generate even greater profits. The financial-market innovations that began in 1987 were about to take a few more twists and turns.

Credit ratings were central to the changes, although few financial-market participants understood why at the time. A decade later, credit ratings would be even more important, and would play a central role in the collapse of several companies, including Enron.

The two most prominent credit-rating agencies were Moody's Investors Services and Standard & Poor's Corp., known as S&P. Moody's had been in the business since 1909, when John Moody began publishing ratings of railroad bonds. S&P followed soon thereafter, and Fitch Investors Service—a distant third to Moody's and S&P—began rating bonds in 1924.

The agencies labored in obscurity until 1973, when regulators began tying legal rules to ratings. Because only Moody's, S&P, and Fitch were approved for regulatory purposes, those three agencies had a monopoly lock on the market.[18] Not surprisingly, it was a profitable business. Nearly every company with publicly traded bonds paid the rating agencies directly for the ratings. The typical cost of a rating ranged from $30,000 to $100,000. With thousands of companies needing ratings, business boomed. The legendary investor Warren Buffett invested in Moody's and touted its franchise. By 2002, Moody's would be worth more than Bear Stearns, a prominent investment bank.

As commentator Thomas Friedman put it in 1996, "There are two superpowers in the world today in my opinion. There's the United States and there's Moody's bond rating service. The United States can destroy you by dropping bombs, and Moody's can destroy you by downgrading your bonds. And believe me, it's not clear sometimes who's more powerful."[19]

Why were credit ratings so important? Again, the explanation related to legal rules. Since 1973, regulators had passed dozens of laws that depended on credit ratings, ranging from AAA to D, with BBB being the all-important *investment-grade* dividing line. By the time Allen Wheat arrived at First Boston, just about every major financial business was limited in some way based on these ratings.

In simple terms, a better rating meant better regulatory treatment. For example, certain mutual funds couldn't buy bonds rated below investment grade. Insurance companies had to set aside more capital for lower-rated bonds. Federal loan guarantees required a high rating. And so on.

During the 1980s, no one understood and profited from credit ratings more than Michael Milken and his investment bank, Drexel Burnham Lambert. When Milken was in business school (also at Wharton), he had noticed that bonds rated below the investment-grade level of BBB—now known as *junk bonds*—were undervalued relative to higher-rated bonds. The prices of bonds dropped sharply when the credit-rating agencies downgraded them to a level below BBB.

Building on work by previous scholars,[20] Milken concluded that by buying a portfolio of bonds rated below investment grade, an investor could increase returns without increasing risk. Even though a portfolio of sub-investment-grade bonds might include a few companies that defaulted on their debts, overall the cheap prices of those bonds more than made

WHEAT FIRST SECURITIES I 67

up for the risks. In other words, the sharp divide between investment-grade bonds and non-investment-grade bonds made no sense. To Milken, junk bonds were like $20 bills lying on the ground, and Drexel began trading them, earning huge profits both from holding sub-investment-grade bonds for its own account and from selling them to other investors who had become believers in "junk."

Unfortunately, Drexel became involved in various insider-trading schemes and other alleged violations of securities law, and its bond-trading business deteriorated. When Drexel filed for bankruptcy in February 1990—at exactly the same time Allen Wheat joined First Boston—a baton was passed. Drexel's collapse made credit ratings even more important, and it left a gaping hole in the market for sub-investment-grade bonds.

Like Bankers Trust, Drexel had been active in swaps. Now, banks—and their regulators—were worried about whether Drexel would default on payments owed on its swaps. Regulators and market participants began focusing more on the credit ratings of counterparties in the swap market. And the more they focused on credit ratings, the more important the ratings became.

By combining CSFP's AAA credit rating with the complex deals developed by Bankers Trust, Allen Wheat could create new products and sell them in previously untapped markets. CSFP designed the instruments, but they often were sold through First Boston, which had a more established and better-known sales force than Bankers Trust.

Allen Wheat's marketing pitches were transparently directed at Bankers Trust's derivatives business. One glossy brochure stated, "We solve problems for clients rather than push products on them. In fact, Credit Suisse FP's success can best be understood by focusing on this single underlying theme."

The pitches worked. CSFP earned numerous awards during this time, including "Swap House of the Year," "Options House of the Year," and "Best Derivatives House." Wheat hired more people in 1991, and took over a floor of First Boston's Park Avenue Plaza glass tower. CSFP developed new trades, which "solved problems" for clients, enabling them to make financial bets or hedge risks in increasingly sophisticated ways.

There were two major innovations at First Boston during the early 1990s. One involved *structured notes*—essentially, highly rated bonds whose payments were linked to the same types of formulas Bankers Trust had used in its complex swaps with Gibson Greetings and Procter & Gamble (plus a few new formulas CSFP invented). The other innovation related to *structured finance*—a class of deals in which financial assets were repackaged to obtain higher credit ratings. Within a decade, structured finance would become a trillion-dollar industry, ranging from legitimate deals that enabled institutions to transfer risk more efficiently, to more dubious transactions (including those later involved in the collapse of Enron).

First, CSFP began issuing and selling structured notes. Unlike a typical bond, which has a series of standard coupon payments and then a fixed principal repayment, a structured note's returns might vary wildly, based on different variables. In other words, the bond—or note—was structured so that its payouts were based on any conceivable financial instrument or index. One structured note was even linked to the number of victories by the Utah Jazz, a professional basketball team,[21] although more typical variables were interest rates or currencies. As Richard Deitz, head of structured fixed income at CSFP, put it, "The types of structures we can come up with are infinite."[22]

For example, the first page of CSFP's presentation to a new-associate training program in the early 1990s featured a structured note with a colossal 21 percent coupon and principal redemption leveraged twenty times. These numbers dwarfed those in the Gibson and P&G swaps, and the trades were even more complicated. Lest any new employees feel they could create pricing models for these trades on their own, the last page of CSFP's presentation stressed that it was "necessary to exercise a great deal of care in modeling random yield curve movements" in valuing the trades. The message: don't try this one on your own.

Given Allen Wheat's background in Asia, it was natural for CSFP to focus on structured notes linked to variables in Asian markets. For example, the bank sold huge numbers of what it called Thai Baht Basket-Linked Notes. The idea behind these notes was that the currency of Thailand, called the baht, had been fluctuating in a very narrow band; investors could profit by betting the baht would remain stable.

Although the central bank of Thailand would not admit to buying and selling baht to keep its value within a particular range, the traders at CSFP had determined that a *proxy basket* of three other currencies closely tracked how the central bank of Thailand managed its own currency. Specifically, they said a basket of 84 percent U.S. dollars, 10.15 percent

Japanese yen, and 5.85 percent Swiss francs had moved within a 3 percent range of the Thai baht's actual movements since 1986.

They then created a trade based on the proxy basket. Credit Suisse's New York branch issued the notes, which paid an attractive fixed coupon of 11.25 percent, more than triple the rate the bank typically would pay.

In return for the big coupon, investors took on the risk that Credit Suisse would not repay the full principal amount. Instead of a fixed principal repayment—as was typical for standard notes—the principal amount was linked to a formula based on the Thai baht; specifically, on the difference between the value of CSFP's proxy basket at the time the investor bought the bond and the value at maturity (typically, one year later).

In other words, if the Thai baht went down relative to the proxy basket, the investor would lose money. If the baht stayed in its historical range, the investor would earn huge returns. According to CSFP's research, this structured note had earned an average return of 15 percent since 1986, with the worst return being more than 9 percent. These returns were fantastic, given that most bond investors were earning less than half of that.

Still, the notes were peculiar. Why would investors buy a structured note—and pay a substantial fee to CSFP—instead of just borrowing to invest in Thailand directly? After all, an investor buying a Thai-baht-linked note was making precisely the same bet as an investor simply borrowing money to invest in Thailand. (Either way, the investment did well if the Thai baht remained steady and lost money if the baht devalued.) Why the fancy, AAA-rated, proxy-basket package?

The answer—again—related to legal rules and credit ratings. Just as Japanese insurers couldn't buy stocks, many investors were prohibited by law from investing in Thailand, where even government bonds had a low credit rating. Thailand was a risky place, and U.S. regulators had adopted rules that prevented many money managers from investing there. According to these rules, pension funds (to give but one example) weren't supposed to be speculating on the baht.

But even if a fund manager couldn't buy Thai-denominated investments, he *could* buy a note issued by a AAA-rated bank. What was wrong with a one-year note issued by Credit Suisse? It was a perfectly legal investment, and it would look safe to a regulator, a shareholder, or even a boss, who hopefully would not see the fine print describing how principal redemption was linked to the Thai-baht proxy basket. Thus, CSFP's

Thai Baht Basket-Linked Notes allowed regulated U.S. investors to play in Thailand, just as Bankers Trust's equity derivatives had allowed Japanese insurers to play in their own markets.

With trades like this one, Allen Wheat's optimism about CSFP was justified. The fees were comparable to those Bankers Trust charged for complex swaps. Credit Suisse's New York branch set up a borrowing program—called a *medium-term note facility*—to use in issuing these notes. Setting up the facility was like putting securities on the shelf. CSFP could then *take down* structured-note issues when it wanted, just as Bankers Trust had taken down its private placements.

How optimistic was Wheat? The size of the medium-term note facility for the Thai-basket notes—the maximum dollar value of notes that could be issued—was $1.5 billion. As long as the Thai baht remained steady, both CSFP and its investors would get rich, and no one else would need to know exactly how they had done it.

The idea of structured notes quietly spread throughout Wall Street during 1990. Twenty billion dollars' worth were sold in 1991, $30 billion the next year, and $50 billion the next.[23] By the end of 1993, every major bank sold structured notes. They were the rage among large institutional investors, and one of the hottest products among corporate and government treasurers.

Who bought these notes? The better question was, who *didn't* buy them? The list included major mutual funds, insurance companies, pension funds, and corporations. Many were less sophisticated than Gibson and P&G. State and local governments—even some school districts—bought the notes. One of the biggest buyers was the elderly treasurer of otherwise-conservative Orange County, California. The most common structured notes resembled the Bankers Trust swaps; essentially, they were hidden bets that interest rates would stay low.

Investment banks soon found that—with their meager, single-A credit rating—they could not compete with AAA-rated CSFP for structured note issues, or for related swaps. To get a higher rating, they set up derivatives subsidiaries with their own capital. In a typical deal, a bank created a subsidiary and gave it several hundred million dollars of seed capital. Then the subsidiary agreed to strict limits on what it was permitted to do. A bank promised not to do business on behalf of the subsidiary, or to intervene in its transactions. With these protections, the credit-rating agencies agreed to give subsidiaries much higher ratings than their parent banks, typically the highest rating of AAA. As business shifted to these special-

purpose subsidiaries, credit-rating agencies became even more important. One Merrill Lynch employee remarked, "We can't blow our noses
without getting approval from them."[24]

Other structured-note issuers included U.S. government-supported
agencies and well-known corporations. (The *issuers* were the institutions that were using the notes to borrow money; the *sellers* were the
banks that marketed the notes to their investors.) The Federal Home
Loan Bank was the 700-pound gorilla, issuing tens of billions of dollars
of structured notes.[25] Two government-sponsored mortgage agencies—
known as Fannie Mae and Freddie Mac—were big players, as were
quasi-governmental entities, including the World Bank. For example,
one of CSFP's very first deals in New York was a $252 million structured
note for Sallie Mae, the government-sponsored entity that makes student
loans.[26] By issuing structured notes, some of these agencies sometimes
borrowed at lower rates than even the U.S. Treasury, which wouldn't
soil its name by participating directly in these markets.

The most active corporate issuers of structured notes included new
financial subsidiaries of many industrial companies, such as General
Electric, IBM, and Toyota. DuPont Co. issued more than $1 billion of
structured notes during the early 1990s.[27] By issuing structured notes,
these companies could save a half percent or more in interest costs. The
companies didn't really care if the note payments were linked to a complex formula involving interest rates or currencies—or some other wild
bet—because the investment bank selling the structured notes always
agreed to hedge the issuer's risks with swaps, in the same way Bankers
Trust had agreed to hedge the Canadian bankers' risks in the Japanese
markets. Companies often preferred raising money through structured
notes instead of issuing stock or taking loans, both of which were typically more expensive.

Structured notes quickly transformed these issuer companies. Even as
early as 1991, 10 percent of GE Capital's borrowing consisted of structured notes. By 1993, almost half of GE Capital's medium-term-note program was in structured notes.[28] GE Capital was especially savvy about
credit ratings, adding a ratings *trigger*—stating that if a counterparty's
rating fell below a certain level, the swap was automatically unwound
and settled—to many of its deals, beginning in April 1992.[29] IBM and
Toyota had similar approaches. The big three U.S. car makers also were
involved, as were many insurance companies, especially American International Group.

Shareholders of these companies were largely oblivious to these new instruments, because the securities laws did not require disclosure. Moreover, the notes were issued by financial subsidiaries, not by the parent company, and disclosure rules applied primarily to the parent. As a result, many of the details of the financial subsidiaries of major corporations—GE, IBM, and others—were kept secret.

Likewise, the purchasers of structured notes—including many mutual funds, pension funds, and government-treasury departments—did not tell anyone about them. Public filings did not require descriptions, and fund managers certainly weren't talking.

The term *structured note*—ubiquitous in finance today—was not even mentioned in a major newspaper or business magazine during this period. The first listing in the general-news database of Lexis-Nexis, a computerized information service, was on April 27, 1992, in an article by Michael Liebowitz, of the specialty publication *Investment Dealers' Digest,* noting in passing that First Boston had hired Tom Bruch to become the firm's second structured-note trader. There were no substantive discussions of structured notes until well over a year later. The first reference to "structured note" in the *New York Times* was not until June 16, 1994; *BusinessWeek* on May 16, 1994; *Fortune* on November 29, 1993; and the *Wall Street Journal* on August 10, 1993. As a result, even a sophisticated, well-read investor following the markets during the early 1990s would not have heard of structured notes.

Although structured notes were very profitable for the banks at first, just as complex swaps had been, inevitably the business became more competitive and margins declined. To maintain their profit margins, bankers needed to invent new versions of the notes, new structures that could not easily be copied, with margins that would last.

CSFP liked to describe itself as solving problems for clients. However, a closer analysis reveals that CSFP was not so different from Bankers Trust in its approach to client relationships. Many of the "problems" CSFP was solving involved enabling clients to avoid regulation.

Bankers Trust had demonstrated that regulation-avoiding trades were not only very profitable—they had staying power. And as long as clients couldn't accurately value the trades and were using them to avoid legal rules, they would pay a premium. CSFP was about to take Bankers Trust's approach to a new level of complexity.

One of CSFP's most innovative trades was called a *Quanto*, a turbo-charged version of the structured notes the bank already had been marketing. A version of this trade was awarded "derivatives trade of the year" in a 1991 survey by *Institutional Investor* magazine. CSFP was widely credited with inventing the Quanto concept, which it first marketed to Japanese companies, although the concept grew from earlier deals Wheat did at Bankers Trust, and it resembled the swaps sold to Gibson Greetings and P&G.

In a Quanto, the investor received payments based on foreign interest rates, with the unique twist that all payments were in the investor's home currency. In other words, a U.S. investor could bet on European interest rates, but receive payments in U.S. dollars. In one typical deal, the Federal Home Loan Bank of Topeka, Kansas, issued $100 million of notes paying a coupon of twice U.S. LIBOR, minus British LIBOR plus 1.5 percent, all payable in U.S. dollars.[30]

This twist—putting all payments in one currency—looked simple enough. But in reality, it was unimaginably complex.

In most trades, the impact of the risk of different economic variables could be analyzed separately. An investor could first consider the effect of changes in interest rates, and then worry about currencies. Interest rates and currencies affected each other—they were correlated—but, in a typical trade, the correlation didn't matter. If the correlation didn't matter, it was safe to analyze the risks separately. For example, it was difficult to value Andy Krieger's currency options or Bankers Trust's structured swaps, but neither posed a correlation problem; the interest rate and currency risks of these trades were separated.

The Quanto's risks could not be separated, because—unlike the payoffs of the other trades—the payoffs of a Quanto depended on the correlation of interest rates and currencies. In simple terms, the amount to be converted at maturity into U.S. dollars (the currency variable) depended on the value of, say, British LIBOR (the interest rate variable). Interest rates and currency rates affected each other, not only in the real world, but also in the Quanto. They could not be separated.

At the time, correlation risk was new, and could not be hedged or traded directly. So banks had to come up with ways of pricing the risk on their own. Bankers Trust developed some techniques; CSFP mastered them. The techniques were sufficiently complex that most clients had no hope of accurately evaluating Quantos. Worse, traditional risk measures understated the amount of risk in correlation-based trades, so that even a sophisticated client—trained in the state of the art of risk analysis at the time—might underestimate the risk of a Quanto.[31]

Investors weren't likely to obtain much comfort by phoning other banks, as they might have for other structured trades, because many banks didn't understand correlation risk any better. In 1991, the banks selling Quantos disagreed so much about what the trades were worth that their quoted prices differed by as much as half a percent, a huge amount. By late 1993, the differences had narrowed to one-fifth of that, but still were substantial.[32] During this period, it took a typical bank an entire weekend to produce a report assessing correlation risk. (A decade later, relatively inexpensive software programs could calculate these risks almost instantaneously.)

Investors didn't seem bothered by correlation risk, and they bought Quantos in droves. Either they were oblivious to the fact that their investments now depended on correlations of various interest rates and currencies, or they didn't care. CSFP sold over 100 Quanto swaps in 1990 and 1991, more than any other bank.

The Quanto was the perfect trade for Japan. Many companies believed interest rates outside Japan would fall, but wanted their investments denominated in Japanese yen. Similarly, Quantos also fit U.S. investors who sought higher yields, but did not want to receive a currency other than U.S. dollars.

Still, it seemed odd that investors would be so eager to buy Quantos, especially when they were unable to assess correlation risk. If currency rates moved the wrong way, the investor still would lose money; it wouldn't help that the money paid in a Quanto was in U.S. dollars instead of foreign currency. Moreover, investors who wanted to bet on foreign interest rates could easily buy foreign bonds and exchange whatever foreign currency they received at maturity, thereby avoiding correlation risk. Yet they wanted Quantos anyway. Why?

The answer: legal rules, yet again. The true driving force behind Quantos was that they allowed investors who, by law, were not permitted to speculate in a particular currency, to do so indirectly, without being noticed. Many investors—especially U.S. insurance companies, major clients of CSFP—could not buy large amounts of non–U.S. dollar instruments. But they arguably could buy as many Quantos as they wanted, because their payments were denominated in U.S. dollars.

James M. Mahoney, writing in the *Federal Reserve Bank of New York Economic Policy Review,* put the issue clearly:

Some individuals and institutions use derivative securities to circumvent (sometimes self-imposed) restrictions on holdings. For instance, the investment committee of a pension fund or insurance company may require all investments to be denominated in the domestic currency. While this rule would prohibit direct foreign capital market holdings, the managers of these investments could gain exposure to foreign debt or equity markets through correlation products such as diff swaps or quanto swaps.[33]

("Diff swaps" were based on the difference between two interest rates; P&G's second swap with Bankers Trust—the one based on U.S. and German interest rates—was a typical example.)

Eventually, the Quanto market, too, became competitive. Banks did billions of dollars of such trades. The U.S. government–supported agencies also got involved, as issuers. Pension funds, insurance companies, and other regulated institutional investors bought Quantos, and—as with other structured notes—did not disclose the risks. Investors had no way of knowing whether they owned companies that speculated using Quantos or similar instruments.

A fund manager considering Quantos faced enormous temptation. Consider this deal: in January 1992, the Student Loan Marketing Association sold $150 million of three-year notes with a Quanto-style interest rate. The rate was twice the Swiss franc version of LIBOR minus twice the U.S. version of LIBOR. As was typical of a Quanto, the interest rates were in different currencies, but payments would be only in U.S. dollars.[34]

Why would a fund manager be tempted to buy this structured note? The first interest rate was set at 7.6 percent, an incredible teaser, given that U.S. interest rates were very low and European interest rates were falling. The note had a three-year maturity; but, for a fund manager focused on the upcoming year, the first-year return would outperform just about any other fund (perhaps except funds that were buying similar notes). It wasn't clear what would happen in years two and three. But, by then, the fund manager would have a stellar reputation and likely would have opportunities to leave for other firms.

Fund managers loaded up. And when they tired of correlation trades based on European currencies—which were converging as part of the planned move to a single currency—they began doing trades based on more exotic interest rates and currencies, including those of Hungary, Mexico, and Brazil. No computer program could model the correlation risks in those markets.

. . .

The second major innovation at CSFP—after structured notes such as Quantos—involved structured finance, the repackaging of financial assets to reallocate risks and obtain higher credit ratings. Structured finance generated great benefits for many institutions, enabling banks to repackage and sell off their exposure to home mortgages, credit-card loans, and other assets. Before the mid-1980s, companies had done *factoring* transactions, in which they sold their receivables—rights to payments owed by other parties. Examples included uncollected debts or the rights to various lease payments. Structured finance was simply a modern version of factoring.

Although economists applauded structured finance, the practice was—at its core—contrary to economic theory. Why would investors pay more for repackaged receivables than the amount the companies holding those receivables thought they were worth? Did investors really prize these new financial assets so much that they would value them more highly than the company that was owed the money, which invariably was in a better position to manage the risks associated with the loan? Economists long had argued that the lowest-cost manager of risk would (and should) bear it.[35] Why would an individual investor buy the rights to car-lease payments from General Motors, when General Motors obviously was in a much better position to be sure that the people leasing cars continued to pay? According to economic theory, if General Motors was in a position to extract the greatest value from leases, it would (and should) hold and monitor them.

Yet investors, nevertheless, began buying deals that enabled them to take on the risks associated with receivables owed to other companies. The companies were happy to rid themselves of the risks, and investors got a new set of investments, potentially with lower risk and higher returns than the available alternatives, such as government bonds. For example, banks began issuing securities backed by auto loans or credit-card payments. Leasing companies sold their risks to investors. The deals were complex, but essentially they involved transferring the rights to payments to a newly created company or trust, which issued bonds backed by the rights. First Boston was a leader in these markets, and did the first deal with a financial affiliate of a car manufacturer, General Motors Acceptance Corporation (GMAC), in 1985.[36] Volvo later did a

$300 million lease deal with First Boston.[37] Sperry Lease Finance Corp. sold securities backed by a portfolio of equipment leases.[38] And so forth.

Instead of buying bonds, investors could now buy shares of a trust backed by credit-card payments. A bank would create the trust, and payments by people who held that bank's credit cards would flow into the trust, instead of to the bank. The legal documents establishing the trust provided for a cushion of credit-card payments, in case people defaulted or delayed payment for several months. Unlike the payments of a bond, which were backed by the issuer of the bond, the payments of the trust were backed only by the trust's assets. In addition, investors in the trust were protected from the bank's financial problems: even if the bank filed for bankruptcy protection, the trust's assets would be secure. Because the trust was isolated from the bank, it was more attractive to investors.

One of the main reasons investors rushed to buy these new structured-finance instruments was that the trusts typically received very high credit ratings. For example, GMAC's bonds were rated in the second highest category by Moody's and S&P. That meant most institutional investors could buy them, and because the bonds paid a higher return than comparably rated investments, most institutional investors *wanted* to buy them. They were a new form of investment with a high return, and the demand for these instruments outweighed the fact that investors were not in a good position to monitor the various obligations. Even if General Motors was in the best position to ensure that car leases were repaid, the investors perceived greater value from a new, highly rated investment than the benefit of having General Motors monitor the leases.

The process of transferring receivables to a new company and issuing new bonds became known as *securitization,* which became a major part of the structured-finance industry. After 1985, the race was on to securitize every asset bankers could find.

First Boston had entered this market years before Allen Wheat arrived. The investment bank securitized credit-card payments, equipment-lease payments, auto loans, commercial mortgages, and other instruments. Other banks also did these deals, which became more exotic over time. Eventually, banks would securitize every contractual right imaginable, from repackaged Latin American debt to David Bowie's rights to royalty payments from his rock albums.

One of the most significant innovations in structured finance was a deal called the *Collateralized Bond Obligation,* or CBO. CBOs are one of the threads that run through the past fifteen years of financial markets, ranging from Michael Milken to First Boston to Enron and WorldCom. CBOs would mutate into various types of *credit derivatives*—financial instruments tied to the creditworthiness of companies—which would play an important role in the aftermath of the collapse of numerous companies in 2001 and 2002. Although it wasn't apparent during the early 1990s, even the relatively primitive CBO deals developed at First Boston posed serious regulatory questions, especially related to accounting.

In simple terms, here is how a CBO works. A bank transfers a portfolio of junk bonds to a *Special Purpose Entity*, typically a newly created company, partnership, or trust domiciled in a balmy tax haven, such as the Cayman Islands. This entity then issues several securities, backed by the bonds, effectively splitting the junk bonds into pieces. Investors (hopefully) buy the pieces.

In a simple CBO, there were three pieces, divided according to risk, and payments on the bonds held by the SPE flowed to the various pieces in order of seniority, just as credit-card payments had flowed to investors in the GMAC deal. The *senior* piece was paid first, and had a yield of, say, one percent more than government bonds. Once the senior piece had been paid in full, the *mezzanine* piece would be paid next, and had a yield of perhaps three percent more than government bonds. The bottom piece would be paid last—after both the senior and mezzanine pieces were paid in full—and received whatever was left, an unspecified yield that would be very high if the junk bonds didn't default, but could be zero if they did.

The top two pieces were easy to sell, because the rating agencies gave them favorable ratings. Typically, the senior piece would receive one of the very top ratings; the mezzanine piece would receive a lower, but still respectable, investment-grade rating. These pieces had higher yields than any comparably rated investment, so fund managers who could only buy highly rated bonds could make more buying CBO senior pieces than in almost any other way.

The lowest-rated piece was the most difficult to sell. Sometimes, the owner of the junk bonds would keep this *junior* piece. But more often, an investment bank would need to sell it. This was where First Boston's sales force stepped in. If a salesman could sell a junior piece, that sale would drive a huge CBO deal, which was very profitable for the bank. One deal typically generated several million dollars in fees.

CBOs were the brainchild of Fred Carr, the head of an insurance company called First Executive Corp., and one of Michael Milken's biggest customers during the 1980s. CBOs were based on the same logic Milken had applied to the junk-bond market: low-rated bonds outperformed less risky bonds, in part because of the legal rules that made low-rated bonds less attractive, and therefore cheaper.

In a CBO, the sum of the pieces was more than the whole, like a nuclear reaction that released energy by splitting apart atoms. Investors were willing to pay more for the three pieces separately than they would pay for the underlying junk bonds on their own. The credit ratings "added value" to the bonds, by enabling institutional investors to buy pieces of them, which they otherwise could not have done. CBOs were a kind of high-finance fission: top credit ratings made the two safest pieces so attractive that a bank could unlock hidden value in junk bonds simply by dividing them.

The first CBO was TriCapital Ltd., a $420 million deal sold in July 1988. There were about $900 million of CBOs in 1988, and almost $3 billion in 1989.[39] Notwithstanding the bad press junk bonds had been getting, analysts from all three of the credit-rating agencies began pushing CBOs. They were very profitable for the rating agencies, which received fees for rating the various pieces.

Fred Carr did the most ingenious CBO of all in 1989. When regulators began requiring First Executive to keep financial reserves to back all of its bonds, Carr responded by converting his junk bonds into CBOs. But instead of selling the pieces for more than the bonds' value, First Executive kept *all* of the pieces.

Why? Once the top two pieces were highly rated, Carr could argue that First Executive no longer needed to keep financial reserves to back them. If only the most junior piece appeared to be risky, only that piece required full reserves. It was as if the owner of a three-story house had claimed it was really three pieces with only the ground floor subject to property tax. Yet the regulators bought the argument, and Carr saved First Executive $110 million of reserves.[40]

Of course, First Executive denied that the purpose was to avoid regulatory requirements. It was doing CBOs simply because the market valued the pieces more highly than the whole. But that begged the question: should the bonds really be worth more packaged in a CBO than they were worth on their own?

Fred Carr's idea spread to Thomas Spiegel, the founder of Columbia Savings & Loan, a client of both Michael Milken and First Boston.

Columbia, based in Beverly Hills, held billions of dollars of junk bonds. When Spiegel became embroiled in the savings-and-loan fiasco of the late 1980s, he resigned, and began working with First Boston on a CBO of Columbia's junk bonds.[41] (Meanwhile, Spiegel was delighted when a federal jury in Los Angeles acquitted him—he even hugged his attorneys.)

First Boston gained expertise on this deal, and then began setting up more CBOs based on a wide range of financial assets, including Brady bonds—the restructured debt of several Latin American countries. CBOs were good for First Boston, not only because they generated fees, but also because the bank made money buying and selling the junk bonds that went into them. In 1990, First Boston raised $255 million for a CBO called Delaware Management Co., and used the proceeds to buy junk bonds, buoying the market.[42]

Not surprisingly, some CBOs didn't do well, especially during 1990. After several of the fifty junk bonds held by one deal, CBC Holdings, either defaulted or were downgraded, Moody's announced it was considering a possible downgrade.[43] But the rating agencies were reluctant to downgrade these deals, because the consequences were so dire. For CBC Holdings alone, $200 million of bonds carried high Moody's ratings, and if Moody's downgraded the bonds too much—and investors had to sell them—the CBO and junk-bond markets might enter a death spiral. (In 2002, several corporate defaults would lead to just such risks; more on that in Chapter 11.)

With the various types of structured-finance deals, a trend began of companies using Special Purpose Entities to hide risks. From an accounting perspective, the key question was whether a company that owned particular financial assets needed to disclose those assets in its financial statements even after it transferred them to an SPE. Just as derivatives dealers had argued that swaps should not be included on their balance sheets, financial companies began arguing that their interests in SPEs did not need to be disclosed.

The Financial Accounting Standards Board began debating the SPE question during the late 1980s. The issue was controversial and was referred to the group's Emerging Issues Task Force, which decided in 1990 that if an outside investor made a substantial investment in, and controlled, the SPE, then the other assets and liabilities of the SPE did not need to be included on a firm's balance sheet. In 1991, the acting chief accountant of the SEC, concerned that companies might abuse this accounting standard, wrote a letter saying the outside investment had to be at least three percent.

The initial substantive residual equity investment should be comparable to that expected for a substantive business involved in similar [leasing] transactions with similar risks and rewards. The SEC staff understands from discussions with Working Group members that those members believe that three percent is the minimum acceptable investment. The SEC staff believes a greater investment may be necessary depending on the facts and circumstances, including the credit risk associated with the lessee and the market risk factors associated with the leased property.

This letter—which came to be known as the *three-percent rule*—stuck like glue, even though it wasn't a rule at all, and some securities regulators had opposed it at the time. Ultimately, companies would do mind-boggling numbers of structured deals—trillions of dollars in all—assuming that if they found an outside investor to buy three percent, they could keep the details off their balance sheets. The deals ranged from basic structured-finance transactions (credit-card and car-loan deals) to CBOs to more complex off-balance-sheet partnership structures, including the infamous deals at Enron. As more companies relied on the three-percent rule, it became more difficult to change it.

In January 1992, E. Gerald Corrigan, president of the New York Federal Reserve Bank, expressed concern about these deals in a closely followed speech: "If this sounds like a warning, that is because it is. The growth and complexity of off-balance sheet activities and the nature of the credit, price, and settlement risk they entail should give us all cause for concern." Wheat pooh-poohed Corrigan's remarks at a Paris conference of derivatives dealers, and instead warned of a "credit gridlock," in which regulated dealers would fill up all of their credit lines and find themselves unable to transact, unless they could do substantial off-balance-sheet financing.[44] He argued that regulations needed to be loosened, not strengthened.

In fall 1993, Allen Wheat took over as president and chief operating officer of CS First Boston. As one of the firm's senior bankers put it at the time, "I think this is now really Wheat's baby. We'll either fly with Wheat or we'll go down with Wheat."[45]

Wheat flew to London to give a 45-minute address to the firm's management committee. According to one former colleague, "He told us that he had accepted the job, because he saw it as a great way to vastly increase his personal wealth and that he would make us all incredibly rich. He never once mentioned the clients."[46]

Perhaps he should have. The clients' fees already had made Wheat incredibly rich. CSFP had earned about $125 million per year in 1991 and 1992.[47] The London bank's return on equity was reported to be 40 percent, double that of Bankers Trust, then the most profitable bank in the United States.[48] CSFP employees reportedly earned twice as much as their counterparts at other banks, and by 1992 there were nearly 500 of them.[49] Wheat made $9 million a year, leading many competitors to rebrand First Boston as Wheat First Securities, the name of a small regional brokerage firm headquartered in Richmond, Virginia.

But a chill wind blew through the firm. Infighting continued and morale ebbed. Even in good years, employees reportedly were tearing up million-dollar bonus checks and tossing the confetti in their bosses' faces.[50] Wheat didn't seem optimistic that the firm's culture would change anytime soon. After his promotion, he compared First Boston to a patient emerging from heart surgery who "then gets up and tries to run a marathon."[51]

Wheat's inner circle was small and the key positions were held by former Bankers Trust employees.[52] Wheat maintained only superficial relationships with outsiders, many of whom felt jilted, especially around bonus time. One former colleague said, "He appears to be a nice guy. You talk to him, joke with him and feel close to him. Then he blows you away." Wheat wasn't sympathetic about employee bonus complaints. He told an interviewer, "At bonus time, I look at people and think, 'Why are you upset?' They can't really answer. They constantly look at the next guy and say, 'I am better than him, I am worth more than him.'"[53]

In 1994, CSFP made $240 million in profits, whereas the entirety of First Boston—with thousands of employees—made just $155 million.[54] Wheat was underwhelmed by the riffraff outside of CSFP. That year, First Boston made a controversial decision not to give many of its employees any bonus at all, even though they had worked for the entire year. The bank fired hundreds of employees and asked departing personnel to sign a sweeping release that barred them from disclosing confidential or proprietary information "to anyone," including their own lawyers.[55]

Wheat's seeming disdain for some employees was consistent with his overall view that the "skills" of most investment bankers were vastly overvalued. Wheat frequently derided the benefits of financial sophistication, noting at one point that "it has tended to be the very sophisticated guys in very sophisticated instruments who have been burned."[56] A few years later, Wheat would finally bare his soul, in a candid interview with Helen Dunne of the *Daily Telegraph:* "OK. If I am being honest with you then yes, let's whisper it, but the truth of the matter is that all of us are over-paid. There is nothing magical about what we do. Anybody can do it."[57]

Chris Goekjian, one of Wheat's inner circle from Bankers Trust, described him as "looking for arbitrage in the widest sense of the word. He responds to inefficiencies in the market by responding to client needs."[58] Clients valued Wheat's approach to structured notes, Quantos, structured finance, and other derivatives, because CSFP enabled them to place bets they otherwise could not have made, thereby creating new products to profit from limits in the markets.

But there wasn't as much magic at First Boston and some other banks, which were limited by their lack of vision and—believe it or not—by their managers' relatively conservative approaches. In contrast, at Salomon Brothers, another investment bank, there were no limits, and one enigmatic trader approached the recent wave of financial innovation from a radically different perspective. Whereas Wheat profited from arbitrage by selling risk to clients, this unobtrusive man exploited the risks on his own. His small group of traders bet more than anyone else and they made a lot more, too. Their bosses at Salomon gave them absolute freedom and virtually unlimited capital, and their performance was—well—magical. The man's name was John Meriwether and his traders were known as the Arbitrage Group. For many years, they were the highest-paid people on Wall Street.

UNRECONCILED BALANCES

John Meriwether could have been Andy Krieger's older brother. They were similar in appearance, with floppy hair and wiry builds. Meriwether was a superb golfer and won a scholarship to Northwestern University; Krieger played professional tennis. Their first jobs out of business school were at the same firm—Salomon Brothers. At Salomon, they sat just two seats apart.

Meriwether's father was an accountant, like Krieger's.[1] Both worked during business school at a Chicago financial firm. For business school, Meriwether attended the University of Chicago, not Wharton, but that was simply because Meriwether, like Krieger, chose to attend a school close to home. If Meriwether had grown up in Philadelphia, not on Chicago's South Side, he likely would have attended Wharton, too.

But in business, the similarities ended. Krieger lasted barely a few years at Salomon and Bankers Trust, and ran a modest, if profitable, trading operation after that. Meriwether, for the better part of two decades at Salomon, was arguably the best performing trader in the world.

Meriwether joined Salomon Brothers in 1973, twelve years before Krieger, the same year Black, Scholes, and Merton published their famous options-valuation formulas. By 1977, Meriwether had created a small team at Salomon called the Domestic Fixed Income Arbitrage Group, known as just the Arbitrage Group.

During the next several years, Meriwether and his group of about a dozen other traders were responsible for much of Salomon's bottom line. In 1981, the Arbitrage Group made $100 million, one-third of Salomon's profit.[2] By the late 1980s, Meriwether's group was consistently making more than half a billion dollars a year.[3]

Of course, the Arbitrage Group was only a small part of a growing and diversified, full-service Wall Street firm. Like Bankers Trust and CSFP, Salomon sold equity derivatives in Japan and structured notes in the United States. It traded long-maturity options and pitched Collateralized Bond Obligations. It underwrote securities and advised on mergers and acquisitions. It even set up a derivatives subsidiary to obtain a higher credit rating. But in terms of trading profit, the focus of the firm was the Arbitrage Group, and the most important trader at Salomon Brothers from 1977 until the day he left was John Meriwether.

In early 1990, at about the same time Allen Wheat was leaving Bankers Trust for CSFP, the executive committee of Salomon Brothers was meeting to discuss bonuses for the year. Committee members did not know that Meriwether secretly had persuaded Salomon's chairman, John Gutfreund—who had been dubbed the "King of Wall Street" in a *Business Week* cover story—to set aside 15 percent of the Arbitrage Group's profits as bonuses. The committee members were paging through a document listing Gutfreund's recommended compensation for each group, as they did every year at bonus time.

When they turned to the Arbitrage Group's page, they were stunned. It listed bonuses ranging from $3 million at the *low* end to $23 million for Lawrence Hilibrand, who had a Ph.D. from the Massachusetts Institute of Technology and was one of the most mathematically astute and aggressive traders in the group. (Hilibrand was the trader who sat next to Andy Krieger a few years earlier, before Krieger left Salomon for Bankers Trust.) Meriwether, who by this time was the number-three person at Salomon, was to receive $10 million. The bonuses would dwarf the money anyone previously had made at any Wall Street firm. By comparison, Gutfreund, Salomon's chairman, would be paid a mere $2.3 million,[4] exactly one-tenth of what Hilibrand would make.

The fact that Meriwether had secretly negotiated such lucrative bonuses enraged many bankers at Salomon, especially young Paul Mozer, who had been in the Arbitrage Group until Meriwether asked him to leave to head government bond trading in 1988.[5] Meriwether remained Mozer's boss, and they kept a close relationship, but Meriwether had not included Mozer in the secret bonus deal. Mozer was irate, and realized that he was now on his own. For him to compete with Lawrence Hilibrand, he would have to find a new and spectacular way to make money trading government bonds.

Mozer wasn't the only one who resented the special treatment for the Arbitrage Group. A selfish culture was spreading throughout Salomon, along with word about the 1990 bonuses. Chairman Gutfreund announced that the Arbitrage Group's deal was a model for the rest of the firm, and that compensation would be tied more directly to profits. One executive recalled, "After that, it was every man for himself."[6]

Like Bankers Trust and CSFP, Salomon developed new products and practices in a rapidly evolving, unmanageable, and unregulated marketplace. Whereas Bankers Trust developed over-the-counter options and complex swaps, and CSFP created structured notes and Collateralized Bond Obligations, Salomon was a pioneer in complex arbitrage strategies and mortgage instruments. Beginning in the mid-1980s, Salomon's Arbitrage Group invented new ways of buying low and selling high, supposedly with little or no risk.

A close examination of Salomon's practices from the mid-1980s until 1994 reveals that the firm was completely out of control. Paul Mozer was engaged in a hugely profitable scheme to rig the government's billion-dollar Treasury-bond auctions. Salomon's blunders in valuing its own derivatives made Bankers Trust's mistakes look like rounding errors. Salomon's mortgage inventions led to huge losses, at Salomon and elsewhere. Chairman John Gutfreund's only control over John Meriwether was an occasional, "If this doesn't work, you're fired."[7] Meriwether had a modicum of control over his subordinates, but rarely exercised it. When one trader asked Meriwether for permission to double the size of a losing mortgage trade, Meriwether waved away the details, saying, "My trade was when I hired you."[8]

Meriwether's Arbitrage Group consistently made money from 1977 until the early 1990s, when the group totally dominated Salomon, generating 87 percent of the firm's profits.[9] In 1991, Meriwether was forced to resign from Salomon—along with chairman John Gutfreund—for failing to supervise Paul Mozer's activities in Treasury-bond auctions. But Meriwether's traders continued to prosper. In 1991 and 1992, the Arbitrage Group made over a billion dollars a year,[10] more than the entire profits of many Wall Street banks. A few years later, Meriwether would persuade the traders to join him at a new firm, called Long-Term Capital Management, where they would carry on the Arbitrage Group's legacy.

. . .

John Meriwether attended the University of Chicago in the early 1970s, just as efficient-market theory was taking over the study of financial markets. So-called *Chicago School* economists were almost religious in their belief that markets were efficient. (The economist in the joke about the $20 bill was always from the University of Chicago.) The Chicago faculty included Eugene Fama, whose empirical research corroborated efficient-market theory, and Merton Miller, who argued that financial innovation was driven by a desire to reduce regulatory costs.

Miller had the greatest impact on Meriwether, with his arguments that economically equivalent financial assets should have the same value. Financial economists following Miller took his argument a step further, concluding not only that similar assets *should* have the same value, but that they *would* have the same value. This conclusion was the proposition known generally as the Law of One Price.

Meriwether accepted Miller's premise, but rejected the conclusion. Sure, markets *should* be efficient. Everyone knew, for example, that if gasoline at one station was too expensive, people would buy cheaper gas at the station next door. But when Meriwether began working at Salomon, he found that many markets were not even close to efficient. Similar assets had radically different values, and it seemed to stay that way for long periods of time. People were foolishly buying the expensive gasoline, and continuing to do so for months and months. Of course, similar assets *should* be worth similar amounts. But they were not.

When Meriwether found such inefficiencies, he simply bought the cheap asset, sold the expensive one, and waited for the values to converge. They almost always did. This was proof that the University of Chicago economists had reached the wrong conclusion. They had assumed that someone would be in the markets buying the cheap assets and selling the expensive ones. But where was that someone? It seemed incredible, but there were $20 bills lying around all over the place. All Meriwether and his traders had to do was reach down and pick them up.

Traders at Bankers Trust and CSFP had learned that arbitrage opportunities didn't last long. Charlie Sanford and Allen Wheat had struggled to reinvent themselves every year, finding new ways to profit from financial innovation. The only profits that persisted for very long were those due to legal rules (as in the Japanese insurance companies buying equity derivatives) or sophistication gaps between the buyer and seller (as in the complex deals Gibson Greetings, P&G, and others bought). Other than these two situations, mispricings disappeared quickly.

Meriwether understood this experience, and his traders exploited legal rules and sophistication gaps beautifully. The conventional wisdom about Meriwether's success is that he and his traders took advantage of market inefficiencies created by imbalances in the supply and demand for particular financial assets. In the beginning, this was true. But over time, Meriwether and his traders increasingly profited by exploiting legal rules and by taking advantage of less sophisticated clients. The more they did so, the more profitable their strategies became.

Most of Meriwether's trading strategies have remained a secret, even though the leading financial journalists of the past decade—including Michael Lewis, Roger Lowenstein, and Martin Mayer—have covered Meriwether and Salomon in great detail. All of the major business magazines and newspapers have had lengthy front-page stories about Meriwether at some point, and Meriwether and his traders have been the topic of several books. But even after years under the microscope, the details of the trading strategies are a mystery. Meriwether wanted it this way: he swore his traders to secrecy, fearing that if anyone discovered the strategies, profits would disappear.

Here, briefly, is what is known. In 1977, Meriwether's arbitrage strategies were simple. For example, he discovered that Treasury-bond futures—contracts that had just begun trading on exchanges in Chicago—were economically similar to Treasury bonds, but frequently had very different values. Meriwether bought whichever was cheaper, and sold whichever was more expensive. He made money, but—not surprisingly—these price differences didn't last long.

Meriwether also found inefficiencies among Treasury bonds of different maturities. The U.S. Treasury paid different rates on its bonds, depending on their maturity, just as a homeowner typically paid different rates for a 30-year mortgage compared to a 5-year mortgage. For example, long-term Treasury bonds would have a high yield if investors expected inflation. Short-term bonds would have a low yield if the Federal Reserve was keeping interest rates low. In such a situation, which was common, the graph of the yields for different bonds compared to their maturities—called a *yield curve*[11]—would slope upward from left to right.

Meriwether noticed that this yield curve was not smooth. There were kinks, where one bond had a higher yield than a bond of nearby maturity. Where there were kinks, there were opportunities for arbitrage. As with futures, Meriwether could profit by buying the cheap bond and selling the expensive one. Meriwether made money, but when others discovered the strategy, the kinks—and the arbitrage opportunities—disappeared.

The example most frequently given of Meriwether's approach was something called the *on-the-run/off-the-run* Treasury-bond trade. The idea was that at certain times investors flocked to newly issued on-the-run Treasury bonds with a 30-year maturity, ignoring other off-the-run long-term bonds that the Treasury previously had issued, including those with a similar maturity of, say, 29¾ years. Meriwether (and many others) observed that 30-year bonds were more expensive than 29¾-year bonds, a price difference that made no sense, given the bonds' similarities. Still, some clients—particularly Japanese investors—stubbornly refused to buy anything but the most recently issued government bonds. Meriwether bought the cheap bonds, sold the expensive bonds, and waited. As the bonds aged, their prices converged, and Meriwether unwound his positions at a profit.

The on-the-run/off-the-run trade was easy to do. It wasn't complicated, and it didn't even require a computer. Traders at many investment banks made this bet, and although Meriwether was widely credited with doing the trade in substantial size, he didn't discover it. In fact, the on-the-run/off-the-run trade has been very common during the past two decades, and Meriwether wasn't even the first person to do the trade at Salomon.[12]

Meriwether's strategies became more sophisticated in 1984, when he met Eric Rosenfeld, then a professor at the Harvard Business School. In his study of options, Rosenfeld had discovered some flaws in the assumptions of the Black-Scholes option-pricing model, which traders at both Bankers Trust and CSFP had used. For example, the model assumed the volatility of underlying financial assets was constant. It also assumed there were no costs of transacting and no market discontinuities (in other words, no *kinks*). Most important, it assumed that the distribution of returns on assets was bell-shaped, like the normal distribution of grades in the courses Rosenfeld taught. This key assumption—the gospel among most financial economists—was the source of the *random walk* hypothesis, which said that the movements of the market up and down were essentially random.

However, to anyone with experience in the options markets, these assumptions were demonstrably false. Volatility changed over time, options were expensive to buy and sell, and there were kinks throughout the markets, where the supply and demand of particular options were unbalanced. Moreover, returns were not normally distributed; there were periods of manias and dramatic crashes, which did not fit a bell-shaped curve. Asset prices followed a random walk some of the time, but not all of the time.

Eventually, financial economists would abandon these assumptions and seek more-nuanced models of price behavior. In 2000, even Burton Malkiel, the well-respected economist and author of *A Random Walk Down Wall Street,* would conclude in a revised edition of his book that "More recent work, however, indicated that the random-walk model does not strictly hold."[13] But during the late 1980s and early 1990s, economists were not focused on assumptions, and traders using flawed models routinely misvalued options.

Meriwether recognized that options were more complicated than futures. If Salomon could approach options pricing in a more sophisticated way than its competitors, it might obtain a sustainable advantage. He seized the opportunity by hiring Rosenfeld and several other academics who understood the flawed assumptions of the models. He even brought on Myron Scholes and Robert Merton as consultants. Scholes developed new models, and helped to create Salomon's AAA-rated derivatives subsidiary, known as Salomon Swapco.[14] Merton, who had been Rosenfeld's mentor, offered big-picture advice about options arbitrage.

Meriwether also hired Victor Haghani, Gregory Hawkins, and Larry Hilibrand (the aggressive trader who would receive a $23 million bonus in 1990). These three H's became the Arbitrage Group's most profitable traders. Haghani had a master's degree in finance from the London School of Economics and found arbitrage opportunities in Japan, especially in convertible bonds. (Haghani had done research for Andy Krieger when Krieger was trading currency options at Salomon a few years earlier.) The other two were Ph.D.s from MIT:[15] Hawkins was an expert in mortgages (more about them later); Hilibrand was an expert in everything. These were the people whose 1990 bonuses would enrage Mozer and other employees outside the Arbitrage Group; all of these people were closely bound to Meriwether, and they became a family.

Meriwether's "quants" put the nerds of Bankers Trust to shame. He gave them a special place in the middle of the trading floor at Salomon, where they stood like geeks in the middle of a high school party. This group of traders was known as the best finance faculty in the world.

When currency options were introduced, Meriwether's group began trading them at the same time Andy Krieger was trading currency options at Bankers Trust. Like Krieger, Meriwether's traders looked for options that, according to the group's computer models, were mispriced relative to economically equivalent portfolios. As options traders at other firms were using sledgehammers to bludgeon each other with one-way directional bets and misdirection strategies, Meriwether and Rosenfeld were using a scalpel to dissect minor mispricings in dozens of options markets throughout the world.

The Arbitrage Group designed the first pricing systems using a high-speed network of personal computers, while other traders at Salomon were stuck waiting in line to use the firm's one, relatively slow, mainframe.[16] Meriwether set up trading desks in London and Tokyo with similar analytical firepower, to exploit opportunities in options markets abroad.[17]

Victor Haghani found arbitrage opportunities in the Japanese convertible bond market. The owner of a convertible bond has the option to convert the bond into a specified number of shares of stock, and effectively has the choice between two investments—bond or stock—depending on the price of the stock. In other words, a convertible bond can be thought of as two investments: a bond plus an option to buy stock. When a company's stock price is low, a convertible bond is really just a plain-vanilla bond with fixed interest payments; the stock-option component has little or no value. But as the stock price rises, the stock-option component of the convertible bond becomes more valuable. When the stock price is high enough, the holder of the convertible bond is better off *converting* the bond into shares. At that point, the bond portion of the convertible bond evaporates, and the holder simply owns stock.

The Japanese government restricted the amount of stock companies could issue, in an attempt to limit supply and keep share prices high. There were no similar restrictions on issuing convertible bonds. However, few investors were buying Japanese convertible bonds—in part because they didn't like buying both the bond and stock components—and they were relatively cheap. That meant the options embedded in the bonds also were cheap—cheaper than they should have been in an efficient market. The legal rules restricting stock issuance in Japan, and the reluctance of investors to buy convertible bonds, had created an arbitrage opportunity. If Haghani could somehow buy just the cheap stock-option component of the convertible bonds and then sell similar stock options to investors at a higher price, he could make virtually risk-free profits.

Haghani bought the convertible bonds, so that he effectively owned a bond plus a stock option. He then eliminated the interest-rate risks associated with the bond component of the convertible bonds, using interest-rate swaps, so that he remained exposed only to the stock-option component of the convertible bond. Then, in the over-the-counter market, Haghani sold new stock options to investors. These new stock options were designed to mimic the risk that Haghani faced in the stock-option component of the convertible bond. In other words, Haghani would simply pass along his remaining risks to investors. The beauty of this deal was that, because the convertible bonds were cheap, Haghani could buy the stock-option component for less than investors were willing to pay for the new stock options. Effectively, Haghani bought a convertible bond made of two pieces, and then sold the pieces for more than the whole—like buying a cheese sandwich for $3, and then selling the cheese and bread for $2 each.

Haghani made hundreds of millions of dollars for Salomon using this strategy. In 1992, when he was just 30 years old, Salomon paid him a $25 million bonus as a reward for finding these trades.[18]

The Arbitrage Group did similar trades when the options embedded in bonds were misvalued because companies did not understand them. For example, when short-term interest rates were falling during the late 1980s, many corporate treasurers recalled high interest rates during the late Carter and early Reagan administrations, and wanted to lock in lower rates. They bought interest-rate caps—options that made money if short-term interest rates rose. But the treasurers didn't have good models for evaluating the options, and, as a result, Salomon was able to make money selling overvalued short-term options.

At the same time, companies were issuing long-term callable bonds, which they could redeem, if interest rates declined, by returning the investor's principal investment. The coupon payments of these bonds— the semi-annual interest payments investors received—were higher than those of non-callable bonds. In effect, the companies issuing the bonds were purchasing options from investors, paying them above-normal coupons instead of an upfront premium. But companies didn't necessarily want to buy these long-term options, any more than they had wanted to be exposed to an increase in short-term interest rates. Instead of keeping the risk associated with these long-term options, the companies sold offsetting options to Salomon. Again, the companies did a poor job of assessing the value of these options, and Salomon was able to make money buying undervalued long-term options.

Salomon didn't want to keep the risk associated with the short-term options they had sold and the long-term options they had bought. Instead, traders sought to buy short-term options and sell long-term options to offset their risks; even if those options were fairly priced, Salomon could pocket the difference between buying low and selling high. Sometimes, Salomon's traders found counterparties willing to take on these risks in the over-the-counter market, just as Victor Haghani had done. When traders could not find anyone willing to take on the offsetting risk, they bought and sold options on Treasury bonds that carried roughly the same risk as their options on corporate bonds. Managing these risks was a complicated task, but Salomon's traders seemed to know what they were doing.

Salomon's options arbitrage extended outside the United States. When German investors were interested in buying call options on Boeing Co., the American airplane manufacturer, Salomon simply sold the options on its own, instead of asking Boeing to issue the options—which would have required extensive negotiations.[19] Boeing didn't even need to know about the trade. Salomon hedged its risks from the sale by buying Boeing stock—on the New York Stock Exchange—and by buying put options on Boeing stock—in the over-the-counter markets. As Andy Krieger's misdirection-play showed, a call option was roughly equivalent to an investment in an asset—in this case, stock—plus a put option. That meant Salomon was hedged, and could pocket a riskless fee.

Salomon also found a new way to arbitrage Nikkei 225 options, trading on the difference between the stock market in Tokyo and the stock-index future market in Osaka, Japan. Investors were so bullish on stock-index futures—contracts to buy and sell all of the stocks in the Nikkei 225 index, traded in Osaka—that those futures were worth more than the underlying stocks in Tokyo. Salomon could buy the stocks in Tokyo, sell the Osaka index, pocket the difference, and wait for the two to converge.[20] If Osaka investors were too pessimistic, Salomon would take the opposite positions. (This trade utilized the same strategy Nick Leeson later would tell his bosses he was employing in the Singapore office of Barings Bank.)

A final example of a non-U.S. strategy was when Salomon's traders learned that, although the German tax system rewarded German companies for buying German stocks, foreigners actually wanted to buy those stocks more than Germans did. Salomon created a trade whereby the German companies bought the stocks, but entered into a swap agreement to pay out the stock returns to the foreigners. No one paid tax, and everyone was better off (except German citizens, who lost out on tax revenue, but that wasn't Salomon's concern).[21]

The "magic" behind these various, complex trades was that they made money even though Salomon was neither selling deals to clients nor taking on much risk. The trades were driven by legal rules or by the actions of unsophisticated parties, or by both. Unlike previous methods of arbitrage, these innovations generated profits for Salomon that were sustainable over a period of years.

As the Arbitrage Group's profits increased, Salomon's top managers were unable to monitor the risks the firm's traders were taking, especially in derivatives, and the reports they received about trading risks were inaccurate and incomplete. Although it was not widely known at the time, Salomon's supposedly sophisticated risk-management systems could not accurately value the firm's trading positions. Salomon had the same problem as Bankers Trust: its own employees could not assess the firm's risks. Bankers Trust and Salomon were two of the most sophisticated participants in the derivatives markets, yet during the late 1980s and early 1990s, those banks were not able to figure out what their own derivatives were worth.

In 1993, Salomon's managers decided to overhaul the firm's internal risk-management systems, just as many Wall Street firms were doing the same. As employees in New York began reviewing these systems, they discovered tens of millions of dollars of mistakes. Forty Salomon employees spent the next eighteen months, full-time, trying to track down the firm's hidden losses. Ultimately, Salomon found $87 million of "unreconciled balances" in New York, and another $194 million of errors in London.[22] The losses had been building up undetected in an outdated accounting system since 1989. The mistakes resembled those Bankers Trust made during the Andy Krieger incident, but over a much longer period of time, with more than double the losses.

Salomon's accounting firm at the time was Arthur Andersen, the prestigious firm that would be involved in numerous accounting scandals later in the decade, including Enron, Waste Management, and others. If Bankers Trust, with Arthur Young, and Salomon Brothers, with Arthur Andersen, couldn't control and understand these financial risks, how could anyone else be expected to do so? As one well-respected stock analyst, Perrin Long of Brown Brothers Harriman, said after Salomon finally announced the losses in 1995, "You have to ask, 'What the hell is going on?'" Another analyst asked, "When does it end?"[23]

Ironically, it turned out that poor supervision and controls were the Arbitrage Group's major advantages over its competitors. Meriwether's traders could allocate more capital to their bets when they spotted arbitrage opportunities, because no one above Meriwether was carefully monitoring the group's risks and use of capital.

Meriwether had a close and informal relationship with Salomon's chairman, John Gutfreund. Unlike Charlie Sanford of Bankers Trust, Gutfreund did not impose controls on employees based on RAROC (the risk-adjusted return on capital). Instead, Gutfreund kept track only of revenues, not costs, even with respect to new products.[24] If Sanford had permitted Andy Krieger to place billion-dollar currency bets, imagine what Gutfreund would permit Meriwether to do.

Fortunately, Meriwether was a sophisticated risk manager, and while Gutfreund was ignoring the details about risk and cost of capital for Salomon as a firm, Meriwether was setting profit targets based on these factors within the Arbitrage Group. In rough terms, each of Meriwether's traders needed to make at least $60 million a year for the firm; otherwise, the trader would need to find a job somewhere else.[25] In other words, Meriwether recognized that the Arbitrage Group's traders were taking such large positions, and potentially putting so much of Salomon's capital at risk, that if a trader couldn't make at least $60 million doing so, it wasn't worth it for Salomon as a firm.

Gutfreund's laissez-faire approach had one other advantage. Because Meriwether was not subject to strict controls, he could leave his trading positions in place for long periods of time, long enough for price discrepancies to converge. At other banks, senior managers became nervous when trades turned bad, and forced traders to liquidate positions that eventually might have become profitable. In contrast, Meriwether could "let his bets ride." The result was counterintuitive: the more out of control the Arbitrage Group became, the more money it could make.

One example was Meriwether's response to the stock market crash of

1987. For the first ten months of 1987, the Arbitrage Group had been up $200 million. After losses from the crash, they were suddenly back to even for the year.[26] Many of the traders were terrified. Their computer models, which looked at *standard deviation* as a measure of the likelihood of particular events, had failed. (A one-standard-deviation event happened about a third of the time. A two-standard-deviation event happened only about five percent of the time. And so on.) According to the computer models, the 1987 stock market crash was a vastly improbable *twenty*-standard-deviation event,[27] less likely than a hundred perfect storms.

But Meriwether kept his cool, and turned to the reliable on-the-run/off-the-run trade. In the panic, investors had rushed to the safety of 30-year Treasury bonds, making them more expensive than off-the-run bonds with similar maturities. The arbitrage opportunity—previously competed away—suddenly reappeared. Unlike his peers at other banks (who were panicking over losses, worried their firms might not survive), Meriwether didn't need special approval to do this trade "in size." Meriwether bet that the gap between bonds would close, and made $50 million on that trade alone.[28]

Gutfreund's hands-off approach also encouraged traders to engage in strategies designed to skirt legal rules. In addition to the strategies already mentioned, the Arbitrage Group structured trades to profit from regulations, such as those that encouraged European banks to invest money in government bonds, rather than lend money to companies. Meriwether's traders also structured deals in Italian government bonds to convert government tax subsidies into trading profits. When Paul Mozer had worked in the Arbitrage Group, he did several trades designed to reduce Salomon's own tax obligations. These opportunities to avoid legal rules persisted so long as the legal rules persisted.

One commentator described Mozer's tax-avoidance trades as "dirty jobs."[29] In one example, Mozer created sham transactions to minimize Salomon's taxable earnings. In these transactions, Salomon bought and sold bonds at artificial prices to generate what appeared to be losses— thereby concealing more than a hundred million dollars of taxable earnings—when in reality the trades had no economic effect. (By the late 1990s, there would be billions of dollars of such tax-avoidance trades— especially among energy and telecommunications companies such as Enron and Global Crossing—with no economic purpose other than avoiding legal rules, including taxes.)

Not surprisingly, traders who were consistently designing transactions to avoid legal rules—and who were paid millions of dollars for doing so—developed a culture of supremacy and disdain. Mozer and other traders began to disparage other firms in the same way salesmen from Bankers Trust had derided their clients. Salomon's customers were important to the Arbitrage Group, because they provided precious information about supply and demand that traders needed to spot inefficiencies. But many of Meriwether's traders began to take that information for granted, and to view their customers as fools. Paul Mozer was said to "turn on the charm on sales calls. But then he'd turn around and say something about what a moron the person was."[30]

Although Mozer rankled some of his colleagues and their clients, he was a consistent source of trading profits. When Mozer's predecessor on the government-bond desk was involved in a Treasury-bond auction, dozens of people would stand behind and watch. But when Mozer took over, anyone who tried to watch him—even Chairman John Gutfreund—was castigated with "get away from here" or "get out of here."[31] Salomon's chief legal counsel, Donald Feuerstein, thought Mozer had an "attitudinal problem."[32] Nevertheless, Meriwether and Gutfreund strongly supported Mozer, and the fact that he was abrasive didn't matter much. Mozer made $3 million in 1988, $4 million in 1989, and $4.75 million in 1990.[33]

When Mozer learned that Salomon had paid Hilibrand $23 million in 1990—five times Mozer's compensation—something snapped. As one executive described it, "Mozer looked at Larry Hilibrand and thought, he got 23 million; I want to get 23."[34] In a bank full of bonus-obsessed traders, Mozer was unusually neurotic about his pay.

For his plan to "get 23," Mozer returned to the on-the-run/off-the-run trade idea. Again, the original idea was that many clients—particularly foreign insurance companies—always wanted to hold the most liquid Treasury bonds. As a result, the newest bonds often were worth more than slightly older bonds. That was the arbitrage opportunity: a trader could buy the cheap bonds, sell the expensive ones, and wait for the prices to converge. In Mozer's case, the bonds that fit into his new plan were 2-year notes, not 30-year bonds, but the idea was the same.

A group of investment banks had created a *when-issued* market, in which traders could buy and sell future rights to the newest 2-year notes. In this market, Mozer could agree today to sell notes that did not yet exist but would be created in a few weeks "when issued" by the

Treasury in its next auction. The Treasury approved of this market, for the same reason regulators allowed *price talk* for new issues of stock: the early market minimized surprises and gave traders more confidence in bidding for the actual notes at auction.

Because companies were eager to buy new notes, prices tended to rise during the when-issued period, and then fall when the Treasury auctioned the notes (companies then would begin looking forward to the next auction and a fresh batch of notes). That predictable price decline presented an arbitrage opportunity: traders could sell in the when-issued market, and then buy a few days later at the Treasury auction. The major government-bond dealers all did this trade, selling billions of dollars of when-issued notes and buying at auction to cover their positions.

Mozer had a diabolical idea: if he could control the Treasury auction, he could *squeeze* the other dealers doing the arbitrage, who were counting on the new notes to satisfy their obligations to sell in the when-issued market, forcing them to pay a premium to buy the precious, recently auctioned bonds. Mozer wasn't the first person to think of this manipulative scheme: some of the clients Mozer so disdained—including Japanese insurance companies—had attempted to squeeze the Treasury market several years earlier. But Salomon was the largest of the handful of dealers approved to participate in Treasury auctions, so Mozer would be in a much better position to execute a big squeeze.

Nevertheless, Mozer's first attempts failed. In May 1990, he tried to corner a Treasury auction by boldly bidding for more than 100 percent of the notes. By submitting more bids than there were bonds for sale, Mozer improved the chances that he would receive most, if not all, of the bonds being auctioned, just as some Wall Street traders placed reservations to buy, say, twelve cars when they learned that a dealership was receiving a shipment of ten of the latest model. (When the Mazda Miata was introduced, traders held the rights to buy many of the new cars—rights they were able to sell at a profit, even if they had no interest in buying a Miata.)

The U.S. government frowned on traders submitting such large bids, because they didn't want one investment bank to be able to control the price of recently auctioned bonds. Michael E. Basham, a deputy assistant secretary of the Treasury, called Mozer immediately after receiving Mozer's bid and reminded him of a "gentleman's agreement" between the Treasury and Wall Street that no firm would bid for more than 35 percent of a Treasury auction. The Treasury wanted the dealers to compete, so that the government could borrow at lower rates. Although the auctions were only loosely regulated, the Treasury did not want to encourage anti-competitive behavior by dealers. Basham said the Treasury wouldn't discipline Salomon this time, but cautioned that Mozer should take care to comply with the informal 35 percent agreement in future auctions.

After this incident, Mozer's bad attitude got worse. He lashed out at Basham, admonishing him not to get in the way. He warned that John Gutfreund, Salomon's chairman, would call the secretary of the Treasury (Nicholas Brady, a close friend of Gutfreund's) if Basham interfered again.[35] The nerve of a "lowly" government official getting in the way of a top trader from Salomon!

Mozer ignored Basham's warning, and submitted a bid for 240 percent of the next month's auction. Basham called again, saying, "Paul, quite frankly the nature of the process is designed to encourage you to bid a higher price than the next guy, not to try to game the system. We would prefer that you not do it again."[36] Basham asked the Federal Reserve, which managed the auctions, to adjust Mozer's bid down to 35 percent.

Frustrated, Mozer again ignored Basham and bid for 300 percent of the notes in the next auction. Again, Basham ensured that Salomon's bid was adjusted down to 35 percent. A few weeks later, on July 10, 1990, the Treasury converted the 35 percent "gentleman's agreement" into a formal rule.[37] Basham had not consulted Wall Street regarding this new rule, and government-bond traders were surprised by it. At the next day's auction, Mozer angrily entered eleven separate bids for 35 percent each, a total of 385 percent of the auction.[38] He assailed the Treasury, over the phone and in the media, telling the *New York Times* that "the Treasury had been rash in making their decision without any prior consultation with the primary dealers. The Treasury has tied the hands of large dealers who time in and time out are the ones who underwrite the Treasury's debt."[39]

At this point, Mozer had to be reined in. Thomas Strauss, the number two person at Salomon (junior to Gutfreund, senior to Meriwether), insisted that Mozer apologize to the regulators, and then go to London for a few weeks to calm down.[40]

Mozer apparently spent the next months contemplating ways to circumvent the new 35 percent rule, just as he previously had helped Salomon dodge paying taxes. On February 21, 1991, Mozer submitted a bid in Salomon's name for precisely 35 percent of the auction, dutifully in compliance with the new Treasury rules.

But he also submitted a bid for 35 percent of the auction on behalf of Mercury Asset Management, a subsidiary of S. G. Warburg & Co., then the top securities firm in England, and a Salomon client. And he submitted yet another bid for 35 percent in the name of Quantum Fund, the hedge fund run by billionaire George Soros (where Andy Krieger had worked briefly). Warburg and Quantum hadn't authorized the bids, but Mozer—who derided clients anyway—didn't seem to care. They would never know about the bids, and Mozer would simply keep the extra notes for Salomon, effectively avoiding the Treasury's 35 percent rule.

The strategy worked as planned, and Salomon controlled well over half of the notes sold at auction. After the auction, Mozer executed fictitious trades in which Warburg and Quantum "sold" their notes—more than a billion dollars' worth—to Salomon at less than their market price.[41] Salomon made a huge profit, and Mozer was on his way to catching Hilibrand and "getting 23."

However, even the brainiest criminals frequently make one critical mistake. For Mozer, it was his failure to consider the possibility that a Salomon client might independently submit a bid in the auction. Mozer had entered bids for Mercury Asset Management and Quantum Fund at exactly the 35 percent limit, so even a small independent bid would put one of these clients over the limit, and in violation of the Treasury rule. There was no room for error.

Unfortunately for Mozer, Warburg—the parent company of Mercury Asset Management—entered a relatively small, $100 million bid of its own in the February 21, 1991, auction. This bid pushed Warburg over the 35 percent limit, and red lights began flashing at the Treasury. After several weeks of investigation, Treasury officials sent a letter questioning the bids to Warburg, with a copy to Mozer, who regulators knew had submitted the bid on behalf of Mercury Asset Management.

In an attempt to cover his tracks, Mozer immediately called a senior manager at Mercury Asset Management and tried to explain that the $3.15 billion bid he had submitted in Mercury's name was merely a clerical error. Mozer asked, please, would he keep the matter confidential?

That same day, April 24, 1991, Mozer showed Meriwether the letter. Meriwether told Mozer his "behavior was career-threatening" and called to arrange a meeting with his own boss, Thomas Strauss, and Salomon's general counsel, Donald Feuerstein.[42] The three men met the next morning, discussed Mozer's actions, read the Treasury letter, and decided they needed to speak to Salomon's chairman, John Gutfreund, who was out of town. But they did not reprimand or discipline Mozer.

Meanwhile, that very day, Mozer was busy violating the 35 percent rule yet again, in the April auction. Mozer submitted a 35 percent bid for Salomon, along with a smaller authorized bid on behalf of Tudor Investment Corporation, a hedge fund run by Paul Tudor Jones. But Mozer couldn't resist adding an extra $1 billion—unauthorized—to Tudor's bid. This time, he was careful to leave some cushion, so that Tudor would not appear to have violated the 35 percent rule; in reality, Salomon was bidding the extra $1 billion, furtively putting itself over 35 percent. Mozer succeeded, and Salomon kept the additional $1 billion in notes, falsely purchased on behalf of Tudor, at a substantial profit.

A few days later, Gutfreund finally met with Meriwether, Strauss, and Feuerstein. Meriwether described the Warburg incident as an "aberration" and said he hoped it would not end Mozer's career at Salomon. Even Feuerstein—who reportedly loved converting "chinks in the regulators' armor"[43] into advantages for the firm—thought Mozer had gone too far. He thought Mozer had committed a crime, and said Salomon should tell the government about it, although he noted that there probably was no legal duty to do so. They debated whether to notify the Treasury, or perhaps the New York Federal Reserve (Chairman E. Gerald Corrigan and Strauss were friends). They did not mention disciplining Mozer or limiting his activities.[44]

Perhaps nothing could have stopped Mozer at this point. He had submitted billions of dollars of false bids, including a $1 billion bid as a practical joke on a retiring Salomon salesperson from San Francisco.[45] His reckless trading had not remained confidential, and when several hedge-fund managers learned about it, they hopped on Mozer's wagon. Two large hedge funds—Caxton Group and Steinhardt Partners—had been involved in squeezing the April auction, too, and they were interested in participating, through Salomon, in the upcoming May auction.[46] Julian Robertson, the famed head of Tiger Management, another hedge fund, also wanted in on the action.

In all, Mozer bought 86 percent of the May auction. Mozer included Tiger in his bid for the May 22, 1991, auction, and added $500 million for Salomon—unauthorized, of course—to Tiger's bid. Caxton and Steinhardt bought even more notes. This time, Mozer also bought 2-year notes in the when-issued market, and did not disclose those purchases, as Treasury rules required.[47] With these secret purchases, Mozer was swinging for the fences, hoping he could sell all of these positions at a huge profit.

The big squeeze was on. The price of the 2-year notes skyrocketed, and the holders of the notes made $30 million.[48] Mozer had hit a home run. Yes, he was out of control, but if he could just hold on until the end of the year, he would earn a huge bonus, perhaps even set a new record at Salomon. It seemed unlikely that regulators would catch him, and inconceivable that he would go to jail.

Arbitrage wasn't the only profitable business at Salomon. The firm also was a pioneer in the market for complex mortgage bonds, financial instruments based on interest and principal payments made by home-owners. Lewis Ranieri of Salomon was a crusader for mortgage bonds in the same way Michael Milken was a crusader for junk bonds. They visited the same accounts and gave the same forceful sales pitches. Ranieri illustrated how homeowners' payments of principal and interest flowed through a U.S. government agency into a specially created trust, and then into some lucky investor's portfolio. Ranieri was just as colorful as vice chairman of Salomon as he had been as a mail clerk at the firm who was promoted to supervisor after he "got the brilliant idea one day to put a map of the U.S. on the wall and outline the postage zones in Magic Marker."[49] One of his favorite comments to investors was that "mort-gages were so cheap your teeth hurt."[50]

Mortgage bonds and junk bonds had much in common: they were undervalued relative to plain-vanilla bonds, they were more difficult to evaluate than most other investments, and there were hundreds of bil-lions of dollars of them. Just as First Boston had securitized junk bonds in CBOs, Salomon would securitize mortgage bonds in similarly com-plex deals.

Mortgages had one key advantage over junk bonds: they were rated AAA by the major credit-rating agencies. The U.S. government felt that home mortgages were important and it subsidized them, not only by allowing taxpayers to deduct interest payments, but by implicitly back-ing the payments on mortgage bonds.

This AAA rating didn't mean mortgage bonds were risk-free, of course. What the bonds lacked in credit risk, they more than made up for in interest-rate risk. Because homeowners could refinance their mort-gages anytime they wanted, the owner of a mortgage bond never really knew if the bond would last for 30 years or 30 months. If interest rates declined and everyone refinanced, the purchaser of a long-term, 10 percent mortgage bond might have her principal back in a year, when available investments paid a much lower rate. This risk—known as *prepayment risk*—was very difficult to quantify, and was one reason mortgages were cheap.

Salomon stripped these mortgages into pieces in the same way First Boston had stripped junk bonds. Salomon created a trust (typically backed by a U.S. government agency), transferred a pool of mortgages into the trust, and then created a structure to separate the mortgages into different *tranches*. Mortgages could be split in various ways: interest and principal, short-term and long-term, West Coast and East Coast. They also could be separated based on prepayment risk, with a risky set of bonds immunizing others. For example, one tranche of bonds might suffer first from prepayments, and the second tranche would not be prepaid until all of the first tranche had been.

These strips of mortgages generally were known as Collateralized Mortgage Obligations, or CMOs, and the different varieties had fantastically colorful acronyms, from *interest-only bonds* (IOs) and *principal-only bonds* (POs) to PACs, TACs, IOettes, VADMs, and Z-bonds. In most cases, the wilder the name, the riskier the bond. The riskiest versions were sometimes just called "nuclear waste." Salomon became the biggest mortgage dealer in the world (although First Boston—the long-standing expert in securitization—had been the first firm to create a CMO). Salomon made money from mortgage bonds in three ways.

First, it earned a fee from setting up mortgage deals. The more complex the tranches, the higher the fee.

Second, Salomon made a commission selling mortgages to clients, especially those who wanted to take risks but were restricted by law to highly rated instruments. For example, regulated financial institutions, such as savings and loans, which were permitted by law to buy only highly rated instruments, could nevertheless buy CMOs, even though they were riskier than plain-vanilla bonds. Ranieri understood the importance of legal restrictions on investors, and he refused to accept state-imposed limits on mortgage investing. As one of his traders put it, "If Lewie didn't like a law, he'd just have it changed."[51]

(From a fund manager's perspective, Salomon's mortgage bonds resembled CSFP's structured notes. They had very high credit ratings and their returns were potentially higher than any comparably rated investment.

But even the more sophisticated fund managers didn't understand mortgages much better than they understood structured notes, and they paid substantial fees to Salomon and other sellers as a consequence. Typically, fund managers *did* understand that mortgages had a much greater upside than other highly rated government bonds, and they stuffed their government-bond funds with risky mortgages—whatever the fee—hoping to outperform their peers; more on the effects of these risks in the next chapter.)

Third, Salomon made money trading mortgages for its own account. Chairman John Gutfreund was not any better at managing the risks associated with mortgages than he was with any other area of trading. Neither was Lewis Ranieri, who ran the mortgage desk, and had trouble keeping tabs on the multiplicity of CMO structures. As a result, many of the firm's mortgage risks were essentially unmanaged. On a typical day in the mid-1980s, Salomon had as much as $5 billion—more than twice its capital—tied up in mortgages it was hoping to securitize; yet, according to commentator Martin Mayer, nobody in upper management even knew it.[52] Ranieri's group made money simply by holding mortgages, which increased in value as interest rates declined.

Meriwether's arbitrage group had a more sophisticated approach, speculating on the relative values of different mortgage tranches. Traders in the Arbitrage Group took advantage of differences between the values of options embedded in mortgages and similar options in other bonds. These trades were huge and volatile; sometimes they lost a fortune, but generally they made money. For example, Lawrence Hilibrand lost $400 million on one mortgage bet, but he was permitted to hold on to the bet, and it eventually made money.[53]

Greg Hawkins had been on Salomon's mortgage desk before he began working in Meriwether's Arbitrage Group. Hawkins had a Ph.D. in finance, and created computer models to assess the risk of mortgage prepayment. He found that the prepayment options in mortgages were overpriced, because investors didn't understand prepayment risk and wouldn't pay much for mortgages with these risks.[54] As a result, certain mortgage instruments were cheap, and Hawkins could buy them, hedge their option-related risk in other markets, and pocket the difference.

Salomon dodged a bullet when one of its newly minted star traders, Howard Rubin, left for Merrill Lynch. Ranieri had called Howard Rubin "the most innately talented trader I have ever seen."[55] Rubin's story is a typical example of how quickly the practices within one investment bank could flow out to the rest of Wall Street. Just as Bankers Trust's derivatives innovations spread to First Boston along with Allen Wheat, some of Salomon's mortgage expertise flowed along with Howard Rubin, when he left Salomon for Merrill Lynch. Merrill would wish it hadn't.

In his first year out of Salomon's training program in 1986, Rubin made $25 million for the firm, an astonishing amount for a novice trader.[56] But that year, Salomon refused to pay first-year traders more than $90,000, including salary and bonus, regardless of how much money they had made for the firm.

The next year, Rubin made $30 million for the firm, but Salomon also capped the overall pay of second-year employees, this time at $175,000.[57] That was not enough for Rubin, and he left Salomon for Merrill Lynch, which guaranteed him $1 million a year, plus a percentage of his trading profits.[58] By hiring Rubin, Merrill was hoping to buy some insight into how Salomon had been making so much money trading mortgages.

It didn't work out as planned. Howard Rubin's mortgage desk at Merrill lost $377 million—all on a single day in April 1987. Rubin had been trading mortgages for less than five years at that point, and it turned out he wasn't a wunderkind after all.

Rubin's loss was eerily similar to Andy Krieger's gain that year. They had both started at Salomon. As Krieger was leaving for Bankers Trust, Rubin was off for Merrill Lynch. Both traded instruments whose value depended on the volatility estimates: currencies for Krieger, mortgages for Rubin. Rubin was just a few years older, 32, at the time of his losses. Both had placed huge bets with their firm's capital, and their results were of the same order of magnitude. Both left their jobs soon thereafter. The main difference was that Krieger won his bet, while Rubin lost.

How had Merrill lost the money? Principal-only bonds were the culprit. Merrill had purchased $935 million of 11 percent bonds issued by the Government National Mortgage Association (called Ginnie Mae). It split the bonds into interest and principal, and sold the interest-only portion of the mortgage (the IOs) to savings-and-loan associations. But Merrill kept the principal-only pieces (the POs).

Meanwhile, Rubin had done an additional $800 million of a similar deal, without telling his bosses. He kept the POs of that deal, too. That left Merrill with about $1.7 billion of POs.

An owner of POs essentially is betting that interest rates will go down. A PO is a discount instrument, meaning that its price is only a fraction—say, 20 percent—of its principal amount. If rates go down, and homeowners prepay their mortgages, the owner of the PO receives an early windfall—an extra 80 percent today, instead of several years in the future. But if rates go up, and homeowners don't prepay, the PO might not pay anything for 30 years. POs are among the most volatile financial instruments available.

Unfortunately for Rubin, interest rates went up. As with Bankers Trust, rumors immediately began swirling about Merrill's trading, including reports—never confirmed—that some of the records had been hidden in desk drawers. But unlike Bankers Trust, Merrill quickly admitted the truth, and the losses were front-page news a day later.[59] The firm's press statement said the losses were due to "significant unauthorized activity by a recently discharged senior trader and subsequent market volatility." Merrill's stock fell about six percent.

Surprisingly, Merrill still found a way to avoid reporting a loss for the quarter, by recognizing offsetting gains from sales of some businesses. Those sales seemed coincidental, but were far more plausible than the $80 million entry for reduced compensation at Bankers Trust. Several Merrill executives said the firm planned to record several large "one-time gains" in the quarter.[60]

The Securities and Exchange Commission suspended Rubin from the securities industry for nine months in 1990, and he was soon working at another investment bank, Bear Stearns. Merrill Lynch did not face any charges relating to the way it avoided reporting a loss from Rubin's trades. The message—as with Andy Krieger—was clear: traders involved in complex financial schemes would not be punished. Ironically, a few months after Merrill fired Rubin, Salomon also fired Rubin's mentor, Lewis Ranieri, who no longer could compete with younger and more sophisticated traders. Difficulties with mortgages would resurface during the next several years. During the early 1990s, investors with a wide range of expertise would use mortgage instruments to place bets that interest rates would remain low, just as Gibson Greetings and P&G had used structured notes to place similar bets. Beginning in 1994, all of those bets would become losers. Salomon would suffer greatly during this period.

But the firm's most serious problems in 1991 related to government bonds, not mortgages. It remained unclear what regulators would do about Paul Mozer gaming the various Treasury auctions.

• • •

By the time John Gutfreund finally imposed some controls on Mozer, telling him not to bid for too many notes in the June 1991 auction, it was too late. Nevertheless, Gutfreund seemed to believe Salomon might get away with the profits from Mozer's "big squeeze" in the May 1991 auction. When Gutfreund met with Treasury officials in June, he brazenly suggested that Salomon had behaved properly in that auction. Gutfreund neglected to mention that he had known for months about Mozer's false bids in the February 1991 auction.[61]

When regulators began requesting documents about Salomon's role in the auctions, Gutfreund hired lawyers from Wachtell, Lipton, Rosen & Katz, but gave them a limited mandate, to investigate only the May 1991 auction (much as Enron later would give a special committee formed to investigate its collapse a limited mandate to look only at a few questionable trades). But the lawyers soon discovered Mozer's earlier bids, and the investigation inevitably expanded. In early August 1991, the law firm reported its conclusions to Salomon's top brass—Gutfreund, Strauss, Meriwether, and Feuerstein. The report was damning, and Salomon was forced to issue a press release describing "irregularities" in its Treasury auction bids.

Thomas Strauss had considered telling his friend E. Gerald Corrigan, the head of the New York Federal Reserve, about Salomon's problems, back in April, but had not done so. Instead, Corrigan learned about Mozer from reading the newspaper on Monday morning, August 12.[62] Right away, Corrigan demanded "managerial and other changes" at Salomon. For Gutfreund, Strauss, Meriwether, and Feuerstein, the end was very sudden. A few days later, all four top officials had resigned.[63]

Ironically, at precisely the same time (August 15), Michael Basham, the Treasury official who had met with Salomon officials several times as Mozer executed his scheme, also resigned, to begin working as a managing director at Smith Barney, the securities firm that soon would merge with Salomon.[64] At that point, no one knew better than Basham how to deal with the Treasury's approach to the bond markets. Before his two-year stint at the Treasury, Basham had been a junior employee in the government-bond department at Wertheim Schroeder. Basham's moves were typical of the revolving door between government and Wall Street. Gerald Corrigan was about to leave his Fed post for a senior position at Goldman Sachs; later, Robert Rubin, co-chair of Goldman Sachs, would become a senior government official.

Meanwhile, Warren Buffett—the Omaha-based multibillionaire—was concerned about his firm's $700 million investment in Salomon. Buffett had invested in Salomon's convertible preferred stock in 1987, to help the firm fend off a takeover threat from financier Ronald Perelman. Now, his investment was in danger. Buffett flew to New York, to try to save the struggling investment bank (just as years later he would consider rescuing Long-Term Capital Management, John Meriwether's hedge fund). Buffett brought much-needed credibility to Salomon, and the investment bank soon recovered.

Through September 1993, the Treasury scandal had echoed the recent changes in financial markets at other firms. Salomon had become much more technologically sophisticated, so much so that senior managers lost the ability to control key employees. The Arbitrage Group traded in deregulated markets, and took advantage of legal rules. The remaining question was whether prosecutors would punish anyone from Salomon, to send a message to financial market participants that the government would not tolerate manipulative practices.

After a few years of negotiating with prosecutors, Mozer finally confessed to his critical mistake in the February 1991 auction, and pled guilty to submitting false bids on behalf of Warburg and Quantum. Although the criminal statutes specified a maximum prison term of 10 years—the sentence Michael Milken had received—federal sentencing guidelines allowed for departures downward from that maximum, depending on several factors, including the defendant's cooperation. Hoping for a lighter sentence, Mozer told prosecutors about Salomon's $100+ million tax-avoidance schemes. They appreciated this information, which they could use in their case against Salomon.

At the sentencing hearing, Mozer—with his wife, parents, and siblings behind him—told Judge Pierre Leval he was "truly sorry" for his conduct. His lawyer asked that any time be served at home.

Judge Leval said Mozer's crime was an "extremely foolish, arrogant, insouciant offense," but imposed a fine of only $30,000 and sentenced Mozer to just four months in a minimum-security prison in Florida. Judge Leval concluded the hearing by saying that "in the world of financial crimes, deterrence of others is an extremely important aspect of sentencing."[65]

But actions spoke louder than words, and Mozer's punishment was unlikely to deter much misconduct. Like Michael Milken (who was convicted only of books and records violations) and Al Capone (who was convicted only of tax evasion), Mozer was not convicted of the most serious allegations: manipulating the Treasury market. Instead, he pled guilty only to making false statements to the government, a serious offense, but an offense that—because it did not cover financial crimes more generally—would not likely deter financial malfeasance *unless* it involved lying to the government. (The same issue would arise in 2002, when prosecutors would choose to indict Arthur Andersen for obstruction of justice, for shredding documents related to the collapse of Enron, but not for any underlying fraud.) The implicit message was: go ahead and commit financial fraud, but don't you dare lie to the U.S. Treasury.

Regulators forced Salomon to pay a huge penalty—a $290 million fine—but that came from the firm's shareholders (including Warren Buffett), not from any former executives. Buffett was not happy with this result. As he put it, "Mozer's paying $30,000 and is sentenced to prison for four months. Salomon's shareholders—including me—paid $290 million, and I got sentenced to ten months as CEO."[66]

Mozer later was fined $1.1 million and banned permanently from the finance industry in a civil action for securities fraud. Remarkably, much of this fine was for insider trading: Mozer had made $500,000 when he exercised some employee stock options, and then sold Salomon stock just three days before the firm disclosed the "irregularities" in its Treasury bids and, predictably, its stock price plunged.[67] Prosecutors typically loved insider-trading cases, which were much easier to prove than complex financial fraud; but, nevertheless, they did not charge Mozer with a crime related to this conduct.

In all, four months in a minimum-security prison seemed like a small price to pay for the millions of dollars Mozer made. In 2001, Mozer was enjoying his wealth—relaxing, and raising his eight-year-old daughter. He spent much of his time managing his own money and playing golf.[68] Mozer's treatment raised an interesting question: what would most people have done in his situation—assuming they *knew* in advance they would be caught and spend four months in a low-security prison—if they also knew that, afterward, they would retire as a multimillionaire, all before their fortieth birthday?

Compared to Mozer, his supervisors received mere slaps on the wrist. Gutfreund, Strauss, and Meriwether paid fines of $100,000, $75,000, and $50,000, respectively—just a few days' pay, at their salaries.

Gutfreund was barred from running an investment bank for life, although he technically was permitted to work at a lower level than chairman. Of course, the "King of Wall Street" couldn't be anywhere but the top, and, after the Treasury scandal, most highly regarded firms didn't want Gutfreund as their leader. He became president of Gutfreund & Co.—no mean feat—and ultimately found a job as chairman of Nutrition 21, Inc., a vitamin company.[69] Gutfreund also sneaked back into Wall Street in late 2001, at the age of 72, as a senior managing director of C. E. Unterberg, Towbin, a small and struggling investment firm run by Thomas Unterberg.[70] Unterberg and Gutfreund had been friends for 60 years, and Unterberg returned from retirement to chair the firm, something Gutfreund was barred from doing. As Gutfreund put it, "All of the geriatrics are calling me for jobs."[71]

Thomas Strauss, the number-two person at Salomon, was suspended from the industry for six months. After that, he began running Ramius Capital, a successful multibillion-dollar hedge fund named for the renegade captain in Tom Clancy's novel, *The Hunt for Red October*.[72]

Meriwether was suspended for just three months. He sued Salomon for lost compensation, and received $18 million in a settlement. All things considered, Meriwether did pretty well.

After Meriwether resigned, he worked on his golf game and thought about how he might replicate his Arbitrage Group elsewhere. Although his group had depended on Salomon for capital, it was an otherwise self-contained operation. With the right staff, he didn't need the support of a full-service investment bank. Meriwether began recruiting former employees and talking to potential investors. To re-create the autonomy he had at Salomon, he would require that investors commit their capital for a long period of time, perhaps several years. Given this requirement, he had the perfect name for his new investment fund: Long-Term Capital Management.

Meriwether's loyal traders were happy to leave Salomon to join him. Their work environment would change radically: instead of sitting in the middle of Salomon's cramped trading floor in Manhattan, they would rent offices in a relaxed, private office park in Greenwich, Connecticut.

By August 1993, Meriwether had recruited Eric Rosenfeld, his first academic hire at Salomon, along with Victor Haghani and Greg Hawkins. Larry Hilibrand—the $23 million man—joined a few months later. Meriwether persuaded the famed economists Myron Scholes and Robert Merton—who had worked as consultants at Salomon—to join Long-Term Capital as partners, along with a couple of Meriwether's golfing friends.

Meriwether wanted some new blood, too, especially someone who could navigate difficult regulatory issues. When David W. Mullins Jr.'s term as vice chairman of the Federal Reserve Board ended in February 1994, Mullins also agreed to join. Mullins was a perfect addition, especially given the importance of legal rules in Meriwether's strategies. Mullins was one of the most powerful banking regulators in the world, next to Alan Greenspan. Moreover, as a past critic of derivatives markets, Mullins had credibility with other regulators, especially those outside the United States.

The new group drafted a "confidential private placement memorandum" to give to investors interested in Long-Term Capital. The memorandum had few details. It described the on-the-run/off-the-run trade, which every smart trader on Wall Street already knew, but little else. Meriwether was selling his fund based solely on the reputation of his traders. Long-Term Capital was just as mysterious as the Arbitrage Group at Salomon had been.

It was expensive, too. Whereas typical hedge funds charged a fee of 1 percent annually, plus 20 percent of the profits, Long-Term Capital was asking for a 2 percent fee, plus 25 percent. It was outrageous, really, and numerous investors said no at first. But when a few of Salomon's competitors agreed to invest, including the CEOs of Merrill Lynch, Bear Stearns, and PaineWebber, the money started to flow. As word spread, Long-Term Capital became known as the "hot" investment, and everyone wanted in, from movie stars and professional athletes to major university endowments and international pension funds.[73] The list ranged from Hollywood agent Michael Ovitz to partners in the McKinsey consulting firm, from Nike CEO Phil Knight to Italy's central bank.[74] The initial investments topped $1 billion.

February 1994 was an eventful month. Bankers Trust was preparing to close another complex swap with Procter & Gamble. First Boston was preparing to fire hundreds of employees. Long-Term Capital was preparing to begin trading in a few weeks. Paul Mozer—now permanently excluded from Meriwether's inner circle—was preparing to spend several months in a Florida prison. But few people were prepared for what Alan Greenspan, chairman of the Federal Reserve, was planning. Greenspan was about to turn over a rock, revealing just how much the markets had changed during the years since Andy Krieger.

A NEW BREED OF SPECULATOR

On February 4, 1994, Alan Greenspan and the Federal Reserve raised overnight interest rates from 3 percent to 3.25 percent. To most investors, the change seemed insubstantial. Greenspan's reasoning was sound: the economy was growing very quickly, and although slightly higher interest rates would hurt investments, they also would help contain inflation. The markets fell in response, but the move was not unusual. Stock prices declined about two percent; bond prices dropped half a percent.

But behind the scenes, it was pure panic.

Most individual investors did not yet know of the swaps Bankers Trust had done with Gibson Greetings and Procter & Gamble, or of the complex financial strategies First Boston and Salomon Brothers had engineered. And no one realized how far and quickly those strategies had spread beyond those firms.

By early 1994, hundreds of money managers and treasurers—from Robert Citron, the 70-year-old treasurer of Orange County, California, to Worth Bruntjen, the aggressive mutual-fund manager at Piper Jaffray in Minneapolis—had secretly bet hundreds of billions of dollars using strategies and instruments that were near copies of those described in the previous chapters. Although the trades were complex, most of them—at their core—were bets that interest rates would stay low. Collectively, these managers had placed the largest secret wager in the history of financial markets. When the Fed raised rates on February 4, they lost.

Imagine a casino full of gamblers betting on a roulette wheel. Spin after spin, the ball lands on a red-colored number. The gamblers bet on red numbers and win, doubling and feverishly redoubling their bets. As the cheers grow louder, they begin ignoring the fact that the wheel has just as many black numbers as red. They believe they have entered an incredible new world where the roulette ball only lands on red numbers. They bet everything on the next spin of the wheel.

Substitute "low interest rates" for "red numbers" and you have a description of the early-1990s financial markets. Fund managers had been placing huge bets on a financial-market roulette wheel, where the ball kept landing on low interest rates. They insisted interest rates would remain low and increased their bets, frequently borrowing huge sums to do so. Egged on by the Fed's commitment to keep interest rates down in order to boost the economy, they imagined a new world where short-term interest rates were always three percent. Inevitably, on February 4, the ball landed on black.

Why didn't investors learn about the losses that day? One reason was that the bets involved largely unregulated and undisclosed financial instruments, such as structured notes, swaps, and other derivatives. Another was that many fund managers simply hid the losses, not only from investors, but from their bosses as well. After February 4, those managers were scurrying like a colony of ants whose cover had just been kicked over. Given the complexity of the instruments and the lack of regulation, they would be able to hide for quite a while. The public would discover the losses only in dribs and drabs during the year.

In contrast to investors, Wall Street bankers immediately knew the damage caused by the rate hike, for two reasons: first, they had created the various fund-managers' bets, so they knew the hidden details; second, Wall Street traders had hedged the bets by taking "mirror" positions in the market. Traders closely monitored these hedges, and—with a few glaring exceptions, such as Bankers Trust and Salomon Brothers— bank managers generally knew their traders' positions. Various sources estimated the total damage to the bond market at around $1.5 trillion. That made the rate hike more costly than any other market debacle since the 1929 stock-market crash. The *New York Times* took note of the panic among financial specialists on February 5, the day after the rate hike, saying the Fed's action sent "an Arctic blast through Wall Street."[1]

During the next few months, the fund managers—one by one—would admit their losses. David Askin was first. His fund, Askin Capital Management, was one of the largest and most sophisticated investors in mortgage securities. Askin was a respected trader—formerly of Drexel Burnham Lambert, Michael Milken's firm—and he was among the most active traders of complex mortgage derivatives. Often, Askin *was* the market. Yet Askin's $600 million fund evaporated within weeks after the rate hike, and Askin filed for bankruptcy on April 7 (more on the details later).

Five days later, Gibson Greetings and Procter & Gamble admitted to losses on their previously hidden bets with Bankers Trust, and rumors swirled about similar losses at other companies. Air Products and Chemicals lost $113 million, Dell Computer lost $35 million, Mead Corporation lost $12 million, and so on.

Various congressional committees immediately held hearings, with much fanfare (just as they would after the collapses of Long-Term Capital Management and Enron). On April 13, the House Banking Committee called on George Soros, the billionaire investment guru who briefly had employed Andy Krieger. Soros warned that many fund managers were using financial alchemy to make otherwise-prohibited bets. Regarding new financial instruments such as derivatives, he said, "There are so many of them, and some of them are so esoteric, that the risks involved may not be properly understood even by the most sophisticated investors."

To average investors, the public discussion of these new instruments was impossibly complicated. Professor Jonathan Macey of Cornell Law School suggested that for the ordinary citizen contemplating these new instruments, "it is rational to remain ignorant."[2] The costs of learning about financial innovation were simply too great, relative to the potential benefits. But as the floodgates opened, and investors learned of billions of dollars of losses at brand-name companies, mutual funds, pension funds, government treasuries, and other organizations, the costs of remaining ignorant began to rise. Even investors who didn't understand any of these new instruments still had to put their money somewhere.

As news spread, it appeared that many of the biggest losers were no more sophisticated than the average investor. The most surprising losses were in the treasurer's office of Orange County, California, and at Piper

Jaffray, the Minneapolis mutual fund. Orange County and Piper were well-respected, supposedly conservative, institutions. Yet the individuals who were blamed for the losses—Robert Citron of Orange County and Worth Bruntjen of Piper—were surprisingly inexperienced and unsophisticated. Citron and Bruntjen didn't have college degrees, much less Ph.D.s, and they lacked the financial training necessary to understand the details of structured notes and mortgage derivatives.

Nevertheless, they had bought billions of dollars of these instruments, feeding the Wall Street firms that created them, and—for many years—generating positive investment returns for their constituents. Citizens of Orange County counted on Citron as a reliable and trustworthy steward of public funds. For investors in Minneapolis, Bruntjen was practically a hero. Citron was the top-performing municipal treasurer in the United States; Bruntjen was the top-performing U.S. government-bond fund manager. In February 1994, citizens of Orange County and investors in Piper had no idea how far their men had fallen.

The story of Orange County, California, was well publicized during late 1994 and early 1995. Everyone read newspaper stories describing the record losses of $1.7 billion; assessing the antics of eccentric Robert Citron, the 70-year-old treasurer whose investment strategy had led to the county's bankruptcy; and speculating about the uncertain future of the wealthiest county in the United States.

But even after all the media coverage, most investors remained baffled by the Orange County story, and few people could explain exactly what had happened, or even answer basic questions about what went wrong with the county's investment strategy. How could an elected official have been secretly gambling with so much public money for so long? And how could he have lost so much money, given that he technically was operating within the county's conservative investment guidelines?

The reason the Orange County debacle made no sense was that few people understood its context. Orange County's losses were the inevitable result of the recent spread of new financial instruments and strategies from Wall Street to much less sophisticated venues. To understand Orange County's collapse, you had to understand the recent wave of financial innovation at Bankers Trust, First Boston, Salomon Brothers, and other Wall Street firms. With that perspective in hand, Orange County's story was a reasonably simple one.

Robert Citron was about as far from the high-tech Arbitrage Group at Salomon as a person could get. He was a University of Southern California dropout who had been to New York only four times in his life. He kept investment records on index cards and a wall calendar, and used his wristwatch calculator more than any financial software. Instead of developing computer pricing models, he consulted psychics and astrologers for advice about interest rates.

Citron had spent his entire career in Orange County's treasury department. After several decades, he held the elected position of treasurer—with no term limits. Throughout the 1980s and early 1990s, Citron had outperformed every other county investment manager, sometimes by several percentage points. While some counties were earning just two or three percent, Citron was earning almost 10 percent. The voters loved Citron and reelected him, over and over.

By the early 1990s, Citron was one of the largest investors in the country, managing $7.4 billion of Orange County taxpayers' money. But instead of investing the money in plain-vanilla Treasury bonds, he bought structured notes—the same instruments with embedded formulas that Allen Wheat and First Boston had sold by the billions. Citron bought a few of these notes from First Boston, but most of his purchases were from other banks, especially Merrill Lynch. By this time, structured notes had spread to every major investment bank, including Merrill.

Merrill's structured notes looked just like First Boston's: they ranged in maturities from 3 to 5 years (as Orange County's guidelines—which Citron had helped to write—required), and were issued by highly rated entities, such as the Federal Home Loan Bank (as Orange County's guidelines required). On paper, they looked like very safe, AAA-rated investments.

But the structured notes contained formulas that essentially were a big bet on interest rates remaining low. For example, one $100 million note paid a coupon of 10 percent minus LIBOR, the short-term interest-rate index. So if LIBOR were 3 percent, Orange County would receive a 7 percent coupon. As interest rates rose, Orange County's coupon went down, and vice versa. By buying these *inverse floaters,* Citron effectively was borrowing at short-term rates and investing at longer-term rates. Most of the notes were based on U.S. rates, but Citron also bet that European rates would remain low; he even purchased $1.8 billion of structured notes tied to Swiss LIBOR.[3]

Citron quickly came to believe that $7.4 billion was not a big-enough bet, so he borrowed as much as he could—about $13 billion—from various banks, including Merrill Lynch. He invested that money in structured notes, too. In all, by early 1994, Citron had made a $20 billion bet on low short-term rates.

In many ways, Robert Citron was simply a big, public version of Jim Johnsen of Gibson Greetings, the company that had unknowingly paid more than $10 million in fees for the interest-rate bets it bought from Bankers Trust. Like Johnsen, Citron wanted to gamble on interest rates, but was constrained by investment guidelines that permitted only highly rated, short-maturity bonds. Like Johnsen, Citron did not understand how to evaluate the derivatives embedded in structured notes, and he paid more for them than he should have, especially because he frequently didn't bother to shop around. That made Citron an extremely valuable client to Merrill Lynch. From 1990 to 1993, Merrill Lynch earned profits of $3.1 billion, more than it had earned during its 18-year history as a public company, and a big chunk of the profits—about $100 million—came from Orange County.[4] Merrill earned $62.4 million from Orange County in 1993 and 1994 alone.

Thus placed in its proper context, the story of Orange County's losses was simple, and all too familiar. Citron used structured derivatives to bet on low interest rates, just as Gibson Greetings had, and he lost his bets when the Federal Reserve raised rates on February 4. The only difference between Orange County and Gibson Greetings was the size of the bet: millions of dollars for Jim Johnsen, billions for Citron.

Who was to blame for the losses? Obviously, Citron was at the top of the list. He made all the decisions and hid all the risks. On January 17, 1995, he told a special committee of the California State Senate, "I was an inexperienced investor. In retrospect, it is clear that I followed the wrong course. I will carry that burden the rest of my life."

Many public accounts also blamed Merrill Lynch. Michael Stamenson, the top salesman in Merrill's San Francisco office, didn't help Merrill's media relations when he publicly praised Citron's investment acumen. No one thought Stamenson genuinely believed, as he testified, that "Mr. Citron is a highly sophisticated, experienced, and knowledgeable investor. I learned a lot from him."

But while Stamenson may have engineered Citron's gambling, the structured notes Merrill sold to Orange County were no different from tens of billions of dollars of similar instruments sold by numerous banks to numerous investors. To the extent there were problems with structured notes, they weren't specific to Merrill; they were endemic to the financial system. If Merrill was to blame for Orange County, then all of Wall Street was to blame for billions of dollars of losses in 1994.

In fact, Merrill seemed less culpable than other banks, especially Bankers Trust. Merrill had warned Citron on at least eight occasions, from 1992 to 1994, to reconsider his risky interest-rate bets. But Citron ignored all warnings, including those from prestigious Goldman Sachs, which disapproved of Citron's risks and refused to sell him any structured notes. When Goldman criticized Citron, he responded with an angry letter, saying, "You don't understand the type of investment strategies that we are using. I would suggest that you not seek doing business with Orange County."

The central problem for Merrill and other banks was not necessarily selling structured notes (as troubling as it might seem for Merrill to be selling securities with complex embedded formulas to an antediluvian client like Citron). Instead, the problem was that Merrill had played a dual role of derivatives salesman and bond underwriter. In this second role, Merrill and other banks had arranged new Orange County bond issues and sold them to the public. Unfortunately for Merrill, the public disclosures related to those bond issues did not mention Citron's risky interest-rate bets. That meant that even if Merrill had dealt properly with Citron in selling structured notes, it arguably had violated the securities laws by failing to disclose risks associated with Orange County's bonds.

The other blameworthy parties were the credit-rating agencies. Just as Standard & Poor's and Moody's had been critical to the development of new financial instruments at First Boston and Salomon Brothers, the agencies had played a central role in the collapse of Orange County.

First, they had given AAA ratings to the structured notes Orange County bought, even though the market risks of those notes were much greater than those of more typical AAA-rated investments. That enabled Robert Citron to fit his large interest-rate bets within the technical boundaries of Orange County's investment guidelines, even though the structured notes he bought were riskier than any highly rated bond in existence when the guidelines were written.

Second, both Standard and Poor's and Moody's gave Orange County *itself* their highest ratings through December 1994, when the county filed for bankruptcy. These high ratings gave confidence not only to Orange County residents, but also to investors in the county's bonds.

Investors in many conservative bond mutual funds—including those at Franklin Advisors, Putnam Management, Alliance Capital, Dean Witter, and many others—had purchased Orange County's bonds, precisely because of the high credit ratings.[5]

The rating agencies collected substantial fees for rating Orange County's bonds (S&P made more than $100,000 from Orange County in 1994 alone).[6] They collected even greater fees for rating structured notes. These fees raised questions about whether the agencies had been objective in assessing Orange County's risks. More than six months before Orange County's bankruptcy, the agencies had learned about Citron's losses on structured notes, but they kept this information secret, and didn't adjust their ratings in response.

For example, according to notes taken by a rating-agency analyst, on a telephone conference call with the rating agencies on May 9, 1994—seven months before the agencies downgraded Orange County's debt—Matthew Raabe, Citron's assistant treasurer, candidly discussed the county's risks, noting "DISASTER" and "danger!" and concluding that if interest rates rose one percent, Orange County's collateral would be "gone."[7] At another meeting, officials from the rating agencies learned about large numbers of "inverse floaters."[8] In addition, Raabe explained that Orange County was not "marking to market" its portfolio, meaning that it wasn't recording changes in value over time, even as interest rates increased.[9] In other words, if Orange County had paid $20 billion for structured notes in 1993, they were still recorded as being worth $20 billion in 1994, even though the Fed's rate hike had decimated their value.

Even if the agencies hadn't been privy to this information, they knew of numerous public warning signs about Citron, including Citron's own remarks from the previous year. In July 1993, when Citron was asked how he knew that interest rates would not rise, he replied, "I am one of the largest investors in America. I know these things." In a September 1993 report to the County Board of Supervisors, Citron wrote, "Certainly there is nothing on the horizon that would indicate that we will have rising interest rates for a minimum of three years." These statements were red flags showing how important the level of interest rates was to Citron's investment strategy, and how naïve Citron was. In spring 1994, John Moorlach, an accountant from Costa Mesa, California, launched an aggressive campaign to unseat Citron. Moorlach warned voters that the county was taking on huge risks and predicted a billion-dollar loss. But Citron won reelection, the losses remained hidden, and the rating agencies stayed mum.

Finally, on December 1, 1994—long after it was clear Orange County had lost more than a billion dollars—Standard & Poor's finally said it *might* lower Orange County's credit rating.[10] The agencies finally downgraded Orange County during the second week of December 1994, as the county was preparing to file for bankruptcy. The downgrades were much too late. Robert Froelich, director of bond research at Van Kampen Merritt, said, "If rating agencies can't keep track of one of the largest counties in the U.S., what is the value of their ratings on other counties?"[11] Or, he might have said, other companies?

As Orange County fell into bankruptcy, the major derivatives dealers swooped down to feed on its carcass. First, they made sure their loans would be repaid. In early December, First Boston sold $2.6 billion of collateral the county had posted for its loans.[12] Chapter 11, the relevant section of the bankruptcy laws for companies and individuals, would have prohibited such a sale, but First Boston's lawyers argued it was permitted under Chapter 9, the little-known and little-used section for municipalities. Other banks liked this argument, and sold collateral *after* the filing, something most experts agreed was prohibited.

Freed from the loans they had made to Orange County, the banks began feasting on the county's structured notes. In 1994, dealers bought back about $20 billion of structured notes, roughly one-fifth of the total outstanding in the entire market.[13] They repackaged the notes and sold off their risks, using swaps and securitizations, the recent innovations by First Boston and other Wall Street firms. They commonly earned fees of about a half percent from these deals, which meant profits of another $100 million.

Notably absent from these dealings was Salomon Brothers. By this time, its Arbitrage Group had disbanded, and the firm was slow to enter the Orange County fray.[14] Now under the control of Warren Buffett, Salomon was taking fewer risks and having a terrible year; it was well on its way to losing $400 million in 1994.

Given the spread of financial innovation, the collapse of Orange County seemed, with hindsight, to have been entirely predictable. It was dangerous to have someone like Robert Citron managing billions of dollars, especially when Wall Street firms were inventing new financial instruments to help fund managers place aggressive bets without regard for investment restrictions. Moreover, many of these new instruments were largely unregulated, so there were no ground rules to prevent fund managers—even municipal treasurers—from putting other people's money at risk. There weren't even disclosure requirements related to the new instruments. Given these circumstances, Orange County's collapse was not only understandable, it was practically unavoidable.

Orange County emerged from bankruptcy intact, but it wasn't the only municipality to buy complex derivatives. Municipal officials throughout the country had wanted to gamble on interest rates during the early 1990s, and because they couldn't evaluate derivatives properly, they paid high fees, just like Orange County and Gibson Greetings. The same factors that led Michael Stamenson to pitch structured notes to Robert Citron also led other Wall Street salesmen to pitch complex derivatives deals to various city and county treasurers throughout the United States. As one example, brokers called Joseph Flowers, the controller of Escambia County—in Florida's panhandle—four or five times a day, until he finally put 15 percent of Escambia's $45 million portfolio into structured derivatives.[15]

Some municipal treasurers said no. Charles Cox, finance director of the city of Farmers Branch, Texas, reasoned, "If I don't understand it and I don't know how it works, I'm not going to invest in it." David Bronner, head of the Alabama state pension fund, added a Southern sensibility: "Why should I invest in something I can't even spell?"[16] (In 1992, Orange County officials had bragged to Bronner about their returns and called him "antiquated.")

But many more said yes, and there were dozens of Orange County debacles, writ small. Every municipality imaginable—from San Diego County to the Municipal Electric Authority of Georgia, from Auburn, Maine, to Lewis & Clark County, Montana—was invested in structured notes and Collateralized Mortgage Obligations. In 1994, the House Banking Committee heard testimony by officials from Odessa College in Texas, Charles County in Maryland, and the Eastern Shoshone Tribe in Wyoming about why they had invested public funds in mortgage derivatives. Dozens of schools and townships across the country were gambling in derivatives. Eighteen Ohio municipalities lost $14 million; the Louisiana state pension fund lost $50 million; City Colleges of Chicago lost $96 million, almost its entire investment portfolio.[17] Even the Sarasota-Manatee Airport Authority lost money on inverse floaters. Derivatives had come a long way, baby.

Of course, public officials weren't the only ones betting on interest rates. As individual investors were about to learn—much to their horror—for every municipality gambling in derivatives, there was a mutual fund doing precisely the same thing. Dozens of mutual funds, including supposedly safe money-market funds, had been speculating in even riskier instruments than Orange County had bought. One mutual-fund manager in particular had put hundreds of millions of dollars, invested in a purportedly conservative fund, into the riskiest mortgage derivatives Wall Street had been able to imagine. His story was even more disturbing than Robert Citron's.

Of all the mutual fund managers gambling on interest rates through February 1994, Worth Bruntjen of Piper Jaffray led the pack. Bruntjen's arrival at Piper's headquarters in Minneapolis in 1988 was like a tornado touching down.[18] He appeared at sales meetings dressed as General Patton. He demanded that other managers move their desks to make more space for him and his subordinates. He created his own fiefdom, even reconstructing Piper's floor plan to seal him and his staff into private quarters, behind a frosted-glass door. This special work area was known as "the vortex."

Bruntjen managed Piper's flagship mutual fund, the Piper Jaffray Institutional Government Income Portfolio. When Piper first introduced the fund in 1988, it was extremely low risk, and invested almost exclusively in U.S. Treasury bonds and plain-vanilla government-agency mortgage securities. Piper had been a well-respected fund manager since 1913, and it advertised Bruntjen's fund as more of the same: safe and secure.

Beginning in 1991, when new rules made it for difficult for banks and thrifts to buy risky mortgage derivatives, Bruntjen decided to step in to fill the void. He began planning to invest in various types of mortgage derivatives—in particular, Collateralized Mortgage Obligations, the mortgage derivatives Salomon had pioneered—in an effort to boost Piper's returns. CMOs were highly rated mortgage bonds backed by the U.S. government, so they technically fit Bruntjen's investment mandate. On a paper list, all CMOs looked basically the same as government bonds: the name of a government agency, a rating of AAA, and a few numbers and letters designating the code for the particular security. However, CMOs ranged widely, from very conservative—safer even than plain-vanilla mortgages—to unbelievably volatile. Some were much riskier than anything Bruntjen's fund previously had purchased.

During the summer of 1991, Piper held a conference in Sun Valley, Idaho, for its top salespeople. Bruntjen's low-tech presentation at the conference—just a few slides on an overhead projector—was difficult to follow. In explaining his plan to invest in mortgage derivatives, Bruntjen used so many unusual words and acronyms that some of the salesmen felt he was "speaking another language." It seemed clear that Bruntjen was expanding from plain-vanilla mortgages to more exotic investments, but the salespeople didn't get all the details about inverse IOs (more on them later). There were repeated whispers of "Did you understand that?" and when Piper's top-performing salesman was asked about Bruntjen's new strategy, he said it seemed "like magic."

And it was. From 1991 through early 1994, Bruntjen's fund was the top-rated short-term government-bond fund in the United States. Bruntjen generated annual returns of more than 13 percent—*double* the average of other short-term government-bond funds—with little volatility. During this period, Bruntjen simply blew away Piper's competition.

How did Bruntjen do it, given that the fund's stated investment objective—conservatively seeking high income while preserving principal investment—never changed? Was he exploiting some market inefficiency, like Meriwether's traders at Salomon? Or was he just placing big bets, like Andy Krieger at Bankers Trust?

The answer was: a bit of both. Bruntjen bought the complex mortgage derivatives that First Boston and Salomon Brothers had invented in the 1980s, and that other banks such as Kidder Peabody and Bear Stearns had begun selling by the billions of dollars. Many of these investments—known on Wall Street as *nuclear waste*—involved risks that required advanced mathematical training to understand. Because of these complexities, these instruments occasionally would be undervalued, or at least Bruntjen hoped they might be. But whereas the Arbitrage Group at Salomon had captured that value by buying cheap mortgage derivatives and hedging the risks in other markets, Bruntjen just bought the mortgage derivatives outright, without such hedges.

Essentially, Bruntjen's investment strategy was a huge bet that interest rates would remain low, although it also carried other risks. For example, Bruntjen bought a special kind of mortgage derivative, called an *inverse IO*. An IO, on its own, was the right to receive the interest-only portion of payments on home mortgages. An inverse IO was an IO with a twist: instead of paying a coupon that corresponded to the interest payments homeowners actually paid, an inverse IO paid a coupon that moved in the opposite direction of interest rates.

The inverse IO had a formula just like a structured note. For example, the coupon might be 25 percent, minus four times the short-term interest rate. So if the short-term rate were three percent, the inverse IO would pay 25 percent minus 12 percent, or 13 percent (the amount Bruntjen was earning in his fund). If short-term rates went up, the coupon, based on the formula, went down.

This formula made the inverse IO doubly hard to assess. On one hand, the inverse IO seemed to become less valuable when interest rates declined, because individuals prepaid their mortgages and the inverse IO lost some of its payments. On the other hand, the inverse IO seemed to become more valuable when interest rates declined, because the coupon formula— which moved in the opposite direction of rates—actually went up.

In other words, an inverse IO was a whipsaw. There were two risks— maturity and coupon—that went in opposite directions. It paid a higher coupon when interest rates dropped, but it also shortened in maturity because of mortgage prepayments; it paid a lower coupon when interest rates rose, but it also lengthened in maturity because of few prepayments. Thus, the inverse IO had two faces, neither of which was very attractive. It was a short-fused explosive when interest rates were low, and a long-fused dud when rates were high. This was why inverse IOs were known on Wall Street—quite appropriately—as nuclear waste. It was unclear whether *any* mutual-fund managers really understood all of this.

All things considered, an interest-rate hike would be especially damaging to an owner of inverse IOs. Although few homeowners would refinance their mortgages if rates were higher, the owner of inverse IOs wouldn't benefit from the additional payments of interest in the future, because as rates went up the coupon on the inverse IOs would go down. In fact, a significant rate increase would send the coupon plummeting to zero, leaving the owner stuck with a 30-year investment that did not pay anything at all.

As Bruntjen loaded up his fund with inverse IOs, he was moving far, far away from the fund's original strategy. Although investors did not realize it, by March 1993, more than 93 percent of the fund's net assets were invested in CMO derivatives.[19]

Although the securities in the fund were complex, the pitch to investors was simple: put your money with Worth Bruntjen and get a better return. Bruntjen didn't directly solicit investors, but he gave numerous presentations regarding his investment strategy. For important clients, salespeople were told to "bring 'em in to talk to Worth." Brokers hinted to corporate clients that if they invested a substantial amount in the fund, they might improve their investment-banking relationship with Piper, and perhaps even persuade one of Piper's respected stock analysts to begin following their companies. (Such hints would become a reality when Internet-securities offerings heated up several years later.) Bruntjen was poised and articulate during these presentations, and clients left feeling swept away in the whirlwind of his enthusiasm and expertise.

Less sophisticated investors didn't need to visit Piper's offices or hear Bruntjen talk about the fund. They knew enough just by looking at the fund's advertisements: THIRTEEN PERCENT RETURNS! Even better, Bruntjen's fund had top ratings from Morningstar and Value Line, the two rating systems for mutual funds (although this wasn't surprising, given that those ratings were simply based on the fund's historical returns).

It wasn't hard for Piper's brokers to sell 13+ percent returns with a top Morningstar rating. A good broker could bring in over a million dollars per month of new investments into the fund. Individual investors were greedy, just like the managers at Gibson Greetings and Procter & Gamble, and with double the returns of any other comparable investment, the fund basically sold itself.

The small companies and individual investors who bought the fund didn't ask many probing questions about the 20 percent of the fund invested in inverse floaters, or even about the 33 percent invested in principal-only strips and Z-bonds (essentially, these were CMOs with a very long maturity, well beyond the fund's stated limit of three-to-five years). Even if investors had read the prospectus carefully, they had no reason to ask about the fund's CMOs, which on paper looked just like any other AAA-rated U.S. government-backed obligation—the details weren't disclosed, but even if investors had asked, they wouldn't have gotten any answers. The top brokers at Piper didn't understand what Worth Bruntjen was buying, either.

To expand Piper's investor base, Piper's lobbyists drafted legislation—known as the Piper amendment—that permitted Minnesota towns and counties to invest in Piper funds. With this amendment, the tiny Orange County wannabes throughout the Midwest could enter Piper's casino, too. About sixty government bodies did so, including cities such as Eden

Prairie, Moorhead, Maple Grove, and Mound. Even the Metropolitan Sports Facilities Commission—which operates the Metrodome stadium, where the state's beloved football team, the Minnesota Vikings, plays—put millions into Bruntjen's fund.[20]

The fund's performance attracted $500 million of new investment during 1992 and 1993. As money flowed into the fund, investors from all over the world spoke with awe of Piper's investment acumen. Bruntjen became a media celebrity, and was called the "Wizard of Mortgages." Tad Piper, an heir to the Piper family of funds, was overjoyed that Bruntjen had given the Minneapolis firm a national profile. He rewarded Bruntjen by taking him on a ski vacation.

In retrospect, Tad Piper and his sales force might have been more skeptical about how Bruntjen was generating such stellar returns. When Bruntjen bragged in a December 6, 1993, cover story in *Business Week* that "We buy government-agency paper that has a higher interest rate than the 30-year bond but has an average life of only three to five years," it sounded too good to be true. Bruntjen was buying highly rated government bonds, and beating all of his peers, year after year. But instead of being subject to scrutiny, or punished for taking excessive risks, he was promoted to senior vice president at Piper, and was personally charged with managing almost a third of Piper's $12 billion in assets.

Worth Bruntjen's fate was intimately tied to that of David J. Askin, a soft-spoken and scholarly fund manager, with an ego as big as his oversized spectacles.[21] Askin had been a successful banker at Drexel Burnham Lambert, but as Drexel was failing, in 1990, Askin looked to start his own firm. When Edwin Whitehead, a wealthy investor who ran Whitehead/Sterling Advisors, died that year, Askin found his opportunity. He bought one of Whitehead's funds, whose investors included various charities related to Whitehead, along with Whitehead's estate.

In January 1993, Askin renamed Whitehead's fund Askin Capital Management. Like Piper, Askin told investors his fund would purchase only the "highest credit quality" securities. Askin also said the fund would employ a "market neutral investment strategy to hedge against market volatility." Unlike Bruntjen, Askin wasn't planning to make outright bets. Instead, the fund's investments would be "hedged so as to maintain a relatively constant portfolio value, even through large interest rate swings."[22]

Askin's strategy sounded just like that of Salomon's Arbitrage Group.

Askin told investors the fund had "proprietary analytic models" that identified mispricings among complex mortgage securities, such as Collateralized Mortgage Obligations. The fund then bought the cheap CMOs and sold the expensive ones, just like Greg Hawkins of Salomon Brothers.

The funds within Askin Capital Management had rock-solid names, such as Granite Partners and Quartz, and solid returns, too, which attracted hundreds of millions of dollars of investment. New investors ranged from Nicholas J. Nicholas Jr., former CEO of Time Warner, to the 3M Employee Retirement Income Plan.[23] General Electric and its chairman, Jack Welch, also were involved in Askin through Kidder Peabody.

Askin bought many of the same securities Worth Bruntjen of Piper bought, including hundreds of millions of dollars of inverse IOs, sold by Kidder Peabody, which General Electric owned. By 1994, Askin had become such a big player that the market for exotic mortgage derivatives simply could not function without the fund. Bruntjen was dependent on Askin's trading of complex CMOs; without it, the market would dry up, and the price of the securities would plummet.

After the rate hike, Bruntjen's fund had lost a great deal of money, but Askin was in much worse condition. The fund was stuck with long-maturity securities that paid virtually nothing, and Askin had borrowed money to leverage its positions. As the markets went down, Askin needed to sell CMOs to repay some of the loans. But when the firm began selling, the sales created a downward spiral in the CMO market, with prices dropping so low that many dealers refused to trade at all.[24]

Askin also was a victim of the same kinds of valuation problems that had plagued Bankers Trust and Salomon. When the Fed raised rates on February 4, the Granite fund used its own computer models to determine the value of its mortgages, instead of looking to the market for values. As the markets declined, Granite's computer models said that the market was wrong, and that the mortgages were still valuable. Granite did not mark to market its securities based on reliable, outside data. Instead, it valued its portfolio based on the computer's outputs.

Askin survived briefly because of the fund's cozy relationship with brokers. The brokers made millions from Askin's purchases, so they gave the fund favorable lending terms, and even allowed Askin to take possession of securities he had not yet paid for. As described in the previous chapter, the value of a mortgage derivative depended greatly on assumptions about how quickly homeowners were prepaying their mortgages; with this flexibility, brokers could give Askin favorable mark-to-market numbers, to help justify relying on the fund's computer outputs, and thereby smooth the fund's income and, potentially, hide losses. In describing the special consideration David Askin received, one investor called him "the Hillary Clinton of the bond market."[25] (This was a reference to Hillary Clinton's foray into cattle-futures trading, where she netted $100,000, allegedly because her broker had allocated only winning trades to her account.)

The special treatment helped at first. When Askin reported its February 1994 results to investors, there appeared to be only a two-percent loss. But a few weeks later, when Askin obtained some less friendly marks from other dealers, the loss was 20 percent. In late March, Askin told investors the loss was 35 percent.[26]

At this point, it appeared that Askin might not be able to repay its loans. Askin's brokers—fair-weather friends—abruptly abandoned the fund and began issuing *margin calls,* demanding that Askin repay the money it had borrowed. When Askin couldn't repay the loans, brokers sold Askin's CMOs—just as Orange County's brokers had sold its structured notes. The CMO markets crashed, destroying not only Askin, but Worth Bruntjen and numerous other investors. By April 7, all $600 million of Askin's fund was gone.

Throughout this time, Askin was paying huge fees for the CMOs it purchased. Either Askin was overpaying its brokers and hoping for favorable treatment, or it was no more sophisticated than Worth Bruntjen. The first possibility raised troubling questions about conflicts of interest. But the second possibility—that the Askin fund's emperor had no clothes— was more likely. It was difficult for any fund to impersonate Salomon's Arbitrage Group, and Askin apparently had failed.

Taped conversations among salesmen at Kidder Peabody, then the leading CMO dealer, confirmed this second view. After the Fed's rate hike, Kidder's mortgage salesmen were hurting, because trading in complex mortgages had declined. The salesmen passed the time by mocking Askin, just as Bankers Trust salesmen had mocked Procter & Gamble. Kidder had sold Askin hundreds of millions of dollars of CMOs during the weeks before *and after* the Fed's rate hike, just as Bankers Trust had sold swaps to P&G during February 1994, and Kidder had made even more money than Bankers Trust from the sales.

Here is a record of one conversation alleged to have taken place between William O'Connor, the Kidder salesman who covered Askin, and his assistant, Jay Pappas, on March 25, 1994, just seven weeks after the

Fed's rate hike, in the heat of the uncertainty about whether Askin would survive:

> PAPPAS: Just pull the plug if Askin doesn't pay.
> O'CONNOR: You don't seem to understand. We can't pull the plug. We are in bed with these guys. OK? Last thing in the world we want to hear is that Askin can't meet a margin call and we got to liquidate the nuclear waste they bought.
> PAPPAS: A lot of it's nuclear waste?
> O'CONNOR: It's all nuclear waste, come on. You get paid a plus [1/64 of one percent] for selling a Ginnie 7 [a plain-vanilla mortgage security]. You get paid a plus for selling a long bond. What do you think these are? We get paid a point [one percent]. Nuclear waste.
> PAPPAS: You got a point and a half, two points on some of them.
> O'CONNOR: Yes.
> PAPPAS: Did you know that when you sold them?
> O'CONNOR: Of course I did.[27]

To translate: Wall Street was making just as much money from sales to Askin as it was making from sales of similar instruments to municipalities and mutual funds. Interestingly, the brokers fed on Askin, as it lay dying, just as they had picked at Orange County after its bankruptcy. Howard Rubin—the trader who had lost $377 million for Merrill Lynch in 1987 and then resurfaced, unpunished, at Bear Stearns—was one of the vultures, along with traders from Kidder Peabody. It appeared that Kidder Peabody and Bear Stearns were "cooperating" to buy Askin's bonds at fire-sale prices, just as the structured note dealers seemed to have colluded in buying Orange County's bonds. William O'Connor of Kidder reportedly said that "basically we told Howie Rubin, we'll bid all your bonds, you got to bid all ours, we just need legal for court later on."[28] The dealers apparently had plenty of "legal"—meaning they believed they could defend each other's low valuations as lawful and appropriate—and they were never punished for these actions. Howard Rubin and Bear Stearns allegedly made $20 million in a few days, buying and then reselling Askin's CMOs.[29] Askin filed for bankruptcy a few days later. The fund had been able to survive pretending to be Salomon's Arbitrage Group for only about a year.

Askin's troubles were terrible news for Worth Bruntjen, who was struggling to evaluate the damage done to his fund. By March 1994, Piper was unable even to determine end-of-day prices of the assets in Bruntjen's fund on a daily basis, as required by law. Bruntjen and his staff had switched to a weekly pricing procedure—comically dubbed "Pricing Thursdays"—in which they would attempt to evaluate the prices of all of their instruments by calling various financial institutions and plugging data they often didn't understand into computer models.[30] During early April 1994, the pricing procedure took most of the day.[31]

Like Askin, Piper did not disclose the risks associated with these complex instruments, or the difficulties of pricing them. At Piper, the problems were not even disclosed to employees outside Bruntjen's circle, or to many of the salesmen who had sold so many millions of dollars' worth of Bruntjen's fund to their accounts. Piper employees later would express shock when they learned that Bruntjen had not been such an expert in mortgage derivatives. Many people had assumed that Bruntjen's background was similar to those of the traders and Ph.D.s at Bankers Trust, First Boston, and Salomon Brothers. But the reality was that Bruntjen was far from a "rocket scientist"—he did not have a college degree, and he certainly did not have the training necessary to understand complex CMOs.

The supposedly ultra-safe mutual funds Worth Bruntjen managed at Piper were the worst-performing bond funds in the entire market in 1994. Bruntjen was down 28 percent for the year, an inexplicable loss for a short-term government-bond fund that advertised preservation of principal. John Rekenthaler, editor of Morningstar—which had given Piper its highest ratings—said that although Piper had claimed Bruntjen's fund was short-term in nature, "the fund had to be a hell of a lot longer."[32] Yet these longer-maturity risks, embedded in highly rated CMOs, had been invisible to fund investors.

In September 1994, CEO Tad Piper maintained that the instruments Bruntjen owned were still undervalued, and said he believed the fund would come back. He admitted that the fund "got caught in a market that we thought we understood,"[33] but insisted that "we have great confidence in Worth."[34] He did not explain how a conservative government-bond fund could lose 28 percent in less than a year, or how it previously could have averaged returns of more than 13 percent for several years. In any event, Tad Piper would not be taking Worth Bruntjen on any more ski vacations. Bruntjen would continue to work for Piper only until just after the lawsuits against his firm were resolved. Bruntjen settled the SEC's case against him by agreeing to be barred from the industry for five years. He paid a $100,000 fine.[35]

. . .

Like Orange County and the various municipalities, Piper was far from the only mutual fund at the gambling tables. In the early 1990s, managers of many of the largest mutual funds in the world had placed similar, hidden bets, using various types of derivatives. The bets included not only structured notes and mortgage derivatives, but novel variations on the currency derivatives Andy Krieger had pioneered. For example, the Alliance North American Government Income Fund—then one of the largest and best-performing bond funds in the world—had placed large bets on the Mexican peso, which had remained stable relative to the U.S. dollar for several years. For years, the bets had paid off, and Alliance's fund was the best performer in its category. (The aftermath of the peso devaluation of late 1994 is covered in Chapter 8.)

The major money-market funds—which had bet on U.S. interest rates, just as Orange County and Piper had—did not fare as well. Money-market funds were supposed to be ultra-safe, basically a substitute for cash or a checking account. Yet several banks were forced to prop up the money-market funds they managed, in order to avoid losses, including such major funds as BankAmerica ($68 million), First Boston ($40 million), Merrill Lynch ($20 million), and PaineWebber ($268 million).[36] As if Kidder Peabody's bad year selling mortgages hadn't been bad enough for Jack Welch, the chairman of General Electric—Kidder's parent company—Welch also had to spend $7 million to cover derivative-related losses in five of Kidder's money-market funds.[37] Atlantic Richfield Company's ARCO managed a $400 million money-market fund, and lost $22 million.[38] United Services Advisors lost $93 million,[39] Fleet Financial Group lost $5 million. And so on. In September 1994, a money-market fund called Community Assets Management Inc., in Denver, was liquidated, and there was no parent company to make up for losses. Community Assets became the first-ever money-market fund to lose money for its shareholders.

On June 1, 1994, Edward C. Johnson III, chairman of the Fidelity family of mutual funds, sent a letter to all of Fidelity's bond investors, explaining the funds' use of derivatives and blaming the recent losses on the interest-rate hike and the role of leveraged hedge funds, which he said "were caught by surprise by the magnitude of the rise in interest rates and the decline in bond prices and were forced to sell to meet margin calls."[40] Fund giant Vanguard distributed a similar notice in a bulletin called "Plain Talk About Derivatives."

The losses at mutual funds affected millions of investors. Moreover, now that commercial banks were increasingly engaging in the securities business, it was difficult for investors to separate a risky investment in derivatives from a simple deposit at their local bank. Consider Nations-Bank, for example. In 1993, NationsBank received permission to begin operating a securities firm, called NationsSecurities, which immediately began selling *Term Trusts* to NationsBank clients.[41] Term Trusts were 10-year-maturity bond funds that paid an extra one percent or more above the 10-year U.S. Treasury Yield. To a bank customer with money in a checking account or a certificate of deposit, this was a huge increase in yield.

Of course, the increase didn't come without risk. Unlike a bank deposit, return of principal was very much at risk. The Term Trusts achieved a high yield by investing up to 40 percent of their assets in inverse floaters, which—as Orange County made clear—were not without risk.

NationsSecurities made the Term Trusts its first focus product, creating monetary incentives for its representatives to sell them. In the first months of the program, through February 1994, NationsSecurities sold more than $300 million of the Term Trusts, generating more than $16 million in fees. Sales representatives pitched the Term Trusts to investors in traditional Certificates of Deposit, telling NationsBank customers who never had invested in anything other than CDs that Term Trusts were as safe as CDs, but better because they paid more. NationsSecurities paid Nations-Bank employees referral fees for sending these customers.

The sales representatives were given detailed prospectuses with fine print describing the various risks associated with Term Trusts, but apparently they either ignored them or did not read them very carefully. Instead, the sales representatives told clients, as they had been told during presentations, that the Term Trusts were backed by the U.S. government and would not lose principal. On several occasions, a sales manager held up a picture of a Term Trust brochure with a picture of the U.S. Capitol Building on the cover, and said, "If the Capitol is standing in 10 years, these people will get their money back." The representatives fed these pitches to their customers during "call nights," when they emphasized the Term Trusts' safety, predictability, and return. Some Texas representatives told customers that "until now you had to be Texas A&M or have the wealth of Ross Perot, to get access to this quality of management." Some representatives even told customers that because the Term Trusts would return *all* of the principal payment in 10 years, there was no fee (in reality, the sales commission was a whopping 5.5 percent). These representatives didn't discuss the details about all the inverse floaters the Term Trusts held.

NationsSecurities blurred the line it was supposed to maintain between itself and NationsBank. Even the names were almost interchangeable. NationsSecurities sent a mass mailing about the Term Trusts to more than a million NationsBank customers, in envelopes bearing the Nations-Bank logo and colors. Representatives were taught to call the Term Trusts "accounts at the bank"—rather than securities—and to say they were calling "from the bank."

Not surprisingly, the Term Trusts did not perform very well. Recall that inverse floaters decline in value when short-term interest rates rise. After the Fed's rate hike, the Term Trusts declined in value by more than a third. So much for protection of principal. (NationsSecurities later was censured by the SEC and fined $4 million.)[42]

The spread of financial innovation to more traditional and conservative financial intermediaries—particularly, money-market funds and commercial banks—created new dangers. How could individual investors discern the risks of these new menus of investment possibilities? The Securities and Exchange Commission had taken the position that stock and bond mutual funds should be able to invest in whatever they wanted, so long as they disclosed the risks. But what constituted adequate disclosure? And even with adequate disclosure, should an elderly banking client who had never bought anything other than a CD really be purchasing inverse floaters under any circumstances? The questions were not merely theoretical. NationsBank was one of several large banks entering the securities business to sell new financial products to millions of individual banking customers.

In addition, paying bonuses based on performance skewed the incentives of fund managers and bank salespeople. If they performed well, they made a lot of money for themselves. If they performed poorly, they lost someone else's money. Federal law generally barred investment advisers from receiving incentive compensation for sales to small clients (people with less than $1 million of net worth or $500,000 in investments). But there was an exception for mutual funds, and financial institutions had shown, in recent years, a great ability to drive trucks through even small exceptions. Mutual funds had to compete with Wall Street for talent, and if they couldn't pay big bonuses, they wouldn't be able to attract the best managers. The more Wall Street traders made, the higher the fund managers' compensation would have to be.

Still another problem was the lack of sophistication among fund managers. The data showed that most active managers underperformed market indexes. The Arbitrage Group at Salomon Brothers had been able to spot inefficiencies and outperform their peers, year after year. But not many fund managers were like John Meriwether's traders. Certainly Robert Citron and Worth Bruntjen didn't measure up. And the greatest damage had come from the smartest manager, David Askin.

Fund managers all seemed to be buying the same financial instruments, like gamblers all betting on red at a roulette wheel. *Fortune* magazine conducted a detailed survey and found only four money managers who had outperformed the major bond-market indices in 1994.[43] It was remarkable, but nearly every professional money manager during the early 1990s had been speculating that interest rates would remain low.

The Federal Reserve had fueled this speculation by committing to keep interest rates low. In 1989, short-term rates had been higher than long-term rates, which were around eight percent. By 1992, short-term rates were three percent, while long-term rates were still near eight percent. As long as this interest-rate environment held, it was easy to make money, with just a little bit of (relatively painless) math.

Suppose you use $1,000 of savings to buy long-term bonds. If long-term rates are eight percent, you make $80 in a year, if rates don't change. Not bad.

Now suppose that you also borrow $10,000 and invest the entire $11,000 amount in long-term bonds. You still make $80 on your $1,000 of savings. But now you also make $800 on your $10,000 of borrowings—$880 in all. If short-term rates were only three percent, you would only have to repay $300 of interest on a 1-year loan, so you would keep $580—a return of more than 50 percent on your money. And, in that example, your leverage—the ratio of your borrowings to your savings—was only 11-to-1. Financial institutions typically had leverage in the range of 25 to 1. Throughout the early 1990s, financial institutions could do this simple *carry* trade—borrowing short-term and investing long-term—and make a fortune. ("Carry" refers to the difference between short-term and long-term rates.)

The incredible thing about the carry trade was that *everyone* did it—not only mutual funds, but also hedge funds, the unregulated investment funds that often did everything but hedge. *Hedge fund* was a generic term that referred to any unregulated investment fund; *mutual fund* referred to a regulated U.S. fund. (Hedge funds could avoid U.S. regulation if they had 100 or fewer U.S. investors.) Managers of the biggest hedge funds had them borrow money to place huge bets on various currencies, interest rates, and other securities. George Soros was a prime example. So was David Askin.

During the early 1990s, nearly every hedge fund bet on the carry trade. As Stan Jonas, a well-regarded trader at Societe Generale/FIMAT, described it, looking back on 1994, "If a Martian came to the U.S. and looked at the universe of hedge fund managers, he'd see the same person. Many of these managers are interrelated by blood, by hobbies, by education. They're all competing, checking what the other one's doing."[44] And they all made the same bets.

Unfortunately, the Federal Reserve didn't understand hedge funds very well, and didn't realize how much financial institutions had borrowed to bet on interest rates using unregulated derivatives. The spread of this leverage was the reason the Fed's rate hike had had such far-reaching, unanticipated effects.

By early May 1994, the Fed had raised rates another half a percent, and the carnage was more visible. Three of the biggest hedge-fund managers—Leon Cooperman of Omega Partners, Julian Robertson of Tiger Management, Michael Steinhardt of Steinhardt Partners—lost billions of dollars. Banks and securities firms also were hit hard, with Bankers Trust finally experiencing its first loss, and Salomon Brothers reporting a pretax loss of $371 million for the first half of 1994, most of it from bond losses. The life insurance industry lost about $50 billion on bonds in 1994; property and casualty insurers lost $20 billion, more than they paid in claims for Hurricane Andrew.[45] (These losses didn't show up in financial statements, either, because insurance companies recorded their bond investments at their historical cost.)

A few prescient firms abandoned their bets just before February 4, 1994. For example, AIG Financial Products made more than $1 billion on derivatives between 1988 and 1992, but AIG's chairman, Maurice "Ace" Greenberg, decided in 1993 that his firm was taking too many risks, and the head of AIG Financial Products, Howard Sosin, left the firm, along with a reported $200 million in compensation. Sosin had joined AIG from Drexel Lambert in 1987, and he avoided the frenzy of Wall Street's trading culture by operating out of an office in Westport,

Connecticut, with a fifty-foot saltwater fish tank. Long-Term Capital Management—which was just opening its doors as the Fed was raising rates, in a similarly relaxed setting in Greenwich, Connecticut—took advantage of the collapse of various investment funds by hiring several dozen employees with strong quantitative backgrounds.

Joseph Erickson, a partner at Peat Marwick and a consultant on derivatives, derided fund managers who didn't understand the derivatives they bought, saying: "If you don't understand, you might as well place it all on red at Atlantic City or Las Vegas, because at least there you get free drinks."[46] Erickson was missing the point. Sophisticated or unsophisticated, understanding or not, drinks or no drinks, everyone had bet on red.

In 1995, Brandon Becker and Jennifer Yoon, of the Securities and Exchange Commission, compiled a list of institutions that had lost money in the various new financial instruments during the previous year. The list included virtually every kind of institution, from every sector of the economy. To get a sense of how far these new instruments had spread by then, take a glance at this paragraph, which includes a selected "top 100" from the list. (You might even recognize a few that lost some of your money.)

ABN AMRO; Air Products and Chemicals; Allied-Lyons; American International Group; AmSouth Bancorp; Askin Capital Management; Atlantic Richfield; Auburn, Maine; Banc One; Bank of Montreal Harris Trust & Savings; Baptist Missionary Association of America; Barings; Barnett Banks; Benjamin Franklin Federal Savings and Loan; Berjaya Industrial; CS First Boston Investment Management; Capital Corporate Federal Credit Union; Cargill Investor Services; Caterpillar Financial Services; Chemical Bank; China International Trust and Investment; City Colleges of Chicago; Codelco; Collier County, Florida; Colonia Asset Management; Common Fund; Community Bankers Fund; Connecticut State Pension Fund; Constitution State Corporate Credit Union; Corporate One Credit Union; Credit Lyonnais; Cuyahoga County, Ohio; Dell Computer; Eastman Kodak; Escambia County, Florida; Federal Farm Credit System; Federal Paper Board; Fidelity; First Boston; Fleet Financial; Florida operating fund; Franklin Savings; Fundamental Family of Funds; Gibson Greetings; Glaxo; Gothaer Life Insurance; Hammersmith & Fulham; Independence Bancorp; Indiana Corporate

Federal Credit Union; Investors Equity Life, Hawaii; J. P. Morgan; Japan Airlines; Joplin City, Missouri; Kanzaki Paper Manufacturing; Kashima Oil; KeyCorp Bank; Kidder Peabody; Mead; Mellon Bank; Meritor Savings Bank; Merrill Lynch; Metallgesellschaft; Mutual Benefit Life Insurance; National Fisheries, South Korea; New England Investment; Northern Trust; Norwest; Odessa College; Ontario Province, Canada; Orange County; PaineWebber; Piper Jaffray; Pittsburgh National Bank; Postipankki Bank, Finland; Procter & Gamble; Robert W. Baird; Salomon Brothers; Sandusky County, Ohio; Seamen's Bank for Savings; Sears Roebuck; Shanghai International Securities; Showa Shell Sekiyu; Silverado Banking Savings and Loan; Sinar Mas; Soros Fund Management; Southwestern Federal Credit Union; Southwestern Life; St. Lucie County, Florida; St. Petersburg, Florida; Tokyo Securities; Union Bank; UNIPEC; Virginia state pension fund; West Virginia Consolidated Fund; Western Corporate Federal Credit Union; Wilmington Trust; Wimpey Group; Wisconsin State Pension Fund; Yamaichi Securities.

The list was impossible to ignore. The stories of investors losing money on derivatives were not isolated incidents; they evidenced an epidemic. Just a few years earlier, structured notes did not exist, and complex CMOs were merely the wacky idea of a few traders. But by 1994, the financial innovations of Bankers Trust, First Boston, and Salomon Brothers had spread so far that it was hard to find someone who *didn't* own these instruments. The news was bewildering and overwhelming for average investors, who barely had time to follow the media coverage of the losses, and certainly did not have the resources to understand all the details. In this new world, how could a person keep tabs on his or her investments?

As average investors learned about the losses, they became upset with Wall Street, and bankers briefly became pariahs, as they occasionally do. The number of top business-school graduates seeking finance jobs dropped by half. The media portrayed wealthy bankers as villains. And the inevitable cartoons appeared, one picturing a man in a three-piece suit, holding a briefcase and a cup for begging, next to a sign that said "Dabbled in Derivatives." Another had a caption, "Hey, there's always tomorrow. Well, unless you're in derivatives." For the 1994 holiday season, Trimedia, a public-relations firm, sent out a card depicting Santa and his reindeer crashing into a building, with the legend, "Don't worry. He's got a derivatives contract from Bankers Trust. Happy Holidays!"

The bankers didn't seem to care about all the fuss. They knew it would go away soon, as it always did. Instead, they disclaimed any responsibility, and blamed investors for making stupid bets and for failing to supervise their investments. Besides, in December 1994, there was little chance of getting bankers to focus on anything other than the upcoming bonus check.

After several years of being spoiled by skyrocketing bonuses, bankers threw tantrums when they learned overall pay would be down 20 percent for 1994. Many angrily tore up their bonus checks, took unannounced vacations, quit, or otherwise behaved as one might expect of youngsters losing their million-dollar allowances. A trader from Lehman Brothers sent an impostor to perform his jury service while he skipped out on a trip to Milan.[47] (Reportedly, when the judge began routinely questioning the surrogate, he said he wasn't the trader, asked to visit the men's room, and never returned.) *New York* magazine reported on other bankers' attempts to "get even" by billing expensive consumer items to their firms, including groceries, home furnishings, Brooks Brothers shirts, and even Chanel suits. One banker said, "Given what they put me through, they owe me." The greatest abuses involved limousine services, which cost firms millions of dollars in waiting time alone. Bankers called for cars at odd times, made drivers wait, and then billed the fees to their firms, or to clients. One Goldman Sachs banker sent a briefcase—just the briefcase— home to Connecticut in a limo.

As investors learned about these stories, they became angrier, still. This clash between Main Street and Wall Street created the ideal atmosphere for legislators to create new legal rules governing the various new financial instruments and strategies. Investors are typically too diffuse to mount intense lobbying efforts, especially compared to banks, which have well-funded trade organizations and dedicated lobbyists. But in 1994, investors were crying for reforms, and there were signs they were being heard. Congressional staffers began drafting new legislation, judges were hearing lawsuits related to the losses, securities regulators were preparing rules to improve disclosure, and prosecutors were considering bringing criminal cases against various perpetrators. As the year closed, with Orange County filing for bankruptcy, investors found little comfort, except perhaps the hope that governmental officials would punish the wrongdoers and create a new regulatory framework to stop the wave of undisclosed risk-taking of 1994 from spreading even further. Instead, the regulators were about to do precisely the opposite.

INCUBATION

MORALS OF THE MARKETPLACE

The two most prominent people managing the regulatory response to the financial fiascos of 1994 were Arthur Levitt Jr. and Mark C. Brickell. Levitt was the chairman of the Securities and Exchange Commission, the primary regulator of financial instruments in the United States—a federal agency that advertised itself as "the investor's advocate." Brickell was a vice president of J. P. Morgan and the top lobbyist for the derivatives trade group, called ISDA, that had persuaded lawmakers to allow the unregulated derivatives markets to grow unchecked since 1985. It was surprising how much the two men were in sync.

Levitt was an unlikely candidate to be the investor's advocate. During the 1960s and 1970s, he had been a Wall Street broker, eventually rising to become president of the predecessor firm to Lehman Brothers. To the extent he focused on individual investors, he was persuading them to buy stocks. In 1981, he even wrote a book of investment advice called *How to Make Your Money Make Money*. (When Levitt testified before Congress on the collapse of Enron in January 2002, one admirer sitting in the second row of a packed room in the Hart Senate Office Building was clutching a tattered copy of Levitt's book, presumably seeking an autograph.)

After working as a stockbroker, Levitt spent twelve years as chairman of the American Stock Exchange (the smaller sister of the New York Stock Exchange), where he advocated on behalf of major Wall Street firms and even ran a derivatives-trading business. Levitt had plenty of experience with derivatives, stretching back to as early as 1985, when he chaired a conference on futures and options.[1]

Notwithstanding his Wall Street background, Levitt served the longest term of any SEC chair—nearly eight years—acquiring a reputation as an effective regulator (a reputation that this chapter will show is mostly undeserved). In 2002, after Levitt finally stepped down, some members of Congress even apologized for ignoring some of the proposals Levitt advanced late in his term.

Levitt was a fish in a barrel for Mark Brickell, an aggressive banker who, beginning in 1976, spent more than two decades at J. P. Morgan. J. P. Morgan—like Bankers Trust—was transforming itself from a stodgy commercial bank into a sophisticated risk manager and trader of new financial products. Brickell had studied politics at the University of Chicago and, although he also had attended Harvard Business School and worked in swaps, he only began to thrive at J. P. Morgan when he returned to politics, lobbying on behalf of his bank and other derivatives dealers as chairman of ISDA.

When Brickell's colleagues said he was good at "working" Washington, they vastly understated the case. Many legislators and regulators dreaded Brickell. He was both condescending (saying officials couldn't possibly understand derivatives) and reassuring (saying Wall Street had everything under control). But even Brickell's enemies admitted that he was a success. Brickell and ISDA had kept lawmakers away since the mid-1980s, and in early 1994 over-the-counter derivatives were largely unregulated.

After the Fed raised interest rates in February 1994, Brickell became a pit bull, telling legislators that although recent derivatives losses looked bad, regulators couldn't possibly understand or control the situation any better than market participants. He said new legislation would cause unforeseen damage, potentially imperiling not only Wall Street and the derivatives industry, but—by implication—campaign donations as well. (ISDA's members were major political contributors.)

Throughout 1994 and 1995, Brickell and Levitt worked to protect the finance industry from new legislation. In early 1994, lobbyists waited for investors to calm down from the shock of how much money-fund managers and corporate treasurers had lost gambling on interest rates. When legislation was introduced, Brickell fought it and Levitt gave speeches saying the financial industry should police itself. The issues were complicated, and the public—once so angered by the various scandals—ultimately lost interest. Instead of new derivatives regulation, Congress, various federal agencies, and even the Supreme Court created new legal rules that insulated Wall Street from liability and enabled financial firms to regulate themselves. Under the influence of Levitt and Brickell, regulators essentially left the abuses of the 1990s to what Justice Cardozo had called the "morals of the marketplace."[2]

As a result, most of the financial dealings described in previous chapters—even obvious malfeasance—went unpunished. Regulators stretched the existing law to bring a questionable case against Bankers Trust, but the result was a relatively small fine for Bankers Trust and no prison time for any bank employee. No one in the Orange County debacle did prison time for any conviction, either. Piper was much the same: Worth Bruntjen continued to manage money, his only punishment being a regulatory slap on the wrist.

The best illustration of this new self-regulatory approach was the response to a $350 million loss incurred by Orlando Joseph Jett, a trader at Kidder Peabody—the investment bank owned by General Electric that sold mortgage derivatives to Worth Bruntjen and David Askin. Prosecutors attempted to bring cases against the key parties at Kidder Peabody, but the facts were too complex, and the law was too unfriendly. (The basic pattern of the "Joseph Jett" story would be repeated several times during the next decade, including by Kent Ahrens of the Common Fund, which lost $138 million on stock-index options and futures at about the same time as Jett's loss,[3] and by Nick Leeson of Barings Bank, which lost a billion dollars trading options and futures in Singapore a few months later—more on Leeson in Chapter 8.)

Where the regulators failed, the markets succeeded in a limited way, by punishing the shareholders of firms that had engaged in questionable schemes. For example, the Joseph Jett scandal destroyed Kidder Peabody and embarrassed Jack Welch, the chairman of General Electric. The message to shareholders was: watch your investments carefully, because without the help of securities regulators—including the supposed "investor's advocate"—you are on your own.

After almost thirty years working in finance, Arthur Levitt Jr. wanted to cap off his Wall Street career with a Cabinet-level political appointment in the Clinton administration: secretary of commerce or perhaps even treasury. Levitt was an unlikely nominee for chairman of the Securities and Exchange Commission, a lower-level position requiring substantive knowledge of securities regulation. The typical SEC chairman had been a distinguished lawyer or law professor.

After majoring in English at Williams College, Levitt had ambled through several low-prestige sales jobs in the 1950s, including life insurance and cattle (ironically enough, he had sold cattle to William Casey, who later became chairman of the SEC),[4] until Sandy Weill—the later chairman of Citigroup—gave Levitt a job as a stockbroker. Levitt was moderately successful under Weill's tutelage and, although he wasn't always liked or respected, he made a fair amount of money.

But throughout this time, Levitt was unable to satisfy his political ambitions, which stemmed from his father, a respected senior statesman and long-time New York State comptroller. Levitt took on a few minor political appointments, including chairman of President Carter's "White House Conference on Small Business," but nothing compared to what Arthur Levitt Sr. had accomplished.[5]

The second Reagan administration considered Levitt for a position, but he still lacked both experience with policy issues and political connections. Besides, he was a Democrat. In 1989, Levitt improved his résumé by taking a quasi-political job as chairman of the American Stock Exchange, where he developed connections with both politicians and Wall Street leaders. He also bought a controlling interest in Roll Call, the newspaper that covered insider scoop on Congress.

During the 1992 presidential campaign, Levitt made campaign contributions in the six-figure range, ensuring that several candidates would consider him for an appointment. He gave money to a few unsuccessful presidential candidates, took various politicians on Outward Bound expeditions, and even made a small contribution to Pete Domenici, a Republican on the Senate Banking Committee. But his focus was on William Jefferson Clinton. When Clinton won the Democratic primary, Levitt helped raise $3.5 million for him, and made a personal gift of $40,000 to the Arkansas Democratic party.

When Clinton won the election, the only remaining question for Levitt was whether Clinton would be willing to give a senior appointment to a former stockbroker. During the previous twelve years, Republicans had been cautious about naming Wall Street executives to positions of power, fearing that the public would criticize them for having the fox guard the henhouse. Democrats historically had been even more reluctant to appoint financial executives.

But Bill Clinton had experienced an epiphany about Wall Street during the presidential election. Before 1992, experts had predicted that Clinton would be an unsympathetic president to Wall Street. But Clinton had learned about the power of the financial lobby when he suffered after criticizing Wall Street during the campaign. As president-elect, he famously said, "You mean to tell me that the success of the economic program and my reelection hinges on the Federal Reserve and a bunch of fucking bond traders?" When Clinton discovered that voters cared much more about whether the stock market was going up than other economic issues, he increased support for Wall Street—a then-current and potential future source of substantial campaign contributions—and committed to continue the deregulatory policies of the previous Republican administrations. Clinton appeased the populist anti-corporation forces by making a campaign pledge to halt the allegedly excessive pay of corporate executives.[6]

Levitt waited to receive a call about a Cabinet position. But there were too many potential nominees with more distinguished backgrounds, including Robert Rubin, who was a much bigger name than Levitt on Wall Street and had been co-chairman of Goldman Sachs, an even bigger campaign contributor. In April 1993, Clinton nominated Levitt to be chairman of the SEC.

Levitt was disappointed. Still, it was an important post and might be a stepping stone to the Cabinet, so Levitt took every measure to ensure the Senate's approval. Numerous securities lawyers objected to Levitt, for numerous reasons, not the least of which was that Levitt didn't have legal experience or even a law degree. (Only two previous SEC chairmen since the 1930s had been non-lawyers.) He tried to assuage their concerns, as he firmed up his Wall Street support, meeting with senior banking officials at the annual dinner for the new governors of the American Stock Exchange, and speaking at a conference held by a major securities lobbying group, the Securities Industry Association.[7]

Levitt also sold his majority stake in Roll Call—for an estimated $8 million to $10 million[8]—after officials suggested, quite sensibly, that Levitt couldn't both negotiate with members of Congress and report on them. Levitt didn't see the conflict of interest right away, but eventually agreed to sell the stake. There also were allegations that Levitt had possessed inside information when he bought Roll Call, but he denied them.[9] (Ironically, conflict-of-interest issues—ranging from accountants offering consulting advice to securities analysts receiving compensation based on the banking business done with firms they covered—would play a prominent role during Levitt's last years at the SEC.)

Levitt's confirmation hearing before the Senate Banking, Housing and Urban Affairs Committee was set for July 13, 1993. Levitt's testimony was perfectly engineered. He began by introducing his wife and children, who were there to show support. Levitt then told the senators what they wanted to hear. Republican senators Pete Domenici and Lauch Faircloth had recently held hearings on abusive securities lawsuits, and Levitt showed support, an odd position for a candidate to be the lead securities cop. He assured them, "I have experienced the pain and the cost of this litigation. I will work to see if we can come up with a solution."[10] Levitt also could point to his credentials as founder and chair of the American Business Conference, a group that supported laws curbing securities suits. The earlier gift to Senator Domenici probably didn't hurt, either.

There were a few tense moments, especially when Levitt dodged questions about accounting for stock options. Companies were not required to record as an expense the cost of stock options they gave executives, and several prominent legislators were opposed to a recent proposal to add that requirement. Levitt said that, although "as a recipient of options, I know how important options are, nonetheless, I must share with you a nagging reservation about the process of passing legislation to set accounting rules." He suggested a compromise position: more complete disclosure about options compensation as an alternative to requiring that companies include them as an expense.

When asked about derivatives, Levitt said he worried that companies might be playing with fire: "I am not persuaded that all managements of firms totally understand their impact."[11] Levitt later repeated his concern when Lou Dobbs, anchor of the Cable News Network television show *Moneyline,* asked him about derivatives, saying, "I think there is a lack of understanding in terms of how to use them and a lack of understanding in terms of the ways they can be used."[12]

But apart from these questions, Levitt skated through the hearing. His confirmation was a yawn compared to that of Dr. Joycelyn Elders, the nominee for surgeon general, who had distributed condoms in Arkansas public-health clinics and schools. With the media focused on Elders, the Senate voted to approve Levitt; he quickly returned the favor, appointing Republicans to most of the key SEC positions: director of enforcement, general counsel, and even spokesman.[13] No one even asked about *Roll Call.*

. . .

The first few months of Levitt's term were quiet, and the Clinton administration was hands-off. Financial-market regulation was split between Levitt's SEC (which had jurisdiction over "securities") and the Commodity Futures Trading Commission (which had jurisdiction over "futures"). The two agencies had fought over turf for decades. In January 1993—just days before President Clinton took office—departing CFTC chair Wendy Gramm delivered her "farewell gift" to the derivatives industry, signing an order exempting most over-the-counter derivatives from federal regulation. (A few months later, she would receive her own farewell gift, being named a director of Enron, which was an active trader of natural gas and electricity derivatives.)

Levitt decided not to press the issue, even though it remained unclear whether many derivatives fit under SEC or CFTC jurisdiction. Wendy Gramm's swap exemption was based on a 1992 law that allowed the CFTC to exclude from regulation any swaps that involved individually negotiated contracts among sophisticated parties. The CFTC's swaps exemption had expanded to include virtually all swaps, including those that were standardized and involved less sophisticated parties. Nevertheless, no one in the Clinton administration opposed this expansion. The new CFTC chair, Sheila Bair, kept the exemption in place, saying, "We have a strong affinity for derivatives at this agency. We like them."[14] On October 28, 1993, Levitt appointed Howard Kramer to the newly created SEC post of associate director for derivatives, but the SEC didn't propose any major initiatives related to new financial products.

Meanwhile, there were two major government studies of derivatives under way. In 1992, Congress had asked the General Accounting Office to consider whether derivatives regulation was necessary. Derivatives dealers were nervous about what the GAO and its director, Charles Bowsher, might say. At the same time, Representative Jim Leach of Iowa was probing the derivatives markets, asking some uncomfortable questions of Mark Brickell and the ISDA lobby; Leach's staff on the House Banking Committee also began preparing a report.

As the leading Republican on the Banking Committee, Jim Leach was an unlikely critic. Why was Leach so different from his colleagues, who were uninterested in derivatives regulation? Why was Leach alone in publicly warning that derivatives markets were out of control and might cause a system-wide collapse? The only discernible difference between

Leach and other members of Congress was that Leach did not receive financial support from Wall Street and members of the ISDA. Because he refused to accept contributions from political action committees, Leach could speak with an independent mind. By contrast, Senator Alfonse D'Amato—Representative Leach's counterpart for financial issues in the Senate—received $1.7 million in PAC money from the financial industry from 1987 to 1995.

Mark Brickell had lobbied Leach unsuccessfully, and when his efforts failed, he tried to isolate Leach from the rest of Congress. Brickell was reportedly furious when ISDA invited Leach to speak at a 1993 conference, and he began bad-mouthing him, questioning his motives, and saying that Leach and his staff didn't know what they were doing.[15]

Under Leach's direction, the House Banking Committee staff issued a 900-page report on financial derivatives in November 1993—more than three months *before* the Fed's rate hike.[16] The staff had met with all of the major federal regulatory bodies, several of the major banks, numerous lobbyists (including ISDA), and even the two largest credit-rating agencies, Standard & Poor's and Moody's. The report addressed every major issue confronting the markets for derivatives, which Leach called both "the new wild card in international finance" and a "house of cards."

ISDA's lobbyists tried to minimize the impact of Leach's report. Joseph Bauman of ISDA told a *Washington Post* reporter, "I have a tough time conceiving of any event that would make derivatives the culprit of something that really crashed the system."[17] Derivatives were an abstract issue, and the public paid little attention. The GAO was still working on its report as the Fed raised interest rates in early 1994.

After the Fed's rate hike, Wall Street's lobbyists mobilized. They met with regulators and lawmakers immediately. ISDA held an "end-user" meeting to try to neutralize the companies and mutual funds that had lost money on derivatives. In April 1994, the group named Brickell—who already had served as chairman—to be vice chairman, so that he would remain involved. As the media reported on the various scandals, ISDA especially needed Brickell to assist with a public-relations nightmare. Brickell was skilled at deflecting criticism: for example, when Neil Cavuto, the CNBC television news anchor, began a May 25, 1994, interview by telling Brickell, "People don't like you guys for some reason," Brickell responded by saying, "Well, our clients do."

Fortunately for ISDA, Jim Leach became distracted during early 1994 by an investigation into President Clinton's involvement in the Whitewater scandal in Arkansas. This investigation was a political priority and temporarily shifted Leach's attention away from derivatives.

During this time, Arthur Levitt was involved only at the periphery. Instead, Treasury Secretary Lloyd Bentsen led the administration's response. He reassembled the president's Working Group on Financial Markets—a group of financial officials who had analyzed the causes of the 1987 market crash—to consider the 1994 losses. Levitt was a member, but the Working Group did little substantive work, and instead actually served to ease ISDA's task by concentrating the lobbyist's efforts on a smaller number of designated officials. In one day, senior bankers could make all of the required rounds in Washington. Consider March 15 as one example. Officials from one firm (in this case, Morgan Stanley) met with senior Treasury officials, the chief economist and several lawyers from the Senate Banking Committee, several House of Representatives legislative directors, a lawyer with the House Banking Committee, and the staff director of the House Small Business Committee, all in one day.

Arthur Levitt gave a few speeches warning investors about derivatives during the months following the rate hike. In March 1994, he called for mutual-fund directors to pay more attention to their investments in derivatives: "With millions of inexperienced investors leaving the safety of bank CDs for the expectation of higher returns in the mutual fund market, we can ill afford even the perception of conflict."[18] In April, he told Congress that until they learned more about derivatives, "we're shooting in the dark in terms of the amount of risk involved." But Levitt made few substantive proposals.

In contrast, Richard C. Breeden, the former SEC chairman who oversaw the deregulation of the early 1990s, during the first Bush administration, immediately began warning corporate directors and officers about the dangers of derivatives. He wrote an opinion piece in the *Wall Street Journal* on March 7, entitled "Directors: Control Your Derivatives," in which he scolded corporate managers using derivatives and warned that they needed to shape up or face a "one-way ticket to financial disaster." Breeden also questioned whether companies that said they used derivatives to hedge really were speculating.[19] Even as a former SEC chair, Breeden was exerting more influence over the markets than Levitt.

In May, Arthur Levitt admitted to a group of 1,500 mutual-fund executives that the SEC didn't have the resources to police the mutual-fund industry, and he instead blamed the funds for the losses, saying, "In the final analysis, compliance is the principal responsibility, not of the commission, but of each investment company." Instead of adopting new rules, the SEC sent the funds a letter advising them to sell certain types of structured notes, including inverse floaters. The SEC's list of "dangerous" structured notes included many instruments investors had never heard of; Antony Michels of *Fortune* magazine advised, "Don't bother asking what these things are, but if a fund owns them, don't buy it."[20] Levitt tried to suggest to the public that the mutual-fund losses—which involved so many major funds—were isolated, even though the deluge of media coverage of fund losses indicated otherwise. He naively told Congress, "Our inspections to date suggest that the use of derivatives by most funds is limited."[21]

Also in May, the GAO finally released its two-year, 195-page study of derivatives.[22] The GAO was a strong supporter of free markets, but it found many serious problems related to derivatives, including regulatory gaps, antiquated accounting practices, and uncontrolled risk-management. It recommended a sweeping overhaul of derivatives regulation, including "federal regulation of the safety and soundness of all major OTC derivatives dealers."

Levitt opposed the GAO's recommendations, as did most federal regulators, who distanced themselves from GAO leader Charles Bowsher. ISDA immediately issued a point-by-point attack of the report, saying that although some of the facts in the report were correct, the GAO's conclusions were flawed. For example, ISDA noted that requiring companies to mark to market their derivatives would introduce "artificial volatility into the financial statements of commercial and industrial companies."[23] ISDA also argued that the actual amount of money at risk in derivatives was only two percent of their stated (or *notional*) value. In other words, it was misleading to talk about $50 trillion of derivatives when a mere $1 trillion was at risk.

The GAO seemed to have the better argument. Mark-to-market procedures had been the sources of trouble at financial institutions since the days of Andy Krieger at Bankers Trust. The problem with companies keeping derivatives on their books at historical cost was that, as valuations changed, investors had no idea of the changes. ISDA was correct that marking to market would make corporate earnings more volatile, but that was because corporate earnings *were* more volatile. Hiding the fluctuations didn't make a company any safer. ISDA's argument that only a fraction of the face value of derivatives was at risk also was correct. In fact, only a fraction of any investment—in derivatives or in stocks, bonds, or even real estate—was typically at risk at any point. But that didn't mean the investment was safe, or that the markets were small. Moreover, ISDA's two-percent number had ballooned after the Fed's rate hike, reflecting the losses from the rate hike. By March 1995, the percentage would be closer to four, or almost $2 trillion—arguably, more money than was at risk at any point in the entire U.S. bond market.[24]

Nevertheless, investors were too diffuse and poorly organized to counter ISDA's arguments. Economists and political scientists had long predicted that small, well-organized groups (such as ISDA) would prevent diffuse and poorly organized groups (such as investors) from achieving legislative reforms in their best interests.[25] Whatever the merits of the debate, investors never had a chance.

As one show of ISDA's power, some of its lobbyists even persuaded journalists to stop using the word "derivatives," which now had a negative connotation among the investing public. ISDA monitored the media carefully, and distributed press clippings on derivatives to all of its members. When ISDA's watchdogs found that *Wall Street Journal* reporters were continually using the "d-word" in covering the various derivatives scandals of 1994, they implored them to say "securities" instead.

For example, *Wall Street Journal* reporters originally had referred to Orange County's structured notes as "derivatives," but stopped doing so at ISDA's suggestion. An ISDA director noted in a letter to Byron E. Calame, deputy managing editor of the *Journal,* that the "problem" had been corrected, and "that in your report about promising developments in Orange County's situation, the reporter never once used the word derivatives, referring to them only as securities." When another reporter referred to complex instruments linked to the Mexican peso as "derivatives," ISDA admonished Calame, "Because we read your newspaper and know that a lot of people rely on it to increase their understanding of financial activity, we think it's important that financial activities are accurately and consistently reported."

The "d-word" began appearing much less frequently, especially in the *Wall Street Journal.* This was true even though the groups within banks that sold the financial instruments at issue—including those related to Orange County and the Mexican peso—actually called themselves "derivatives" groups and referred to the financial instruments as "derivatives." But investors didn't like that word, and ISDA wanted it expunged from the public record. (Ironically, ISDA had just added the word "derivative" to its own title, when it changed its name in 1993 from the International Swap Dealers Association to the International Swaps and Derivatives Association, in an attempt to show ISDA was more than just a lobbying vehicle for the top swap dealers.)[26]

The derivatives lobby occasionally was as inaccurate as it was aggressive. For example, Warren Heller, director of a research firm called Veribanc Inc., quickly became popular among derivatives dealers when he published a study in the fall of 1994 saying that banks were not at risk from their derivatives activities. It turned out that Heller had made a glaring error, counting only the contracts on which banks had a net gain, not those on which the banks had a net loss.[27] But few investors had the resources to find the error, and point it out.

Jim Leach was one of the few members of Congress who consistently stood up to the lobbyists at ISDA (others included Democratic Representatives Henry Gonzales and Edward Markey). In 1994, he introduced derivatives legislation, based on his staff's 900-page study of the market. Mark Brickell battled Leach, making arguments—to various members of Congress and the media—that included serious misstatements of fact. For example, Brickell said that Leach's bill would impose a suitability standard on derivatives "that is not applied to any other area of finance"; in fact, the standard was no different from the applicable standard in other areas, such as the rules for banks and savings and loans. Brickell also complained about the Leach bill's supposed capital standards for swaps, when in fact the bill contained no such provisions.

At a July 12, 1994, hearing on the bill, Representative Leach finally lost his patience with Brickell. Congressional hearings are typically scripted, calm affairs, but this time Leach blasted Brickell, accusing him of lying about provisions of the derivatives bill Leach had proposed.[28] Leach said, "You are quoted yesterday in the *American Banker* that banks could become liable for every derivatives contract that loses money. Well, I would like to know where in my bill it says that. That is a very powerful statement and one that is false. What section of the bill is this in? I mean, I and my staff wrote the bill. I don't recall putting it in." Leach said his bill's provision on suitability was the same as the standards already imposed by the Office of the Comptroller, and he noted that capital standards for swaps were not even in the bill. He admonished Brickell, "If you're going to be a constructive engager in making recommendations to this Congress that carry weight, I would recommend that you state valid objections."[29] When Brickell attempted to defend himself by noting that Leach's bill treated derivatives differently than other securities, Leach lashed out again, telling him that "derivatives are new, they are off balance sheet, they are a totally different dimension, and your bank has been in the lead in suggesting that."[30]

Brickell said he didn't take the attacks personally, but he gave up trying to persuade Leach. Instead, Brickell shifted his focus to other legislators. Brickell had alienated a few staff members of the Senate banking committee, who refused to meet with J. P. Morgan officials until they were assured Brickell was out of town (they were worried Brickell "might cause a scene in the halls").[31] But he persuaded many other members of Congress that Leach's bill was premature and would be counterproductive. He argued that regulation of derivatives, including swaps, was unnecessary, and focused on how derivatives were used to hedge, ignoring their speculative uses. He said, "Swaps guys may be clever characters, but we haven't been able to invent new kinds of risk. What swaps have allowed us to do is tear apart different sorts of risk, isolate them, and manage them independently."[32]

Brickell had plenty of help from Arthur Levitt, who suggested, in August 1994, that it would be better for the top derivatives dealers to regulate themselves. Levitt urged the dealers to form a self-regulatory "Derivatives Policy Group," and said legislation should wait until that group had decided on a plan.

Brickell also received help from several former and soon-to-be-former regulators. Gerald Corrigan, who had issued so many warnings about derivatives as head of the New York Fed, had just left for a much-higher-paid position at Goldman Sachs, and he was named co-chairman of the Derivatives Policy Group, which was lobbying for self-regulation. Wendy Gramm, the former CFTC chair and board member of Enron, praised Brickell and said that he and ISDA "could have been even tougher in terms of their position."[33] Gramm wrote an opinion piece in the *Wall Street Journal* entitled "The Good Derivatives Do," in which she argued, "If another major default or market shock occurs, we must all resist the urge to find scapegoats, or to over-regulate what we just do not understand." Frank N. Newman, the Treasury undersecretary for domestic finance, lobbied Congress in a September 16, 1994, letter, to "indefinitely postpone" derivatives legislation in light of the progress being made in the private sector. (Newman's comments were a job interview of sorts; he would soon leave to become the head of Bankers Trust, where he would be paid more money than former chairman Charlie Sanford had ever dreamed of making.)

With this assistance, Brickell and ISDA stopped the derivatives legislation. Brickell was obviously pleased and confident, calling the opposition to derivatives regulation a "consensus."[34] He belittled members of Congress who had continued to support new laws during the 1994 hearings on the legislation, and who failed to draw a distinction between structured notes and swaps, saying, "I don't know how they even realized it during the hearings, but none of the investors were talking about the use of swaps."[35] Just before the 1994 elections, Brickell predicted a Republican victory, saying, "I suspect that after Nov. 8, we'll be dealing with a very different Congress."[36]

Many prominent regulators were surprised that more members of Congress hadn't supported some new legislation, given the magnitude of the losses and the widespread, unseemly behavior of many Wall Street bankers. As David Mullins Jr., former vice chairman of the New York Fed and later a partner of Long-Term Capital Management, put it, "Given the steady stream of reported losses and all the publicity, there's been surprisingly little steam for legislation." *Institutional Investor* magazine, a prominent Wall Street publication, gave the credit to ISDA.[37]

In 1995, the prospects for new derivatives legislation declined even more. President Clinton appointed Robert Rubin—the ex-chairman of Goldman Sachs—to replace Lloyd Bentsen as Treasury secretary, and Rubin joined the band of regulators opposing new laws.

Four bills were proposed during the 1995 Congress. Jim Leach introduced a new version of his 1994 bill, proposing a "Federal Derivatives Commission" to regulate the markets.[38] Henry Gonzales introduced a bill requiring companies to disclose their derivatives investments, and coordinating federal regulation of derivatives.[39] Democratic Senator Byron L. Dorgan, of North Dakota, introduced a bill to prevent federally insured banks from speculating using derivatives.[40] And Democratic Senator Edward Markey, of Massachusetts, introduced a bill to bring derivatives dealers into a regulatory framework similar to that for securities generally.[41]

All the bills died. Brickell's prediction about Congress becoming more sympathetic had come true. By 1995, the losses from the Fed's rate hike were a distant memory. There had been no obvious financial crisis. The markets hadn't crashed. And derivatives reform was not part of the "Contract with America," the agreement among Republicans who now controlled Congress. Perhaps most important, the private sector had responded to Arthur Levitt's request for self-regulatory reforms. On March 9, 1995, the Derivatives Policy Group—the six top Wall Street firms in the over-the-counter derivatives markets—agreed to a "Framework for Voluntary Oversight," a document in which the dealers pledged to improve internal controls and risk management, and to report more quantitative data privately to federal regulators.

Although Congress supported self-regulation by derivatives dealers, it sharply questioned efforts by a private self-regulatory accounting group to create new disclosure requirements for some financial instruments. Many of the questionable accounting practices that would plague the financial markets during the late 1990s and early 2000s grew out of these failed efforts.

Since 1973, the Financial Accounting Standards Board had set accounting policy for U.S. companies, telling them what information they needed to disclose to their investors. In the alphabet soup of accounting, FASB established GAAP (*Generally Accepted Accounting Principles*), the basic rules of accounting practice, which were a key factor in persuading investors that the stock prices of companies traded in U.S. markets were fair and accurate.

For their first two decades, FASB and GAAP worked reasonably well. But by the early 1990s, accounting rules had fallen well behind financial innovation. Many experts said that if you asked all of the Big Five accounting firms a question about a complex accounting issue involving new financial instruments, you would get five different answers.

Anyone who had looked at a corporate annual report understood the problem. According to a survey by Ernst & Young, the length of an average annual report had increased from thirty-five pages, when FASB first began setting accounting rules, to sixty-four pages in the early 1990s. The number of footnotes was up from four to seventeen. Ray J. Groves, the chairman of Ernst & Young, warned that "we can expect to see even fatter and more unreadable annual reports in the future. Readers will decide to ignore them, as many people already do."[42]

Even as the amount of disclosure increased, the reports became less useful, especially as to complex financial products. In response to a question raised at an ISDA conference, Ethan M. Heisler, a vice president at Salomon Brothers, expressed skepticism that even sophisticated securities analysts could draw anything of value out of financial disclosures about derivatives: "Show me an equity analyst who has taken the disclosures that you currently have on derivatives and made any kind of meaningful use out of those disclosures. I would challenge you to find it. I have never seen it."[43]

Nevertheless, when FASB proposed new rules for derivatives, in an attempt to make financial statements more accurate, the financial lobby and many members of Congress opposed—and killed—them. There were two notable examples of proposed rules during the mid-1990s: accounting treatment of options and mark-to-market requirements for derivatives more generally.

The regulatory treatment of stock options became a hot issue in the new Clinton administration. The issue arose out of President Clinton's campaign promise to do something about allegedly excessive corporate-executive pay. In reality, CEO compensation was not excessive, based on historical measures, and was trivial compared to other corporate expenses, at roughly one-sixteenth of one percent of an average shareholder's annual returns in 1992.[44] But voters had been moved by various television programs on CEO pay, as well as Graef Crystal's exposé, *In Search of Excess*.[45] Following up on his promise, Clinton pushed Congress to limit the tax deduction for the salaries of top corporate executives to $1 million.[46] Never mind that only forty-nine CEOs had base salaries of more than $1 million.[47] The law had popular appeal and easily passed.

However, the tax deduction contained a loophole large enough to fly a private jet through. The $1 million cap didn't apply to "performance-based compensation," which Internal Revenue Service regulations said required "objective performance goals."[48] The stated purpose of the regulations was to remove discretion from the corporate directors who determined the pay of top executives. Instead of trusting directors to make judgments based on qualitative factors, the rules required directors to follow quantitative ones, based on metrics easily measured by the market. The prime example of performance-based compensation was a stock-option plan.[49] The value of a stock option was based, at least in part, on a simple objective factor: the price of the company's stock. In response to the new regulations, companies began shifting executive compensation from salary to stock options, in part to preserve the rather small tax deduction but, more important, to assure shareholders and commentators that they were following the letter of the new law.

This relatively minor legal change would have unanticipated, insidious effects. As companies shifted to stock options and other forms of market-based compensation, executives began to focus almost exclusively on those quantitative factors. The more a CEO could increase the company's stock price (or its earnings per share, or some other objective measure), the more money he would make, regardless of how the board thought he had performed. As the board's power was reduced, a mercenary culture developed among corporate executives. Corporate executives began managing their company's earnings, buying potentially higher-growth companies, and in too many cases even committing accounting fraud, all of which resulted in higher compensation. Much of the crisis of confidence in the financial markets in 2002 could be traced back to the cultural change that began in 1993, with new tax rules encouraging performance-based executive compensation.

This tax change was reinforced by the FASB accounting rule for stock options, which did not require companies to include options as an expense. This rule—established in October 1972—said the cost of an option to a company was the difference between the market price and the exercise price at the time the option is granted.[50] In other words, if a stock is trading at $10, a company can give an executive the right to buy stock for $10 with no accounting charge. To an investor looking at a company's financial statements, such options would appear to be "free."

Just a few months after this rule was established, economists Fischer Black, Myron Scholes, and Robert Merton had published research showing how options could be valued. The accounting rule was demonstrably wrong, and stock options had an ascertainable value. Yet even as traders began using financial models to track changes in the value of stock options on a minute-by-minute basis, the 1972 rule remained unchanged.

FASB officials knew that the $1 million cap on non-performance-based pay would lead companies to switch to stock options, and they were concerned that investors wouldn't understand how much those stock options were costing the company. The officials began considering a proposal to require that companies include, as a compensation expense, an estimate of the value of the stock options they awarded to executives. The proposal seemed reasonable enough: the options clearly had a cost, and options models such as Black-Scholes had been churning out options valuations for two decades.

But companies—especially high-technology companies in Silicon Valley—didn't want to include the options as an expense, because it would limit their ability to match executives' pay to the performance of their stock. It also would hurt the value of their stocks. In theory, the accounting change shouldn't have mattered—efficient-market theorists said that as long as the options compensation was disclosed in footnotes or appendices to financial statements, the stock price would reflect that compensation. (Existing disclosure rules for stock options and other compensation required companies to describe all compensation in a footnote, including a summary compensation table and performance graphs, but did not require companies to include the cost of stock options in their financial statements. Theoretically, these rules should have had the same effect as requiring that companies include stock options as an expense in both financial statements and footnotes.)[51]

Yet the difference mattered. Corporate CEOs—especially those from Silicon Valley—lobbied aggressively against FASB's proposal. They obviously did not think markets were efficient, or that stock prices reflected the costs of stock-option compensation. They were afraid the proposal would hurt their stock prices, and they told regulators about their concerns. They claimed that, without favorable treatment of options, they wouldn't be able to attract top executives, because they didn't have enough cash to pay them. Lobbyists sent out hundreds of comment letters and distributed thousands of "Stop FASB Action Kits."

Again, individual shareholders were powerless to lobby against such forces. The day before FASB was to issue its new rule for options, Senators Joseph Lieberman, Barbara Boxer, Dianne Feinstein, and Connie Mack introduced a bill to force FASB to drop the proposal.[52] Senator Carl Levin was a lonely voice in Congress supporting FASB, although he had plenty of company among accounting and finance experts. Arthur Levitt—who earlier had expressed concern about stock-options accounting during his confirmation hearing—abruptly caved in, and announced his opposition to the FASB options proposal. In May 1994, the U.S. Senate passed a resolution condemning the proposal, by a vote of 88 to 9. Facing this opposition, FASB backed down. Arthur Levitt would later describe his timid flip-flop on the accounting proposal as his "greatest mistake."

Senator Lieberman's position was that, "As a matter of abstract accounting theory, FASB's approach to stock option accounting may be defensible. But from a public policy, job creation, and competitiveness perspective, it simply is unnecessary and unusually disruptive."[53] Lieberman certainly was correct in arguing that some options—particularly complex, long-term options—were difficult to value, as the losses at Bankers Trust and Salomon Brothers established. But if companies couldn't figure out what long-term stock options were worth, should they really have been giving those options to their CEOs, instead of simply paying them in stock, which had an obvious value?

The next chapter describes the effect of large stock-option grants on the behavior of corporate executives. It isn't pretty. For now, it is sufficient to note that the increase in the use of stock options coincided with a massive increase in accounting fraud by corporate executives, who benefited from short-term increases in their stock prices. More than half of the profits from some major high-technology firms were from the accounting treatment for options. The accounting treatment of stock options also was a dangerous precedent in allowing companies to use stock to affect their own income. When Jeffrey Skilling, formerly Enron's CEO, was challenged at a congressional hearing to name one example of when a company was entitled to use its own stock to affect its income statement, he cited the accounting rules for stock options.

A second example of a FASB proposal failing in the face of well-funded lobbying involved the question of whether derivatives contracts should be marked to market, so that companies would record changes in value over time. With such a requirement, corporate financial results would be more volatile, but investors would receive more accurate and timely information. For example, investors would have known more about the losses stemming from the Fed's rate hike. In October 1994—after forty-five months of work in the face of intense lobbying—FASB still couldn't agree on rules, and it adopted only a watered-down "interim" proposal, which gave companies great discretion in deciding which instruments to mark to market.[54]

Banking regulators, including Alan Greenspan, consistently opposed these changes, saying they would introduce too much volatility. Commentator Martin Mayer was skeptical of the regulators' motives, and said, "The Fed has no interest in honest mark-to-market accounting and never has. Their interest is that they, and they alone, should value the banks' portfolio. They don't want the market to do it."[55] Senator Lauch

Faircloth from North Carolina—home state to First Union, Bank of America, and Wachovia—played the role of Senator Lieberman in this debate, introducing a bill to prevent FASB's new rules from taking effect. FASB's mark-to-market proposal died, just as its options proposal had.

FASB later resurrected both proposals. In the aftermath of Enron's collapse, Congress and FASB again began debating the issue of accounting for stock options, and some change appeared likely in early 2003. The mark-to-market proposal actually passed, in a grossly mutated form, as part of an 800-page set of rules (called Financial Accounting Standard 133) so watered down and complex as to be incomprehensible. FAS 133 now requires companies to add several more garbled pages to their annual reports, but few analysts pay attention to those disclosures, because they do not accurately portray a company's derivatives risks. If you think you really understand a company whose stock you own, a perusal of the section of its annual report discussing FAS 133 probably will change your mind.

The SEC, to its credit, proposed some regulatory changes to improve disclosure of derivatives risks,[56] and many of these changes were adopted in 1997.[57] After surveying the annual reports of 500 public companies, the SEC staff found that companies accounted for derivatives with similar economic characteristics in different ways. They also focused on the section of companies' reports entitled "Management's Discussion and Analysis of Results and Operations," known as MD&A. With some prodding by the SEC, companies began telling investors a bit more about their accounting procedures related to derivatives, but not enough for investors to know with certainty how much of a particular company's profit was from volatile financial businesses.[58]

Moreover, the SEC's new MD&A rules didn't exactly flush out information. Companies were only required to disclose material information, and "materiality" was a very loose term. The SEC tried to clarify the definition by requiring that companies examine future earnings, fair values, and cash flows from "reasonably possible" near-term changes in market rates or prices. But that term wasn't any clearer, so the SEC advised in a footnote that "reasonably possible" meant that "the chance of a future transaction or event occurring is more than remote but less than likely."[59] These definitions weren't encouraging anyone to make useful disclosures.

The difficulties posed in these regulatory debates centered around the problem that new legal rules would simply encourage private parties to figure out ways around them, or even move offshore. The first four chapters of this book described numerous instances of such "regulatory arbitrage." Those practices didn't change during the mid-1990s. For example, in 1995, when FASB adopted new rules requiring companies to account for certain foreign-exchange hedging, Bankers Trust quickly developed a way around the rules, by creating a financial contract with an unlikely contingency related to a company's offshore activities.[60] Accounting for derivatives continued to be open to novel interpretations because, although accounting is based on the notions of assets and liabilities, derivatives are not really either.[61] In other words, many accounting concepts were too crude to be useful in modern finance.

Some academics—most notably Professors Henry T. C. Hu and Lynn A. Stout—argued that, because unregulated derivatives markets had flaws, legal rules might improve market imperfections, but these scholars were in the minority.[62] In 1995, Alan Greenspan testified: "It would be a serious mistake to respond to these developments by singling out derivative instruments for special regulatory treatment. Such a response would create artificial incentives to structure transactions on the basis of regulatory rules rather than of the economic characteristic of the transactions themselves." Joseph A. Grundfest—a former SEC commissioner—described "an escalating cycle in which regulatory initiatives inspire financial innovations that trigger further regulations that in turn give rise to additional rounds of innovation. At the end of this cycle, the rule books are thicker, but the capital markets often restructure themselves to block the regulatory regimes' goals."[63]

The stealth nature of derivatives also made government economic policy difficult. Although the Federal Reserve Board—which sets monetary policy in the United States by controlling short-term interest rates—employs numerous top economists and devotes a great deal of time to discussing derivatives at its meetings (at least according to meeting minutes),[64] Fed officials said that derivatives made it impossible to predict how its short-term rate changes would affect markets.

Although the Fed controlled short-term interest rates directly, long-term rates were the key factor affecting the economy and long-term economic planning. Before 1994, Fed economists thought they understood the relationship between short-term and long-term rates. But when the Fed raised short-term rates in 1994, long-term rates increased by almost *triple* the amount Fed economists had predicted.[65] One reason for the widespread losses at mutual funds and corporations in 1994 was that the Fed had slammed on the brakes too hard, not realizing how slippery the road had become. As the markets skidded along, even Alan Greenspan was realizing how little power he wielded when compared to modern financial markets.

Without new legal rules, the only way for regulators to punish the financial malfeasance of the previous years was to bring cases under existing law. Unfortunately, by this time, many of the best and the brightest prosecutors had left for the private sector. For example, the two key securities-enforcement officials from the Drexel Burnham/Michael Milken era of prosecutions left for jobs at prestigious private law firms. Gary Lynch, formerly director of enforcement at the Securities and Exchange Commission, left for the New York law firm of Davis Polk & Wardwell, and Bruce Baird, formerly chief of the securities fraud unit of the U.S. Attorney's Office in Manhattan, left for the Washington, D.C., law firm of Covington & Burling. (During the following years, both would ably represent defendants in several high-profile derivatives disputes.)

Many securities prosecutors remained, but they found it difficult to obtain support for criminal cases against major banks and corporations, especially after the bombing of the World Trade Center in 1993. Prosecutors were much more interested in high-profile terrorism trials, or cases against the Mafia or drug dealers, which were easier to prove than financial fraud. The SEC instituted about 500 formal enforcement actions each year, many of which involved straightforward cases of fraud or insider trading. Arthur Levitt indicated a preference for high-profile cases that were "signature" in some way, and he made it clear that only those investigations "we believe are most relevant" or present a "broad public danger" would receive support.[66] But without the support of the Department of Justice, the SEC could not bring criminal charges, which would result in jail time. This was another major change since the late 1980s, when prosecutors from the Department of Justice had policed the markets by bringing high-profile cases against Michael Milken and numerous insider traders. On its own, the most the SEC could do was impose a fine and a cease-and-desist order—a slap-on-the-wrist enforcement remedy Richard Breeden, the previous SEC chairman, had requested in 1990 to "permit the Commission to resolve cases without protracted negotiation or litigation . . . [and to] provide the Commission with an alternative remedy against persons who commit isolated infractions and present a lesser threat to investors."[67] The derivatives losses of 1994 hardly fit this definition; they weren't isolated and they already had proven a threat. Yet on its own, the SEC could do no more.

The SEC devoted much of its resources to the highest-profile cases—such as Bankers Trust—leaving other cases to the discipline of private, civil lawsuits. This approach would work only if the high-profile cases persuaded other bankers that they, too, were at risk of prosecution if they broke the law. But it turned out that neither was true: prosecutors lost many of the high-profile cases, and other bankers—quite rationally—perceived the probability of going to jail for financial fraud as virtually zero. Here is an assessment of these cases, beginning with Bankers Trust. The regulators' inability to prosecute these misdeeds provided great comfort to anyone considering committing financial fraud during the mid-to-late 1990s.

When federal regulators began investigating Bankers Trust, they uncovered a mountain of damning evidence. In taped conversations, Bankers Trust employees admitted giving Gibson Greetings false valuations; one employee said, "We told him $8.1 million when the real number was $14 million."[68] Then there was the infamous quote from another Bankers Trust employee, describing the derivatives business: "Funny business, you know? Lure people into that calm and then just totally fuck 'em." These statements were ideal fodder for a criminal jury trial. Yet not a single person from Bankers Trust did any jail time, the principal actors were not charged with crimes, and most of the people involved in the cases continued to work on Wall Street. Even the fines were minimal.

Kevin Hudson—the Bankers Trust salesman who had made millions selling complex swaps to Procter & Gamble—was not punished at all. In fact, Hudson's last appearance in the news was on November 5, 1994, when, in the midst of the Bankers Trust prosecutions, he and Allison Bernhard—the saleswoman he had regaled with stories about his exploits—were married in Greenwich, Connecticut. The next day, the *New York Times* took a break from its coverage of the various derivatives fiascos to run a society-desk article about the wedding, complete with a photograph from UV Studios. The happy couple moved to London, where they continued to work for Bankers Trust.

Gary Missner—the Bankers Trust salesman who had covered Gibson Greetings—agreed to settle SEC charges by paying a fine of $100,000 and agreeing not to work in the securities industry for five years.[69] Mitchell A. Vazquez, the other salesman covering Gibson, paid $50,000 and was barred for four years.[70] The SEC charges in those cases were harsh, alleging that "Missner knowingly provided Gibson with values that significantly understated the magnitude of Gibson's losses, and that as a result, Gibson remained unaware of the actual extent of its losses from derivatives transactions and continued to purchase derivatives from BT Securities,"[71] and that Vazquez "participated in providing Gibson with valuations which materially understated Gibson's losses from derivatives transactions."[72]

But because they settled their cases out of court, neither Missner nor Vazquez even admitted guilt. In fact, Missner disputed the charges, in a letter to *Fortune* magazine that was hardly contrite: "Whatever you wish to conclude from the regulatory consent decrees entered into by Bankers Trust, I never lied to Gibson Greetings at any time about anything, including the extent of Gibson's losses on derivatives contracts entered into with Bankers Trust. Bankers Trust stood ready to transact with Gibson at the tear-up prices [that is, prices for terminating swaps] quoted to Gibson from 1991 to 1994, without exception. The fact that the quoted tear-up prices did not always agree to a theoretical model price is not only not unusual but reflects a practice that, at least until recently, has been common among derivatives dealers."[73]

Vazquez remained quiet, and in 1999—before his four-year SEC ban had expired—reentered the finance business, as president of an investment fund called Global Capital Investment LLC.[74] Vazquez and GCI sold over-the-counter currency options—the same contracts Andy Krieger had traded at Bankers Trust more than a decade earlier. But instead of dealing with other Wall Street traders, Vazquez offered these financial contracts to the public, in "mini accounts" of as little as $250, with leverage of up to 200 times the original investment (in other words, $250 could control $50,000 of currencies). Vazquez and GCI transacted almost $2 billion per month through an Internet website.

Vazquez's case demonstrated the limitations of existing federal regulation. First, although the SEC had brought Vazquez's case in the Bankers Trust matter, the CFTC—which regulated futures instead of securities—pursued Vazquez the second time. The SEC case had related to violations of securities law, whereas the CFTC case involved rules related to the illegal sale of futures. The CFTC investigators didn't seem to notice that Vazquez had violated the SEC's four-year ban; but, even if they had, Vazquez could have argued that the SEC couldn't bar him from a business regulated by the CFTC.

Second, there was some question whether Vazquez's actions had been subject to any regulation at all. Years earlier, Wendy Gramm, the previous CFTC chair, had exempted many derivatives from regulation, and there were nagging questions about the CFTC's jurisdiction, given the turf battle with the SEC. It was all very complicated; but, ultimately, Vazquez abandoned the issue and submitted to the CFTC's jurisdiction.

The SEC and CFTC were like Keystone Kops. The CFTC fined Vazquez $100,000 and barred him from CFTC-regulated businesses for five years; but, by this time, his SEC ban had lapsed, so he was permitted to sell securities again. In theory, he could even approach Gibson Greetings with more structured swaps if he wanted.

Brooksley Born, the former head of the CFTC, said in 2002 that she favored merging the SEC and CFTC in order to ensure federal regulators would have the power and sophistication to oversee the OTC derivatives markets and to maintain the necessary independence from the industry, although she recognized that the split in congressional jurisdiction over the agencies might make a merger politically impossible, and she expressed concern that the able staff of the CFTC would suffer a loss of autonomy and power in a merged agency. Meanwhile, the new leaders of the CFTC were gutting the agency from within, relinquishing authority and deregulating markets, even claiming that the collapse of Enron did not involve derivatives. After a few more years of such "leadership," a merger wouldn't matter—the CFTC would be an empty shell.

Guillaume Fonkenell—the Bankers Trust trader who had made last-minute changes in the values of P&G's first swap—was charged with falsifying the bank's books and records, but ultimately was cleared of the charges, eight years later. Fonkenell's case was a huge embarrassment for banking regulators, who almost never lose cases brought before administrative-law judges. Yet administrative-law judge Walter J. Alprin of the Office of Financial Institution Adjudication, which handles Federal Reserve cases, found that "Fonkenell has not been proven to have violated any law, rule or regulation or to have engaged in any unsafe or unsound banking practice."[75]

This dismissal gave a green light to managers and traders looking to use volatility to manipulate their financial results. Even though an expert had testified in the Fonkenell case that financial institutions other than Bankers Trust tried to use some objective measure of volatility—such as the "mid-market" point, between where traders were buying and selling options—the Fed declined to require any objective practice. Instead, traders would be permitted to use any volatility within a "reasonable" range. The judgment concluded that marking to market involved a "number of judgment calls," and closed by instructing: "Management's assessment of risk may well take into account the variation in value that can result from choosing one volatility rather than another equally defensible one." This judgment was a road map for Enron employees to follow when they later manipulated their trading results, and it provided a solid defense for bankers who manipulated the values of their options positions.

Jack Lavin—the derivatives boss who allegedly had responded to Kevin Hudson's news about Bankers Trust's trade with P&G by saying, "I think my dick just fell off"—aggressively defended his case, which was tied up for years in a dispute about whether the SEC could use tapes of conversations between Lavin and his wife. The dispute was the subject of lengthy opinions in the District of Columbia federal courts in 1996 and 1997.[76] Lavin's case remained unresolved in 2002, and federal investigators would not comment on its status.

Securities regulators settled a case against Bankers Trust itself, although the SEC was arguably outside its jurisdiction in charging Bankers Trust with violating the securities laws in its trades with Gibson Greetings. The swaps arguably were not securities, and the instruments on which the swaps were based—currencies and interest rates—clearly were not securities. However, Bankers Trust decided it was in no position to raise this jurisdictional issue, and the firm agreed to pay a $10 million fine and reform some of its practices.[77] The SEC also pursued Gibson Greetings, which agreed to cease and desist from violating the law, but did not pay any fine.[78] Treasurer Jim Johnsen was subject to a cease-and-desist order, but no fine or criminal charge.

Charlie Sanford wasn't prosecuted or fined, but his reputation was tarnished forever. He deserved credit for having the vision and intelligence to transform Bankers Trust from a dying, old-line commercial bank into a sophisticated risk manager. But in implementing this dramatic change, he had turned the ship too far, creating the mercenary culture that led to the aggressive practices of the early 1990s. Sanford had wanted Bankers Trust's board of directors to appoint his chosen successor, Eugene Shanks—the assistant he had chosen over Allen Wheat several years earlier. But when the board refused to give Sanford the last word, Sanford resigned.

For the sake of balance, the board insisted on replacing Sanford with Frank Newman, the Treasury official who had opposed derivatives regulation in an earlier "job interview." Compared to Sanford, Newman was a feeble and short-sighted manager who seemed more interested in his own personal gain than in the future of the bank. While he was CEO, Bankers Trust was directionless and sustained huge losses, especially in Russia in 1998. It also pled guilty to a crime: illegally diverting funds from various accounts, although Newman was not implicated in any way in that case. When Deutsche Bank offered to buy Bankers Trust for $10 billion in 1999, Newman eagerly supported the deal, and when Deutsche Bank refused to let Newman make any high-level business decisions, he happily resigned,[79] a consensus failure in every way except one: Newman had very skillfully negotiated a guaranteed 5-year pay package of $55 million—which would be paid regardless of whether he was working for Bankers Trust or not—in addition to millions of dollars of compensation he already had received, plus a multimillion-dollar payment he was due for selling Bankers Trust to Deutsche Bank, plus a multimillion-dollar severance payment.[80] Even with the derivatives scandal, Sanford had been a much better value.

The prosecution of Piper Jaffray and its employees didn't go any better than the Bankers Trust cases. The SEC investigated Piper's misconduct for more than four years, compiling more than one million pages of documents and taking thirty-seven days of deposition testimony.[81] The hearing in the case took eight weeks in 1999, and involved more than forty witnesses and over 1,000 exhibits. The hearing transcript was 4,969 pages.[82]

The issues in the case against Piper were especially difficult, because the mortgage derivatives Piper had bought were incredibly complex. Essentially, the SEC was arguing that Piper had misrepresented the instruments' unusual payoff profile. For example, one issue that took a great deal of time in the case revolved around *negative convexity*, a concept resembling deceleration in physics. (If you must know, negative convexity is essentially the tendency of a portfolio to become volatile by a greater amount when interest rates rise than the amount by which it becomes less volatile when interest rates fall.)

The case against Piper did not involve criminal charges, did not involve a federal prosecutor, and was not even heard before a U.S. district court judge. Instead, the SEC brought the Piper case before an administrative-law judge, H. Peter Young, who did not have the authority to order criminal sanctions. Judge Young found that Piper employees had committed minor securities-law violations in valuing their mortgage derivatives in early April 1994, when the markets were collapsing as Askin Capital Management fell into bankruptcy. Piper was fined $2 million for these violations. Judge Young also found that Worth Bruntjen had lied to the SEC about his educational background, and imposed an additional $5,000 fine for this misrepresentation.[83] In March 1996, Piper also paid a $1.25 million fine in a separate case brought by the National Association of Securities Dealers, which charged Piper with improper sales practices. In total, the fines were about the same size as the fee on one large derivatives deal.

The SEC also brought a civil suit against NationsSecurities for selling Term Trusts that owned risky inverse floaters under the guise of a safe investment managed by NationsBank. But the punishment was a civil censure and a penalty of just $4 million. Again, no one went to jail.

The Orange County prosecutions were the least effective of all. The SEC had interviewed Treasurer Robert Citron and knew about his investment strategies several months before the county collapsed, but decided it did not have jurisdiction to take any action at that time. Although the financial instruments involved in the Orange County collapse were similar to those Bankers Trust had sold, the SEC and the Department of Justice decided not to press the issue of whether Orange County's structured notes were "securities," and instead conceded that the federal government did not have jurisdiction to prosecute anyone for Orange County's losses. Whereas ISDA had persuaded the *Wall Street Journal* that the structured notes Orange County bought were merely securities, not derivatives, the federal securities regulators decided the opposite. (The SEC did have jurisdiction over the sale of Orange County's bonds, and it sued the investment bankers involved in the offering and sale of those bonds for securities fraud.)[84]

That left state prosecutors to bring cases against Robert Citron and his assistants. In April 1995, Citron pled guilty to state securities fraud, and faced up to fourteen years in prison. But his attorney asked the court to be lenient, telling the judge that Citron had suffered from dementia for several years.[85] Instead of serving prison time, Citron agreed to work in a jail commissary during the day for nine months, as part of a state work-furlough program.[86]

Prosecutors had no success against anyone else at the county. A jury found Assistant Treasurer Matthew Raabe guilty of securities fraud and misappropriation, and he was sentenced to three years in prison; but, an appeals court overturned the conviction in 2001, and the district attorney dropped the case, returning the $10,000 fine Raabe had paid.[87] In the prosecution of Citron's budget director, a jury was hung in favor of acquittal. No one working at any of the investment banks, credit-rating agencies, or government institutions involved in the Orange County debacle spent time in jail. Raabe was the only person to do any time—the forty-one days he had spent in jail before he was released on bail, pending appeal.

The examples of Bankers Trust, Piper, NationsSecurities, and Orange County were typical. Most cases of financial malfeasance were complex, and the defendants had plausible arguments about why what they had done was legal or fell outside the scope of existing law. Prosecutors did not bring many criminal cases, and they lost when they did. The only individuals criminally punished for the losses of 1994 were those who had engaged in truly blatant fraud. For example, James Martignoni, a 27-year-old Australian trader at ABN AMRO Bank, was convicted of fraud in a New York federal court for buying currency options, inflating their volatility, and recording false profits (much as Bankers Trust was alleged to have done regarding Andy Krieger's trades). Martignoni left a clear trail of proof; he even had concealed losses by asking his assistant to move a decimal point in a trade one to the right, magically turning a $1.8 million sale into an $18 million sale.[88] Similarly, Nicholas Leeson of Barings Bank was sentenced to serve six years in a Singapore prison for a fraudulent scheme that involved Leeson using a pair of scissors to cut and paste false profit reports (more on Leeson in Chapter 8). But those guilty few were the exceptions.

With the paucity of criminal cases, most of the disputes among various parties to the losses of 1994 were left to be resolved in civil lawsuits. In litigation related to Bankers Trust, Piper, and Orange County, there were only a few written judicial opinions resolving the cases, but defendants nevertheless agreed to pay hundreds of millions of dollars to settle the claims. To the extent anyone was deterred from aggressive sales practices related to derivatives, it was these lawsuits—not any government prosecution—that created the potential threat of liability.

Several clients of Bankers Trust, including Procter & Gamble, sued to recover their losses. P&G and Gibson Greetings weren't the only clients to settle with Bankers Trust on favorable terms. Bankers Trust had made about $25 million in profits from a series of derivatives deals with Sandoz Corp., the first of which was especially ill-timed, on January 31, 1994, just five days before the Fed's rate hike. Bankers Trust had then persuaded Sandoz to amend the derivative nine times, each time taking out a fee. Sandoz reached a confidential settlement with Bankers Trust, as did Jefferson Smurfit Corp., a company that amended its swap agreement eleven times before it was finally unwound at a loss in September 1994. Bankers Trust also paid $67 million to settle its dispute with Air Products and Chemicals.

The litigation revealed that some supposedly sophisticated companies—such as P&G—were, in fact, babes in the woods. Edwin Artzt, formerly P&G's chairman and CEO, had stated publicly, "Derivatives like these are dangerous and we were badly burned. We won't let this happen again." In handwritten notes that were discovered in the litigation between P&G and Bankers Trust, Artzt wrote about P&G's treasurer, "Didn't penetrate—didn't ask the right questions. Simply went to sleep." The treasurer, Raymond Mains, took early retirement in 1994, at P&G's suggestion. These discoveries prompted Michael D. Greenbaum, a general partner of the O'Connor Partnerships (the Chicago firm Andy Krieger had first worked for during business school), to write a letter to *Forbes* magazine, saying, "As a general partner of a firm specializing in derivatives trading, I don't attempt to make soap, and therefore think it only equally smart for the treasurer's office of Procter & Gamble to avoid trying to make derivatives a profit center."[89]

In the most notable written decision in any derivatives case to date, an Ohio judge, John Feikens, in the *Procter & Gamble v. Bankers Trust* lawsuit, found that the swaps were not securities, and therefore were not subject to federal regulation.[90] This decision was not binding on the New York courts, where most financial disputes were litigated, but it was a noteworthy success for derivatives dealers, who—now that they had a favorable legal ruling on the books—quickly settled remaining disputes, before a judge in another case issued a conflicting ruling.

Piper spent more than $100 million resolving its lawsuits. Once they were resolved, Bruntjen left immediately. (Companies frequently keep employees involved in questionable schemes on their payroll during litigation, so they have some control over the employees' testimony, and because firing them looks like an admission of guilt.) Once the suits were resolved, Piper was an attractive acquisition target, and U.S. Bancorp bought Piper the next month for $730 million.

The investment banks that had sold structured notes to Orange County paid hundreds of millions of dollars to settle their lawsuits.

Orange County also sued McGraw-Hill Companies, owner of the Standard & Poor's rating agency, but S&P defended itself by arguing that the First Amendment protected its ratings as free speech. In assessing these arguments, Judge Gary L. Taylor wrote that "S&P's expression is entitled to First Amendment protection."[91] Judge Taylor allowed some of Orange County's claims to proceed; but, ultimately, the county settled its suit against S&P for fractions of pennies on the dollar.

Orange County also sued the Student Loan Marketing Association, known as Sallie Mae, arguing that Sallie Mae failed to disclose to Orange County all of the profits being made on $913 million of structured notes the county bought.[92] Sallie Mae had disclosed an "underwriting discount" of 15 to 50 basis points as the compensation for Sallie Mae and Merrill Lynch, which underwrote the notes. But, in reality, Merrill Lynch had reimbursed this fee, and made its money the same way Bankers Trust profited from the deals with Gibson Greetings—on related swap transactions.

The Sallie Mae case raised an issue that would become crucially important during the upcoming years. Securities rules required borrowers to disclose compensation to underwriters, including "all other items that would be deemed by the National Association of Securities Dealers to constitute underwriting compensation for purposes of the Association's Rule of Fair Practice."[93] The NASD Rule of Fair Practice 44(c) stated the compensation must be fair and reasonable and that "all items of value . . . which are deemed to be in connection with or related to the distribution of the public offering . . . shall be included."[94] The rules also stated that compensation in addition to the underwriting discount had to be referenced in a footnote on the cover page of the offering.[95] Just as Merrill Lynch had not disclosed all of its fees, numerous investment banks would receive undisclosed kickbacks from clients who bought IPOs (Initial Public Offerings) at sweetheart prices. According to the allegations in the Sallie Mae case, those undisclosed kickbacks also were illegal. In fact, CS First Boston would later pay $100 million to settle a case related to the kickbacks, and similar dealings would plague numerous investment banks in 2002.

The various derivatives disputes were mostly resolved on terms favorable to investors. However, during the mid-1990s, there were numerous obstacles thrown in the path of plaintiffs in future cases. By the end of

1995, corporate defendants would be much better protected from litigation than they had been in 1993. Ironically, government officials chose to make securities lawsuits more difficult at precisely the time such lawsuits were most needed to deter financial misconduct.

A major obstacle to lawyers pursuing financial fraud cases came from the U.S. Supreme Court in 1994. The Court ruled in a case called *Central Bank of Denver v. First Interstate Bank of Denver*[96] that plaintiffs could not sue accounting firms, investment banks, and law firms for aiding and abetting securities fraud. In the future, these "gatekeeper" firms would be immune from secondary liability, and a plaintiff could recover from them only by showing they were primarily liable for fraud, something that was much more difficult to do.

The Central Bank case was argued in November 1993, and the justices had completed much of their work on the case before the Fed's rate hike, so it seems unlikely that they were influenced by the losses of early 1994. It was a radical decision, and the Supreme Court largely ignored hundreds of judicial and administrative proceedings over sixty years, when parties had assumed that accountants could be liable for aiding and abetting securities fraud.

Instead, the case focused on the potential abuses of securities litigation. In a 5-to-4 decision, Justice Anthony Kennedy argued for the majority that liability for securities fraud demanded "certainty and predictability," citing testimony that in 83 percent of cases, accounting firms paid $8 in legal fees for every $1 paid in damages to investors. Just a few years after the decision, few people would have such a sympathetic view of accounting firms.

In 1995, Congress joined the Supreme Court in limiting securities lawsuits. The legislative limitations had been in the works since 1991, when Richard C. Breeden, the previous SEC chairman, had testified before Congress that "because baseless securities litigation amounts to a 'tax on capital,' which undermines economic competitiveness, there is a strong public interest in eliminating meritless suits." In 1992, Representative W. J. "Billy" Tauzin, a Democrat from Louisiana, had introduced legislation limiting liability for securities fraud.

Arthur Levitt supported these limitations. In January 1994, Levitt began arguing in speeches that abusive litigation imposed tremendous costs on issuers of securities. He said the legal system failed to distinguish between strong and weak cases. Many lawyers viewed Levitt—in his words—as "the single greatest threat to the continued viability of private remedies against fraud."[97]

The proposed legislation was directed at one lawyer in particular, Bill Lerach, a well-known and much-feared litigator in the San Diego office of the law firm known as Milberg Weiss. Lerach had recovered billions of dollars for shareholders, although his reputation had been tarnished by some less meritorious suits. Companies commiserated about being "Lerached," which meant they had been sued by Bill Lerach for securities fraud. As the cost of defending these suits increased, the support for restrictions increased.

(Surprisingly, Lerach and Milberg Weiss were largely missing from the lawsuits related to derivatives. The cases were extremely complicated and costly to pursue, and it wasn't at all clear they would succeed. At the time, Lerach preferred simpler suits involving insider trading or blatant financial fraud.)

When Republicans captured the House of Representatives in November 1994—for the first time since the Eisenhower era—securities-litigation reform was assured. In a January 1995 speech, Levitt outlined the limits on securities regulation that Congress later would support: limiting the statute-of-limitations period for filing lawsuits, restricting legal fees paid to lead plaintiffs, eliminating punitive-damages provisions from securities lawsuits, requiring plaintiffs to allege more clearly that a defendant acted with reckless intent, and exempting "forward looking statements"— essentially, projections about a company's future—from legal liability.[98]

The Private Securities Litigation Reform Act of 1995 passed easily, and Congress even overrode the veto of President Clinton, who either had a fleeting change of heart about financial markets or decided that trial lawyers were an even more important constituency than Wall Street. In any event, Clinton and Levitt disagreed about the issue, although it wasn't fatal to Levitt, who would remain SEC chair for another five years.

The PSLRA, as the law became known, made securities-fraud suits more difficult for plaintiffs to sustain. Many legislators believed that result was a positive one; investors' advocates thought it was a negative. Although there were arguments on both sides, it seemed that, with the government no longer aggressively pursuing criminal prosecutions for financial fraud, and with new limits on plaintiffs' lawyers, corporations and their managers would be governed more by their own moral values and reputations than any legal constraint.

One money manager, James S. Chanos, was skeptical that the markets alone would provide sufficient discipline to Wall Street, major corporations, accounting firms, and lawyers. Reflecting on the dramatic increase in financial fraud from 1995 through 2001, he told the House Energy Committee that the PSLRA was responsible for many of the abuses that followed: "That statute, in my opinion, has emboldened dishonest managements to lie with impunity, by relieving them of concern that those to whom they lie will have legal recourse. The statute also seems to shield underwriters and accountants from the consequences of lax performance."

The losses at Kidder Peabody were a prime example of how legal rules did not prevent or deter financial manipulation. They did not create incentives for managers to control their employees at the outset, and they did not punish them for failure to supervise them after damage was done. As Kidder Peabody showed, the only remaining penalty was the destruction of the corporation, a penalty that was imposed more on shareholders than on the perpetrators who caused the loss.

The $350 million of losses at Kidder were even more troubling than the hundreds of millions of dollars in unreconciled balances at Bankers Trust and Salomon Brothers, for two reasons. First, they involved much more straightforward financial instruments than Bankers Trust and Salomon had traded, instruments for which there was a liquid market and there were even daily quotes in the newspaper. Second, unlike Bankers Trust and Salomon Brothers, whose shareholders understood that those firms' focus was on financial markets, Kidder Peabody was owned by General Electric, whose shareholders considered that firm to be primarily industrial in focus. GE shareholders never imagined the company was taking speculative bond positions in the range of $40 billion, twenty times the biggest trades Andy Krieger had made at Bankers Trust.

The news about Kidder was a black mark on the record of John F. Welch Jr., the longtime chairman of General Electric. Welch had a reputation for building top businesses, slashing costs, and producing consistent profits. When he began running General Electric, Welch fired one in four employees, even as he spent $25 million on a new guest house and conference center at GE's corporate headquarters.[99] He became known as "Neutron Jack" for his practice of buying firms and leaving the buildings intact while eliminating all the people.[100] His strategy was to be first or second in a business, or abandon it. He set firm quarterly and annual targets for his businesses, and managers met them—or else. The strategy seemed to work: for fifty-one straight quarters, GE's earnings were higher than those of the previous year.

Welch was also legendary for his brusque temper and management style; not surprisingly, he was livid about the losses at Kidder. General Electric had purchased Kidder in 1986, when the investment bank was suffering through a series of 1980s insider-trading scandals. (Martin Siegel, Kidder's investment-banking superstar, did time in prison.)

After GE bought Kidder, Welch provided special support for Kidder's personnel, including Edward Cerullo, the head of bond trading. Welch was reportedly "intense" in his determination to fix Kidder, although analysts questioned his obsession with bond trading, and wondered why it was so "critical" or "vital" to a company like General Electric.[101] But Welch knew of the profits at Bankers Trust, First Boston, and Salomon Brothers. Although shareholders still thought of General Electric for its lightbulbs, in reality GE under Welch already had become much more like an investment bank. It increasingly depended on GE Capital, the subsidiary that had issued billions of dollars of structured notes. By 1993, GE Capital was responsible for more than a third of GE's earnings. Although Welch lacked experience in modern finance, he had great confidence in his employees, and he gave them free rein to meet his performance targets.

At first, GE seemed to have turned Kidder around, cutting costs and even acquiring Drexel Burnham Lambert's trading floor when that firm went under in 1990.[102] Kidder's employees were well paid and morale was high. Ed Cerullo stressed that Kidder would reward people based purely on their performance. Two of Cerullo's top hires fit this performance focus: Melvin Mullin, a mathematics Ph.D. who built Kidder's structured notes and options businesses into profitable lines that made $58 million in 1993,[103] and Michael Vranos, a shy mathematics undergraduate who turned Kidder into one of the top mortgage-trading firms on Wall Street. By 1993, Kidder would succeed Salomon Brothers as the top mortgage-trading firm; it was the firm that sold Worth Bruntjen and David Askin many of their inverse IOs.

Jack Welch didn't meddle in the details of Kidder's business, but he provided unwavering support, giving the firm more than a billion dollars of capital, and introducing Kidder bankers to GE's top clients. Throughout the late 1980s and early 1990s, Jack Welch sent one simple message to Kidder employees: "stretch goals."[104] Welch wanted GE to be the dominant firm in *all* of its businesses. With Kidder, Welch could add a top Wall Street trading operation to GE's diverse mix of businesses.

Several experts questioned whether Welch was asking for trouble by combining a hands-off approach with a relentless focus on producing profits. Samuel Hayes, a professor at Harvard Business School, said Welch "has built a culture of individual fiefdoms, and that decentralized responsibility leaves a firm like GE vulnerable."[105] Edward Lawler, director of the Center for Effective Organizations at the University of Southern California, said, "Welch is intimidating, tough. GE's culture is results oriented, and that's the reason they do well and also break rules. It's the opposite side of the same coin."[106]

Welch began learning about some of these broken rules in early 1994, even before the Fed raised rates. In January, Kidder fired Clifford Kaplan, a 28-year-old derivatives vice president who had made a laughingstock of the firm, not only by costing Kidder almost $2 million in cost overruns on a botched derivatives deal involving Italian government bonds, but also by showing that he could keep a job at Kidder while also being employed by the U.S. unit of La Compagnie Financière Edmond de Rothschild Banque, of Paris.[107] Kidder had paid Kaplan a $500,000 bonus the previous year, even though he did not even have a securities license while he was marketing the Italian deal.

Then Kidder discovered that one of its swaps traders had hidden $11 million in losses on a bond derivatives deal with NationsBank, and that one of its options traders had hidden $6 million in losses on French and Spanish government-bond options. It looked like no one was minding the store, and Jack Welch seemed concerned. He told *Fortune* magazine, in a March 7, 1994, interview about Kidder, "Things tend to grow to the sky, get momentum. 'Let's make it a little higher, a little higher.' I think we've learned a lot about that."

Some employees blamed the problems on 46-year-old Melvin Mullin, the math Ph.D. who had developed Kidder's derivatives businesses and then ran its government-bond trading desk. But in many instances, Mullin appeared to be simply following his marching orders from Jack Welch. When Clifford Kaplan said, "Mel was totally 'hands off.' Mel was purely driven by profit—profit, always profit," it wasn't clear if the comment was praise or criticism.[108]

Was it a negative when Mullin permitted Kaplan to work on a derivatives deal without a proper securities license? Was it a negative when Mullin ignored warnings about a deal that violated Japanese banking laws? Was it a negative when he hired and supervised his wife, helped her determine her own bonus of $900,000, and then inadvertently double-hedged her options portfolio, costing Kidder $2 million?[109] Okay, the last one was obviously a negative, but the others were arguably consistent with the culture Jack Welch was trying to create, and Mullin's "hands-off" approach seemed to be generating profits.

In 1991, Mullin took the step that would destroy his career, as well as the career of his boss, Edward Cerullo, and would bring down Kidder Peabody. He hired a young bond trader named Orlando Joseph Jett. When Melvin Mullin interviewed Joseph Jett, he said Jett "seemed like a hard worker with quantitative skills." Kidder wasn't bothered by the fact that First Boston had just fired Jett, or that he had lasted only a short time before that at Morgan Stanley, his first job after graduating from Harvard Business School. Jett began working at Kidder in July 1991.

Mullin assigned Jett to trade long-maturity U.S. government bonds called "STRIPS."[110] STRIPS were *zero-coupon* Treasury bonds, meaning obligations of the U.S. government that repaid principal at maturity but did not pay any coupons in the interim. STRIPS were created from the Treasury bonds traders like Paul Mozer, at Salomon Brothers, bought through a federal-government program called "Separate Trading of Registered Interest and Principal of Securities" (hence, the acronym STRIPS).

The "stripping" resembled the separating of interest and principal on mortgages, except that the Federal Reserve Bank of New York did all the hard work. As a trader at Kidder, Jett could simply buy a Treasury bond and present it to the Fed. In return, he would receive a collection of STRIPS: one small STRIPS for each semi-annual interest payment, and one big STRIPS representing the repayment of principal. Each one gave him the right to receive a single payment in the future, but no interim coupons. For example, if Jett presented a $1 million, 30-year bond that paid 10 percent interest on a semiannual basis, he would receive sixty coupon STRIPS representing the right to receive $50,000 every six months ($100,000 per year), and one principal STRIPS representing the right to receive $1 million in 30 years.

Jett could also reverse the transaction. If he gathered up the sixty-one

STRIPS necessary to "reconstitute" the Treasury bond, he could present all of those STRIPS to the Fed, and receive the actual Treasury bond in exchange.

Because STRIPS represented rights to receive just a single payment in the future, they always traded for less than their face value (the amount the holder would receive at maturity). For example, a STRIPS representing the right to receive $1 million in 30 years might be worth $200,000 today. A STRIPS with a maturity of three years might be worth $800,000 today.

Traders of STRIPS were very active, and the business was extremely competitive. In theory, a trader could buy a bunch of cheap STRIPS, reconstitute them, and then sell the new Treasury bond at a profit. (Or buy the bond, split it up, and sell the STRIPS at a profit.) In reality, such "arbitrage" opportunities were rare. These trades were easy to do and their costs were low. The Chicago economists who had predicted efficient markets could cite STRIPS as Exhibit A. There were no $20 bills lying around the STRIPS market.

Jett was assigned to trade STRIPS of ten years or longer.[111] He had no training in STRIPS (he had been in mortgages at First Boston), and Mullin expected him to learn on the job. During the first few months, Jett's results were discouraging, and Mullin was concerned. Then, on September 20, 1991, Jett had his eureka moment.

Jett knew that STRIPS traded at a discount to their face value. In the above example, the 30-year STRIPS were worth $200,000; the 3-year STRIPS were worth $800,000. Over time, the value of STRIPS approached their face value. In other words, the day before maturity, the $1 million face value of STRIPS might be worth $999,900. This made sense: a person would pay a lot more to receive $1 million tomorrow than to receive it 30 years from now. STRIPS increased in value over time, just as money in the bank did.

On September 20, Jett noticed that Kidder's accounting system allowed him to record a STRIPS transaction in which the purchase and sale of bonds would occur, not right away, but instead at some future date. In other words, rather than buying STRIPS today, reconstituting them, and selling the resulting bond today, Jett could agree today to do the same transaction six months in the future.

Why would he agree to do the reconstitution in the future, instead of today? This was the eureka. When Jett entered a future trade—a *forward reconstitution*—into Kidder's accounting system, it produced an automatic profit. Why? Recall that a reconstitution involved a sale of

STRIPS and a purchase of the corresponding bond. To make a profit, Jett needed to be able to buy cheap STRIPS. Kidder's accounting system guaranteed that Jett could always buy cheap STRIPS, because it was misprogrammed to record the fact that STRIPS became more valuable over time, and to give the trader credit for that increase—not in the future—but *today*.

In other words, Jett could buy STRIPS today for, say, $200,000, and agree to sell them in six months as part of a forward reconstitution. Kidder's accounting system would record the sale price of the STRIPS as if time had moved forward by six months, when the STRIPS would be worth, say, $250,000. In this example, the system would record $50,000 as profit—the difference between the "forward price" and the current price.

In reality, there was no profit at all. If Jett bought STRIPS today and committed today to sell them in six months, he would make nothing at all today. The value—in today's terms—of the STRIPS he had bought was exactly equal to the value—again, in today's terms—of the STRIPS he had agreed to sell in the future. Jett *might* make money over time, if he held on to those positions, depending on changes in interest rates. He might lose money, too. But he clearly would *not* make money up front. The accounting system was comparing forward values to today's values, something that was as mathematically false as subtracting four from four and getting one.

Jett did a few forward reconstitutions, and Kidder's accounting system magically showed that he had made a profit. Suddenly, after four months of poor performance, Jett was making money. For November and December 1991, his forward reconstitutions showed a $265,000 gain. Not bad.

Melvin Mullin was pleased with Jett's turnaround. Another STRIPS trader complained to Mullin about Jett's trading practices, and accused Jett of mismarking his positions. But Mullin brushed off these complaints. After all, the accounting system showed a profit. (Notwithstanding his mathematics Ph.D., Mullin later would claim he hadn't understood Jett's transactions.) A few months later, Jett ensured that the complaining trader would be fired, by delivering to Edward Cerullo a tape of a conversation in which the trader sought employment at another bank. Ironically, this trader ended up at First Boston, where he became a successful STRIPS trader in a group that made millions of dollars trading with Jett.

Nevertheless, Mullin was cautious about Jett. In a year-end performance evaluation, Mullin gave Jett the next-to-lowest mark for "Overall

Rating," but the highest mark for "Performance Trend." Mullin wrote that Jett had had a "lower start than anticipated" but "seemed to be improving." The improvement wasn't enough to justify any big money, though. Jett received a token bonus of $5,000.

In 1992, Jett finally began to impress Mullin, and he began trading in forward reconstitutions at a frenetic pace. At the end of the year, Kidder's accounting system recorded profits of $32 million for Jett, well above what anyone at Kidder had ever made trading STRIPS. Mullin was ecstatic, and recommended that Jett be promoted to senior vice president. In reality, Jett had lost $10 million. His profits were false, although apparently no one at Kidder knew it. Jett received a bonus of $2.1 million. He was a new man.

A few months later, Edward Cerullo—the head of bond trading—told Mullin he wanted Mullin to run a new derivatives desk. Other banks—including Bankers Trust, First Boston, and Salomon Brothers—were making a fortune in derivatives, and Kidder wanted to be involved, too. The only question was who should replace Mullin? The two men decided on Jett, and in 1993—after less than two years at the firm—Jett became head of government-bond trading, supervising about twenty traders. Jett began reporting directly to Cerullo.

Again, Jett didn't disappoint, at least on paper. In 1993, he showed trading profits of nearly $151 million—more than a quarter of the profits in Kidder's entire bond-trading operation. In reality, he had lost almost $100 million dollars, but Cerullo didn't know it. Cerullo decided to pay Jett a record bonus of $9.3 million—more than triple what Andy Krieger had earned at Bankers Trust a few years earlier. If any managers at Kidder questioned how Jett, previously a total flop, had become the firm's wunderkind, they didn't voice their concerns. Instead, Jett was a hero and was named Kidder's "Man of the Year."[112] At Kidder's annual retreat, in Boca Raton, Florida, Jett gave an intense motivational speech, which Kidder's general counsel described as "an emotional let's-go-out-and-win kind of thing."[113]

When Jett began 1994, he was out of control. In the first two months of 1994—even as fund managers including Robert Citron, Worth Bruntjen, and David Askin were imploding—Jett set another record: $66 million of profits. Finally, his bosses began to ask some questions. How was Jett making so much money? When Cerullo looked at Jett's trades and discovered more than $40 *billion* of forward reconstitutions—in some cases, more than the entire amount outstanding of a particular U.S. government bond—he was stunned.

Cerullo's first reaction was that he wanted to be sure those transactions wouldn't appear on the firm's financial statements. Even General Electric wasn't a big-enough company to have one trader with so many assets and liabilities. An extra $40 billion of entries on GE's balance sheet would jeopardize its AAA credit rating, and investors would bail out of the stock. As Kidder looked at ways of avoiding disclosure of these trades, no one focused on the issue of whether the profits were real. Everyone assumed they were real; they just wanted to hide the size of the bets. Jett apparently believed Kidder's senior management supported his trading as a way of "window dressing" the firm's balance sheet.[114] The forward reconstitutions were classified as a type of over-the-counter derivatives transaction, and—remember—those were largely unregulated and did not need to be disclosed. For GE, they were safely "off balance sheet."

Finally, in late March 1994—just as Worth Bruntjen was struggling to evaluate his inverse IOs and David Askin was receiving margin calls—one of Cerullo's deputies discovered the accounting glitch. Cerullo demanded that Jett explain his trading strategy in writing. The explanations made no sense, and Cerullo's deputies calculated that Jett had lost about $350 million. Now, Cerullo had to tell Jack Welch.

Welch was advised that Kidder had a "reconciliation problem," but, ten days later, Kidder officials still could not figure out what had happened. The $350 million loss caused GE to report only $1.068 billion in profits for the first quarter of 1994, less than the $1.085 billion in 1993, the first time in fifty-two otherwise-perfect quarters that earnings were less than those of the previous year.[115] At this point, it is possible that even Robert Citron, the Orange County treasurer, heard Jack Welch scream.

Welch could barely contain himself in public, stammering, "This reprehensible scheme . . . has all of us damn mad." When a *Wall Street Journal* reporter asked Welch to respond to comments that he had lost his management touch, he shot back, "Who says that? Be sure and quote them by name."[116]

Welch immediately hired Gary Lynch, the former Securities and Exchange Commission enforcement lawyer who—in another demonstration of how little the circles of Wall Street extended—had investigated Kidder Peabody's Martin Siegel during the 1980s. When asked whether Kidder should have tighter controls, Welch—referring to Lynch—snapped, "I'm paying a lot of bright people a lot of money to find out."[117]

After firing Jett on April 17, Cerullo left Kidder in July with a $10 million severance package, only $50,000 of which he paid to the SEC to settle the case against him (he didn't admit liability and was barred from the industry for one year).[118] Mullin resigned the next month, and Kidder suspended several other officials. Welch had no more patience for his tarnished bond-trading firm—which no longer was the number one or two business in its area. He quickly sold Kidder to PaineWebber, which kept some of Kidder's employees and assets, but deleted the firm's name.[119] Twenty-five hundred employees were offered a harsh severance package that included just two weeks' pay for each year of employment, and that required them to agree not to publish any books related to their experience.[120]

Lynch's report criticized Kidder's lax oversight, and described a culture in which employees were unwilling to ask questions about a successful rising star. It focused the blame on Jett, and didn't criticize Jack Welch or General Electric. Several senior partners from Lynch's law firm had spent months working on the report, billing huge numbers of hours. For GE, it was worth every penny.

Welch later admitted that he and his managers hadn't really understood Kidder's business. In one interview, he described getting into a business they didn't understand, and stressed the importance of culture: "Culture counts. When I got into one I didn't understand, we screwed it up. We were lucky it was small enough. We sold it and got out. And got out alive. But it could have eaten us up if it were a bigger thing." Not surprisingly, Welch didn't focus on Kidder or Jett in his 2001 autobiography, except to note that when he learned of the losses, he vomited.

Jett remained a mystery. If he had intended to engage in a fraudulent scheme, he had done so very foolishly. Jett had conducted his trades openly on Kidder's accounting system, which many other traders used and numerous employees could access. Jett also had recorded the trades in large "red books," ledgers he kept on his desk. He even had helped Kidder's auditors with inquiries into his trading (they said Jett "was more helpful than most other managers").[121] Jett also had kept all of his cash bonuses—millions of dollars—in accounts at Kidder, where they were immediately frozen when his bosses discovered the losses. By 1996, Jett was down and out, moving from one friend's apartment to another, unable even to afford the $500-a-month rent for a tiny studio in Hell's Kitchen, spending most of his time preparing his legal defense.[122]

Jett ultimately was acquitted of securities fraud, showing how difficult it was for prosecutors to send any participant in an alleged fraudulent financial scheme to jail. (He was found guilty of the lesser charge of false record keeping and fined $200,000.) Jett also avoided damages from civil lawsuits, which General Electric settled for $19 million. Ironically, the publicity surrounding Jett's failed prosecution enabled him to revive his career. As of 2003, he was the chief investment officer of a multimillion-dollar offshore investment fund, which even advertised Jett's experience at Kidder Peabody managing "roughly 10% of the assets of Kidder's parent, General Electric." If you are impressed by this, and want to invest your money with Jett, you can do so at www.josephjett.com.

The collapse of Kidder Peabody raised troubling new questions. It seemed virtually impossible to design a system of controls that would catch a rogue trader. Although Jett's remarkable turnaround might have generated suspicion in a different industry, it was very common for traders to find a new product or strategy that produced unusually large returns. How could a manager tell if Jett was different from one of John Meriwether's traders at Salomon?

Even more troubling, the structure of Wall Street compensation seemed to encourage traders to take excessive risks, or even to defraud their firms. In cataloguing many of the instances of "rogue trading" during this period, Professor Jerry W. Markham noted that traders were motivated to expose their firms to as much risk as possible to maximize their own compensation: "There is very little downside when taking on more risk, and the upside is much greater. There is also little motivation to protect the firm's capital from excessive risk. The trader is motivated to be successful, but that motivation lends itself to taking on risk and earning short-term profits, even if this requires illegal or improper conduct."[123] Consider Jett's financial incentives. In his short time at Kidder, his compensation grew from $5,000 to $2.1 million to $9.3 million. He was a poster child for traders looking to make a quick buck.

In July 1994, international regulators from the Basel Committee of international supervisors had warned banks not to tie the bonuses of derivatives traders too closely to their profits, because such links could create excessive risks.[124] But, as usual, the banks ignored the regulators. If they took any message from the fiascos of 1994, it was that they needed to link compensation even more closely to performance. Traders who reported huge profits would make millions; traders who did not report huge profits would be fired.

Finally, Jett's losses exposed how much companies such as General Electric depended on high finance. Treasurers of industrial companies had begun operating as profit centers, taking on huge risks, and receiving compensation based on their success. Many treasury officials believed that they should not tell their managers about the risks they were taking on, in order to preserve their flexibility.[125] Just as the managers of banks had lost control over their traders, the CEOs of major companies were losing control over their treasury operations.

Shareholders of these companies were just as ignorant of their treasurers' activities as the residents of Orange County had been of Robert Citron's. Companies weren't about to tell their shareholders about these practices, either. More than a third of CEOs surveyed by *Fortune* magazine said they thought shareholders were being told enough already.[126]

SEC chairman Arthur Levitt ended his term unconcerned with the question of which company would be next, largely oblivious to the revolution in markets that had occurred under his watch. In one final interview with Hal Lux, senior editor of *Institutional Investor,* Levitt arrived in the midst of his Christmas shopping, loaded with packages from expensive Madison Avenue boutiques.[127] When Lux asked him what his legacy was, as the longest-serving SEC chair in history, Levitt was hard-pressed to come up with an answer: "investor education" was the best he could do, although he did mention several failed initiatives. (Later in the interview, he mentioned Regulation FD—the rule that prohibited senior managers from selectively disclosing non-public information to securities analysts—as one of the "landmark attainments of this Commission," saying, "I don't know why I forgot that.") Levitt admitted that it had been a mistake for him to recommend his chief of market regulation, Richard Lindsey, for a job at Bear Stearns while the SEC was supposedly conducting a serious investigation into that firm's clearing unit. But, throughout a lengthy and substantive interview, covering many topics—including the challenges facing his successor—he did not mention derivatives.

For more than seven years, Arthur Levitt was a long-standing sideshow to the Clinton administration. Levitt's interaction with Clinton was, in his words, mostly "social." President Clinton—a notoriously prolific letter and memo writer—had written only one note to Levitt in all that time: a one-liner about an article in the *New York Times*.[128]

In contrast to Levitt, Mark Brickell—the ISDA lobbyist from J. P. Morgan—remained engaged in the issues, and continued his run of successes, arguing on July 22, 2000, to the House Banking and Financial Services Committee, that swaps should be permanently exempt from regulation because of their custom-tailored nature. In reality, most swaps were not custom tailored and, instead, were as standardized as government bonds. Nevertheless, the permanent exemption became Congress's "farewell gift" to the derivatives industry, on its last day of the session in December 2000, during the heat of debate about the Florida ballots in the presidential election.

As luck would have it, at this hearing Brickell was seated next to Shawn Dorsch, cofounder of Blackbird Holdings. Blackbird had been trading derivatives on a high-tech, Internet-based system since September 1999. It held seventeen patents pending, more than many biotechnology and pharmaceutical firms, and experts regarded Blackbird—and other automated systems like it—as the future of financial trading, and the enemy of Wall Street. Compared to most derivatives dealers, Blackbird had superior technology and significantly lower costs. Brickell and Dorsch found common ground, and Brickell agreed to oppose Wall Street for the first time since the 1970s, by signing on as CEO of Blackbird.

William O. Douglas, Supreme Court justice and SEC chairman, had famously advised that, in financial markets, "Government should keep the shotgun, so to speak, behind the door, loaded, well oiled, cleaned, ready for use." With Levitt and Brickell in charge, the shotgun, now 60 years old, had gone missing, empty of shot, dry, and dirty.

Douglas had understood that there were certain inevitable risks associated with a market economy, and some firms and individuals would end up bearing those risks. As William Donaldson, chair of the NYSE (and future nominee to chair the SEC), put it in 1992, "No matter how much hedging is done, somebody winds up holding the hot potato when the music stops."[129] The goal of the law was to ensure that the people who could best bear the risks would, in fact, end up bearing them, so that the hot potato landed in the right place. But as the derivatives markets were beginning to show, risks in modern financial markets were moving in the opposite direction, migrating progressively to less sophisticated investors: first, Bankers Trust, First Boston, and Salomon Brothers; now, Procter & Gamble, Piper Jaffray, and General Electric.

The deregulatory response to the losses of 1994 led to two dramatic changes in financial markets. First, corporate executives in the United States became much more willing to "cook the books," inflating income and hiding expenses. At first, many of these accounting schemes were relatively simple, short-lived, and easy to understand. Most executives—especially those willing to commit accounting fraud—did not yet comprehend how recent financial innovations could be used to further their schemes. (In other words, the really big trouble was still a few years away.)

Second, financial innovation moved abroad. In foreign venues, the risks of these instruments spread in fantastic and unanticipated ways, leading to several market crises in Latin America, Europe, and Asia.

The first set of changes—the wave of bald-faced accounting fraud in the United States—is covered in the next chapter. The second set—the migration of financial innovation abroad—is covered in Chapter 8.

MESSAGES RECEIVED

The regulatory changes of 1994–95 sent three messages to corporate CEOs. First, you are not likely to be punished for "massaging" your firm's accounting numbers. Prosecutors rarely go after financial fraud and, even when they do, the typical punishment is a small fine; almost no one goes to prison. Moreover, even a fraudulent scheme could be recast as mere *earnings management*—the practice of smoothing a company's earnings—which most executives did, and regarded as perfectly legal.

Second, you should use new financial instruments—including options, swaps, and other derivatives—to increase your own pay and to avoid costly regulation. If complex derivatives are too much for you to handle—as they were for many CEOs during the years immediately following the 1994 losses—you should at least pay yourself in stock options, which don't need to be disclosed as an expense and have a greater upside than cash bonuses or stock.

Third, you don't need to worry about whether accountants or securities analysts will tell investors about any hidden losses or excessive options pay. Now that Congress and the Supreme Court have insulated accounting firms and investment banks from liability—with the Central Bank decision and the Private Securities Litigation Reform Act—they will be much more willing to look the other way. If you pay them enough in fees, they might even be willing to help.

Of course, not every corporate executive heeded these messages. For example, Warren Buffett argued that managers should ensure that their companies' share prices were accurate, not try to inflate prices artificially, and he criticized the use of stock options as compensation. Having been a major shareholder of Salomon Brothers, Buffett also criticized accounting and securities firms for conflicts of interest.

But for every Warren Buffett, there were many less scrupulous CEOs. This chapter considers four of them: Walter Forbes of CUC International, Dean Buntrock of Waste Management, Al Dunlap of Sunbeam, and Martin Grass of Rite Aid. They are not all well-known among investors, but their stories capture the changes in CEO behavior during the mid-1990s. Unlike the "rocket scientists" at Bankers Trust, First Boston, and Salomon Brothers, these four had undistinguished backgrounds and little training in mathematics or finance. Instead, they were hardworking, hard-driving men who ran companies that met basic consumer needs: they sold clothes, barbecue grills, and prescription medicine, and cleaned up garbage. They certainly didn't buy swaps linked to LIBOR-squared.

And yet they were at the center of financial schemes that were even bigger than the derivatives scandals of 1994.

Over time, commentators have dismissed these four CEOs, and dozens like them, as just "bad apples." But the metaphor is false, as abundant evidence and economic theory show. Instead, the stories of these four men symbolize a cultural change among corporate executives during the 1990s that flowed predictably—even inevitably—from the earlier regulatory changes. The apples fell because the tree was rotten.

This claim may seem counterintuitive at first. Most investors had supported the regulatory changes of 1994–95 to deter specious litigation, and there was evidence that, paradoxically, even more securities lawsuits were being filed under the restrictive 1995 securities law.

Moreover, economists had long argued that corporate executives would never systematically take advantage of investors, because their reputations would be destroyed if they did. As the argument went, CEOs would secure reputations for honesty and hard work by keeping accurate books, refusing overly generous options pay (or at least disclosing the options they received), and hiring only independent accountants and bankers, regardless of changes in law. If they failed to do these things, investors would flee the company's stock, and when the stock price dropped, the CEOs would lose their wealth—and their jobs. In other words, CEOs were rational economic actors just like any other member of the species homo economicus; they avoided fraud for the same reason they avoided any other bad business decision: it didn't pay.

It became clear during the 1990s that this argument, although perhaps sound in theory, was wrong in practice. CEOs manipulated their companies' earnings, paid themselves huge amounts of options, and established cozy relationships with their accountants and securities analysts, but they did not acquire bad reputations—at least not until several years later. Instead, CEO reputations—at least in the short run— depended almost entirely on the performance of their firms' stock prices, which in turn depended on whether CEOs were able to meet the quarterly expectations of analysts, and do so—on television—with a charming smile. Few investors or analysts paid attention to the details of particular business units or financial disclosures. As *The Economist* magazine put it, "it was easier to follow the jockeys than the form."[1]

Investors trusted the charismatic CEO who assured them earnings would be up next quarter, and then announced he had beaten the earlier target by a penny a share. If the CEO told a good story (think Michael Armstrong of AT&T, Kenneth Lay of Enron, or Jack Welch of General Electric), investors flocked to the stock. When the stock price went up, the CEO became even more alluring, and more investors joined in, all regardless of what the company actually was doing, and regardless of whether the company's reported numbers were accurate.

Although some economists insisted that such an irrational cycle was impossible—just as they previously had insisted that arbitrage opportunities did not exist, and that no $20 bills were lying on the ground—a new group of academics were creating a new field, called *behavioral finance,* to describe the mountain of evidence inconsistent with classical theory.[2] According to these new theories, stock markets weren't efficient—not even close—and stock prices could (and did) diverge wildly from reality. Arbitrageurs who sold overpriced stocks wouldn't close the gap between perception and reality, because anyone betting against a company that could artificially inflate its earnings for several years would likely go broke before the scheme unraveled.

Previous chapters of this book have tracked the spread of risk from a few Wall Street traders to hundreds of less sophisticated money managers. As companies recovered during the aftershock of the losses of 1994, many of them temporarily abandoned these complex financial innovations (although plain-vanilla derivatives markets, overall, continue to grow, especially outside the United States). With a few notable exceptions, the financial innovations described in the first chapters of this book lay dormant during the mid-to-late 1990s, and did not figure prominently among the major accounting frauds of the period.

Instead, at this point, the major changes in financial markets took a new turn. The financial virus spreading through the markets, which previously had involved primarily new *risks,* broke through a significant barrier and began to involve new methods of *deceit*. This was the beginning of the time Alan Greenspan was referring to when he told the Senate Banking Committee in 2002, "An infectious greed seemed to grip much of our business community."

In a few years, new financial instruments would return to U.S. corporations—often in transmuted form—and the mix of risk and deceit would prove even deadlier. Until then, simple deceit alone would do plenty of damage.

During the previous two decades, Walter Forbes had built the world's largest consumer-services company, CUC International, with 68 million members of various auto, dining, shopping, and travel clubs. CUC was the "middleman" between consumers and manufacturers—like a gigantic corporate Avon Lady—and it made money primarily by selling club memberships, which—like Avon, or even Costco or the Book-of-the-Month Club—entitled the holder to new products and discount prices. Its biggest club was called Comp-U-Card (hence the name "CUC"), but Forbes also had partnerships with major catalog retailers, including Sears. Probably half of the readers of this book have been members of some CUC-related club.

From the beginning, Comp-U-Card executives faced a difficult problem: how should they record revenues and expenses associated with membership sales? Suppose CUC sells a 3-year membership that costs $60 per year, payable quarterly. How much revenue should CUC recognize in its next quarterly financial report? The entire $180 it expected to receive during the three years of membership? Or just the $15 it expected to receive in the first quarter? Or some intermediate amount, perhaps adjusted for expected cancellations, interest rates, or inflation? Expenses weren't any easier. How much of CUC's salaries, overhead costs, and other solicitation expenses should it allocate to a membership it sold? And when?

CUC managers developed a grid to project how much revenue and expenses to reflect over time, based on the company's experiences with cancellations and costs. The goal was to match membership-sales revenues with corresponding expenses. Such a grid was precisely what investors and analysts would expect from a company facing thorny questions about revenues and expenses. So long as CUC used the grid consistently, it would be possible to track the company's business accurately over time.

However, Walter Forbes and CUC's executives wouldn't necessarily benefit from disclosing accurate earnings. By 1994, CUC's membership growth was slowing, and earnings were volatile. If CUC could "manage" its earnings to meet the expectations of analysts and investors, its stock would be more valuable. Here is why.

Major investment banks had securities analysts who rated stocks, typically in one of three categories: buy, hold, or sell. Investors followed these ratings, and higher-rated stocks were more valuable. Analysts (and investors) wanted to see earnings that increased, year to year, and they didn't like surprises. The more predictable corporate earnings were, the more investors would trust the analysts, the more money the analysts would make, the more "buy" ratings they would issue, and the higher stock prices would be. In 1994, companies ranging from AT&T to Enron to General Electric were managing their earnings, and there were a lot of happy analysts; only about one percent of ratings were "sells." There were a lot of happy investors, too.

To please the analysts, CUC began manipulating its grids, adding "allocation" columns, so that executives could manually shift revenues from one period to another.[3] But CUC executives took earnings management a step farther, sometimes ignoring the grids entirely and, instead, simply typing into the computer spreadsheet new numbers that tracked CUC's earnings to better match the expectations of analysts. Those numbers magically became the firm's revenues and expenses for a given period. Over time, CUC's accounting system began to resemble the one Joseph Jett used at Kidder Peabody, recognizing false profits today and pushing losses off until tomorrow, disguising the reality that CUC was losing money.

CUC's executives refined their earnings-management scheme during the mid-1990s, until they were recognizing tens of millions of dollars in additional revenues prematurely and pushing similar amounts of expenses into the future. For example, when Comp-U-Card members cancelled memberships during the fourth quarter of a year, CUC would hold that cancellation off the books until the following year. Executives also began stretching expenses associated with memberships across three years, instead of recognizing them within the year they were sold.[4] If the expenses associated with a membership were $30, CUC would switch from recording an expense of $30 in the first year to recording $10 per year for three years, thereby pushing two-thirds of its expenses into the next two years.

These tricks worked very nicely in the short run. However, investors and analysts expected CUC's earnings to continue to grow, and after a few years CUC executives had milked its membership sales for as much as they could. The accounting firm of Ernst & Young—the successor to Arthur Young, the firm that was implicated in the cover-up of Andy Krieger's $80 million of missing profits at Bankers Trust—had approved of CUC's prior financial statements, but the accounting firm was only willing to go so far. By 1996, the deferred expenses were coming due, and there were no real profits to offset them. CUC would either have to declare a loss or find another source of additional false profits.

Walter Forbes considered his options—both literally and figuratively. CUC had granted Forbes millions of stock options, and if CUC declared a loss, he would lose tens of millions of dollars. However, if he could find a merger partner, he might be able to buy more time by hiding the losses elsewhere, and perhaps even pick up more stock options from the merger.

Forbes met with Henry R. Silverman, founder and CEO of HFS International, a company that owned hotels (Days Inn and Ramada), real estate (Century 21 and Coldwell Banker), and other franchises (HFS stood for Hospitality Franchise Systems). Wall Street loved Henry Silverman. He had banking experience at the prestigious Blackstone Group, and analysts loved the predictable earnings of his brand-name franchises (never mind that many of them were near bankruptcy). HFS was one of the best-performing stocks in the rapidly rising market of the mid-1990s.

Forbes and CUC presented an intriguing opportunity for Silverman. Forbes's club members were potential customers of Silverman's franchises, and vice versa. CUC members could buy homes through Century 21; guests at Ramada hotels could sign up with Comp-U-Card. In addition, HFS could partner with CUC's Internet website, called Netmarket.com, which Forbes claimed "will sell 90% of what you'd want in your home."[5]

CUC's new "online mall" was attractive to HFS for two reasons. First, Netmarket.com already had 700,000 members who had bought

$1.2 billion of consumer products.[6] Those were people who might use HFS franchises. Second, Internet retailing seemed to be a brilliant new business model, and Forbes and Netmarket were among the very few firms in this new "space." Amazon.com—which in a few years would become a dominant Internet retailer—had just sold its first book in 1995; auction site eBay.com was just a start-up company. Netmarket.com was in position to be the market leader (although it seemed implausible that members would pay the advertised $69.99 annual fee, given that introductory memberships were available for $1).

The merger seemed attractive to everyone. The combined firm—to be called Cendant—would have more than 35,000 employees, operations in 100 countries, and would be among the 100 largest U.S. corporations. Its shares would be worth almost $40 billion.[7] Walter Forbes would have 9.4 million stock options, worth more than $65 million, in a company that was better than his current one. Silverman would receive even more stock options, enough to bump his personal wealth above $100 million.

Most important for CUC, a merger with a company the size of HFS would give it the opportunity to use a new scheme to hide its rapidly building losses—permanently. CUC had just tried this scheme on a smaller scale, and it had worked beautifully. Here is how it would work: Cendant, the merged company, would record an expense called a *merger reserve*, to reflect the cost of the merger. Analysts would view the merger reserve as separate from operating expenses, and it would be listed separately in Cendant's financial statements. According to the analysts' models, Cendant's stock price was based on how much money it was expected to make in the future, and the one-time costs of a merger—such as legal expenses, banking fees, and severance payments—would not affect future operations.

The trick was to inflate the value of the merger reserve. Cendant could then draw from this inflated value to offset its accumulating operating expenses. Sure, the merger might look really expensive, but the analysts wouldn't focus on that. Instead, they would look at earnings, which would appear to be growing, smooth as ever.

In previous mergers, CUC had experimented with puffing its merger reserve, to great success. It wasn't rocket science. In one deal, CUC executives estimated the total merger reserve, and then simply doubled it.[8] CUC's Ideon reserve—which related to a merger with a firm called Ideon

Group, Inc.—was overstated by $135 million. By drawing on this reserve, CUC magically deflated its accumulating operating expenses by $135 million. With these mergers under his belt, Walter Forbes was looking for the "mother of all merger reserves," a deal with HFS that would wipe out all of CUC's mounting expenses.

Unfortunately for Forbes, CUC never got the chance to use the merger-reserve trick again. Cendant was formed in December 1997, but, within a few months, HFS executives discovered what their due-diligence advisors had failed to uncover prior to the merger: that CUC had been a shell game. When Henry Silverman learned that CUC executives had been typing in their own versions of income and expenses, and abusing earlier merger reserves—and that therefore he might lose his hard-earned $100 million—he was understandably upset. None of the watchdogs supposedly monitoring CUC's managers had barked. That included the twenty-eight members of Cendant's unwieldy board of directors, half of whom had been directors of CUC. It included Ernst & Young, CUC's accounting firm. And it included three of the most prestigious investment banks: HFS had hired Bear Stearns and Merrill Lynch, and CUC had hired Goldman Sachs—and these banks undertook a due diligence investigation that lasted several weeks.

After learning of the apparent fraud at CUC, the directors on Cendant's audit committee immediately met to appoint an accounting firm to investigate. The directors needed a world-class group of auditors with an impeccable reputation and no conflicts of interest. Ernst & Young was out. The directors chose the accounting firm Arthur Andersen.

Andersen's accountants easily unraveled the fraud, perhaps because it was so basic, perhaps because they had seen similar schemes at other companies. In hindsight, it seemed obvious that CUC's earnings could not have been growing at such a rapid pace without a substantial amount of accounting puffery. But investors and analysts had focused instead on Walter Forbes's story about CUC's future on the Internet and the fact that CUC consistently beat earnings estimates. They hadn't probed the details until it was too late.

In April 1998, Cendant finally disclosed that it had discovered accounting "irregularities." Its stock price fell by half, and then half again. Suddenly, a $40 billion company was a $10 billion company. In all, CUC had artificially overstated its earnings by nearly one-third.[9]

Notwithstanding the limitations on securities lawsuits from 1995, more than seventy lawsuits were filed during the days after Cendant's announcement, including eight lawsuits brought on behalf of purchasers of $1 billion of bizarre securities Cendant had just issued called FELINE PRIDES (more about them later in this chapter). Ultimately, these lawsuits led to the largest securities-fraud settlement ever: more than $3 billion.

Henry Silverman didn't fare badly, though. The money for the settlement came from insurance and from Cendant shareholders. In September 1998, the compensation committee of Cendant's board of directors approved a program to *reprice* the options held by executive officers of Cendant so that they didn't lose any money. For example, a 10-year option to buy stock for $40 a share was very valuable when the stock was at $40; it wasn't so valuable when the stock was at $10. But it would be valuable again if Cendant transformed it into a right to buy stock for $10 a share. By repricing the options, Cendant protected its executives from financial loss. Shareholders were outraged by the repricing. Why hadn't the board made up for *their* losses?

Cendant also took care of Walter Forbes, paying him a severance package of $35 million, plus $12.5 million worth of stock options. In 2000, Forbes was living the good life, developing the new Queenwood Golf Club, west of London, and raising money for a business called LivePerson, which provided Internet customer service and sales support.[10] Netmarket.com was still running in 2002, indistinguishable from about a million online buying guides, and still ostensibly charging $69.99 for a membership (although trial memberships were still available for $1).

Although CUC was not able to use the Cendant merger reserve to cover up its operating expenses, Forbes tried to use it as a slush fund to cover his own costs. He requested reimbursement for $596,000 of air-travel expenses for 1995 and 1996—travel that had occurred before the HFS merger was even contemplated—and noted that the expense should be charged to the reserve related to the HFS merger.[11] Cendant's audit committee later found that Walter Forbes had overbilled his expense account by more than $2 million.[12]

It was unclear whether Forbes would be punished for CUC's fraud. Prosecutors persuaded several former Cendant employees to plead guilty to securities fraud, and—in exchange for leniency—they agreed to testify that, between 1995 and 1997, their supervisors had instructed them to manipulate accounting figures to increase profits.[13] With this testimony in hand, prosecutors indicted Walter Forbes for fraud on February 28, 2001, and he was still awaiting trial in 2003.

The Cendant case was a wake-up call for government officials, who finally recognized that they would need to bring more criminal prosecutions in the financial area, to make up for the increase in fraud following the regulatory changes of 1994–95. As former SEC director of enforcement Richard H. Walker put it, "There is a growing awareness that committing a fraud by cooking the books results in the same, if not greater, harm than pulling up to a bank and putting a gun in a teller's face. But civil remedies and injunctions simply were not sufficient to achieve the kind of deterrence to stop people."[14] For Cendant's investors, even a $3 billion settlement was too little, too late.

Like Walter Forbes, Dean Buntrock was not well-known. (Neither man had ever been mentioned in People magazine or The New Yorker, for example.) In 1955, Dean Buntrock was selling insurance in Colorado, when his father-in-law, Peter Huizenga, died. Buntrock had little business experience, but he was needed to help run his in-laws' family business, a garbage collection company called Ace Scavenger Service, which operated fifteen dump trucks.[15]

Meanwhile, one of Buntrock's wife Elizabeth's cousins, Wayne Huizenga, had dropped out of Calvin College in Michigan and wandered down to Fort Lauderdale, Florida, where he purchased a garbage truck and began working a $500-a-month route. Within a few years, Wayne Huizenga had twenty trucks of his own, and he and Buntrock—cousins by marriage—decided to merge.[16] They named their new venture Waste Management.

The men borrowed a "tremendous amount of money" from banks and sold stock to the public in 1971.[17] During the next decade, they bought more than a hundred local dumping companies and landfills, and made generous political contributions. They won a city cleaning contract for Riyadh, Saudi Arabia, in 1976, and followed that with over a billion dollars' worth of contracts with major foreign cities. Over time, as hundreds of U.S. landfills closed due to environmental concerns, Waste Management's remained open. As state and local governments bowed out of the distasteful business of garbage collection, they effectively gave Waste Management a monopoly. As one company official, Phillip Rooney, put it, "Regulation has been very, very good for the business."[18]

Wayne Huizenga stepped down from Waste Management in 1984,

when he began a string of successful business ventures (the video rental company Blockbuster, which he sold to Viacom; AutoNation, the largest U.S. auto dealer; Boca Resorts, a luxury-resort chain; and a somewhat less successful stint as owner of several Florida professional sports teams).[19] Buntrock became chairman and CEO of Waste Management.

Under Buntrock's leadership, Waste Management's executives had been accused of every crime or infraction imaginable, from bribing local officials to denying competitors access to dumps to violating numerous environmental regulations.[20] The company had been a defendant in seven antitrust cases, and had paid tens of millions of dollars in fines related to its illegal storage and improper handling of carcinogenic polychlorinated biphenyls (PCBs).[21] The phrase "No job is too dirty for Waste Management" stuck to the firm, yet criminal charges did not. Unlike some of its employees, the company—and Dean Buntrock—had never been convicted of a crime.

Given its aggressive approach to the law, it is not surprising that Waste Management—like CUC—began managing its earnings during the 1990s. The garbage business was becoming less profitable—in part due to a glut of dump capacity—and Waste Management sought to inflate its earnings and push expenses into the future.

Waste Management was assisted in its effort to manipulate earnings by its accounting firm, Arthur Andersen—the firm that Cendant's audit committee had hired to investigate CUC's books. Andersen had audited Waste Management for two decades, and it regarded the company as a "crown-jewel" client. During the 1990s, Andersen billed Waste Management $7.5 million for audit work, and another $18 million in other fees, including fees from Andersen's consulting business. During this time, Andersen and Waste Management built a close relationship. Every chief financial officer and chief accounting officer at Waste Management had previously worked at Andersen. Fourteen former Andersen employees worked at Waste Management during the 1990s.[22]

Beginning in 1994, Andersen auditors identified numerous adjustments they thought were necessary to correct misstatements in Waste Management's books. The firm had been pushing expenses into the future, much as CUC had done. Waste Management refused to correct the misstatements and, after some debate, Andersen's partners apparently decided that the problem was temporary. They signed off on Waste Management's 1994 annual report, but wrote a memorandum specifying the minimum steps Waste Management "must do" to correct the problems. Andersen also identified Waste Management as a "high risk client."

Notwithstanding this warning, nothing changed. As Andersen's auditors reviewed Waste Management's financial statements in 1995, they worried that Waste Management had not "taken the pill" yet. Waste Management had continued to roll forward its expenses. Moreover, in December 1995, it recorded a gain of $160 million by exchanging shares it owned in a limited partnership called ServiceMaster for shares of ServiceMaster's parent. It was merely a paper transaction—Waste Management retained the same economic interest in ServiceMaster after the deal—but company officials wanted to use this "gain" to offset accumulating expenses.

Accounting rules clearly prohibited the offset. One-time gains from deals such as the ServiceMaster transaction had to be separated from operating expenses, so that investors could get an accurate picture of the company and understand that it was losing money, generally, but had booked a substantial gain on one financial transaction.

However, Andersen concluded that even though the offset was improper, it was not "material" and, therefore, did not need to be disclosed. This interpretation was dubious at best. The legal test for whether information was material was whether an investor would consider it important in the total mix of information about the company. The $160 million offset was obviously important; its disclosure would have caused Waste Management's stock to plummet. Andersen officials wrote another memorandum, this time noting that they had "communicated strongly to WMX [Waste Management] management that this is an area of SEC exposure." But Andersen nevertheless signed off on the firm's 1995 financial statements.

In 1996, Waste Management was even more aggressive. It continued to push expenses into the future and it netted other one-time gains against various expenses. It even conducted a "sweep" of its field offices, in which it asked controllers to try to find some extra reserves the company could claim as income. At the last minute, one day before releasing its earnings, Waste Management came up with an additional $29 million of such income—an extra four cents a share, which greatly pleased investors and analysts. Again, Andersen signed a statement that Waste Management's annual report presented an accurate financial view of the company.

As with Cendant, this sort of accounting at Waste Management didn't remain hidden forever. Rumors spread about the aggressive practices, and Dean Buntrock stepped down in 1996. The next year, former SEC chairman Roderick Hills joined Waste Management's board and audit committee, and ordered a thorough audit, which revealed that the company had overstated its earnings by $1.43 billion, twice as much as Cendant had.[23] In February 1998, Waste Management announced this finding to the public—the company had lost almost as much money as Orange County had lost a few years earlier. At the time, it was the largest corporate financial restatement in history.

Andersen again issued its unqualified approval of the firm's financial statements, which—this time, at least—were accurate. The SEC wasn't impressed, and fined Andersen $7 million for approving Waste Management's earlier, inaccurate financial statements.[24]

Like Cendant, Waste Management was sued for securities fraud, but Dean Buntrock wasn't indicted or found personally liable. His reputation suffered, but he did just fine financially. He had earned a salary of about a million dollars for several years, and had received huge grants of stock options (one grant in 1995 was for options on 205,505 shares). As one sign of Buntrock's wealth, he was able to donate $26 million to his alma mater, St. Olaf College, where the student center was now called Buntrock Commons. A St. Olaf philosophy professor said he planned to use the fraud at Waste Management as an example in class: "I'm not saying Buntrock did anything. But this issue would be a good one."[25]

The Waste Management saga ended like a bad horror film, with the perpetrator rising from the dead to commit another wicked act. The plotline was similar: after a smaller garbage company, USA Waste Services, bought Waste Management in July 1998,[26] the new executives failed to tell investors about yet another round of accounting problems. The company—still called Waste Management after the merger—failed to meet its earnings estimates, and the stock plunged from $54 to $34 in one day. The board of directors immediately ousted the new management and began yet another investigation, which revealed an additional $1.2 billion of charges. Was anyone really that surprised? With the stock around $20, shareholders were awaiting Waste Management III.

When Sunbeam Corporation announced it had hired Al Dunlap in July 1996, the company's shareholders, directors, and securities analysts were

thrilled. Sunbeam's shares went up 50 percent on the day of the announcement. As far as investors knew, Dunlap was a master cost-cutter, with the
credentials and credibility to turn the failing company around.

For Sunbeam, the key fact about Al Dunlap was that he had become
CEO of Scott Paper, where he had earned the nickname "Chainsaw Al"
by firing 11,200 people—one in three of the firm's employees. Scott
Paper's stock was up, and shareholders loved Dunlap, even if employees
didn't.

In 1996, Sunbeam was in the same predicament Scott Paper had been
in a few years earlier. It was bloated and inefficient, and needed similarly
radical reforms. To Sunbeam's board, Dunlap seemed like the perfect
person to come in and start cutting.

They couldn't have been more wrong. Within two years, the board
would fire Dunlap, the SEC would begin an investigation into massive
accounting fraud at Sunbeam, and the company would be headed for
bankruptcy. There would be numerous parallels to Cendant and Waste
Management.

In fact, if Sunbeam's board had asked more questions about Dunlap's
past, they might not have hired him at all. Dunlap's résumé had not
listed the fact that Max Phillips & Son had fired him in 1974, or that
Nitec Paper Corporation had fired him in 1978, allegedly for overstating
profits.[27] (In 1982, Nitec Paper filed for bankruptcy after some executives accused Dunlap of a massive accounting fraud.)[28] Nor did Sunbeam's directors hear from executives who had worked with Dunlap
when he ran an Australian firm called Consolidated Press Holdings; they
alleged similar improprieties.[29] If the board members had known how
many times Al Dunlap had been fired, they might have found his eagerness to fire others suspicious.

In any event, Dunlap didn't disappoint the shareholders' expectations: he fired half of Sunbeam's 12,000 employees right away, and shut
down numerous plants. These actions had substantial one-time costs,
but the hope was that, with lower future expenses, Sunbeam finally
would look attractive to investors and analysts.

At the end of 1996, Sunbeam took a huge one-time restructuring
charge of $338 million. Executives padded this charge by $35 million, in
the same way Cendant and Waste Management had padded their reserves.
In accounting parlance, Sunbeam created a "cookie-jar" reserve. By overstating one-time expenses, it created a $35 million stash from which it
could take a cookie when necessary.

In addition, executives front-loaded as many expenses as they could into 1996, in an effort to guarantee that 1997 would be a good year. For example, at the end of 1996, Sunbeam understated the value of inventory it was planning to sell in 1997, thereby guaranteeing that it would make more money when the inventory was later sold. It also recognized expenditures made for 1997 advertising as a 1996 expense.

In 1997, Sunbeam engaged in a variety of accounting games to inflate its income, including *channel stuffing*—stuffing its distribution channels with so many advance sales that there would be little revenue left in future periods. For example, just before the end of the first quarter, Sunbeam booked $1.5 million from sales of barbecue grills, even though it had promised the purchaser it could return any grills it did not sell (in fact, six months later, all of the grills were returned unsold).[30] Sunbeam also began rewarding customers for agreeing to buy products before they needed them, so that Sunbeam could book the revenue earlier (again, purchasers had the right to return unsold products). Throughout 1997, even with these adjustments, Sunbeam just barely beat analysts' earnings estimates, by a penny or two per share. By the end of 1997, it appeared that even with all of the accounting games, Sunbeam's earnings nevertheless would "miss" analysts' estimates. Like Cendant, it was running out of schemes.

How could Sunbeam conceal more of its expenses, to meet the estimates? As Cendant had shown, mergers were the only answer. Sunbeam began negotiating to buy Coleman (camping gear), First Alert (fire alarms), and Signature Brands (Mr. Coffee), each of which might enable Sunbeam to overbook merger reserves and, thereby, artificially reduce future expenses. Dunlap hurriedly met with financier Ronald Perelman, who owned 82 percent of Coleman, but Perelman wanted $30 per share, and Dunlap was only willing to pay $20. Dunlap again showed he was a tough guy, stomping out of Perelman's house in Palm Beach, Florida, reportedly screaming, "Fuck you! And fuck your company."[31]

Meanwhile, Arthur Andersen—Sunbeam's auditor—began questioning the firm's aggressive accounting policies and proposing some changes to the financial statements, just as it had done with Waste Management. But Sunbeam rejected the changes, and Andersen nevertheless issued an opinion that Sunbeam's 1997 financial statements were fair, even though 16 percent of Sunbeam's 1997 income was from sources Andersen deemed improper.

On January 28, 1998, Sunbeam announced its annual results, calling its earnings a "record" compared to previous years. But on Wall Street, the only relevant benchmark was what analysts were expecting, and this time Sunbeam fell short by three cents per share. Investors were no longer thrilled with Al Dunlap; the stock fell almost 10 percent.

The first quarter of 1998 was desperate. Sunbeam had borrowed too much from future earnings by channel stuffing, and now senior managers were receiving reports that customers held up to eighty weeks of Sunbeam's inventory—that meant those customers wouldn't need to buy anything else from the company for well over a year.

Dunlap returned to Perelman and agreed to exchange $30 worth of Sunbeam's shares for each of Perelman's Coleman shares. It also borrowed money to buy First Alert and Signature Brands. But by the time the merger negotiations had ended, there was not enough time for Sunbeam to conjure false profits from its merger reserves before it had to disclose results for the first quarter of 1998. This time, the news was awful: Sunbeam had actually lost money. The stock dropped by 24 percent that day.

Al Dunlap tried to persuade investors that it was just a one-time problem. He was just as surprised as they were. But his story that he had believed "until the very end of the quarter" that Sunbeam would exceed its results from the first quarter of 1997 seemed implausible. It had taken several years, but investors finally had learned they could not trust Al Dunlap.

In April 1998, an analyst at PaineWebber, Andrew Shore, downgraded Sunbeam's stock from "buy." When other analysts followed, and began questioning the company's accounting practices, Sunbeam's board hired a headhunter to find a replacement for Dunlap.

Dunlap was furious, and refused to leave. When *Fortune* magazine reporter Patricia Sellers asked Dunlap if he was afraid of losing his job, he told her to "get goddamn serious!" and said he would be staying as CEO for another three years. At a meeting before 200 analysts and investors, Dunlap tried to explain why Sunbeam's stock had lost half of its value since March. He blamed Sunbeam's troubles on a recently departed junior executive and on the recent El Niño–related weather ("People don't think about buying grills in a storm"). When Andrew Shore, the PaineWebber analyst, questioned Dunlap at the meeting, Dunlap confronted him afterward, called Shore a "son of a bitch," and threatened, "If you want to come after me, I'll come back at you twice as hard."[32]

Dunlap never got the chance to come back. The board of directors fired him on June 13, 1998. Ironically, Waste Management had considered hiring Dunlap several months earlier, when the height of that firm's troubles coincided with the height of Dunlap's glory. Now, of course, Dunlap was an untouchable. But he had used the possibility of a job at Waste Management to persuade Sunbeam's board to double his salary and pay him even more stock options.[33]

Stock options had given Dunlap an incredible incentive to pump up Sunbeam's stock price. When Dunlap joined Sunbeam in July 1996, he had received 2.5 million 10-year options to buy Sunbeam shares—a meatier signing bonus than most professional athletes received. Dunlap received another 3.75 million options in February 1998. At Sunbeam's peak stock price of $52, Dunlap's options were worth well over $100 million dollars, based on the Black-Scholes option-pricing model. In November 1998, when Sunbeam finally issued accurate financial statements for the previous year—reducing its 1997 income by half—the stock fell, and at a stock price of just $7, Dunlap's options were worth close to zero.

Ultimately, Sunbeam would file for bankruptcy. The lawsuits against Al Dunlap for Sunbeam's fraud were covered by insurance. Arthur Andersen paid $110 million to settle securities-fraud suits in 2001 (Andersen also had insurance, through a complicated self-insurance program established by the major accounting firms.) The SEC brought civil cases against several Sunbeam executives, as well as the former lead partner at Andersen for the Sunbeam audits, but the settlements did not include jail time or large fines. Dunlap settled civil charges with the SEC in September 2002, and his $500,000 fine didn't hurt much. He remains in retirement—a wealthy, if disgraced, man.

On May 5, 1989, Martin L. Grass—the 35-year-old heir apparent to Rite Aid, his father's retail drugstore chain—boarded the firm's nine-seat corporate jet and flew to Cleveland, Ohio.[34] He had worked for Rite Aid since he was 13, and had just been named president of the firm.

Grass was planning to meet with Melvin Wilczynski, a member of the Ohio Pharmacy Board, which represented local drugstores. Two months earlier, Rite Aid had purchased Lane Drug, a local pharmacy that previously had hired Wilczynski as a consultant. The Ohio Pharmacy Board was unhappy about Rite Aid's intrusion into the state, and had penalized Rite Aid for security violations related to the Lane Drug deal.

When Martin Grass arrived in Cleveland, he went directly to a room at the Sheraton Hotel near the airport and met with Wilczynski. Wilczynski had asked for a meeting, and knew that Rite Aid's managers wanted him to resign from the Pharmacy Board. Grass gave Wilczynski a check for $33,249.93, and a form guaranteeing him four years of health-care coverage, along with six letters of resignation from the Ohio Pharmacy Board. Wilczynski could sign the letter he liked best, and keep the check and the health insurance.

Grass didn't know they were being videotaped—Wilczynski had contacted the police to complain that Grass was trying to bribe him—and, moments after Wilczynski signed one of the letters, Grass was arrested. The case went to trial in Cuyahoga County—which, coincidentally, was about to lose millions of dollars on leveraged derivatives—and a judge ultimately dismissed the charges. Grass's lawyers had argued that the Ohio bribery law covered only a person's actions as a public official, not that person's decision whether to remain a public official.[35] In other words, Grass did not commit bribery simply by paying Wilczynski to resign. After the charges were dismissed, Grass sued Wilczynski for defamation, and agreed to dismiss the suit in exchange for the return of the $33,249.93 check and a letter of apology.[36] Grass kept the apology letter framed on his wall, as a message to anyone who questioned his authority and willingness to retaliate against opponents.

By 1995, Martin Grass and Rite Aid were managing 2,717 stores, and preparing to buy Revco, which operated another 2,000 stores. Rite Aid was such a sprawling enterprise that, in order to keep in touch with store managers, Martin Grass hosted a talk show on Rite Aid's internal television network (he discussed issues ranging from where to put perfume racks to current profit reports).[37]

Rite Aid's accounting scheme began in 1996, when it sold 189 stores for a $90 million gain. Instead of recognizing the one-time gain from the sale, it used the $90 million to absorb operating expenses. It was the same game Cendant, Waste Management, and Sunbeam had played; the one-time gain and the operating expenses should have been listed separately. Ninety million dollars was a substantial sum for Rite Aid; it represented more than one-third of the company's 1996 income. Yet Rite Aid's annual report stated that "gains from drugstore closings and dispositions were not significant."[38]

When this 1996 accounting scheme seemed to work, Rite Aid began a systematic effort to inflate its profits and reduce expenses. Rite Aid's overstatement was almost as large as those at Cendant, Waste Management, and Sunbeam—combined. In all, Rite Aid overstated its income by $2.3 billion.[39]

The Rite Aid accounting adjustments were too widespread to describe in detail, even for the SEC, which provided only a summary in its 2002 description of the charges. The charges read like a condensed version of the charges against Cendant, Waste Management, and Sunbeam—as if the SEC lawyers understood that the reader had heard all of this before and needed only a summary. The fraud included inflated revenues, reductions of previously recorded expenses, inflated deductions for damaged and outdated products, and unwarranted credits to various stores at the end of particular quarters.

The Rite Aid charges included one new element that would haunt the financial markets after Enron's collapse: *related-party transactions*. Martin Grass was a "related party" to Rite Aid, and he had been dealing with Rite Aid accounts as if they were his own, borrowing from and lending to the company using other "related parties." For example, Rite Aid did not disclose the fact that Grass had financial interests in properties that Rite Aid leased as store locations. In January 1988, Rite Aid transferred $2.6 million to a real-estate partnership controlled by Grass and a relative; the partnership then purchased an 83-acre parcel of land to be used for Rite Aid's new headquarters, and paid off some of Grass's debts. When the deal unraveled, Grass allegedly tried to conceal it, and repaid the money from his personal account. In another instance, in September 1999, Grass reportedly signed false minutes from a Rite Aid finance-committee meeting purporting to approve a stock pledge that was a prerequisite for a loan Rite Aid needed. In fact, the meeting Grass swore to had never occurred. Like Walter Forbes, Martin Grass reportedly sought reimbursement for various expenses, but whereas Forbes (and Buntrock and Dunlap) had merely used a private jet, Grass commuted daily from Baltimore County to Harrisburg, Pennsylvania, by helicopter, with the majority of the costs paid by the firm.[40]

Rite Aid's accounting firm was KPMG, one of the so-called Big Five. In auditing Rite Aid, KPMG behaved no differently than Ernst & Young in auditing Cendant or Arthur Andersen in auditing Waste Management and Sunbeam. Grass treated KPMG's auditors like low-level employees. When KPMG auditors raised questions about Rite Aid's accounting practices, Grass reportedly began threatening them. He told the KPMG partner with primary responsibility for Rite Aid's audit that "skeletons would come out of KPMG's closet" if Rite Aid suffered from an audit. At the same time, Grass also offered KPMG a lucrative consulting contract, in addition to the fees associated with the Rite Aid audit. KPMG graciously accepted.

Throughout this time, Rite Aid granted millions of options to Martin Grass. For example, in 1999 he received one million options with a value of about $12 million. At their peak, Grass's options were worth in the range of $100 million.

Charges against Rite Aid and Martin Grass were brought in June 2002. Prosecutors intended to make an example of Grass, just as they were trying to do with Walter Forbes of Cendant.

Fortunately for the prosecutors, Grass hadn't learned his lesson about recording in sting operations from the Ohio Pharmacy Board incident. Rite Aid's former president, Timothy Noonan, secretly recorded conversations with Grass and a Rite Aid lawyer in which they allegedly discussed submitting false information to the FBI, fabricating contrived explanations for certain events, back-dating documents, and destroying the computer that generated them.[41] Grass argued that the tapes should be suppressed, but in early 2003 the judge overseeing his case decided to permit prosecutors to use the tapes at trial. In June 2003, Grass pleaded guilty to conspiracy to defraud and obstruction of justice, and agreed to pay $3.5 million in fines and forfeitures. The 1990s stock bubble had ended.

The list of companies manipulating their earnings during the mid-to-late 1990s goes on (W. R. Grace, Livent, Oxford Health Plans, and Xerox, for example), but you get the point. Over a hundred companies filed financial restatements in 1997. In a 1998 survey of chief financial officers of major corporations at a *Business Week* conference, 12 percent admitted they had "misrepresented corporate financial results," and 55 percent said they had been asked to misrepresent results but had "fought off" the demand.[42] In other words, two-thirds of CEOs were asking their assistants to misrepresent financial statements. And even these numbers were probably too low; not everyone was willing to admit to fraud in a survey, even a confidential one.

In sum, the system of financial controls had broken down, and it stayed broken for several years. Corporate executives created fictitious earnings, and no one caught them or even asked serious questions. There were numerous parties to blame. Accounting firms had become conflicted by high audit fees and revenues from their consulting businesses. (To his credit, Arthur Levitt finally began complaining about these conflicts.) Securities analysts covering these companies had become conflicted by the investment-banking revenues the companies paid their firms. Boards of directors and members of audit committees failed to ask hard questions. Corporate lawyers not only created the deals that generated false profits or hid losses, but also set up programs to deter the hostile takeovers that had dominated the 1980s. Because of legal defenses against takeovers, the threat of a corporate raider buying a company's stock and ousting a selfish CEO was virtually nil.

Yet investors seemed oblivious to the breakdown of controls, and the markets continued to rise, so much so that Alan Greenspan of the Federal Reserve felt compelled to intervene. Some investors believed that the markets had entered a new phase—bolstered by technology—in which the returns from investing in stocks had doubled. (The technology-and-Internet bubble and its bursting are addressed in Chapter 9; for now, suffice it to say that investors either didn't read or didn't believe *The Economist* magazine, which was posting warnings about the speculative bubble practically every week.) From Greenspan's perspective, stock-price increases posed the same kinds of inflationary dangers as increases in the prices of consumer goods. He was determined to change investors' minds before the markets spun completely out of control.

However, Greenspan had learned from the interest-rate hikes of 1994 that, with so many undisclosed financial arrangements floating in the system, the Fed could no longer accurately anticipate the effect of changes in monetary policy. Instead of raising interest rates, he decided to use his bully pulpit. Perhaps he could jawbone investors into greater rationality by talking the markets down to more reasonable levels.

In December 1996, Greenspan gave a speech in which he famously asked, "How do we know when irrational exuberance has unduly escalated asset values?" This term—*irrational exuberance*—instantly became part of the vocabulary of average investors, who bristled at the accusation that they were behaving irrationally. If the stock market continued to go up by 20 percent every year, was it really so irrational to put more money in? And even if the market was just a speculative bubble, didn't it make sense to continue to invest, so long as you could get out before the bubble burst?

The classical economic models couldn't explain market behavior during the mid-1990s, so economists proposed two major revisions. First was the theory of *downward-sloping* demand for stocks. The idea was that the price of a stock depended on its demand, just as the price of gas at a particular station depended on how many people wanted to buy gas there. (In other words, a graph of quantity on the horizontal axis versus price on the vertical axis would slope downward from left to right.)

Although this idea sounds like common sense, it was a radical departure from classical theory, which assumed that all investors behaved similarly, so that demand was flat at a single price. For example, in the classical model, if Sunbeam stock were worth $50 per share, no one would want to buy for $60 and everyone would want to buy an infinite amount for $40. The equilibrium price for all investors would be $50.

In the newer models, some people would buy at higher prices— perhaps because they were unwilling to expend the resources necessary to learn the stock was really worth $50, or because they had different expectations about the company's future prospects and believed it was worth more. Other people would not buy even at $40, again because of laziness or differing beliefs. In the classical theory, demand was flat at $50; in the new theory, demand sloped down from $60 to $50 to $40, with more people demanding stock as the price declined. Law professor Lynn Stout has labeled this theory "heterogeneous expectations," to note the differences among investors in the model.

This theory is heresy to a classical financial economist, but it easily explained the 1990s bubble. The demand for stocks increased because more individuals began investing in markets. As these individuals began buying more stocks, demand and prices moved up. Moreover, these new investors were more optimistic (or, perhaps, naïve) than previous investors, and so they were willing to pay more for particular stocks.

The reason this theory was heresy was that stocks were thought to have some value at a particular time, given the available information about the company at that time, and if the stock price diverged upward from that value, an arbitrageur could make money by selling the stock and waiting for the price to return to "normal." Economists argued that heterogeneous-expectations theory made no sense in a market with arbitrageurs. If Sunbeam's price increased to $60 (or even $50.01), one of John Meriwether's traders would sell millions of shares until the price went back to $50.

The second revision to the classical theory was a response to this argument. What if there were limits to arbitrage? For example, if companies engaged in accounting fraud, so that many investors were persuaded that a stock was worth $60—even though it really was worth only $50—then arbitrageurs might bet against the stock and lose money, year after year, until the fraud was revealed. In a perfect market, the information about the fraud would come out right away, but the past few years had demonstrated that markets were not perfect. That made long-term bets against stocks very risky, which was why Salomon Brothers—and other major banks—rarely made them. Instead, arbitrageurs focused on shorter-term bets, such as mergers, where any price gap was virtually guaranteed to close within a month or so.

Another limitation on arbitrage was the difficulty of taking a position that would increase in value when the stock went down. The basic problem was that, although it was easy to bet in favor of a particular stock, it was difficult and expensive to bet against it by shorting stock. Moreover, put options often were unavailable, too expensive, or expired too soon.

In this way, the stock market was just like pari-mutuel betting at a horse race. It was simple to bet on a horse: you walked up to a window and bought a ticket. But how could you bet against a horse? You could try to find someone in the stands who wanted to bet on the horse, and bet with them. But that was time-consuming, and—unlike the cashier standing at the pari-mutuel window—you couldn't be assured that a random person you found would pay if she lost. Or you could do something more complicated: find someone who already had bet on the horse, borrow their ticket, and sell that ticket to someone else, promising to pay that person if the horse won, in which case she would give you the ticket, which you then would return to the first person, along with a fee. This second plan had problems, too. Not only did it have several complex steps, but a random person betting on the horse might not be persuaded that *you* would pay if she won.

In the stock market, someone wanting to bet against a stock generally had to use this second, convoluted plan. The first plan—finding another person who wanted to buy the stock and transacting with that person—was theoretically possible in the unregulated over-the-counter market, but it was too expensive to be worthwhile, except for very large institutions doing very large trades. That left the more complicated version: borrowing stock from a broker, selling it to another investor, promising to pay that investor if the stock went up in value, and promising to return the stock to the broker at a future time. This complicated transaction was known as *shorting* a stock.

There were numerous limitations on shorting, in addition to its complexity and costs. Legal rules established in the 1930s restricted short sales. For example, you could only short a stock when the last trade in the stock had been at a higher price than the previous trade. This *uptick rule* was intended to prevent short sellers from manipulating the price of a stock downward. In addition, to short a stock you actually had to find shares to borrow. Because each company had a finite number of shares, it sometimes was difficult to find shares to borrow for a shorting transaction. This was true even for stocks with millions of shares traded. Some companies required employees to own stock, but prohibited them from lending it out, to limit the pool of shares available for shorting.

Given the structural obstacles to betting against stocks, it seemed entirely predictable that markets would have an upward bias, at least on occasion. This was true in horse racing, where each horse typically was "overvalued"—meaning that the odds payable on particular horses would have been higher if there had been a two-way market of people betting both for and against. It was less frequently true in stocks, but there was ironclad evidence that it was true at least some of the time. For example, for several weeks 3Com stock was worth less than the stock of its more fashionable subsidiary Palm (maker of Palm Pilot handheld organizers)—even though 3Com owned 95 percent of Palm. How was it possible for a piece of the pie to be more valuable than the pie itself? Simple: there weren't enough Palm shares for arbitrageurs to sell short. And put options, which would enable investors to bet against Palm, were too expensive and had limited terms. Investors who really loved Palm drove its demand—and stock price—to "irrationally" high levels.

Because of these limitations, short selling was a dying business, especially in the rising stock markets of the mid-1990s. In total, dedicated short-selling firms had only $2 billion total under management—less than one medium-sized hedge fund.[43] Interestingly, Raymond L. Dirks, an insurance analyst who, in the 1970s, had warned his clients about a massive fraud at Equity Funding, was leading the attack on short sellers. He established a "Shortbusters" club at RAS Securities, where he found stocks that many people had shorted, and issued buy recommendations, hoping to squeeze the shorts into selling at a loss, much as Paul Mozer of Salomon had tried to squeeze the market for Treasury bonds.[44] (If anyone knew the consequences of betting against stocks, it was Ray Dirks. Regulators had rewarded him for uncovering the Equity Funding scandal by prosecuting him for tipping insider information to his clients, who then bet against Equity Funding's stock; Dirks was convicted, but later exonerated by the U.S. Supreme Court.)[45]

With these limitations, stocks could remain overpriced for long periods of time. If these new theories about the limits of arbitrage were correct, then stock markets weren't nearly as fair and efficient as regulators thought (most of them had been taught by the market-efficiency theorists of the classical school). It no longer seemed plausible to argue that market prices must be fair because, if they were not, someone would have shorted the stocks until the prices declined. Because of accounting misstatements and omissions, arbitrageurs never learned that stocks such as Cendant, Waste Management, Sunbeam, and Rite Aid were overpriced. And even if someone knew about these stocks, she might not be able to make money, because some investors would persist in believing in the higher valuation, and because shorting the stocks was both expensive and difficult.

Arthur Levitt realized much of this in 1998—five years into his term as chairman of the SEC. As more accounting schemes were disclosed, he reached what Carol Loomis of *Fortune* magazine described as "the gag point."[46] In 1997, 116 companies had needed to correct or restate their financial statements, and more companies were issuing such restatements in 1998. These disclosures woke up Levitt, and he began taking the actions that finally would form the basis for his mostly undeserved reputation as the investors' advocate.

In September 1998, Levitt gave the most important speech of his career—entitled "The Numbers Game"—in which he described various abuses and announced that the SEC would be clamping down on accounting fraud. With phrases such as "Managing may be giving way to manipulation; integrity may be losing out to illusion," Levitt was trying to sound like John F. Kennedy—or perhaps Arthur Levitt Sr. He concluded, "It's a basic cultural change we're asking for. Nothing short of that."

After Levitt's speech, the SEC sent letters to 150 companies that had taken restructuring charges in 1998. SEC enforcement lawyers brought cases against Cendant, Waste Management, Sunbeam, and Rite Aid, all relatively simple instances of fraud. (None involved derivatives, for example.) The choice to prosecute simpler cases was understandable. Even though the SEC enforcement division had more than a thousand lawyers, it did not have the resources to prosecute every financial fraud. A complex accounting-fraud case against a major corporation required years of work, and dozens of lawyers and other staff. It was difficult for SEC officials to persuade federal prosecutors to bring criminal cases, and a major case was hardly worth the work if it merely resulted in a cease-and-desist order. Plaintiff's securities lawyers behaved similarly: they were busy enough with simple fraud cases against medium-sized corporations, and so they avoided the complex cases against major corporations.

As a result, the criminal convictions for accounting fraud and related shenanigans through 2000 did not exactly resemble a Who's Who of corporate America: Cendant, McKesson HBOC, Livent, Underwriters Financial Group, Donnkenny, California Micro Devices, Health Management, Home Theater Products International, FNN, Crazy Eddie, Towers Financial, Miniscribe, and ZZZZ Best. The only true "household name" on the list was Bankers Trust, back for a second round of fraud accusations after the derivatives fiascos of 1994. Bruce J. Kingdon, who ran securities processing at Bankers Trust, pled guilty to falsifying bank records in September 2000, but did not receive jail time (although he was ordered to see a therapist once a week for three years and to perform 450 hours of community service, which his attorney—reflecting the culture of Bankers Trust—said was for "cerebral palsy or muscular dystrophy or something like that").[47] At that time, Walter Forbes and Martin Grass had not yet been indicted; Dean Buntrock and Al Dunlap had apparently skated by.

By focusing on simple fraud cases, the SEC sent a message to major corporations engaging in complex fraud that they were likely to avoid punishment. Companies such as Enron and WorldCom were obviously managing their earnings, but were not the target of any investigations. All SEC officials had to do was compare the earnings a company reported to shareholders to the income it reported to the Internal Revenue Service. A huge gap was likely a sign of accounting fraud, tax fraud, or both. Between 1996 and 2000, this gap widened at numerous companies. Enron told shareholders it made $1.8 billion, but told the IRS it lost a billion. WorldCom told shareholders it made $16 billion, but told the IRS under a billion.[48]

A spokesman for General Electric was smug about accusations of earnings manipulation, saying, "You have to have the earnings to be accused of smoothing them."[49] General Electric, in particular, received special treatment. Many of the SEC's cases had been prompted by financial journalists' exposés of wrongdoing. Ultimately, those reports led to the bankruptcy of Enron and WorldCom, and prosecutions of officials at both firms. But, notwithstanding numerous reports since 1994 of careful timing of capital gains, and creative restructuring charges and reserves, at General Electric, the SEC did not bring a case against that firm or its officers.

In hindsight, it is obvious that stock options were a key factor in the major corporate fiascos of the mid-to-late 1990s. As noted in the previous chapter, the rise of stock options was due primarily to regulatory changes: a $1 million cap on tax deductions for executive salaries, with an exception for performance-based compensation (which included stock options), and an accounting rule that said stock options were essentially free.

Professor Kevin J. Murphy, one of the leading scholars studying executive compensation, has estimated that option grants in industrial companies more than doubled from 1992 to 1996.[50] Compared to the average worker's pay, CEO compensation in 1996 was three times higher than it had been before 1990. Including stock options, the average CEO made 210 times more than the average worker.[51]

There were many arguments in favor of options, most notably that they aligned the incentives of managers and shareholders. However, options only aligned incentives in one direction. Managers who held options had a limited downside, whereas shareholders were not so protected. That meant that both managers and shareholders benefited when shares went up, but managers were more willing to gamble because of their limited downside. This was especially true when companies, such as Cendant, repriced executives' stock options when the stock went down, lowering the price at which they could buy stock, or when companies *reloaded* executives' stock options by issuing new options when an executive cashed in some options before their maturity.

In other words, executives who owned *stock* were aligned with shareholders—for good or for ill—but executives who owned *options* were less aligned with shareholders because their downside was limited. The difference between a CEO with stock and a CEO with options was like the difference between a captain who was prepared to go down with the ship, and a captain with the only lifeboat (or, better yet, a helicopter) set aside for times of danger. The best way to align the incentives of executives and shareholders was to put them in the same boat, which stock options did not do.

Some economists worried that CEOs were too risk-averse, and therefore favored stock options precisely because they encouraged CEOs to take on more risk. This argument was more speculative. Before the mid-1990s, CEOs had taken on plenty of risk without the incentives of huge, 10-year stock-option grants—Walter Forbes, Dean Buntrock, Al Dunlap, and Martin Grass were all examples. Moreover, when the stock price declined, options could lead CEOs to take on too much risk.

Besides, if companies really wanted to "incentivize" their CEOs, they could do so in two ways that made much more economic sense. First, they could pay CEOs more in stock, based on their performance. For example, Jack Welch had received hundreds of millions of dollars of *restricted stock*—stock that could not be sold in the market for a period of several years. This stock carried many of the regulatory benefits of stock options, but forced executives to think more about downside risk.

Second, they could pay CEOs in stock options that were based on how well their company did relative to its competitors or an index, so that CEOs were rewarded for outperforming the market and not merely for being in office as the tide rose.

Many companies offered restricted stock, but the percentage of stock held by CEOs—ignoring stock options—actually declined throughout the mid-1990s.[52] Only one in 1,000 firms offered *indexed* options—based on how well its stock did relative to other stocks. Why? The only plausible explanation was legal rules: these two alternatives were better economically, but they forced companies to record an expense. (Unlike standard stock options, *outperformance* options had to be disclosed as an expense, because the 1972 accounting rule had created exceptions only for options with a fixed-exercise price.)[53]

Stock options had other drawbacks. They diluted the value of shares, because if the price of a stock went up and executives exercised their right to buy shares, there would be more shares outstanding and each shareholder would own a smaller fraction of the company. Companies were required to disclose this dilution in their financial statements, although many companies tried to minimize dilution by repurchasing from shareholders enough stock to set aside for executives when they exercised their options. The problem with repurchases was that they required companies either to spend cash that could have been used in more valuable projects, or—if they wanted to repurchase shares and do the projects—to borrow money, thereby increasing their debt.

Options also were a very expensive form of compensation, because the cost of the stock options granted to executives, in terms of how they were valued in the market, was much greater than the value to the executives themselves. An economically rational CEO would much rather have $1 million in a diversified portfolio (or in cash) than $1 million of stock options. In order to pay a CEO $1 million of value (to the CEO), it would cost the company either $1 million of cash or, say, $2 million of options. The reason was that CEOs had so much invested in their companies—reputation, other compensation, pensions, and so forth—that a concentrated position in stock options was just about the least valuable form of compensation they could receive. One of the central tenets of modern finance is that a diversified portfolio is worth more than a concentrated one, because it is less volatile. CEOs valued diversification, like anyone else. Some studies showed that, in rough terms, a typical CEO valued stock options at half their market value.[54] In other words, it was twice as expensive for companies to pay their CEOs in stock options as it was to pay them cash.

Another odd consequence of stock options was that they advantaged CEOs who were already rich or who liked risk, because they placed a higher value on stock options than their middle-class, risk-averse counterparts. Again, the explanation was diversification. A rich CEO would have only a small part of her wealth in options, whereas a middle-class CEO would have a much more concentrated position. According to Professor Murphy, a CEO with 90 percent of her wealth in her company's stock options would value those options only *a fifth* as much as a wealthy CEO with the same options, if those options represented only half of her wealth. In other words, companies might prefer to hire rich CEOs because they didn't have to pay them as much.

The list of problems with stock options goes on and on. Because options do not receive dividends, CEOs who receive large stock-option grants have an incentive to reduce dividends. In fact, the dividends paid by public companies decreased dramatically during the 1990s. Before that, dividends—not capital gains—accounted for three-fourths of the returns from stocks, and companies signaled that they were doing well, not by increasing reported earnings to meet expectations, but by paying high cash dividends.[55] (Another reason not to pay dividends is that they are taxed, but this feature did not change during the same period.)

But the biggest problem with options granted during the 1990s was that they were hard to value. Most options granted during the 1990s had long maturities, and restrictions that limited the use of option-pricing models, such as the Black-Scholes model. For example, 83 percent of options had 10-year terms, and most executives could not cash in the options for several years. That meant the maturities of most executive stock options were more than twice as long as the options Bankers Trust and Salomon Brothers had been unable to value. Options models did not work well for long-maturity options, primarily because the variables—especially the key variable, volatility—change so much over time. Moreover, the restrictions on cashing in options were very difficult to incorporate into an options-pricing model. By one estimate, the true value of a typical executive stock option was only about half of the value estimated by the Black-Scholes model.[56]

In other words, the opponents to the FASB rule requiring companies to include stock options as an expense—particularly Senator Joseph Lieberman—had a valid point: these options were quite difficult to value. Consultants to corporate boards gave a wide range of valuations for options, and some directors used a rough rule of thumb that the value of a typical option was about one-third of the value of the stock. But given the uncertainty about value, was it really a responsible business decision to give executives options in the first place? Even with a rough rule of thumb, it was easy to see that the stock options were of very high value. By this measure, one million options on a stock with a price of $60 were worth about $20 million. Walter Forbes, Dean Buntrock, Al Dunlap, and Martin Grass had millions of stock options, each. And they were not alone: with the dramatic increase in stock-option grants to corporate executives in the mid-to-late 1990s came greater temptation for corporate executives to commit fraud.

The corporate frauds of the mid-to-late 1990s likely would not have occurred without the dramatic increase in stock-option grants to corporate executives. Three conclusions from this period are indisputable: first, legal changes in the early 1990s led companies to give unprecedented amounts of stock options to their CEOs; second, those stock options became much more valuable if companies inflated profits and hid losses for a few years; third, many companies, in fact, engaged in accounting fraud.

As stock options were on the rise, other new financial instruments were coming back to life after a brief post-1994 hibernation. The over-the-counter derivatives markets continued to grow, and with them the concern that corporate executives who wanted to manipulate earnings might move beyond simple accounting tricks to use derivatives in schemes of unimaginable complexity.

One reason these new instruments hadn't appeared in a major accounting scandal yet was that top-level corporate executives—whose involvement typically was required—didn't understand them. *Risk* magazine, a leading financial-industry publication, harshly concluded, "Top management, whether corporate or otherwise, failed to understand the nature of the products being used in their treasuries or trading operations."[57] Whereas the derivatives scandals of the early 1990s had come from the bottom (salesmen and traders at Bankers Trust, First Boston, and Salomon; junior treasurers at Gibson Greetings and Procter & Gamble), where at least some of the people understood derivatives, the more recent accounting scandals had come from the top, where most CEOs did not.

Even several years later, corporate boards still had a lot to learn about financial engineering. According to partners at several major accounting firms, most board members had only a cursory grasp of their risk exposures in 1996.[58] In response to the fiascos of 1994, most boards had approved policy statements dealing with derivatives, but not much more. A traditional audit was of little value in assessing financial risk, and members of corporate-audit committees often didn't even know the right questions to ask. Corporate directors attempted to insulate themselves from liability for any future problems by implementing corrective procedures and controls, but that didn't mean they actually understood any of the details themselves.

Corporate directors of many of the top companies in the world— from Aetna to Dow Chemical to General Electric—did not spend much time focusing on these new financial risks. Barbara Scott Preiskel, a member of the board of General Electric, told *Derivatives Strategy* magazine, in 1996, "At GE, we've never had a full board discussion about derivatives."[59] That was a shocking admission, given that General Electric had made (and lost) huge amounts of money on new financial instruments, and its financial subsidiary, GE Capital, had been involved in derivatives markets for many years. Clayton Yeutter, former chairman of the Chicago Mercantile Exchange and a member of half a dozen major boards, agreed that corporate directors rarely discussed or understood new financial techniques: "It's a rare occurrence where the board is in a position to dispute the presentation of a senior financial officer on risk management matters."[60] No wonder so many CEOs were walking away with $100 million of stock options.

Directors of companies felt—perhaps quite rationally—that their role was to put procedures in place, and then rely on others to do their jobs. But, as a result, the responsibility for ensuring that shareholders were not exposed to undue or undisclosed risks fell on senior executives and their accountants—precisely the same people who had just completed a round of unprecedented accounting fraud.

There were some signs, even in the early accounting scandals, of new financial instruments lurking in the background. To give one example, one of Cendant's first acts after the merger of CUC and HFS was to issue $1 billion of new financial instruments bizarrely called FELINE PRIDES. A few months later, owners of these FELINE PRIDES would become embroiled in litigation surrounding Cendant, as yet another victim of the company's fraud. But the Byzantine structure of these instruments—the very nature of the FELINE PRIDES—raised troubling questions about the state of U.S. financial markets.

The name FELINE PRIDES was a mouthful of acronym. "FELINE" stood for Flexible Equity-Linked Exchangeable Security; "PRIDES" stood for Preferred Redeemable Increased Dividend Equity Securities. The bizarre acronym had an even stranger history, one that illustrates how much financial markets had changed during recent years. The lineage of FELINE PRIDES reads like an Old Testament family tree, with a stray cat thrown into the mix. If this discussion seems esoteric, remember this: by 2002, most public companies used these types of instruments—undoubtedly companies whose stock most investors own.

In the beginning, there was equity and debt. Equity consisted of shareholders who owned a company. Debt consisted of bondholders whom the company owed. Together, equity and debt supplied all of the capital available for a company to invest. Debt was at the bottom of a firm's capital structure; equity was at the top. Bondholders received interest and were repaid their principal at maturity. Shareholders received dividends plus any other increase in the value of the company.

Then, *preferred stock* was created, a hybrid of equity and debt. Preferred stock had an infinite life, like equity, but was paid a fixed rate, like debt. Some preferred stocks could be converted into regular stock (called *common stock*) at a future date, at the option of the preferred stockholder. Other preferred stocks had a cumulative dividend—an obligation that accumulated when it wasn't paid (unlike a common-stock dividend, which was at the company's discretion). Thus, preferred stock sat in the middle of a company's capital structure, above debt but below equity.

The key questions about preferred stock involved legal rules. When the rules for debt and equity were different, how would preferred be treated? For example, interest on debt was tax deductible, but dividends on equity were not. Could a company deduct payments to its preferred shareholders for tax purposes? What about the rating agencies, which were always critical to the financial markets, as the first chapters demonstrated? In assigning ratings, they looked at the ratio of debt to equity. How would they assess preferred stock? And what about the all-important accounting rules? Analysts compared companies by looking at the relative amounts of equity and debt on their balance sheets. Where would preferred stock fit?

Financial engineers at investment banks were very good at answering these questions. They designed novel types of preferred stock to take advantage of tax deductions and favorable credit ratings, and to minimize the amount of debt disclosed in financial statements.

First, creative bankers noticed that common stock was really composed of two pieces: dividends, plus any change in stock price. They separated these two pieces—just as they split apart the interest and principal payments on mortgages—by putting them into a common-stock trust (one well-known 1980s version was called Americus Trust), which issued two securities: one conservative security, that received dividends plus some of any increase in the stock price; and one riskier security, that received any additional increase in stock price. Such instruments were used in the United States, Europe, and Japan.

In 1988, Morgan Stanley created a security called PERCS, based on the more conservative piece of the Americus Trust deals. PERCS stood for "Preferred Equity-Redemption Cumulative Stock," and resembled a preferred stock, with cumulative dividends that were higher than the dividends paid on common stock (a "perk" for the investor, in case that reference wasn't obvious). The key twist was that, in three years, PERCS *automatically* converted into common stock, according to a specified schedule. For example, PERCS would convert into one share of common stock if the common stock was at $50 or lower, but convert into fewer shares if the price was above $50, so as to limit the upside of PERCS. Essentially, an investor buying PERCS committed to buy a company's stock in three years, and also sold some of the upside potential of that stock by selling a three-year call option (similar to those Andy Krieger was trading at Bankers Trust). The company bought the three-year call option from the investor, and paid the investor a "premium" in the form of a cumulative dividend for three years.

PERCS were quite complex, and one might imagine that only the most sophisticated companies and investors would use them. But the first PERCS deal, in July 1988, was done by Avon Products, Inc.[61] Avon's common stock had fallen to around $24, but was still paying a $2 dividend. Avon wanted to cut the dividend to $1, but doing so would infuriate investors and drive down its share price even more. The brilliant solution was to offer to exchange common shares for PERCS, which would still have a $2 dividend but would convert into common shares in three years. The price cutoff for converting PERCS into common stock declined during the three years, wiping out any gain from the additional dividend—but that was much more subtle than simply slashing the dividend by $1. Investors didn't complain. If Avon's common stock were below $32 in three years, the PERCS would each receive one share of common stock; otherwise, they would get less.[62] The company received some favorable regulatory treatment: the rating agencies treated PERCS as equity, as did Avon's accountants, although the dividends on PERCS were not tax deductible.

Without the tax benefit, PERCS lacked mass appeal. The idea was really not that new, and investors preferred to buy either common shares, which kept all of the upside, or corporate bonds, which were safer. The main advantage was that a company could "borrow" money using PERCS without increasing its debts (at least in the minds of rating agencies officials). In the early 1990s, a few debt-laden companies whose credit ratings were lower than their competitors' issued PERCS, instead of debt: Citicorp, General Motors, Kmart, RJR Nabisco, Sears, and Tenneco.[63] The credit-rating agencies did not seem to care that these companies' short-term obligations were increasing, and they did not count these securities as debt in their analyses. The companies protected their credit ratings, and were willing to pay large fees for the deals. Morgan Stanley doubled its income in 1991, due in large part to the sale of about $7 billion of PERCS.

Then, in 1993, Salomon Brothers introduced DECS (for Dividend Enhanced Convertible Stock), which added a twist to PERCS, to give the investor more upside. PERCS had two payout zones: above and below a specified exercise price—below that price, the investor received one common share for each PERC; above that value, the investor received a diluted number of shares, capping the investors' upside. DECS added a third zone, at a higher stock price, above which the investor received the upside of common stock.

For example, Salomon did a DECS deal for First Data Corp., the data-processing subsidiary of American Express. If you bought 100 DECS, your payout in three years would fall into one of three zones, divided by common stock prices of roughly $37 and $45. If the common stock were below $37 in three years, you would receive 100 common shares. Between $37 and $45, you would receive fewer shares, to maintain a constant value of $37—that meant that if the price went up to $40, you would still only receive $37 worth of shares per DECS; if the price reached $45, you would receive only 82 common shares. However, in the new third zone, when the price increased above $45, you would still receive 82 shares—no more dilution—regardless of how high the price went. This new upside was the only economic difference between PERCS and DECS.

For American Express and First Data, the regulatory benefits of the DECS were enormous. First, because American Express had agreed to pay the first three years of dividends, the credit-rating agencies gave the DECS a high rating, based on American Express, not First Data Corp.[64] The rating agencies also treated the DECS as equity in their analyses. Second, Salomon had obtained an opinion that the three years of payments— called "dividends" for PERCS but "interest" for DECS—were tax deductible.[65] In other words, tax lawyers were willing to call DECS "debt" for tax purposes. Third, accountants did not include DECS among the financial statement's other debts and obligations, even though everyone else was calling them debt. Salomon had created a financial chameleon that could appear to be equity or debt, depending on the regulator. *Investment Dealers' Digest* labeled the DECS for American Express "Deal of the Year" in 1993, and Salomon was paid an incredible $26 million,[66] roughly the same fee Salomon would have received from advising Bell Atlantic on its planned $21 billion takeover of Tele-Communications Inc.—the largest announced takeover since the RJR Nabisco deal in 1989—if that deal had not collapsed in 1993.[67]

In 1994, as the Fed was raising rates and losses were spreading throughout the financial markets, every major investment bank was copying Salomon's mousetrap. Merrill Lynch had Preferred Redeemable Increased Dividend Equity Securities (PRIDES), Goldman Sachs had

Automatically Convertible Enhanced Securities (ACES), Lehman had Yield Enhanced Equity Linked Securities (YEELDS), and Bear Stearns had Common Higher Income Participation Securities (CHIPS).[68] For a time, having a facility with acrostics became more important on Wall Street than mathematical training.

For the next two years, Wall Street made substantial fees from these deals; and companies raised billions of dollars while propping up their credit ratings, reducing their taxes, and hiding their debts. A company's financial statements would not reflect changes in its obligations on these new instruments as the companies' share prices changed, even though the value of the obligation depended on which of the three zones the company's stock was in.

Accountants at the SEC began questioning this accounting treatment in 1996, after they examined a Merrill Lynch PRIDES deal for AMBAC Inc. When they told officials at Merrill that AMBAC would need to record an ongoing expense for the PRIDES, the deal collapsed.[69] Then Goldman Sachs invented a security called MIPS, for Monthly Income Preferred Securities, which purported to qualify as equity for accounting purposes but debt for tax purposes. Enron was a major issuer of MIPS, and even won a battle with the Internal Revenue Service in 1996 over the tax treatment of such preferred securities.

In 1997, Merrill added the FELINE twist to its PRIDES, thereby inventing a nearly perfect financial mousetrap. Instead of the company itself issuing the PRIDES securities, Merrill would create a special-purpose trust to issue securities resembling the original PRIDES. The trust would give the money it received from investors to the company in exchange for securities that matched the trust's obligations on the new securities it had issued. In other words, the trust was simply a middleman: cash would flow from investors through the trust to the company, and the obligations would flow from the company through the trust to investors. The economics of the deal were essentially the same as those of the original PRIDES, with a few bells and whistles added to target specific investor profiles, and a maturity that was extended to five years. By March 1997, Merrill had completed its first FELINE PRIDES deal for MCN Energy Group Inc., through a special-purpose entity called MCN Financing III, which was created especially for the purpose of new issue.[70] The new hybrid securities would be tax deductible, would be treated as equity for credit-ratings purposes, and would neither be included as a liability nor dilute the common shares on a company's balance sheet.[71]

On February 25, 1998, just weeks before Cendant's massive accounting scam was uncovered, Cendant announced the public offering of 26 million units of FELINE PRIDES, worth about $1 billion in aggregate. Essentially, investors would buy a preferred stock that would pay a dividend of 6.45 percent for five years and then automatically convert into Cendant common stock, according to a specified schedule. The FELINE PRIDES were tax deductible, received an investment-grade credit rating, and were not included as debt or equity on Cendant's balance sheet. Merrill Lynch—which had represented HFS in the Cendant merger—created the FELINE PRIDES and was one of the lead underwriters for the Cendant deal. This deal was Cendant's last gasp for breath, an attempt to raise money to fund its money-losing businesses without disclosing any new debt or jeopardizing its credit rating.

The fact that Cendant did a FELINE PRIDES deal just before its collapse is significant for two reasons. First, it shined a bright light on these new financial instruments. There were numerous related lawsuits, and the publicity presented an obvious opportunity for SEC accountants and, perhaps, even experts at the Internal Revenue Service and the credit rating agencies, to reexamine the impact of these new financial techniques, now that—please indulge one jab at the acronym—the cat was out of the bag.

Second, Cendant's deal made it clear that the investment bankers were facing serious conflicts of interest in their various businesses, conflicts that became more intractable as financial instruments became more complex. Merrill Lynch had advised HFS in the Cendant merger negotiations and, supposedly, had performed due diligence on CUC at that time. It also had created Cendant's FELINE PRIDES, so it should have performed due diligence at the time of that deal, too. In addition, Merrill Lynch brokers had been involved in selling Cendant stock to investors, and Merrill's analysts had recommended Cendant stock. Merrill had earned substantial fees from all of these various sources, just as it had pocketed huge fees from its role in the Orange County debacle as derivatives salesman, bond underwriter, and cleanup crew. Was it really any surprise that Merrill had not uncovered the accounting problems at Cendant?

The scandals in the United States during the mid-1990s raised troubling questions about the conflicted role of accountants and investment bankers, and the inability of regulators to police them. Top accounting firms were involved in approving accounts that later turned out to be fraudulent. Top investment banks were closely advising the firms engaging in these schemes. In 1998, regulators finally began pursuing accounting fraud in a few cases, but they largely ignored the more complicated schemes, sending yet another message that complex financial crime did, indeed, pay. Meanwhile, the financial innovations of the early 1990s, having been nurtured in a warm, comforting, deregulated environment, were about to multiply and spread throughout the markets. Their next stops would be outside the United States, where no one was prepared for the consequences. Soon enough, they would return home.

EPIDEMIC

THE DOMINO EFFECT

The Société Générale Super Bowl parties were a reminder to financial market participants in the United States that they were not alone. Beginning in 1992, traders from the French bank—one of the biggest options dealers in the world, with $80 billion in currency options alone[1]— gathered on Super Bowl Sunday with hundreds of their clients in a custom-built derivatives trading pit at the Equitable Building in Manhattan. The floors were covered with AstroTurf and white yard lines. Several big-screen television sets showed the pregame festivities.

A 27-page rule book explained the various ways participants could trade derivatives, pegged to which team won and by how much. Traders could buy options that the Washington Redskins would win by 10 points, or futures on the Buffalo Bills leading at a particular time. French employees wearing striped referee shirts explained the rules; options traders wore red, white, and blue smocks; and futures traders wore pink. Hall of Fame football players—including Howie Long, Roger Staubach, and Walter Payton—advised the traders, who made more than 100,000 trades during the game.

The bank's head of options sales, a Frenchman, turned up his nose when asked whether the betting was legal: "A triple-A rated French bank would never do anything that has any possibility of being related to gambling."[2] Société Générale also planned derivatives trading events in Europe based on international rugby matches, and in Japan based on sumo wrestling.[3]

The Super Bowl parties were a microcosm of the financial markets: global in scope, frenzied in pace, and steeped in risk taking. It was fitting that a non-U.S. bank was sponsoring them. Participants came from throughout the world. Every year, when they weren't trading, they could discuss a new international financial crisis, each one more severe than the last. On December 20, 1994, just before the 1995 Super Bowl party, corporate treasurers, who finally had recovered from the Fed's interest-rate hike, were stunned by the crash of the Mexican peso. The next year, Barings—the 233-year-old British bank—collapsed after Nick Leeson, one of the bank's derivatives traders, lost more than a billion dollars. In 1997, the Central Bank of Thailand abandoned its support for the Thai currency, called the baht, and numerous currencies in Asia plunged. In 1998, financial problems in Russia and Brazil led to an international crisis in which the markets briefly froze, and then moved downward in lockstep. Incredibly, during this last crisis, Long-Term Capital Management, the much-admired hedge fund managed by John Meriwether and his rocket-scientist traders from Salomon Brothers, lost nearly all of its investors' money in a period of weeks.

Financial innovation and derivatives were at the center of these crises, and the proliferation of unregulated financial instruments both contributed to the problems and exacerbated their effects. The Mexican and Asian currency crises led to unexpected losses at various corporations and investment funds that had secretly bet on currencies, much as the Fed's rate hike in the United States had flushed out interest-rate speculators. Nick Leeson's trading involved offshore derivatives in Singapore and Japan; Long-Term Capital Management held more than one *trillion* dollars of derivatives.

There were three key lessons from the various international crises. First, governments had created incentives for investors to take on excessive risks by bailing out investors or companies in times of crisis. The Mexico and East Asia bailouts, and the indirect role the Federal Reserve Bank of New York played in the private bailout of Long-Term Capital, led investors to take on additional risks under the assumption that governments would help rescue them. These bailouts created *moral hazard* among investors—the taking of excessive risks in the presence of insurance.[4]

Second, it became increasingly difficult to measure and monitor cross-border risks. Barings and Long-Term Capital collapsed primarily because their owners improperly assessed their risks. Even the sophisticated models at Long-Term Capital did not work as predicted. Moreover, many investors did not realize the extent of their exposure to particular risks, such as the risk of currency devaluation in Latin America and East Asia.

Third, financial derivatives were now everywhere—and largely unregulated. Increasingly, parties were using financial engineering to take advantage of the differences in legal rules among jurisdictions, or to take new risks in new markets. In 1994, *The Economist* magazine noted, "Some financial innovation is driven by wealthy firms and individuals seeking ways of escaping from the regulatory machinery that governs established financial markets."[5] With such innovation, the regulators' grip on financial markets loosened during the mid-to-late 1990s. Central banks could not defend themselves against speculators who could access over-the-counter currency options and futures markets. Legislators could not restrict investment, because if they did it would simply move elsewhere. Regulators found it impossible to predict how a crisis in one market would spread to another. And when one financial regulator—Brooksley Born, chair of the Commodity Futures Trading Commission—suggested that government should at least study whether some regulation might make sense, a stampede of lobbyists, members of Congress, and other regulators—including Alan Greenspan and Robert Rubin—ran her over, admonishing her to keep quiet.

Derivatives tightened the connections among various markets, creating enormous financial benefits and making global transacting less costly— no one denied that. But they also raised the prospect of a system-wide breakdown. With each crisis, a few more dominos fell, and regulators and market participants increasingly expressed concerns about *systemic risk*—a term that described a financial-market epidemic. After Long-Term Capital collapsed, even Alan Greenspan admitted that financial markets had been close to the brink.

Financial innovation was not limited to the United States. London was a hub of derivatives activity, and a close second to New York in terms of profits. The London markets benefited from a more efficient regulatory system than the one in the United States. British regulators merged into a single financial-market regulator (after deciding that "there are too many cooks in the regulatory kitchen"),[6] and British judges seemed to understand when to take a "hands-off" approach, and when a proper whipping was in order. The London market had survived a scare in 1990, when a British court found that the Council of the London Borough of Hammersmith & Fulham (a municipality like Orange County) had entered into seventy-two interest-rate swaps "for the purpose of trading and not for the purpose of interest rate risk management."[7] The court found that this trading purpose was unauthorized and outside the powers of the Council, and declared the swaps null and void. The banks that were owed hundreds of millions of dollars on these swaps were understandably upset about the decision. But it clarified important legal boundaries in the market; and, in response, banks took careful measures to establish whether a client was authorized to purchase particular instruments.

Similarly, although regulators in the United Kingdom generally were more permissive than U.S. regulators regarding derivatives trading, they took a much harder line in questioning the "suitability" of complex derivatives, such as structured notes. Laws in both the United States and the United Kingdom required that a seller of financial instruments take into account the sophistication of the buyer, and not sell "unsuitable" financial instruments. For example, Morgan Stanley lost a high-profile case in which a well-respected British judge ruled that the currency-linked structured notes it had sold to an Italian client were not suitable. Morgan Stanley was forced to swallow the losses on the instruments and pay a fine.[8] The case was especially notable because the instruments at issue—called PERLS, for Principal Exchange Rate Linked Securities—were relatively straightforward instruments compared to the derivatives at issue in cases in the United States. Whereas U.S. regulators took a one-size-fits-all deregulatory approach, British regulators distinguished between markets that were limited to the major derivatives dealers and markets that involved less sophisticated participants.

But like their U.S. counterparts, British prosecutors had largely abandoned criminal prosecutions. England's equivalent of Drexel and Michael Milken—the "Guinness Case," probably the most prominent criminal securities trial to occur outside the United States—had been in 1990, the same year Milken was sentenced. Four prominent British businessmen, including Ernest Saunders, were found guilty of a conspiracy to prop up the price of Guinness shares so that its bid (in shares) for Distillers Co. would be more attractive.[9] Although the facts in that case were relatively simple, at least compared to the new financial transactions in London, the trial lasted 113 days. There were odd parallels between Milken and Saunders, both of whom were flayed by the media and sentenced to lengthy prison terms. Both also left prison early, became gravely ill, and miraculously recovered. (Milken overcame cancer; Saunders was diagnosed with Alzheimer's, which he incredibly conquered after he was released early from prison—apparently, the proper diagnosis had been curable pseudo-dementia; or, as many British newspapers argued, prevarication.) There had been few criminal prosecutions for financial fraud in either the United States or England since those two cases in 1990.

International regulators, often based in Europe, followed the British practice of distinguishing between segments of the financial markets, although their focus was on major banks and derivatives dealers. The Basel Committee of the Bank for International Settlements published reports on the derivatives positions of major banks. In July 1993, the Global Derivatives Study Group of the Group of Thirty—called the G-30, for the thirty countries who were members—issued a report on derivatives practices and made a set of recommendations, although they related primarily to specific questions for major dealers, such as whether a swap contract would be enforceable, rather than any broader concerns related to investors or markets more generally.

In contrast, Japan's regulators were both fragmented and largely dysfunctional. The powerful Ministry of Finance and the Bank of Japan, the central bank, split jurisdiction, but the Ministry of Finance—called the MOF—was dominant. Any firm planning to deal in a new type of derivative needed to obtain prior approval from the MOF, although firms often would obtain approval for a generic transaction, and then add bells and whistles without the MOF's knowledge.

Because the MOF tightly restricted Japanese companies, but barely even winked at foreign ones, non-Japanese banks operating under the regulators' radar dominated the Japanese markets, selling derivatives to Japanese institutions that were willing to pay high fees to skirt the MOF's often-nonsensical legal rules. Allen Wheat's salesmen at Bankers Trust and First Boston had pioneered deals designed to enable Japanese institutional investors to avoid legal requirements or to create false profits. By 1994, many other banks—especially Salomon Brothers and Morgan Stanley—were doing the same. Even as Jack Welch was preparing to sell off Kidder Peabody, Kidder's salesmen were pitching a deal in Japan with two pieces, one of which was virtually guaranteed to make 20 percent, the other of which was virtually guaranteed to lose 20 percent. The Japanese company buying the deal would recognize the 20 percent gain, but hide the 20 percent loss—a blatant accounting scam.[10] Other banks did similar deals.

Not surprisingly, Japan had its share of derivatives victims in the early 1990s. In 1992, Yukihusa Fujita lost $1.1 billion trading currencies for a Japanese subsidiary of Royal Dutch/Shell.[11] Kashima Oil, a Japanese firm, lost $1.5 billion on currency derivatives. Tokyo Securities lost one-third of its value trading currency options—about $325 million—in November 1994.[12]

When the Fed raised rates in 1994, the losses spread well beyond investors in the United States, especially to Asia. In Indonesia alone, dozens of major companies lost millions of dollars on derivatives linked to interest rates, including major conglomerates such as Indah Kiat, Indocement Tunggal Prakasa, Tjiwi Kimia, and the Dharmala group.[13] Two Indonesian companies—PT Adimitra Rayapratama and PT Dharmala Sakti Sejahtera—lost more than $100 million combined. Berjaya Group, a Malaysian property developer, insurer, and bicycle manufacturer, lost $14 million on a complex swap with CSFP, the derivatives subsidiary of First Boston that Allen Wheat had created.[14] Berjaya disputed the losses, and the case resembled the Gibson Greetings–Bankers Trust dispute; First Boston settled the case by writing off half the losses.[15] Several Chinese trading firms lost over $100 million on swaps, and then refused to pay Lehman Brothers and Merrill Lynch.[16] Taiwan's Overseas Chinese Bank lost $20 million on five Quanto swaps (the complex trade pioneered by CSFP) it bought from Union Bank of Switzerland.[17]

Of course, there were plenty of losers in Europe, too. Major European banks lost millions, and were involved in disputes with their own clients over structured notes and mortgage derivatives. Glaxo Holdings, the British drug maker, lost more than $100 million on complex derivatives, including structured notes and Collateralized Mortgage Obligations.[18] Carlton Communications, a British media company, lost money on structured notes it bought from Bankers Trust.[19] Balsam, a German floor manufacturer, borrowed nearly a billion dollars from various German banks, and then lost most of it trading in interest-rate derivatives and selling currency options.[20] And this was all *before* the various international crises began in late 1994.

Europeans had learned about the dangers of derivatives in 1993 when

Metallgesellschaft, a German conglomerate, lost $1.4 billion on oil derivatives. The losses at Metallgesellschaft illustrated the difficulty of distinguishing between *hedging* (reducing risk) and *speculating* (increasing risk with the hope of higher returns), and also foreshadowed future problems in the energy markets, including the electricity crisis in California and the related collapse of Enron. Unfortunately, few people saw the parallels.

Like any oil refiner, Metallgesellschaft was exposed to the risks of changes in the price of oil and oil-related products. If oil prices went down, the firm would buy cheaper oil, but probably would earn less from selling refined products. If oil prices went up, the opposite would be true. Thus, the major risk facing the firm was the difference between the price of unrefined oil at the time of purchase and the price of refined oil products at the time of sale.

During the early 1990s, a U.S. subsidiary of Metallgesellschaft agreed to sell millions of barrels of oil products at fixed prices for up to ten years. Was the firm hedging or speculating? On one hand, the long-term contracts looked like hedges because they locked in a price. On the other hand, the contracts created a new risk: now if prices rose, the firm would pay more for unrefined oil, but would not capture any price increase from its sale of unrefined products.

Metallgesellschaft hedged part of this exposure to rising oil prices by buying short-term oil futures on the New York Mercantile Exchange (NYMEX), the exchange that would figure prominently in Enron's collapse. It also bought over-the-counter oil derivatives in unregulated markets. What about these trades? Were they hedging or speculating?

In late 1993, oil prices dropped and Metallgesellschaft began losing money on its futures positions. Theoretically, the firm could make up for these losses by selling oil-related products in the future at the prices it had locked in on its long-term contracts, which were now higher than prices available in the market. But as the losses on the short-term oil hedges increased, the firm had to pay hundreds of millions of dollars right away, years before the future gains from its long-term contracts. On December 17, 1993, directors of the firm's German parent took control of the hedging operation and began selling off the short-term contracts, at huge losses.[21] By January 1994, the firm had lost more than a billion dollars.

Experts disagreed about who was to blame for the German refiner's collapse, and whether the hedging strategy was, in reality, just speculation. Christopher Culp and Merton Miller (the Chicago economist who had argued that derivatives were used to avoid regulation) maintained that the trades were hedges and made economic sense; they blamed the German directors for abandoning the hedging strategy. John Parsons and Antonio Mello concluded that the hedging strategy was an over-hedge that was so big it was speculative.[22]

U.S. regulators cracked down on Metallgesellschaft more than they did against U.S. firms in similar situations. (This was typical: unless a case created political tensions, financial regulators in one country gener-ally preferred to bring harsher charges against a foreign company than against one of their own.) The Commodity Futures Trading Commission charged Metallgesellschaft's U.S. subsidiaries with trading illegal futures contracts and with having inadequate controls, and imposed a $2.5 mil-lion fine. Regulated futures contracts—like regulated securities—had to be registered with the CFTC or exempt from registration, and firms that dealt in futures were required to have adequate controls in place, as a prudential measure to protect parties dealing with firms in futures. Sev-eral members of Congress criticized the charges, as did former CFTC chair Wendy Gramm, who by that time was working as a director of Enron.[23]

Like Metallgesellschaft, the state of California (and its electric utili-ties) also faced a potential mismatch between the long-term cost of elec-tricity production and short-term revenues from electricity consumers. Because short-term rates were capped by law, California was vulnerable to an increase in electricity prices unless it entered into a long-term con-tract to purchase electricity. At first, the state of California did not hedge, and it lost billions of dollars when electricity prices increased—in part, it was alleged, because energy companies were manipulating prices in markets similar to those Metallgesellschaft had used. Later, California locked in long-term electricity prices by entering into swap contracts with various energy companies. The Metallgesellschaft and California examples showed that it was very difficult for an institution to control its hedging operations, and that it was very easy to lose a billion dollars or more in the energy-derivatives markets.

The German central bank warned investors in October 1993 that derivatives trading "could cause a chain reaction and endanger the entire financial system."[24] Dutch, German, and Belgian authorities pros-ecuted a few criminal cases against various derivatives firms in 1994, in an attempt to reduce the chance of more serious problems in the future.[25] In January 1995, Netherlands Central Bank Governor Wim

Duisenberg remarked, "What's needed is that companies that use derivatives tightly control their use and the risks taken. You shouldn't give sophisticated weapons to children." Investors and regulators outside the United States apparently were cognizant of the risks associated with financial innovation. But they were unprepared for the financial crises beginning in December 1994.

During the summer and fall of 1994, investors from the United States, Europe, and, especially, Japan, poured money into investments in Mexico, even though the Mexican central bank was under pressure and political tensions were rising. The Mexican central bank was the key to understanding how Mexico's currency system worked. The value of the Mexican peso was established primarily by supply and demand, but the central bank periodically intervened, buying pesos when it thought the value was too low and selling when it thought the value was too high.

Specifically, the Mexican central bank established a *currency band*—a range of peso values it promised to maintain. The band expanded over time; but, for illustrative purposes, assume it was between 3.0 and 3.5 pesos per dollar. That meant that if the peso moved to 3.0, the central bank would enter the market, selling pesos—which it could print anytime it wanted—and buying U.S. dollars. The value of the peso would never move to 2.9, so long as the central bank was willing to transact at 3.0. Likewise, if the pesos moved to 3.5, the central bank would enter the market, selling U.S. dollars—from an accumulated reserve—and buying pesos. The value of the peso would never move to 3.6, so long as the central bank was willing to transact at 3.5.

For several years, the peso had been at the "top" end of this range— 3.0 pesos per dollar, where the peso was more valuable. (To see that the peso was more valuable at a rate of 3.0 than a rate of 3.5, consider what someone in Mexico could get for 30 pesos in each case: $10 at a rate of 3.0, but less than $9 at a rate of 3.5.) Mexico's "strong" currency policy had made the country attractive to foreign investors, who could earn high returns on Mexican government bonds and stocks, and not be hurt by a weakening currency.

Over time, the peso began moving to the "bottom" end of the range— closer to 3.5 pesos per dollar—and the central bank became obligated to buy pesos in exchange for U.S. dollars at the rate of 3.5. The downward movement of the peso was due to a variety of factors, the most important of which was that inflation rates and interest rates were higher in Mexico than in the United States. This differential encouraged investors to borrow in U.S. dollars and invest in pesos. If the central bank hadn't established a currency band, investors might have worried that their gains from such a strategy would be wiped out by a decline in the value of the peso relative to the U.S. dollar. But because the central bank had committed to prop up the value of the peso—buying at the rate of 3.5—investors were assured of easy profits.

The only problem was that the peso was becoming overvalued at 3.5. In the long run, currency rates are determined primarily by the difference in inflation rates between the two countries—a currency is a measure of prices, just as the Consumer Price Index is a measure of inflation. If prices were rising more quickly in Mexico, one would expect the peso to decline in value. For example, if the price of wheat in Mexico were increasing faster than the price of wheat in the United States, people would buy wheat from the United States, and this additional demand for U.S. dollars would make it more expensive, relative to the peso. The same was true of other goods and services. In other words, higher prices in Mexico would put downward pressure on the currency.

During the early 1990s, inflation in Mexico was very high, much higher than in the United States, so there was downward pressure on the peso. However, the Mexican central bank had committed to keep the peso at 3.5 and no lower. Moreover, in 1994, investment funds bought billions of dollars of short-term Mexican government debt, including record amounts of unusual U.S. dollar–linked bonds, called Tesobonos. As a result, the Mexican government soon would need to sell tens of billions of pesos in order to buy U.S. dollars to repay investors, while at the same time the Mexican central bank would need billions of U.S. dollars—to buy the pesos of people wanting to sell pesos at a rate of 3.5. The overvalued peso was a ticking time bomb.

It was unclear how long the central bank would be able to support the peso, but Wall Street analysts—who should have known all of the above facts—continued to issue optimistic reports about Mexico through the end of 1994. Many investors believed the reports, ignored the risks, and continued to put money into Mexico. Their so-called hot money had flowed into Mexico-related funds based primarily on double-digit historical returns, not on any close analysis of the risks associated with an investment in Mexico. In fact, many investors did not even know their investment funds were betting on the Mexican peso. For example, major U.S. mutual funds—including Fidelity and Alliance Capital Management—owned huge amounts of peso-linked derivatives, including structured notes and options, and did not disclose the details of these risks.[26] About 20 percent of Alliance's flagship fund—the North American Government Income Trust—was in peso-denominated debt. As a result, U.S. mutual-fund investors would be the biggest losers from a crisis in Mexico.

Meanwhile, Mexican companies, especially banks, were using new financial techniques to create false profits and to avoid taxes and other regulation. Banco Serfin and Banamex did derivatives deals resembling the Collateralized Bond Obligations invented by First Boston and Salomon Brothers; these deals enabled the Mexican banks to borrow money without recognizing a loss on bad investments. Nacional Financiera, Mexico's state-owned development bank, did an unusual $500 million PRIDES deal with Merrill Lynch, selling securities that in four years automatically converted into shares of Telefonos de Mexico, the state telephone company.[27] This deal was very profitable for Merrill Lynch, but made it difficult to understand Nacional Financiera's financial disclosures.

In sum, the financial risks in Mexico were largely hidden from view, and most people were surprised when the Mexican government announced it was abandoning its currency band on December 20, 1994. The peso instantly fell by 15 percent. For a U.S. person investing in Mexican pesos, it was worse than the 1987 stock-market crash. The peso continued to collapse during the following weeks, ultimately dropping by more than half. Investors throughout the world lost billions of dollars. Many Wall Street firms also remained exposed to failing Mexican companies and banks, through loans and derivatives deals, although economist Rudi Dornbusch accused major U.S. banks of "using the back door," selling off their own positions in Mexico before the crisis, even as they sold peso-linked derivatives to their clients.[28]

As the peso crashed, U.S. regulators were just recovering from the Fed's interest-rate hike. Secretary of the Treasury Lloyd Bentsen was nervous about another crisis, and was concerned that U.S. investors would panic. He immediately called Arthur Levitt and told him, "I'd like you to close the markets. Don't open them." Levitt described being intimidated as just "a junior chairman of an agency talking to the Secretary of the Treasury," but he managed to respond, "Well, that's a very serious step. I don't think that's a very good idea." Eventually Robert Rubin, former co-chairman of Goldman Sachs and then chairman of the National Economic Council, calmed Bentsen, and the U.S. markets remained open. Reflecting on the events seven years later, Arthur Levitt said, "A combination of my inexperience, the suddenness of the event, the drama of how Lloyd Bentsen postured this thing made me think about it. I never would have shut the markets down, never."[29]

Individual investors did not panic, in part because they did not realize, at first, how much money they had lost. The peso-related losses were just as hidden as the earlier interest-rate-related losses, and ranged from a trader at Chemical Bank, who lost $70 million trading Mexican pesos, to a fund manager at the State of Wisconsin Investment Board, who lost $95 million on derivatives, much of it on trades linked to the Mexican peso. Many manufacturing companies also were hurt by the Mexican peso's decline, which made the goods Mexicans imported from the United States—ranging from auto parts to electrical equipment to children's toys—more expensive. For example, Mattel announced just two weeks after the peso devaluation that it would lose at least $20 million from the peso's plunge.[30]

During the previous Mexico crisis, in the early 1980s, U.S. regulators had known precisely what troubles faced the Mexican government and its banks, because they could look at a record of assets and liabilities, and immediately grasp the risks. Now, the world was much more complicated, and these institutions were using so many new financial instruments that regulators could not understand the scope and nature of their risks, or even how the different institutions and markets were connected.[31] They believed the losses would be in the tens of billions of dollars, but they couldn't be sure about much more than that.

Wall Street lobbied the U.S. government to bail out the Mexican government with loans, and the Clinton administration—especially Robert Rubin—supported the idea. President Clinton sought approval from Congress for loans to Mexico, but when Congress did not indicate any interest, Clinton acted on his own. On January 31, 1995, he determined that the economic crisis in Mexico posed "unique and emergency circumstances" that justified the use of the obscure Exchange Stabilization Fund to provide loans to the government of Mexico.[32] A handful of congressional leaders issued a joint statement agreeing with the president's determination.

The Exchange Stabilization Fund had been created in 1934, as part of the New Deal, for the U.S. Treasury to use in protecting the value of the dollar in foreign currency markets. But President Clinton obviously wasn't using the fund to prop up the dollar, which had just gone *up* relative to the peso. Instead, he wanted to lend money to the Mexican government, to help it avoid a default on its debt, much of which was held by U.S. investors.

Some members of Congress weren't happy with President Clinton secretly disbursing money without their approval, and they accused members of the Clinton administration—including Treasury official Lawrence Summers, an economist from Harvard—of concealing information about problems in Mexico before the peso devaluation.[33] They also tried to prevent Clinton from using the Exchange Stabilization Fund, arguing that the president did not have the constitutional authority to lend money to Mexico without the approval of Congress. They had a good argument.[34] The U.S. Constitution gave Congress the "power of the purse," and the law establishing the Exchange Stabilization Fund arguably did not permit a multibillion-dollar bailout.

Nevertheless, on February 21, 1995, Mexico and the United States signed financial agreements for loans of up to $20 billion, to be structured as swaps between the two countries, in which the United States would give Mexico money up front and Mexico would agree to make payments over time. Mexico agreed to open its economy to foreign investment, and the United States began cutting checks. The amount owed on the swaps varied over time, but was in the range of $13 billion.

The most surprising aspect of these swaps was the low interest rate Mexico would pay. The U.S. Treasury only charged Mexico rates that were "designed to cover the cost of funds to the Treasury and thus are set at the inception of the swap based on the Treasury Bill rate."[35] For example, Mexico borrowed $3 billion, on March 14, 1995, at an interest rate of 7.4 percent. Even before the crisis, dollar-denominated interest rates in Mexico had been higher than that; dollar-denominated rates shot up to 40 percent after the crisis. In other words, the Clinton administration had given Mexico an incredible sweetheart deal, like a credit-card company offering a temporarily low rate to a high-risk borrower. The economic cost of the loan, in foregone interest, was several billion dollars.

Mexico ultimately repaid the swaps in 1997, three years ahead of schedule, and President Clinton declared the policy a victory. By this time Robert Rubin was secretary of the Treasury and Lawrence Summers was his deputy. The administration claimed the United States had made $580 million on the loans, even though this "profit" represented a below-market interest rate. When many journalists seemed to accept this argument, the Treasury officials were in good spirits. Summers joked with Rubin that he would settle for just one percent of the Treasury's interest, and Rubin responded, "Larry, anything you can negotiate, I'm happy to split with you."[36]

The Clinton administration glossed over the key problem with the bailout: the message it sent to investors who had foolishly pumped money into Mexico without much thought. The bailout defined "moral hazard"—if investors could count on the government to provide insurance, by stepping in if the market crashed, they undoubtedly would increase their bets. Imagine what gamblers at a roulette wheel would do if they believed the government would cover their losses. Not surprisingly, the Mexico bailout would lead investors throughout the world to take on unwarranted risks, in the same way federal deposit insurance had led U.S. savings and loans to gamble during the 1980s.

Many economists were highly critical of the Mexico bailout. They argued that moral hazard distorted markets and should be avoided whenever possible. Economist Paul Krugman questioned whether future bailouts would go as smoothly. The fact that Mexico had repaid its loans on time didn't mean every borrower would be able to do so. Krugman claimed the Clinton administration "got very lucky" in resolving the Mexico crisis, and warned that "it was a mistake on everybody's part to assume they would always be so lucky in the future."[37] The British regulators would be tested next.

Nicholas William Leeson was an unlikely rogue derivatives trader. He failed A-level mathematics in high school in Watford, a cheerless suburb of London.[38] He did not attend college or business school. Friends described him as "just a normal bloke who likes all the ordinary things like football."[39] With his mediocre record, he was fortunate to find a job as a low-level financial clerk. After a few years, Barings hired him. It was 1989, just before Allen Wheat joined First Boston and set up his derivatives firm, CSFP, in London.

Barings was a prestigious bank, the oldest in England, and it served clients ranging from the queen to prominent British industrial companies. Leeson began at the bottom, processing trade records, and his early career in London was undistinguished. Barings shipped him to Singapore to help with the back-office settlement of the firm's derivatives trades there. The Singapore office was lightly staffed, and Leeson also took over a routine, low-margin trading operation, designed to profit from small price differences between Nikkei 225 futures contracts (recall that these are financial instruments based on the value of the Japanese stock-market index), which were traded in both Singapore and Osaka, Japan. If the prices in Singapore were lower, Leeson would buy there and sell in Osaka (and vice versa). This arbitrage trading was not very risky, or very sophisticated. Salomon Brothers had done the trades years earlier, and now First Boston, and other banks, already had begun selling much riskier trades based on the Nikkei 225 index. It didn't seem necessary to supervise Leeson very closely, and Barings did not.

When one of Leeson's clerks made a small error on twenty futures contracts (selling futures—when he had instructed her to buy), he tried gambling in the futures markets to make up the $30,000 loss.[40] It worked. When no one at Barings questioned why he had made these trades, he began speculating more often. Unfortunately, he was not a very good trader, and the more he strayed from the low-risk arbitrage strategy, the more money he lost. Over time, Leeson became more aggressive, trading "in size," and even selling options, betting that Japanese markets would remain within a narrow range. He lost these bets, too. By the end of 1994, he was $285 million in the hole.

Leeson hid his losses by entering losing trades into an error account, labeled #88888, which was not connected to the rest of the Barings computer network. As with those of Joseph Jett at Kidder Peabody, Nick Leeson's losses were hidden for a time because of a flawed accounting system. It also helped that Leeson's supervisors permitted him to act both as trader and as back-office manager, so that he could control both the execution of trades and the processing of trade records.

The senior managers at Barings didn't see the $285 million of losses. Instead, their accounting reports showed that the back-office boy in the Singapore office had somehow made $30 million in 1994, nearly 20 percent of the bank's total profit.[41] Leeson's trading had grown from a handful of futures contracts to tens of thousands of contracts, representing billions of dollars of bets, almost half of the trading in Nikkei 225 futures in Singapore. The managers didn't know precisely how Leeson was making so much money, but they liked it, and they were planning to reward him: Leeson's bonus for 1994 was to be $680,000, more than triple his pay from the previous year.[42] He was 28 years old.

Ron Baker, the head of financial products at Barings, was proud of Leeson. Several hundred managers from offices of Barings around the world were gathering for a year-end conference, and Baker asked Leeson to give a speech summarizing his trading strategies, much as Joseph Jett had done at Kidder Peabody. On December 9, 1994, Baker introduced Leeson to his fellow managers, saying, "Nick Leeson, whom most of you know and all of you have heard of, runs our operation in Singapore, which I want all of you to emulate. You'll hear later from Nick about how he does it, but I just want to drive home to you guys that if you could all think about Nick and perhaps come up with ideas to follow his footsteps, Barings will become one of the most successful operations in the derivatives business."[43]

It wouldn't be long before they would be hearing all about how Nick had done it. At the time of the conference, Leeson had sold tens of thousands of call and put options on Japanese stocks, betting billions of dollars that the Japanese stock market would not move much. If the markets remained calm, Leeson would keep the option premiums, and this profit would help him crawl out of his hole. Selling "naked" options was a very risky strategy (so risky Andy Krieger of Bankers Trust had refused to do it).

On January 17, 1995, a serious earthquake hit near Kobe, Japan, and Japanese stocks crashed. As Leeson's options positions plummeted in value, he increased his bets, desperately doubling down to try to get back to even. He began buying Nikkei 225 index futures, betting that the Japanese stock market would go up after the earthquake. When other traders questioned the huge increase in Leeson's trading, he reportedly claimed to be acting on behalf of financier George Soros; in truth, Soros had bet, against Leeson, that the Japanese stock market would fall, and made $320 million.[44]

In early February, the Japanese stock market briefly recovered, and Leeson climbed to within a few hundred million dollars of even. At this point, his positions essentially consisted of a $7 billion bet that Japanese stocks would go up and a $22 billion bet that Japanese bonds would go down. If the bets would only move a little more in his favor, he would be out of the hole.

When Japanese stocks plunged again, and bonds went up, Leeson's game was up. Given the size of his bets, it would be surprising if he only lost a billion dollars. He and his wife flew to the island of Borneo and hid in a hotel room in a Malaysian resort called Kota Kinabalu. They watched the news about the collapse of Barings on television.

Needless to say, the senior executives at Barings were surprised to discover, on February 23, that their back-office boy in Singapore had lost $1.4 billion, more than the bank's capital. Just two days earlier, they had received a *Value At Risk* report for Leeson's trading. Value At Risk, or VAR, was a statistical technique designed to show the maximum probable loss for a particular portfolio of investments. The report listed the VAR for Leeson's portfolio as "ZERO."[45] All of Leeson's long positions appeared to be matched by short positions, as one would expect in a low-risk arbitrage strategy. In other words, the firm's accounting system had totally failed to pick up Leeson's speculative bets. The managers might have learned about the bets if they had asked some hard questions about how, exactly, Leeson had suddenly made $30 million. But they had not. A few months later, Leeson would tell interviewer David Frost, "A couple of the people who were in the core places within Barings that should have been administering a high level of control had what I would describe as almost no understanding of the fundamentals of the business."[46] Ironically, a few months earlier, the penny-wise bank had decided not to buy a $50,000 computer-software system that continually tracked traders' positions, because it was too expensive.[47]

Bank of England officials learned of the losses at Barings and met with a group of senior bankers, but the British regulators—having just watched the U.S. bailout of Mexico—wisely decided to let Barings slip into receivership on February 26, 1995. International Nederlanden Groep (ING) bought the venerable bank for the princely sum of one British pound.

Leeson flew to Frankfurt, Germany, where police detained him until the Singapore authorities faxed a national arrest warrant. He was extradited to Singapore and sentenced to serve six-and-a-half years in a Singapore prison.[48] The lesson: you could commit financial fraud in the United States, but don't you dare do it in Singapore. In prison, Leeson wrote a book about his experience, which Miramax made into a 1999 movie entitled *Rogue Trader*. He had come a long way from Watford.

After the television program *60 Minutes* aired a segment on Barings and derivatives on March 5, 1995, Mark Brickell, the pit-bull Wall Street lobbyist, and Arthur Levitt, the SEC chair, were suspiciously defensive in response. Brickell appeared on Charlie Rose's television program on PBS and insisted that the collapse of Barings had little to do with derivatives.[49] Arthur Levitt phoned reporters from South Africa, saying, "The Barings issue, again, is not a derivatives issue—they could have been trading in cabbages."[50] These comments were odd, given that Barings obviously had lost the money on various types of options and futures.

Brickell and Levitt were trying to reframe the collapse of Barings to deemphasize these new financial instruments and to persuade the media and regulators not to fan the derivatives flames in the United States with new scandals abroad. Their argument was that the various financial fiascos abroad were caused more by the unique lack of controls at foreign banks than by the instruments themselves. In other words, deceit mattered more than risk.

But this argument ignored the fact that deceit and risk were feeding off of each other: simply put, it was easier to commit financial misdeeds with derivatives. It was no coincidence that many of the control problems at non-U.S. banks during the mid-1990s involved new financial instruments. Barings was far from alone. Britain's National Westminster Bank lost more than $80 million on options trades that senior managers were unable to evaluate in an incident that was eerily similar to earlier valuation difficulties at Bankers Trust and Salomon Brothers.[51] Deutsche Bank, Germany's largest bank, also suffered from lax controls, and fired a rogue trader in March 1995, although its losses were only about $15 million.[52] Union Bank of Switzerland's "crown jewel"—its sophisticated equity-derivatives group—lost $240 million on long-dated stock options.[53]

During this time, Sumitomo Corporation and Daiwa Bank—two Japanese firms—also experienced billion-dollar-plus scandals involving complex trading strategies. In each case, a rogue trader placed large bets, allegedly without the knowledge of supervisors. Several major Wall Street dealers were involved.

Sumitomo reported the largest derivatives loss to date: $2.6 billion, in unauthorized trading of copper futures by the firm's chief trader, Yasuo Hamanaka. The Sumitomo debacle was unfathomably complicated and provoked a Dickensian legal battle, ranging from a prosecution by the CFTC, alleging manipulation, to numerous lawsuits against Sumitomo to a dispute between Sumitomo and J. P. Morgan over alleged loans. J. P. Morgan reportedly paid $125 million to settle a suit by Sumitomo alleging that Morgan had given Hamanaka an off-balance-sheet loan so that he could continue his trading (J. P. Morgan later would make similar loans to Enron, before Enron collapsed). Sumitomo blamed Hamanaka for doing

2,000 unauthorized deals a year for ten years, and for forging records and signatures needed to give him the authority to trade. Hamanaka was charged with forgery and manipulating copper prices, and was sentenced to an eight-year prison sentence in Tokyo. Merrill Lynch was charged with contributing to the manipulation, and agreed to pay a $15 million fine.

At Daiwa, Toshihide Iguchi's story was similar to Nick Leeson's, but it lasted four times longer. In 1984, Iguchi lost about $200,000 while trading U.S. Treasury bonds at Daiwa's New York branch. During the next eleven years, Iguchi made about 30,000 unauthorized trades in an attempt to dig out of the loss. He was quite possibly the worst trader in history. From 1984 until 1995, he lost an average of almost half a million dollars a day, $1.1 billion in all.[54] He covered up the losses simply by not booking the sales of securities he sold at a loss. No one knew the bonds had been sold, because Iguchi—like Leeson—was involved in the back-office booking of trades. The bonds were held on Daiwa's behalf by Bankers Trust, and Iguchi had obtained some Bankers Trust letterhead, and printed forged financial statements on that, just as Leeson had forged his own position reports.[55]

During this time, U.S. banking regulators had examined Daiwa ten times and had never spotted the losses, even though the trading involved simple financial instruments issued by the U.S. government. The banking regulators ignored various "red flags," including the fact that Daiwa lied to the Federal Reserve in 1993.[56] One can only imagine what might have happened if complex derivatives had been involved.

Iguchi was an unlikely rogue trader, and he lacked formal training in finance. He had moved to the United States from Kobe, Japan, to attend college at Southwest Missouri State University, in Springfield, Missouri, a school known more for its proximity to Lake of the Ozarks than for any programs in finance. Iguchi studied psychology and art, and was a cheerleader.[57] After graduating in 1975, he worked at a car dealer before joining Daiwa's back office, the same first job as Nick Leeson.

Yet Iguchi wasn't even an unusual hire for Daiwa, which also hired Mohamad Sotoudeh, a trader whose experiences demonstrated the close connections among various financial scandals. Managers at J. P. Morgan, where Sotoudeh worked before Daiwa, reportedly had asked him to resign when they discovered a $50 million discrepancy in the monthly mark-to-market values of his trades in mortgage derivatives, the same risky instruments that had destroyed Askin Capital Management and Worth Bruntjen.[58] When Daiwa hired Sotoudeh in 1992 to be its first mortgage-derivatives trader, Andrew Stone, head of Daiwa's mortgage group, remarked, "We have a lot of people with unusual backgrounds and work histories. He won't stand out much."[59] Compared to Toshihide Iguchi, it was true.

In July 1995, Iguchi wrote a 30-page confessional letter to his bosses, saying, "After 11 years of fruitless efforts to recover my losses, my life is filled with guilt, fear and deception." His bosses responded by immediately trying to cover up the losses, too. When officials at the Japanese Ministry of Finance discovered the losses, they, in turn, also tried to cover up the losses, this time from U.S. regulators. A few months later, when U.S. regulators finally learned of the scandal, they returned the favor, prosecuting Daiwa and Iguchi with a vengeance. Iguchi was sentenced to four years in prison, where—like Leeson—he wrote a book about his experiences. In *The Confession,* Iguchi alleged that other traders at Daiwa also had engaged in unauthorized trading, and claimed that his bosses in the United States had promised to protect him so long as he agreed to hide his losses from the firm's Japanese managers.[60] Daiwa ultimately resolved its sordid case by paying a $340 million penalty, the largest fine for financial fraud in U.S. history.

It was embarrassing for Europe and Japan that Barings, National Westminster, Deutsche Bank, Sumitomo, and Daiwa were their elite financial institutions. But even Barings and Daiwa ran tight ships compared to companies and governments in East Asia during the 1990s. Managers of companies in Indonesia, Malaysia, the Philippines, and Thailand borrowed billions of dollars, which they invested in largely frivolous new projects, especially in real estate.

Governments encouraged the borrowing by propping up their currencies, in the same way Mexico had supported the peso. For example, the government of Thailand committed to maintain the value of its currency, called the baht, at an overvalued level based on a basket of several other currencies. Recall that it was this basket that formed the basis of the Thai baht-linked structured notes sold by CSFP, Allen Wheat's firm, during the early to mid-1990s.

Individual investors were drawn to the apparently high returns in these "Asian Tiger" economies until 1997, when some traders finally questioned the dubious nature of corporate investments in East Asia, and predicted that governments would not be able to sustain overvalued currencies for much longer. These traders used over-the-counter derivatives to bet tens of billions of dollars against those currencies until July 2, 1997, when Thailand—in a repeat of Mexico a few years earlier—finally gave up trying to maintain the value of its currency. The baht devalued by 15 percent in one day, just as the Mexican peso had fewer than three years earlier. Other countries soon followed.

Investors in East Asian companies hadn't paid much attention to the fact that they were not entitled to the protections available to shareholders in the United States and England.[61] They generally could not file private suits, and securities regulators were much less effective. Boards of directors did little to monitor managers, and the threat of a corporate takeover was minimal.[62] In international rankings of the rule of law, countries in East Asia consistently received the lowest ratings.[63]

One reason was the concentrated family ownership of East Asian companies. Buying a million dollars of stock in an Indonesian conglomerate was like buying a single share of a small family business in the United States or England: you might make money, but your investment really depended on how much the family decided you should receive. Outside shareholders, even in aggregate, had little influence on family-controlled corporations, even in countries with strong legal protections.

In Indonesia, the Philippines, and Thailand, ten families controlled half of the corporate sector.[64] The Suharto family in Indonesia controlled 417 listed and unlisted firms through business groups led by children, other relatives, and business partners.[65] The Marcos family controlled almost one-fifth of the value of all stocks in the Philippines. Although commentators complained about Japan's "keiretsu," which bound together firms with cross-ownership, ownership of Japanese companies was highly diversified compared to ownership in East Asia, where a handful of mostly corrupt families controlled many of the largest companies in the region.

Not surprisingly, managers at these firms didn't always tell investors the truth about their investments. For years, companies hid bad loans and failed real-estate projects, while borrowing more money, often in surprisingly unsophisticated ways (the "commercial paper" markets in Indonesia and Thailand included postdated checks and notes scribbled on the backs of envelopes).[66] As more foreign investment arrived, the value of shares increased, but the value of the projects underlying those shares declined.[67]

It was an ugly picture, and yet money continued to flow in. Why? The simple explanation was that investors were irrationally optimistic, swept up into the first stage of a cycle of manias, panics, and crashes economic historian Charles P. Kindleberger had argued applied generally to financial crises.[68] Mutual funds investing in East Asia generated double-digit returns in the mid-1990s, and those returns attracted new money, driving up the value of stocks. The markets weren't efficient, in part because it was too difficult, expensive, and risky for sophisticated investors to bet against stocks. Shorting stocks was even more difficult in East Asia than it was in the United States, and even an outside investor betting against an obviously overvalued company might lose money, temporarily, if wealthy and powerful families—or even the government—provided temporary support. As a result, manic investors, instead of sophisticated ones, drove prices, and stocks were temporarily overvalued.

But that explanation was only part of the story, because sophisticated investors, including major hedge funds and investment banks, also were putting money into these countries, not betting against them. Why would sophisticated investors believe they could make money by providing loans to East Asian companies and governments, even if those institutions were in poor shape? This is where the central banks enter the picture.

If interest rates in Thailand were 15 percent, an investor from the United States could borrow at, say, 5 percent, lend money in Thailand, and keep a profit margin of 10 percent, so long as Thailand's currency did not devalue. Even if some of the borrowers defaulted, a U.S. lender would still make money, so long as the Bank of Thailand (the central bank) continued to support the baht. This strategy—borrowing in U.S. dollars and lending the money in another country's currency—was called a carry trade, and it resembled the strategy many investors followed within the United States during the early 1990s, borrowing at low short-term rates and investing at higher long-term rates, hoping to earn the difference. Foreign carry trades began in Malaysia in 1991, and followed in Thailand and Indonesia in 1993.[69]

The increase in these carry trades might not have been problematic if they had been disclosed and monitored by investors and regulators. But because of restrictions on borrowing and lending in East Asia, much of the trading was done in the over-the-counter derivatives markets, where there was no centralized information and no requirement that trades be reported on companies' financial statements.[70] As a result, no one knew how much money particular East Asian companies or countries had borrowed. It was difficult to predict when a company had borrowed so much that it would be unlikely to repay, or when a government spent so much of its reserves that it would no longer be able to defend its currency.

In fact, the derivatives used in East Asia during this time were even more hidden from view than they had been a few years earlier, because banks were selling structured derivatives transactions with a new twist: the Special Purpose Entity, a company or trust created specially for a particular transaction. Like derivatives, SPEs could be used for good or ill. An SPE could be a necessary component of a deal to build a new power plant in Indonesia, or to distribute interests in leases to new investors; or it could be an otherwise useless add-on that enabled a company to create false profits, hide losses and liabilities, and remove the details of various risks from its financial statements.

During the early 1990s, banks had enabled institutional investors to bet on various currency rates by purchasing structured notes or entering into currency swaps. (Remember, a structured note was simply a debt, issued by a highly rated company, with payments that were linked to financial variables, such as the value of a foreign currency; a swap was an agreement between two parties to exchange payments linked to such variables.) These were the instruments Bankers Trust had sold to various investors, including many in East Asia.

But structured notes and swaps had drawbacks for banks, including the risk of being liable for "unsuitable" sales, as the losses of 1994 had shown. Federal regulators in the United States had sued Bankers Trust for selling complex swaps to unwitting customers, even though the extent to which U.S. law covered them was unclear. In private legal disputes regarding structured notes and swaps, purchasers had argued that the selling bank was responsible for their losses, either on suitability grounds or because the bank had breached some agreement or duty. Buyers had obtained favorable settlements in these disputes in the United States, and had even won in court in England.

By using a Special Purpose Entity, a bank could ostensibly avoid these problems, and—depending on the type of SPE—create a deal that wasn't taxable or that avoided disclosure requirements. The SPE could be domiciled in a tax and regulatory haven—Cayman, Jersey, Labuan, and so forth—countries whose financial regulations had been shaped by years of transactions in illegal narcotics and money laundering. In simple terms, a bank could put an SPE between itself and an investor, and thereby keep the details of a transaction hidden from view, while avoiding the problems that had arisen in earlier derivatives deals.

During the mid-1990s, banks began offering elaborate webs of transactions so complicated that it was difficult even to explain the roles of various parties. Economically, the bank was still the seller, but the diagrams and documents for the deals described the bank's role in minimal terms. The buyers dealt directly only with the SPE, not with the bank and, as a result, the bank disclaimed any responsibility. In simple terms, the buyer entered into a swap with the SPE, who entered into a swap with another entity, who entered into a swap with the bank. If the deal went bad and the buyer sued, the bank now had defenses to the arguments that had been raised in earlier cases: the bank didn't breach any contract or duty because there was no relationship between the buyer and the bank. Economically, the bank was the seller, but on paper it was merely a swap counterparty to an SPE, who was a swap counterparty to the buyer.[71] And all of these details remained hidden from anyone except the parties to a particular transaction.

In early 1997, as rumors spread that many borrowers in Thailand were in or near default, sophisticated investors reversed their positions in Thailand, betting that the baht would collapse.[72] But U.S. banks continued to sell investors derivatives linked to the Thai baht, using SPEs. In May 1997, several large Thai corporations began selling baht and buying U.S. dollars, to ensure they would have currency on hand to satisfy their debts. With all this downward pressure on the baht, the Bank of Thailand itself began entering into over-the-counter derivatives transactions to support its currency. On May 8 and 9, the Bank of Thailand sold $6 billion of forward contracts on the baht, roughly one-fifth of its net foreign-currency reserves. After a few weeks of selling forward contracts, the Bank of Thailand was obligated to deliver $26 billion—all of its U.S. dollar reserves. At that point, it should have been obvious that the Bank of Thailand would not have any money left to support the baht, and that therefore a collapse of both the currency and stock prices was inevitable. (Stock prices would decline following a devaluation of the Thai baht, because Thai companies would need to repay their obligations using less valuable currency.) Investors who knew all of this could have sold off their investments in May 1997. However, neither Thai companies nor the Bank of Thailand disclosed their derivatives positions, and investors in Thailand did not learn the details until it was too late. Even now, investors do not know the details of derivatives structured using SPEs during this time.

The rating agencies—which had performed so abysmally in the United States, downgrading Orange County only after it was obviously bankrupt—did not warn investors about the various financial problems in East Asia. In fact, both Moody's and S&P continued to give a single-A rating to the bonds of the government of Thailand for several months *after* the devaluation.[73] Standard & Poor's did not even put Thailand on its "credit watch" until August, and did not downgrade Thailand's credit rating until late October 1997.

After the Bank of Thailand abandoned its defense of the baht on July 2, investors began worrying about similar problems throughout East Asia. Indonesia, the Philippines, and Malaysia faced similar predicaments and abandoned their currencies a few weeks later. The Malaysian central bank, known as Bank Negara, blamed foreign investors speculating in derivatives. It certainly had reason to know: it had made and lost billions of dollars speculating in currencies, and allegedly had even played a role in Andy Krieger's trading years earlier. In fact, the Malaysian complaints were a near-perfect replay of the supposed battle between Andy Krieger and New Zealand's central bank, the only change being an increase in the size of the bets from billions to tens of billions of dollars.

The International Monetary Fund—led by the United States—engineered a $17 billion bailout for Thailand and a $42 billion one for Indonesia,[74] thereby compounding the moral-hazard problems of the Mexico bailout. The economies of Indonesia, Malaysia, the Philippines, and Thailand all soon recovered, as Mexico's had, and investors quickly returned, confident that they would be rescued if another crisis hit.

John Meriwether's firm, Long-Term Capital Management (known as LTCM), was the "Rolls-Royce" of hedge funds, and its expenses justified the name.[75] LTCM charged a two percent annual fee (double the going average), plus 25 percent of any profits, and the fund required a minimum investment of $10 million. Moreover, investors would not be able to withdraw their money for three years, hence the name "Long-Term." The idea was that LTCM—unlike other investment funds with a time horizon of, perhaps, a few days—could weather a financial storm, keeping bets it believed in even if they turned bad for months.

LTCM employed many of the top minds in finance: John Meriwether; Robert C. Merton and Myron Scholes, two of Meriwether's finance professors (who later would win the 1997 Alfred Nobel Memorial Prize in Economic Sciences for their work in options theory); David Mullins, a former vice chairman of the Federal Reserve and Merton's first research assistant; a former senior Italian treasury official;[76] and a cadre of traders from Meriwether's Arbitrage Group at Salomon. With this staff, investors approached Meriwether more than he approached them. As Roy Smith, a professor at New York University and the author of several important finance books, put it, "Investing in this thing was done on the basis of networking, wanting to do the cool thing and trusting the superstars."[77]

The men from LTCM knew they were superstars, too. During one early meeting, Andrew Chow, the head of derivatives at Conseco, an insurance company, questioned whether LTCM really could be very profitable, given how competitive the financial markets had become. When Chow told Myron Scholes he didn't think there were enough "pure anomalies" for LTCM to succeed, Scholes snapped back, "As long as there continue to be people like you, we'll make money."[78] Conseco didn't invest, but plenty of others did. By early 1994, Meriwether had raised $1.5 billion.

In addition, several major Wall Street banks agreed to lend billions of dollars to LTCM, often through *zero-margin* loans, in which LTCM would not even post collateral to assure banks that it would repay the loans. Individual investors had to post collateral of at least 50 percent, and even other hedge funds posted a few percent, but Wall Street was starstruck, too, and gave LTCM special deals. James Cayne, the CEO of Bear Stearns, a second-tier securities firm, was so taken by LTCM that he not only agreed that Bear Stearns would serve as the *clearing agent* for most of LTCM's trades—transferring money and various securities to the parties who were owed them—but he also invested $13 million of his personal funds, even though he had never even met John Meriwether.

LTCM began trading on February 24, 1994, just after the Fed's rate hike. Its prospectus permitted the fund to do just about anything, and warned investors about the volatility of its strategies. The prospectus described *relative-value* and *convergence* trades—essentially, buying a temporarily cheap asset, selling a roughly equivalent, temporarily expensive asset, and waiting for the two to converge in price—and cited a few examples of such trades from Salomon's Arbitrage Group, noting that new strategies were expected and could not be specified in advance. It also mentioned that the firm was permitted to make directional bets ("Directional trades will tend to occur opportunistically and at times may involve positions of significant size"), although the fund didn't plan to engage in much outright speculation.

In a rare statement, David Mullins explained: "We're not directional investors. We don't take highly leveraged bets in the direction of markets. This is a long-term activity which could last a year or two, although we fine tune the hedging during this period. It's very intensively research oriented, with state of the art valuation models which relate various securities to each other. Normally, we only pursue 10 of these plays a year, so it's not frenetic trading."[79] The prospectus also noted that LTCM intended to form "strategic relationships" with important organizations throughout the world. Mullins would be the point man in these dealings.

LTCM lost money during its first month of trading, but in April 1994 it began an incredible four-year run of profits. It made money during the market chaos of 1994, buying mortgage derivatives that Askin Capital Management and Worth Bruntjen were dumping, and betting that temporarily cheap bonds would move back to their historical levels. In ten months of trading in 1994—a terrible year on Wall Street—LTCM made 28 percent.[80]

Beginning in 1995, LTCM traded every financial instrument imaginable: arbitrage between Japanese options and stocks, bets that shares of the same company sold in different markets would converge in price, bets that the price difference between French and German government bonds would diverge, bets that interest rates of U.S. swaps were too high compared to interest rates on U.S. Treasury bonds, and even a bet on long-dated British government bonds that, because it was made using over-the-counter derivatives, actually exceeded the size of the entire market. LTCM's trades frequently were in the range of $10 billion to $25 billion[81]—ten times the size of Andy Krieger's trades at Bankers Trust.

LTCM's bets were astute, but the fund often got lucky, too. For example, when LTCM followed the earlier Salomon Brothers strategy of buying cheap options embedded in Japanese convertible bonds, it had expected to make small amounts of money over a long period of time, as the bonds matured. Instead, the options skyrocketed in value when the Kobe, Japan, earthquake hit in January 1995, causing volatility to increase 50 percent.[82] (This was the same earthquake that had decimated Nick

Leeson's bets on Japanese stocks.) With a combination of skill and luck, the fund made 59 percent in 1995.

Over time, LTCM began taking on the complex risks that other banks shunned. As horror stories spread about how Bankers Trust, and then Salomon Brothers, had been unable to evaluate their complex portfolios, the top managers at many banks instructed their traders to unload such positions.[83] LTCM bought them, betting that its finance specialists could manage the risks better than anyone else. Banks continued to sell complex derivatives deals to clients, but instead of keeping all of the fees, they often paid LTCM to take on the more esoteric risks. In other words, the successors to Gibson Greetings were unknowingly buying their trades from LTCM, with the major Wall Street banks acting merely as an intermediary.

But LTCM's most lucrative trades weren't from skill or luck but, instead, from its cozy relationships with central bankers and government officials, which provided the opportunity for the fund to learn about *regulatory arbitrage* trades—essentially, buying and selling to profit from mispricings due to various countries' legal rules and regulations. These strategies hardly required a Ph.D. in finance. For example, the fund took advantage of a quirk in British tax law that treated high-coupon and low-coupon government bonds differently, even though they were economically similar. It also used its connections in Japan to short bonds, even though the Bank of Japan had rules discouraging such practices.[84] These strategies were a few of the small number of trades David Mullins had described as requiring so much research and time.

Much of LTCM's activity was in Italy, where it had extraordinary connections. Not only did LTCM employ the former Italian treasury official responsible for debt management, but the Bank of Italy, the country's central bank, had invested $100 million with LTCM. (This investment was highly unusual; imagine if Alan Greenspan invested the Fed's money in a foreign hedge fund.) Meriwether and Mullins also had connections in Italy, and Merton was a near-deity there.

It was no coincidence, then, that in one trade LTCM purchased an estimated $50 billion of Italian government bonds—a bet bigger than any previously described in this book, including Joseph Jett's trading in STRIPS. LTCM owned 25 percent of one segment of the Italian government-bond market. In other trades, LTCM benefited from an Italian tax loophole for foreign investors, and from the prospect of Italy's entry into the European monetary system, about which it had very good information.

LTCM even found regulatory advantages in its trading with clients. When Union Bank of Switzerland, known as UBS, expressed an interest in buying a stake in LTCM in 1996, long after the fund had closed to new investors, Myron Scholes designed an over-the-counter options deal that enabled the Swiss bank to invest while reducing the taxes of LTCM's partners. UBS bought shares in LTCM, but sold a seven-year option to LTCM's partners. When LTCM's partners eventually exercised the option, they would pay tax at the low, long-term-capital-gains rate, instead of the high, personal-income-tax rate.[85]

In all, 1996 was another fantastic year, and the fund made 44 percent. Investors already had doubled their money, with little apparent risk. Fund managers were often measured by the *Sharpe ratio*—essentially, the fund's average returns divided by its risks. For a good fund manager, the relevant percentages of returns and risks might be about the same, so that the Sharpe ratio was 1.0. A Sharpe ratio of 2.0 was excellent, and probably not sustainable for long. LTCM's Sharpe ratio, in its first three years, was an astronomical 4.35.[86]

There were some signs of trouble in 1997. The fund paid investors just 17 percent, after fees. By this time, LTCM employed 25 Ph.D.s,[87] but even with this brainpower, the fund had moved from highly quantitative arbitrage trades to outright gambling on currencies and stocks. Myron Scholes questioned whether LTCM really had an advantage in such areas, and wondered whether the fund was assessing its risks properly. The partners agreed that they would reduce the size of the fund by about $3 billion, because of concern that they might not be able to find enough good investments, given the limited number of regulatory-arbitrage opportunities. By the end of 1997, LTCM had about $4.7 billion of equity, which it used to borrow $125 billion and enter into another $1.25 trillion of derivatives. LTCM's ratio of debt-to-equity, an important measure of the riskiness of a firm, was almost 27 times ($125 billion of debt divided by $4.7 billion of equity). Firms with a high debt-to-equity ratio were said to have greater leverage, and were more likely to have trouble repaying their debts.

Some investors whose money was returned were upset to lose the cachet of LTCM. But anyone who thought carefully about what LTCM was doing would have spotted the danger signs; and, indeed, a few investors called the fund to express concerns. The number of hedge funds had grown by about 20 percent every year since 1988; and, by 1996, there were almost 5,000 of them, with $300 billion under management.[88] The markets had become so competitive that even the most sophisticated hedge-fund operators were questioning whether it still was possible to find the tiny arbitrage-profit opportunities that remained.

David Shaw, a computer scientist, who had founded a hedge fund called D. E. Shaw in 1988 and had generated 18 percent annual returns, with low volatility, for eight years, said the markets were so competitive that if he were considering starting up a hedge fund in 1996, he'd "probably stay out of the business altogether."[89] Victor Niederhoffer, a peculiar hedge-fund manager, who was frequently barefooted or reading obscure philosophy tracts, and who had a track record of 30 percent annual returns for fifteen years, lost all of his investors' money—more than $100 million—in 1997. First, Niederhoffer lost $50 million in the East Asia crisis. Then, he "doubled down" by selling put options on U.S. stocks, betting that the market would not go down. When U.S. stocks fell seven percent on October 27, he lost everything that day.[90]

Investors in these hedge funds hadn't known about their risks, because the funds did not disclose details. LTCM, D. E. Shaw, and similar funds said they needed to keep their strategies secret or other investors would mimic them, thereby eroding the profit opportunities. Many investors could not understand these complex strategies, anyway. One of David Shaw's investors said, "With most of the investments I have, I understand exactly what's going on. I don't with David."[91]

The same was true of LTCM. LTCM split its trades among numerous banks, so that no one would be able to see its trading strategies. It might do one side of a trade with one bank, and another with a different bank. It told its investors very little about its strategies, and never released the details of specific trades.

The President's Working Group on Financial Markets later concluded that "financial firms did not fully understand LTCM's risk profile and that some may not have adequately contemplated the market and liquidity risks that would have arisen if LTCM had defaulted. As the complexity, volume, interrelationship, and, in some cases, the leverage of transactions increased, the existing risk management procedures underestimated the probability of severe losses."[92] But during the months before LTCM collapsed, most regulators were more hostile to regulation. After the Commodity Futures Trading Commission considered issuing a "concept release," addressing the regulation of the over-the-counter derivatives LTCM and various banks traded, the President's Working Group on Financial Markets held a meeting at which Treasury Secretary Robert Rubin discouraged the CFTC from issuing any release, arguing that the "CFTC was utterly without jurisdiction over the over-the-counter derivatives market." Arthur Levitt meekly agreed. When pressed for an explanation of why the federal law granting authority for regulating derivatives to the CFTC did not apply, neither Rubin nor his general counsel could offer any legal analysis supporting their position. The CFTC boldly decided to issue the concept release anyway, against the objections of Greenspan and Rubin, and when one Treasury official discovered the CFTC's plans, his reaction was, "Oh, no. The big banks won't like that."

In theory, investors didn't need legal rules for protection, so long as they could trust LTCM's traders to manage their risks appropriately. In early 1998, LTCM's traders carefully checked the fund's risk exposures by using its Value-At-Risk computer models, which estimated the maximum daily loss the fund would suffer with a 95 percent level of confidence, based on historical data. After crunching the numbers, the traders concluded that the fund's VAR was $45 million—less than one percent of its capital. The models said that it would take LTCM several billion times the life of the universe before it would lose all of its capital on just one day.[93]

Unfortunately, the VAR models were wrong, and became even less accurate as LTCM lost money on bets in foreign bond and currency markets during May and June 1998. The fund lost 16 percent during that time—the first time it lost money in consecutive months.[94] The traders decided to reduce their one-day exposure, based on their VAR models, from $45 million to $35 million, just to be safe. However, when they sold off some of their less attractive positions, and rechecked the models, the VAR measures had gone *up*, to over $100 million. The firm's computer models were going haywire. It seemed that the traders had not properly accounted for liquidity risk—the risk that their bets would become more difficult to sell as trading dried up. Illiquid markets moved down much more quickly than liquid ones—think of trying to sell a million-dollar home when no one is buying—and LTCM's sophisticated experts had not correctly modeled that risk.

In July 1998, Salomon Brothers decided it had become too difficult for its Arbitrage Group to make money, and shut its remaining traders down. Meanwhile, LTCM not only remained open, but pursued trades far removed from the Arbitrage Group's original strategies, which had become less profitable as other traders learned of and implemented them. For example, LTCM had begun betting on whether particular corporate takeovers would be completed. The rationale was that after a company announced it was taking over another company, but before the takeover was completed, there was a small gap between the price of the shares of the target company and the value the target shareholders would receive at the time of the takeover. LTCM could buy shares of the target, sell shares of the acquirer, and wait for the values to converge.

In reality, it was more like *praying* for the values to converge than merely waiting. The reason for the price gap was that the companies might abandon the merger, and if they did, the value of the target shares would plunge. That was why the target's shares would trade for $99 per share even after the acquirer had announced that it was planning to buy those shares for $100. The strategy of buying for $99 with the hope of getting $100 was sometimes labeled *risk arbitrage*—the ultimate finance oxymoron, for true arbitrage did not involve risk.

Nevertheless, LTCM embraced the strategy. It lost and then recouped $100 million on the takeover of MCI Communications: first betting that British Telecommunications would succeed as an acquirer, and then— when that takeover failed—betting that WorldCom would buy MCI.[95] In August 1998, LTCM had made a large bet that Tellabs would complete its takeover of Ciena, and was "waiting" for the values to converge.

A glance at LTCM's trades showed how much the firm had changed. It was no longer simply betting on the convergence of different financial assets to their historical levels; it also had begun speculating, not only on corporate takeovers, but in various international markets. It bet on bonds in so-called *emerging markets,* including Russia. It sold options on various European stock indices, making essentially the same outright gamble in Europe that Nick Leeson had made in Japan.

Selling options was a highly risky, but relatively simple strategy. The seller received cash today and kept the cash so long as markets did not move much. But if the markets were volatile, the seller's potential losses were unlimited. It was the same desperate trading strategy Victor Niederhoffer—and before him, Nick Leeson of Barings—had tried. Selling options was far from the kind of complex, quantitative strategies that had earned Meriwether and his traders their reputations. Myron Scholes owed an apology to Andrew Chow, the derivatives manager from Conseco who had questioned whether LTCM could continue to find arbitrage opportunities. It could not.

In mid-August, Russia defaulted on some of its debts and devalued its currency, just as Mexico had in 1994, and Thailand had in 1997. Numerous hedge funds lost billions of dollars in total. George Soros's fund was the big loser, at $2 billion.[96] LTCM's Russian losses were smaller.

The Russian collapse quickly infected other markets, as various hedge funds, banks, and other financial institutions that had borrowed to buy Russian bonds were forced to sell other investments to raise cash. Unfortunately, many of the institutions that owned Russian bonds also owned essentially the same other instruments: stocks and bonds in Latin America, Eastern Europe, and—again—East Asia. Once again, everyone had made the same bet on the financial roulette wheel. Just as investors in the early 1990s had bet in unison that interest rates would stay low, various institutions in 1998 had gambled on emerging markets. Memories of losses from the crisis in East Asia had barely lasted a year.

Banks worried that hedge funds might not be able to repay their debts, so they refused to lend them more money, forcing the funds to sell even more investments. Half of the two dozen so-called emerging markets were down by more than 35 percent in 1998, through August. Interest rates shot up as high as 40 to 80 percent in Brazil, Mexico, and Venezuela, countries that still did not have long-term bond markets and therefore were vulnerable to short-term investment outflows.[97] The Mexican peso—which had stabilized around eight pesos per dollar (less than half its 1994 value)—fell to below ten pesos per dollar. The Malaysian government imposed controls on currency trading, to try to avoid another collapse. The Republic of Korea restricted the amount of money its large conglomerates—*Chaebols*—could borrow. Markets in Hungary, Poland, and the Czech Republic collapsed. *The Economist* magazine announced, "A contagious disease continues to spread through emerging markets," and labeled the disease "Emerging-Market Measles."[98]

LTCM had a diversified portfolio of investments, and its computer models had calculated that losses in some of these investments would be offset by gains in others. However, as investors bailed out of various risky assets, almost every market—except the most liquid U.S. Treasury bonds—went down in lockstep. Meriwether's traders hadn't anticipated this correlation. They had believed their portfolios were sufficiently diversified to survive even if the ball on the roulette wheel landed on black several times in a row. But now, all of LTCM's supposedly uncorrelated bets were going down, at the same time. The ball was landing on black, over and over again.

In mid-August, LTCM lost money on bond investments in various emerging markets. On August 20, LTCM lost $100 million on its bet on the Tellabs-Ciena takeover, when analysts speculated the merger might be canceled. On August 21, LTCM lost $550 million on its basic convergence bets, as investors bailed out of relatively safe plain-vanilla interest-rate swaps, seeking the ultimate security of U.S. Treasury bonds. Suddenly, the fund had lost 44 percent for the year.[99]

LTCM was down to about $2 billion of capital, and it still had $100 billion of debt. That debt had been manageable when the fund had $4 billion of capital. But now its leverage ratio was up to 50-to-1. Such leverage made LTCM's returns hair-trigger sensitive to small changes in markets. Earlier, LTCM's predicament had been analogous to trying to sell a million-dollar home when no one was buying; now, it was like trying to sell the same home with a mortgage of $980,000. How long could LTCM's sliver of capital last? John Meriwether tried to refinance LTCM's positions, to reduce the fund's leverage ratio, but at this point no one was interested in giving LTCM any more money. He hurriedly sent a letter to investors blaming the collapse in Russia for the liquidity crisis, and assuring investors that LTCM was still alive.

Other traders smelled blood at LTCM, and began betting against the hedge fund, trying to weaken its positions, just as Andy Krieger had traded against the central bank of New Zealand. LTCM was known as the "central bank of volatility," and it began experiencing a classic run on the bank. John Meriwether, who rarely gave interviews, told reporter Michael Lewis, "It was the trades that the market knew we had on that caused us trouble."[100] Although the firm's investors were locked in and couldn't withdraw their money, LTCM's once-starstruck lenders were finally considering whether they should call in their billions of dollars of loans.

The final blow came in September, when volatility in nearly every market spiked upward, and LTCM sustained massive losses from its sales of long-dated stock options, mostly on the French and German stock indices. All the world's markets were moving in lockstep, and LTCM was losing on nearly all of its trades. On September 21, the firm's trades were worth less than $1 billion, and with leverage of more than 100-to-1, it would go under if the market even flinched.

Under the "gentle pressure" of the Federal Reserve, which was concerned that LTCM's failure might trigger a sequence of global defaults that would cause the entire banking system to unravel, LTCM's lenders met in the offices of the New York Federal Reserve Bank. Fed chief Alan Greenspan already had remarked that the financial crisis surrounding LTCM was the worst he had ever experienced; Treasury Secretary Robert Rubin said in September that "the world is experiencing its worst financial crisis in half a century." U.S. government officials didn't want to bail out LTCM, so they bullied the banks to do so instead.

On September 23, 1998, after a potential buyout, involving billionaire Warren Buffett, fell through, fourteen major banks—including the banks that had given LTCM sweetheart terms on its loans—agreed to contribute $3.6 billion in return for a 90 percent stake in LTCM.[101] With the regulators watching, and the alternative of a widespread international crisis, the bankers didn't have much of a choice. It was incredible, but no one had seen it coming.

Many commentators criticized U.S. regulators for assisting with another bailout, but the more troubling issue was the fact that the Fed had seemed powerless to do much more than offer cookies and a meeting room, as Alan Greenspan later admitted. The minutes of the Federal Open Market Committee, from September 29, 1998, stated, "The Committee discussed the limited role of the Federal Reserve Bank of New York in facilitating a private-sector resolution of the severe financial problems encountered in the portfolio managed by Long-Term Capital Management L.P. The size and nature of the positions of this fund were such that their sudden liquidation in already unsettled financial markets could well have induced further financial dislocations around the world that could have impaired the economies of many nations, including that of the United States. Against this background, the Federal Reserve Bank of New York had brought together key interested parties with the aim of increasing the probability of an orderly private-sector solution to the hedge fund's difficulties."

To their credit, the regulators had learned at least a partial lesson about the moral hazard created by earlier bailouts. This time, they were involved only indirectly, and no government funds went to support either the Wall Street banks or John Meriwether's traders.

Meriwether and his crew kept their jobs, but lost most of their personal stakes in LTCM. In all, the fund had lost more than 90 percent of its value during 1998: less than 10 percent of the losses were from emerging markets; $1.3 billion was from selling options, and $1.6 billion was from the convergence strategies that had generated 87 percent of the profits at Salomon Brothers just a few years earlier.[102]

From Mexico to Barings to East Asia to LTCM, the international financial crises of the mid-to-late 1990s had become progressively more complex and far-reaching. By 1998, it was obvious that global markets were linked more closely than anyone had anticipated, so that a problem in Russia could lead to the collapse of a hedge fund in the United States. Now investors had plenty to talk about at Super Bowl parties, regardless of who was hosting. The open question was: where could they possibly put their money?

No one doubted that new financial instruments had created great benefits by enabling investors and corporations to manage risks more efficiently. But the instruments also had increased the frequency and potential severity of market crises, in part because they were so hidden from view. Commentators argued about whether the changes were for better or worse, but the argument was moot: the changes were permanent, and investors and regulators would need to deal with the new risks, or else.

Even the strongest supporters of deregulation recognized that market participants were not adequately monitoring their risks. The President's Working Group on Financial Markets blamed Wall Street for these risk-management failures, although it stopped short of recommending new rules. The Working Group's report on LTCM rebuked major U.S. banks for being complacent during good times, and warned them not to let the lessons of LTCM recede from memory. As a Sword of Damocles, the Working Group listed "Direct regulation of derivatives dealers unaffiliated with a federally regulated entity" as a "potential additional step."[103] Meanwhile, the derivatives activities of the top investment banks remained outside the scope of U.S. law.

These unregulated financial institutions were LTCMs-in-waiting. In many ways, the top investment banks looked just like LTCM. They had an average debt-to-equity ratio of 27-to-1—exactly the same as LTCM's (and that did not include off-balance-sheet debt associated with derivatives—recall that swaps were not recorded as assets or liabilities— or additional borrowing that occurred within a quarter, before financial reports were due).[104] They did many of the same trades, and used the same risk models. Now that LTCM was laying off employees, some investment banks would even hire the same traders.

The various international crises highlighted the fact that market participants were no longer able to assess their own risks. Investment funds didn't have a good understanding of the risks in Mexico or Thailand. Executives at Barings had no clue about Nick Leeson's trading. And, worst of all, the traders at LTCM had used computer models that simply did not work. When the President's Working Group on Financial Markets surveyed financial firms to see how they were managing risks, it reached the following chilling conclusion, buried in an appendix to its report on LTCM: "Most models do not incorporate all products traded by the firm. Firms initially included products they believed presented the highest risks to them, with the intent of including other credit sensitive products at some future date. Some firms do not have an ability to calculate and monitor aggregate exposure limits across all product lines in a VAR-based environment. For instance, some firms only include derivative and foreign exchange transactions, and not repurchase agreements, mortgage backed securities and forwards. A firm's inability to evaluate exposures across all product lines could considerably underestimate credit exposures during periods of extreme market volatility."[105]

In other words, even firms that used Value At Risk—which calculated the maximum daily loss with a 95 percent confidence interval, based on historical data—were not able to track their own risks. In truth, VAR was dangerous. It gave firms a false sense of complacency, because it ignored certain risks and relied heavily on past price movements. In some markets, VAR actually increased risk, because every trader assessed risk in the same flawed way. In other markets, traders calculated VAR measures that varied "by 14 times or more."[106]

Risk management was more art than science, and risk could not be boiled down to a single VAR number. LTCM's VAR models had predicted that the fund's maximum daily loss would be in the tens of millions of dollars, and that it would not have collapsed in the lifetime of several billion universes. Askin Capital Management's VAR had been only about $15 million just before it collapsed.[107] Barings's VAR models said its risk was zero.

Yet even after LTCM collapsed, more than 80 percent of financial firms said they used VAR with a 95 percent confidence interval.[108] This was true even though, in 1998, almost anyone could buy much more sophisticated computer models—which would have required an army of Ph.D.s in 1994—for just a few thousand dollars, as a plug-in to a computer spreadsheet such as Microsoft Excel. But instead of using more sophisticated models, most firms used a simple VAR model. Companies paid Bankers Trust a million dollars each for access to the firm's VAR model, called RAROC 2020, based on the risk-adjusted rate of return Charlie Sanford had introduced at Bankers Trust many years earlier. In 1997, the credit-rating agencies—always slow to the game—finally adopted J. P. Morgan's benchmark model, called CreditMetrics, which relied on historical data and VAR.[109] The names were fancy—VAR, RAROC 2020, CreditMetrics—but all these models really did was compare historical measures of risk and return. They were the models the President's Working Group on Financial Markets had said were seriously flawed.

Why were so many firms using such faulty models? Once again, the primary explanation involved legal rules. Although some firms stuck with VAR because they didn't know any better, the major reason firms used VAR—and even disclosed VAR measures in financial statements—was that regulators required them to do so. Just as regulators had inadvertently led CEOs to become mercenaries by tinkering with the rules for executive compensation and stock options, they were now inadvertently encouraging firms to misstate their own risks.

On January 28, 1997, the SEC had adopted a rule[110] requiring companies to disclose more information about derivatives, and gave them three options, the easiest of which was to disclose a VAR measure with a 95 percent confidence interval. Likewise, the Bank for International Settlements also recommended the use of VAR, as did many international-banking regulators, including the Federal Reserve. Not surprisingly, companies used VAR.

Fed Chairman Alan Greenspan opposed any additional regulation. Although Greenspan publicly mouthed support for laws prohibiting financial fraud, in private he was willing to disclose his true opinion—that he believed there was no need for anti-fraud rules, either. In one lunch meeting in his private dining room at the Fed, he told a senior regulator, "We will never agree on the issue of fraud, because I don't think there is a need for laws against fraud." Greenspan said his experience trading commodities early in his career had persuaded him that anti-fraud rules were unnecessary, because participants in the markets inevitably would discover fraud. Market competition alone—without any regulation—was sufficient, because no one would do business with someone who had a reputation for engaging in fraud.

Given Greenspan's power and strong opinions, any new financial regulations were going to be market-based. Regulators began allowing financial institutions to use their own versions of models to assess whether they were complying with rules that required them to reserve a sufficient cushion of capital based on the risks they took. In simple terms, banks had been required to keep eight cents in reserve for every $1 of loans they made. That requirement was easy to administer when all banks did was make loans. But banks were now engaged in more complex businesses, and they weren't the only financial institutions with capital requirements. How much capital should a securities firm reserve against an inverse IO? What about an insurance company that owned a slice of a Collateralized Bond Obligation? How should a bank treat a complex swap with a hedge fund such as LTCM?

These were more difficult questions, and regulators knew that if they created specific rules for particular instruments, they would be drawing lines in the sand, where financial innovators would quickly find economically equivalent instruments that fell on the other side. So, instead, regulators abdicated to the market and permitted companies to use their own models—flawed or not—to determine whether they were in compliance with minimum capital requirements. In reality, there wasn't much they could do. As one regulator put it, "For $112,000 a year, we can't hire someone who can check the models of kids making ten times that."[111]

All of these issues were much too complicated for average investors. Even if they scoured financial statements to assess a company's leverage and derivatives, and examine its VAR measures, they still wouldn't have an accurate picture. If Wall Street banks couldn't even get an accurate sense of their investments, or gauge their own risks, and if a sophisticated hedge fund such as LTCM could collapse because it had been using bad computer models, what hope did individuals have of accurately assessing the risks of their investments? In 1994, it hadn't made much sense to read lengthy corporate annual reports. Now, it didn't even seem worth bothering to look at anything other than the company's name, or perhaps its website.

In such a hopelessly complex environment, with all the various international crises, companies involved in speculative ventures related to the Internet and other new technologies seemed like reasonable investments.

If the alternatives were established companies that either were lying about their accounting data or were unable to manage their own risks, just about any new investment looked attractive. When technology companies began issuing shares to the public in Initial Public Offerings that shot up by hundreds of percent during the first day of trading, and then continued going up, these stocks looked like sure things.

THE LAST ONE TO THE PARTY

Frank "Frankie" Quattrone grew up in a small, two-story row house in a working class neighborhood in south Philadelphia, where the movie *Rocky* was filmed.[1] As Rocky Balboa was running past Quattrone's home, and up the seventy-two steps of the Philadelphia Museum of Art, on his way to winning the heavyweight boxing championship, the bookish Quattrone was acing his high school exams and standardized tests, on his way to winning a scholarship to Wharton—the same school Michael Milken, Charlie Sanford, Allen Wheat, and Andy Krieger had attended. After Wharton, Quattrone worked for two years as an investment banker at Morgan Stanley in New York,[2] moved to Palo Alto, California—where he graduated from Stanford's business school—and then returned to Morgan Stanley, this time in the firm's California office, not far from Stanford. It was 1983.

At the time, a group of technology "nerds" in the Silicon Valley area—many from Stanford—were starting up companies with strange and unfamiliar names, such as Cisco and Netscape. Quattrone fit right in, befriending and advising hundreds of these young entrepreneurs. They loved the fact that a Wall Street banker would wear ugly sweaters instead of expensive suits, and entertain clients at karaoke bars by singing "Rocky Raccoon."[3] Quattrone was smart and offbeat, and his thick, black, center-parted hair and bushy mustache were about as far as it got from a Wall

Street look. As Will Clemens, CEO of Respond.com, put it: "He looks like a guy who could be towing your car."[4]

Many start-ups in Silicon Valley hired Quattrone, and Morgan Stanley promoted him to managing director in 1990, the year the investment bank did Cisco's IPO—the Initial Public Offering in which the privately owned technology firm first sold shares to the general public. In 1995, Quattrone did the IPO for Netscape—the software company that created Netscape Navigator, which enabled individuals to access the Internet—and this deal marked the beginning of the Internet boom. By that time, Morgan Stanley was involved in the lion's share of technology deals, and Quattrone reportedly was making $10 million a year.[5]

After a few control-related disputes with Morgan Stanley's president, John Mack, and a run-in with a Morgan Stanley technology research analyst who had rated one of Quattrone's clients a "hold" instead of a "buy,"[6] Quattrone quit in 1996 to join Deutsche Bank's investment banking division (called Deutsche Morgan Grenfell). Deutsche gave Quattrone everything he wanted, including more staff, a greater share of profits, and control of research analysts.

Quattrone's success and offbeat approach continued at Deutsche. His "pitch book" for the IPO of Amazon.com, an Internet bookseller, looked like a real hardcover book; Deutsche won that deal—and many others. But like Rocky Balboa, Quattrone was a restless superstar. Notwithstanding the fact that he had doubled his annual pay to a reported $20 million, he considered moving to another firm.[7] When rumors spread in 1998 that he might leave Deutsche, he wrote a letter to clients assuring them, "We are here to stay. Please trust us."[8] Then he promptly quit to join CS First Boston—Allen Wheat's firm—taking along the best bankers from his group, capturing even greater control and an even more lucrative pay package.

At CS First Boston, Quattrone dominated the market for technology IPOs, and CS First Boston made $718 million in fees for IPOs of technology companies alone, much more than any other bank.[9] (Incredibly, as it would turn out, that amount included just the firm's *disclosed* fees, which were only a fraction of the money it really made from those IPOs.) In two years, Quattrone took CS First Boston from the 19th-ranked technology investment bank to number one.[10]

Quattrone also continued his antics. When Peter Jackson, the CEO of Intraware, complained that soliciting investors during his company's IPO was going to make him "feel like a mule," CS First Boston actually delivered a live mule to Intraware's lobby the next morning, complete with a sign urging the company to hire CS First Boston. Intraware hired Quattrone, and Jackson later admitted that the mule "may have made the difference."[11] Quattrone bristled when others attempted to grab the limelight. When Katrina Garnett, the 38-year-old Australian founder and CEO of CrossWorlds Software—whose board Quattrone served on—tried a marketing gimmick of her own—appearing in advertisements in *Vanity Fair* and *The New Yorker* magazines wearing a black size-4 cocktail dress and a seductive pose, as part of a million-dollar advertising campaign—Quattrone resigned in a huff, protesting that he had not been informed of the campaign.[12]

During the late 1990s, Quattrone was the highest-paid person on Wall Street, at a reported *$100 million* a year. Other bankers weren't far behind. Wall Street firms made tens of billions of dollars in the late 1990s, and paid roughly half of their revenues to employees. Hedge-fund managers who bought shares in technology IPOs could make even more money, as share prices increased by hundreds of percent. Looking back, Andy Krieger's $3 million bonus in 1988 seemed like peanuts. In response to a claim that $6 million was an impressive bonus in the late 1990s, one industry veteran said, "What he thinks of as a lot of money isn't a lot of money. He thinks that people who are worth $50 million are rich guys. In this world, lots of people have that kind of money. Nobody's impressed when they hear you have guys in the firm making $6 million."[13]

Investors didn't do nearly as well. Unfortunately, the mania in technology stocks ended badly: by 2002, 99 percent of all IPOs of Internet companies were trading below their first-day closing price, and more than half of such companies were worth less than $1 per share.[14] In addition to the hundreds of billions of dollars lost on Internet companies, roughly a trillion dollars of money invested in telecommunications companies was squandered during the late 1990s, and nearly half a million people working in the telecommunications industry lost their jobs.

Although most investors now know these facts all too well, what is not widely understood is how intimately this technology boom and bust was connected to earlier changes in financial markets. It is tempting to blame the bubble on investor greed or banker venality. But the story is not that simple. Human *nature* didn't change; human *behavior* did, as a natural response to the changes in the structure of financial markets and legal rules during the previous decade.

Three groups of people—investors, bankers, and corporate executives—formed the key connections. Investors succumbed to incentives for increasingly risky behavior and, given the complexity of financial reporting, decided it no longer mattered whether companies made money; they rushed to buy stocks without earnings, anyway. Bankers substituted for accountants as the primary facilitators, responding to investor demand, deregulation, and the limited prosecution of financial fraud by pumping stocks in return for fees. Frank Quattrone and his ilk were not evildoers; they were simply the most skilled in responding to new circumstances, like the strongest lions of the pride after a kill. Young corporate executives engaged in deceitful practices, just as their elder counterparts at Cendant and other companies had a few years earlier; but, in a new milieu—technology—where it was even more difficult to distinguish fraud from mere puffery. Their behavior, too, made perfect sense, given the upside associated with "free" stock-option grants and the low probability of punishment.

In short, the "dot.com" era was not some bizarre anomaly in which investors briefly went insane. Nor was the bubble created solely by the nefarious "pump-and-dump" schemes of a few greedy bankers and corporate executives. Instead, the era followed, inexorably and seamlessly, from the earlier changes in markets and law. Investors, Wall Street, and corporate executives were all participants; but, given the incentives facing each group, their behavior—if not excusable—should not have been surprising, either.

First, as markets became more complex, individuals became intoxicated by what economist John Maynard Keynes called the "animal spirits" of markets.[15] The various international bailouts were only the most recent incentive for investors to take on more risk. During the two decades before 1990, individuals actually had taken money out of the market. But then, in 1991, the stock market went up 30 percent, and individual investors began buying stocks, fueled a few years later by the media—especially television network CNBC—which expanded coverage of financial markets. Individuals began trading based on anything from a whim to a trend to a tip from a relative, coworker, or Internet chat room. *Day trading*—making numerous stock trades throughout the day—became a popular pastime, even though nearly all day traders lost money. As investors focused less on detailed financial statements, they became open to investing more speculatively—in, say, shares of an Internet bookseller or a provider of wireless telephone products.

Year after year, more people became investing experts, and devoted innumerable hours to comparing stock prices and financial ratios. Everyone knew about the Netscape IPO, even though most investors had not heard of either Netscape or IPOs a few years earlier. Even teenage tennis-star Anna Kournikova and N.F.L. football tight-end Shannon Sharpe were discussing P/E ratios in television advertisements for Charles Schwab. And who could forget on-line broker E*TRADE's commercial about the emergency-room patient with "money coming out the wazoo"?

Almost anyone who invested in stocks during the 1990s made money. It was the longest bull market since World War II, and the numerous financial debacles of the decade seemed far removed from most investors' lives. So what if Orange County declared bankruptcy, or Procter & Gamble lost a hundred million, or Barings failed? Why agonize over a few bad apples at Cendant and Waste Management? And why worry at all about international crises? The various crises of the 1990s led to bailouts, which encouraged investors to take on excessive risk. Economists from Morgan Stanley wrote an essay entitled "It Started in Mexico," in which they reported, "Our analysis of correlation between markets and investment styles points to the Mexican bailout as a factor that set the stage for increasing investor confidence worldwide and helped to ignite the growth market of the late 1990s, along with a strong U.S. economic expansion."[16]

A few disasters might occur here and there, but in the long run, you couldn't afford *not* to be in stocks.[17] The numbers spoke for themselves: as Jeremy Siegel argued in his 1994 book, *Stocks for the Long Run*, stocks had been chronically undervalued throughout history. The trend continued through 1999: an investment in the Standard & Poor's 500—the index of the largest U.S. stocks—returned an average of more than 16 percent per year. If you had put just $75,000 into stocks in 1984, you would have over a million dollars by the end of 1999.

Were investors behaving rationally during this period, or not? One view was that higher stock prices were justified because of a technology revolution of the scale of the industrial revolution, in which new Internet and telecommunications tools would—at some future date—lead to record corporate profits, just as the railroads had revolutionized business a hundred years earlier. The other view was that investors were simply manic, or "irrationally exuberant." There was evidence supporting both views. It was undeniable that consumers were using new technologies, especially wireless telephones and the Internet. But hundreds of telecommunications companies were competing in markets that, like the railroad industry, would support only a handful of leading firms. And it was difficult to imagine, paradigm shift or not, that very many of the hundreds of on-line consumer websites would ever make any money.

As investors were rushing to buy stocks in a rising market, several experts were demonstrating how the second view—of investor mania—was the correct one. Experiments by Daniel Kahneman, Richard Thaler, and Amos Tversky—which showed that people overestimated their own skills, overvalued items they owned, were shortsighted, greedy, and occasionally even altruistic—were an assault on the citadel of efficient-market theory that well-regarded economists such as Paul Samuelson and Eugene Fama had been putting forward since the 1960s. More than a generation of business and government leaders had been taught that markets were efficient and that stocks were "rationally" priced; based on these teachings, they had implemented a deregulatory approach to financial markets since the 1980s.[18] But as the markets continued to soar, these new studies were evidence that the prior assumptions about markets had been wrong.

At first, finance theorists dismissed the new studies as mere anecdotes—just evidence looking for a theory—because they did not have the mathematical rigor of previous rationality-based efficiency theories. Moreover, in a market with "arbitrage," where sophisticated investors could buy and sell mispriced securities, stocks arguably would be "rationally" priced even if some investors were irrational. It might be true, as some new experiments showed, that 80 percent of car drivers thought they were of above-average skill, or that most gamblers took greater risks when playing with *house money* (money they already had won). But, the argument went, the same irrational behaviors didn't matter in financial markets, because sophisticated, rational investors could make money trading with irrational investors until arbitrage opportunities were gone, and stocks were no longer mispriced.

When a few economists—led by Andrei Shleifer—translated the experimental data about irrational human behavior into the language of advanced mathematics, the study of irrational investing got a name, *behavioral finance,* and some credibility.[19] Behavioral finance offered a retort to the powerful arguments about arbitrage. As the traders at LTCM had found, arbitrage—buying low and selling high, until a stock was correctly valued—had limits,[20] including the difficulty of shorting stocks and the impossible problem of predicting how long investor irrationality would last. Behavioral-finance theorists expressed these limits in mathematical terms, and concluded that, although arbitrage theoretically would drive prices in the long run, it was inevitably risky in the short run, when irrational investors could drive stock prices instead. In other words, sophisticated investors betting that irrational ones would regain their senses might have to wait for the long run—and, as John Maynard Keynes famously quipped, "This long run is a misleading guide to current affairs. In the long run, we are all dead."[21]

Behavioral finance quickly found a following, including many banking and securities experts who had been arguing for a decade that unregulated financial markets didn't allocate risk in an efficient or fair manner. Instead, these people had argued, risks were like hot potatoes being passed to the people least able to hold on to them. According to author Martin Mayer, in unregulated banking markets, *credit risk*—the risk that a borrower would not repay—moved from banks, who knew how to assess risk, to other investors, who did not. William Heyman, former head of market regulation at the SEC, argued, "In manufacturing, the market price is set by the smartest guy with the best, cheapest production process. In securities markets, the price is set by the dumbest guy with the most money to lose."[22] Those ideas, in essence, were behavioral finance.

The most powerful evidence supporting these new theories began accumulating on August 9, 1995, when Frank Quattrone did the billion-dollar Initial Public Offering of shares of Netscape Communications, the provider of Internet-access software. Netscape originally had planned to sell shares for about $13 each, but investors were so eager to get into the deal that Quattrone and Morgan Stanley raised the IPO price to $28, and increased the number of shares by half.[23]

The day of the IPO was a wild ride. The shares were sold to investors in the IPO for $28, but there was so much demand that Netscape shares began trading at $71—five times their anticipated price just a few weeks earlier. During the morning of August 9, Quattrone and his bankers had planned to raise $1 billion for Netscape. At the peak of trading that day, those shares were worth $3 billion. At four P.M., when trading closed, the shares were down to $2 billion, but still up 107 percent for the day. These violent moves suited the "bucket-shop" trading of the 1920s more than a modern stock market.

The Netscape IPO sparked investors' attention and prompted numerous questions. By any objective account, Quattrone had massively underpriced the deal. Historically, the average first-day IPO return had been in the range of six percent. During the early 1990s, first-day returns had doubled.[24] But Netscape's first-day return of 107 percent set a new standard. Was it a mistake? Incredibly, Jim Clark, the founder of Netscape, wasn't upset about underpricing the IPO by a billion dollars. Nor was Frank Quattrone, who apparently had given up tens of millions of dollars in IPO fees, which were set at a standard seven percent of the initial proceeds of the deal. (On a two-billion-dollar IPO, a seven percent fee would have been $140 million, but on a one-billion-dollar deal, the fee was a mere $70 million.)

These men apparently were willing to leave huge amounts of money on the table, and they weren't alone. Bankers continued to underprice IPOs, and by 1999 the *average* first-day IPO return was 70 percent.[25] There were various theories about why corporate executives would allow bankers to sell IPOs at such low prices: the young executives were inexperienced and negotiated bad deals; they were getting so much money they didn't care; they wanted to feed a market frenzy so that their stock prices would be even higher in six months, when they finally were permitted to sell their shares (in an IPO, the insiders typically were not allowed to sell their own shares for 180 days, a restriction known as a *lock up*). Whatever the reason, instead of selling stock in an IPO for, say, $25, firms were selling for $15—over and over again.

Post-IPO prices remained high throughout the first year of trading. Historically, only about half of IPOs had gone up during their first year; but, in 1995, IPOs began performing much better than the historical average. Netscape, a typical example, was up from the IPO price of $28 to a price of $171 by the end of the 1995. As more Internet companies issued shares whose values doubled—and then doubled again—Alan Greenspan issued his warning about irrational exuberance, and some commentators admonished investors to avoid a market bubble. In an efficient market, the warnings shouldn't have been necessary; sophisticated investors should have been able to short these stocks, and drive prices down to rational levels. Instead, as behavioral-finance theory predicted, the "sophisticated" investors who bet against Internet stocks were eaten alive.

Consider Palm, the subsidiary of 3Com that made handheld Palm Pilots. When Palm issued five percent of its shares to the public, Palm's shares had a higher value than 3Com's, even though 3Com still owned

95 percent of Palm.[26] Strangely, the part was worth more than the whole. Two factors made this anomaly possible, both explained by behavioral finance: first, individual investors flocked to high-profile companies such as Palm, and were willing to buy shares at exorbitant prices; second, sophisticated investors who might have been willing to bet against Palm, thereby bringing Palm's price down to a more reasonable range, could not do so because of regulations restricting short selling, and because of the limited supply of Palm shares available to sell short. As a result, the anomaly persisted. As behavioral-finance theories predicted, the upward bias of overly optimistic investors determined stock prices more than the grounded views of sophisticated experts.

After Netscape, media coverage—especially on CNBC—fed investors' desire to buy "hot" technology IPOs, which began occurring nearly every day: Amazon, Yahoo!, eBay, and then lesser-known start-ups such as Gadzoox, GoTo.com, and VA Linux. According to John Cassidy of *The New Yorker,* "CNBC didn't create the stock-market boom, but it did perpetuate and amplify it. To borrow a term from biology, the network acted as a 'propagation mechanism' for the investing epidemic."[27] The media began covering the NASDAQ—the National Association of Securities Dealers Automated Quotation system, where most technology stocks were traded—even more than the New York Stock Exchange. (By 2002, the average volume of NASDAQ had surpassed that of the NYSE.)

One of the thorniest issues related to investor mania and the media was the role of the securities analysts who recommended stocks. Many economists argued that these analysts were the key players making stock markets efficient. Investors trusted securities analysts to make accurate and informed assessments of companies, just as they previously had trusted accountants. These analysts began appearing regularly on television, and many investors followed analyst recommendations, word for word. Why shouldn't they?

On December 16, 1998, in the midst of the holiday-shopping season, 33-year-old Henry Blodget, an unknown securities analyst at CIBC Oppenheimer, a second-tier firm, predicted that Amazon would nearly double, to $400 a share, within a year. The stock suddenly shot up from $243 to $289. Investors believed Blodget's prediction, even though he had only been issuing analyst reports on Amazon for two months, and didn't have any unique insight into Amazon's business plan, or any inside information. Blodget was more like Peter Jennings than Peter Lynch, more television personality than investment guru. He was clean-cut and articulate and had a degree from Yale—and that seemed to be enough for most investors. If such a nice young man said Amazon stock would be worth $400, then it was a steal at $250.

That day, Blodget received more than fifty media calls, and he immediately began appearing on CNBC on a regular basis. Less than a month later, Amazon hit $400, just as Blodget had predicted, and his credibility was confirmed. Investors were justified in relying on Blodget; he was the one who had made so many people rich on Amazon. Blodget capitalized on his new-found value, moving to Merrill Lynch in 1999, with a guaranteed combined annual salary and bonus of $3 million.[28] Looking back on his Amazon prediction, Blodget said, "It was like touching a match to a bucket of gasoline. I was shocked."[29]

After Blodget's prediction came true, the floodgates opened. From 1999 through March 2000, there was a deluge of new Internet IPOs as the overall NASDAQ market more than doubled in value. Blodget made hundreds of television appearances, recommending stocks that, for the most part, went up.[30] Day trading increased to 15 percent of the volume on NASDAQ, even more in hot Internet stocks.[31]

In 1999, three-quarters of all IPOs increased in price during their first year. An investor who bought into every 1999 IPO would have tripled her money; even an investor who bought at the end of the first day of trading would have made 81 percent.[32] All of these companies were supported by securities analysts shouting "buy," including not only Blodget but a few "superstar" analysts—notably Mary Meeker of Morgan Stanley and Jack Grubman of Salomon Brothers (more on him in Chapter 11)—who were nearly as well compensated as Frank Quattrone. Investors listened and obeyed when Henry Blodget said to buy Pets.com, or Frank Quattrone's analysts at CS First Boston said to buy mortgage.com, or when Jack Grubman said to buy Global Crossing or WorldCom. Investors did it and, more often than not, the analysts were right. Until 2000, anyone betting against these analysts' recommendations would have lost money.

Charles Mackay wrote in the preface to his 1852 book, *Memoirs of Extraordinary Popular Delusions and the Madness of Crowds*, "Men, it has been well said, think in herds; it will be seen that they go mad in herds, while they only recover their senses slowly and one by one."[33] For almost five years, from August 1995 until March 2000, investors joined in a fanatic stampede, oblivious to the fact that they were approaching a cliff. But the cliff was always there—as Alan Greenspan, *The Economist* magazine, and many others had warned—and, by 2002, most investors had lost everything they had made during the earlier madness, and more. After news of repeated corporate bankruptcies and frauds, individual investors would only slowly recover their senses.

In reality, bankers and securities analysts had been corrupted by precisely the same forces that had corrupted accountants: pressure from corporate executives, limitations on liability, and conflicts of interest related to their own firms. Although investors hadn't noticed, there were signs during the mid-1990s that Wall Street had begun to behave very badly. First were the various derivatives fiascos, with Bankers Trust leading the pack. Then there were a series of scandals in the NASDAQ market, where most technology stocks were traded. In 1994, economists William Christie and Paul Schultz reported that NASDAQ traders were conspiring to charge investors high commissions (the securities dealers later settled disputes related to the conspiracy for more than a billion dollars.)[34] In March 1995, several traders from Morgan Stanley allegedly manipulated the markets for several technology stocks—including Dell Computer, Novell, Sybase, and Tele-Communications Inc.—in order to profit from a complex scheme related to NASDAQ options (Morgan Stanley later was fined $1 million and the traders involved in the scheme were fined and suspended, although all of the fines were reduced substantially on appeal).[35] Bankers also advised on technology-related mergers, which increased from $12 billion in 1992 to $150 billion in 1997,[36] and wrote "fairness opinions"—that these mergers were fair for shareholders, even though the deals made no more sense than the disastrous conglomerate mergers of the 1960s.

In the late 1990s, two schemes in particular—one involving IPOs, one involving securities analysts—enabled investment banks to make billions of dollars at the direct expense of their clients and investors. Through these two schemes, Wall Street hid important facts from investors, facts that might have sobered those drunk on animal spirits. Frank Quattrone was the key figure in the IPO scheme; Henry Blodget was the key figure in the analysts scheme.

An Initial Public Offering is the most lucrative transaction any Wall Street firm can arrange for a corporate client. It is a special time in a company's life: the moment it finally "arrives" in the public financial markets; the time when the corporate executives and venture capitalists who have invested money, time, and sweat finally raise money from large numbers of individual investors and establish a public market in which they later will be able to sell their shares. IPOs warranted high fees because they were risky and required more work than a typical deal. Securities regulators drew a bright line between private and public companies, and required that any company doing an IPO file an especially lengthy set of financial statements describing the company's risks.

The fees for almost all IPOs were set at exactly seven percent, ten times the fees from most structured derivatives transactions, and much more than the fees from any other investment-banking deals. Some economists were suspicious of these seven percent fees, and argued that they were evidence of an antitrust conspiracy among banks to charge high fees and avoid competition. They were right to be suspicious, but wrong about the argument. In reality, the seven percent fee was just a fraction of the fees the top banks made from IPOs. This was the IPO scandal. Here are some examples of how it worked.

CS First Boston did more IPOs for technology companies in 1999 and 2000 than any other securities firm, thanks mostly to Frank Quattrone's relatively small group. Consider one example: in July 1999, CS First Boston was the lead underwriter for the IPO of Gadzoox Networks, an Internet company.[37] That meant that Frank Quattrone and his group were the bankers charged with primary responsibility for selling shares of Gadzoox to the public, including the *road show* during which they described the company to various institutional investors. Frank Quattrone didn't directly call the little old lady in Peoria to solicit an order; individual brokers at CS First Boston did that. But Quattrone created the "story" for the company, which individual brokers would then use in selling shares.

CS First Boston had about 3.4 million shares of Gadzoox to sell. The key issue, other than the story, was price. How should Quattrone advise Gadzoox about what the IPO price should be? The Gadzoox insiders wanted the price to be as high as possible, because all of the money raised in the IPO, less fees, went to the company. But CS First Boston's clients wanted the price to be as low as possible, so they could buy at the cheap IPO price and then sell later at a higher price. CS First Boston was conflicted: it wanted a higher IPO price so that its seven percent fee would be higher, but it wanted a lower IPO price so that it would be sure to sell all of the shares. Historically, IPOs had been priced at a slight discount to the price the bankers believed the stock would trade at during its first day, as a compromise among the company doing the IPO, the bank, and its clients. As noted above, by 1999 this "IPO discount" had increased from a few percent to an average of 70 percent. It appeared that companies were agreeing to give up proceeds in return for rewarding the bank's clients.

The Gadzoox IPO was a mirror of the Netscape IPO in 1995, which had gone from $28 to $71 the first day. On July 20, 1999, CS First Boston sold Gadzoox shares in the IPO for $21, and by the end of the day, the shares were trading for $74, an increase of more than 250 percent.[38] The lucky clients who had bought in at the IPO price appeared to have made—in aggregate—more than $180 million. The Gadzoox IPO was not unusual for CS First Boston; the bank did a similar IPO the very next day for MP3.com, an Internet music distributor, in which it sold 7.2 million shares in the IPO at $28. Shares of MP3.com were trading at $63 by the end of the day, generating a one-day gain of more than $250 million for clients.

During the days surrounding these two IPOs, some of CS First Boston's clients began behaving strangely, and it was this type of behavior that tipped off a few reporters, and ultimately the Securities and Exchange Commission, to the IPO scheme. For example, one client who received 4,000 shares of Gadzoox and 10,000 shares of MP3.com, and therefore had a one-day profit of more than half-a-million dollars, began frenetically trading tens of thousands of shares in unrelated stocks, such as Allstate, Coca-Cola, Conoco, and Philip Morris, all at the very high commission rate of $1 per share, all at the same time as the IPOs.[39] Another client who received 2,500 shares of Gadzoox and 5,500 shares of MP3.com traded 180,000 shares of various unrelated companies, paying commissions to CS First Boston on those trades of $124,000. Still another received 7,200 IPO shares and traded 210,000 shares with CS First Boston at high commissions. And so on.

In addition, CS First Boston allocated shares to the venture-capital investment funds that sent their best corporate clients to CS First Boston. For example, Technology Crossover Ventures, a firm with close ties to Quattrone, was allocated 50,000 shares in the December 1999 IPO for VA Linux. Those shares went up by more than $10 million the day of the IPO.[40]

This pattern was repeated in numerous IPOs arranged by CS First Boston, such as El Sitio, OTG Software, and Selectica. The most infamous example was the December 1999 IPO of VA Linux, which went from $30 to $239.25 the first day, an increase of nearly 700 *percent*. One "lucky" client received 13,500 shares of VA Linux at $30, for a total cost of $405,000. By the end of the day, those shares were worth $3.2 million. This grateful client immediately placed a trade for 2 million shares of Compaq at a total commission to CS First Boston of $1 million.

Why were clients engaging in such strange behavior? In simple terms, clients of CS First Boston were buying underpriced IPO shares, pocketing substantial one-day profits, and then trading hundreds of thousands of unrelated shares with CS First Boston at very high commission rates. The commissions were as high as $3 per share—compared to the standard commission rate of six cents per share—and clients typically sold the stock they bought through CS First Boston immediately, sometimes simultaneously. In each case, the value of the commissions paid to CS First Boston was one-third to two-thirds of the client's IPO profits. In aggregate, these payments represented as much as one-fifth of the firm's *total* revenues from commissions.[41]

It didn't take the SEC long to conclude that clients were paying CS First Boston kickbacks through high commissions in return for shares in an IPO. In fact, CS First Boston employees left little doubt that the IPO scheme was bribery, pure and simple. There was extensive evidence that CS First Boston employees told clients they were expected to repay a portion of the IPO profits in the form of excess commissions. CS First Boston tracked the percentage profits of various clients and told them they should maintain a ratio of 3-to-1 IPO profits to commissions. In early 2000, a senior executive at CS First Boston reportedly told a fund manager, "You get $3—we get $1."[42] Another senior executive described a client as being on "the 4 to 1 plan which is generous." Other salesmen told customers they were expected to repay CS First Boston 50 percent of their profits from IPOs or they would not receive IPO shares in future deals.[43]

Some clients were told to kick back to CS First Boston as much as 65 percent of the money they made on IPOs. One salesman reported to his boss that he had informed a client "that he was very far behind on his commissions and that we expect a 65% return on all money that we make him. I said that he still owes us for the VA Linux deal not to mention the deals that have come since then. I then stated that he can do trades to increase his commissions but he will be further cut from any syndicate in the future." One especially slick salesman told a client, "Okay we got another screaming deal and I weasled [sic] you guys some stock we've yet to see any leverage out of your guys for the free doughre-me does it make sense for me . . . to continue to feed your guys with deal stock or should I take the stock to someone who will pay us direct for the allocations."[44]

Some clients who received IPO shares in so-called "Friends of Frank" (Quattrone) accounts were CEOs of technology firms who were in a position to give those banks investment-banking business. These deals were not limited to CS First Boston; indeed, bankers later would defend them as standard custom and practice in the industry. Bankers regarded IPO allocations as no different from frequent flier miles: if you transacted enough times, you would receive a reward.

In any other industry, federal regulators with evidence of these schemes would have impaneled a grand jury, shut the firm down, and prepared to send the perpetrators to jail. There was plenty of proof of a kickback scheme, and the victims were clear: individual investors who did not receive preferential treatment and, instead, bought at higher prices in the market. But the SEC did not have the authority to bring a criminal case; it had to persuade the Justice Department to do that. And the Justice Department didn't have much of an appetite for complex financial cases, given the deluge of criminal activity in other areas, including the illegal-drug trade, health-care fraud, and terrorism.

Instead of cooperating with the SEC, Allen Wheat, who had been running CS First Boston for three years at this point, casually dismissed the investigation. Anyone who had worked on Wall Street during the 1990s knew that the government rarely brought criminal cases alleging complex financial fraud; besides, given the aggressive ethos at CS First Boston, why would employees think they had done anything wrong? Wheat had created the same kind of mercenary culture that had pervaded his previous firm, Bankers Trust. He constantly asked employees, "How much did you make for us today?"[45] (just as Charlie Sanford, Allen Wheat's boss from Bankers Trust, had relentlessly questioned employees, "What's next?"). Because the answer for compliance officers—the employees at banks who were supposed to police the traders and salesmen—was "nothing," they were treated with disdain. On the other hand, CS First Boston paid bankers who generated profits more than any other bank, in part because its best employees constantly threatened to leave unless Wheat upped their pay. One managing director at CS First Boston said, "The only culture here is greed. You come to work 50 weeks a year for the one day when you are told how much your bonus will be."[46]

Wheat was a gambler and, in 1998, when CS First Boston lost about $3 billion in Russia, Wheat had bet on Quattrone, giving him not only a cut of profits, but also his own fiefdom, complete with salespeople, media relations, and research analysts. Until 2001, the bet on Quattrone had paid off, and was responsible for a good chunk of Allen Wheat's personal fortune of several hundred million dollars. Wheat wasn't about to remove his bet on Quattrone, now that a few regulators were sniffing around.

By giving Quattrone special treatment, Wheat created an environment rife with conflicts of interest. For example, Wheat gave Quattrone and other members of his group $25 million a year to invest in potential clients. In June 1999, Quattrone and a few partners invested $126,000 in a private Internet software company called Interwoven, Inc. Four months later, they did an IPO for the company, and then later sold their shares—near the stock's peak—for more than $2 million,[47] a return that surpassed even Hillary Clinton's profits on cattle futures.

As news about the SEC's investigation leaked, CS First Boston tried to blame three stockbrokers in the San Francisco office where Quattrone worked—Scott Bushley, Michael Grunwald, and John Schmidt. CS First Boston issued a press release on May 1, 2001, saying that Frank Quattrone was not responsible for overseeing IPO allocations, brokerage accounts, or commissions, contradicting Randall Smith, a top reporter for the *Wall Street Journal*, who had covered Quattrone for several years, and who called him a "control freak" who was involved in every step of the IPO process.[48] The press release also was contrary to evidence later submitted by the Commonwealth of Massachusetts, indicating that Quattrone had the ability to "hire and fire" research analysts and determine their compensation.[49]

In June 2001, instead of disciplining Quattrone or his bankers, CS First Boston fired the three brokers in the San Francisco office, and issued a press release saying the firings had followed an "extensive internal review" and noting that the firm had "informed the appropriate regulators of our action."[50] But CS First Boston was merely shooting the messengers: Scott Bushley was a junior employee; Michael Grunwald was a recent hire from Lehman Brothers, who was simply following past practices at CS First Boston; and John Schmidt was a conservative, bookish sales manager whose actions were approved by his bosses and by firm lawyers.[51] It hardly seemed plausible that these three men had orchestrated the firm-wide scheme.

When the National Association of Securities Dealers—the self-regulatory organization that governs securities dealers—began investigating the IPO scheme, CS First Boston submitted a 121-page argument in defense, claiming that the fees it made from the commissions—although perhaps high, at three percent—were perfectly appropriate, because they were less than a bright-line five percent rule for excessive commissions.[52] The filing was made confidentially before the NASD, but two reporters from the *Wall Street Journal*—Susan Pulliam and Randall Smith—obtained a copy.

In the filing, CS First Boston essentially admitted to the IPO scheme, but defended it as consistent with established rules and practice. Consider the following statement, from the filing: "There is absolutely nothing written in any guideline, rule, regulation, case or speech by a regulatory official that forbids the voluntary payment by clients of large commissions to CSFB to demonstrate that such clients are good enough customers to deserve being given IPO allocations." Or this one: "The practice of rewarding better customers is neither new or unknown in the industry or investing public."[53] CS First Boston was using the classic teenager's defense: everyone's doing it. Average investors who were not "good enough" to deserve IPO allocations were not happy to learn about their lowly positions.

Lukas Muehlemann, the chairman of Credit Suisse, which controlled CS First Boston, wasn't happy about how Allen Wheat was handling the investigation. Wheat had brushed with regulatory authorities all over the world, and had paid little attention to the details of controls or compliance. For Credit Suisse, the IPO scheme was the last straw. Muehlemann told his managing directors, "We have been perhaps a little careless in the past. Now we will not tolerate that."[54] Allen Wheat was fired in July 2001.

Wheat's replacement was John Mack, who had battled with Frank Quattrone years earlier, and who had just lost his own battle for control of Morgan Stanley. Mack captured the culture Allen Wheat had created at CS First Boston when he called an early conference of the firm's managing directors and showed a video clip of John Belushi from the movie *Animal House*.[55] As Mack put it, "This firm has a history of tolerating cowboys. I don't like cowboys."[56]

Not surprisingly, Mack committed to reinforce the firm's compliance and legal departments. He immediately hired Gary Lynch, the former Milken prosecutor who had written the report for Jack Welch about Joseph Jett's losses at Kidder Peabody. Lynch became the general counsel of CS First Boston, and a member of the firm's board of directors. Mack and Lynch understood that if prosecutors filed criminal charges against CS First Boston for the IPO scheme, the firm probably would not survive (just as criminal charges brought against Arthur Andersen later assured the death of that firm). Lynch was charged with settling the case right away.

After the terrorist attacks of September 11, 2001, and the collapse of Enron, the media coverage of the IPO scheme slipped from the front pages. On October 3, 2001, Mack and Quattrone sat down to have a little chat, over steaks in Kansas City, Missouri. The details of their conversation remain secret, but two conclusions were clear; first, Mack somehow persuaded Quattrone to give up his hefty pay package;[57] second, Quattrone and CS First Boston would settle the investigation of the IPO scheme as quickly and quietly as they could. After that, Quattrone could find something else to do at the firm, or elsewhere.

Gary Lynch negotiated the settlement beautifully. The public documents omitted the most serious allegations; instead, CS First Boston was charged with a technical violation of mislabeling the extra payments it had received from clients as "commissions" instead of as "IPO fees," which they really were. The implication: if CS First Boston had simply disclosed that it was receiving a 65 percent IPO fee, its actions would have been perfectly legal.

Prosecutors dropped the criminal case against CS First Boston. The firm's $100 million fine represented roughly one year of pay for Quattrone, and only a fraction of the fees technology companies paid to CS First Boston the previous year.[58] Lynch happily signed the settlement agreement in January 2002.

The media portrayed the case as a significant victory for securities regulators, and any criticism seemed to come from an undistinguished peanut gallery. Even John Gutfreund—the chairman of Salomon Brothers who had been forced to resign during the Paul Mozer scandal—emerged from the shadows to complain about CS First Boston's settlement, saying he was "dismayed" and that the fine was just a "slap on the wrist."[59] (It was less than the fine Salomon paid in 1992, after Gutfreund resigned.)

More than a thousand private lawsuits were filed, by investors in 263 companies.[60] Those cases were a thorn in John Mack's side, although CS First Boston would benefit from the legal changes of the mid-1990s that made such lawsuits more difficult. CS First Boston suffered from a decline in IPO fees, which plunged almost 100 percent, but that was primarily due to a widespread decline in the market. During the first six months of 2002, the firm did just one IPO, for Simplex Solutions, Inc., and made just $3.4 million, barely one week's worth of compensation for Frank Quattrone.

Some commentators have called Frank Quattrone the Michael Milken of the 1990s. There were a few similarities, but in some respects the comparison wasn't fair to Milken. Both men were Wharton grads who quickly rose to the top of their firms and negotiated similar compensation packages. Quattrone symbolized the mania associated with Internet stocks in the same way Milken symbolized the 1980s obsession with corporate raiders and takeovers. Regardless of whether Quattrone "measured up" to Milken, Milken's punishment arguably was too harsh, while Quattrone's treatment arguably was too generous.

The scheme involving securities analysts was closely related to the IPO scheme, but was much simpler to describe. In fact, three words were enough: "pump and dump." Securities analysts at investment banks pumped up stocks, especially those recently issued in IPOs, with overly optimistic reports. Individual investors believed the hype and stock prices remained high until the 180-day lockup period during which corporate insiders were prohibited from selling shares. After the lockups expired, insiders dumped their shares.

It wasn't always this way. Before 1990, securities analysis was a respected profession, and investors valued the quality of analysts' research and the independence of their opinions. Analysts told investors not only when to buy but, even more important, when to sell. Today, business journalists uncover most financial fraud; ten years ago, that was the job of securities analysts.

As markets became more efficient, and information began flowing more quickly and inexpensively, it became difficult for research analysts to add much value. Investors weren't willing to pay for research reports if the market price of a stock already reflected the information. Consequently, analysts faced pressure to add value in other ways: by helping investment bankers solicit business from the companies they covered.

In 1990, Clayton J. Rohrbach III, a senior officer of Morgan Stanley, suggested in an internal memo that analysts' compensation should be tied to how much business the companies they rated gave to Morgan Stanley. Rohrbach suggested that analysts themselves receive explicit ratings of A to C. Morgan Stanley never formalized this policy, because it presented obvious conflicts of interest, but analysts at the firm reported that their pay was based on this grading. Most Wall Street firms, including CS First Boston, adopted similar systems of linking investment banking and research.[61]

These systems remained secret for a decade, until the market finally collapsed and analysts began confessing their sins. In 2002, Gretchen Morgenson of the *New York Times* persuaded several analysts to tell her about their experiences on condition of anonymity. They spoke of being "not so much an analyst as a marketing machine" and said analysts' pay was tied to the investment-banking business they brought in.[62] Charles Gasparino of the *Wall Street Journal* uncovered documents that offered analysts "1% to 3% of the firm's net profit per transaction" or 8.5 percent of revenues that "the analyst is clearly instrumental in obtaining," or that stated "Banking Related Compensation: You will be paid banking related compensation. . . ."[63]

Bankers and clients also pressured analysts to avoid making negative or controversial comments. For example, when David Korus, an analyst at Kidder Peabody (just before the firm went under after Joseph Jett's losses), questioned some of Dell Computer's currency trading, the company threatened to sue Kidder, and barred Korus from meetings.[64] It is not surprising, then, that according to a May 1998 survey by the First Call Corporation, just under two-thirds of analyst recommendations were "buy" or "strong buy," one-third were "hold," and just one percent were "sell." In 1990, there were fifteen times more "sell" recommendations than "buys."[65] It wasn't that analysts had some evil intent; they were simply responding to an incentive system that rewarded them financially for making positive comments, and punished them for making negative ones. Analysts began inflating ratings for the same reason children acquire good manners.

In addition, as financial statements became more complex, analysts— like investors—didn't have time to scrutinize financial statements. By the late 1990s, even an experienced stock analyst would need at least a day to read an annual report carefully. But a typical analyst covered fifteen or more companies, and spent most of the day on the telephone or in meetings with investors and clients. The easy way out was to accept a company's own profit estimates and label it a "buy."

By 1998, most investment bankers recognized that a high-profile securities analyst could help them get business. After Frank Quattrone arrived at CS First Boston, he noted, "We don't compete against Morgan

Stanley—we compete against Mary Meeker." Mary Meeker was an Internet analyst who consistently received top rankings from *Institutional Investor* magazine, which rated analysts based on a poll of fund managers, just as *U.S. News & World Report* ranked colleges and graduate schools. Experts criticized these rankings, but they were the most credible and simple rankings available, and individuals trusted them. Just as Princeton University attracted students based on its number-one ranking, Mary Meeker attracted investors.

A cozy relationship with a company helped a top analyst, too. Company officials "selectively disclosed" certain information to their favorite analysts, but not to the general public. Companies also prepared their favorite analysts in advance of public announcements, so that they could adjust their expectations and accurately predict corporate-earnings announcements,[66] almost like magic.

In short, corporate clients wanted a high-profile analyst to do the "pumping" before they did the "dumping." This scheme didn't bother investors as long as stock prices continued to increase. When the analysts said "buy," they generally were giving good advice, at least in the short run.

The key difference was that now it was the analysts who were lying, instead of the companies. Years earlier, analysts had accurately predicted the "numbers" for Cendant, Waste Management, Sunbeam, and Rite Aid, too. But in those cases, companies had lied to both the analysts and to investors. Investors could continue to trust analysts, even if they did not trust the companies.

Now, the greed that earlier had consumed corporate executives was spreading to securities analysts. If CEOs and investment bankers could make tens of millions of dollars per year, why couldn't analysts do the same? All they had to do was rate companies higher than they otherwise would and persuade those companies to do business with their banks. With the links between banking and research, they could then claim the right to a ten-million-dollar-plus bonus. The downside was limited: criminal liability seemed out of the question, and they could always claim they genuinely believed in a company and were surprised—no, shocked—to see a company go under. Besides, federal regulators had shown no interest in pursuing analysts, who were, according to traditional economic theory, providing an important service to financial markets.

The analysts hadn't counted on Eliot Spitzer, the attorney general of New York. Although federal securities regulators had primary jurisdiction over financial markets, state regulators also had the ability to prosecute financial fraud. Federal and state prosecutors in New York had fought turf battles for decades, and often negotiated parallel investigations, with the U.S. attorney for Manhattan taking one case and the New York district attorney taking another.

This time, there were no negotiations. Spitzer was politically ambitious and the federal regulators—led by Harvey Pitt, the new chairman of the Securities and Exchange Commission—were not aggressively pursuing many cases. Pitt was an able lawyer, but was constrained by perceived conflicts of interest from his previous job representing the major accounting firms and Wall Street banks. That left an opening for Spitzer.

Spitzer issued subpoenas for the e-mail records of analysts at several Wall Street banks, including Merrill Lynch, where Henry Blodget—of Amazon fame—was the top Internet analyst, with a guaranteed annual compensation in 2001 of $12 million.[67] Blodget was one of the most popular Internet analysts, and Merrill had done numerous high-profile Internet deals, including eToys, Excite@Home, InfoSpace, Internet Capital Group, iVillage, Pets.com, Quokka Sports, and Webvan. Needless to say, these companies hadn't done very well, and were the subject of numerous lawsuits.

Spitzer uncovered documents confirming that the greed infecting corporate executives had spread to securities analysts. In short, the e-mails were the "smoking gun."

Spitzer submitted an affidavit to a New York court excerpting some of these e-mails. Investors read edited versions of some of them in the newspapers; others were not fit to print. But, as a whole, the lengthy affidavit was a powerful indictment of how analysts were behaving at Merrill Lynch. If other firms were the same, the system of securities ratings was totally rotten.

Like most banks, Merrill Lynch had a stock-rating system, ranging from 1 to 5. A rating of 1–1 was the highest, then 1–2, 1–3, and so forth. A rating in the general category of 1 or 2 was positive. A 3 was neutral. Merrill's Internet group never ranked companies a 4 or 5; instead, they simply stopped covering the stock.[68]

The e-mails showed that analysts were publicly issuing high ratings while privately ridiculing the same stocks. For example, analysts privately described stocks with a neutral 3 rating as "crap" or a "dog" or "going a lot lower."[69] Stocks with a positive 2 rating were repeatedly described as a "piece of shit" or "such a piece of crap."[70] Internet Capital Group, Inc., with a 2–1 rating, was described as "Going to 5." Info-Space, which Merrill gave its highest rating of 1–1, was nevertheless described in e-mails as a "piece of junk" and a "powder keg."[71]

On April 8, 2002, just after the affidavit was filed, Merrill issued a statement that "E-mails are only one piece of a continuous conversation, isolated at a single point in time—not an end conclusion." A Merrill spokesperson cautioned investors not to take these e-mails out of context, and disputed Spitzer's allegations.

But in context, the e-mails made Merrill look even worse. Consider the "Going to 5" comment about Internet Capital Group. Merrill had maintained a positive 2 rating for Internet Capital Group and kept the stock on its "top-ten" list of technology stocks, even though Henry Blodget was predicting privately that "there really is no floor to the stock."[72] But as the stock's price fell from $200 to $15, Blodget was upset by the pressure to maintain a high rating, and he threatened to start "calling the stocks like we see them, no matter what the ancillary business consequences are."[73]

Or consider the "piece of junk" and "powder keg" comments about InfoSpace, which Merrill rated a 1–1. Blodget was pressured to maintain the high rating even as InfoSpace's stock fell 80 percent, and Blodget expressed "enormous skepticism" about the stock and complained that "I'm getting killed on this thing." Why? InfoSpace was planning to buy another Internet company, Go2Net, for more than a billion dollars, and Merrill—which represented Go2Net—would earn substantial investment-banking fees from the deal. After the deal was done, Blodget finally reduced his rating.

Perhaps the most damning example—in context—was Merrill's coverage of GoTo.com, an Internet search company now known as Overture Services, Inc. In 1999, Merrill lost its pitch to do GoTo's IPO, and Merrill's analysts did not issue a rating for GoTo's stock. In 2000, Merrill again solicited investment-banking business from GoTo, and dangled a stock rating from Henry Blodget as a carrot. In September 2000, GoTo finally agreed to give Merrill some business, arranging for a European deal, and Merrill promised that Blodget would begin covering GoTo. When a fund manager asked Blodget, "What's so interesting about GoTo except banking fees?" Blodget responded, "Nothin'."[74]

It would have been very time consuming for Merrill to prepare its initial research report on the company from scratch, so GoTo executives supplied the data and comments, and actually typed changes into the draft report. They even supplied the full text of particular sections. When Kirsten Campbell, a junior Merrill research analyst, questioned whether GoTo would become profitable before 2003, and suggested it deserved only a 3 rating, she became embroiled in a dispute with GoTo's executives, who argued that the company would become profitable in 2002 and deserved a 2 rating. Campbell e-mailed Blodget that she did not "want to be a whore for f-ing management" of GoTo.

A decade earlier, Campbell would have been respected for her interest in ensuring an accurate rating. But in 2000, she was merely causing trouble by raising concerns: "We are losing people money and I don't like it. John and Mary Smith are losing their retirement because we don't want Todd [Tappin, GoTo's chief financial officer] to be mad at us." No one wanted to hear Campbell's complaints that "the whole idea that we are independent from banking is a big lie."[75] And no one supported her opinion that GoTo should be rated 3–2 at the highest.

Meanwhile, GoTo's stock had fallen below $10 a share. There was a brief circus as Merrill—which was prohibited by law from issuing new ratings on stocks with a price below $10—tried to decide what to do. Blodget, showing off his Yale education, said, "Waiting for $10 is waiting for Godot." On January 10, the price briefly hit $10, and Blodget immediately announced coverage of GoTo at a rating of 3–1, higher than Campbell had recommended.

Campbell left Merrill a few months later and, after she left, Blodget upgraded GoTo to a 2–1, and the stock rose 20 percent. Blodget then joined a group of investment bankers sponsoring a road show for a new stock issue GoTo was planning. Merrill hoped to be named lead manager for the deal, which would mean substantial investment banking fees.

When GoTo indicated it was leaning toward CS First Boston and Frank Quattrone, instead of Merrill, Blodget was irate. He immediately began preparing to downgrade GoTo from the rating of 2–1. A Merrill banker complained, "Not only did Henry Blodget show leadership by initiating on the stock near its low point but he recently upgraded it and sponsored a set of investor and Merrill sales force meetings for management in New York, which dramatically moved the stock price." One of Blodget's assistants began drafting a memorandum explaining that Merrill was downgrading the stock *on valuation,* meaning that the price had risen too much (he noted that "I don't think I've downgraded a stock on valuation since the mid-90's"). The downgrade was held in reserve until GoTo decided who to name as lead manager for its offering. During the morning of June 6, 2001, GoTo filed its stock-offering documents, listing CS First Boston as lead manager. A few hours later, Henry Blodget issued a notice that he was downgrading GoTo to a 3–1.

Blodget left Merrill a few months later, with a severance package reportedly worth $2 million.[76] Merrill ultimately agreed to pay a $10 million fine and to reform its approach to research. But many major investment banks and analysts continued to assert that their high ratings may have been wrong in hindsight, but were perfectly legal. For example, Mary Meeker, the Morgan Stanley analyst, had not been accused of any wrongdoing and continued to receive big bonuses for 2002 (although perhaps not the eight-figure bonus she had received at the peak of the Internet boom).

The final group of people profiting from the technology bubble was the most obvious: corporate executives. CEOs in 1999 were no different from CEOs a few years earlier, and all responded to the incentives created by earlier changes in law. Executive compensation rules continued to encourage stock-option grants, and CEOs with millions of options sought to increase share prices in the short run, even if they knew their actions jeopardized the long-term health of their companies. Likewise, limits on securities lawsuits continued to insulate executives, and their accountants and bankers, from liability. Not surprisingly, technology firms aggressively manipulated their financial statements, just like their predecessors at Cendant, Sunbeam, Waste Management, and Rite Aid.

There were numerous "new-economy" examples of fraud allegations, ranging from Lernout & Hauspie to W. R. Grace, from Livent to Yahoo!, from Lucent to Navigant, from MicroStrategy to Xerox. But the stories were essentially the same. To the extent the problems at these companies differed from previous frauds, SEC lawyers tried to put the problems within one of the simple categories of fraud SEC chair Arthur Levitt had outlined in his 1999 "Numbers" speech.

Consider MicroStrategy Inc., one of the many high-flying companies that did an IPO in 1998 and then crashed in 2001. Michael Jerry Saylor and Sanjeev Bansal cofounded MicroStrategy to provide custom software for companies to use in analyzing large databases. Their products were successful, and they had large corporate clients such as Kmart and NCR Corporation.

MicroStrategy's stock price told an interesting story. In June 1998, six months before Henry Blodget's Amazon prediction, MicroStrategy did an IPO at $6 per share. The stock price went up 75 percent the first day—a huge increase, but merely average compared to other IPOs at the time. For more than a year, the stock price traded in a range of $10 to $18. Suddenly, in October 1999, the shares took off like a shot, doubling within a month and reaching $110 by mid-December. By March 2000, the peak of the Internet bubble, MicroStrategy was worth $333 per share.[77] Then the stock collapsed, and by summer 2002 was back down to its IPO price of $6.

The abrupt boom and bust caused alarm bells to ring at the Securities and Exchange Commission. But interestingly, there were no sudden increases in reported profits to match the increase in stock price beginning in October 1999. Instead, MicroStrategy actually reported lower net income during the last quarter of 1999—when its stock price shot up—than in the previous quarter. Before then, net income had been increasing slowly and smoothly since 1997. In other words, Micro-Strategy's stock price was being driven by factors other than simple accounting fraud. Aggressive analysts were a likely possibility, but such a theory was outside Arthur Levitt's box.

Instead, the SEC brought a simple case, arguing that MicroStrategy had been manipulating its financial statements, typically at the end of a quarter. Some of the violations were very minor. For example, Micro-Strategy recognized $17.5 million of revenue from one contract for the quarter ended September 30, 1999, even though the contract was not signed until the early hours of October 1. A $5 million contract signed on January 3, 2000, was booked in the quarter ended December 31, 1999. A $1 million contract signed on April 2, 1999, was booked in the quarter ended March 31, 1999. These were minor instances of earnings management. In 2000, the SEC would have found similar problems at just about any company.

The SEC found some evidence supporting more serious allegations. Like Cendant, MicroStrategy was booking revenue upfront for service contracts that involved payments over time. In aggregate, the accounting manipulation led MicroStrategy to report gains, when in reality it was losing money throughout 1998 and 1999. The SEC enforcement attorneys had seen all this before, and the case moved quickly. By December 14, 2000, the top officers settled the case by agreeing to pay fines of $350,000 each.

Done this way, the MicroStrategy investigation, like other instances of accounting fraud at technology firms, became an easy case. Micro-Strategy's officers were lightly punished, but the SEC forced them to undertake some reforms, and it could claim yet another victory in the fight against corporate fraud. The case became another "win" to be presented to Congress when it considered the SEC's funding requests. In a related strategy, the SEC ran a series of nationwide Internet fraud "sweeps," in which it brought enforcement actions against people who used the Internet in various fraudulent schemes.

However, as the SEC brought more simple, easy-to-prove cases, it sent two signals to corporate executives. First, blatant accounting fraud would be punished, but only lightly. The officers of MicroStrategy, like those of other technology companies involved in similar schemes, were not charged criminally, did not go to jail, and the fines they paid were insignificant compared to the fluctuations of their stock-options positions. Second, more complex fraud would likely go unpunished. Arthur Levitt had mentioned only the easiest and most common methods of fudging numbers, methods corporate executives had been using for decades. Noticeably absent from the list were schemes involving the more complex financial instruments that chairman Levitt had repeatedly ignored during his term. Sophisticated companies were using various types of swaps, as well as Special Purpose Entities and new financial instruments called credit derivatives, to take undisclosed risks and hide losses. By sending the message that the SEC was policing a handful of straightforward accounting schemes, the SEC—perhaps inadvertently—sent a message to more sophisticated firms that they could manipulate their financial statements, as long as they did it in a way that was sufficiently complex.

These more complex schemes would haunt the financial markets after the collapses of Enron and Global Crossing. But there was a hint of additional complexities in the MicroStrategy case, buried in a section of the SEC's charges labeled "Other Accounting Issues." MicroStrategy had recognized $5 million of revenue from a deal with Sybase, Inc., in which the companies essentially swapped $5 million of software. Was it illegal for a company to record revenue from such a swap? The SEC asserted that MicroStrategy should not have recorded any revenue until it either actually used the software or sold it to another party. But how would those rules apply to other swaps, such as an agreement to deliver natural gas over a several-year period, or an agreement to exchange fiber-optic capacity over several years? In the future, such hidden arrangements would cause much greater damage to shareholders than simple accounting fraud.

Corporate executives profited from the technology boom in other ways, too. In particular, CEOs in "old-economy" businesses began buying technology companies in an attempt to increase the growth rate of their earnings. AT&T, WorldCom, Global Crossing, and others made massive investments in telecommunications infrastructure. Industrial companies—such as Enron—began shifting to an Internet platform, in an attempt to persuade investors that they, too, deserved the lofty valuations of Internet companies. Companies such as Enron also set up venture-capital subsidiaries, which they used to invest in start-up companies, just like Frank Quattrone at CS First Boston. For example, both Enron and WorldCom were major early investors in Rhythms NetConnections, which did an IPO with Salomon Brothers on April 6, 1999. One of the "lucky" investors who received shares at a price of $21 in the IPO was Bernard J. Ebbers, the CEO of WorldCom. The stock went up 229 percent the first day. WorldCom had invested $30 million and owned 8.6 percent of the company; Enron had a similar stake.[78]

During his last years as SEC chair, Arthur Levitt tried to repair the damage done earlier, primarily by attacking accounting fraud. The SEC passed several well-intentioned measures during that time. In 1998, the SEC began requiring that financial filings be written in plain English and even published a "Plain English Handbook" on its website to help companies with grammar rules. In 1999, the SEC passed rules requiring additional disclosure and prohibiting corporate executives from intentionally misstating financial results, even if the misstatements were small—or *immaterial*—relative to the size of the company. Companies had been omitting disclosures that involved less than five percent of their revenues or earnings, calling them immaterial, but the SEC stated that "exclusive reliance on this or any percentage or numerical threshold has no basis in the accounting literature or the law." In 2000, the SEC established Regulation FD, for "Fair Disclosure," which prohibited companies from selectively disclosing information to securities analysts.[79] According to this rule, known as "Reg FD," if managers wanted to disclose material information, they needed to disclose it to everyone, at the same time.

These changes were cosmetic at best, and financial statements did not become more readable or accurate, because the punishments for violating the SEC's rules were insubstantial. Corporate executives either ignored the full-disclosure rule—Reg FD—or used it as an excuse to avoid disclosing information. Moreover, Reg FD made illegal the one positive role securities analysts potentially had played: gathering hard-to-get information from companies. Not surprisingly, the quality of information about companies began to decline.

Arthur Levitt's last act as SEC chair was to oversee the passage of the Commodity Futures Modernization Act in 2000. Among other things, this law made clear that over-the-counter derivatives were exempt from regulation. It specifically included an exception for the trading of energy derivatives, a provision strongly supported by Senator Phil Gramm, whose wife Wendy had initially deregulated swaps in 1993 and had continued to serve as a member of Enron's board of directors since then.

Anyone who imagined that members of Congress, or their staffs, drafted laws regarding derivatives would have been surprised to peek inside the offices of the House Agriculture Committee during the time Congress was considering the CFMA. Instead of seeing members of Congress at work, you would have seen Mark Brickell, the lobbyist from ISDA, writing important pieces of the legislation. The legislative process has sometimes been compared to sausage-making; in the case of derivatives, the sausage makers were actually writing the law. The role of Congress was simply to look over the shoulders of the finance lobby, and nod.

Without any serious oversight, the financial markets entered a period of frenzy. The animal spirits became ubiquitous. It was as if the bartender, instead of announcing "last call," had begun giving free drinks. Until March 2000, there was a boisterous party in the financial markets. Unfortunately for most individual investors, they were the last ones to arrive, long after the securities analysts, bankers, accountants, and corporate executives already had drunk their fill. Soon, as President George W. Bush would later remark, the hangover would begin.

The first splitting headache for investors would be Enron, which had been the darling of financial markets as it grew from a modest oil-and-gas company into a global energy-and-technology behemoth. In its collapse, Enron would change the way investors thought about financial markets, although often not for the right reasons. The details of Enron's collapse were not widely understood, and investors' knee-jerk reaction to Enron was more like an alcoholic's vow never to binge again than any rational decision about the merits of Enron as an investment. Nevertheless, the fall of Enron—more than the various international crises or the bursting of the dot.com bubble—was the key signal that the market merry-making of the 1990s had ended.

THE WORLD'S GREATEST COMPANY

By now, most people have heard the basic story of Enron; how three radically different characters—the professorial founder Kenneth Lay, the free-market consultant Jeffrey Skilling, and the brash financial whiz Andrew Fastow—converted a small, natural-gas producer into the seventh-largest company in the United States, on the way generating fabulous wealth for Enron shareholders, employees, and especially insiders, who cashed out more than $1.2 billion. Most people also know about Enron's spectacular fall into bankruptcy, the thousands of layoffs, the imploded retirement plans, the controversy surrounding political contributions, and even the details of Enron executives' personal lives, such as Cliff Baxter's suicide and Rebecca Mark's alleged sexual exploits.[1]

But the basic story is unsatisfying, because by focusing on just a few transactions and people, it ignores crucial details and fails to place Enron in perspective. Was Enron a unique surprise, a "perfect storm" of financial misdealings that, although it was devastating for Enron shareholders and employees, did not matter much to the general health of financial markets? Or was Enron the tip of an iceberg of financial risk and greed, a sign of serious sickness among public corporations? To answer these questions, it was necessary to understand where Enron fit within the major changes in financial markets since the 1980s.

Simply put, fifteen years ago, Enron could not have happened. Enron was made possible by the spread of financial innovation, loss of control, and deregulation in financial markets. Enron's managers—with the assistance of accountants at Arthur Andersen and several Wall Street banks—used complex financial instruments and engineering to manipulate earnings and avoid regulation. Enron's shareholders lost control of the firm's managers, who in turn lost control of employees, especially financial officers and traders. And Enron operated in newly deregulated energy and derivatives markets, where participants were constrained only by the morals of the marketplace. By 2001, modern financial markets had changed so radically that Enron was playing on an entirely new field, in a new body designed for a new sport.

Enron's officers combined the risky strategies of Wall Street bankers with the deceitful practices of corporate CEOs in ways investors previously had not imagined. Even after more than a year of intense media scrutiny, congressional hearings, and other government investigations, most of the firm's dealings remained unpenetrated. A special committee appointed to decipher Enron's collapse spent several months reviewing documents and interviewing key parties, but its two-hundred-page report covered just a few of Enron's thousands of partnerships and was filled with caveats about its own incompleteness. The U.S. Congress held dozens of hearings, but barely scratched the surface. Incredibly, after Enron's bankruptcy, the firm's own officials were unable to grasp enough detail to issue an annual report; even with the help of a new team of accountants from PricewaterhouseCoopers, they simply could not add up the firm's assets and liabilities.

A close analysis of the dealings at Enron leads to three key conclusions, each counter to the prevailing wisdom about the company. First, Enron was, in reality, a derivatives-trading firm, not an energy firm, and it took on much more risk than anyone realized. By the end, Enron was even more volatile than a highly leveraged Wall Street investment bank, although few investors realized it.

Second, Enron's core business of derivatives trading was actually highly profitable, so profitable, in fact, that Enron almost certainly would have survived if key parties had understood the details of its business. Instead, in late 2001, Enron was hoist with its own petard, collapsing—not because it wasn't making money—but because institutional investors and credit-rating agencies abandoned the company when they learned that Enron's executives had been using derivatives to hide the risky nature of their business.

Third, Enron, arguably, was following the letter of the law in nearly

all of its dealings, including deals involving off-balance-sheet partnerships and now-infamous Special Purpose Entities. These deals, which
blatantly advantaged a few Enron employees at the expense of shareholders, nevertheless were disclosed in Enron's financial statements, and
although these disclosures were garbled and opaque, anyone reading
them carefully would have understood the basics of Enron's self-dealing
or, at a minimum, would have been warned to ask more questions before
buying the stock. To the extent Enron, its accountants, and bankers were
aggressive in transactions designed to inflate profits or hide losses, they
certainly weren't alone. Dozens of other companies were doing precisely
the same kinds of deals—some with Enron—and all had strong arguments that their deals were legal, even if they violated common sense.

In sum, relative to many of its peers, Enron was a profitable, well-run,
and law-abiding firm. That does not mean Enron was a model of corporate behavior; it obviously was not. But it does explain how Enron could
have happened. Although the media seized on Enron as the business
scandal of the decade, the truth was that Enron was no worse than
Bankers Trust, Orange County, Cendant, Long-Term Capital Management, CS First Boston, Merrill Lynch, and many other firms to follow,
including Global Crossing and WorldCom, which collapsed soon after
Enron. Enron's dealings were not illegal; they were *alegal*; and Enron
was a big story, not in itself, but as a symbol of how fifteen years of
changes in law and culture had converted reprehensible actions into
behavior that was outside the law and, therefore, seemed perfectly
appropriate, given the circumstances.

After Ken Lay received a Ph.D. in economics from the University of
Houston's night school,[2] he quickly climbed the executive ladder in the
energy industry, switching among various firms and specializing in
"bricks-and-mortar" projects, such as the conversion of a trans-gulf
Louisiana-to-Florida natural-gas pipeline. In 1985, Lay—with the assistance of Michael Milken's firm, Drexel Burnham Lambert—arranged
for Omaha-based InterNorth, one of the largest natural-gas companies
in the world, to acquire Lay's firm, Houston Natural Gas, for $2.3 bil-
lion.[3] It was a medium-sized merger by 1980s standards, but, for Ken
Lay, it was the greatest opportunity of his career. He was selected to run
the merged company, which was to be called Enteron. Fortunately, at the
last minute, someone noticed that "Enteron" meant "intestine," and the

name was quickly abridged to Enron, which—as a spokeswoman said—"has no meaning other than what we make it mean."[4]

To help move Enron from bricks and mortar to the more exciting and lucrative business of trading energy products, Lay turned to Jeffrey Skilling, a partner at the prestigious consulting firm, McKinsey & Company. Skilling was more urbane than Lay, with an M.B.A. from Harvard and experience at a London investment bank; and he provided excellent advice about how Enron could create and profit from new energy markets. Both men were zealots for deregulation and free markets, and they became close friends. Lay also relied on Michael Milken of Drexel, who provided merger advice and helped Enron sell $180 million of junk bonds. Enron became the biggest client of Drexel's eight-person Houston office.[5]

As Andy Krieger, the currency-options trader, was beginning his career at Salomon Brothers, Enron was setting up an oil-trading business, called Enron Oil, in Valhalla, New York. From 1985 to 1987, the two men who ran the operation—Louis J. Borget and Thomas Mastroeni—reported nearly as much profit from oil trading as Krieger reported from currency options. When Charlie Sanford of Bankers Trust hired Krieger and gave him hundreds of millions of dollars to use trading, Ken Lay did the same thing with Borget and Mastroeni. The limit on their trading—twelve million barrels of oil—was about a third of the value of Krieger's limit, a huge amount, given that Enron was a medium-sized energy firm, not a Wall Street bank.

For Ken Lay, trading was a dream business compared to the dirty and dull pipeline projects of his past, and an entrée into the upper echelon of corporate America. He rewarded his energy traders with a total of $12.5 million in performance bonuses in 1985 and 1986, not much below Andy Krieger's pay during the same time.[6]

A few months before Charlie Sanford learned the bad news about Krieger's trading profits, Ken Lay discovered a problem of his own at Enron Oil. As the stock market was crashing in October 1987, Lay learned that Borget and Mastroeni had positions of more than *eighty* million barrels of oil, almost seven times their limit. These positions represented roughly three months of output from the entire North Sea oil province, far more than Lay had imagined Enron Oil would trade.[7] Lay also learned that the two men had been bilking Enron for millions of dollars.

Borget and Mastroeni's scheme presaged the financing structures Enron would use a decade later. The men had set up four Panamanian companies known by the acronym "SPIT" to enter into trades with Enron, much as Andy Fastow later would set up several partnerships to do business with Enron. Borget and Mastroeni used the SPIT companies to hide huge volumes of Enron's trades and to redirect funds to themselves. The SPIT companies paid inflated fees to a London broker called Rigoil (a rather unfortunate name, given the rigged nature of the trades), which kicked back a portion of the fees to Borget and Mastroeni.[8] In all, the two men diverted more than $5 million from Enron to themselves and related parties.[9]

But the real damage was done when Enron officials tried to unwind the eighty million barrels of oil positions. The losses from those trades were around $140 million, wiping out the year's profits and nearly destroying the firm.[10]

In 1987, financial frauds were still being prosecuted with a vengeance, and a tough young federal prosecutor named James B. Comey got the case (fifteen years later, Comey would be the U.S. attorney in Manhattan, the lead federal prosecutor charged with investigating the unprecedented number of financial frauds). Comey obtained convictions, although Borget was sentenced to just one year in prison, and Mastroeni to two years' probation and 400 hours of community service.[11]

Enron's reputation was sullied, but only briefly. Yes, the company's first three years of financial reports had been false, but Enron was in good company, with Bankers Trust and Merrill Lynch, which had lost even more money during 1987 from their own trading scandals. Investors shrugged off these losses, blaming them on a few rogue traders. Enron's core energy business seemed sound, and Ken Lay even found a silver lining in the scandal, saying, "We put in place probably the best risk management and control system, not just in our business, but in any industry." Until 2001, it appeared that Ken Lay genuinely had, as he said, "learned a lot" from the experience.[12]

In addition to a control system, Lay obviously needed some new talent and, within a few months in 1990, he got it, making the two most significant hires of his career: Jeffrey Skilling and Andrew Fastow. Skilling left McKinsey, at the age of 36, to run a new finance division at Enron. Fastow, just out of Northwestern's M.B.A. program, quit his job at Continental Bank in Chicago, where he had been using some of the new structured-finance techniques that were spreading through the markets. Skilling had plans to revolutionize Enron by focusing on new markets for energy products, and by demonstrating that a modern corporation could be based on intellectual capital instead of physical assets.[13] Fastow knew less about energy, but was eager to use his creativity and expertise in structured finance. Skilling and Fastow also became friends, and soon would join Ken Lay's inner circle.

Skilling and Fastow developed relationships with dozens of commercial and investment banks, and met regularly with bankers. During the early 1990s, when Bankers Trust, First Boston, or Salomon Brothers invented a new product, it wasn't long before Enron learned about it. Enron developed especially close relationships with commercial banks, such as Citibank, J. P. Morgan, and Chase Manhattan, which were aggressively pitching investment-banking-type deals, now that regulators were permitting them to do so.

Like most oil companies, Enron created partnerships—with the assistance of major banks, accounting firms, and law firms—to do its major projects, such as oil wells and pipelines.[14] These partnerships—not Enron—borrowed money, purchased assets, and entered into leases and other contracts. There were numerous reasons for Enron to use partnerships instead of doing deals directly. By using partnerships (or other legal entities, such as trusts or corporations), Enron could create *non-recourse financing*—meaning that the company could borrow money for a project based solely on the assets of the partnership; investors in the partnership could not hold Enron responsible for the partnership's debts. Moreover, so long as Enron controlled no more than 50 percent of the partnerships, accounting rules did not require that Enron *consolidate* the partnerships' assets and liabilities; in other words, any debts belonged to the partnerships, not to Enron, and they would appear only in a footnote to Enron's financial statements, not on its balance sheet. By keeping debt off its books, Enron would appear healthier, and the all-important credit-rating agencies would give Enron a higher rating.

Enron also began using offshore Special Purpose Entities to do various over-the-counter derivatives deals, including swaps, that enabled Enron to borrow money without recording the debt. For example, in 1992 Enron and Chase Manhattan did a swap using a company called Mahonia, which had been incorporated in 1986 in the island of Jersey, a regulatory haven in Europe. Chase effectively controlled Mahonia, so in reality Enron was doing the swap with Chase (the legal independence of Mahonia potentially protected Chase from liability, an issue that would be hotly disputed beginning in 2001). At first, Enron used Mahonia to do deals that reduced its taxes. After several years, Enron also borrowed billions of dollars in *prepaid swaps* with Mahonia, organized by Chase and—after Chase's merger with J. P. Morgan—J. P. Morgan Chase (more on these prepaid swaps later).

As Enron's deals became more complex, Skilling and Fastow took over responsibility from Lay. Skilling traveled the world to sell investors on Enron's new concepts, and Fastow stayed in Houston to deal with the nuts and bolts of various financial issues. Meanwhile, Lay developed connections among business and political leaders. Lay chaired the 1992 Republican National Convention in Houston and sat with George H. W. Bush in the presidential box.[15] After Bush lost the election in 1992, Lay maintained strong ties to the Bush family, hiring two of Bush's former cabinet ministers and his former director of operations. Bush's sons lobbied on behalf of Enron: Neil and Marvin in Kuwait and George W. in Argentina.[16] Lay also rewarded Wendy Gramm, Bush's chair of the Commodity Futures Trading Commission, with a position on Enron's board, just weeks after she had pushed through the regulatory exemption for over-the-counter derivatives, which were becoming an important part of Enron's business.

By 1993, Enron was an active participant in derivatives markets, along with just about every other company, investment fund, and governmental entity in the United States. As Gibson Greetings was buying complex swaps from Bankers Trust, Orange County was buying structured notes from Merrill Lynch, and John Meriwether was soliciting investors in Long-Term Capital Management, Enron was arranging the complex deal that the public would seize on as the cause of Enron's demise. It was called the Joint Energy Development Investments Limited Partnership, or JEDI. Enron's equal partner in JEDI was the California Public Employees' Retirement System, known as CalPERS. Enron and CalPERS each invested $250 million, and they shared control.

As with its other partnerships, Enron excluded JEDI from its financial statements. Again, the well-accepted rationale was that, because Enron controlled only 50 percent of JEDI, accounting rules did not require that Enron consolidate JEDI's assets and liabilities. Instead, some of JEDI's numbers were included in a footnote to Enron's annual report.

According to efficient-market theory, it shouldn't have mattered where JEDI appeared in Enron's annual report. As long as it was disclosed somewhere, the value of JEDI—positive or negative—should have been reflected in Enron's stock price. In other words, Enron's executives didn't need to feel any qualms about burying JEDI in a footnote, because sophisticated investors would spot the disclosure and buy or sell Enron stock until its price was accurate. Thus, efficient-market theory reinforced a culture of following the bare letter of the law in complex financial transactions. Doing more simply wasn't necessary.

For efficient-market theorists, Enron was a poster child: a profitable, flexible, and efficient firm operating in new, unregulated markets. On December 9, 1997, economist Myron Scholes, then at Long-Term Capital Management, delivered a lecture in Stockholm, Sweden, after he received the Alfred Nobel Memorial Prize in Economic Sciences for his work in options pricing. He singled out two companies—General Electric and Enron—as having the ability to outcompete existing financial firms, and noted, "Financial products are becoming so specialized that, for the most part, it would be prohibitively expensive to trade them in organized markets." According to Scholes, Enron's trading of unregulated over-the-counter energy derivatives was a new model that someday would replace the organized securities exchanges.

Enron was every bit as sophisticated and aggressive as General Electric, and both companies were expanding outside the United States during the mid-1990s, just as financial risks were spreading to Mexico, East Asia, and beyond. Enron borrowed billions of dollars to fund overseas ventures ranging from a Brazilian electric plant to a United Kingdom water company.[17] (Ultimately, Enron would lose much of that money.)

The daisy-chain deals overseas were just as complex as the structured transactions developing in the United States. For example, in 1996, Enron Europe, with the help of Goldman Sachs and J. P. Morgan, sold a stake in a power plant to an entity called Thornbeam, which sold the stake to a Dutch company called Strategic Money Management, which then issued AAA-rated notes, backed by the power plant's assets, to a leading bank.[18] Andy Fastow also created a complex structured transaction in which Enron used a partnership called Marlin to put money into the Atlantic Water Trust, one of Enron's many subsidiaries, which in turn invested in Azurix, a subsidiary that owned a majority of the facilities of a United Kingdom water company known as Wessex. In an interview with *CFO Magazine,* Fastow boasted about the deal: "What we did is we set up a trust, issued Enron Corp. shares into the trust, and then the trust went to the capital markets and raised debt against the shares in the trust, using the shares in the trust as collateral."[19] In other words, instead of borrowing money, Enron was using its own shares to pay for its overseas investments, a controversial practice contrary to the spirit of accounting rules, even though it was quite common and, arguably, within the letter of the law. No worries for Enron, though, Fastow assured *CFO Magazine*'s readers: "We have disclosures about it in the footnotes, which help our investors and the rating agencies understand all of this."

The legal changes of 1994 and 1995—including restrictions on securities lawsuits, incentives for companies to compensate executives with stock options, and various forms of deregulation—enticed Enron executives to take advantage of accounting rules, and contributed to the company's developing mercenary culture. In 1994, Enron created an entity called Enron Capital LLC, incorporated in the regulatory haven of the Turks and Caicos, to deal in financial markets without complying with U.S. securities laws.[20] In 1996, the Federal Energy Regulatory Commission began deregulating energy markets, in response to lobbying from Ken Lay and other energy firms. The more Enron did deals in the shadow of the law, the less legal rules seemed to matter. At the same time, most Enron executives received substantial numbers of stock options, which rewarded them for pushing short-term accounting profits. The options grants ranged from five percent of annual base salary to hundreds of thousands of options for top executives, far more than their counterparts at Cendant, Waste Management, Sunbeam, and Rite Aid. In all, Enron's executives would make more than a billion dollars from these options.

Enron's risk-management manual explicitly encouraged employees to adhere to the letter of accounting rules, even if they were contrary to economic reality. It stated: "Reported earnings follow the rules and principles of accounting. The results do not always create measures consistent with underlying economics. However, corporate management's performance is generally measured by accounting income, not underlying economics. Risk management strategies are therefore directed at accounting rather than economic performance." In other words, Enron managers were encouraged to focus on the accounting effect of their decisions more than their real economic impact. This was true even when Enron was dealing with issues of risk, where real economic impact should have mattered more to the company than accounting disclosures.

As Enron's board of directors became more international, to reflect the company's new global businesses, it became less effective in monitoring

Enron's management. Lord John Wakeham, former leader of the British House of Commons, and minister of energy, previously had permitted Enron to build England's largest power plant at Teesside, and now received even more money as a consultant to Enron than as a board member—both at the same time.[21] The five-member audit committee of Enron's board of directors was hardly full of watchdogs, either. Ronnie C. Chan, chairman of the Hang Lung Group in Hong Kong, and Paulo V. Ferraz Pereira, a senior officer of Group Bozano in Brazil, lived outside the United States and had little experience with U.S. accounting. Wendy Gramm, the former chair of the Commodity Futures Trading Commission, was conflicted as a direct beneficiary of Enron's political and charitable largesse. Her free-market policy group in Washington, D.C., received $50,000 from Enron and another $10,000 from a foundation set up by Ken Lay. Her husband, Texas senator Phil Gramm, received $97,350 of aggregate donations from Enron, plus additional funds raised by Mark Brickell, the J. P. Morgan lobbyist, one of Wendy Gramm's comrades.[22] (Not surprisingly, the newspaper *Barron's* called the Gramms "Mr. and Mrs. Enron.") John Mendelsohn, president of the Anderson Cancer Center at the University of Texas, benefited indirectly from Enron's $1.6 million of donations to the Center.

That left the chair of the audit committee, Robert K. Jaedicke, a respected emeritus professor of accounting at Stanford. In spite of his accounting expertise, Jaedicke did not grasp the complex disclosure issues presented by the managers he was supposed to oversee and control. Jaedicke also made nearly $1 million from Enron stock—a lot of money for an accounting professor, even one who had been the dean at Stanford Business School during the 1980s.

Enron's anything-goes atmosphere was ideal for Jeff Skilling and Andy Fastow. Skilling was promoted to president and chief operating officer, and became Ken Lay's clear No. 2 man in 1997. After Fastow raised more than $5 billion for Enron in 1996, in dozens of financings, Lay promoted him to senior vice president of finance, where he became the youngest member of Lay's inner circle, at the age of 35. Incredibly, Enron—now a large multinational firm—still did not have a chief financial officer, so Lay quickly created the position and put Fastow in it.

With Skilling and Fastow at the helm, Lay disengaged even more, turning to his social and political circles, and lobbying his friend, Texas governor George W. Bush. When Lay and Skilling were together, it often was merely for public appearances: for example, they posed for photographs while playing basketball with members of the Houston Rockets, who periodically stopped by Enron's headquarters during the lunch hour to play on a special court set up in the street in front of Enron's building.

Meanwhile, Enron was changing its face. In 1997, Jeff Skilling unveiled a major new advertising campaign, complete with television advertising during the Super Bowl and a newly redesigned corporate logo (the one that later became known as the "crooked E"). Skilling described the ad campaign as the beginning of a process "to take Enron from being one of the least well-known large companies, to joining McDonald's, Coca-Cola and American Express as one of the most recognized names in the world."[23] Enron even purchased the rights to name the Houston Astros' baseball stadium, which became Enron Field.

As the Internet IPO market began its boom, Enron strived to look like a dot.com, and began betting its future on technology and the Internet. Television monitors scattered throughout Enron's headquarters in downtown Houston flashed the company's stock price. Inspirational messages played inside the elevators. There was an on-site gym, and even a subsidized Starbucks coffee shop. Enron was named one of the best companies to work for in the United States. The retirement plan was generous, especially given that the stock price was rising. Every year, young executives received big bonuses and more stock options. And every year, the number of new Porsches and BMWs in the Enron garage multiplied.

Enron's board increased the incentives for executives to bet shareholders' money on speculative ventures by granting huge numbers of stock options. In 1998, Enron granted almost 16 million options to its employees and executives.[24] In 1999 and 2000, those grants more than doubled, to roughly five percent of Enron's outstanding shares. By Enron's own estimate, these options would have reduced Enron's earnings by almost ten percent if their cost had been reflected in Enron's financial statements.[25] (Fortunately for Enron, Congress had defeated the proposal to include stock options as an expense.) Moreover, because options were a one-way bet, unlike stock, they created incentives for the options holders to take risks that shareholders might not support, and to reduce dividend payments, which benefited only holders of stock, not options.

In addition to granting these options, Enron entered into derivatives deals to ensure that it would have adequate shares to cover the options by agreeing to purchase its own shares in the future. These *forward purchases* of its own shares were like a cash repurchase of shares in the open market, except that they didn't require any cash. Moreover, because these forward purchases involved over-the-counter derivatives, not actual securities, they did not need to be disclosed in Enron's financial statements. By agreeing to buy its own shares in the future, Enron—and its executives—had made a huge, secret bet on Enron stock, without using any of Enron's precious cash.

Unfortunately, beginning in 1997, Enron lost most of the risky bets it made, costing the firm billions of dollars. First, Enron bet on the Internet by setting up a venture-capital firm to invest in Internet-related companies, and by putting its own trading operations on an Internet platform. Second, Enron expanded its trading from natural-gas and electricity derivatives—its primary areas of expertise—to new products such as fiber-optic capacity for telecommunications and even derivatives based on the weather. Third, Enron permitted employees to create and invest in new partnerships that did business with Enron, and to use these partnerships to manipulate Enron's financial statements. For Enron, these deals were three strikes.

The great paradox of Enron was that, notwithstanding these awful decisions, Enron's core business—natural-gas and electricity derivatives trading—generated enough money to offset its other failed efforts, including billions of dollars in profits during Enron's last years. By August 1999, Enron had withdrawn entirely from oil and natural-gas production. Instead, Enron made money by exchanging billions of dollars of long-term natural-gas and electricity derivatives, in which it committed to buy or sell energy products of various types for up to ten or more years. Enron's traders routinely took speculative positions that were much riskier than those Louis Borget and Thomas Mastroeni had taken at Enron Oil more than a decade earlier. In the developing energy markets, Enron's traders were in basically the same position Andy Krieger had been in years earlier: there were no organized exchanges for trading long-term energy contracts, and Enron traders could make huge sums trading with relatively less sophisticated market participants and taking advantage of market inefficiencies. Enron shareholders supposedly didn't need to worry too much about the risks of these trading operations, because Ken Lay had learned his lesson about trading risks with Enron Oil, and had committed to improved controls.

From the managers' perspective, the problem with Enron's derivatives trading was that even successful trading firms were not highly valued in the market. Investors generally believed that markets were efficient, and that trading made big money only when traders took on substantial risks.

Simply put, investors didn't value firms that took on substantial trading risks. Whereas a trading firm might have a price/earnings ratio of 10 or perhaps 15, a typical technology firm had a P/E ratio of 60 or more. To maximize its stock price, Enron executives needed to make it appear to investors that earnings were increasing because of the firm's successes in a range of technology businesses, not because of profits from its core business of derivatives trading. To the extent Enron appeared to be a technology firm, not a trading firm, its stock price would rise, and the executives' options would be worth more money.

As Enron shifted to new technology businesses, while hiding its derivatives trading, the perception of the firm's technology investments and the reality of its trading business were in intractable conflict. As a technology firm, Enron needed to borrow billions of dollars to pay for new investments and infrastructure. But as a trading firm, it needed to keep debt low, to maintain a high credit rating. This conflict eventually would tear Enron apart.

In the late 1990s, Enron Capital, the company's venture-capital fund, began investing in start-up technology companies, just as Frank Quattrone's fund at CS First Boston had bought shares of his clients' start-up companies before they did IPOs. For example, in March 1998, Enron invested $10 million in Rhythms NetConnections, an Internet service provider and a potential competitor of Netscape, the company whose IPO had marked the beginning of the Internet boom.

Enron's point man for Rhythms NetConnections was Ken L. Harrison, the former CEO of Portland General, an energy company Enron had just acquired. Harrison had just joined Enron's board and, after Enron invested in Rhythms NetConnections, he joined that board, too. Harrison was an ideal overseer, given that he had been named as a defendant several years earlier in a major financial-fraud case related to Bonneville Pacific, an energy company in which Portland General owned a substantial stake. Bonneville Pacific had raised several hundred million dollars, allegedly manipulated its earnings by using off-balance-sheet vehicles, and then declared bankruptcy—the same things Enron later would do. Portland General had settled the litigation while Ken Harrison was CEO. Given that both Ken Lay and Ken Harrison had been through painful financial scandals, it seemed likely that Enron would be safe from any similar scheme related to Rhythms NetConnections.

Enron originally had purchased shares of Rhythms NetConnections for less than $2. On April 6, 1999, Rhythms NetConnections did its IPO with Salomon Brothers, offering shares to the public for $21. At the end of the first day of trading, the stock was at $69, a big jump even for a late-1990s IPO. Enron had made 35 times its money on a $10 million investment—the same payoff as betting on a single number on a roulette wheel—and suddenly it had a $300 million gain, which represented almost half of its earnings from the previous year. (WorldCom and its CEO, Bernard J. Ebbers, made even more money from the IPO[26]—more on that in the next chapter.)

The huge paper gain put Enron in an awkward situation. Enron couldn't realize the gain right away, because as an insider of Rhythms NetConnections, it was prohibited from selling the shares during a lock-up period of 180 days. But even if Enron could have sold the shares, it wouldn't have wanted to do so. Why? A $300 million gain on a speculative Internet stock was not the kind of steady growth from technology investments Enron wanted to show investors. Securities analysts and credit-rating agencies wanted to see increases in income from operations, not one-time speculative gains. Solid earnings would help Enron's share price, but a several-hundred-million-dollar roulette win would not.

Andy Fastow, having sharpened his creative skills in structured finance with JEDI and other deals, had the solution. The road map came from a deal he had just done in 1997 to buy out CalPERS, the original investor in JEDI (CalPERS insisted that Enron buy its share of JEDI before it would do JEDI II, a sequel). Recall that Enron had kept JEDI off its balance sheet because CalPERS—an independent party—owned and controlled half of it. Fastow proposed replacing CalPERS with a newly created partnership called Chewco Investments L.P. (named after Chewbacca, the furry Wookie from the movie *Star Wars,* a foolish choice, given that Chewco and JEDI—names derived from the same movie—were supposed to be independent). Chewco would own and control 50 percent of JEDI, so that Enron could keep JEDI off its books.

The machinations of the JEDI-Chewco deal were widely publicized, but the rationale for the deal was not. For more than a decade, creative financiers had been dealing with the recurring problem of finding an independent source of funding, so that a company could move liabilities off the balance sheet. The problem generally arose in the context of leases, and by 1997 it applied to nearly every financial asset. Enron's attempt to find an independent investor in Chewco was an object lesson

in how apparently obscure legal rules were causing new financial products to mutate in wild and unanticipated ways. The solution to the problem involved the Special Purpose Entity.

In the 1980s, airlines often entered into long-term leases for their airplanes, instead of borrowing money to buy them. If the other party to
the lease bore a substantial amount of risk with respect to the value of
the leased planes, it didn't seem fair to require the airline to record the
entire value of the planes as an asset and the entire value of the amount it
owed on the lease as a liability. Instead, the lease would remain "off balance sheet."

But what if the outside party bore little risk, so that the airline essentially owned the airplanes even though it technically had entered into a
lease? If accountants permitted *any* lease to be off balance sheet, companies would start doing leases in droves, and investors would never know
what companies actually owned and owed. To provide some guidance to
leasing companies, the Emerging Issues Task Force of the Financial
Accounting Standards Board—the same board that unsuccessfully proposed that companies count the value of stock options as an expense—
issued an opinion called EITF 90-15, which said, essentially, that
companies could move leases off their books if outsiders bore at least
three percent of the residual risk of the lease.

This accounting opinion came to be known as the *three percent rule,*
and companies began applying the opinion to transactions other than
leases, arguing, for example, that companies did not need to record their
dealings with a partnership if an outsider owned more than three percent. Some creative financiers argued that if the rationale applied to an
existing partnership, a company also should be able to create a *new*
partnership, sell an outside interest of three percent, and then remove
the related assets and liabilities from its books.

The Securities and Exchange Commission was uncomfortable with
three percent as a one-size-fits-all bright line. Why not five percent? Or
why not a higher percentage for risky deals, and a lower percentage for
less volatile ones? Notwithstanding these concerns, the SEC's Office of
the Chief Accountant wrote a guidance letter in 1991, sanctioning the
three percent rule, but noting that "a greater investment may be necessary depending on the facts and circumstances."

With that mixed blessing, the three percent rule became like law, even
though there was no real law or even any clear pronouncement by securities regulators supporting it. Instead, parties relied on letters from private

law firms opining that it was appropriate in a given deal to remove assets and liabilities from a company's balance sheet, citing EITF 90-15 and the 1991 SEC guidance letter. The three percent rule was an unsteady foundation for trillions of dollars of structured transactions, but that was precisely what it supported. For companies eager to use newly created SPEs to repackage and sell off mortgages, car loans, and numerous other financial interests, the three percent rule was plenty of justification for moving debts off their balance sheets. A typical SPE closely tracked the rule, with 97 percent debt and three percent stock. The three percent stock was supposed to be owned by an independent, outside party, although frequently it was held by a charitable trust or other entity related to the parties doing the deal. As SPEs became more common, financial firms pushed the envelope on the definition of "independent, outside investment."

Chewco's "outside" investors were not really independent of Enron, but they arguably satisfied the rules. Enron cobbled together a three percent investment from Barclays Bank and some partnerships related to an Enron employee, Michael Kopper, and his domestic partner. The investment was not really at risk, because Enron put up cash collateral to guarantee repayment. And the investment was not really independent, because Michael Kopper worked for Enron. But in the new financial-market culture, reality didn't matter. The key question was whether the deal technically satisfied the rules. Technically, Barclays and the partnerships controlled Chewco. And technically, their money was labeled an outside "equity" investment, even though it was not really at risk.

With these arrangements, Enron could at least argue that Chewco had an outside investor with control. This argument might seem a thin reed, but it was entirely reasonable given how other companies were using supposedly "outside" investors in SPEs. Moreover, it wasn't up to Enron to decide whether a deal satisfied the SPE rules. That was the job of Enron's auditor, Arthur Andersen. Andersen's decision to approve of the accounting treatment for JEDI and Chewco was mired in controversy, and Andersen later claimed it would have made a different decision if Enron had disclosed key details regarding the collateral for the Barclays loan and the role of Michael Kopper and his domestic partner. But at that time, Andersen advised Enron that Chewco qualified as an SPE and, based on this advice, Enron continued to exclude JEDI from its financial statements, reporting its 50 percent ownership only in a footnote.

The bottom line of all these intricate dealings was simple. Enron substituted one outside investor in JEDI for another. And it kept JEDI—which it could now continue to use to make various energy investments—off its balance sheet.

Enron's dealings in JEDI and Chewco later horrified many individual investors, but the truth was that they were arguably legal, not especially unusual, mostly disclosed, and largely irrelevant to Enron's collapse. There were enough key details about JEDI and Chewco in the footnotes to Enron's financial statements to warn off any investor who read them. And even if Enron had included JEDI in its financial statements, its reported income still would have been almost a billion dollars a year, and its reported debt would have been at reasonable levels. Indeed, after Enron later revised its financial statements to include JEDI, the effects were insubstantial compared to the magnitude of Enron's derivatives trading. To the extent that Enron's financial statements were inaccurate, the primary reason was not that Enron was violating the rules; instead, it was that the rules of the game had changed so much that companies were permitted to create a fictional accounting reality, which didn't need to comport with economic reality.

After the JEDI-Chewco deal, Fastow began developing even more complicated transactions, with strange names such as Enron Cash Co. No. 2 or, more creatively, Obi-1 Holdings LLC and Kenobe Inc., keeping with the *Star Wars* motif.[27] Fastow was obviously good at structured finance. In 1999, he received a major award for excellence as a CFO, which stressed his "unique financing techniques."[28]

With his new-found expertise, Fastow finally had the road map for dealing with Enron's $300 million gain on Rhythms NetConnections, and for making himself some easy money. Fastow's fingerprints were all over his newest partnership, called LJM; even the initials stood for the names of his wife and two daughters. Fastow would be directly involved in LJM, even though the securities laws would require that Enron disclose his involvement. In the Chewco deal, Michael Kopper, not Fastow, had been directly involved, because Kopper was a lower-level employee who fell outside the scope of disclosure rules.[29] But Kopper and the related partnerships had made $10 million on a $125,000 "outside" investment—why should Kopper, Fastow's assistant, make all the money?[30]

Fastow persuaded Enron's board of directors that LJM would be of great value to Enron as a purchaser of Enron's assets, a partner with Enron in new investments, and a counterparty to derivatives agreements to help Enron hedge its risks.[31] Fastow also asked the board to give him permission to keep a percentage of the profits from LJM's deals, even though it created a blatant conflict of interest.[32] The proposal sailed through Enron's hands-off board, with a minimal requirement that Enron officers review LJM's transactions. The directors later approved a second, similar partnership called LJM2 Co-Investment, L.P. They apparently never imagined that Fastow would make more than $45 million from the partnerships.[33]

The details of the two LJM partnerships were unknown to Enron's shareholders, but they were palpable among Wall Street firms, which funded the bulk of the partnerships' outside investment. LJM was a relatively small partnership, with just two outside investors putting in $7.5 million each: ERNB Ltd., a partnership set up by CS First Boston, and Campsie Limited, a partnership set up by National Westminster, a British bank.[34] Fastow also invested $1 million of his own money, bringing the total amount of money raised for LJM in 1999 to $16 million.

LJM2 was more than twenty times the size of LJM, with several hundred million dollars of outside investment from a Who's Who of the financial markets: investment banks such as Merrill Lynch; commercial banks such as J. P. Morgan Chase; insurance companies such as American International Group; charitable institutions such as the John D. and Catherine T. MacArthur Foundation; retirement funds such as the Arkansas Teacher Retirement System; and even several wealthy individuals such as Leon Levy, former chairman of the Oppenheimer mutual funds, John Friedenrich, a prominent Silicon Valley lawyer, Jack Nash, a New York hedge-fund manager, and even ninety-six employees of Merrill Lynch.[35]

LJM used its $16 million to purchase from Enron the rights to 3.4 million Enron shares, worth $276 million. Of course, LJM didn't have $276 million in cash to pay for the shares, so it agreed to make payments over time. Enron imposed a restriction on the shares, so that LJM could not sell them for four years, and therefore deemed that the restricted shares were worth only 60 percent of their value in the market. That restriction, and the resulting discount, were a substantial windfall to LJM. Assuming LJM was willing to hold the Enron shares for four years, they would be worth 40 percent more than it had paid for them, even if Enron's share price only remained constant.

Then, Enron entered into several derivatives deals with LJM and an LJM subsidiary called "Swap Sub," purportedly to hedge the risk of Enron's stake in Rhythms NetConnections. Enron was still barred from selling the Rhythms NetConnections stock during the six-month lockup period, but nothing prevented it from buying a put option from Swap Sub, which would give Enron a five-year right to sell 5.4 million shares of Rhythms NetConnections if its price fell below $56 per share. Effectively, the put option—the right to sell the stock—was an insurance policy on Enron's investment.

These deals seemed to benefit both Enron and LJM. Enron unlocked some of its gains from Rhythms NetConnections. When the lockup period expired, Enron unwound the deals with Swap Sub and cancelled the put option. But, this time, Enron calculated the value of the put option assuming the shares were unrestricted, so that LJM and Swap Sub received the higher, unrestricted value; in other words, LJM made money when Enron was moving in, and when it was moving out. Although Arthur Andersen apparently allowed Enron to make this calculation based on the higher unrestricted value, which obviously took money from Enron and gave it to LJM, Andersen required that subsequent deals be done using the restricted value.[36]

All of these transactions were, essentially, just Enron trading with itself, because LJM's ability to pay Enron depended on the price of the rights to the 3.4 million Enron shares it originally received, and continued to hold, as its major asset. In other words, if Enron's stock price declined, so would LJM's assets, and then LJM would not be able to repay its debts to Enron. This was why accounting rules typically did not allow companies to use their own stock to influence their earnings: from an economic perspective, such deals were a sham. Nevertheless, Arthur Andersen permitted Enron to treat the LJM partnerships at arm's length, and to keep the deals with LJM off its books. Technically, Enron wasn't using its stock—it was using derivatives instead (the rights to receive its stock in the future).

The Rhythms NetConnections deal was just one of dozens of transactions Enron entered into with LJM and LJM2. They were deals involving various assets, debt, stock, loans, and derivatives, including put and call options. Many of these trades also were sweetheart deals for investors in the LJM partnerships. For example, in 1999, when Enron purchased a portfolio of corporate loans and repackaged them in a Collateralized Loan Obligation—a deal similar to the Collateralized Bond Obligations pioneered by First Boston and Salomon Brothers—Enron could not find a buyer for the riskiest securities in the deal, so it sold those securities to LJM2. When the transaction later deteriorated, Enron repurchased those securities at their full value.[37]

Several of Fastow's employees also became involved in the LJM transactions. Ben Glisan, Enron's treasurer, and Kristina Mordaunt, an Enron lawyer who worked for Fastow, each invested $5,800 in a partnership called Southampton Place—after an exclusive Houston neighborhood. Southampton Place was involved in several dubious deals with the LJM partnerships: it bought CS First Boston and National Westminster's stakes in LJM and repaid some of LJM2's loans, using Enron's backing and even a new subsidiary of Southampton Place, called Southampton K ("K" for Michael Kopper).[38] Southampton Place made so much money that, within a year, it paid Glisan and Mordaunt each $1 million for their shares.[39] Their annualized return was more than 16,000 percent. With those returns, it wasn't hard to find "outside" investors.

The last step in the evolution of Fastow's structured finance deals involved four partnerships appropriately named "Raptors," for the highly evolved species of dinosaur that appeared in the movie *Jurassic Park* (Enron's officers apparently had decided to switch from *Star Wars*). There were four Raptors, which were used in various daisy-chain deals with LJM2. The myriad Raptor deals involved various types of complex derivatives and were almost incomprehensible; they were a major reason Enron was unable to produce an annual report for 2001. To give an example, one Raptor deal involved Enron lending money to Kafus Industries Ltd., a Vancouver paper-products company, in exchange for shares of Kafus, which Enron sold to SE Thunderbird LP, which was controlled by Blue Heron I LLC, which was controlled by Whitewing Associates LP, which was controlled by Whitewing Management LLC, which was controlled by Egret I LLC, all of which were listed among more than 3,000 affiliated firms in Enron's annual report filed in 2001—but without enough detail to enable an investor to figure out what Enron was doing.[40]

The Raptors satisfied the three percent rule with a neat trick: by having LJM2 act as their "outside" investor. It was a diabolical and intricate scheme. First, Enron invested in the Raptors by contributing derivatives based on Enron shares—or, in the case of Raptor III, shares of The New Power Company, a technology stock Enron had purchased before its IPO in October 2000. Then, LJM2 "invested" $30 million, in each Raptor, in exchange for a promise to repay the $30 million, plus $11 million of interest. Next, the Raptors sold a put option to Enron, giving Enron the right to sell its shares to the Raptors. Enron paid each Raptor $41 million for this put option, which the Raptors then forwarded to LJM2, thereby satisfying the Raptor's obligation to repay the $30 million plus interest. The initial $30 million "investment" by LJM2 remained within the Raptor.

In other words, the LJM2 "investors" were not investors at all; they had no money at risk and were simply temporary placeholders to satisfy the three percent rule. Their $30 million made a quick round-trip through Enron, picking up an extra $11 million along the way. For their willingness to "lend" $30 million to LJM2, they made $11 million—a 35 percent return—virtually overnight.

The accounting treatment of the Raptors was a hotly debated topic within Arthur Andersen. One Andersen partner, Carl Bass, said the Raptors had "no substance," and argued that Enron should be required to report the transactions. Enron's chief accountant, Richard A. Causey, complained about Bass, and Andersen removed him from Enron's account in March 2001.[41] Enron and Andersen ultimately decided that the $30 million "outside" investment remaining in the Raptors satisfied the SPE rules.

Enron used the Raptors to inflate the value of its own assets by selling a small portion of those assets to a Raptor at an artificially high price, and then revaluing the lion's share of the assets Enron still held, at that high price. As with the other partnerships, Enron disclosed some details about these deals in the footnotes to its financial statements, albeit in a convoluted way. For example, anyone who cared to scrutinize page 49, footnote 16, of Enron's annual report for 2000 would find the following two sentences: "In 2000, Enron sold a portion of its dark fiber inventory to the Related Party in exchange for $30 million cash and a $70 million note receivable that was subsequently repaid. Enron recognized gross margin of $67 million on the sale."[42] Anyone who thought carefully about these sentences would be very worried about the nature of Enron's *Related Party* deals, and would be skeptical of whether Enron really was making money in its new telecommunications business.

The Related Party was LJM2, although it wasn't necessary to know that detail to be worried. The evident bottom line was that Enron had sold something called "dark fiber" for $100 million—$30 million in cash, plus $70 million in a note that would be paid over time—and made $67 million on the sale. In other words, Enron had sold something it valued at $33 million for *triple* its value. And it had sold that something to a Related Party.

Dark fiber referred to telecommunications rights Enron had begun trading as part of its foray into the broadband business. In this business, Enron traded the right to transmit data through various fiber-optic cables, more than 40 million miles of which various companies had installed in the United States.[43] Only a small percentage of these cables were *lit*—meaning they could transmit the light waves required to carry Internet data; the vast majority of cables were still awaiting upgrades, and were "dark." As one might expect, the rights to transmit over dark fiber were very difficult to value.

It was difficult to triple the value of a short-term investment in any business, especially telecommunications, which was struggling at the time. It was apparent that Enron had sold dark fiber at an incredibly inflated price. The inevitable conclusion was either that Enron had found a chump to buy some of its assets, or that Enron was engaging in some dubious, undisclosed side deal with LJM2.

Andy Fastow and LJM2 certainly were not chumps. Instead, LJM2 was persuaded to pay an inflated price for the dark fiber, because Enron entered into a *make whole* derivative deal with LJM2: protecting it from a loss by agreeing to pay LJM2's investors with additional Enron stock. In other words, when the dark fiber inevitably declined from its inflated value, the LJM2 investors wouldn't care, because Enron would make them whole.

This meant that Enron retained the economic risk associated with the dark fiber. As the value of dark fiber plunged during 2000, Enron would be obligated to deliver more stock to LJM2, offsetting Enron's illusory gain from the original sale of dark fiber to LJM2. Yet, because LJM2 was an SPE—like Chewco and JEDI—Enron would not have to report the loss on its make-whole derivatives contract—that remained hidden inside LJM2. Instead, Enron would report only the gain from its purported sale of dark fiber to LJM2 at the inflated price. Thus, Enron and LJM2 became a financial hall of mirrors, where Enron looked profitable regardless of which way investors looked.

In all, Enron committed to deliver almost $4 billion worth of its own stock in make-whole derivatives deals.[44] With the stock price near its highs, these obligations amounted to just a few percent of Enron's outstanding shares. But if Enron's stock price fell, the obligations would increase, substantially diluting the holdings of Enron's shareholders by requiring Enron to give more shares to its partnerships. Because the deals were unregulated derivatives with SPEs, Enron would not need to report the details of these transactions in its financial statements.[45]

Enron's sale of dark fiber to LJM2 also magically generated the appearance of a fair market price, which Enron then could use in valuing any *remaining* dark fiber it held. Enron could pretend that the sale to LJM2 was just like any other sale in the market. LJM2 had, in a sense, "validated" a higher price for the dark fiber in Enron's inventory, and Enron could then use that inflated price to make its assets appear more valuable.

Suppose Enron sold one unit of dark fiber to LJM2 for $30—triple its actual value—using this scheme. Now, Enron had an argument that each remaining unit of dark fiber also was worth $30. If Enron's assets were difficult to value—as dark fiber was—Enron could inflate the value of its assets in reliance on the "market" prices established by the deals between Enron and LJM2.

Legally, the valuation might be defensible. Economically, the valuation was preposterous, and Enron, eventually, would need to recognize a loss to offset the false profit it had booked. Until then, as Enron's risk-management manual had instructed, accounting numbers were more important than economic reality.

The inflated value of the dark-fiber deal between Enron and LJM2 would be the basis for a much larger, $500 million dark-fiber swap between Enron and Qwest Communications, the dominant telephone company in the western part of the United States.[46] During the second quarter of 2001, Enron had been negotiating to sell its dark-fiber capacity to a *real* company—not one of its Related Party partnerships—so that it could *really* avoid a loss on its foolish telecommunications investments. However, talks with Qwest and Global Crossing had broken down. Late during the third quarter of 2001, Qwest finally became desperate for a deal that would generate some reported revenue. On September 10, Qwest had reduced its profit forecast by half a billion dollars and, by the end of September, it was obvious that it wouldn't meet that lower estimate, either.

On September 30, 2001—the last day of the quarter—Enron and Qwest agreed to the swap. Qwest would buy $308 million of Enron's dark-fiber capacity, including lines running from Salt Lake City to New Orleans. Enron would buy some of Qwest's lines for $196 million. It was unclear why Qwest—which had just announced plans to fire 4,000 employees—needed the new 5,500 miles of dormant capacity, especially in New Orleans, far away from its primary customers. But it was absolutely plain why Qwest was doing the deal: it booked $86 million of the amount Enron paid as revenue in the third quarter. Enron recorded the revenue from its sale of dark fiber, just as it had done on the previous deal with LJM2. It was all eerily similar to MicroStrategy's swap a few years earlier.

Arthur Andersen, which audited both Enron and Qwest, blessed this accounting treatment, and both Enron and Qwest marked to market the value of their positions, recording an accounting profit even though they were not receiving any cash. It appeared that both companies were planning to record the expenses related to these deals in later quarters, but neither would survive for long enough to know for sure. (In late 2002, Qwest would admit to other swaps and reduce its reported profit even more.) The Enron-Qwest swap illustrated the accounting professor's admonition that profit is an opinion, but cash is a fact.

Accounting numbers were especially important at EnronOnline and Enron Energy Services, two Enron businesses that appeared to generate revenues and profits but, in reality, were losing money. EnronOnline was Enron's Internet platform for computerized trading of virtually any commodity. Compared to Enron's SPE schemes, which were abstrusely disclosed, EnronOnline was transparent. Nothing at EnronOnline was off balance sheet; indeed, the point of EnronOnline was that everything was *on* balance sheet, including "revenues" that arguably didn't belong.

The idea of EnronOnline was simple: Enron would set up a website for trading various commodities and derivatives, and its clients would use it. Enron would use the website to match buyers and sellers, just like an exchange, except that the transactions would take place on-line with Enron. It was like eBay for commodities, except that Enron would act as counterparty to each trade.

Enron booked many of EnronOnline's trades as revenue, even though the money paid by buyers went directly to sellers. It was this "revenue" that propelled Enron to seventh on the Fortune 500 list of top U.S. companies, which was based on revenue, even though most experts agreed that revenue was a poor measure of the true size of a company (profit or share value were better). Without EnronOnline's sham revenues, Enron would have been perceived to be a much smaller company.

EnronOnline was the brainchild of Louise Kitchen, a junior Enron executive who had worked after hours developing the Internet platform with key employees in Enron's commercial, legal, and technical departments. Kitchen's secretive approach to EnronOnline made sense given the mercenary culture at Enron, where an aggressive manager might try to steal a good idea, and where top employees such as Kitchen were encouraged to pursue new business lines on their own. Kitchen even protected herself by obtaining patents for the trading system—in her name.

Just a few weeks before she was ready to launch EnronOnline, Kitchen finally told Jeff Skilling about it. He was enthralled, and immediately took credit for the idea, launching EnronOnline on November 29, 1999. A year and a half later, when the site had completed its one millionth transaction, Skilling would proudly proclaim: "With the power of the Internet, we believe the potential for extending our business model to new markets is limitless."

Like much of Enron's dealings, EnronOnline functioned outside the scope of U.S. financial regulation. EnronOnline was exempt under U.S. law because all of its trades were judged to be "bilateral contracts" between the two parties trading on Enron's website, and such over-the-counter derivatives were unregulated, thanks to the new law passed by Congress in December 2000, with Senator Phil Gramm's involvement, cementing the derivatives exemption Wendy Gramm had pushed through in 1993. It was a sign of Enron's political influence that U.S. legal rules permitted the firm to set up an unregulated website to trade energy derivatives when prosecutors were bringing cases against other firms doing precisely the same thing with other financial instruments. (Recall from Chapter 6 that, in 2002, federal regulators shut down just such a website set up by Mitchell Vazquez, the former Bankers Trust salesman who had covered Gibson Greetings.)

The theory behind EnronOnline was that trading networks based on long-term relationships among a small number of market participants were too costly. Instead, EnronOnline was an open, transparent market, which—it was argued—would be cheaper and fairer than alternatives. Any member of the network could offer to buy and sell any amount of any trade at any time, and all trades would be posted on the website.

Unfortunately, the theory was flawed. Trading networks often failed *because* they were transparent. Numerous studies showed that electronic trading networks were more expensive than exchanges run by human beings, and sophisticated investors—given the choice—frequently chose less automated systems. For example, the clean and computerized Tokyo Stock Exchange had higher trading costs than the loud and frenetic New York Stock Exchange and, in both markets, when sophisticated investors wanted to sell large blocks of shares, they typically did it privately, through a Wall Street bank, not with the stock exchange. Notwithstanding the advances in computer technology and artificial intelligence, trading networks seemed to work best when real people were directly involved. Even eBay, the Internet auction site, allowed for human interaction.

Moreover, even if EnronOnline succeeded, and lowered the costs of transacting, it was unclear why it would generate profit for Enron. If anything, it would sabotage Enron's other profitable trading operations by commoditizing Enron's businesses. Enron might capture more trading "revenues," but its profits from trading would decline.

Nevertheless, EnronOnline sounded good, and investors and securities analysts seemed to like the idea. Enron's employees stressed EnronOnline's flexibility. A presentation by EnronOnline manager Mike McConnell began with Charles Darwin's quote: "It is not the strongest of the species that survives, nor the most intelligent, but the one most responsive to change."

EnronOnline could have used more strength and intelligence. Without much serious thought, Enron first used the EnronOnline model for natural-gas trading, and then copied it to cover the trading of virtually any commodity. It was simply a matter of creating another link on the website. First, traders branched out from oil to steel to plastics, commodities that already were traded on various exchanges in Chicago. In these cases, the only significant advantage of EnronOnline over the exchanges was its ability to avoid U.S. regulations. Not surprisingly, EnronOnline's revenues increased, but its profits narrowed. In response, traders began searching out more exotic markets to trade—retail energy services, fiber-optic bandwidth, and, finally, weather derivatives—which they hoped would have higher margins.

Ironically, on-line bets on the weather (which the media later mocked as a sign of Enron's murky dealings) were one of the few successes of EnronOnline. Weather derivatives—essentially, bets on changes in the weather over a period of time—already were traded in the over-the-counter markets among private parties. These contracts might have seemed like lunacy at first, but they actually fulfilled an important economic function. Many businesses—such as farming, leisure, insurance, and travel— faced risks based on the weather. Weather derivatives allowed parties to hedge risks they previously had not been able to hedge.

Trading in weather-related contracts had not become standardized in

any way, and Enron was a leader in creating a standardized trading platform. The contracts were based on the minimum or maximum temperature, the inches of rainfall or snowfall, the amount of streamflow or
storm activity, or the level of perceived temperature (wind chill or heat
index). With Enron, if you wanted to bet that the temperature in Houston on August 1 would be above 100 degrees, you could do so.

Enron completed more than 5,000 weather-derivatives deals, with a
value of more than $4.5 billion. Those numbers were impressive, but
Enron's weather-derivatives business suffered the same fate as the rest of
EnronOnline: revenues increased, but as the market became competitive, margins declined.

Enron Energy Services, the division of Enron known as EES, was even
more of a letdown than EnronOnline. EES sought contracts to reduce
the energy costs of individual and corporate customers by improving
their energy efficiency. For example, EES might claim that it could
change the way a company used lightbulbs to save it $1 million per year.
EES would enter into a contract to do this, and then book all the revenues from the contract upfront—another example of how mark-to-
market accounting stressed opinions about profit over facts about cash.
Not surprisingly, EES deals were very difficult to value upfront, and EES
employees were constantly trying to correct their mistaken over- and
under-valuations. EES used these difficulties to its short-term advantage.
According to one trader, when EES officials found that they had misvalued a winning deal, they added the correction to Enron's financial statements. But when they found that they had misvalued a losing deal, they
simply put it on a list. The losses at EES steadily accumulated, hidden
from view. According to one source, EES lost $700 million in 2001.

EES was a good example of how Ken Lay had not followed through
on his promise to implement the "best risk management and control system, not just in our business, but in any industry." Traders from different regions sent in hundred-page faxes listing the details of trades, and
the numbers were keyed by hand into a Microsoft Excel spreadsheet. Up
until 2000, Enron was running the multibillion-dollar operation out of
Microsoft Excel, which was not designed for such purposes. According
to one former employee, the system was so inefficient that some billing
reports cost more than $10,000, and the average cost of an invoice for a
new customer was $7—a significant percentage of a typical energy bill.

Incredibly, investors and securities analysts continued to rave about
EnronOnline and EES. Enron's annual report for 2000 prominently fea-

tured both businesses. They were important to Enron's managers, because shareholders valued technology businesses more than they valued trading firms. But the reality was that the new businesses were losers, and were supported by Enron's huge and hidden profits from derivatives trading. Just as Andy Krieger had feigned betting that currencies would fall when his real bet was that they would rise, Enron was pretending to be a technology company when its real business was derivatives trading.

The billions of dollars Enron lost in virtually all of its new businesses should not have been fatal, because Enron was making up for the losses in its North American natural-gas and electricity derivatives-trading operations. Enron disclosed more than $1 billion of income from trading in 2000; but, in reality, the firm's traders were making much more money than they were disclosing. The true numbers may never be known, but several sources established that Enron made billions of dollars trading in 2000 and 2001. Total trading profits for 2001—Enron's final year—were estimated at $3.8 billion.

In fact, Enron was making so much money trading derivatives that its traders decided to implement precisely the opposite scheme that Cendant and other companies had used to front-load their profits a few years earlier. Enron's traders actively manipulated their accounts to *reduce* their profits, which were embarrassingly large. Ironically, it remains unclear whether Enron's top officials were aware of this fact or, instead, whether Enron's traders were duping Ken Lay and Jeff Skilling at the same time those men were trying to persuade investors that Enron was a technology firm, not a trading firm.

There were several reasons for Enron's traders to want to reduce their reported profits. One was to "manage" Enron's earnings by shifting profits from trading to Enron's other ailing businesses. Another was to smooth Enron's trading profits over time, so that they appeared less volatile. But the most important reason, in late 2000, was the California energy crisis. California officials claimed that Enron had been manipulating energy markets and profiting at the state's expense. If Enron disclosed huge trading profits for 2000, it would only fan those flames.

In all, Enron reduced its trading profits by as much as $1.5 *billion* in late 2000 and early 2001, during the peak of the crisis in California.[47] Enron's internal trading records state that the firm lost over a billion dollars trading during a three-day period in December 2000—$550 million on a single day. It remains unclear whether these losses were real (from market volatility) or imagined (from manipulation of reserves). Either way, the short-term swings in trading profits were larger than any ever reported, by any company. The story of how Enron's traders hid their profits is one of the least known and understood aspects of the Enron scandal.

During Enron's last few years, the main trading floor at its headquarters in Houston (the sixth floor) was less of a zoo than a typical Wall Street trading floor, in part because the traders were in laid-back Texas, not Manhattan, and in part because business was so good. Yes, Enron's traders ogled their secretaries and staged eating contests. Yes, they gambled on sporting events and frequently blasted AC/DC or some other hard rock band. Yes, they mercilessly pursued trading profits and drove expensive cars. But the machismo at Enron was muted. Traders wore casual clothes—khakis and blue shirts were the uniform—and they politely tossed Nerf footballs across the trading floor. Morale and pay were high, and there was no need to engage in the gratuitously bloodthirsty antics that were typical among Wall Street firms. When one Enron trader vomited on the floor after failing to eat ten large hamburgers on a bet—an easy feat for a well-trained Wall Street trader—everyone actually felt sorry for the guy.

John Lavorato was one of the more intense traders at Enron. Lavo, as he was known, was in his early 30s, just under average height, with a stocky ex-football player's build and auburn hair. Although his gaze seemed perpetually fixed, he had a nervous tic, repeatedly grabbing the corner of his shirt when he spoke.

If Lavo was nervous about his trading, other traders didn't know it. He had moved to Houston after a successful stint running Enron's trading operation in Canada, and he quickly became one of Enron's most profitable traders, earning multimillion-dollar bonuses.

According to fellow traders, Lavo was known for making huge profits and then keeping those profits in reserve for the future. One day his profit-and-loss statement would be zero, and then, suddenly, a multimillion-dollar gain would appear. These practices were unremarkable to other traders, who shrugged them off, saying only, "Oh, Lavo's doing something again." Indeed, Enron and others later would argue that taking such reserves was standard practice, although an investigation of the firm's trading practices was open as of early 2003, and it remained unclear whether Lavorato or other traders would be implicated.

In fact, Lavo was far from alone. Numerous Enron traders hid their profits, saving them for the future. Their primary motivation in doing so was to smooth their trading profits over time. If they tucked away some profits, they could make a few million dollars of gain magically appear at some point in the future, to offset losses in a bad quarter. Traders who made smooth, consistent profits received bigger bonuses, because they were perceived as making more money per unit of risk. In aggregate, a trading operation that made smooth, consistent profits would be more highly valued in the market, for the same reason.

The primary measure of the riskiness of Enron's trading operation was Value At Risk, the statistical measure of the greatest amount of money Enron would expect to make or lose from *all* of its trading operations in a day, with a 95 percent level of confidence. For 2000, Enron reported a Value-At-Risk number for its trading operations of $66 million, meaning that investors could expect Enron to make or lose no more than $66 million on 95 percent of its trading days. Unfortunately, because VAR was based on historical data, it often understated risks, as Long-Term Capital Management's use of VAR had demonstrated. Even worse, Enron's VAR measure was based on the inordinately smooth profits its traders reported; in reality, the volatility of its trading operation was much greater. In fact, traders frequently made and lost more than their reported VAR; on a single day during 2000, traders made $500 million.[48] On December 12, 2000, they lost $550 million.

Enron's traders used two basic methods to manipulate their profits. Here is how they worked.

First, some Enron traders used dummy accounts, called *prudency reserves,* to hide profits. Enron's derivatives traders kept records of their profits and losses in a spreadsheet format. For some trades, instead of recording the entire profit in one column, traders split the profit into two columns. The first column reflected the portion of the actual profits the trader intended to add to Enron's current income. The second column—labeled "prudency reserve"—included the remainder.

To understand this concept of a prudency reserve, suppose a derivatives trader earned a profit of $10 million from a trade. Of that $10 million, the trader might record $9 million as profit today and enter $1 million into "prudency." A trader might have prudency reserves of several million dollars.

Enron's prudency reserves did not depict economic reality, nor could they have been intended to do so. Instead, prudency was a slush fund that could be used to smooth out profits and losses over time. The portion of profits recorded as prudency could be used to offset any future losses.

In essence, the traders were saving for a rainy day. Prudency reserves would have been especially effective for long-maturity derivatives contracts, because it was more difficult to determine a precise valuation as of a particular date for those contracts, and any prudency cushion would have protected the traders from future losses for several years going forward.

As luck would have it, some of the prudency reserves turned out to be quite prudent. In one quarter, some derivatives traders needed so much accounting profit to meet their targets that they wiped out all of their prudency accounts.

Saving for a rainy day is not necessarily a bad idea, and it seems possible that derivatives traders at Enron did not believe they were doing anything wrong. Prudency reserves, properly used, can be an accurate measure of the portion of the traders' profit that they might not be able to collect from trading counterparties. However, that is not how Enron was using prudency reserves. Instead, its traders were misstating the volatility and current valuation of their trading positions, and thereby misleading the firm's investors. Such practices thwarted the very purpose of Enron's financial statements: to give investors an accurate picture of a firm's risks.

It remains unclear who at Enron was aware of the use of prudency reserves. Traders said Enron's president, Greg Whalley, was aware of the practices. Enron's chief accounting officer, Richard A. Causey, claimed that he had informed Enron's directors about prudency reserves, but the directors denied any such knowledge, as did Lay and Skilling.[49] If Lay and Skilling did not know that their traders were hiding profits, they may genuinely have believed that Enron's future profits would come from other areas, including its new technology business. On the other hand, how could Lay and Skilling have thought Enron was still profitable during the second and third quarters of 2001, as they claim to have believed, if they did not know about the huge profits from trading?

The second method of misreporting derivatives positions at Enron was less brazen than prudency, and remains largely a mystery. In simple terms, Enron's traders misstated their profits by mismarking *forward curves*—the various rates at which commodities were trading for delivery at specified future dates. For example, a natural-gas derivatives trader could commit to buy natural gas to be delivered in a few weeks, months, or even years. The rate at which a trader could buy natural gas in one year was the one-year forward rate. The rate at which a trader could buy natural gas in ten years was the ten-year forward rate. The forward curve for a particular natural-gas contract was simply a graph of the forward rates for all maturities.

Forward curves are crucial to any derivatives-trading operation because they determine the value of a derivatives contract today, much as interest rates determine the value today of money to be received in the future. Like any firm involved in trading derivatives, Enron had risk-management and valuation systems that used forward curves to generate profit-and-loss statements.

Forward curves in some markets were easily susceptible to manipulation; others were not. For example, the forward curve for short-term natural-gas contracts traded on NYMEX was publicly available every day. Anyone who wanted to check whether a trader had mismarked a NYMEX trade could simply look in the newspaper. In contrast, natural-gas contracts with a term of more than six years were traded in an over-the-counter market with no transparency, and only infrequent trading. Just as years-earlier traders at Wall Street banks such as Bankers Trust and Salomon Brothers had misvalued derivatives without being caught, Enron's traders did the same in long-term natural-gas markets. At Enron, some forward curves remained mismarked for as long as three years.

Moreover, because Enron's natural-gas traders were compensated based on their profits, traders had an incentive to hide losses by mismarking forward curves. In some ways, prudency reserves and forward curves were two sides of the same coin. Traders who had made money might use prudency reserves, to reduce gains, in order to save profits for the next year; traders who had lost money might mismark forward curves, to create gains, in order to offset their losses. The extent of mismarking at Enron remains unclear, although several traders said the inaccuracies were more than a billion dollars.

In some instances, a trader would simply manually input a forward curve that was different from the market, just as the officials from Cendant had typed false numbers into their spreadsheets. For more complex trades, a trader would tweak the assumptions in the computer model used to value the trades, in order to make them appear to be more valuable. Complex computer models were especially susceptible to mismarking, as had been illustrated by the 1994 collapse of Askin Capital Management, the firm that had used such models to value mortgage derivatives.

Some traders even mismarked forward curves to understate their profits, as they had using prudency reserves. For example, one trader who already had recorded a substantial profit for the year, and believed any additional profit would not improve his bonus, reduced his recorded profits for that year, so he could push them forward into the next year, which he wasn't yet certain would be as profitable.

Enron's auditors from Arthur Andersen did not carefully audit Enron's forward curves. Instead, they took the forward curves as a given, and simply spot-checked the day-to-day change in the values of trades. Even then, the auditors failed to catch traders who suddenly moved forward curves by as much as three cents in one day—an adjustment that might not have seemed significant, but that nevertheless could impact profits by as much as $20 million.

These rigged-valuation methodologies and false profit-and-loss entries were systematic, and occurred over several years, beginning as early as 1997. Like many employees of public corporations during the late 1990s, Enron derivatives traders faced intense pressure to meet quarterly earnings targets imposed directly by management, and indirectly by securities analysts who covered Enron. Enron's risk-management manual instructed them that accounting numbers were more important than economic reality. It is not surprising, then, that traders manipulated the reporting of their "real" economic profits and losses in an attempt to fit the "imagined" accounting profits and losses that drove Enron's increasing stock price.

Interestingly, although Enron sought to avoid disclosing huge gains during the electricity crisis in California, the bulk of Enron's trading gains were not from traders in its West region. Enron traders made more money trading in the Northeast, and made hundreds of millions of dollars in other regions. Nevertheless, it obviously was important to Enron officials that they not be perceived as profiting from the plight in California.

Even given the inflated prudency reserves, Enron reported a profit increase of one-third during the last quarter of 2000, the peak of the California energy crisis. Few people believed Jeff Skilling when he told analysts on a conference call, on January 22, 2001, "Now for Enron, the situation in California had little impact on fourth-quarter results. Let me repeat that. For Enron, the situation in California had little impact on fourth-quarter results."[50]

More than a year later, it was discovered that, in fact, Enron traders around the country had been profiting from trading strategies that took advantage of the situation in California. The fact that these strategies had names like "Death Star" and "Fat Boy" didn't help Enron's public relations, but experts concluded that the strategies were perfectly legal. For example, Enron traders sold California electricity out of state, where it was more valuable; they created the false appearance of congestion, which increased prices; and they bought power in California, sold it to out-of-state parties, repurchased it, and then sold it back into California at higher prices. One Enron trader, Timothy N. Belden, was charged with manipulating these markets in October 2002, and the Department of Justice was busily deposing other traders at the end of 2002.

California officials expressed horror at these practices and disparaged Enron's "greedy" traders. But being greedy was what traders were paid to do, and the opportunities for trading profits were created by legal rules in place in California, in particular, a cap on the price of in-state electricity. The poorly constructed regulatory system didn't excuse illegal behavior, but it did explain its rationale. As one Enron trader put it, "It's like if you were trying to sell your car and California puts a cap on car prices. But you're thinking, 'Hey, it's worth more than that. There's a guy in Nevada willing to pay three times as much.' There's no law in California against selling in Nevada. So what are you going to do? Suck it up and sell it in California? No."[51]

Notwithstanding the accounting games, Enron's trading operations remained hugely profitable on paper—right up until the end. According to one source, Enron's North American trading operations were up $2.9 billion during the first eight months of 2001, when Jeff Skilling resigned. Several sources confirmed that Enron made more than $1 billion in 2001 trading natural-gas derivatives alone. One trader, John Arnold, made an incredible $750 million in 2001—nearly three times Andy Krieger's profits for Bankers Trust.[52] Ironically, most of Arnold's profit came during the third quarter of 2001, when Enron's stock price was declining, as investors began to lose confidence, and when energy prices in California were falling, as the crisis calmed; fortunately for Arnold, he had bet billions of dollars that prices would fall.

After October 2001, Enron's trading operation finally floundered, as banks refused to extend them credit. When Enron sold its derivatives-trading business to UBS, the Swiss bank, Enron kept the billions of dollars of derivatives its traders already had purchased. John Lavorato, having received a $5 million bonus for 2001, left to run the trading operation at UBS, where he would be just as successful as he had been at

Enron. The derivatives profits lingered at Enron even after its bankruptcy, when all of its derivatives traders were gone. The derivatives Enron retained after Lavo and his colleagues departed steadily paid off; and, by July 2002, the bankrupt company was awash in an incredible $6 billion of cash, according to a reporter at the *New York Times*—a reminder that although the company had died, its heart had been healthy throughout.

Unfortunately, even these massive trading profits weren't enough, and Enron ultimately was forced into bankruptcy. Even given the extensive media coverage, it was difficult to capture the breathless pace of the firm's collapse. From an insider's perspective, the last few days were a blur.

October 23, 2001, was a relatively quiet day throughout most of Houston. Harris County officials announced the successful test of a new $25 million electronic voting system for the upcoming elections. At Enron Field, the Houston Astros were interviewing candidates to replace Larry Dierker, the baseball manager who had resigned the previous week after leading the team to four National League Central Division titles in five years.

It had been just six weeks to the day since the terrorist attacks of September 11, and the 1.8 million residents of Houston were numb to bad news. A Texas National Guard office was closed after an officer discovered white powder on a stack of papers, but few people were alarmed and the powder tested negative for anthrax. The Union of Concerned Scientists released a long-awaited report projecting a seven-degree temperature increase in fifty years, but after another 100-degree summer, no one really believed Houston could get any hotter.

Meanwhile, at 1400 Smith Street, Enron's headquarters, all hell was breaking loose. For Ken Lay, it was the beginning of the end.

Lay spent much of the morning on a conference call with investors and analysts, trying to explain some recent troubles. During a previous Enron conference call, months earlier, investors had asked some heated questions about Enron's finances, and Jeff Skilling had responded to one analyst, Richard Grubman of Highfields Capital Management, by saying, "Well, thank you very much, we appreciate that. Asshole." Skilling had resigned in August, citing personal reasons. Now, Ken Lay was the target.

For many of the listeners, Enron had been a solidly performing investment. During 2000, as high-flying Internet stocks had lost almost all of their value, Enron's stock had stayed in a range of more than double its

1999 price. Enron hit its all-time high of $90.56 in August 2000, and closed the year at $80.

Then, the California energy crisis struck and, by summer 2001, Enron's stock price had been cut in half. California officials blamed Enron for everything from price gouging to manipulating the price of electricity. Just before Skilling resigned, he was mobbed by angry protestors, one of whom hit him in the face with a pie. Many investors assumed that California was the primary reason for the decline in Enron's stock price. California regulators had taken over some electricity contracts, and fewer people were trading electricity, all of which should have meant lower profits for Enron. Investors did not know that Enron was having a record year trading natural-gas and electricity derivatives, notwithstanding the problems in California. During the summer, several analysts finally focused on the cryptic disclosures in Enron's annual report about its dealings with various "Related Parties." They noticed disclosures, from months earlier, that Fastow and his partnerships were the Related Parties, and that Fastow was paid based on how the LJM partnerships performed. Anyone who closely read Enron's public filings from 2000 and 2001 would have spotted the description of Fastow's involvement and compensation.

The analysts were furious, and demanded that Enron remove Fastow from the partnerships and end the firm's relationships with LJM and LJM2. Lay asked Vinson & Elkins, the firm's primary outside legal counsel, to investigate these issues; and, in an October 15, 2001, letter to Enron's general counsel, the law firm wrote, "The facts disclosed through our preliminary investigation do not, in our judgment, warrant a further widespread investigation by independent counsel and auditors." According to its lawyers, Enron's actions were legal.

The next day—Tuesday, October 16—Enron announced that it was removing Fastow from the LJM partnerships, and taking a $35 million charge related to "early termination" of its dealings with those partnerships. The firm also announced a $1.01 billion one-time charge to reflect losses in its broadband, retail-electricity, and water investments. These announcements were portrayed as terrible news, which undoubtedly would cause Enron's stock price to plummet.

Instead, Enron's stock price went *up* about two percent that day. Sophisticated investors didn't seem to care much about Enron's announcement of a billion-dollar charge. Enron's stock price didn't budge on Wednesday, either, and trading was calm. By this time, at the latest, the price of

Enron stock should have reflected all of the information related to the LJM partnerships and the billion-dollar charge. The information was out, and markets usually don't take very long to react to news. In an efficient market, a few minutes is a lifetime, and most news is reflected in stock prices within seconds. But in Enron's case, the markets didn't react immediately to the news; instead there was a two-day calm before the storm.

Finally, on Thursday, October 18, Enron's stock price began spiraling down, out of control. On Thursday, trading volumes in Enron's stock doubled, and the price dropped to $29. On Friday, volumes tripled, and the stock dropped $3 more. On Monday, 36.4 million shares traded— more than any other stock that day, more than double Friday's volume, and more than any other single day in Enron's history—leaving Enron's closing price at around $20, a quarter of its value nine months earlier.

What accounted for the frenzied trading and nosedive in price? Enron gave investors a partial answer on Monday, when it disclosed an "informal inquiry" by the Securities and Exchange Commission into transactions between Enron and the LJM partnerships. Investors shuddered at the words "informal inquiry." If the SEC started digging, who knew what they might find? Ken Lay began calling in his political chits. Enron officials had meetings with Vice President Dick Cheney's staff, and Lay called his good friend, Commerce Secretary Donald Evans (although both men later claimed they did not discuss any of Enron's problems).

But none of this helped, and Lay had no choice but to arrange the October 23 conference call. As the call began, the participants asked what Lay was going to do about the fact that the stock price, which months earlier had fallen from $90 to a plateau of $35, was now falling off a cliff.

The stock analysts listening in on the call had issued buy recommendations on Enron stock, and were even more upset than the investors. (In October 2001, sixteen of seventeen securities analysts covering Enron called it a strong buy or buy.)[53] Given recent allegations about conflicts of interest among analysts—specifically, that they were making unjustified buy recommendations in exchange for lucrative investment-banking business for their firms—they wanted to be sure they got accurate information about companies they were covering. No one had questioned the analysts' conflicts as stocks were rising, even though they consistently rated nearly every stock a buy. But now that prices were falling, investors and regulators were raising eyebrows. Now, analysts were subject to greater scrutiny—a few had even been fired, and New York attorney general Eliot Spitzer had begun investigating various analysts and their firms. He was about to file an affidavit describing incriminating e-mails from Merrill Lynch. The analysts wanted to be sure they were making an accurate call on Enron.

In fact, the analysts' ratings finally looked like they made some sense. Enron might not really have been a strong buy at $80 just a few months earlier, but at $20 it seemed to be reasonably valued.

During the call, Lay admitted that having a chief financial officer run partnerships that did business with Enron was an "inherent conflict of interest." But he defended Enron, saying the company had set up procedures, which officials rigorously followed, to ensure that shareholder interests weren't compromised. He said, "There was a Chinese Wall between LJM and Enron," and noted that Enron was not obligated to do deals with the partnerships. Indeed, Lay said, the partnerships only did deals when it was in *Enron's* best interests.

From the analysts' perspective, the phrase "Chinese Wall" was the last straw. Wall Street investment banks had defended themselves for years with "Chinese Walls" between businesses that were subject to conflicts of interest. For example, analysts were not supposed to talk to investment bankers about confidential information. "Bringing someone over the wall" was supposed to be a significant event, when a person finally was entitled to learn secrets associated with a company or transaction. In reality, "Chinese Walls" were about eighteen inches high; bankers often compared them to the miniature Stonehenge in the movie *This Is Spinal Tap*.

Lay's use of the "Chinese Wall" defense raised suspicions about other partnerships and investments. Analysts asked about arrangements with Whitewing, Atlantic Water Trust, and other SPEs Enron partially owned. Enron officials assured listeners that the company had access to enough capital to carry out normal operations, although they warned of the risk that the credit-rating agencies might downgrade Enron's debt. Any mention of credit ratings always created a hush among the crowd, and the explanations of these commitments in particular were cryptic, and seemed to involve several triggering events. When pressed, Lay finally told callers he was limited in what he could say about the LJM partnerships because of the SEC inquiry.

Having earlier demanded Andrew Fastow's resignation from the partnerships, the analysts listening to Lay began demanding Fastow's head.

David Fleischer, an analyst from Goldman Sachs, said Enron's credibility was seriously in question, and called on Lay to do everything in his power to explain to investors that Enron's dealings were "aboveboard." He said, "I, for one, find the disclosure is not complete enough for me to understand and explain all the intricacies of all those transactions." Jeff Dietert, an analyst from Simmons & Co. International in Houston, said, "I had hoped to get a little bit more out of the call." For many others, that was an understatement.

As the call ended, it appeared that Ken Lay was not being entirely truthful with the investing community. Lay said he and his board of directors continued to have "the highest faith and confidence" in Fastow, the CFO. For the skeptical analysts, these words sounded like the kiss of death. No one expected Fastow to survive the year at Enron. In fact, Lay fired Fastow the next day.

Meanwhile, at the Houston offices of accounting firm Arthur Andersen, October 23 was even more frantic. Enron was Andersen's most important client in Houston, and had paid Andersen $52 million in fees in 2000 alone—more than half of which was for consulting, not audit, advice. The ties between the firms were very close, and many Enron employees—including Richard Causey, the lead audit supervisor—had spent time working at Andersen. As one former risk manager at Enron put it, "You couldn't swing a dead cat without hitting a manager from Andersen."

The focus of Andersen's work for Enron had changed markedly in recent years. A decade earlier, Andersen had performed only audit work for Enron, and not much else. Because Andersen had been independent, and had not relied on Enron to pay it for any other services, investors believed that Andersen would scrutinize Enron's financial statements very carefully. Even if they couldn't trust Enron, at least they could trust Andersen.

But Andersen had become less independent during the past few years, as it had expanded the consulting services it provided to corporate clients, including Enron. By 2000, the audit business was dying, and dreadfully boring. An annual audit required thousands of hours of tedious work. Consulting—especially consulting for an innovative company such as Enron—was glitzy and arguably more profitable.

While Ken Lay was spinning a tangled web during his conference call, employees at Andersen had powered-up the firm's shredders. David Duncan, the lead Andersen partner on Enron's audits, called a meeting to organize an "expedited effort to dispose of Enron-related documents." The document destruction quickly became document carnage, and continued until November 9, when Duncan's assistant finally issued a memorandum directing Andersen secretaries to "stop the shredding." During that short time, Andersen deleted thousands of e-mail messages and disposed of garbage bags' worth of shredded documents.

Andersen later would attempt to distance itself from Duncan, issuing a statement that the shredding "was undertaken without any consultation with others in the firm." Duncan must have anticipated that he would be left without friends in upper management, because he took at least six boxes of documents home before Andersen fired him on January 15, 2002. Those boxes contained important documents the investigators otherwise might not have seen.[54] Ultimately, prosecutors decided that Duncan's story would be useful in bringing a case against Andersen, and they appreciated the helpful documents, so they offered Duncan a deal: if he agreed to testify against Andersen at trial, he could plead guilty to obstruction of justice, and prosecutors would recommend a lenient sentence, perhaps with no jail time at all. After lengthy deliberations, a Houston jury convicted Andersen of obstructing justice, in part based on Duncan's testimony, in which he admitted to committing a crime.

On October 31, Ken Lay asked William Powers Jr., the dean of the University of Texas Law School—a well-known and respected figure in the legal profession—to join Enron's board and to oversee a special committee investigating Enron's losses. Powers then hired William McLucas, a former head of the SEC's enforcement division, and a dogged prosecutor with an impressive track record of victories.

Lay also continued to call in favors owed by various Bush administration officials. He had just raised more than $100,000 for Bush's election campaign as one of 214 so-called "Pioneers," and had been an adviser to Bush during the transition after the election as well.[55] In October and November, Lay called Treasury Secretary Paul O'Neill, Commerce Secretary Don Evans, Federal Reserve Chairman Alan Greenspan, and Robert McTeer, president of the Dallas Federal Reserve. Enron President Greg Whalley made several calls to Peter Fisher, the undersecretary of Domestic Finance, who had been involved in the private bailout of Long-Term Capital Management.[56] But none of these men would agree to help Enron; and, on November 6, the stock price fell below $10 per share.

During this time, the key issue in Enron's survival was its investment-grade credit rating. Enron had noted, in its most recent annual report, that "continued investment grade status is critical to the success of its wholesale business as well as its ability to maintain adequate liquidity."[57] A downgrade would be a double whammy for Enron. First, most financial institutions would refuse to extend additional loans to Enron because of the low rating. It wasn't merely that its cost of borrowing would increase; with a sub-investment-grade rating, Enron simply would not be able to borrow enough money at any rate.

Second, many of Enron's loans had credit-rating *triggers,* so that even though payment might not be due on its debt for several years, the terms of the debt specified that payments would be accelerated, following a downgrade to below investment grade. Specifically, if the credit-rating agencies downgraded Enron to below investment grade, Enron *immediately* would owe $690 million, and its various partnerships *immediately* would owe $3.9 billion.[58] Given Enron's deteriorating financial situation, it would not be able to cover these obligations—which meant that Enron's fate was in the hands of the credit-rating agencies.

In early 2000, Moody's supposedly had "exhaustively" reviewed Enron's off-balance-sheet activities and made a decision to change Enron's rating, based on what it found: it had *upgraded* Enron one notch, to Baa1.[59] (The lowest investment-grade rating on Moody's scale was two notches lower, at Baa3.) Moody's didn't raise the issue of credit-rating triggers, which were not unique to Enron. Although companies—including Enron—typically did not disclose these triggers in their financial filings, the credit-rating agencies were aware of them. Moreover, all three rating agencies had closely followed Enron throughout the tumult of the California energy crisis, Jeff Skilling's resignation, the revelations about Andy Fastow, Enron's public announcement of a billion-dollar-plus charge, and Ken Lay's firing of Andy Fastow after the hellish conference call on October 23. And yet, with Enron's stock price down from $80 to below $10, all three agencies still gave Enron's debt an investment-grade rating.[60]

In early November, Citigroup and J. P. Morgan Chase each agreed to give Enron an additional $1 billion in secured loans. The banks were in a tough spot, having loaned $8 billion to Enron through prepaid-swap deals, all of which were now in jeopardy. They committed to put more money into Enron, just as they had with Long-Term Capital Management.

Citigroup's co-chairman, Robert Rubin, who had been the Treasury secretary during the Mexico bailout and the collapse of Long-Term Capital Management, called Peter Fisher at the U.S. Treasury Department, to request that Fisher ask the credit-rating agencies to find an "alternative" to downgrading Enron. Rubin reportedly began the call by saying, "This may not be the best idea, but . . ."[61] Fisher declined.

In a filing with securities regulators on November 8, 2001,[62] Enron restated its financial statements, saying that its profits had been overstated by almost $600 million over four years. The culprits were JEDI, Chewco, and the LJM partnerships, which Enron had used to inflate its profits. Under the scrutiny of the special committee investigating Enron's partnership deals, Enron finally was forced to disclose some of its hidden losses. The media gasped at the numbers; but, even as revised downward, Enron's net income was substantial and its debt manageable. Even the restated numbers showed a profitable company, which should have easily survived.

However, the restatement made it clear that Enron's investment-grade credit rating was undeserved, and should be lowered a notch or two. Such a downgrade would kill Enron, because it would make it impossible for its traders to borrow money. The sluggish rating agencies were under pressure to respond, or else risk permanently soiling their own reputations. Enron had paid substantial fees directly to the credit-rating agencies for almost two decades, and agency officials didn't want their downgrade to send Enron into bankruptcy. Nevertheless, the officials were worried about maintaining *some* credibility, so that regulators would not punish them or, even worse, open the market for credit ratings to competition. Based on historical data, the lowest investment-grade rating suggested that the probability of Enron defaulting on its debts within the next twelve months was just 0.33 percent.[63] That probability was too low for Moody's, which finally began planning to downgrade Enron to a rating of below investment grade.

Moody's would have downgraded Enron then, had it not been for entreaties from Dynegy, one of Enron's competitors—and Dynegy's investment bankers, including Richard Fuld, the chief executive of Lehman Brothers.[64] On November 9, Dynegy told Moody's it would agree to merge with Enron if Moody's would maintain an investment-grade rating on Enron's debt. The ostensible rationale was that, if the merger were completed, Enron would be financially stronger and would be more likely to be able to repay its debts. (In reality, the rating agencies soon would be downgrading Dynegy, too.) Less than an hour before Moody's was planning to announce it was downgrading Enron to sub-investment grade, Moody's capitulated and agreed to give Enron's debt the lowest possible investment-grade rating. With that concession, Charles Watson, the CEO of Dynegy, agreed that day to a merger with a desperate Ken Lay. At this point, Enron was hanging by a thread.

Ten days later, on November 19, Enron again restated its third-quarter earnings, and its stock fell to the lowest level in a decade. Enron extended by a few weeks the deadline on the $690 million of debt that would have been triggered by a downgrade, but the extension didn't inspire the firm's investors. Enron's stock price fell to $3.

The last straw for the credit-rating agencies was the revelation about derivatives deals Enron had used to dress up its financial statements, including $8 billion of prepaid swaps with J. P. Morgan Chase and Citigroup, and several deals designed to generate last-minute accounting profits at the end of the year. In the prepaid swaps, the banks paid money up front to Enron, in exchange for Enron's promise to repay that money over time. The banks used Special Purpose Entities to do the deals—J. P. Morgan Chase used Mahonia, the Jersey company Chase had created years earlier. Enron and its accountants had argued that there were sufficient technical differences between the prepaid swaps and traditional loans that Enron could keep the swaps off its balance sheet.

When U.S. Senate investigators later uncovered the details about Enron's prepaid swaps, the politicians professed outrage. Senator Carl Levin interrogated officials from J. P. Morgan Chase, demanding that they accept responsibility for the prepaid swaps. He said, "They were just simply loans from these two banks that were covered up through a series of transactions. These were phony prepays. They were not real."[65]

These deals might have been phony, but they were both common and, arguably, legal. Numerous companies used prepaid swaps to borrow money off balance sheet, and prepaid swaps—like FELINE PRIDES and other structured finance deals—were part of mainstream corporate life, even though few investors had heard of them. Yes, these deals did not fit economic reality, but in a world governed by accounting standards, economic reality was barely relevant.

J. P. Morgan Chase had pitched prepaid swaps with the understanding that they would be used to avoid liabilities. In a November 1998 e-mail, a Chase employee stated, "Enron loves these deals because they are able to hide funded debt from their equity analysts . . . they can bury it in their trading liabilities." A Chase pitch book described the deal as "Balance sheet 'friendly'" and said, "Attractive accounting impact by converting funded debt to deferred revenue or long-term trade payable." Chase also noted that, from a tax perspective, the transaction would be treated as a loan. When one Chase employee expressed surprise that Enron had billions of dollars of prepaid swaps, another employee wrote in response, "Shut up and delete the e-mail."

J. P. Morgan Chase vigorously defended the prepaid swaps, and a spokesperson said, "If they were being marketed to other companies, it's because they were perfectly legal transactions in accordance with generally accepted accounting principles." In fact, J. P. Morgan Chase also marketed prepaid swaps to numerous companies, including Equitable Resources, Kerr-McGee, PG&E, Devon Energy, Dominion Resources, Duke Energy, and Phillips Petroleum.[66]

Citigroup was equally active in prepaid swaps, marketing them to Williams, El Paso, Mirant, Dynegy, American Electric Power, Reliant Energy, and others.[67] Enron did $4.8 billion of prepaid swaps with Citigroup. In one deal, called "Roosevelt," Enron orally promised to repay $500 million Citigroup had advanced to Enron as part of a natural-gas swap; Enron later honored the oral promise, making the transaction appear to be a loan.[68] Congressional investigators later uncovered e-mails from Citigroup showing that Enron had "agreed to prepay" and warning, "The papers cannot stipulate that as it would require recategorizing the prepaid as simple debt."[69] Given that Enron had disguised $8 billion of "loans" as cash flow from operations, the company had much more debt than the rating agencies had imagined when they gave Enron an investment-grade rating. Enron's bankruptcy examiner would later discover more than $25 *billion* of debt.

Enron also engaged in numerous other structured finance deals in addition to its infamous SPEs, none of which the credit-rating agencies had managed to uncover. For example, in December 1999, Enron had been desperate to sell its interest in some Nigerian barges that were mounted with electricity generators. Enron had planned to sell the interest to an Asian investor, but when that deal fell through, Jeffrey McMahon, a senior Enron executive, tried to find another buyer, so that Enron could recognize a profit from the sale before the end of the firm's 1999 reporting year. McMahon approached Merrill Lynch, which reportedly agreed to "buy" Enron's interest in the barges after Andy Fastow orally promised that, by June 2000, Enron would "make sure Merrill Lynch was relieved of its interest."[70] It was illegal for Enron to "park" securities with a bank—booking a gain—even though it planned to repurchase the securities later; and, as promised, LJM2 repurchased Merrill Lynch's interest in the barges in June 2000. But Enron had never committed in writing to repurchase the interest, and Merrill defended the deal as a "real transaction, with real risk." Merrill said it "would never knowingly engage in a transaction that threatened our reputation."[71] This Nigerian barge deal was one of many similar transactions.

As the rating agencies learned the facts, they finally decided that Enron was not the investment-grade company they had imagined. The agencies delivered the death blow to Enron on November 28, downgrading its debt to below investment grade. Enron's stock price dropped from $3 to $1 within a few minutes of the downgrade—the largest one-day percentage decline in the company's history. There was no other important news that day, except the fact that Moody's, Standard & Poor's, and Fitch/IBCA were lowering their ratings on Enron's debt. Now that Enron was sub-investment grade, it was locked out of the capital markets and could no longer sustain a trading operation. With the stroke of a pen, the rating agencies had put Enron out of its misery.

The rating agencies apparently were unaware that Dynegy, Enron's prospective merger partner—also barely above investment grade—had done similar off-balance-sheet deals with Citigroup, including one, called Project Alpha, in which Dynegy paid an incredible $33 million in fees to Citigroup and Vinson & Elkins, also Enron's law firm, in order to inflate its own reported cash flow. Dynegy had booked mark-to-market profits on its derivatives trades, but had not yet received cash. Most experts believed that, although companies could use derivatives to manipulate their recorded income or debt, they could not use them to affect operating cash flow—the key variable in assessing the profitability of a company. Dynegy proved the experts wrong. Project Alpha enabled Dynegy to report it had received more operating cash, even though the deal did not affect Dynegy's actual operations.[72]

Dynegy described some aspects of Project Alpha in its annual report, but not in enough detail for anyone to understand. Later, when investors were trying to understand why Dynegy also collapsed, instead of explaining the details about Project Alpha, they simply pointed to Enron as the paradigmatic example of an energy company engaged in complex financial deals.

In November 2001, Dynegy's complex deals were not yet public, and the company sought to avoid being dragged down by Enron. After Dynegy's officers learned the credit-rating agencies had downgraded Enron, they immediately terminated the merger. Without a partner, Enron had to suspend all payments, except those necessary to maintain its core operations. Enron's credit was no longer good, and it could not find any more sources of money. Having lived just above the cusp of investment grade for more than a decade, Enron was about to die just below it.

For Matt McGrath,[73] a natural-gas derivatives trader at Enron, the last few days of Enron's life were a surprise. Like many traders, McGrath had earned huge profits for Enron during 2001; but, given the firm's trajectory, he had assumed a big bonus was unlikely. Bonuses for a given year typically weren't paid until January or February of the next year, and McGrath wasn't sure he would remain employed at Enron until then. Enron didn't look like it would survive for much longer, and McGrath—like many traders—had begun looking for work elsewhere.

When the credit-rating agencies downgraded Enron, all trading halted, and the high-tech trading floor became lifeless. Frenetic traders, with as many as nine computer screens stacked in front of them, took a break. A visitor to Enron's trading floor would have seen a line of casually dressed young men and women, leaning back in their black-leather chairs, watching daytime television. There were few jokes or eating contests—not even ogling. The traders' telephone turrets, with dozens of direct lines, were silent. No one was tossing Nerf footballs or listening to AC/DC.

During Friday morning, some of the employees who worked on the fourth floor—two floors below the traders—decided to liven up the place and ordered several kegs of beer, to celebrate what might be their last day at the firm. The kegs were delivered around ten A.M., Styrofoam cups were passed around, and the traders from the sixth floor made multiple trips downstairs and back up. McGrath had just returned to the sixth floor when an attractive woman, with an Ally Sheedy haircut, stopped behind him and whispered, "Hey, I need you to come to meet me in a conference room. I'll call you with directions. Wait by the phone." McGrath was a little tipsy, but he recognized the woman as an employee from Enron's human-resources department. He wondered if he was about to be fired.

A few minutes letter, a phone line buzzed. The woman said, "Come down the hallway behind the trading floor. Knock on the last door on the left. If I come and open the door, you're at the right place." McGrath went to the hallway, and walked past the glassed office of John Lavorato, the senior trader known as Lavo. He had never been farther down this particular hallway, which was light and airy, with glass doors and windows throughout—except for one closed door made of dark wood, on the left, at the end of the hallway. The door appeared to lead to the only private room on the trading floor. McGrath had never seen it before.

When the door opened, McGrath saw that the room was empty except for a twenty-foot oval conference table made of hickory and surrounded with black-leather chairs. The table was empty except for two pieces of paper. The woman told him to read them, and sign. One was a confidentiality agreement, requiring that McGrath not disclose any information he knew about Enron. The other was a check with more zeros than McGrath had ever seen. He quickly signed the agreement, took the check, and rushed to the bank.

When he returned, he told the other traders what had happened. For the next several hours, the remaining traders sat by their phones and waited.

Enron had decided to pay $55 million in advance bonuses to a handful of energy-derivatives traders who had had a spectacular year in 2001. Enron called the payments "retention bonuses," and required that the traders remain at the firm for a few months. Indeed, Enron needed its top traders to stay at the firm, under contract if possible, so it could sell its trading business to another firm as an ongoing concern. Without the traders, Enron's trading business was virtually worthless.

Few people understood that these "retention bonuses" were the same amounts that Enron ordinarily would have paid the traders a few months later, as their year-end performance bonuses. The difference was that Enron was paying them early—ostensibly to get the traders to stay—but, in reality, because Enron was about to run out of money. The huge payments—such as $5 million for John Lavorato and $8 million for John Arnold, the trader who reportedly made $750 million of profits for Enron in 2001—were well deserved. During 2001, these traders had generated record profits for Enron, of several billion dollars, and had kept the company alive as it plunged into a series of ill-advised and conflicted investments. However, it wasn't clear whether Enron legally could pay $55 million of bonuses and then file for bankruptcy. Such last-minute payments typically were not permissible. That was one reason why the traders were running so quickly to the bank with their checks.

Anyone who doubted the supremacy of the derivatives trader in modern financial markets needed only to take a peek inside Enron on November 30. The company's stock had plunged from $90 a share to pennies. Thousands of employees were out of work. Thousands more had watched helplessly as their retirement plans evaporated; they couldn't sell their Enron shares during October and November because Enron was changing pension-fund administrators and had locked employees out of their plans.[74] And yet, that Friday afternoon, one by one, a few top derivatives traders were called into secret meetings where they received seven-figure bonus checks in exchange for agreeing to stay at the firm just three months longer (and for agreeing to keep quiet about what they knew).

December 2—two days later—was a busy Sunday for Enron: the company filed for bankruptcy protection, fired 4,000 employees, sued Dynegy for $10 billion for breaching its merger agreement, and procured $1.5 billion more in financing from J. P. Morgan Chase and Citigroup, so it could attempt to sustain a skeleton operation. Incredibly, Enron's two big banks continued to lend the firm more money, even in bankruptcy.

Ultimately, Enron sold its trading operations to Union Bank of Switzerland. According to some of the licensing agreements associated with this venture, UBS received all of Enron's assets (including a long list of hardware and software) and did not assume any liabilities. The price for the deal: zero. UBS paid nothing for Enron's trading operations, one British pound less than what ING (International Netherlanden Groep) had paid for Barings Bank six years earlier.

The collapse of Enron led to numerous lawsuits, government investigations, and criminal prosecutions. But the question remained: were the direct participants really responsible for Enron's collapse?

Ken Lay, who finally stepped down in January 2002, benefited financially from Enron's schemes; in all, he sold $144 million of Enron stock. Lay also received loans from Enron, and public records from Texas indicated that several members of Lay's family had purchased million-dollar homes during late 2000 and 2001. (Texas has a homestead exemption, which protects homes from being taken as part of the penalty in a criminal prosecution—however, as of early 2003, it was unlikely that prosecutors would be able to sustain charges against Lay or any members of his family.) Although Lay was not directly involved in the deals that ruined Enron, he helped to fashion the firm's trading-focused culture. Especially after August 2001, when he learned the details of Enron's partnerships, he should have been more engaged in Enron's business, and more forthcoming with investors. But even then, Ken Lay really did not seem to understand what was happening at his company.

Jeff Skilling also benefited from Enron's schemes—selling $76 million of stock—and some people questioned whether Skilling's reasons for resigning on August 14, 2001, were truly "personal." However, Skilling had been CEO for only six months when he resigned, and it seems unlikely that he would have learned much startling new information during that time that would lead him to resign. Moreover, Skilling had effectively been running Enron for several years before he became CEO, and he was a reasonably hands-on person during this period. Instead, it seemed more likely that Skilling was telling the truth when he testified before Congress that, after several months of scrutinizing Enron's dealings, he still believed that Enron's financial statements had been accurate, and that accounting rules had permitted the various off-balance-sheet transactions. He clearly was right about Enron's trading profits, which were substantial when he resigned. Indeed, there was a strong argument that Skilling was correct about the SPEs, too, and that, although Enron's practices made little economic sense, they were, nevertheless, perfectly legal.

Andy Fastow benefited directly from Enron's schemes, selling $30 million of stock, and making another $45 million from the LJM partnerships in two years. In July 2001, Fastow made an undisclosed amount from selling his interests in the LJM partnerships to Michael Kopper, just after Kopper resigned from Enron.[75] Fastow told board members he had spent only a fraction of his time working on the LJM partnerships, but it seemed that he had spent a great deal of time engineering the partnerships' deals with Enron. According to several sources, Lay, Skilling, and Enron's board members were stunned when they learned how much money Fastow had made from the partnerships.[76] But many financial institutions permitted their employees to engage in deals with related partnerships—the involvement of ninety-six employees from Merrill Lynch as investors in LJM2 was not unusual, by Wall Street standards—and Fastow was nowhere near the highest-compensated person at Enron. If Enron's board hadn't agreed to compensate him from the LJM partnerships, Fastow could have quit Enron and made nearly as much money somewhere else. Most important, Fastow's compensation didn't prove that the SPE deals were illegal, or that Fastow possessed criminal intent. Fastow was indicted for various schemes related to the SPEs, and the allegations of kickbacks were damning. But as for the vast majority of the SPEs Fastow created, he arguably was playing within the rules of a game whose very structure and purpose had been corrupted.

Some of the highest-paid senior executives at Enron were less known, but more directly involved in the company's most spectacular failures. Lou Pai, who ran two ruinous businesses—Enron Energy Services, the firm's retail energy flop, and NewPower Holdings, one of Enron's failed dot.coms—sold $270 million worth of Enron stock. Thomas White, the vice chairman of Enron Energy Services—who then became secretary of the army—made $5.5 million a year, and sold $12 million of stock during the months before Enron's bankruptcy. Ken Harrison, the former CEO of Portland General, who also was on the board of Rhythms NetConnections, sold $78 million of stock.[77] In terms of Enron's failed business operations, these three men deserved just as much blame as Lay and Skilling.

After Enron's bankruptcy filing, Jack Welch, former CEO of General Electric, blamed the firm's trading culture for the losses, comparing Enron to the Kidder Peabody scandal involving Joseph Jett, which occurred under his watch: "I think what happened was they got into a culture they didn't understand, and culture counts. When I got into one I didn't understand, we screwed it up. We were lucky it was small enough. We sold it and got out. And got out alive. But it could have eaten us up if it were a bigger thing. This thing at Enron got bigger than the core business and it ate them up."[78]

But Welch had it backwards. The problem at Enron wasn't the trading culture; Enron had been a trading firm since the beginning, and it was a profitable one. Welch had the wrong image in his mind when he spoke of moving "from people in overalls and wrenches who ran pipelines and utilities to a trading business where people wore suspenders and had $10 million salaries." Enron's traders didn't make $10 million, and they certainly didn't wear suspenders. John Arnold, the 27-year-old who made $750 million for Enron and was the highest-paid trader, at $8 million, was by all accounts a calm, low-key math whiz who was simply a better trader than his peers—he arguably deserved a *bigger* bonus. No, the people who were most to blame for Enron's collapse weren't the traders. Instead, it was the corporate executives who had run Enron's non-trading businesses, all of which were utter failures. They were the ones running off with the serious money.

Enron's bankers and lawyers had not exactly behaved admirably, but it was difficult to pin much blame on them. Enron paid several hundred million dollars in fees to banks for work on various financial aspects of its business, including fees for derivatives transactions and loans masquerading as prepaid swaps, and yet none of those firms pointed out to investors any of the derivatives problems at Enron.[79] Enron's bankers faced serious conflicts of interest, and many were even investors in Enron's partnerships. Recall, also, that as late as October 2001, sixteen of seventeen securities analysts covering Enron rated it a strong buy or buy.[80] Enron paid more than ten million dollars in legal fees to its primary outside firm, which previously had employed Enron's general counsel, yet that firm failed to correct or disclose the problems related to derivatives and Special Purpose Entities. But the bankers and lawyers weren't accountants, and it was difficult to hold them responsible for accounting mistakes. The deals they had structured had a financial and legal justification, even if they were dubious from an accounting perspective.

Arthur Andersen was responsible for auditing Enron's financial statements and assessing Enron management's internal controls on derivatives trading. Most people blamed Andersen for Enron's collapse, and even Andersen's top auditors seriously considered the fact that they might be responsible for Enron's malfeasance, when they met in January 2001 to discuss Enron's account. They discussed these risks but, ultimately, decided that Enron was a large enough client that it was worth the downside.

However, the case against Andersen was a difficult one, too. When Andersen signed Enron's 2000 annual report, it expressed approval, in general terms, of Enron's system of internal controls from 1998 through 2000.[81] Andersen certainly could have done a better job of independently verifying Enron's valuations of complex trades; but most of the information relevant to Enron's questionable deals was contained in Enron's financial statements, even if it was hard to understand. (In Enron's 2000 annual report, it stated that the firm's derivatives-related assets and liabilities had increased five-fold during one year alone,[82] a flashing red light to anyone reading the report.) Although Andersen was convicted of obstruction of justice, it would have been much more difficult to convict the firm of securities fraud. The strongest argument that Andersen was to blame for Enron's collapse was one few commentators had made: Andersen had been willing to opine that Enron's internal controls were adequate when it was obvious, based on Enron's financial statements alone, that the firm was spinning out of control.

Investors, prosecutors, plaintiffs' lawyers, and members of Congress have blamed the various direct participants in Enron's collapse. But, in reality, it was difficult to assign blame to any of these parties, and it was likely that most—if not all—would avoid successful prosecution for fraud. Instead, it was the parties outside Enron that were most to blame: the credit-rating agencies that had propped up Enron's credit rating and then pulled out the carpet at the end; the investors who had not scrutinized Enron's public filings; and the legislators and regulators who not only had passed the rules Enron used to rationalize its dealings, but then stood by for years while those rules distorted the dominant corporate and financial culture so much that Enron's dealings, which should have been reprehensible, became permissible.

Enron was the culmination of the decade's key developments in financial markets. First, Enron's financial instruments were so complex—and so many of its deals were so explicitly designed to skirt legal rules—that few people understood the company, and even its accountants and bankers did not have an accurate picture of Enron's finances. Second, control and ownership of Enron were so far separated that shareholders and the board of directors could not stop, or even effectively monitor, the self-interested activities of Enron's managers. Third, the markets Enron participated in—including both the energy and derivatives markets—were mostly deregulated; no corporate executive, accountant, or banker perceived a substantial risk of punishment for misleading investors, in part because prosecutors hadn't been punishing complex financial fraud, but also because their activities arguably complied with the letter of the law.

Enron reinvented the U.S. corporation, trading every commodity imaginable, not just natural gas, but also electric power, plastics, metals, bandwidth, pollution, and even complex bets on the weather. Enron moved this trading to the Internet, where traders completed more than a million on-line transactions. In 2001, Enron was worth more than AT&T, and its top officers were prosperous, prominent members of the Houston community. The firm's lower-level employees were wealthy, too; Enron awarded them so many stock options that many already were millionaires, and most others expected to be millionaires soon, given Enron's soaring stock price. It didn't even seem like hubris when an enormous banner was put up at the firm's headquarters, proclaiming Enron "The World's Greatest Energy Company on the Way to Becoming the World's Greatest Company."

Then—poof—Enron was gone. It was only a few weeks from the time of Ken Lay's October 23 conference call, when Enron seemed to face only a minor crisis, until the company filed for bankruptcy protection.

Enron's focus on markets resurrected an important question Ronald Coase, the Nobel Prize–winning economist, had first posed fifty years earlier: markets or companies?[83] According to Coase, markets and companies were alternative ways of doing business—you could buy a widget in the market or you could produce it in a company—and rational economic actors would choose whichever method was cheaper and more efficient. Someone had to make the widget, but that person didn't necessarily need to operate within a corporate structure. In other words, companies existed only when it was cheaper to provide a service or produce a good within a company than in the market.

The dominant belief during the 1990s was that markets would dominate companies, which were no longer able to change at the pace and scale required in the new economy. Enron was the definitive representation of this belief.

But for Enron, the victory of markets over companies was a Pyrrhic one. Enron was destroyed, in part, because it became too costly for it to engage in its own businesses within a corporate structure. The costs of a company, compared to the costs of the market, included not only a building, computers, and paper clips, but also the very real *agency* costs associated with human behavior.[84] At Enron, there were too many conflicts of interest within those agency relationships, too many temptations for personal profit, and too many ways to use other corporate entities—such as partnerships and Special Purpose Entities—to hide details from shareholders. These were all costs of putting so much activity within a single corporate structure. In the end, Enron was evidence that the answer to Ronald Coase's question, increasingly, *was* markets, although that answer was the death knell for companies such as Enron.

Although some of Enron's businesses were profitable, the fact that they were housed within a large and costly corporate structure marked Enron for doom. Ironically, this conclusion was precisely what Jeff Skilling had been preaching, in substance, since he had joined Enron in 1990. Skilling had argued that Enron should strip itself of hard assets and focus, instead, on making money as a market intermediary, profiting from individuals and institutions that traded in organized markets, rather than from producing the items those traders might buy or sell. To the extent that it focused on markets—including acting as a market intermediary trading energy derivatives—Enron was a success. To the extent that it abandoned markets—dealing in opaque disclosures and Related Party transactions in other businesses—Enron was a failure.

During the months after Enron's demise, numerous shareholders of other companies would decide that the corporate structure was too costly for their other businesses, primarily due to the costs associated with monitoring complex financial transactions. Those companies— Global Crossing, WorldCom, Adelphia, Tyco, and so on—would fail, just as Enron had. Other companies would nearly fail. The next era of markets would be defined by an effort to untangle the web of conflicted relationships within various corporate structures, and to hunt for—and avoid—companies, like Enron, that simply cost too much to justify their existence.

As time passed, investors learned that Enron—which many journalists had labeled the biggest business story of the decade—was merely the first public notice of a much bigger story about how much the playing field of investing had changed. During Enron's life, it had evolved from a bricks-and-mortar firm into the perfect design for modern markets: an agile firm focused on technology and trading, with finances too complex to describe in the traditional language of finance. Perhaps it was fitting that Enron's officials became the scapegoats for investors seeking an explanation of why their double-digit returns were ending. But Enron was not merely about a few bad guys, and anyone who believed it was would miss the important connections between Enron's collapse and the even bigger bankruptcies that were about to follow it.

HOT POTATO

Just as the interest rate hikes of early 1994 had uncovered hundreds of derivatives bets at major institutions, the collapse of Enron exposed widespread risks and deceitful practices at the world's leading corporations. Any investor who read a newspaper in 2002 knew about financial scandals at companies ranging from Adelphia to WorldCom, from Anadarko to Xerox.

By the end of 2002, the surfeit of information about complex dealings and surprise losses became, for many investors, like financial white noise. On average, one company restated its financials every day. There was a billion-dollar collapse every few weeks. Congressional inquiries into the Enron, Global Crossing, and WorldCom scandals were televised incessantly.

At first, public officials blamed corporate executives and accounting firms. Jeffrey Skilling of Enron was publicly assailed, while other former CEOs, including Bernard Ebbers of WorldCom, invoked their Fifth Amendment right against self-incrimination. Arthur Andersen was convicted of obstructing justice, PricewaterhouseCoopers was charged with violating rules requiring auditor independence, and Congress established new penalties for top corporate executives and additional oversight of accounting firms. Over time, the emphasis shifted from CEOs and accountants to Wall Street, as it became clear that major banks—especially Citigroup and J. P. Morgan Chase—were intimately involved in the various schemes.

The range of financial malfeasance and manipulation was vast. Energy companies, such as Dynegy, El Paso, and Williams, did the same complex financial deals Andy Fastow had engineered at Enron. Telecommunications firms, such as Global Crossing and WorldCom, fell into bankruptcy after it became clear they, too, had been cooking their books. Financial firms were victims as well as aiders-and-abettors. PNC Financial, a major bank, settled SEC charges that it abused off-balance-sheet deals and recklessly overstated its 2001 earnings by more than half. A rogue trader at Allfirst Financial, a large Irish bank, lost $750 million in a flurry of derivatives trading that put Nick Leeson of Barings to shame. And so on, and so on.

These firms were closely connected, and Enron was at or near the center of the web. During the previous decade, the financial world had become even more incestuous than Hollywood, with its "six degrees of Kevin Bacon" (one degree was being in a movie with Kevin Bacon, two degrees was being in a movie with someone who was in a movie with him). In 2001, "two degrees of Enron" was more than sufficient to link most major corporations and financial firms. Enron did dubious deals directly with Global Crossing, WorldCom, and many other firms. Enron officials marketed earnings-management strategies to other companies, ranging from AT&T to major utility companies. Enron also did deals with Citigroup, J. P. Morgan Chase, Merrill Lynch, and other prestigious banks; those banks, in turn, transacted with nearly every public company.

The top energy and telecommunications firms did the most notorious transactions, including questionable round-trip swaps with each other, many of which were arranged by Wall Street's top banks and blessed by Big Five accounting firms. Some of these swaps merely inflated the companies' revenues, without affecting the bottom line; others puffed up profits. Like Enron's partnership transactions, many of these deals were arguably legal, but they were contrary to economic reality and common sense, and when investors learned about them, they dumped the companies' stocks, without regard for whether the practices could be defended in court.

As with the prior financial scandals, substantial losses were related to over-the-counter derivatives. There were prepaid swaps, in which a company received an up-front payment resembling a loan from a bank, but did not record its future obligation to repay the bank as a liability. There were swaps of Indefeasible Rights of Use, or IRUs, long-term rights to use bandwidth on a telecommunications company's fiber-optic network, which were similar to the long-term energy derivatives Enron traded—and just as ripe for abuse. And there were more Special Purpose Entities, created by Wall Street banks.

As news of the various corporate fiascos spread, there was more evidence of the inefficiency of stock markets, where individual investors played, especially as compared to the markets for bonds and derivatives, where more sophisticated institutions dominated trading. Invariably, when bad news appeared about a company, that company's bonds and derivatives were hit first, as financial institutions quickly sold their holdings and bet against the company. In contrast, stock markets reacted only gradually, in a kind of slow-motion crash, as individual investors sluggishly realized they should sell. For example, on the day Enron CEO Jeffrey Skilling resigned, the price of Enron's stock—supported by individual investors—barely moved, even though the resignation was obviously awful news. In contrast, the cost of a derivatives contract insuring against a default by Enron spiked by 18 percent that day.[1] The stock markets eventually caught up with the derivatives markets and by August 2002 had lost more than a quarter of their value, destroying more than $7 trillion of wealth built during the 1990s—roughly $70,000 of losses for each U.S. household.[2]

The last ones to react, in every case, were the credit-rating agencies, which downgraded companies only after all the bad news was in, frequently just days before a bankruptcy filing. Nevertheless, investors continued to trust the credit-rating agencies, and regulators continued to rely on them.

To any close observer of the changes in financial practices since the late 1980s, the collapse was not a surprise. New forms of risk and deceit now permeated every corner of the financial markets. Financial instruments had continued to develop in complex ways, and no one—including accountants, bankers, directors, regulators, or even plaintiffs' lawyers—was in a position to exercise even a modicum of control. New instruments called credit derivatives enabled banks to transfer and repackage risks, making themselves safer and more profitable, but pushing trillions of dollars of risk into the dark corners of the financial markets. Individual investors, having jumped into stocks without understanding what they were buying, were now suffering unprecedented losses associated with these new instruments, often without realizing it.

There was one unexpected twist. Compared to the sophisticated financiers involved in the complex schemes of the 1990s—ranging from the nerds of Bankers Trust to the rocket scientists of Long-Term Capital Management, many of whom had attended the Wharton business school or had Ph.D.s in finance—the leaders of the companies involved in the major scandals of the early 2000s were uneducated in finance and had little experience in the businesses they ran. Consider Gary Winnick and Bernard Ebbers, the heads respectively of Global Crossing and WorldCom. Both graduated from college in the late 1960s, and took mundane first jobs. Both lacked advanced training in business or finance. Both knew little or nothing about telecommunications before they stumbled upon their respective companies.

And yet these two men were billionaires, and leaders of the telecommunications industry. By 2002, they also would be proof that you didn't need a business degree from Wharton to watch over a billion-dollar financial fraud.

For Wall Street bankers, Winnick and Ebbers were the ideal clients: colorful, hands-off personalities who paid hundreds of millions of dollars in banking fees. Each of their companies was built around one simple idea. Winnick of Global Crossing sold a telecommunications network crossing under the Atlantic Ocean. Ebbers of WorldCom sold a low-cost, long-distance service. These plans seemed plausible enough during the stock-market boom of the late 1990s and, with the help of Jack Grubman, a respected analyst from Salomon Brothers, the stock prices of Global Crossing and WorldCom surged. The companies then used their highly valued stock to acquire more than 100 companies, each time paying hefty investment-banking fees.

Their business plans were simple enough for television sound bites, but they weren't very good long-term strategies, especially given the difficulties of integrating so many different acquisitions. Nevertheless, as the telecommunications industry was collapsing, Global Crossing and WorldCom continued to perform well—at least on paper. Their earnings met analysts' expectations and revenues continued to grow.

In late 2001, as investors finally discovered the truth about Enron, they began to question the financial statements of Global Crossing and WorldCom, too; and, by 2002, investors had learned of accounting gimmicks at these companies. Now, Enron was no longer the largest bankruptcy in history. If investors who had bought stock in Global Crossing and World-Com had known the stories of those companies in any depth at all, they would have thought twice about trusting Gary Winnick and Bernard Ebbers with their money.

Gary Winnick was a native of Long Island, New York, and graduated from the C. W. Post Campus of Long Island University in 1969 with a degree in economics.[3] C. W. Post had been founded a decade earlier, by the Post cereal family, to educate World War II veterans living on Long Island.

Winnick obviously loved the school. In remembering his C. W. Post days, he reflected, "I am a true Long Island boy, born and bred, and very proud of it. My experience at C. W. Post helped shape my success, and the school remains a very important part of my life." Winnick and his wife gave $10 million to C. W. Post in 2001, and the school agreed to name its center for academic, cultural, and administrative activities "Gary Winnick House."[4]

After graduation, Winnick began working as a furniture salesman for a store owned by his brother in-law.[5] In 1972, he got his first break, and joined a New York securities firm called Burnham and Co. as a trainee. Winnick was relentlessly focused on making money, and the firm needed confidence and loyalty more than intelligence—a trader named Michael Milken supplied plenty of brainpower. After a 1977 merger, Burnham became Drexel Burnham Lambert, and Winnick became a part of Milken's original twenty-man trading operation in New York. In 1978, Milken moved his closely knit group—including Winnick—from Wall Street to new offices in Beverly Hills.[6]

For the next seven years, Winnick worked by Milken's side at his famous X-shaped trading desk. Winnick was brash—some called him a "blowhard"—but he was reliable, and was promoted to head of Drexel's convertible-bond group, which led the industry. Winnick made millions of dollars, as did everyone in Milken's inner circle.

Winnick left Drexel at the perfect time, in 1985, just before prosecutors began investigating the firm for securities fraud. Nevertheless, he remained at risk of prosecution and his record wasn't entirely clean. For example, Winnick allegedly was involved in a questionable junk-bond deal involving Rooney, Pace, a defunct securities firm.[7] But in December

1989, any questions about Winnick's dealings at Drexel became moot, when prosecutors granted him immunity from prosecution after he agreed to testify against Milken. (They ultimately did not call him as a witness, in part because of time constraints imposed on both sides by Judge Kimba M. Wood.)[8]

With the taint of his Drexel experience, Winnick wasn't a viable candidate for a senior position at a major corporation. Not yet, anyway. Instead, he decided to set up his own investment firm, called Pacific Asset Holdings—funded with a large investment from Milken. *Business-Week* called the firm a "Little Drexel,"[9] and the ties to Drexel remained strong. Winnick did various financial deals with Drexel beginning in the late 1980s, including a bid to acquire Western Union. That bid failed in part because of Winnick's connections to Drexel, which by then was under intense investigation.[10] It was as close as Winnick came to running a telecommunications firm—before he joined Global Crossing a decade later.

Although Winnick was frequently credited as the genius behind Global Crossing, in fact the idea of building a network of telecommunications lines under the Atlantic Ocean was not his. Instead, some business partners suggested the idea, and Winnick agreed to invest $15 million of his own money.[11] He was persuaded that, given the increased demand for global telecommunications networks, a company with a "global crossing" would have a valuable franchise. He bought an instructional video that showed how to lay undersea cable, and in 1997 Global Crossing was formed.

Winnick began relentlessly selling the idea of Global Crossing to anyone who would listen. Jack Grubman, who had been an executive vice president of AT&T's consumer and small-business division, and was now an analyst at Salomon Brothers in New York, heard the message loud and clear. Global Crossing had a catchy name and a reasonably interesting idea, and it didn't take much more than that to persuade investors to buy a stock during the late 1990s. Moreover, Grubman knew that if he became a close adviser to Winnick, he could persuade Global Crossing to make numerous acquisitions, and to direct investment-banking business to his firm.

Grubman was so successful that, thanks in part to Global Crossing, he made $20 million a year from 1998 to 2001, more than almost anyone on Wall Street except Frank Quattrone of CS First Boston. Salomon had guaranteed Grubman such huge bonuses to keep him from leaving to join Goldman Sachs as a partner; when that firm later did its Initial Public Offering, partners made tens of millions of dollars each. Grubman proved to be well worth Salomon's money. For Salomon, and many banks, telecommunications advisory work was even more profitable than Internet IPOs. Overall, telecommunications firms paid Wall Street $13 billion in fees from 1998 to 2001. Of that amount, Global Crossing paid more than $420 million,[12] twenty times more than a similarly sized company would pay in a typical year. A big chunk of those fees went to Salomon.

Salomon did Global Crossing's Initial Public Offering in August 1998, along with Merrill Lynch, a few months before Henry Blodget's prediction that Amazon.com would hit $400 per share. Compared to speculative Internet IPOs, Global Crossing was practically a sure thing: even continents filled with telecommunications networks still had to be connected to each other. And although Global Crossing's undersea network had not been built, it was at least a real thing that *could* be built. The IPO was successful, and Winnick—who owned 27 percent of the company—was suddenly worth more than a billion dollars. Many of Winnick's friends were also involved in Global Crossing's management, and they also made millions of dollars, but Winnick made the most money and was obviously in charge. He and his friend Lodwrick M. Cook, a former CEO of ARCO, were ostensibly co-chairmen of the company, but Winnick's official title was "chairman," whereas Cook's was "co-chairman."

Now that Global Crossing's shares were worth several billion dollars, Winnick could use them as currency to buy other companies. If securities analysts approved of the deals, Global Crossing's stock would rise even more. Winnick went on a buying spree, acquiring dozens of telecommunications companies, with Jack Grubman advising on the deals, attending a critical board meeting, and promoting the stocks as an analyst—and with Salomon serving as the firm's primary investment banker. With these acquisitions, Global Crossing was doing much more than building a fiberoptic line under the Atlantic Ocean; it was acquiring one of the largest land-based telecommunications networks, too.

With all of the acquisitions, it was becoming more difficult to interpret Global Crossing's financial statements. Just as mergers had enabled Cendant to inflate its assets, dozens of mergers presented the same opportunity for Global Crossing. Moreover, for technology companies involved in large numbers of acquisitions—such as Cisco and Global Crossing—investors relied on analysts to interpret the detailed financial-statement data. For example, what should investors conclude from the fact that almost one-third of Global Crossing's $22 billion in assets were recorded as *goodwill*—an accounting term representing the difference between the price Global Crossing paid for a company's shares and the value that company previously had recorded for its assets in its financial statements. Investors looked to Jack Grubman to translate these numbers and, not surprisingly, Grubman gave Global Crossing his highest marks. Why wouldn't he? Grubman had practically arranged the deals himself.

During this time, Winnick and other top executives milked Global Crossing for unprecedented perquisites and personal financial gain. Global Crossing engaged in Related Party transactions that made Enron look like a nunnery. It agreed to pay a subsidiary of Winnick's Pacific Capital Group, PCG Telecom, a full two percent of its revenues in exchange for advice.[13] It agreed to buy an on-line voice-transmission system from Withit.com, an Internet company—run by the son of the firm's senior vice president for finance—which had no substantial clients.[14] There were several questionable real-estate deals involving entities related to Winnick. Global Crossing even avoided paying taxes by incorporating outside the United States; although the firm's headquarters was in Los Angeles, its corporate address was Wessex House, in Hamilton, Bermuda.[15]

And then there were the insider sales: in all, Gary Winnick cashed in $735 million of stock, and other insiders sold $4.5 billion, four times more than similarly situated people at Enron.[16] Early investors in Global Crossing who later sold at a huge profit included former president George H. W. Bush, who took stock in lieu of a speaking fee, and Terry McAuliffe, the former chairman of the Democratic National Committee, who invested $100,000 in 1997 and cashed out for $18 million after the IPO. Many of these shares were sold when Global Crossing was near its peak in February 2000, when the market value of the firm's shares was $47 billion, almost as much as Enron's value.

In 1999, as Enron was exploring the idea of expanding into telecommunications, Global Crossing and Enron began discussing deals they might do together. In December 1999, Enron did its first trade of broadband fiber-optic capacity—a monthly contract between New York and Los Angeles on one of Global Crossing's new networks.[17] The relationship would last until just before Enron's collapse; Gary Winnick and Jeff Skilling spoke about one end-of-quarter deal just before Skilling resigned in August 2001.[18]

Global Crossing and Enron were a natural fit. Fiber-optic networks were laid along the path of natural-gas pipelines, so there were reasons for Enron and Global Crossing to do legitimate business together. Enron was more interested in financial techniques than bricks-and-mortar projects, and Global Crossing's executives quickly learned that financial engineering could be more profitable than any other form of engineering the firm had used. The dealings between the two firms quickly became focused more on accounting numbers than economic reality, just as Enron's risk-management manual had instructed: accounting numbers were the important measure of performance.

As Global Crossing and Enron developed a relationship, Enron also was advising other companies about how to create phantom revenue and earnings. For example, in July 2000, Enron visited AT&T to pitch its expertise in various complex structured transactions. Enron's pitch book was audacious: Enron claimed to have replicated its capabilities in natural gas and energy in the telecommunications sector, and said it would be "the world's largest buyer and seller of bandwidth," "the world's largest provider of premium broadband delivery services," and would "deploy the most open, efficient network with broad connectivity." These were bold claims to be making to AT&T, which had long been the leading telecommunications company. But AT&T was dying, and although Michael Armstrong, the firm's leader, had tried numerous financial tricks—from spinning off various divisions to issuing *tracking stock,* whose value was based on the performance of particular business lines—AT&T's stock price was at a low. Enron officials thumbed their noses at AT&T's hard assets, arguing that they could simply "swap" into fiber-optic networks, buying the rights to use other firms' capacity, and thereby become a leading telecommunications firm overnight, without wasting the time and resources necessary to build its own network.

Enron offered AT&T a variety of complicated transactions designed to improve AT&T's financial numbers. These were essentially turbocharged versions of the simple schemes Cendant and others had used to "borrow" profits from future years.

One idea related to AT&T's practice of selling rights to its bandwidth in exchange for a prepaid amount from a customer. Customers did long-term deals with AT&T, and instead of agreeing to pay a fixed rate over time, they agreed to prepay a discounted amount up front. For example, if a customer bought 20-year rights to AT&T's bandwidth, the cost might be $5 million per year, or $100 million in all spread over 20 years.

Instead of agreeing to pay over time, the customer would agree to pre-pay some discounted amount up front—say, $40 million.

The problem with such a deal, according to Enron, was that account-ing rules required AT&T to spread out the income from the $40 million up-front payment over the 20-year period, so that it reported earnings of just $2 million per year. That made economic sense, given that AT&T would incur costs from its obligation to provide broadband services dur-ing the 20-year period. But Enron claimed it could arrange a deal so that AT&T reported the full $5 million per year instead.

Here is how it would work. Enron created a Special Purpose Entity, and the customer prepaid $40 million to the SPE instead of to AT&T. AT&T then entered into an over-the-counter derivative with the SPE in which AT&T received a "loan" of $40 million and agreed to pay inter-est during the 20-year period. Enron then entered into derivatives with both the SPE and AT&T, in which Enron received the full $5 million per year from the SPE and passed that amount on to AT&T. It was a com-plex daisy chain; but, essentially, AT&T borrowed money from itself, and recognized the additional borrowed amount—an extra $3 million per year—as income. According to Enron, AT&T arguably received $5 million in "income" per year from the SPE, and the "loan" with the SPE was an over-the-counter derivative that did not need to be reported (remember, such derivatives transactions were unregulated and fell out-side the scope of traditional accounting rules).

AT&T had frittered away tens of billions of dollars of shareholder value through failed investments in telecommunications, and financial gimmickry, but this scheme was too much—even for AT&T. The com-pany rejected Enron's proposal, even though it seemed unlikely that reg-ulators would detect these deals. Even if they did, they likely would not understand them. Still, the pitch book for the AT&T deal gave a picture of Enron's overall dealings, and Enron sold similar products to other companies, reportedly including Lucent, Owens Corning, and even a handful of utility companies.

Then there was Global Crossing.

In March 2001, a little over a year after Enron's first deal with Global Crossing, the two firms entered into a long-term swap. On the surface, the swap appeared to be a fiber-optic deal, in which Enron paid for eight years of access to Global Crossing's fiber-optic network and Global Crossing purchased something called "network services" from Enron.[19] Enron paid

$17 million up front, whereas Global Crossing agreed to make monthly payments for eight years.

In reality, the fiber-optic and network-services rights roughly cancelled each other, leaving only a $17 million "loan" from Enron with monthly "interest" payments to be made by Global Crossing. Global Crossing reported earnings from selling rights to its fiber-optic network, but did not report the "loan" as a liability. Enron reported $5 million of gains from the sale of network services, but did not record the fact that Global Crossing owed it $17 million. Both companies benefited from the appearance of high volumes of transactions in network rights.[20] It was exactly the same as the $8 billion of prepaid swap deals Citigroup and J. P. Morgan Chase had sold to Enron, except that now Enron was playing the role of a bank, arranging the deal on its own with Global Crossing.

This swap, and others like it, were designed to help Global Crossing "manufacture" earnings, especially at the end of a financial quarter. Like the Wall Street banks, Enron disclaimed any responsibility for how Global Crossing accounted for the swap on its financial statements. One Enron executive reportedly said, "We were selling them bullets; they could use them any way they wanted." Enron executives argued that there was nothing wrong with manufacturing earnings, and defended the swap with Global Crossing, because "[e]veryone was over-reporting their numbers back then."[21]

During the time of these trades with Enron, Global Crossing also began entering into swap transactions with other firms, to trade rights known in the telecommunications industry as Indefeasible Rights of Use. IRUs were created at AT&T, which had trained many of the executives running various telecommunications companies. Now, many of these executives' companies were inflating their revenue and earnings with IRU swaps—telecommunications executives from AT&T included Joseph Nacchio, CEO of Qwest; and Robert Annunziata and Leo Hindery Jr., who had been CEOs of Global Crossing. Even Jack Grubman, the analyst from Salomon, had come from AT&T.

In an IRU swap, two telecommunications companies agreed to exchange the rights to use bandwidth on different parts of their fiber-optic networks. One company might exchange the rights to use lines in New York for rights of roughly the same value in Kansas.

The beauty of IRUs, from the perspective of a telecommunications company, was that accounting rules arguably permitted companies to treat the two legs of the swap differently, recording the revenue leg up front, while deferring the expense leg over time. In 1999, the SEC had published "Staff Accounting Bulletin No. 101" in an attempt to standardize the way companies recognized their revenues, and to ban revenue recognition practices that had deceived investors during the late 1990s (recall Al Dunlap's "channel stuffing" of barbecue grills at Sunbeam). This bulletin set forth the requirements for when certain revenues should be recognized and for when certain costs should be spread over time. The bulletin was lengthy and complex; but, essentially, Global Crossing and other companies were using one portion of the bulletin to justify up-front recognition of revenues, while using another portion of the bulletin to justify spreading expenses over time. Global Crossing could argue that the incoming payments from the IRU were revenues, to be recognized right away, while the outgoing payments were a capital expense, to be spread over a period of several years.

Not everyone in Global Crossing's accounting department agreed with this interpretation. Roy Olofson, a vice president of finance at Global Crossing, believed the legs of the swap should be treated equivalently. But any support he had—within Global Crossing or among the firm's auditors at Arthur Andersen—evaporated in May 2000, when Global Crossing hired Joseph P. Perrone as a senior vice president of finance. Perrone had been at Arthur Andersen for thirty-one years, where he audited Global Crossing, was involved in discussions about how to account for IRUs, and even suggested some restrictions on Global Crossing's accounting practices.[22] Winnick lured Perrone with a huge guaranteed bonus and 500,000 stock options, worth millions of dollars.[23] (In addition, it was Perrone's son who ran Withit.com, the Internet company that did its first major deal with Global Crossing.) With Perrone at Global Crossing in 2000, Arthur Andersen received $2.3 million in audit fees and $12 million for non-audit work. Not surprisingly, Global Crossing's executives listened to Perrone more than Olofson.

Olofson began reporting directly to Perrone during mid-2000, and the two men immediately clashed over accounting policies. However, the disputes lasted only a few months, because Olofson was diagnosed with lung cancer and took a leave from the firm beginning in January 2001.

While the cat was away, the mice began to play. Global Crossing's executives proposed to use IRU swaps in March 2001—the end of the firm's first financial quarter—to generate revenues and earnings that the company needed to meet analysts' expectations. Global Crossing's accountants wanted employees entering into these swaps to be sure the swaps contained the correct language, so that they would receive appropriate accounting treatment. On March 8, 2001, they circulated a memorandum stressing, "It is important for GX [Global Crossing] to classify these purchases as a capital lease versus a pre-paid service, because the classification affects how the expense impacts our EBITDA [earnings] calculation. A capital lease expense is excluded from our EBITDA calculation, while a service expense is included as a deduction in our EBITDA." In other words, the accountants wanted to ensure that the cost of deals was spread over time, not included as an immediate expense. (EBITDA is an acronym for one important measure of accounting earnings: Earnings Before Interest, Tax, Depreciation, and Amortization.)

One $100 million IRU swap was with Qwest, a telecommunications company that had outbid Global Crossing for U.S. West, one of the regional Bell companies created by the breakup of AT&T. Qwest then used the IRU swap technique on its own. During the first three quarters of 2001, Qwest sold $870 million of capacity and bought $868 million of capacity—to and from the same parties.[24] These swaps appeared to be round-trip transactions, which served no purpose other than to inflate Qwest's revenues. A year later, on July 28, 2002, Qwest would file a billion-dollar-plus restatement, admitting that it had improperly recorded revenues from these trades.

Meanwhile, Global Crossing did IRU swaps with other companies. When Olofson returned to work in May 2001, he expressed concern about the financial statements Global Crossing had filed for the first quarter of 2001. Olofson told Perrone he believed Global Crossing had done illegitimate end-of-quarter swaps to achieve revenue and earnings targets. Global Crossing conducted a study to assess the value of the firm's swaps, and concluded that less than 20 percent of the swaps actually could be added to Global Crossing's network.[25] In other words, Global Crossing found it was doing swaps that had no real business use.

Nevertheless, the firm continued doing IRU swaps, and continued booking revenue up front and spreading expenses over time. According to Olofson, $720 million of Global Crossing's $3.2 billion in revenue during the first half of 2001 was from illegitimate swaps.[26] Olofson also claimed that thirteen of eighteen of these swaps occurred during the last two days of the quarter,[27] making it appear that Global Crossing was using the IRU swaps as a last-minute way to create fictional earnings it needed to meet quarterly expectations.

On August 6, 2001—at almost exactly the same time an Enron employee, Sherron Watkins, was warning Ken Lay about the firm's accounting practices—Olofson sent a five-page letter to James Gorton, Global Crossing's 39-year-old general counsel and "Chief Ethics Officer," warning him that the firm had engaged in misleading accounting practices.[28] The letter closely resembled Sherron Watkins's letter to Ken Lay, and even discussed similar issues.

After consulting with Global Crossing outside counsel, Gorton responded that the company already knew of these accounting practices and then resigned a few days later, citing "personal reasons."[29] Apparently, Global Crossing's top managers did not send the letter to its auditors or board of directors. Olofson was fired from Global Crossing in November 2001.

According to a February 4, 2002, press release by Global Crossing, the firm did not inform Arthur Andersen or its audit committee about the contents of the letter until January 29, 2002, the day after it filed for bankruptcy, when the *Los Angeles Times* reported the existence of Olofson's letter.

Global Crossing later dismissed Olofson's allegations as the rantings of a disgruntled former employee, notwithstanding the fact that Olofson was not fired until three months after he sent his pivotal letter. It was true that Olofson was embroiled in a legal battle with Global Crossing and Gary Winnick related to his dismissal. But you didn't need to believe Olofson to spot Global Crossing's accounting machinations. Congressional investigators and prosecutors were uncovering the same facts, and much of what Olofson alleged was plain from Global Crossing's public disclosures. All you needed to do was read Global Crossing's most recent annual report.

Anyone looking carefully at Global Crossing's annual financial filing for 2000 would find $350 million of revenue on page 29 listed under "Sales Type Lease Revenue," the term Global Crossing used for swaps of fiber-optic capacity. There was no corresponding line item for the expenses associated with these revenues. Instead, on page 32, there was this statement: "In addition, depreciation and amortization includes non-cash cost of capacity sold resulting from capacity sales that meet the qualifications of sales-type lease accounting." In other words, in 2000, Global Crossing was recognizing revenue up front from these transactions and spreading the associated expenses over time. This accounting treatment matched Roy Olofson's allegations.

Global Crossing apparently was concerned about continuing to follow these accounting practices, because it changed its reporting in 2001 in a way that made the firm's quarterly filings look like financial reports from Wonderland. Suddenly, no "Sales Type Lease Revenue" was listed at all. Instead, Global Crossing downplayed the firm's *actual* revenues and expenses—which were plummeting, along with those of the rest of the telecommunications industry—and encouraged investors and analysts to focus, instead, on something it called "Cash Revenue," which was defined as the firm's actual revenue plus "revenue" from IRU swaps. In other words, "Cash Revenue" was neither cash nor revenue. The additions were substantial: $551 million for the second quarter of 2001.[30]

The firm then used the "Cash Revenue" number to calculate another accounting fiction, "Adjusted EBITDA," a manufactured number that included EBITDA—the measure of accounting earnings—plus the "non-cash cost of capacity sold" and the "cash portion of the change in deferred revenue," terms that referred to IRU swaps. In other words, Global Crossing's "Adjusted EBITDA" was a measure of the firm's income that included up-front revenue from the IRU swaps, but spread expenses over time. This also matched Olofson's allegations.

The securities analysts covering the telecommunications industry were aware of the bizarre accounting practices related to IRUs.[31] They shouldn't have cared whether Global Crossing recorded the costs up front or spread them over time, or whether the firm wanted to use make-believe terms such as "Adjusted EBITDA." As long as they knew what the firm actually was doing, they should have been able to figure out what it was worth, and then either recommend the stock to investors, or not. In an efficient market, sophisticated investors would trade Global Crossing's stock until its price was accurate, selling if uninformed investors had driven up the price. However, the market for Global Crossing stock did not seem to be an efficient one; it was dominated by investors who loved the idea of Global Crossing, but did not understand IRUs and did not even bother to read Global Crossing's financial filings. They overestimated Global Crossing's value, and their frenetic buying drove the price of the stock. An informed investor who tried betting against Global Crossing's stock might be correct, but she was stepping in front of a speeding train.

Meanwhile, Global Crossing's executives were stumbling over each other to sell stock before reality struck, and the firm was awarding unprecedented pay packages to a rapid succession of short-lived CEOs.[32] First, Gary Winnick paid Jack Scanlon 3.6 million stock options to take the top job in April 1998. Then, Robert Annunziata, a former AT&T executive, took over in February 1999, with a $10 million signing bonus and 4 million options.[33] Then Leo Hindery was CEO for seven months, and received 2 million options. In October 2000, Winnick promised new CEO Thomas J. Casey, an investment banker from Merrill Lynch, an $8 million loan (which later was forgiven), in addition to a seven-figure salary and bonus, plus options on 2 million shares of Global Crossing stock. Casey lasted less than a year in the job, and so Winnick enticed John J. Legere with the same terms *plus* a $3.5 million signing bonus, an additional $7 million of loans, and an extra 3 million options. Interestingly, these executives were so eager to sign pay packages that they neglected to check the details of when their stock options would become available. Casey's employment agreement omitted one of the option payment dates; as a result, he was not entitled to receive 440,000 options, with a value of millions of dollars at the time they were granted.[34] It is unclear whether anyone at Global Crossing spotted this mistake. Whatever happened to Casey's extra options, it was incredible that, throughout this period, with five CEOs, individual investors nevertheless remained interested in Global Crossing.

The fictitious gains from IRU swaps could not continue indefinitely without real profits to replace them, and on October 4, 2001—less than three weeks before Ken Lay's fateful conference call with Enron's analysts and investors—Global Crossing announced that it would not meet analysts' earnings estimates. As word spread about the way the firm had recorded revenues and expenses from IRU swaps, investors abandoned the stock. Enron's collapse was a bad precedent, and investors watching Enron nervously sold their Global Crossing stock. The end was sudden, and Global Crossing filed for bankruptcy on January 28, 2002—less than two months after Enron. The firm had had a short life as a public company under Gary Winnick—just four years from IPO to bankruptcy. In the end, as in the beginning, the firm took care of its insiders. In addition to forgiving $18 million in loans to its last two CEOs,[35] Global Crossing—like Enron—arranged for its top employees to be paid millions of dollars just before its bankruptcy filing.[36]

Gary Winnick wasn't suffering too much. In 1999, the *Los Angeles Business Journal* had named Winnick "Los Angeles' richest man," worth $6 billion. He was no longer worth that much, but he was still on the Forbes 400 list of the wealthiest U.S. citizens, behind Bill Gates but ahead of Donald Trump. And he still lived in a $40 million mansion in Beverly

Hills, down the street from Barbra Streisand, where he was considering plans for a new 100-car parking garage. He was active with his favorite charities, although he no longer could use Global Crossing's resources for contributions, as he had, repeatedly, as chairman, even offering use of Global Crossing's marine-services division to assist in the rescue of the Russian submarine Kursk in 2000.[37] It seemed likely that Winnick would avoid civil liability and criminal charges. The leaders of C. W. Post still cherished his support, and with a little luck Gary Winnick House—unlike Enron Field—will keep its name.

Since Bernard Ebbers was a child in Edmonton, Alberta, he had wanted to be a basketball player.[38] He played for his high school team in Canada during the late 1950s, but didn't receive any major scholarship offers. He enrolled at the University of Alberta, but after spending a year practicing his jump shot more than studying, he flunked out. Ebbers did odd jobs in Edmonton, including one summer at Edmonton Telephones[39] and a stint driving a milk-delivery truck.[40]

After a few years, he finally found a place where he could play basketball: Mississippi College, a small school affiliated with the Mississippi Baptist Convention, which was consistently listed in the top 100 "character-building" colleges in the United States. Mississippi College was just the kick in the pants Ebbers needed, and he graduated in 1967 with a degree in physical education.[41]

Unfortunately, a Mississippi College degree didn't do much more for Bernie Ebbers at first than a diploma from C. W. Post had done for Gary Winnick. Ebbers coached high school basketball in Mississippi for a year, and then ran a small garment factory.[42] He eventually persuaded some friends to invest with him in a motel and restaurant in a small town in Mississippi. He kept costs low, and over time bought a few more motels.[43] But sixteen years after graduation, he was a long way from becoming a multibillionaire.

One day in 1983, as Ken Lay was ascending the corporate ladder in Houston, Ebbers was sitting in a coffee shop in Hattiesberg, Mississippi, discussing the recent breakup of AT&T with his friends Murray Waldron and William Rector. The men decided they might be able to make money by purchasing long-distance services from the major phone companies and then selling it to small, local companies. Their waitress was listening to their conversation, and suggested Long Distance Discount Services as a name. The men started LDDS, and Ebbers abandoned his hotels to become CEO of the company in 1985.[44]

Like Gary Winnick, Ebbers was an aggressive salesman. But unlike Winnick, Ebbers also was frugal, and his penny-pinching attitude appealed to companies interested in reducing their long-distance bills. During the next decade, LDDS acquired a portfolio of residential and business customers, and expanded by buying a handful of small long-distance companies, just as Ebbers previously had acquired hotels. By 1995, LDDS had become a substantial provider of discount long-distance services, and Bernie Ebbers decided that the waitress from Hattiesberg hadn't been thinking big enough; he changed the company's name to WorldCom.

Like Gary Winnick, Ebbers built up WorldCom, piece by piece, by acquiring dozens of companies. And like Gary Winnick, Ebbers befriended Jack Grubman and Salomon Brothers, relied on Grubman for advice, and used Salomon as his firm's primary investment bank. Grubman had an unusually close relationship with WorldCom's top managers, and even attended three board meetings, where he discussed deals the company was considering (securities analysts typically were not permitted to attend board meetings).[45] With Grubman's help, WorldCom's stock price soared, and Ebbers began considering acquiring larger companies. In all, WorldCom paid Salomon $80 million in fees for these deals and other investment-banking work.[46]

In 1997, at Grubman's urging, WorldCom offered to buy MCI in the highest-profile deal of Ebbers's career, one of the biggest mergers in U.S. history. The media closely followed the deal, and sophisticated fund managers—including Long-Term Capital Management—bet on whether it would succeed. When MCI agreed to terms, WorldCom instantly became the second-largest provider of long-distance telephone services—and a household name.[47] By the late 1990s, investors knew more about WorldCom than they did about AT&T, the dominant telecommunications firm from the prior decade. WorldCom was the fifth most widely held stock in the United States, and its shares were worth $115 billion, double the value of AT&T's shares. Twenty million residential customers used WorldCom as their long-distance carrier.

And yet, looking at the upper management of WorldCom, it was hard to believe this was a major multinational company. WorldCom was a creation of Wall Street, in the same way Britney Spears was a creation of the entertainment industry. Jack Grubman might as well have propped up a cardboard cutout of a CEO. Ebbers still didn't understand World-Com's finances and relied extensively on Grubman. Ebbers also depended almost exclusively on Scott D. Sullivan, his chief financial officer, to "see if the numbers work."[48] Sullivan was bright—a straight-A student at the State University of New York at Oswego—and was knowledgeable about accounting and mergers, but he lacked Andy Fastow's training and experience in complex financial engineering. In contrast to Enron, which had been featured in Myron Scholes's Nobel laureate address, WorldCom's approach to its finances was straight out of *The Complete Idiot's Guide to Finance and Accounting*.

In many ways, WorldCom's simplistic approach to its finances was superior to Enron's. WorldCom had invested three times as much as Enron in Rhythms NetConnections before that firm's Initial Public Offering.[49] That $30 million investment bought 8.6 percent of the company, worth almost a billion dollars at the peak. In 2001, WorldCom bought most of the assets of Rhythms NetConnections, and those assets appeared on WorldCom's financial statements. Investors knew about WorldCom's involvement in Rhythms NetConnections, and WorldCom didn't use elaborate partnership transactions to hide its gains—or, later, its losses.

WorldCom's financial statements were much easier to understand, and appeared to be transparent. By 2001, given the downturn in the telecommunications industry, many investors expected that WorldCom's income would decline. There were no Special Purpose Entities or off-balance-sheet derivatives for the company to use to hide losses or inflate profits. WorldCom's top managers weren't sophisticated enough to use Enron's elaborate schemes or even Global Crossing's IRU swaps. It appeared that Ebbers and Sullivan would have to admit their business was struggling.

To save the day, Scott Sullivan wangled an accounting fix that was even simpler than Cendant's retyping of revenues and expenses. During 2001 and the first quarter of 2002, Sullivan simply transferred some expenses from the firm's operating account to its capital account.[50] The operating account included the day-to-day costs of doing business, such as wages or advertising; the capital account included investments in long-term projects, such as the construction of a new building. Because operating expenses were incurred right away, whereas capital expenses were spread over time, the effect of the transfers was to reduce World-Com's current expenses, pushing them off into the future. With lower expenses, WorldCom showed higher earnings and, thereby, met expectations, even though, in truth, its business was declining.

The expenses involved the firm's payments to other telecommunications companies to access their networks, known as *line costs,* for the right to access a telecommunications line. From an economic perspective, line costs were indistinguishable from the costs of building a network; as Enron had shown, companies could either build their own network or purchase rights to someone else's. But from an accounting perspective, line costs were unambiguously operating expenses, which should have been deducted from WorldCom's revenues during the quarter the expenses were incurred. A student in Accounting 101 who classified line costs as capital expenditures to be spread out over several years would have failed the class, even if she had an argument about why line costs and new network construction costs were equivalent. Yet that was precisely what WorldCom did—for five straight quarters.

In May 2001—in the middle of Sullivan's scheme to defer WorldCom's expenses—WorldCom completed an $11.9 billion debt deal, the largest in U.S. history. The firms arranging the deal were J. P. Morgan Chase and, not surprisingly, Salomon (a division of Citigroup). These banks performed a supposedly thorough due-diligence investigation, as did WorldCom's accountants from Arthur Andersen; yet, apparently, no one spotted the fact that WorldCom *already* had transferred $771 million of line costs from operating to capital expenses during the first quarter of 2001.[51] Even if Sullivan had been acting alone, it was incredible that top banks and accounting firms would understand their client so poorly that they would not notice a $771 million revision.

The credit-rating agencies also performed an extensive investigation of WorldCom before they decided to give the firm's bonds a rating of A minus, well above investment-grade, and they apparently did not spot the errors, either. In fact, the agencies did not downgrade WorldCom to a sub-investment-grade rating until May 9, 2002—two months after the Securities and Exchange Commission publicly announced an inquiry into WorldCom's accounting practices, and more than a week after Bernard Ebbers resigned.

No one spotted the fact that WorldCom used the same scheme to hide billions of dollars of expenses *after* its big debt deal, either: $610 million during the second quarter of 2001, $743 million in the third quarter, $931 million in the fourth quarter, and $797 million in the first quarter of 2002.[52] In fact, on February 6, 2002, Arthur Andersen, WorldCom's auditor, told the firm's audit committee that it had reviewed the processes management was using to account for line costs and found those processes to be "effective," and had "no disagreements" with them.[53]

How could all of the watchdogs have missed such a basic multibillion-dollar accounting mistake? Perhaps they never imagined WorldCom's top executives would attempt such a simple scheme. Perhaps they were blinded by huge fees. Or perhaps they were no longer serving as watchdogs.

Several of WorldCom's banks—including J. P. Morgan Chase and Citigroup, Salomon's parent—also loaned billions of dollars to World-Com, earning still more fees. These loans made it appear that the banks genuinely had not known about the accounting scheme; if they had, why would they have loaned WorldCom so much money? (The answer to that question involved credit swaps—more on them soon.)

After the collapse of Enron and Global Crossing, rumors spread that WorldCom was involved in similar dealings. The SEC began investigating WorldCom's finances and discovered that the company had made undisclosed loans to Bernie Ebbers of $366 million, twenty times the amount Global Crossing had loaned its last two CEOs. Ebbers had used the money to buy WorldCom stock, now below $3 per share, apparently oblivious to the fact that his company was unprofitable. In light of this, WorldCom's board asked Ebbers to resign.

Ebbers had lost much of his fortune, and now his job. Fortunately, he did not have Gary Winnick's profligate lifestyle. Even after advancing from a summer job at Edmonton Telephones to the top position at a leading global conglomerate, Ebbers had maintained frugal habits: a modest home in Brookhaven, Mississippi; an old red Ford pickup with a loose fender; and low-cost hobbies, such as playing pool, drinking beer, and listening to Willie Nelson.[54] If he could avoid doing time in prison, Bernie Ebbers could handle the financial loss. A few days after he was fired, Ebbers told a local radio station, "I feel like crying. But I am a thousand percent convinced in my heart that this is a temporary thing."

John W. Sidgmore, who had been WorldCom's vice chairman, replaced Ebbers on April 29, 2002. Sidgmore wisely had already sold almost $100 million of WorldCom stock. The rating agencies didn't like the fact that Bernie Ebbers had been forced out, and they immediately downgraded WorldCom to a rating of below investment grade, thereby ensuring that the end would come soon. To appease the rating agencies, and other investors and analysts, Sidgmore ordered a thorough internal review of WorldCom's financial statements, to be done by the end of the third quarter of 2002. A few weeks later, he fired Arthur Andersen and hired KPMG as the company's new auditors.[55] Still, no one outside WorldCom knew the details about WorldCom's fallacious financial statements.

At this point, Scott Sullivan was in serious trouble. Although it would take KPMG some time to unravel WorldCom's finances, Cynthia Cooper, an internal auditor at WorldCom, already had begun her own investigation of the company's capital expenditures for line costs. Cooper had discovered that someone had transferred line costs from the operating account to the capital account, so that those costs would be spread over time. Like Sherron Watkins of Enron and Roy Olofson of Global Crossing before her, she was about to blow the whistle on a billion-dollar-plus accounting error.

Cooper confronted Sullivan with her findings on June 11, 2002. According to Cooper, Sullivan said the problems would be corrected and asked her to delay her review, which did not need to be completed until the third quarter—she should be focusing on the second quarter, not the third. Sullivan had only three days to prepare for the next regularly scheduled audit-committee and board meetings, when he would need to present the company's preliminary financial statements for the second quarter, and he couldn't afford to have Cooper sniffing around. He still needed to decide what to tell board members about line costs.

Cooper ignored Sullivan's request for a delay, and immediately contacted Max Bobbitt, the chair of WorldCom's audit committee. Cooper told him she thought the audit committee should be apprised of the facts she had discovered, but Bobbitt said he believed it was premature.

At the meeting on June 14, Sullivan said WorldCom's second-quarter financial statement would be very "complex" and that he was continuing to examine line costs. The board members were not alerted to Cynthia Cooper's discovery that WorldCom had overstated its income by billions of dollars.

There was a flurry of meetings during the next week. On June 20, Sullivan explained to the audit committee that the accounting for line costs had required significant "judgments." Sullivan's judgment had been that the line costs were long-term contracts and that, because WorldCom had not yet made any money from those contracts, it was appropriate to spread the costs over time, instead of incurring them all at once.[56] WorldCom's directors asked Sullivan to take a few days to prepare a memorandum outlining his reasoning (just as a skeptical Ed Cerullo of Kidder Peabody had asked Joseph Jett to explain his bond-trading strategy in writing). WorldCom's directors contacted representatives from Arthur Andersen, who said that Sullivan's reasoning was contrary to Generally Accepted Accounting Principles. Auditors from KPMG agreed. Andersen officials said they had not known about the line-cost transfers, and they said investors should not rely on the firm's written opinion that WorldCom's 2001 financial statements were accurate.[57]

In Sullivan's defense, his argument for spreading out the line-cost expenses made some sense. After all, there was no economic difference between paying money to build your own network—the costs of which *were* spread out over time—and paying money to access the lines on someone else's network, any more than there was an economic difference between leasing a car for a period of time and borrowing money for the same period of time to buy the car. If the "investment" in someone else's lines would yield returns only over a period of years, then it made sense to treat those costs as capital expenditures to be spread over several years. In fact, such a conclusion followed from one of the basic principles of accounting: matching the timing of revenues and expenses. If, as Sullivan claimed, revenues would occur over several years, then it made sense to record expenses over several years, too.

But economic reality didn't necessarily match accounting, as Enron's risk-management manual had instructed. Generally Accepted Accounting Principles were a somewhat arbitrary set of rules that all companies and their officials promised to live by, even if they diverged from economic reality. If the established accounting practice was to treat line costs as operating expenses, including them in the current period, then it was improper to spread those costs over time.

The effect of the reclassification of line costs was devastating. WorldCom had reported 2001 earnings of $10.5 billion. Now, it would need to reduce that number to $6.3 billion, to account for the additional expenses from line costs. The restatement of earnings was five times larger than Enron's. Sullivan was fired the day of the announcement.

Most of the events to follow were predictable: first, WorldCom's stock price plunged; second, once everyone understood the basics, the credit-rating agencies finally downgraded WorldCom; and third, the company filed for bankruptcy. Jack Grubman had hung on until the very end, finally issuing his first negative report about WorldCom on June 21, just days before WorldCom announced its accounting scheme.[58] On August 2, 2002, there were photographs of Scott Sullivan and his assistant, David Myers, on the front page of the *New York Times*—in handcuffs. A few days later, WorldCom announced that it had discovered another $3.3 billion of accounting mistakes—this time, it had artificially inflated the reserves it set aside for future expenses, just as Sunbeam had overstated its massive "one-time" charges so that it would appear to make more money in the future. In late 2002, the company announced billions more of accounting errors—the losses were a bottomless pit.

Previously, officials of many other companies—including Enron—had relied on the letter of the law to support their interpretations of accounting rules, even when they were contrary to economic reality or common sense. Now, they had a paradigmatic case to cite in their defense. How could any company official be expected to stray from the letter of rules in favor of economic reality, when a prominent CFO, Scott Sullivan, had been fired and prosecuted for following economic reality over accounting practice?

Of course, WorldCom's switch had occurred, not so coincidentally, when WorldCom's business was hurting and the company was falling short of analysts' earnings estimates. And although Sullivan had argued that WorldCom's expenses should be delayed along with its revenues, the reality was that WorldCom's revenues weren't merely delayed; instead, they weren't coming in at all, because of trouble in the telecommunications industry. Sullivan's legal defense would be a challenge.

Nevertheless, WorldCom's collapse presented a paradox for prosecutors. To prove a crime, they had to establish that corporate officials intended to commit fraud. But given the gap between economic reality and accounting rules, which people were guilty of criminal intent: those who followed accounting rules over economic reality, or those who followed economic reality over accounting?

WorldCom's bankruptcy filing listed J. P. Morgan Chase as being owed more than $3 billion. Other banks, including Citigroup, were owed nearly as much. These banks also were the major lenders to other failed companies, including Enron and Global Crossing. These sophisticated financial institutions had loaned billions of dollars to the same foolish firms. In 2000, there had been $42 billion of corporate defaults, a record. In 2001, that number tripled. More than 200 companies defaulted, including one of every nine telecommunications firms.[59] And that was *before* Global Crossing and WorldCom.

This all should have been terrible news for banks. Was the U.S. banking system now in danger of collapse?

The answer was no, but few investors understood the reason. The explanation related to the latest innovation in financial markets—credit derivatives—a new twist even the major Wall Street banks did not fully comprehend. Credit derivatives were just emerging in the mid-1990s, when government officials were restricting securities lawsuits, deregulating financial markets, and creating incentives for companies to compensate executives with stock options.

Now, credit derivatives were a rapidly growing $2 *trillion* market, according to 2002 estimates by the Bank of England, and J. P. Morgan Chase, the leading participant.[60] Credit derivatives were a cash cow for Wall Street. In 2001, banks made an estimated $1 billion in profits buying and selling credit derivatives.[61] During some months, J. P. Morgan Chase traded more credit derivatives than actual bonds.[62]

These new instruments were the last piece of an increasingly complicated financial puzzle. They explained why banks were safe, notwithstanding widespread corporate defaults—and why many individuals were at risk.

Credit derivatives essentially were bets on the creditworthiness of a particular company, like insurance on a loan. Like many other derivatives, they were developed first by Bankers Trust and Credit Suisse Financial Products, beginning in the early 1990s, primarily in Japan. John Chrystal—one of the smartest and most innovative derivatives gurus at CSFP—had been focusing on credit derivatives since 1991.[63] But these instruments did not spread widely until the major commercial banks, such as J. P. Morgan and Citigroup, became more active participants during the late 1990s.

There were two basic types of credit derivatives: credit default swaps and Collateralized Debt Obligations. Both were central to understanding the aftermath of the collapse of Enron, Global Crossing, WorldCom, and other troubled firms.

A plain-vanilla credit default swap was a cross between a loan and an insurance policy. In a typical loan, a bank gave money up front to a borrower and the borrower agreed to repay that money in the future. A credit default swap was similar to a loan, except that no money changed hands up front. Instead, the parties to a credit default swap agreed that one would pay the other if a particular borrower—any borrower they specified—defaulted on its loans. In other words, the loans that triggered payment on a credit default swap typically did not involve either of the parties to the credit default swap itself. For example, Bankers Trust and a Japanese insurance company could do a credit default swap based on whether IBM would repay its loans to Citigroup. In such a swap, the Japanese insurance company might take a similar position to Citigroup as lender, hoping to earn money so long as IBM did not default.

In a typical insurance policy, two parties bet on whether a particular event would occur: a car accident, a fire, a death. In a credit default swap, two parties bet on whether a company would default on its loans. The party betting yes was "buying protection," like an individual buying insurance. The party betting no was "selling protection," like an insurance company. If the company they were betting on remained healthy, the buyer of protection would pay the seller an amount resembling an insurance premium. If the company failed to make its loan payments, the seller of protection would pay the buyer a prespecified amount, like the payout on an insurance policy.

Banks used credit default swaps to transfer credit risk, the risk that they would not be repaid money they had loaned to other companies. They bought credit protection from investors by agreeing to pay a fee in exchange for the right to receive payment if a particular company defaulted on its debts. Credit default swaps were ideal for commercial banks, because they enabled them to cut their risks while reducing the regulatory charges they had to pay for loans they already had made. When the Federal Reserve issued guidelines in June 1997 making these regulatory benefits clear, and the Asia crisis followed immediately thereafter, banks such as J. P. Morgan and Citigroup rushed to do credit default swaps, to lower their risks and regulatory costs.[64]

The market for credit default swaps was tested in 1998, when Russia announced a "rescheduling" in its local debt market, and parties disputed whether that announcement was a "default" according to the ambiguous language in some credit default swaps. But the swap dealers tightened the language in response, and the market doubled and then doubled again. By 2002, banks had done hundreds of billions of dollars of credit default swaps based on various borrowers throughout the world. This was why the banks were reasonably safe, even though they had loaned hundreds of billions of dollars to those companies.

For example, banks had done an estimated $10 billion of credit default swaps related to WorldCom.[65] That meant that even though banks still held loans to WorldCom and were owed money in WorldCom's bankruptcy proceeding, they had sold the risk associated with those loans to someone else. The banks didn't have to worry about WorldCom's bankruptcy, because whatever they lost on WorldCom's loans, they made up for with credit default swaps. Whatever happened, they were hedged.

There also were approximately 800 credit default swaps involving $8 billion of bets on Enron.[66] J. P. Morgan did many of them, just as it did credit default swaps based on Global Crossing and Kmart, which also declared bankruptcy in 2002. As a result, J. P. Morgan Chase recorded "only" $456 million in losses on loans to Enron.[67]

Citigroup did even better with respect to its exposure to Enron, albeit in a slightly more complex way. From August 2000 to May 2001, Citigroup created a series of Special Purpose Entities that held AAA-rated bonds and issued a special type of credit derivative that depended on whether Enron defaulted.[68] If Enron paid its debts, the investors would keep the AAA-rated bonds. But if Enron did not pay, Citigroup would take the AAA-rated bonds and replace them with Enron's bonds. By using these transactions, Citigroup hedged its entire $1.2 billion exposure to Enron. Citigroup lost nothing when Enron defaulted in December 2001. Instead, the investors in Citigroup's SPEs were left holding the bag.

From their narrow perspective, bankers and bank regulators undoubtedly were correct. The risk associated with corporate credit no longer stayed with the banks lending corporations money. Instead, these credit risks were passed around the globe like a hot potato. The hundreds of billions of dollars of losses didn't disappear merely because banks had reduced their risks. Instead, someone else bore the losses. The question was: who?

Bankers and bank regulators applauded credit default swaps for their ability to shift risks away from banks. Before credit default swaps, the collapse of Enron alone might have brought down a major bank. The simultaneous bankruptcies of Enron, Global Crossing, and WorldCom would have decimated the banking industry. But even after the myriad defaults of 2001 and 2002, the banks were doing just fine. In a speech on April 22, 2002, Alan Greenspan said credit derivatives "appear to have effectively spread losses from recent defaults by Enron, Global Crossing, Railtrack, and Swissair [other bankrupt companies] in recent months. In particular, the still relatively small, but rapidly growing, credit derivatives market has to date functioned well, with payouts proceeding smoothly for the most part. Obviously, this market is still too new to have been tested in a widespread credit down-cycle. But so far, so good."

Unfortunately, the credit default swaps market was opaque and unregulated, and because disclosure was not required, no one could be sure where the risk had gone. Even the banks pitching credit-derivatives deals made widely different estimates about who was involved in the market. Ten years earlier, companies such as Enron and WorldCom might have had at most a dozen creditors—institutions they owed money. Instead, the bankruptcy filings of those firms listed dozens of *pages* of creditors. But even that list didn't provide much of a clue about the parties to credit default swaps related to Enron, because those parties typically were looking to each other for payment, not to Enron.

As early as 1997, experts within the financial industry had warned that the sellers of credit protection—the institutions betting that companies would not default—might not fully understand the risks of credit default swaps. E. Gerald Corrigan, the former head of the New York Federal Reserve who had issued warnings about derivatives before he joined Goldman Sachs, cautiously remarked, "The unbundling of credit risk probably should be a good thing, assuming that people picking up the elements of credit risk understand what they're doing and the risks they're incurring." Tanya Styblo Beder, a derivatives consultant, warned that the risk models used in evaluating credit default swaps were based on historical default data that could prove invalid.[69]

By 2002, there was evidence that many of the supposedly sophisticated institutions doing credit default swaps had not understood their risks any better than Gibson Greetings had understood its complex swaps with Bankers Trust. The biggest sellers of protection were insurance companies, some in the United States, but also in Europe and Japan. Life insurance companies invested in credit default swaps as assets. Property and casualty insurance companies and reinsurance companies took on credit risk as a liability, and booked the payments as premiums. By one estimate, insurance companies had exposure to one-third of WorldCom's $35 billion of debt.[70] Pension funds and some hedge funds also did credit default swaps.

Insurance companies had an incentive to use credit default swaps for the same reasons banks did: legal rules. In particular, insurance companies could use credit default swaps to avoid legal rules that limited their investments and penalized them for taking on too much risk. For example, insurance companies could use credit default swaps to make leveraged investments they otherwise would not be permitted to make due to rules restricting their ability to borrow money to buy securities. Just as Japanese insurance companies had used derivatives to buy over-the-counter options a decade earlier—arguing that the options fell outside the scope of legal rules—insurance companies throughout the world made the same arguments for credit default swaps. On its face, a credit default swap would appear to a regulator to be a simple transaction with a major U.S. bank. Financial regulators might not even know that behind an insurance company's swap with J. P. Morgan was a leveraged bet on Enron.

Bank regulators, by tightening their focus on banks to reduce their risks and prevent a banking crisis, had pushed credit risks onto other, less regulated institutions. Whereas the United States regulated banks separately, British regulators covered both banks and other financial institutions, and seemed to have both a broader perspective and a stronger grasp of the risks of credit default swaps than U.S. regulators (just as they had better grasped the risks of other over-the-counter derivatives during the mid-1990s). Howard Davies, chairman of the British Financial Services Authority, warned that credit derivatives were being used for "regulatory arbitrage," to shift risks from regulated banks to less regulated insurers,[71] and that "we may be creating, not reducing market instability."[72] Although British banks, which previously had been plagued by bad loans, were now in reasonably good shape, the same was not true of Britain's insurance companies. One of the biggest losers from the defaults of 2002 was Prudential plc—the 150-year-old United Kingdom insurance conglomerate, not the U.S.-based "piece of the rock" company—which announced losses of half a billion dollars on positions related to Global Crossing and other defaulted borrowers.[73] Because U.S. insurance companies were regulated by state insurance commissions, and did not mark to market their positions in the same way as federally regulated securities and banking firms, no one knew with certainty if some of those insurance companies had become insolvent.

Other major players in the credit-derivatives market included non-financial corporations, such as Enron and General Electric.[74] During the 1990s, as banks used financial innovation to lighten their risks, industrial companies began to look more like banks. Yes, the banking system had become stronger, but that was because the risks were no longer held by banks. Morgan Stanley estimated that one-third of financial activity in 2000 occurred at non-financial companies, such as Enron and General Electric.[75] Even companies such as Ford received more than a sixth of their revenue from financial activities.[76]

By 2002, Enron already had died, and there were serious questions about the health of General Electric. General Electric was one of just eight companies retaining a AAA rating from the credit-rating agencies in 2002, but that was little comfort, given the agencies' track record.

In the previous two years, General Electric's shares had dropped by half, wiping out nearly $300 billion of value. The decline was roughly the same as the decline that had immediately preceded Ken Lay's conference call about Enron in October 2001. And although General Electric was rated AAA, its credit default swaps had fallen to values in line with a low double-A rating at best.

In March 2002, Bill Gross of PIMCO—one of the leading bond managers in the world—announced that he no longer would buy General Electric's short-term debt, because he believed the company had too much debt and too little disclosure. General Electric's financial statements certainly looked suspicious. There was one $14 billion entry on the firm's balance sheet for "All other current costs and expenses accrued." As Doug Skinner, an accounting professor at the University of Michigan, said, "Goodness knows what's in there." In addition, General Electric had grown by acquiring huge numbers of companies—more than 100 per year—much more than Cendant or even Global Crossing and WorldCom.[77] With that kind of acquisition growth, it was impossible to understand what really was happening at the company.

Before 2002, investors had simply trusted chairman Jack Welch. But now that Welch had resigned—and had been tarnished not only by the plunge in the stock, but by negative publicity surrounding a high-profile affair he had with the former editor of the *Harvard Business Review*—investors were less trusting of General Electric and, especially, its financial businesses. When investors learned from documents filed in Welch's divorce proceedings that GE was giving him tens of millions of dollars in retirement benefits—including a wine budget of more than many investors' salaries—they wondered if Welch had been truthful about GE's performance.

General Electric was really two companies: GE Industrial and GE Capital.[78] GE Industrial made lightbulbs, airplane engines, and gas turbines, and "brought good things to life"—as the company advertised on television. GE Capital borrowed and loaned money, and was an active player in derivatives. GE Industrial was the General Electric most people knew. But GE Capital was the engine that drove the firm's profits.

GE Capital was created during the Great Depression, with the modest aim of helping consumers finance their appliance purchases. But by 2002, GE Capital essentially had become a bank. It had more assets than all but two U.S. banking conglomerates, six times more than its assets in 1990.[79]

In its 2001 annual report—issued in 2002—General Electric comforted its investors by stating, "As a matter of policy, neither GE nor GECS [GE Capital] engages in derivatives trading, derivatives market-making, or other speculative activities." But in a footnote, General Electric noted that, because of changes in the way it accounted for its derivatives operations, it had reduced its earnings by $502 million, and reduced shareholder equity by $1.3 billion.[80] These numbers were roughly the same as the restatement Enron had made in 2001, yet investors didn't seem to care. General Electric noted, "This accounting change did not involve cash, and management expects that it will have no more than a modest effect on future results." The rating agencies continued to give General Electric a rating of AAA, and Bill Gross remained one of the few investors to express a loss of faith in General Electric. Fortunately for the credit-derivatives market, General Electric did not appear to be in any danger of default.

Some commentators argued that if insurance companies and industrial corporations were taking on credit risk from banks, that was a sign that these companies must be in a better position than banks to hold and monitor such risks. If markets were efficient, the hot potato, by definition, would be passed to the party best able to handle it. As the argument went, Enron, General Electric, and Prudential were in a better position to monitor and bear the risk of corporate loans than the major Wall Street banks.

There were two flaws in this argument. First, because credit default swaps reduced the regulatory costs of banks and insurance companies, both types of firm benefited from swapping positions, regardless of which was in a better position to evaluate and examine the loans underlying the credit default swaps. From a regulatory perspective, both banks and insurance companies lowered their costs by doing credit default swaps with each other. Because credit default swaps were off balance sheet, industrial corporations also achieved regulatory benefits. Second, and more fundamental, banks were in by far the best position to monitor corporate loans. They were the firms that had made the loans, they had relationships with the borrowers, and they uniquely had access to the data and personnel necessary to keep tabs on the company's prospects.

In other words, banks were passing much of their credit risk to insurance companies and industrial corporations, even though banks were in a better position to monitor that risk. Just as interest-rate risk had flowed from Wall Street to Main Street during the early 1990s, now credit risk was being passed to parties less able to bear it. And, once again, the culprit was financial innovation designed to take advantage of legal rules.

According to Martin Mayer, a leading banking expert, credit default swaps sacrificed the greatest strength of banks as lenders: their ability to police the status of a loan.[81] An insurance company—especially one outside the United States—couldn't do much more than look at a borrower's public financial statements. Nor would it have an incentive to monitor the borrower, because each credit default swap represented only a small portion of the borrower's overall debt. Moreover, an insurance company that bought credit risk from a bank might pass it along to another institution, which might pass it on to another, and so on. Because there were no disclosure requirements for credit default swaps, it was impossible to know who ultimately held the risk associated with a particular company's loans. But it required a fantastic leap of faith to assume that the holder of the hot potato was in the best position to keep tabs on the borrower.

Thus, credit default swaps distorted global investment by leading parties to misprice credit risk. Borrowers who were not being monitored tended to take on greater risks, which meant that the banks making new loans to these borrowers would charge higher interest rates. As the cost of capital in the economy increased, companies would take on fewer projects at higher cost, and economic growth would suffer. Moreover, because banks didn't bear the risks associated with loans, they had an incentive to lend more money than they otherwise would. The International Monetary Fund concluded, "To the extent that regulatory arbitrage drives the growth of the market, banks may be encouraged to originate more credit business than they would have done otherwise and then to transfer the risk to non- or less-well-regulated entities . . . such as insurance companies and, to a lesser degree, hedge funds."[82] Regulators in the United Kingdom expressed concern that, with credit default swaps, "There is a risk of mispricing by less sophisticated market participants."[83] And a top credit derivatives expert, Satyajit Das, worried that investors did not understand the risks associated with these instruments: "Unlike other financial products that have remained largely in the professional markets, one of the most alarming things about credit derivatives is the way they have been packaged into numerous deals that have been sold to relatively small institutions and even occasionally to high-net-worth individuals, which I think has the potential to cause problems."[84]

One final problem with credit default swaps was that, as with any insurance policy, payment hinged on the language describing what was covered—the definition of a default. A loan agreement was a lengthy document that typically specified numerous standard events of default. Loan agreements had evolved over decades, based on the experience of parties, under various market conditions. In contrast, credit-swap agreements were slim documents that allowed parties to use any definition of "default"— ranging from the borrower's failure to make payment to the appearance of a newspaper article suggesting the borrower *might* default. Over time, credit default swaps had become more standardized, and bankers tightened contract terms after Russia's "default" in 1998; but, parties to credit default swaps still could, and did, change the terms for particular deals. In their effort to develop highly customized credit default swaps, banks had created unforeseen difficulties. Having done hundreds of billions of dollars of credit default swaps based on simple documentation, the banks finally understood why the underlying loan agreements had been so lengthy.

The consequence was that parties to credit default swaps bore *legal risk* associated with whether obligations had been triggered. A party that believed it was hedged might be whipsawed if the language in one credit default swap required payment while the language in an offsetting swap did not. J. P. Morgan Chase faced this precise problem when Argentina announced a rescheduling of some debts, and ultimately defaulted on some debts but not others. J. P. Morgan Chase had entered into credit default swaps related to Argentina with different clients using different language.[85] The bank recorded $351 million in losses on Argentina in 2002, and the disputes about how much was owed on which swap remained tied up in court as of early 2003.[86]

The use of credit default swaps revolutionized the bankruptcy process. The defaults by Enron, Global Crossing, and WorldCom created enormous uncertainty about which creditors would be paid, and when. Essentially, market participants had tried, by private contract, to opt out of bankruptcy proceedings that were mandated by federal law, leaping ahead of the line of creditors awaiting payment from these defaulted companies. It remains uncertain whether those efforts will be successful.

In his 2003 letter to Berkshire Hathaway shareholders, Warren Buffett warned of the dangers of credit default swaps, calling derivatives "time bombs" and "financial weapons of mass destruction." (Buffett had been burned by credit derivatives buried in portfolios held by General Re, a reinsurance company he had purchased.) While some market participants objected to Buffett's warning, calling it a "serious slur" and "bad judgment," Federal Reserve chairman Alan Greenspan took note.

Greenspan had been resolutely pro-derivatives and anti-regulation. But on May 8, he appeared by satellite at a banking conference in Chicago and gave a very un-Greenspan-like speech. His remarks were lucid and peppered with colorful metaphor, references to wildcat banking, and hard-hitting criticism. He concluded that he was no longer "entirely sanguine with respect to the risks associated with derivatives." Reporters apparently had no idea what to do. Most newspapers ignored the speech; others covered it, but directly contradicted each other.

Greenspan delivered two ripostes to the derivatives industry. First, he cautioned dealers about market concentration, citing "the decline in the number of major derivatives dealers and its potential implications for market liquidity and for concentration of counterparty credit risks." He specifically mentioned concerns about credit default swaps, because some players were exiting the market. As the number of dealers declined, he said, it became even more important that each one remaining stay in the game. Credit derivatives trading, like poker, is not fun with only a few players.

Greenspan cited a single dealer with a one-third market share, and a handful of dealers with two-thirds of the market. If one of those dealers failed, derivatives markets might become illiquid, just as they did during the Long-Term Capital Management fiasco. Even worse, that dealer might be the first of many dominos to fall. Imagine a poker game where everyone at the table is borrowing from everyone else. Now suppose the biggest loser goes bust after losing a big bet with someone not at the table. Suddenly, all of the poker players at the table are insolvent.

The one dealer of greatest concern to Greenspan was JP Morgan Chase (as its new logo). (Greenspan didn't mention the bank by name, but most experts agreed he was referring to JP Morgan.) That bank's 123-page annual report for 2002 listed $25.8 trillion of derivatives, including $366 billion of credit derivatives, in terms of notional value, the value of the underlying loans the derivatives are based on. Even the fair value of JP Morgan's credit derivatives—just a fraction of their notional value—was greater than the bank's combined investment banking fees and trading revenues for 2002, and more than that for any other dealer.

By comparison, Long-Term Capital Management had $1.25 trillion of derivatives, less than five percent of JP Morgan's, yet the Federal Reserve was forced to engineer a bank-led bailout in 1998 because of concerns about such systemic risks. Banking regulators obviously didn't want to do this again. Greenspan's implicit message was that derivatives dealers should be extra careful not to become too exposed to any one of their competitors. He especially seemed to direct this message to anyone dealing with JP Morgan.

Second, Greenspan warned that dealers needed to disclose more information about their derivatives. Financial institutions have lengthy footnotes chock-full of tables setting forth various financial data, including details about derivatives. But their hundred-plus-page annual reports are opaque, even to research analysts covering the industry. Here, Greenspan's language was unusually pointed: "Transparency challenges market participants to present information in ways that accurately reflect risks. Much disclosure currently falls short of these more demanding goals."

For Alan Greenspan, those were fighting words. He and his regulators apparently had been reading the latest round of impenetrable annual reports from financial institutions. If they couldn't understand what was happening at the big banks, who could?

In this case, JP Morgan's disclosures actually were better than those of its peers. The bank reported various risk measures, including "Value-At-Risk," which captured in a single number the firm's highest expected loss under certain assumptions. The bank also said it analyzed worst case scenarios using a more sophisicated system called "Risk Identification for Large Exposures," better known by the not-so-reassuring acronym "RIFLE." Unfortunately, shareholders didn't get a lot of information about RIFLE.

Similarly, the bank reported that 94 percent of its derivatives assets and liabilities were valued based on "internal models with significant observable market parameters." Investors should be nervous about the use of internal models to value derivatives—recall that when Askin Capital Management discovered its internal models were in error its fund collapsed instantaneously. It would be better if banks used only quoted market prices, but those aren't available in many derivatives markets, and will be less available if markets become less liquid. Moreover, "internal models with significant observable market parameters" are better than "internal models with unobservable market parameters." Unfortunately, JP Morgan (like many derivatives dealers) also reported many of those not-so-comforting "unobservable" valuations.

The concentration and disclosure problems Greenspan cited are a double whammy. Just as Long-Term Capital Management unraveled when its lenders finally learned of the daisy chain deals that enabled that firm to borrow so much money at favorable terms, a derivatives dealer's network of contracts might similarly unravel if counterparties—or even shareholders—learned the truth about the dealer's mysterious web of deals.

Greenspan wants banks to become transparent, so that shareholders, analysts, and counterparties can understand their activities. He also wants more competition. In the long run, greater transparency and competition should lead to greater market discipline. In the short run, they might lead to some spectacular failures, as everyone finally learns how credit default swaps have been used to shift risks around the financial world.

The second type of credit derivative—the Collateralized Debt Obligation—posed even greater dangers to the global economy. In a standard CDO, a financial institution sold debt (loans or bonds) to a Special Purpose Entity, which then split the debt into pieces by issuing new securities linked to each piece. Some of the pieces were of higher quality; some were of lower quality. The credit-rating agencies gave investment-grade ratings to all except the lowest-quality piece. By 2002, there were more than half a trillion dollars of CDOs.

The latest innovation—the *Synthetic CDO*—was the ultimate in financial alchemy. A Synthetic CDO was like a standard *cash-flow* CDO, except that a bank substituted credit default swaps for loans or bonds. In other words, the "assets" of the SPE were credit default swaps. As a result, the companies whose debts formed the basis of a Synthetic CDO had *no relationship* at all to the deal; most likely, the companies would not even know about it. Neither the investors in the SPE, nor the banks, ever had to touch the companies' loans or bonds.

Synthetic CDOs might seem like unusual or esoteric side bets, but by

2002 they were a mainstay of corporate finance. In 2001, banks created almost $80 *billion* of Synthetic CDOs. During 2002, even after the bankruptcies of Enron, Global Crossing, and WorldCom—companies whose debts were referenced in the credit default swaps of numerous Synthetic CDOs—financial institutions still were continuing to do these deals.

Credit default swaps had pushed risks to unknown places, and now CDOs were moving them underground. Howard Davies, the British financial regulator, relayed a comment, from an investment banker, that Synthetic CDOs were "the most toxic element of the financial markets today."[87]

In conceptual terms, CDOs resembled the earlier Collateralized *Bond* Obligations pioneered by First Boston (and described in Chapter 3). To understand CDOs, imagine that a chocolate bar represents a typical corporate bond: a decent blend of ingredients; medium richness; almonds, if you wanted. Some chocolate bars contain artificial—or even accidental—ingredients that consumers would prefer not to think about.

Now imagine melting 100 chocolate bars of different types in a pot, and separating their constituent parts. What would it look like? A slice of Maison du Chocolat–quality ganache, some cocoa and milk, a few almonds, and a small pile of remains you might prefer not to eat. Do you think it would be possible to make money by selling the parts separately? You certainly could find buyers of the high-quality pieces, but who would want the remains? Moreover, given that someone already had gone to the trouble of making the chocolate bars from the various ingredients, is there any reason to think you might be able to deconstruct and then resell the parts for more than the cost of the bars themselves?

Substitute corporate debt for chocolate bars and you understand CDOs. In a CDO, a bank would gather a portfolio of, say, 100 different bonds or credit default swaps, and separate the portfolio into tranches of varying qualities, to be sold to investors. Typically, there was a AAA-rated senior tranche, one or more investment-grade-rated mezzanine tranches, and then the remains, which were called anything from the junior piece to preference shares to nuclear waste.

The question was: how could a bank make money doing such an elaborate reconstruction? In economic theory, the Law of One Price said that similar assets should have similar values. If they didn't, someone would buy low, sell high, and earn a riskless profit. If a bank could make money repackaging corporate debt, it must mean there were inefficiencies in the corporate-debt market. But if some of the debt in the portfolio were mis-priced, why weren't people trading it in the market until prices were accu-rate? There weren't the same restrictions on selling-short bonds or credit default swaps as there were for stocks, and the manic individuals who drove up prices of Internet and telecommunications shares were minor players in the corporate-bond and credit default swap markets. Inefficiencies in these markets were unlikely to last long. Why, then, did banks think the whole— sliced in new ways—was worth more than the sum of the parts?

One reason, again, was legal rules: CDOs, like credit default swaps, were driven by banks that wanted to remove loans from their balance sheets, just as Fred Carr—one of Michael Milken's best clients—had repackaged a portfolio of junk bonds to avoid regulatory requirements in 1989. Now that banks were being permitted to engage in the securi-ties business, they wanted to free up their capital to use in attracting new clients. Banking regulations required banks to set aside capital for their loans; if they could get rid of those loans, they could use the capital for something else.

Another reason involved the all-important credit-rating agencies. Beginning in the 1970s, regulators had given up trying to keep pace with modern financial markets. Instead of making substantive decisions about which securities financial institutions should be permitted to buy and sell, the regulators had deferred to the credit-rating agencies, by passing rules and regulations that depended on ratings. Recall from Chapter 3 that, as a result of these rules, there was a sharp divide between the prices of investment-grade and non-investment-grade bonds. Michael Milken of Drexel had spotted this inefficiency, and had profited during the 1980s by buying portfolios of non-investment-grade bonds. The rules regarding credit ratings hadn't changed since his time, and the three major agencies still had an oligopoly lock on the ratings business, as regulators refused to approve any competitors. Not surprisingly, their business boomed. Moody's became a free-standing, publicly traded company worth more than $5 billion.

Anyone looking closely at the credit-rating agencies would find it dif-ficult to justify their importance. The analysts at the three rating agencies were perfectly nice people, but they were not—to put it charitably—the sharpest tools in the shed. Banks snapped up the best analysts, and invest-ment funds hired the second best. Based on their recent track record, the remaining employees would have done a better job if they had simply followed the business section of a daily newspaper. Not only had the rating agencies given Orange County and Pacific Gas & Electric their highest ratings just before those entities became insolvent, they more recently had given high ratings to Enron, Global Crossing, and WorldCom—and stuck to those ratings until just before the companies filed for bankruptcy.

Yet it was the credit-rating agencies' inaccurate ratings of corporate debt and the tranches of CDOs that made the parts worth more than the whole. To see this, suppose the agencies rated only two bonds on a simplified scale, from A to F. Also suppose legal rules required that regulated institutions buy bonds with a rating of A or B. If there were two bonds in the market—one rated A and the other rated F—the regulated institutions would buy only the A bond.

Now suppose a bank repackaged both bonds into a CDO with one tranche of new securities. If the rating agencies gave these new securities a rating of C—the average of A and F—regulated institutions still wouldn't be able to buy it. But what if the rating agencies bumped up the new securities to a rating of B? Now regulated institutions effectively could buy *both* bonds. The new securities of the CDO would be worth more than the bonds sold separately, because now there were more buyers. More demand meant a higher price.

This logic applied equally to more complex structures, with dozens of bonds and multiple tranches. Essentially, the credit-rating agencies made the parts worth more than the whole by *overrating* the CDO tranches. The computer models used to assess CDOs were merely complex ways of justifying higher ratings for the tranches than the overall ratings for the underlying debt in the market. Many of these models had been created by the banks doing the CDO deals, and their nuances were not understood by some rating-agency employees. For example, the ratings generated by a Synthetic CDO model depended on variables—such as diversity scores, weighted average rating factors and spreads, and various "overcollateralization" tests—which determined the scenarios under which the rated tranches of a CDO would lose money. Bank employees privately admitted they could tweak these models to make a CDO deal appear to add value. By the time a rating agency employee understood the bells and whistles of these models, the banks doing CDO deals would hire him or her, at a significantly higher salary.

This attrition wouldn't prevent the rating agencies from continuing to make money—they would do very well. But it indicated that the product the agencies were selling was not their own expertise or even some well-constructed strategy to exploit market inefficiencies. Instead, they were selling an inflated rating methodology that enabled regulated buyers to purchase riskier, higher-yielding investments. The banks controlled the inputs and told the rating agencies what they needed to get a deal done. As a result, the agencies could hire just about anyone to fill in the blanks—and still make money.

The "value" magically created by a CDO was parceled out among the various participants: the buyers of the highly rated pieces were paid a higher yield than on comparably rated bonds; the banks arranging the CDO received a fee; and the buyer of the junior piece had access to a new kind of investment, which otherwise was not available in the markets—a highly leveraged investment in corporate bonds. Essentially, the junior piece was borrowing money from the senior pieces to invest in the debt of the CDO. That meant that the junior piece was very risky and volatile, but also had the potential for high returns.

Of course, there were valid reasons for investors to buy diversified portfolios of corporate bonds, and there were occasions when financial innovation could bridge the gap between the needs of corporate borrowers and the needs of lenders. However, it wasn't necessary to create CDOs to fulfill these purposes. Investors could diversify on their own or through investment funds, and financial institutions had proven more than able to serve as intermediaries when borrower and lender needs weren't matched—the classic example was an interest-rate swap, which enabled a company that wanted to borrow at a fixed interest rate to borrow from a lender that wanted to lend at a floating interest rate, or vice versa. In contrast, CDOs—especially Synthetic CDOs—weren't necessary to fulfill any economic function. Instead, they made sense only because of foolish credit ratings and the legal rules that depended on them.

Put another way, the same thing would happen with chocolate bars if there were chocolate-rating agencies and legal rules that required supermarkets to purchase only approved chocolate products. If the Food and Drug Administration created incentives for people to buy particular blends of products contained in chocolate bars—or if there were mandatory chocolate-bar raters who gave inflated ratings to reconstituted bars—candy companies would engage in the same kinds of dysfunctional behavior as parties to CDOs.

No one had paid much attention to the first warning that CDOs threatened the health of the global economy. In July 2001—two months before Jeff Skilling had resigned from Enron, and long before investors learned about the accounting problems at Global Crossing and World-Com—American Express, the U.S. financial-services conglomerate, had calmly announced that it would take an $826 million pretax charge to write down the value of investments in high-yield bonds and Collateralized Debt Obligations. It all sounded much too esoteric to matter to average investors. The media brushed off the details by focusing on the junk bonds involved in the various deals, and commentators seemed to agree that these losses were just a minor consequence of the explosion in financial innovation.

American Express was a sophisticated financial institution, and it easily could handle a loss of $826 million. From an outsider's perspective, the losses were due to some complex workings within the company; but, the assumption was that someone within American Express understood what was going on.

Then there was the stunning public admission by the chairman of American Express, Kenneth Chenault, that his firm "did not comprehend the risk" of these investments. What?

During 1997, the financial-advisory division of American Express had begun creating CDOs, buying some of the highly rated pieces, and selling the junior pieces to clients. When the bond markets collapsed in 1998, along with Long-Term Capital Management, the buyers of junior pieces disappeared, and those risky pieces were viewed as nuclear waste. Without those buyers, American Express would not be able to create any more CDOs, which meant it would have to give up substantial fees.

At this point, American Express made its big mistake. Instead of exiting the CDO business, at least temporarily, it continued to do CDOs—and began buying the junior pieces for its own account. By March 2001, American Express owned several billion dollars of CDOs.

Unfortunately, there were some corporate defaults during 2001—even before Enron—and American Express sustained losses on its junior pieces due to these defaults. Moreover, as the junior pieces lost money, they provided less protection to the more senior pieces American Express held. Those pieces also lost value, and by the time Kenneth Chenault realized he had a problem, his firm had lost $826 million. The computer models used to calculate these losses were complex, and—at least according to Chenault—American Express had not properly understood them.

Thus, American Express joined the long list of supposedly sophisticated financial experts that had been unable to assess the risk and value of their own investments in derivatives: Bankers Trust, Salomon Brothers, Askin Capital Management, Barings, Kidder Peabody, Enron, and so on. Like many of these institutions, American Express's investments in CDOs had not appeared on its balance sheet. The consequences for American Express were awful, even if the publicity was not: Chenault dismissed several senior financial officers, and the company laid off hundreds of lower-level employees in Minneapolis, Minnesota, where American Express was the largest private employer.

The problems at American Express led some experts to question complex financial dealings at other companies. While the securities analysts at major banks continued to recommend companies involved in off-balance-sheet dealings and credit derivatives, a few independent analysts and investors began asking hard questions of other companies. What were their derivatives risks? Did they have substantial off-balance-sheet liabilities? Were there any suspicious transactions alluded to only in the footnotes to a company's financial statements? How did they use CDOs? Or SPEs? Or any other dangerous acronym they could think of?

These questions about American Express led directly to Enron, which announced significant losses a few months later. Enron was a major participant in the credit-derivatives market, and had done several CDOs. In fact, Enron boasted of its CDO deals in its most recent annual report, a fact few investors had noticed. Those deals, like those of American Express, were incurring substantial losses, hidden from view.

In addition, Enron—along with Global Crossing and WorldCom—was prominently featured in the portfolios of debt and credit default swaps that made up the underlying investments of CDOs. For example, more than three-fourths of the CDOs Standard & Poor's rated in the United States contained WorldCom bonds.[88] Moody's said fifty-eight of the Synthetic CDOs it rated had exposure to WorldCom.[89]

Although the junior pieces of CDOs absorbed the first losses, those pieces were not very large, relative to the entire CDO. In a typical Synthetic CDO, the junior piece represented just two to three percent of the overall portfolio. Once that cushion was gone, the senior pieces would bear any additional losses. A typical CDO had at most 100 companies; and, with so many companies defaulting, the hundreds of billions of dollars of supposedly safe, highly rated senior pieces were at risk of loss. WorldCom alone made up an average of 1.2 percent of Synthetic CDOs.[90] With Enron and Global Crossing also in default—plus new bankruptcies such as United Airlines and US Airways—the $500+ billion CDO market was hanging by a thread.

The rating agencies scrambled to downgrade their CDOs in 2002, in a last-minute effort to maintain credibility. But members of Congress were not impressed. They held hearings on the role of credit-rating agencies, and included in the corporate reform legislation passed in July 2002 a requirement that securities regulators undertake a major study of how credit-rating agencies fit within the framework of financial market regulation. In late 2002, the SEC lined up dozens of experts to testify about this issue. In late 2003, the SEC was still considering what to do about credit ratings agencies.

Although the waves of financial scandals continued, for every company that was destroyed, there were many others continuing the same risky and/or deceitful practices unabated.

Consider a few: In January 2002, during the heat of the debate about Enron, Merrill Lynch and Citigroup did a $1 billion FELINE PRIDES deal for Williams Companies. (Recall that FELINE PRIDES were the complex, three-stage, mandatory-convertible securities Merrill Lynch had invented to take advantage of favorable regulatory treatment by tax authorities and credit-rating agencies.) Fifteen days later, Williams postponed the release of its fourth-quarter earnings and announced that it might have discovered an additional $2.4 billion in liabilities. The company's stock price fell 25 percent in one day.[91] Merrill and Citigroup apparently hadn't spotted the errors during their due-diligence investigation.

During the first quarter of 2002, half of El Paso Corporation's profit was from a network of partnership deals similar to Enron's—called "Project Electron."[92] El Paso had purchased the right to sell electricity at above-market rates; but, instead of recognizing the profit from these high rates over time, it restructured its agreements to recognize all of the profit up front. El Paso claimed it had disclosed these practices, but it was hard to disagree with Carol Loomis of *Fortune* magazine, who called the firm's disclosure—in a footnote to its financial filings—"convoluted" and "impenetrable."[93] El Paso's stock price also fell 25 percent, the day the news about Project Electron was reported.

Dynegy reportedly manipulated its forward curves—the various rates at which commodities were trading for delivery at specified future dates—

in precisely the same way Enron had.[94] Dynegy's stock price plummeted when these manipulations became public.

Dell Computer announced it had sold put options on its own stock in over-the-counter deals with Morgan Stanley and Goldman Sachs. When Dell's stock price fell by half, the company had been forced to spend $3 billion buying back 68 million shares to fulfill the put options.[95]

AOL Time Warner disclosed an investigation by the SEC into how it accounted for advertising sales at America Online. AOL's stock price plunged 15 percent, to a four-year low. Standard & Poor's and Moody's rated AOL's $24 billion of bonds investment grade, even though the cost of AOL's credit swaps doubled in early July 2002.[96]

John M. Rusnak, a 36-year-old trader at the Baltimore branch of Allfirst Financial, desperately sold "deep-in-the-money" currency options—options he almost certainly would have to pay money to satisfy at maturity—to Citibank, Bank of America, Deutsche Bank, and Bank of New York, losing a total of $750 million.[97] Rusnak pleaded guilty to bank fraud in late 2002 and was expected to begin serving a multiyear prison term in 2003.

PNC Financial was a virtual clone of Enron, in that it had bizarrely named Special Purpose Entities (PAGIC I, PAGIC II, and PAGIC III), huge off-balance-sheet liabilities, and hundreds of millions of dollars of losses. PNC Financial entered into a settlement with the SEC related to these SPEs, but did not even pay a fine. The financial press, tired from news of Enron, did not even have the energy to report on the PAGIC deals.

Five officials from Adelphia Communications were arrested, based on charges the company hadn't disclosed extensive Related Party dealings. Adelphia had at least $2.7 billion in off-balance-sheet debt tied to closely held partnerships, and its controlling shareholders—the Rigas family—had used an off-balance-sheet entity, called Highland Holdings, to guarantee loans to themselves, which they then used to buy Adelphia shares.[98]

Xerox admitted to overstating its revenues by almost $2 billion. L. Dennis Kozlowski, CEO of Tyco International, resigned just before he was charged with evading more than $1 million in sales taxes on art. Qwest Communications disclosed it was under criminal investigation. Even Martha Stewart, the popular CEO, was connected to an insider-trading scheme.

Bernie Ebbers and Scott Sullivan were among the lucky few who had received early allocations of Initial Public Offerings, virtually guaranteeing them a huge profit. They received shares of several hot IPOs, including Rhythms NetConnections, the Internet firm that linked WorldCom to Enron, and sent both firms on a billion-dollar Internet roller-coaster ride during 1999 and 2000. Ebbers allegedly made $16 million from shares of Rhythms NetConnections he was allocated before the IPO; four other CEOs allegedly made similar amounts. Ebbers also allegedly received a half-million-dollar check after the Rhythms NetConnections IPO, which he decided to split with Sullivan, even endorsing the check over to Sullivan so he could deposit it.[99] There was a reference to Rhythms NetConnections on the check, a reference that linked Sullivan and Ebbers to Rhythms NetConnections, which was linked to Salomon and Enron, which were linked to innumerable parties in ways that would sicken individual investors when they learned about it.

The list went on.

As the stock market plunged, Warren Buffett—the multibillionaire investor—began selectively buying companies that appeared to be clean. His advice summed up the changes in financial markets during recent years: "When I take a look at a company's annual report, if I don't understand it, they don't want me to understand it."[100] By 2002, financial practices at many companies were so complex that even senior managers did not understand the details. If Buffett wouldn't touch those companies, and managers couldn't explain the risks, why would individual investors want to buy the stocks?

The only good news was that banks appeared to be immunized from the banking panics that had plagued the U.S. markets during the nineteenth and twentieth centuries. Individuals could feel safe about their bank deposits, even if they were only earning one percent interest. The related bad news was that banks were no longer the major source of risk, and because banks didn't bear the risk associated with loans, they had stepped up their lending. The risks previously associated with the banking system were now buried somewhere deep in the books of insurance companies, industrial companies, pension funds, and perhaps even a municipality or two. Individuals depended on those institutions for their livelihoods.

By 2003, there were worries about the banking system, too, from an unlikely source. The financial markets shuddered in June, but not for the reasons most investors might have expected. The financial pages were filled with news about budget and trade deficits, the plummeting dollar, and especially the indictment of Martha Stewart for insider trading. But Wall Street, Congress, and regulators were jolted by Freddie Mac, the government-sponsored mortgage company that finances one in six U.S. homes and is the forth largest U.S. financial institution.

Freddie Mac announced it was firing its president, David Glenn, "because of serious questions as to the timeliness and completeness of his cooperation and candor with the Board's Audit Committee counsel." Lawyers investigating Freddie Mac's accounting practices had asked Mr. Glenn for notes from meetings, and he had admitted that some pages were altered or missing. That cost him his job.

But Freddie Mac's shares didn't fall 16 percent—more than $6 billion—that day because of worries about Mr. Glenn's notes. The concerns were deeper, and replacing an executive didn't make them go away.

Experts had been nervous about Freddie Mac since March 2002, when the company replaced its auditor, Arthur Andersen, which had been implicated in Enron's collapse. Like Enron, Freddie Mac was a major player in the derivatives market. And like Enron, Freddie Mac had been unable to produce audited financial statements for more than a year because its derivatives trading was so complex.

The fears about Freddie Mac stem from its unusual role in the markets. Congress chartered the Federal Home Loan Mortgage Corporation in 1970 to stabilize mortgage markets and expand opportunities for homeownership. Since then, the company has purchased millions of home mortgages from lenders and repackaged them into securities to be sold to investors. After lenders sell one mortgage, they are free to issue another, which also can be repackaged and sold. Homebuyers, lenders, and investors have benefited from the liquid markets resulting from these practices.

More recently, though, the company now known as "Freddie" has been exploiting its federal charter. Although Freddie Mac has private shareholders, Congress has implicitly guaranteed investors in repackaged mortgages that the government will pay if Freddie Mac cannot. Investors believe this guarantee is credible, and credit rating agencies give Freddie Mac their highest ratings. Over time, the company has used its quasi-public status to borrow hundreds of billions of dollars at very low rates, investing the money to earn positive returns. Regulators, including Alan Greenspan, have been complaining about these practices for years. Meanwhile, Freddie Mac's officials have benefited greatly; Mr. Glenn made $5.3 million last year.

Freddie Mac increasingly plays in the unregulated derivatives mar-kets, where its implicit government guarantee gives it an advantage over less creditworthy parties. Freddie Mac's trades might not be of much concern if it disclosed more details about them. But because of its pre-ferred status as a federally chartered institution, it was not required to file the same statements as virtually every other U.S. financial institution. Whereas a leading bank such as JP Morgan must tell shareholders about its eye-popping $25.8 trillion derivatives portfolio, Freddie Mac could disclose less information. (Recently, Freddie has volunteered to disclose more.)

In this way, too, Freddie Mac echoes Enron. Freddie Mac runs a sophisticated derivatives trading operation that is virtually indistinguish-able from that of a Wall Street investment bank, except that Freddie Mac is not regulated as a financial institution; similarly, Enron traded deriva-tives, but was a deregulated energy firm. Freddie Mac's derivatives assets grew by more than 600 percent during 2002; Enron's grew by roughly the same amount during 2000, the year before its bankruptcy.

In the last election cycle, Freddie Mac was the largest corporate con-tributor of unlimited "soft money" donations to the political parties, just as Enron and its chairman, Kenneth Lay, were major donors. As members of Congress started abandoning some of their scandalized donors, they also began calling for hearings on the regulation of Freddie Mac. But the calls for reform died out after Freddie disclosed its most recent "correct" numbers, indicating that the company had earned *more* income than it originally reported.

In 2003, President Bush needed to nominate a candidate to lead OFHEO, the regulator of Freddie Mac and Fannie Mae, another mort-gage bank embroiled in a derivatives dispute. Given the questions sur-rounding the mortgage market, and the recent brouhaha over corporate scandals, their regulator needed to be able to assert credibly that he or she could confront these crises.

Incredibly, Bush selected Mark Brickell, the pit bull lobbyist for JP Morgan and ISDA, who had blocked regulation of derivatives markets for more than a decade. The media seized on Brickell's nomination, and numerous commentators questioned whether he was an appropriate choice, given his background as an unusually aggressive industry lobby-ist. At his confirmation hearing, several senators questioned him about conflicts of interest, and requested that he answer some additional ques-tions in writing (including some he had not satisfactorily answered at the hearing). Senator Paul Sarbanes, coauthor of the corporate reform legislation of 2002, likened Brickell's nomination to putting a fox in charge of the henhouse. As of late 2003, Brickell had not yet answered the additional questions, and it remained unclear whether he would be confirmed.

The collapses of Global Crossing and WorldCom had involved simple men, and simple schemes. But financial markets no longer allowed for simplicity, and the risks associated with those firms and others had been swapped and reconfigured in incomprehensible ways, transferring risks, through credit derivatives and financial institutions, on to individuals who did not even know they were exposed. Investors had been shocked by recent bankruptcies, but the real horror was that the losses went much deeper than the money individuals had lost on stocks. It would be a long time before anyone discovered where the losses from credit derivatives lay. By that time, the financial markets would be on to the next game.

EPILOGUE

During the summer of 2002, Senator Jon S. Corzine—formerly head of Goldman Sachs, and the most financially sophisticated member of Congress—suggested that any legislative action to reform financial markets depended on how much stocks went down. Otherwise, he said, "these can become issues that are hard for people like my mom to understand."[1]

Stocks went down by 25 percent, and members of Congress were pressured to enact reforms, especially given the upcoming elections in November. Congress passed a new law, called the Sarbanes-Oxley Act of 2002, which increased the penalties for financial fraud, required greater independence of corporate directors, and established a new review board to discipline rogue accountants.[2] Senators Joseph Lieberman, Carl Levin, and Fred Thompson had expressed dismay at the slapdash ratings of credit-rating agencies. They had added a provision for studying what to do about credit ratings, and the SEC began this study. But the reforms were largely cosmetic and did not address the profound changes in financial markets.

One reason the new law was so limited was that legislators and their staffs did not have a blueprint to use in explaining where and how the markets had gone wrong. Instead, they were driven primarily by the investing public's desire to blame someone for the losses, punish the "bad apples" among corporate executives, and improve the oversight of accountants. After the largest and longest bull market in history, investors had lost over $7 trillion on stocks. Politicians had rushed their response, and, not surprisingly, it was incomplete and inadequate.

By late 2002, the markets had hit five-year lows, and financial scandals showed no signs of abating. Accounting firms and Wall Street banks rushed to settle disputes related to IPOs and off-balance-sheet derivatives. Previously respected CEOs—including Al Dunlap of Sunbeam, Dennis Kozlowski of Tyco, and even Jack Welch of General Electric—were vilified, their reputations tarnished forever. Investigators continued to build cases against officials of WorldCom, Global Crossing, and other firms involved in questionable deals. Finally, on October 2, Andy Fastow, the CFO of Enron, was indicted, an act regulators hoped would bring to a close the recent spread of what Alan Greenspan had called "infectious greed."

But in 2003, even as the announcements of corporate scandals continued unabated—Freddie Mac and HealthSouth were two prominent examples—investors began returning to stocks. The markets recovered, and memories of recent losses faded. In this environment, senior executives showed little remorse. More than two years after Enron's demise, it remained unclear whether any corporate officers, including Andy Fastow, would do substantial jail time. Meanwhile, executive pay continued to skyrocket. Richard Grasso, who resigned as chairman of the New York Stock Exchange in late 2003, was awarded $140 million in compensation, a record for any Wall Street regulator.

When ten banks agreed to pay $1.4 billion and to reform their research operations as part of a "global settlement" of allegations that analysts had misled investors, they attempted to portray the settlement as a great sacrifice for the benefit of investors. Now, in their view, the markets could move on. Privately, bankers blustered about how they had avoided criminal charges and damning admissions, all for relatively small fines. Once again, they had gotten away with barely a slap on the wrist. When Morgan Stanley CEO Philip Purcell was asked about the global settlement (for which Morgan Stanley had paid $125 million), he gave the same answer most bankers, commentators, and investors were giving: it's no big deal. He candidly remarked that "I don't see anything in the settlement that will concern the retail investor about Morgan Stanley. Not one thing. So far, so good this year. We have maintained our standards in market share as well as our reputation, in my view."

To his credit, William Donaldson, the new SEC chairman, shot back that Purcell showed "a troubling lack of contrition" and "a disturbing and misguided perspective" as to what had gone wrong. But as much as investors wanted to believe the strong-willed Donaldson, the reality was that Purcell was right. The retail investor was not concerned, and the bankers' reputations were clean, or at least clean enough. By the end of 2003, investors were again pouring money into companies with no record of profits and little hope for success, with impenetrable footnotes and multifarious derivatives deals.

The newly converted bulls included John Moorlach, the accountant who had challenged elderly Orange County Treasurer Robert Citron in a 1994 election, and lost. Now, Moorlach was the new treasurer of Orange County, and he was lobbying for the county to end its near-decade ban on doing business with Merrill Lynch, the bank that had played the largest role in the county's bankruptcy. The individual wrong-doers at Merrill were long gone, and Moorlach wasn't fazed by the various prosecutions and lawsuits against Merrill—including allegations related to "POS" stocks its brokers sold to clients. He beseeched county residents, "We're trying to make some money. We're in a financial crunch."

A few county supervisors remembered the debacle of 1994 and opposed Moorlach, but he narrowly won the right to deal with Merrill in June 2003. One opponent, Jim Silva, remarked, "If we save $1 million a year by utilizing Merrill Lynch, in another 873 years we'll be back to even."[3]

The renewed Orange County–Merrill Lynch relationship would not include Henry Blodget, Merrill's infamous Internet stock analyst. Blodget had just been banned for life from the securities industry (and fined $4 million). Nor would anyone be hearing the advice of Jack Grubman of Citibank, the analyst who had propped up WorldCom and Global Crossing. He was banned for life and fined $15 million. Both Blodget and Grubman could afford the fines; more importantly, they avoided prison.

Andrew Krieger, the whiz kid from Bankers Trust, wasn't as fortunate. He was charged with criminal conduct in August 2003—ironically not for any acts related to the financial markets. Instead, prosecutors from Bergen County, New Jersey, charged Krieger with theft and criminal mischief, alleging that in 2002 he and his contractors had bulldozed part of a county-owned nature preserve abutting his $4.2 million French-style mansion in order to build a private tennis court. Krieger faced up to twenty years in prison, more than double the time any modern financial criminal had served. Even the most ardent environmentalist would have a hard time justifying these terms as fair, relative to the meager punishments arising from the recent corporate mega-scandals.

Today, the key issues behind the recent financial scandals are the complex instruments used to skirt legal rules; the rogue employees who managers and shareholders cannot monitor; and the incentives for managers to engage in financial malfeasance, given the deregulated markets. The antiquated system of financial regulation, developed in the 1930s and designed to prevent another market crash after 1929, no longer fits modern markets. Efforts to deregulate pockets of the markets, at the urging of financial lobbyists, have created an admixture of strict rules governing some dealings and no rules governing others. As a result, the markets are now like Swiss cheese, with the holes—the unregulated places—getting bigger every year, as parties transacting around legal rules eat away at the regulatory system from within.

The information and sophistication gap between average investors and the companies whose shares they buy is now bigger than ever, thanks to the changes in markets, law, and culture since the late 1980s. Accountants, bankers, and lawyers continue to use derivatives to avoid regulation. Corporate executives, securities analysts, and investors continue to focus more on meeting quarterly estimates of accounting earnings than on the economic reality of their businesses.

Media coverage of the stock market is as intense as ever; and, though investors are bombarded by information, increasingly they cannot filter it, or find anyone who will tell the truth about a particular company. In the past, when investors followed the hype about technology companies, markets responded to their whims, in part because of limits on betting against stocks. In 2002, the tentativeness of investors has been a factor in the entire market losing a quarter of its value. Whether the stock markets are going up or down, they are not nearly as "efficient" as a generation of economists had taught corporate and government leaders they would be.

Sometimes, markets respond quickly in response to new information. During the first sixty seconds after the first plane hit the World Trade Center, the German stock market fell 5 percent. In 2002, the values of many stocks were quartered within one day. But often the markets respond sluggishly, seemingly unsure of whether corporate news is credible. Just as it took securities analysts months to digest Enron's publicly filed documents during 2001, it took investors most of 2002 to abandon their practice of buying stocks based on a whim, myth, or rumor. The stock market "crash" of the past year took place in slow motion, one company at a time, as investors learned it was virtually impossible for them to understand many of the companies whose stock they had been buying.

In recent years, the markets have withstood losses at Bankers Trust, Procter & Gamble, Orange County, Barings, Long-Term Capital Management, Enron, and others, largely because these collapses did not create widespread panic among investors. The same was true during 2002: investors were upset but calm, even as they learned how irrational and opaque the markets have become. The regulators, too, have remained composed, in part because banks, which now use credit derivatives to reduce their risks, have virtually eliminated the threat of a system-wide banking collapse, the primary concern of regulators in the United States. Unfortunately, as banks pass credit risks along to insurance firms and industrial companies, these other companies become de facto banks, and the rules and oversight that have kept banks safe for decades do not cover these firms. If investors ever come to understand the hidden risks within these non-bank firms, they might very well panic.

Having passed legislation in response to the scandals of 2002, Congress is unlikely to do more. Instead, the key regulator going forward will be the Securities and Exchange Commission.[4] Until November 4, 2002, Election Day, the SEC's chairman was Harvey Pitt, a lawyer who had represented nearly every major accounting firm and Wall Street bank. But Pitt resigned that day, after committing every political error imaginable during fifteen months as chair: he met with executives from companies under investigation; he lobbied for new legislation to raise his own pay and elevate his position to Cabinet rank; he angrily accused the media of not knowing what they were talking about; he backed away from appointing John H. Biggs, an investor advocate, to head a new accounting board after accounting firms complained that Biggs might be too aggressive; and finally he nominated William H. Webster to chair the accounting board, but did not tell his fellow commissioners or White House officials that Webster had headed the audit committee of a company accused of accounting fraud. The Webster nomination was the last straw, and Pitt became only the second SEC chair in history to resign—the other being G. Bradford Cook, who was accused of involvement in a Watergate-related scandal in 1973.[5]

William Donaldson, Pitt's relacement as SEC chair, was a respected

Wall Street banker with political experience and expertise. Donaldson lobbied for, and received, additional resources to hire more regulators and prosecutors. During 2003, Donaldson began the long process of reforming the SEC, proposing new rules, and bringing new cases. But the finance lobby still influenced the SEC's judgment, and the commissioners backed away from requiring, as Congress had ordered, that companies increase their disclosure of the kind of derivatives deals Enron had buried in its footnotes.[6]

More fundamentally, the SEC still lacked the authority to bring criminal cases. That left the responsibility for deterring financial crime with federal and state prosecutors, who increasingly fired rounds at wrongdoers from the wrong guns. Consider the 2003 prosecution of Frank Quattrone. Like Arthur Andersen, Quattrone was accused, not of any financial fraud, but of obstruction of justice. And like the Andersen prosecution, which the government narrowly won on questionable grounds, the Quattrone prosecution was brought under the wrong laws, for the wrong crimes (more on Quattrone in a moment). The WorldCom prosecution was similarly misguided. After federal prosecutors negotiated deals with WorldCom officers, who agreed to testify against their bosses in exchange for leniency, state prosecutors from Oklahoma filed criminal charges against those same officers, including Bernie Ebbers. The risk of prosecution by a state with only attenuated connections to WorldCom (some Oklahoma pension funds had invested in the company) mucked up federal prosecutions, but given the often uninspired federal cases, state prosecutions might be the best hope for real deterrence.

However, the markets arguably would have been well served by Pitt—or someone with Pitt's background—in the top SEC job. Arthur Levitt's ineffectual seven-year-plus term as SEC chair showed that it was critical for the securities markets to have a smart, assertive leader who understood the complexities of modern finance. Levitt had political skills, but was as ineffective as he was popular. Unlike Levitt, who had been disappointed when offered the SEC job and often seemed lost as SEC chair, Pitt had dreamed of chairing the SEC his entire life, and had the ideal skill set. Of course, like any corporate lawyer, Pitt had been a "hired gun" representing the interests of his clients. Pitt even had written an article about Gibson Greetings, the firm that lost money on complex swaps with Bankers Trust, advising corporate executives about how to avoid the scrutiny of federal securities regulators.[7] And Pitt obviously lacked political skills. But he understood more about the SEC's history than most practicing lawyers; he was a founder of the SEC Historical Society. No one knew where more bodies were buried, and no one better understood that the SEC needed a new perspective to avoid becoming obsolete. Notwithstanding Pitt's gaffes, he had the ideal background for the job, and he would be difficult to replace.

Regulators and investors need to rethink their approach to financial markets. The six recommendations that follow are drawn from the major lessons of the intertwined financial fiascos of the past fifteen years. Ultimately, the health of financial markets will depend on whether credible intermediaries and new regulatory approaches can bridge the gap between investors and corporate executives, reducing the costs of the separation of ownership and control of companies, instead of providing tools and incentives for some executives to bilk their shareholders. Without a change in view, and a shift of priorities, the financial markets will continue to teeter on the edge.

1. *Treat derivatives like other financial instruments.*

During the past fifteen years, regulators have treated derivatives differently from other financial instruments, even if they were economically similar. Differential rules led parties to engage in "regulatory arbitrage," using derivatives instead of securities simply for the purpose of avoiding the law.[8] There were numerous instances of the differential treatment of derivatives and equivalent financial instruments: stock options were accounted for differently than other compensation expenses, prepaid swaps and other off-balance-sheet deals were recorded differently than loans, over-the-counter derivatives were exempt from securities rules applicable to economically similar deals, and swaps were regulated differently than equivalent securities. The result was a split between perceived costs (the numbers reported on corporate financial statements) and economic reality (the numbers reported in incomplete or misleading footnotes, or not reported at all).

Derivatives and financial innovation generated great benefits, enabling parties to reduce risks and costs. In theory, some derivatives markets might appropriately have been left unregulated, especially those that involved transactions only among major derivatives dealers. But you couldn't avoid the fact that some derivatives were economically equivalent to other financial instruments. Andy Krieger made money trading options, in part because other traders thought he had sold when he really had bought in a different market. Bankers Trust sold swaps that were really complex trades based on interest-rate indices. CSFP's structured notes were really currency bets. Salomon's Arbitrage Group and Long-Term Capital Management bought cheap options embedded in bonds and then sold equivalent options in a different market. Nick Leeson of Barings bought and sold futures indices on the same Japanese stocks in both Osaka and Singapore.

The problem was that when similar financial instruments were regulated differently, parties were encouraged to use the less regulated version to hide risks or to manipulate financial disclosures.[9] As long as "securities" were regulated, but similar "derivatives" were not, derivatives would be the dark place where regulated parties did their dirty deeds. The only way to reverse the trend was for regulators to apply various rules—prohibitions on fraud; disclosure requirements; banking regulations; and so forth—based on the economic characteristics of the financial instrument, not based on whether the instrument was called a "derivative."

Moreover, it was foolish to deregulate markets simply because large institutions, instead of individuals, were involved.[10] Ultimately, individuals were at risk, as the owners of institutions, and the relevant question was not the size or wealth of an institutional investor, but rather its sophistication relative to the firm selling the derivatives it was buying. As Gibson Greetings and Procter & Gamble had shown, large companies could be babes in the woods compared to Wall Street bankers. It was a well-established economic principle that markets with large sophistication and information gaps—such as the market for "lemon" used cars—did not function very well. It wasn't that Procter & Gamble was defenseless when approached by Bankers Trust's nerdy salesmen; it was that the costs of an unregulated market were too great given the sophistication and information gaps between Procter & Gamble and Wall Street bankers. "Suitability" rules were designed to cover trades with institutions, as well as individuals,[11] although bankers often denied this fact, and courts sometimes believed them.[12]

The derivatives playing field was skewed in favor of Wall Street banks, thanks to financial-market lobbyists, especially ISDA, the International Swaps and Derivatives Association.[13] In February 2002, Jeff Madrick, a financial expert writing in the *New York Review of Books,* expressed doubt that public pressure would lead government officials to change rules applicable to derivatives.[14] He was correct, in part because derivatives were among those issues that were too difficult for people like Senator Corzine's mom. When Senator Dianne Feinstein proposed, in 2002, that energy derivatives should be treated in the same way as similar financial instruments, ISDA launched a massive counterattack, arguing that derivatives "played no essential role"[15] in Enron's collapse. Securities and investment firms had contributed over $18 million to the Democratic and Republican parties during 2000, more than any other industry—including lawyers—with the energy industry close behind.[16] Not surprisingly, Feinstein's proposal never had a chance.

A few government officials expressed worry about derivatives, ranging from Senator Joseph Lieberman, who said he would hold a hearing on the need for derivatives regulation, to Treasury Secretary Paul O'Neill, who suggested that derivatives regulation needed modernizing. As Secretary O'Neill put it, "In this case, I think it's fair to say it may be that our rules and regulations have gotten behind practices."[17]

There were signs that the markets might resolve some of these problems. A few companies followed Alan Greenspan's advice that they voluntarily report stock options as an expense, although these were mostly industrial firms—not technology companies, where options compensation had been more significant. The market for derivatives deals designed to avoid legal rules temporarily thinned during 2002. But as Nobel laureate Merton Miller had argued, as long as legal rules treated derivatives differently than equivalent financial instruments, parties would continue to use derivatives to avoid the costs of legal rules. By 2003, the derivatives market had grown to an astonishing $140 trillion.

Legislators and regulators needed to understand that the more they carved up markets, the harder it was for anyone—regulators and corporate executives—to keep tabs on risks. Simply put, much of the $100+ trillion derivatives market existed because private parties were doing deals to avoid the law. Regardless of whether you favored more or less regulation, that was an unhealthy result.

2. *Shift from rules to standards.*

A similar and related problem was that, during the past fifteen years, regulators increasingly had emphasized narrow rules, in an attempt to provide clarity to market participants. Accounting rules ostensibly told parties exactly what they could count as revenue, or what they must include as a liability on their balance sheets. Securities rules directed parties to disclose particular information every financial quarter. Elaborate guidelines specified how parties could satisfy these disclosure requirements; for example, by disclosing to investors a measure of Value At Risk—the likely maximum one-day loss—for particular investments.

Market participants responded to these narrow rules by transacting around them. There were numerous examples. Paul Mozer of Salomon had engineered bids for clients in an attempt to satisfy the letter of the "35 percent" maximum for U.S. Treasury auctions. The case against Mozer was successful only because he so brazenly bid more than 35 percent. Robert Citron of Orange County had made huge interest-rate bets, while technically in compliance with county investment guidelines, because he bought only short-term, AAA-rated, structured notes. Enron had solicited outside investors to satisfy the "three percent" minimum, so that it could keep partnerships off balance sheet. Global Crossing followed accounting rules in booking up-front revenue from IRU swaps. Specific rules made prosecuting officials of Enron and Global Crossing more difficult, because they could claim they were merely relying on an outside auditor's interpretation of the rule, or on the advice of counsel that the rule permitted their actions.

In sum, these narrow rules had two unanticipated effects. First, by clearly specifying what parties could and could not do, the rules provided a safe haven for anyone doing something not explicitly covered by the rules. Absent a specific prohibition against doing so, companies increasingly recognized revenue up front, moved liabilities off balance sheet, avoided disclosing important facts, or disclosed misleading facts that arguably fit within the applicable rules. For example, Enron's Value-At-Risk disclosures were so dubious that investors did not even flinch when the firm tripled its reported risk in 2000 and even admitted, in a footnote, that its previous VAR models had not worked properly.[18] None of this mattered, because no one imagined that Enron's VAR disclosure was intended to do anything other than satisfy the applicable regulatory requirement.

Second, because specific rules were effectively carved in stone, they ensured that the regulatory regime would become obsolete, almost immediately. Rule changes took a great deal of time; the Financial Accounting Standards Board had spent years debating changes to accounting rules for stock options and other derivatives. In contrast, financial innovation proceeded at a breakneck pace, with banks inventing new deals every day. Specific rules inevitably were left in the dust.

The lesson is that regulators need to shift away from narrow and clear rules, which parties have shown skill in avoiding and exploiting, to broader standards, which would help encourage a culture of honesty.[19] For example, a broad anti-abuse standard could prohibit companies from disclosing information contrary to economic reality, even if a technical accounting rule might permit them to do so. International accounting regulators have developed a few dozen general standards for parties to follow, the notion being that individual parties would exercise judgment to determine whether a particular accounting treatment was appropriate, given the standards. The SEC may follow suit.

It might seem at first that permitting financial actors to use their judgment in determining the regulatory treatment in specific cases would exacerbate the inaccuracies of financial reporting. It is true that accountants, bankers, lawyers, and corporate executives have spent the last decade exhibiting an eagerness to transact in order to avoid the law, in many cases being transformed from the professional "gatekeepers" of financial markets into horse traders and snake-oil salesmen. But one reason they have done so is that specific rules have given them cover. They have not needed to risk their own reputation for honesty; instead, they have relied on the bare letter of the law. In contrast, parties subject to a more general standard would be forced to rely on their own judgment about the "fairness," "risk," or "economic reality" of a transaction; and, if those deals later were scrutinized, the parties would not be able to point to a specific rule as an excuse.

Here are a few examples: recall the three percent rule—the rule that allowed companies to treat Special Purpose Entities as off balance sheet so long as an outside party bought at least three percent of the SPE's capital. In 2002, accounting regulators debated whether some higher number—perhaps ten percent—would be more appropriate.[20] But this path was a slippery slope. Would nine percent be appropriate for some deals? Would later rules specify what counted toward the ten percent? Or what type of outside investor was truly independent? Instead of simply changing the percentage requirement of the specific rule, a better approach would be a general standard that required companies to account for the value of their share of *all* outside investments, regardless of their ownership interest—including their share of the assets and liabilities of SPEs. To the extent companies wanted to explain to investors why they shouldn't worry about the liabilities of a particular SPE, they could do so in foot-notes to their financial statements. But hiding liabilities would no longer be a valid reason to use SPEs. Outside the United States, international accounting standards are moving in this direction, but the U.S. approach remains unclear. The Financial Accounting Standards Board adopted the "ten percent rule," but the new Public Company Accounting Oversight Board, which was set up pursuant to the Sarbanes-Oxley Act to establish future auditing standards, seemed open to a more general approach.

Likewise, proposed rules for calculating the amount of capital fin-ancial institutions must set aside for particular risks—known as the Basel II proposal, due to be adopted in a few years—included both spe-cific rules and general standards, as in a provision for regulators to con-sider the core economic risks of credit-derivatives deals. This second approach—generalized standards based on economic reality—would both discourage deals designed simply to avoid legal rules and encour-age financial institutions to assess their own risks properly.

An approach using general standards also could require that com-panies publish their financial statements to the Internet, and update them over time, based on changes in their businesses, rather than con-tinue to focus on the strict requirement of reporting specified financial results once every quarter. If the reporting periods were more frequent, or perhaps were even staggered across different periods—a week here, a month there—investors and analysts would lose their obsession with end-of-quarter numbers, and the conflicts of interest associated with meet-ing quarterly expectations would dissipate.[21]

The idea of using broad standards in the financial context is not new. In 1969, the well-respected Judge Henry Friendly found, in a case called *United States v. Simon,* that accountants who technically had complied with Generally Accepted Accounting Principles could nevertheless be held criminally liable if the disclosures created a fraudulent or mislead-ing impression among shareholders. In the Simon case, a footnote in Continental Vending's annual report had resembled the opaque disclo-sures in footnote 16 of Enron's 2001 annual report. As Judge Friendly put it, "The jury could reasonably have wondered how accountants who were really seeking to tell the truth could have constructed a footnote so well designed to conceal the shocking facts."[22]

Unfortunately, the Simon case had not influenced many market par-ticipants—in part because the defendants paid small fines and later were pardoned by President Richard M. Nixon.[23] Nevertheless, Judge Friendly's reasoning is wise and powerful advice for regulators considering how to deal with the chaos of modern financial markets.

3. Eliminate the oligopoly lock of gatekeepers, especially credit-rating agencies.

One specific instance of how regulators inadvertently created rules corrupting the financial markets is the pervasive power of gatekeeper institutions—accounting firms, law firms, banks, and credit-rating agencies—even given their abysmal performance in assessing and reporting risks. The securities laws recognize that managers of companies always will have an incentive to be aggressive in reporting their financial data. Instead of trying to dictate what managers can and cannot do, the U.S. regulatory regime creates and subsidizes these gatekeepers, who are supposed to monitor the inevitable conflict between managers and shareholders. This regime assumes that accounting firms actually do audits, law firms and banks actually perform due diligence, and credit-rating agencies properly analyze information about a company's debts. If the gatekeepers do their jobs, investors can look to them for an impartial, third-party perspective on corporate managers.

Gatekeepers benefit greatly from legal rules requiring that companies employ accounting firms to certify their financial statements, banks to underwrite their securities, law firms to examine the underlying documents and opine that they are legitimate, and credit-rating agencies to rate their bonds.[24] Moreover, legal rules permit managers to insulate themselves from liability by involving gatekeeper firms in their transactions.

In other words, gatekeepers do not survive based on their reputation alone, contrary to the assumptions of many academics. Economists have assumed that gatekeepers would not take advantage of investors, because if they did so their reputations would suffer and no one would use their services. That view has proven as naïve as the belief that a $20 bill lying on the ground was not really there. During the past fifteen years, gatekeeper institutions have performed unimaginably disreputable acts, but their reputations have suffered only a little—and their profits have not suffered at all. Gatekeepers will continue to earn substantial profits as long as rules supporting them persist. For example, no matter how poor the credit-rating agencies are at predicting defaults, companies still will pay them for ratings, because legal rules effectively require them to do so. (Recall the importance to Allen Wheat and CSFP of obtaining an

AAA rating.) The same is true, to a somewhat lesser extent, for other gatekeepers.

One possible response to the failure of gatekeepers would be to punish and reform them, as parents might try to change an unruly child. Beginning in 2002, the U.S. government attempted to do this for accountants, by imposing rules that constrained their behavior, and by prosecuting Arthur Andersen.

Such a punitive approach is doomed, unless it also addresses the oligopoly lock gatekeepers have on their respective businesses. Put simply, gatekeepers do not have proper incentives to police corporate managers, because they do not suffer sufficient reputational consequences even when they do a poor job of monitoring. The barriers to entry are too high: most corporate executives will not hire a low-cost competitor to Merrill Lynch, Ernst & Young, or Moody's, because the regulatory system punishes them for doing so, depriving them of an argument that they did their due diligence in a particular deal, or—in many instances—making their securities less attractive to outside investors by removing valuable regulatory entitlements. When prosecutors killed off Arthur Andersen, they only made the franchise associated with a top "Final Four" accounting firm more valuable. In the case of credit-rating agencies, only three are approved for regulatory purposes, so the barrier to entry is insuperable.

The bottom line is that reputation alone does not constrain the behavior of gatekeepers. They can acquire a bad reputation, so long as the structure of the financial system continues to require the use of their services. The legal rules that effectively require companies to hire gatekeepers are the answer to the oft-asked question about why gatekeepers make so much money.

There are two possible solutions. One is to eliminate the legal rules that effectively require that companies use particular gatekeepers (especially credit-rating agencies), while expanding the scope of securities-fraud liability and enforcement to make it clear that all gatekeepers will be liable for assisting companies in transactions designed to distort the economic reality of financial statements. This approach would require that Congress eliminate the regulatory reliance on credit ratings, and remove the restrictions on securities lawsuits imposed during the mid-1990s, so that gatekeepers could be held responsible for aiding and abetting financial fraud. Such changes would encourage new intermediaries to attempt to fill the shoes of the accountants, bankers, lawyers, and credit raters who have failed during the past decade.

The other possibility is to require that gatekeepers act in the public interest as "professionals," and not merely for private gain. This suggestion might seem laughable to accountants and bankers, as the trend during the past decade has shifted from professionalism to profit. But if the markets are to be reformed without radical changes in law, then gatekeepers will need to improve practices on their own, and prove they are deserving of their special place in financial regulation. Only then should the legal rules giving them such special status remain in place.

A reasonable middle-of-the-road approach might be first to open up the market for credit ratings to competition, and to require that regulators use some dividing line other than credit ratings for determining whether specified institutional investors can buy particular bonds. There are numerous available substitutes (the spread between the yield of a bond and a similar, risk-free U.S. Treasury bond, or even the market value of credit default swaps).[25] If the experiment with credit-rating agencies worked well, regulators could consider removing the special entitlements for other gatekeepers. In any event, gatekeepers should not continue to have their cake and eat it, too, by benefiting from legal rules while avoiding responsibility for their actions.

4. Prosecute complex financial fraud.

Prosecutors could relieve some of the burden on gatekeepers by bringing cases against corporate executives for complex financial fraud. Such cases have been notoriously difficult to prosecute, and the government has avoided them during the past decade, thereby creating incentives for executives to commit such fraud.

In general, people are not deterred from criminal activity unless they view it as morally wrong, or perceive that its expected costs—including the possibility of jail time and fines—outweigh the benefits. In the financial markets, the question of whether an action is morally wrong is typically irrelevant; the relevant consideration is profit, with reputation as a secondary restraint on behavior. In other words, participants in the financial markets are rational economic actors: they violate legal rules not because they are evil people, but because it makes economic sense for them to do so. If the gain from cooking the books is substantial, and the probability of punishment is zero, the rational strategy is to cook, cook, cook. Unless the probability of punishment increases, the additional penalties won't do much to deter. Not surprisingly, in 2002, when

Congress doubled the maximum prison term for financial fraud to twenty years, it barely registered in the financial markets. Legislators might as well have added the death penalty, given the low probability of conviction for complex financial fraud.

In the criminal cases brought since 2002, prosecutors did little to persuade market participants that the probability of punishment for complex financial fraud was anything other than zero. Instead, the government reinforced the message that the more complex the scheme, the lower the probability that the perpetrators will be punished. By making the prosecution of Arthur Andersen for obstruction of justice its first case after the financial calamities of 2001, the government killed that firm; but, instead of sending a warning to other accounting firms that they should be more careful in approving controversial accounting treatment for complex transactions, it signaled merely that firms should take more care in their document "retention" policies. Moreover, the government nearly lost the case against Andersen, and the jurors' ultimate verdict was based on an internal memorandum from an Andersen lawyer, which the prosecution had not even featured in its arguments. That verdict hardly frightened anyone involved in a financial scheme, and there was a decent chance it would be overturned on appeal. Likewise, the indictment of Andy Fastow focused on simple kickback schemes, which might be easy to prove, but which would not send a warning to anyone engaged in a more complex fraud.

The May 2003 indictment of Frank Quattrone is an object case. During recent years, no one on Wall Street was higher paid, or more infamous, than Quattrone. But instead of charging him with crimes related to his highly publicized IPO dealings, prosecutors focused on an obscure e-mail exchange related to document destruction.

In simple terms, Quattrone was alleged to have caused other unnamed employees of his investment banking firm, CSFB, to destroy evidence. The facts didn't look great. Richard Char, a CSFB banker, sent Quattrone and others an e-mail eerily similar to the one Andersen's Nancy Temple sent in 2001 telling employees "it would be helpful" if they were in compliance with the firm's document retention policy. Char's message was similar, but more colorful: "Today, it's administrative housekeeping. In January, it could be improper destruction of evidence."[26]

Quattrone wasn't amused. He admonished Char, "You shouldn't make jokes like that on e-mail!" and forwarded to CSFB employees a tamer version of the e-mail, which said, "We strongly suggest that before you leave for the holidays, you should catch up on file cleaning." The criminal complaint alleged that some of those employees destroyed documents during December 2000, after they received the e-mail.

The key questions in the case involved timing and intent. It seemed clear what Quattrone knew and when he knew it. He was informed of three separate investigations by regulators into his technology group's practices of allocating shares in IPOs to favored clients. But it isn't clear whether he had the necessary criminal intent to obstruct justice as of early December 2000. Just the day before the key e-mail flurry, Quattrone asked a CSFB lawyer, "Are the regulators accusing us of criminal activity?"

In addition to these legal and factual weaknesses, the government's case against Quattrone had a more serious flaw. Although U.S. Attorney for Manhattan James Comey said he brought these charges to signal the importance of voluntary compliance with regulatory inquiries, any document destruction was irrelevant to the government's investigation of CSFB.

For years, prosecutors had ample evidence of CSFB's practice of "spinning" IPOs to favored clients who then kicked back a portion of their instantaneous profits after the IPO price shot up during the first day of trading. The government didn't need a few more notes, e-mails, and "pitch books" as proof. As discussed in Chapter 9, key facts establishing the IPO kickback scheme were set forth in a detailed civil suit by the SEC, which CSFB quietly settled for a $100 million fine (paltry, relative to CSFB's profits from "spinning") during the aftermath of September 11, 2001.

Whatever the legality of "spinning"—and if it was illegal, it certainly was widespread—there wasn't any cover-up, certainly not an effective one. The Quattrone criminal complaint describes two IPOs, involving VA Linux and Selectica, Inc. But there were mountains of documents proving CSFB received kickbacks for allocations of other IPOs, too. Even if CSFB had destroyed all of the documents related to VA Linux and Selectica, there still would be plenty of fodder for cases against the firm, as plaintiffs' lawyers suing CSFB have been happily pointing out in related civil cases.

Recall Gadzoox Networks, for example, the Internet company that hired CSFB as the lead underwriter for its IPO. On July 20, 1999, CSFB sold shares in the Gadzoox IPO for $21. By the end of the day, the shares had more than tripled, and the lucky clients who bought at the IPO price (and made $180 million in all) were trading frenetically in stocks unrelated to Gadzoox (Allstate, Coca-Cola, Conoco, and Philip Morris) at sky-high commission rates of $1 per share or more, in order to kickback one-third to two-thirds of their profits to CSFB. Investors who bought at $76 that day were left holding the bag.

The barrier to a "spinning" prosecution wasn't document destruction or lack of evidence. Instead, prosecutors shied from bringing such a case for the same reason they often avoided complex financial prosecutions: they feared being outmatched by clever defense lawyers and bankers who could credibly argue, like a shrewd teenager, that everyone was doing it. Why devote a dozen lawyers to a case you might well lose? In this case, Quattrone's was represented by the legendary John W. Keker, the aggressive lawyer who successfully prosecuted Oliver North in the Iran-Contra trial (and who also represented former Enron CFO Andy Fastow in his criminal case). Not surprisingly, Quattrone pleaded not guilty.

Is "spinning" criminal? No one knows, and the prosecution of Quattrone won't lead to an answer. That is why it is the wrong case. Nabbing Quattrone Al Capone-like (Capone committed every crime in the book, but was nailed only for tax evasion) for causing another person to obstruct justice won't affect the financial markets, except possibly to send a signal that bankers should destroy documents more systematically, and earlier. If prosecutors indeed wanted to try to vilify Quattrone, they should have fought fair, with more than an obstruction of justice prosecution.

If prosecutors believe IPO kickbacks violated the law, they should prosecute willful violations as crimes, with Quattrone at the head of the pack. But if they can't muster such a case, they shouldn't complain that Quattrone caused someone to destroy evidence they never planned to use. Quattrone's case is far from a warning; it sends the message to people committing financial transgressions that they will be punished only if they also engage in some additional, easier-for-a-prosecutor-to-prove crime.

Nor did the government send the right signal by parading handcuffed officials from Adelphia and WorldCom in front of the media. The prosecution of WorldCom executives, in particular, surrounded a simple scheme. Convicting officials from WorldCom, but not the Enron managers who misstated trading profits or abused SPEs, would be like jailing the local dope dealer instead of the Mafia don. Unfortunately, given the legal rules governing Enron's complex transactions, defendants in those cases would be able to argue that, because they relied on specific rules, with the approval of their accountants, bankers, and lawyers, they lacked criminal intent. Thus, prosecutors faced an uphill battle. Paradoxically, it might not be possible for prosecutors to obtain a conviction in a complex financial-fraud case as long as financial markets were governed by highly specific rules instead of more general standards.

5. *Encourage informed investors to bet against stocks.*

Given that the above measures may take some time, regulators should immediately allow and encourage informed investors to bet against stocks when they have reason to do so. This proposal is counterintuitive, but the best way to prevent speculative bubbles that lead to financial crises is to permit smart and informed people to bet against financial assets whenever a bubble starts to build.

Short sellers—people who bet against stocks—have had a bad reputation for decades, and some officials even held them responsible for the market declines of 2001 and 2002. For example, Representative John LaFalce specifically blamed short sellers for the plunge in stock prices in 2002 and asked Harvey Pitt, then SEC chairman, to close down short selling, at least temporarily. There even was evidence—later questioned—that short sellers and options traders had profited from bets against stocks in advance of the terrorist attacks on September 11, 2001.

The bad reputation and blame were undeserved. In fact, legal rules already made short selling difficult and expensive, and these restrictions contributed to the "irrational" upward bias of stock prices during the 1990s. To short a stock, you needed to borrow shares, which often were in limited supply, and you couldn't trade unless the previous trade in the market had been while the price of the stock was rising, because of the so-called uptick rule. Some savvy investors figured out ways to avoid these legal rules, using put options—the right to sell stock—which effectively was a bet against the stock. For example, some hedge funds bought a stock along with a put option, and then sold the very same stock. The effect was to buy the stock once and sell it twice, because the terms of the put option—the right to sell the stock—could be set so that the holder almost always would sell the stock when the option expired. By using these trades, called *bullets*, traders didn't need to borrow stock and could avoid the uptick rule because, technically, these trades were not short sales, even though they were economically equivalent.

However, the bullet rigmarole was complex and expensive, and many traders betting against stocks had lost money during the late 1990s. As the Internet boom demonstrated, it was dangerous to get in front of an investing herd. The result—as new research in behavioral finance confirmed—was that stock prices frequently reflected the trading of optimistic investors more than pessimists, at least until optimists finally learned that the value of a company was lower than they believed, at which point they all sold and prices crashed.[27]

One way to make stock prices more accurate was to do the *opposite* of what Representative LaFalce had suggested: make short selling easier. In fact, Congress had attempted to do just this in December 2000, when it passed a law legalizing the trading of *single-stock futures,* derivatives that essentially were bets on how stocks would perform at future dates.[28] The restrictions on short selling didn't apply to single-stock futures, so investors could more easily use them to bet against stocks. However, the implementation of single-stock futures was dogged by problems related to the first lesson above: treating derivatives like other financial instruments. Unfortunately, the margin requirements for these instruments—which dictated how much money investors in single-stock futures could borrow—differed radically from the requirements for other securities. The rules governing the trading of single-stock futures in the United States were delayed, while regulators considered how to harmonize these regulations. Trading in these instruments finally began in late 2002, and it was an open question whether they would make markets more efficient or more volatile. By late 2003, several new exchanges, including OneChicago and NQLX, offered trading in single-stock futures, and the volume of trading increased.

Another way to encourage betting against stocks would be to permit insiders to tip others as to negative information about their companies. Negative information tended to remain bottled up within companies, in part because of the Supreme Court case that spelled out when it was illegal for insiders to tip others about problems at their companies. In that case, Raymond Dirks, a securities analyst during the 1970s, had been prosecuted for giving his clients negative, but true, information he had learned about Equity Funding, a company involved in a massive financial scam; his clients then profited from trading based on the information. The Supreme Court exonerated Dirks[29] and, a decade later, he was still betting against stocks and advising others to do the same. But the Dirks case cast a shadow over anyone who traded based on an insider's negative tip about a company, and most market participants cautiously avoided such trading.

In the Dirks case, the Supreme Court unintentionally had ensured that stock prices would be less accurate by discouraging individuals who knew negative information about a company from telling outsiders those facts. If Cynthia Cooper of Global Crossing, Roy Olofson of WorldCom, or Sherron Watkins of Enron had been permitted to tip outsiders—including traders—about their companies' troubles, those stocks would have fallen to a lower, more accurate price right away. Many investors still would have lost money, but market prices would have been more accurate, and investors would have avoided the uncertainty and panic during the months when they speculated about worst-case scenarios. Historically, investor panic has proven to be one of the most dangerous elements in financial markets, perhaps even more dangerous than the risk that insiders will abuse negative information in trading their firm's securities.

However, securities regulators have been obsessed with making the investment playing field at least appear to be level, and so instead of permitting insiders to tip others as to negative information, the SEC has done the opposite. The SEC has prosecuted tipping cases and, in 2000, with Arthur Levitt's urging, the SEC passed Reg FD, the fair-disclosure rule, which barred insiders from selectively disclosing *any* material information to particular individuals, unless that information also was broadcast simultaneously to the entire market, typically in a public-television broadcast or on a conference call. Not surprisingly, under Reg FD, companies did not hold press conferences to tell investors bad news about their stocks and, as a result, even more negative information was penned up within companies.

Regulators should reverse this course. Short sellers should be encouraged to bet against stocks, and company insiders with negative information, who are willing to tip outsiders about it, should be allowed to do so, at least under circumstances when the insider is not profiting directly from tipping. It is easy to distinguish negative from positive information, and regulators should not treat them the same.

6. *Encourage investors to control and monitor
   their own investments.*

During the past decade, investors have rushed to participate in financial markets, primarily through various types of investment funds, including mutual funds. Fifty years ago, 97 percent of individual investors held shares directly; now, most people hold shares indirectly, through mutual funds.[30] But many people follow investment strategies—whether through mutual funds or direct ownership of stocks—without doing the research necessary to understand the companies whose securities they hold.

The insights of modern finance suggest that investors are better off with such a passive approach. Trading too much hurts returns; trying to pick stocks hurts returns. Economic theory suggests that, instead, investors should invest in a low-cost index fund that simply buys and holds a diversified portfolio of all of the securities in the market.

Unfortunately, mutual funds have proven disastrous for investors. Most investors have sought out the best-performing funds, whose managers trade too much and try to pick stocks, both of which hurt returns over time. Many funds advertised as "index" funds or "enhanced index" funds are really just actively managed mutual funds in disguise, and the vast majority of actively traded mutual funds have underperformed market indexes, because of their high costs and relatively low comparative advantage.

As the debacles of the past fifteen years have shown, mutual-fund managers don't do much better than individual investors at researching and understanding the nature of the companies whose stock they buy. Most mutual-fund managers have neither inside information nor the sophistication to spot fleeting arbitrage opportunities, and past performance is never a promise of future results (in fact, many studies show that the worst-performing mutual funds are a better bet than the best-performing ones). Moreover, actively managed mutual funds give fund managers incentives to take excessive risks. Investors who buy funds based on past performance are taking on more risk than they think—in many cases, those funds have performed well historically because they invested in companies that had hidden risks or were involved in fraudulent accounting schemes.

It is still a reasonably good strategy to buy a low-cost, diversified, buy-and-hold index fund or an exchange-traded fund—such as the SPDR Trust, known as *Spiders,* which trade on the American Stock Exchange and represent a share of the S&P 500 stocks. But there is an alternative, which, if investors follow it, might generate better returns and create incentives for intermediaries to monitor corporate managers more effectively. This strategy is simple: instead of buying mutual funds, buy two dozen or so different stocks directly and hold on to them. A few dozen different stocks generate almost as much diversification benefit as an index fund and, given the low commissions of Internet brokers, the strategy is comparable in terms of cost.

The do-it-yourself strategy has one major advantage: investors can avoid stocks they believe are most likely to be involved in shady dealings. For example, if you buy an index fund, you are forced to own General Electric stock, even if you are nervous about General Electric's financial statements. By choosing your own stocks, you can avoid General Electric, if you want. If individuals follow this strategy, avoiding particular stocks, the stocks that investors perceive as problematic will suffer, and their prices will be lower. These perceptions will not be reflected in market prices if individuals passively invest in the entire market.

Moreover, if investors take the time to do proper research in directly selecting portfolios of stocks, instead of passively investing through mutual funds, they will create incentives for companies to be more forthcoming about their business. Intermediaries will begin advising investors about which stocks to avoid—soon there will be lists of the top several dozen stocks to include in a diversified portfolio, like *Consumer Reports* ratings. Excluded companies will need to persuade investors and intermediaries that the lists are wrong, and that they actually have viable businesses and transparent finances. Companies might even band together to list their securities together on an exchange, monitoring each other to see that they live up to the standards of the group. Instead of buying mutual funds, people could buy "packages" of a few dozen stocks. There are good companies out there with honest CEOs and good businesses, and if investors engage in serious research in making their investment decisions, they will reward those good companies, and punish the bad ones.

If markets were truly efficient and *someone* were betting against companies involved in fraudulent schemes, then buying the entire market through an index fund might make sense—those companies would have lower stock prices. But if the limits on short selling and the inability and unwillingness of gatekeepers to do real due diligence prevent negative information from impacting market prices, investors will be better off avoiding the *entire* market, with its hidden pitfalls. They will be better off being a little bit less diversified, with a portfolio of a few dozen companies that are the most forthcoming in their financial statements.

As one example, consider Enron and Alliance Capital Management, the gigantic mutual fund. Alliance permitted Alfred Harrison, a 64-year-old portfolio manager, to make a huge bet on Enron, buying shares at prices ranging from $9 to $80. By 2001, Alliance was Enron's largest shareholder, with 43 million shares, worth several billion dollars at the peak. Yet top managers at Alliance admitted that the fund's managers did not dig into Enron's footnotes, and did not uncover key details or even ask key questions. Alliance sold its Enron shares on November 30, 2001, two days before Enron's bankruptcy filing, for twenty-eight cents per share. The massive losses decimated the investors in Alliance's mutual funds, but hardly mattered at all to Alfred Harrison, from a financial perspective: Alliance paid him $2 million in compensation in 2001; his bonus the previous year had been more than $4 million.[31] As James Grant, the well-regarded investment guru, put it, "If a 43-million share investment wasn't enough to command the attention of our leading fiduciaries, what would have been?"[32] And Alliance is one of the *best-run* mutual funds.

Many investors who are afraid to invest directly in companies buy actively managed mutual funds, such as Alliance, instead. But that strategy will work only if a particular mutual-fund manager is doing his or her job, and if—by some miracle—that mutual fund is one of the few that outperformed a market index. For an individual considering an investment in stocks today, there really are only three defensible choices: buy a low-turnover index fund; avoid investing in stocks altogether; or do your own thorough research and buy a few dozen stocks in different industries. Of these choices, the only one that ultimately will put pressure on companies to become more honest is the last.

Fifteen years have passed since Andy Krieger's record year of trading at Bankers Trust, and that bank's efforts to manipulate its financial statements as a result. During those years, a financial virus has worked its way deep into the markets, leading to unprecedented levels of risk coupled with new forms of deceit. These practices first infected Wall Street bankers and accountants, and then—after a brief incubation—spread to corporate executives and investors.

Many warning signs of the resulting epidemic have been lurking in the footnotes of corporate annual reports—Related Party transactions, options compensation, and off-balance-sheet derivatives, to name a few. An astute investor who actually read these reports could have spotted many of the recent financial collapses before they happened. And if corporate managers had believed investors were scrutinizing their filings, they would have been much more careful in their dealings.

Modern financial markets might be impossibly complex, but the business of investing need not be impossible. Ultimately, investors own a share of the earnings of real companies. The financial filings of every public company are available on the Internet for free, and anyone who uses a computer to check e-mail, weather, sports scores, or news can just as easily download these filings. The Securities and Exchange Commission encourages investors to access this information by making it easily accessible through the EDGAR database on its website. If a company cannot explain its financial dealings in plain language in these filings, it is not worth risking any money on it.

Today, there are an astonishing number of individuals buying and selling stocks. Maybe you are one of them. Maybe you have contributed to the volatile and risky nature of these new markets. As you reflect on the story of the last fifteen years of risk and deceit, ask yourself: Did I carefully read the annual reports of the companies whose stocks I bought? Did I really understand what those companies were doing, who their customers were, and how they made money? Did I know how much they were involved in complex financial instruments? Did I resist the recommendations of friends, colleagues, and talking heads on television about the latest hot stock?

If you answered "no," you have one more person to blame, in addition to the accountants, bankers, lawyers, credit raters, corporate executives, directors, and regulators who failed to spot the various financial schemes of recent years. You.

NOTES

Introduction

1. David Evans, "Ex-Merrill Energy Trader Target of Embezzlement Inquiry," *San Diego Union-Tribune,* August 12, 2003, p. C-4.

2. James Grant, "Pecora's Ghost," *Forbes,* March 18, 2002, p. 200.

3. Bryan Burrough and John Helyar, *Barbarians at the Gate: The Fall of RJR Nabisco* (HarperCollins 1991).

4. Kevin G. Salwen, "Year-End Review of Markets and Finance: Follies, Foibles, and Fumbles," *Wall Street Journal,* January 3, 1989, p. 1.

5. Salwen, p. 1.

Chapter 1: Patient Zero

1. The facts in this chapter are based on a series of interviews and correspondence with Andrew Krieger during 2002. Much of Andrew Krieger's background is covered in his autobiographical book, *The Money Bazaar* (Times Books 1992). Gregory J. Millman interviewed Krieger and reported some additional facts in *The Vandals' Crown: How Rebel Currency Traders Overthrew the World's Central Banks* (The Free Press 1995). In addition, Charles W. Stevens of the *Wall Street Journal* wrote several articles about Krieger, including a front-page story, "Change of Heart: Andrew Krieger Made $3 Million Last Year; Why Isn't He Happy?," *Wall Street Journal,* March 24, 1988, p. A1.

2. Krieger, p. 5.

3. Krieger, p. 6.

4. Krieger, p. 27.

5. J. Orlin Grabbe, "The Pricing of Put and Call Options on Foreign Exchange,"

Journal of International Money and Finance, December 1983. Another early academic paper on foreign currency options was Mark B. Garman and Stephen W. Kohlhagen, "Foreign Currency Options Values," *Journal of International Money and Finance, Volume 2* (1983), p. 231. There were numerous other papers published during the time when Krieger was trading at Salomon and Bankers Trust.

6. Krieger, p. 27.

7. Stevens, p. A1.

8. Stevens, p. A1.

9. Krieger, p. 6.

10. Krieger, p. 6.

11. The theory of options pricing was developed in two key articles published in 1973, one coauthored by Fischer Black and Myron Scholes, the other by Robert Merton. Fischer Black and Myron Scholes, "The Pricing of Options and Corporate Liabilities," *Journal of Political Economy, Volume 81,* May–June 1973, p. 637; Robert C. Merton, "Theory of Rational Option Pricing," *Bell Journal of Economics and Management Science, Volume 4,* Spring 1973, p. 141.

12. Peter L. Bernstein, *Capital Ideas: The Impossible Origins of Modern Wall Street* (The Free Press 1992), p. 227.

13. Millman, p. 19.

14. Millman, p. 13.

15. Michael Lewis, *Liar's Poker* (Penguin 1990).

16. Lewis, p. 119.

17. Stevens, p. A1.

18. Bernstein, p. 17.

19. This research ultimately was published in 1970. Eugene F. Fama, "Efficient Capital Markets: A Review of Theory and Empirical Work," *Journal of Finance, Volume 25* (1970), p. 383.

20. A good review of this literature is Stephen F. LeRoy, "Efficient Capital Markets and Martingales," *Journal of Economic Literature, Volume 27* (1989), p. 1,583.

21. Krieger, pp. 33, 38.

22. James B. Stewart, *Den of Thieves* (Simon & Schuster 1991), p. 14.

23. Krieger, p. 38.

24. Krieger, p. 96.

25. Krieger, p. 104.

26. Put-call parity typically is stated as the value of a put (with an exercise price equal to the price of a stock), plus the price of the stock, is equal to the value of a call (with an exercise price equal to the price of a stock), plus the value of the exercise price, discounted by the risk-free rate. In other words, $P + S = C + PV(E)$, where $PV(E)$ is the present value of the exercise price.

27. Krieger, pp. 76, 98.

28. Krieger, pp. 69–70.

29. Michael R. Sesit, "Krieger Returns to Trading Role in Currencies," *Wall Street Journal,* September 12, 1990, p. C1.

30. Sesit, p. C1.

31. Stevens, p. A1.

32. Stevens, p. A1.

33. Lenny Glynn, "The Forex Game," *Institutional Investor,* June 1988, p. 88.

34. Randall Smith, "The Big Casino: How Currency Traders Play for High Stakes against Central Banks," *Wall Street Journal,* September 18, 1992, p. A1.

35. Smith, p. A1.

36. "How Bankers Trust Lied About $80 Million," *Fortune,* September 7, 1992, p. 79.

37. "Bankers Trust Data on Restatement," *New York Times,* July 21, 1988, p. D5.

38. Stevens, p. A1.

39. Stevens, p. A1.

40. Sesit, p. C1.

41. Millman, p. 244.

42. "Bankers Trust Data on Restatement," p. D5.

43. "Bankers Trust Data on Restatement," p. D5.

44. Millman, p. 245.

45. Glynn, p. 88.

46. "How Bankers Trust Lied about $80 Million," p. 79.

47. Robert Guenther, "Bankers Trust Reduces Gain on Fed's Orders," *New York Times,* July 21, 1988, p. C1.

48. Guenther, p. C1.

49. Charles W. Stevens, "Bankers Trust Isn't Expected to Post Big Gains from Currency Trading for the First Quarter," *Wall Street Journal,* April 18, 1988.

50. Glynn, p. 88.

51. Charles W. Stevens, "Stable 1st-Quarter Currency Rates Hurt Most Big Bank Foreign Exchange Profit," *Wall Street Journal,* April 27, 1988.

52. "How Bankers Trust Lied about $80 Million," p. 79.

53. Charles W. Stevens and George Anders, "Options Trading Whiz Krieger Quits Another Job; This Time at Soros Fund," *Wall Street Journal,* June 7, 1988.

54. Kevin G. Salwen, "Year-End Review of Markets and Finance," *Wall Street Journal,* January 3, 1989.

55. Stevens and Anders.

56. Jeremy Campbell, "Wall Street Gamblers Cash In," *Evening Standard* (London), September 18, 1992, p. 2.

57. Margaret Price, "Prescription for Success: Trader Argues for Extensive Use of Currency Options," *Pensions and Investments,* October 15, 1990, p. 21.

58. Gallo, p. 15.

Chapter 2: Monkeys on Their Backs

1. Gary Hector, "Bankers Trust Takes On Wall Street," *Fortune,* January 9, 1984, p. 104.

2. "Up from Savannah: Bankers Trust Taps Sanford," *Fortune,* January 10, 1983, p. 7.

3. Sarah Bartlett, "Bankers Trust: Let's Make a Deal, and Another, and Another, . . . ," *Business Week,* August 11, 1986, p. 51.

4. Wyndham Robertson, "New York City Is Still on the Brink," *Fortune,* July 1977, p. 122.

5. "Wholesale Banking's New Hard Sell," *Business Week,* April 13, 1981, p. 82.

6. Robert M. Garsson, "Sanford Named Bankers Trust's Next President," *American Banker,* June 17, 1982, p. 3.

7. Sarah Bartlett, "Bankers Trust Could Beat the Street at Its Own Game," *Business Week,* April 4, 1988, p. 86.

8. Daniel F. Cuff, "A New President for Bankers Trust," *New York Times,* June 17, 1982, p. D2.

9. Ida Picker, "Bankers Trust's Amazing Risk Machine," *Institutional Investor*, August 1992, p. 29.

10. Brett D. Fromson, "Guess What? The Loss Is Now . . . $20 Million: How Bankers Trust Sold Gibson Greetings a Disaster," *Washington Post*, June 11, 1995, p. A1.

11. Fromson, p. A1.

12. "A Game of Skill as Well; Innovating off the Balance Sheet," *The Economist*, March 21, 1987, p. 39.

13. "In Search of the Crock of Gold: Diversify or Die," *The Economist*, July 21, 1990, p. 18.

14. Glynn, "The Forex Game," *Institutional Investor*, June 1988, p. 88.

15. "In Search of the Crock of Gold: Diversify or Die," p. 18.

16. "In Search of the Crock of Gold: Diversify or Die," p. 18.

17. "Bankers Trust and Salomon Brothers: Noises Off," *The Economist*, February 24, 1990, p. 80.

18. Saul Hansell, "Change at Bankers Trust: Easier Said than Done," *New York Times*, January 15, 1995, Sec. 3, p. 5.

19. Bartlett, "Bankers Trust Could Beat the Street at Its Own Game," p. 86.

20. Bartlett, "Bankers Trust Could Beat the Street at Its Own Game," p. 86.

21. Carol J. Loomis, "A Whole New Way to Run a Bank," *Fortune*, September 7, 1992, p. 77.

22. Bartlett, "Bankers Trust Could Beat the Street at Its Own Game," p. 86.

23. "Bankers Trust; Leaner, Meaner, Keener," *The Economist*, January 24, 1987, p. 73.

24. "Charlie's Angels," *The Economist*, April 10, 1993, p. 14.

25. Fromson, p. A1.

26. Garsson, p. 3.

27. Gary Hector, "Bankers Trust Takes On Wall Street," *Fortune*, January 9, 1984, p. 104.

28. "Bankers Trust; Leaner, Meaner, Keener," p. 73.

29. "Loans for Sale: A New Way to Stretch Bank Dollars," *Business Week*, October 1, 1984, p. 94.

30. Loomis, p. 77.

31. Hector, p. 104.

32. John P. Forde, "Big Firms Involved in Rate Swaps Form Dealers Association," *The Bond Buyer*, March 8, 1985, p. 4.

33. "How AMF Knocked Down Its Debt Load," *Business Week*, January 9, 1984, p. 104.

34. Forde, p. 4.

35. Forde, p. 4.

36. Forde, p. 4.

37. Arthur Walther, an investment banker with Goldman, Sachs & Co., said that in addition to trying to standardize documentation and practices among interest-rate swap deals, the group will also "explore the accounting and regulatory implications" of the off-balance-sheet financings. Forde, p. 4.

38. Forde, p. 4.

39. "Interview with Gary Hector," *Fortune*, March 26, 1990, p. 108.

40. Merton H. Miller, "Financial Innovation: The Last Twenty Years and the Next," *Journal of Financial and Quantitative Analysis*, Volume 21, December 1986, pp. 459–471.

41. Frank Partnoy, "Financial Derivatives and the Costs of Regulatory Arbitrage," *Journal of Corporation Law*, Volume 22 (1997), p. 211.

42. *Gibson Greetings, Inc. v. Bankers Trust Co.*, U.S. District Court, Southern District of Ohio, Civil Action No. 94-620, September 12, 1994, pp. 1–2.

43. *In the Matter of BT Securities Corporation*, S.E.C. Release Nos. 33-7124, 34-35136, 3-8579, December 22, 1994, p. 3.

44. *In the Matter of BT Securities Corporation*, p. 3.

45. Fromson, p. A1.

46. *Gibson Greetings, Inc. v. Bankers Trust*, p. 7.

47. Alfred Steinherr, *Derivatives: The Wild Beast of Finance* (Wiley 1998), p. 76.

48. "Gibson Greeting's Thank-You Card," *Derivatives Strategy, Volume 3*, September 19, 1994, p. 2.

49. Blaise Labriola, "Modeling the Gibson Trades," *Derivatives Strategy, Volume 3*, September 19, 1994, p. 5; *Gibson Greetings, Inc. v. Bankers Trust*, p. 8.

50. *Gibson Greetings, Inc. v. Bankers Trust*, p. 9.

51. "Corporate Hedging, Hard Soap," *The Economist*, April 16, 1994, p. 82.

52. "Gibson Greeting's Thank-You Card," p. 2.

53. *Gibson Greetings, Inc. v. Bankers Trust*, p. 10.

54. *In the Matter of BT Securities Corporation*, p. 1.

55. Jessica Sommar, "Bankers Trust Announces New Managing Directors," *Investment Dealers' Digest*, October 4, 1993, p. 10.

56. Richard Layne, "BT's Bet on Derivatives Business Pays Off," *American Banker*, August 10, 1993, p. 20.

57. John Thackray, "The Two Faces of Kevin Hudson," *Derivatives Strategy*, 1995, p. 1.

58. Thackray, p. 2.

59. Fromson, p. A1.

60. Kelly Holland, Linda Himelstein, and Zachary Schiller, "The Bankers Trust Tapes," *Business Week*, October 16, 1995, p. 106.

61. Fromson, p. A1.

62. Frank Partnoy, *F.I.A.S.C.O.: Blood in the Water on Wall Street* (W. W. Norton 1997), back cover.

63. Thackray, p. 8.

64. *Procter & Gamble v. Bankers Trust*, 1996 U.S. Dist. LEXIS 6435, Southern District of Ohio, May 8, 1996, p. 10.

65. Carol J. Loomis, "Bankers Trust Times; More Dirt about Derivatives!," *Fortune*, November 27, 1995, p. 34.

66. Thackray, p. 5.

67. Holland, Himelstein, and Schiller, p. 106; Loomis, "Bankers Trust Times; More Dirt about Derivatives!," p. 34.

68. Thackray, p. 8.

69. Thackray, p. 8.

70. The facts related to Fonkenell are based on a reported decision in the case of *In the Matter of Guillaume Henry André Fonkenell, a Former Institution-Affiliated Party of Bankers Trust Company*, New York, New York, Docket No. 98-032-B-I, 98-032-CMP-I, Federal Reserve Bulletin, May 1, 2001.

71. Graef S. Crystal, "How Much CEOs Really Make," *Fortune*, June 17, 1991, p. 72.

72. Hansell, p. 5; Loomis, "A Whole New Way to Run a Bank," p. 77.

73. Loomis, "A Whole New Way to Run a Bank," p. 77.

74. Hansell, p. 5.

Chapter 3: Wheat First Securities

1. "CS First Boston: As Many Names as a Russian Novel," *The Economist,* November 3, 1990, p. 90.

2. Frank Partnoy, *F.I.A.S.C.O.: Blood in the Water on Wall Street* (W. W. Norton 1997), p. 21.

3. "CS First Boston: As Many Names as a Russian Novel," p. 90.

4. Helen Dunne, "Wheat's Promise of a Rich Harvest," *Daily Telegraph,* June 6, 1998, p. 32.

5. David Fairlamb, "Bankers Trust's Mr. Fixit," *Institutional Investor,* June 1989, p. 64.

6. Dunne, p. 32.

7. Fairlamb, p. 64.

8. "Bankers Trust and Salomon Brothers: Noises Off," *The Economist,* February 24, 1990, p. 80.

9. Stephen Fiddler, "Anger at Bankers Trust over Defector to CSFB," *Financial Times,* February 15, 1990, p. 35.

10. Dunne, p. 32.

11. Mary Radford, "CS First Boston Creates Unique Swaps Subsidiary," *Investment Dealers' Digest,* July 9, 1990, p. 6; Julian Walmsley, "Credit Suisse Still Out in Front in Derivatives Market," *Extel Examiner,* June 28, 1993, p. 865.

12. Michael Liebowitz, "Credit Suisse Derivative Unit Opens with a Bang in New York," *Investment Dealers' Digest,* October 1, 1990, p. 6.

13. Tracy Corrigan, "Derivatives Newcomer Expects Quick Profits," *Financial Times,* July 17, 1990, p. 29; "City Shop," *The Times* (London), July 17, 1990.

14. Radford, p. 6.

15. *Hazell v. Hammersmith and Fulham London Borough Council,* 2 QB (CA) 697 (1990), p. 801.

16. Liebowitz, p. 6.

17. "Credit Suisse Financial Products Establishes Representative Office in New York," *PR Newswire,* September 26, 1990, p. 1.

18. These agencies were designated "Nationally Recognized Statistical Ratings Organizations." By the late 1990s, only Moody's, S&P, and Fitch had NRSRO status, and the Securities and Exchange Commission consistently had denied applications from competing agencies from the 1970s until 2002. Frank Partnoy, "The Siskel and Ebert of Financial Markets: Two Thumbs Down for the Credit Rating Agencies," *Washington University Law Quarterly, Volume 77,* Fall 1999, p. 619.

19. *The News Hour with Jim Lehrer:* Interview with Thomas L. Friedman (PBS television broadcast), February 13, 1996.

20. Partnoy, "The Siskel and Ebert of Financial Markets: Two Thumbs Down for the Credit Rating Agencies," pp. 619–711.

21. John Eatable and Lance Taylor, *Global Finance at Risk: The Case for International Regulation* (New Press 2000), p. 101.

22. Leslie Scism, "Low Yields Spark Flurry in New Notes," *Wall Street Journal,* October 4, 1993, p. C1.

23. "Structured Products: Background and Investment Opportunities," Morgan Stanley, March 1994, p. 12.

24. Michael Liebowitz, "Can the Triple-A Subs Live Up to their Billing?" *Investment Dealers' Digest,* November 2, 1992, p. 16.

25. "An Issuers' View of the Structured Note Market," *Derivatives Strategy,* February 20, 1994, p. 6.

26. Liebowitz, "Credit Suisse Derivative Unit Opens with a Bang in New York," p. 6.

27. Scism, p. C1.

28. "An Issuers' View of the Structured Note Market," p. 6.

29. Kevin Muehring, "Who Do You Trust?" *Institutional Investor,* May 1992, p. 73.

30. "Once in Jeopardy, Diff Swaps Prove Resilient," *Bloomberg News,* May 7, 1993.

31. James M. Mahoney, "Correlation Products and Risk Management Issues," *Federal Reserve Bank of New York Economic Policy Review,* October 1995, p. 7.

32. Miriam Bensman, "How Do I Get Out of This? New Exit Strategies for the Structured Note Market," *Futures,* October 1993, p. 32.

33. Mahoney, p. 7.

34. "Traders Sell Strategies for Falling European Rates."

35. Ronald H. Coase, "The Problem of Social Cost," *Journal of Law and Economics, Volume 3,* October 1960, pp. 1–44.

36. "A Large Car-Loan Issue," *The New York Times,* December 13, 1985, p. D4.

37. Steven Bavaria, "Fuzzy Line between Private and Bank Debt," *Investment Dealers' Digest,* September 16, 1991, p. 13.

38. Everette D. Hull and Leslie Annard, "Time to Jump on the Securitization Bandwagon?" *ABA Banking Journal,* October 1987, p. 137.

39. David Gillen, "More Junk Bonds May Be Repackaged as High-Grade Securities, Analysts Say," *The Bond Buyer,* February 22, 1990, p. 3.

40. Martin Mayer, "The Latest Junk Bond Scam?" *Los Angeles Times,* January 7, 1990, p. D3.

41. David Gillen, "Columbia to Sell Entire Junk Holdings, Put at $3.5 Billion, through First Boston," *The Bond Buyer,* March 15, 1990, p. 3.

42. Anne Schwimmer, "Chancellor's CBO Pulled as Investor Backs Out," *Mergers & Acquisitions Report,* November 19, 1990, p. 9.

43. "Moody's Affirms the Rating of CBC Holdings CBO," *Asset Sales Report,* September 30, 1991, p. 3.

44. Kevin Muehring, p. 73; "In World of High-Tech Financial Instruments, Compliance Officer to Become King of Bank," *Thomson's Financial Compliance Watch,* March 23, 1992, p. 3.

45. Philip Maher and Ron Cooper, "CS First Boston's Wheat Begins to Exert Control," *Investment Dealers' Digest,* October 11, 1993, p. 5.

46. Dunne, p. 32.

47. Ron Cooper, "In Switch, First Boston Comes to Rescue of CSFB," *Investment Dealers' Digest,* December 7, 1992, p. 5.

48. "CS First Boston, All Together Now?" *The Economist,* April 10, 1993, p. 90.

49. Tracy Corrigan, "Survey of Derivatives," *Financial Times,* December 8, 1992, p. 4.

50. Dunne, p. 32.

51. "CS First Boston's Wheat Plans Strategy after Reorganization," *Bloomberg News,* September 27, 1993.

52. Peter Lee, "Wheat and the Chaff," *Euromoney,* May 1996, p. 46.

53. Dunne, p. 32.

54. Dunne, p. 32.

55. Michael Siconolfi, "CS First Boston Asks Departing Workers to Sign Sweeping Nondisclosure Pact," *Wall Street Journal,* February 27, 1995.

56. "The Market's Revenge," *BusinessWeek,* April 18, 1994, p. 32.

57. Dunne, p. 32.

58. Fairlamb, p. 64.

Chapter 4: Unreconciled Balances

1. Roger Lowenstein, *When Genius Failed: The Rise and Fall of Long-Term Capital Management* (Random House 2000), p. 5.

2. Peter Grant and Marcia Parker, "Hurtling toward Scandal," *Crain's New York Business,* June 1–7, 1992, p. 3.

3. Lowenstein, p. 33.

4. Grant and Parker, p. 3.

5. Lowenstein, p. 19; Nicholas Dunbar, *Inventing Money: The Story of Long-Term Capital Management and the Legends behind It* (John Wiley & Sons 2001), p. 110.

6. Grant and Parker, p. 13.

7. Lowenstein, p. 4.

8. Lowenstein, p. 15.

9. Dunbar, p. 123.

10. Dunbar, p. 123.

11. Dunbar, p. 79.

12. Dunbar, p. 58.

13. Burton G. Malkiel, *A Random Walk Down Wall Street* (W. W. Norton 2000), p. 243.

14. Dunbar, p. 118.

15. Lowenstein, p. 11.

16. Grant and Parker, p. 9.

17. Dunbar, p. 82.

18. Dunbar, p. 107.

19. Robert Lenzner and William Heuslein, "The Age of Digital Capitalism," *Forbes,* March 29, 1993, p. 62.

20. Lenzner and Heuslein, p. 66.

21. Lenzner and Heuslein, p. 62.

22. Neil Bennett, "Salomon Takes $194m Hit over London Errors," *London Times,* February 3, 1995.

23. "Ways of Wall Street, Bad News for Brokerage Accounting," *Bloomberg News,* February 27, 1995.

24. Grant and Parker, p. 4.

25. Dunbar, p. 105.

26. Dunbar, p. 97.

27. Dunbar, p. 95.

28. Dunbar, p. 98.

29. Dunbar, p. 110.

30. Grant and Parker, pp. 3, 13.

31. Grant and Parker, p. 12.

32. *In the Matter of John H. Gutfreund, Thomas W. Strauss, and John W. Meriwether,* Securities Exchange Act of 1934, Release No. 34-31554, December 3, 1992, p. 11.

33. Martin Mayer, *Nightmare on Wall Street* (Simon & Schuster 1993), p. 196.

34. Robert J. McCartney, "Salomon's Mines; What Makes These Traders Tick?" *The Record,* September 29, 1991, p. B1.

35. Mayer, p. 200.

36. Grant and Parker, p. 13.

37. *In the Matter of John H. Gutfreund, Thomas W. Strauss, and John W. Meriwether,* p. 4, note 3.

38. *In the Matter of John H. Gutfreund, Thomas W. Strauss, and John W. Meriwether,* p. 4.

39. Kenneth H. Gilpin, "Credit Markets; Treasury's Rule Upsets Note Sale," *New York Times,* July 12, 1990, p. D1.

40. Grant and Parker, p. 13.

41. *In the Matter of John H. Gutfreund, Thomas W. Strauss, and John W. Meriwether,* pp. 5–6.

42. *In the Matter of John H. Gutfreund, Thomas W. Strauss, and John W. Meriwether,* p. 6.

43. Grant and Parker, p. 14.

44. *In the Matter of John H. Gutfreund, Thomas W. Strauss, and John W. Meriwether,* p. 8.

45. *In the Matter of Paul W. Mozer,* Securities Exchange Act of 1934, Release No. 34-34373, July 14, 1994, p. 3.

46. Mayer, pp. 206–208.

47. *In the Matter of John H. Gutfreund, Thomas W. Strauss, and John W. Meriwether,* p. 10.

48. Mayer, p. 210.

49. Michael Lewis, *Liar's Poker* (Penguin 1990), p. 92.

50. Lewis, p. 111.

51. Lewis, p. 101.

52. Mayer, p. 155.

53. Lowenstein, p. 21.

54. Dunbar, p. 101.

55. Lewis, p. 124.

56. Lewis, p. 126.

57. Salomon ultimately decided to abandon this cap; for example, the firm paid Michael Lewis, author of *Liar's Poker,* more. Lewis, p. 245.

58. Lewis, p. 126.

59. James Sterngold, "Merrill Lynch Puts Bond Loss at $250 Million," *New York Times,* April 30, 1987, p. A1.

60. Sterngold, p. A1.

61. *In the Matter of John H. Gutfreund, Thomas W. Strauss, and John W. Meriwether,* p. 12.

62. Mayer, p. 214.

63. *In the Matter of John H. Gutfreund, Thomas W. Strauss, and John W. Meriwether,* pp. 14–15.

64. "Basham Leaving Treasury Department," *United Press International,* August 5, 1991; Michael Vachon, "Basham to Smith Barney," *Investment Dealers' Digest,* August 19, 1991, p. 15.

65. Susan Antilla, "Ex-Salomon Trader Gets 4 Months," *New York Times,* December 15, 1993, p. D2.

66. "Now Hear This," *Fortune,* January 10, 1994, p. 20.

67. Keith Bradsher, "Former Salomon Trader to Pay $1.1 Million Fine," *New York Times,* July 15, 1994, p. D1; Antilla, p. D2.

68. Katherine Burton and Liz Goldenberg, "Ten Years Ago, Salomon Treasury Scandal Changed Traders' World," *Bloomberg News,* August 9, 2001.

69. Burton and Goldenberg.

70. Peter Woodifield, "Gutfreund Joins Unterberg, Towbin as Senior Managing Director," *Bloomberg News,* November 14, 2001.

71. Ron Cooper, "Return of the King," *Investment Dealers' Digest*, November 19, 2001.

72. Burton and Goldenberg.

73. Dunbar, p. 130.

74. Lowenstein, pp. 37–38.

Chapter 5: A New Breed of Speculator

1. Robert Hurtado, "Fed's Move Jolts Stock and Bond Markets," *New York Times*, February 5, 1994, Sec. 1, p. 37.

2. Jonathan R. Macey, "Derivative Instruments: Lessons for the Regulatory State," *Journal of Corporation Law*, Fall 1995, p. 93.

3. *In re County of Orange*, U.S. Bankruptcy Court, Central District of California, Case No. SA 94-22272 JR, *County of Orange v. Morgan Stanley & Co.*, Complaint, June 11, 1996, p. 27.

4. Laura Jereski, "Merrill Lynch Saw Big Profit on Orange Fund," *Wall Street Journal*, January 26, 1995, p. A4.

5. Tim Quinson, "A Tough Week, and It's Only Wednesday," *Bloomberg News*, December 7, 1994, p. 2.

6. *In re County of Orange*, p. 30.

7. *In re County of Orange*, pp. 41–42, 72.

8. *In re County of Orange*, p. 41.

9. *In re County of Orange*, p. 43.

10. Sallie Hofmeister, "California Fund Woes Worsening," *New York Times*, December 3, 1994, p. C1.

11. Katherine Burton, John Pickering, and Dave Liedtka, "Credit Agencies Dropped Ball, Investors Say," *Bloomberg News*, December 5, 1994, p. 1.

12. "Orange County Crisis: The Fallout—Wall Street Races to Sell $10 Billion in Collateral," *Dow Jones News*, December 8, 1994, p. 2.

13. Laura Jereski, "Salomon's $8.1 Billion Derivative Offer Seen by Other Firms as Latecomer's Bid," *Wall Street Journal*, March 27, 1995, p. A4.

14. Jereski, p. A4.

15. "Orange County Crisis—Local Heroes: Public Finance Chiefs Are Often Very Boring; That's the Good News," *Dow Jones News*, December 8, 1994, p. 3.

16. "Orange County Crisis—Local Heroes," p. 1.

17. "Orange County Crisis—Local Heroes," p. 2.

18. Jill J. Barshay, "Star Struck: How Piper Tied Its Fortunes to a Maverick," *Minneapolis Star Tribune*, February 8, 1999, p. 1D.

19. *In the Matter of Piper Capital Management, Inc. et al.*, Administrative Proceeding File No. 3-9657, November 30, 2000, p. 13.

20. Karen Padley, "Piper Jaffray Lobbied to Let Minnesota Towns Invest in Bond Fund," *Bloomberg News*, August 26, 1994, p. 1.

21. Gary Weiss, "The $700 Million Mystery," *BusinessWeek*, December 18, 1995, p. 76.

22. *ABF v. Askin Complaint*, March 27, 1996, p. 20.

23. Weiss, p. 77.

24. "What Went Wrong at Granite," *Derivatives Strategy*, April 4, 1994, p. 5.

25. "David Askin's Friends," *Derivatives Strategy*, April 25, 1994, p. 5.

26. David Kleinbard, "U.S. Labor Department Investigates Derivatives Use by Two Funds," *Bloomberg News*, October 27, 1994, p. 1.

27. *ABF v. Askin Complaint,* pp. 32–33.

28. *ABF v. Askin Complaint,* p. 61.

29. *ABF v. Askin Complaint,* p. 62.

30. Barshay, p. 1D.

31. *In the Matter of Piper Capital Management, Inc. et al.,* p. 6.

32. Susan E. Kuhn, "He Lost How Much? $800 Million?" *Fortune,* September 19, 1994, p. 38.

33. G. Bruce Knecht, "Piper Manager's Loss May Total $700 Million," *Wall Street Journal,* August 25, 1994, p. C1.

34. Kuhn, p. 38.

35. *In the Matter of Piper Capital Management, Inc. et al.,* p. 6.

36. Knecht, p. C1.

37. Kevin Shinkle and Tim Quinson, "Kidder Spends $7 Mln to Cover Money Market Losses," *Bloomberg News,* August 31, 1994, p. 1.

38. David Kleinbard, "U.S. Labor Department Investigates Derivatives Use by Two Funds," *Bloomberg News,* October 27, 1994, p. 1.

39. Tim Quinson and Matt Rees, "United Services Spends $93 Mln to Shore Up Money Fund," *Bloomberg News,* September 29, 1994, p. 1.

40. Fidelity Investments, "Letter from Edward C. Johnson III, Chairman," June 1, 1994, p. 2.

41. *In the Matter of NationsSecurities and NationsBank, N.A.,* Administrative Proceeding File No. 3-9596, Securities Act Release No. 7532, Exchange Act Release No. 39947, May 4, 1998.

42. *In the Matter of NationsSecurities and NationsBank, N.A.,* p. 375.

43. Al Ehrbar, "The Great Bond Market Massacre," *Fortune,* October 17, 1994, p. 77.

44. "The World According to Stan Jonas," *Derivatives Strategy,* November 1995, p. 38.

45. Ehrbar, p. 77.

46. Matt Rees and Tim Quinson, "Mutual Fund Directors Need More Derivatives Savvy," *Bloomberg News,* May 26, 1994, p. 1.

47. Christian Plumb, "Lehman Brothers VP Charged with Using Jury Imposter," *Bloomberg News,* January 20, 1995.

Chapter 6: Morals of the Marketplace

1. "New School Slates Futures and Options Conference," *Securities Week,* September 30, 1985, p. 9.

2. *Meinhard v. Salmon,* 164 N.E. 545, 546 (N.Y. 1928).

3. "Interim Report to the Trustees and Members of the Common Fund on First Capital Strategists," Cravath, Swaine & Moore, January 4, 1996.

4. Hal Lux, "The Insider: Proposed SEC Chief Arthur Levitt Jr. Knows Almost Everyone on Wall Street—Which Is Good News and Bad," *Institutional Investor,* May 31, 1993, p. 16.

5. Lux, p. 16.

6. Kevin J. Murphy, "Politics, Economics, and Executive Compensation," *University of Cincinnati Law Review, Volume 63* (1995), pp. 713, 738.

7. Lux, p. 16.

8. David A. Vise, "Levitt Set to Sell Stake in *Roll Call,*" *Washington Post,* June 5, 1993, p. C1.

9. Lux, p. 16.

10. Claudia Maclachlan, "SEC Nominee Says He'll Study Curbs on Securities Suits," *National Law Journal,* July 26, 1993, p. 15.

11. "SEC Nominee Says Strict Rules Make U.S. Markets Attractive," *Thomson's International Banking Regulator,* July 19, 1993, p. 2.

12. *Moneyline,* Cable News Network, September 9, 1993.

13. Hal Lux, "Levitt's Last Testimony," *Institutional Investor,* January 2001, p. 74.

14. David Kleinbard, "CFTC Study Finds Little Risk from Derivatives," *Bloomberg News,* October 26, 1993, p. 1.

15. Anne Schwimmer, "When ISDA Comes Calling...," *Investment Dealers' Digest,* November 21, 1994, p. 16.

16. "Financial Derivatives: Market Overview and Supervisory Concerns," A Report Prepared by House Banking Committee Minority Staff, November 1993.

17. Brett D. Fromson, "Some Industry Executives See Dangers of Derivatives Causing 'Meltdown,'" *Washington Post,* October 28, 1993, p. A29.

18. "Levitt Calls for More Fund Oversight by Directors," *Bloomberg News,* March 21, 1994, p. 1.

19. "Now Hear This," *Fortune,* October 31, 1994, p. 21.

20. Antony J. Michels, "Is Your Money Fund Safe?" *Fortune,* October 3, 1994, p. 40.

21. Erick Schonfeld, "A Broken Buck," *Fortune,* October 31, 1994, p. 21.

22. "Financial Derivatives: Actions Needed to Protect the System," U.S. General Accounting Office, May 18, 1994.

23. "The GAO Report on Financial Derivatives: Good Facts and Bad Conclusions," An ISDA Position Paper, May 27, 1994, p. 1.

24. Bank for International Settlements, "Central Bank Survey of Derivatives Market Activity," December 19, 1995, p. 1.

25. Fred S. McChesney, "Economics, Law and Science in the Corporate Field: A Critique of Eisenberg," *Columbia Law Review, Volume 89* (1989), pp. 1530, 1544.

26. Sean M. Flanagan, "The Rise of a Trade Association: Group Interactions within the International Swaps and Derivatives Association," *Harvard Negotiation Law Review, Volume 6,* Spring 2001, p. 238, note 136.

27. Dean Tomasula, "Study Showing Derivatives Profits at Banks Criticized as One-Sided," *American Banker,* October 19, 1994.

28. Lynn Stevens Hume, "Regulators, Industry Give Differing Views on Bill; Leach Blasts Bank Official for Misstating Provisions," *The Bond Buyer,* July 13, 1994, p. 6.

29. Hume, p. 6.

30. Hume, p. 6.

31. Schwimmer, p. 16.

32. Saul Hansell and Kevin Muehring, "Why Derivatives Rattle the Regulators," *Institutional Investor,* September 1992, p. 49.

33. Schwimmer, p. 16.

34. Schwimmer, p. 16.

35. Dean Tomasula, "Congress Expected to Take Heat off the Swaps Market," *American Banker,* October 14, 1994, p. 22.

36. Tomasula, p. 22.

37. Michael Peltz, "Congress's Lame Assault on Derivatives," *Institutional Investor,* December 1994, p. 65.

38. "The Risk Management Improvement and Derivatives Oversight Act," H.R. 20, 104th Congress, 1st Session (1995).

39. "The Derivatives Safety and Soundness Supervision Act of 1995," H.R. 31, 104th Congress, 1st Session (1995).

40. "The Derivatives Limitations Act of 1995," S. 557, 104th Congress, 1st Session (1995).

41. "The Derivatives Dealers Act of 1995," H.R. 1063, 104th Congress, 1st Session (1995).

42. Ray J. Groves, "Here's the Annual Report. Got a Few Hours?" *Wall Street Journal,* August 4, 1994, p. A12.

43. "Derivatives Accounting Disclosure and Market Surveillance," International Swaps and Derivatives Association Conference, September 25, 1996, p. 7.

44. Murphy, p. 726.

45. Murphy, p. 713.

46. Section 162(m) of the Internal Revenue Code was amended by the Omnibus Budget Reconciliation Act of 1993, Public Law No. 103-66, 13,211 (1993).

47. Murphy, note 68.

48. *Code of Federal Regulations, Volume 26,* Section 1.162-27(e)(2).

49. *Code of Federal Regulations, Volume 26,* Section 1.162-27(e)(2)(vi).

50. APB Opinion No. 25 (1972).

51. "Executive Compensation Disclosure," Exchange Act Release No. 33-692, October 21, 1992.

52. Julie Kosterlitz and Neil Munro, "Full Disclosure," *National Journal,* February 23, 2002, p. 5.

53. "Legislation Introduced to Overturn FASB Stock Option Proposal," *Journal of Accountancy, Volume 176,* October 1993, p. 15.

54. Financial Accounting Standard No. 119, October 1994.

55. "Legislation Introduced to Overturn FASB Stock Option Proposal," p. 7.

56. "Proposed Amendments to Require Disclosure of Accounting Policies for Derivative Financial Instruments and Derivative Commodity Instruments," Securities Act Release No. 7250, Exchange Act Release No. 36643, December 28, 1995.

57. Release Nos. 33-7386; 34-38223; IC-22487; FR-48, January 31, 1997.

58. Rahul Jacob, "The SEC Zeroes in on Derivatives," *Fortune,* November 28, 1995, p. 15.

59. Release Nos. 33-7386; 34-38223; IC-22487; FR-48, p. 26, note 67.

60. "BT, BBL Lead with Forex Structures that Skirt FASB Accounting Standards," *Derivatives Week, Volume 4,* March 6, 1995, pp. 1, 11.

61. Todd E. Petzel, "Derivatives: Market and Regulatory Dynamics," *Journal of Corporation Law,* Fall 1995, p. 108.

62. Henry T. C. Hu, "Hedging Expectations: 'Derivative Reality' and the Law and Finance of the Corporate Objective," *Texas Law Review, Volume 73,* April 1995, p. 985; Lynn A. Stout, "Betting the Bank: How Derivatives Trading under Conditions of Uncertainty Can Increase Risks and Erode Returns in Financial Markets," *Journal of Corporation Law,* Fall 1995, p. 53.

63. Joseph A. Grundfest, "The Limited Future of Unlimited Liability: A Capital Markets Perspective," *Yale Law Journal, Volume 102* (1992), pp. 410–411.

64. Minutes of Meeting of the Federal Advisory Council and the Board of Governors, May 13, 1994.

65. Laura Jereski, "Mortgage Securities Weaken Fed's Power," *Wall Street Journal,* August 30, 1994, p. C1.

66. *Frontline* (PBS Interview), May 2001. For a more thorough discussion of the SEC's approach to such investigations, see William R. McLucas, J. Lynn Taylor, and Susan A. Mathews, "A Practitioner's Guide to the SEC's Investigative and Enforcement Process," *Temple Law Review, Volume 70,* Spring 1997, p. 53.

67. "Hearings before the Subcommittee on Securities of the Senate Committee on

Banking, Housing, and Urban Affairs on S. 647 to Amend the Federal Securities Laws to Revise Enforcement Remedies for Civil Violations of Those Laws," 101st Cong. (1990), pp. 56–57.

68. *In the Matter of BT Securities Corp*, S.E.C. Release Nos. 33-7124, 34-35136, December 22, 1994.

69. *In the Matter of Gary S. Missner,* 62 S.E.C. Docket 265, SEC Release Nos. 33-7304, 34-37301, June 11, 1996.

70. *In the Matter of Mitchell A. Vazquez,* 61 S.E.C. Docket 858, SEC Release Nos. 33-7269, 34-36906, February 29, 1996.

71. *In the Matter of Gary S. Missner.*

72. *In the Matter of Mitchell A. Vazquez.*

73. Gary S. Missner, letter to *Fortune,* May 1, 1995, p. 7.

74. *In the Matter of Global Capital Investment LLC and Mitchell Vazquez,* CFTC Docket No. 02-07, February 27, 2002.

75. "Ex-Trader Cleared of Charges," *New York Times,* June 9, 2000, p. C24; *Wall Street Journal,* June 12, 2000, p. A26.

76. *SEC v. Lavin,* 111 F.3d 921 (D.C. Cir. 1997); *SEC v. Lavin,* 937 F. Supp. 23 (D.C. Cir. 1996).

77. *In re BT Securities Corp.,* Exchange Act Release Act No. 35,136, December 22, 1994, p. 1193.

78. *In the Matter of Gibson Greetings,* File No. 3-8866, Exchange Act Release No. 36357, October 11, 1995.

79. Edmund L. Andrews, "Embattled Bankers Trust Chairman Resigns," *New York Times,* June 30, 1999, p. C4.

80. Liz Moyer, "Ex-Bankers Trust Chairman Resigns from Deutsche Bank," *The American Banker,* June 30, 1999, p. 5.

81. *In the Matter of Piper Capital Management, Inc. et al.,* Administrative Proceeding File No. 3-9657, November 30, 2000, p. 9.

82. *In the Matter of Piper Capital Management, Inc. et al.,* p. 9.

83. *In the Matter of Piper Capital Management, Inc. et al.,* pp. 66, 70.

84. *SEC v. CS First Boston Corp.,* Litigation Release No. 15160, November 20, 1996, pp. 1–2.

85. Michael G. Wagner, "Citron Called An 'Abject Failure' in Probation Plea," *Los Angeles Times,* November 28, 1995, p. A3.

86. Jack Leonard, "Raabe Case Tossed Out," *Los Angeles Times,* July 7, 2001, Part 2, p. 1.

87. Jack Leonard, Jean O. Pasco, and Monte Morin, "Orange County Retrial Rejected," *Los Angeles Times,* July 14, 2001, Part 2, p. 6.

88. Matt Rees and Anthony Effinger, "ABN Amro Case Brings Derivatives Nightmare to Life," *Bloomberg News,* November 16, 1993.

89. Michael D. Greenbaum, "Duking It Out," *Forbes,* October 10, 1994, p. 21.

90. *Procter & Gamble v. Bankers Trust,* 925 F. Supp. 1270, 1277 (S.D. Ohio 1996).

91. *In re County of Orange,* U.S. District Court, Central District of California, District Court Case No. SACV 96-0765-GLT, March 18, 1997.

92. *In re County of Orange,* U.S. Bankruptcy Court, Central District of California, Case No. SA 94-22272 JR; *County of Orange v. Student Loan Marketing Association,* Complaint, pp. 11–14.

93. Regulation S-K, Item 508(e).

94. NASD Rule of Fair Practice 44(c)(2)(B).

95. NASD Rule of Fair Practice 44(c)(2)(C).

96. *Central Bank of Denver v. First Interstate Bank of Denver*, 511 U.S. 164 (1994).

97. "Remarks by Arthur Levitt," 22nd Annual Securities Regulation Institute, January 25, 1995, p. 1.

98. "Remarks by Arthur Levitt," p. 1.

99. "The Return of von Clausewitz, A Survey of Management," *The Economist*, March 9, 2002, p. 18.

100. Jill Andresky Fraser, "How GE's Tough Love Saved Kidder," *Institutional Investor*, April 1994, p. 35.

101. Michael Carroll and Ida Picker, "GE Draws a Line in the Sand at Kidder," *Institutional Investor*, July 1994, p. 13.

102. Fraser, p. 35.

103. Michael Siconolfi, "Jettisoned: With Scandal Report Due Today, Kidder Ousts Another Official," *Wall Street Journal*, August 4, 1994, p. A1.

104. Fraser, "How GE's Tough Love Saved Kidder," p. 35.

105. William M. Carley, Michael Siconolfi, and Amal Kumar Naj, "Major Challenge: How Will Welch Deal with Kidder Scandal? Problems Keep Coming," *Wall Street Journal*, May 3, 1994, p. A1.

106. Carley, Siconolfi, and Naj, p. A1.

107. Carley, Siconolfi, and Naj, p. A1.

108. Siconolfi, p. A1.

109. Siconolfi, p. A1.

110. Gary G. Lynch, "Report of Inquiry into False Trading Profits at Kidder, Peabody & Co. Incorporated," August 4, 1994, p. 28.

111. Lynch, p. 31.

112. *In the Matter of Orlando Joseph Jett*, Administrative Proceeding File No. 3-8919, July 21, 1998, p. 3.

113. Fred Vogelstein, "Smoke and Mirrors on Wall St.; Bond Trader Allegedly Learned to Fool System," *Newsday*, May 3, 1994, p. A41.

114. *In the Matter of Orlando Joseph Jett*, p. 16.

115. Carol J. Loomis, "Behind the Bombshells at GE and Procter & Gamble," *Fortune*, May 16, 1994, p 14. This estimate excluded certain accounting adjustments.

116. Carley, Siconolfi, and Naj, p. A1.

117. Carley, Siconolfi, and Naj, p. A1.

118. Michael Siconolfi, "Cerullo Leaves Kidder with Healthy Severance," *Wall Street Journal*, July 25, 1994, p. C1.

119. Gary Weiss, "The Flimsy Case against Joseph Jett," *BusinessWeek*, July 1, 1996, p. 90.

120. "Ex-Kidder Workers Get Severance Pay—With a Catch—They Must Agree to Be Silent on Tenure at Company," *Bloomberg News*, January 13, 1995, p. 1.

121. Weiss, p. 90.

122. "Disgraced Trader Vows to Return," *Daily Telegraph*, July 6, 1996, p. 1.

123. Jerry W. Markham, "Guarding the Kraal—On the Trail of the Rogue Trader," *Journal of Corporation Law*, Fall 1995, pp. 144–145.

124. John Gapper, "Banks Warned on Linking Bonuses to Profit," *Financial Times*, July 27, 1994.

125. "Explaining It to the Board," *Derivatives Strategy*, April 4, 1994, p. 3.

126. Terence P. Pare, "Learning to Live with Derivatives," *Fortune*, July 25, 1994, p. 106.

127. Hal Lux, "Levitt's Last Testimony," *Institutional Investor*, January 2001, p. 74.

128. Lux, "Levitt's Last Testimony," p. 74.

129. Ford S. Worthy, "What We Learned from the '87 Crash," *Fortune,* October 5, 1992, p. 98.

Chapter 7: Messages Received

1. "Fallen Idols," *The Economist,* May 4, 2002, p. 11.

2. Andrei Shleifer, *Inefficient Markets: An Introduction to Behavioral Finance* (Oxford University Press 2000).

3. *In the Matter of Cendant Corporation,* Securities Exchange Act of 1934 Release No. 42933, June 14, 2000, p. 7.

4. *In the Matter of Cendant Corporation,* p. 15, note 10.

5. Susan Jackson, "Point, Click—and Spend," *Business Week,* September 15, 1997, p. 74.

6. Mary J. Cronin, "Business Secrets of the Billion-Dollar Website," *Fortune,* February 2, 1998, p. 142.

7. "Cendant Announces Public Offering of $1 Billion of FELINE PRIDES," *Business Wire,* February 12, 1998.

8. *In the Matter of Cendant Corporation,* p. 10.

9. *In the Matter of Cendant Corporation,* p. 13.

10. Tom Lowry, "Just Going about His Business," *Business Week,* February 28, 2000, p. 138.

11. Amy Barrett, "Who's to Blame," *Business Week,* August 17, 1998, p. 70.

12. *Cendant Corp. v. Forbes,* 99 Civ. 4869 (S.D.N.Y. 1999).

13. David E. Rovella, "SEC 'Goes Criminal' on Fraud," *National Law Journal,* May 7, 2001, p. A1.

14. Rovella, p. A1.

15. Subrata N. Chakravarty, "Dean Buntrock's Green Machine," *Forbes,* August 2, 1993, p. 96.

16. Chakravarty, p. 96.

17. Ralph Blumenthal, "Waste Hauler's Business Acts Faulted," *New York Times,* March 24, 1983, p. B12.

18. Chakravarty, p. 96.

19. Gene G. Marcial, "Big Names at Boca Resorts," *Business Week,* July 2, 2001, p. 110.

20. David Young, "Waste Firm Still Hauling Image Woes," *Chicago Tribune,* October 6, 1991, p. C3.

21. Young, p. C3.

22. *In the Matter of Arthur Andersen LLP,* Exchange Act Release No. 44444, Administrative Proceeding File No. 10513, June 19, 2001, p. 5.

23. Michael Schroeder, "Suit Says Policing Audits Is Conflict for SEC," *Wall Street Journal,* February 22, 2002, p. C1.

24. *In the Matter of Arthur Andersen LLP.*

25. Kristina Torres, "Generosity Can Come with Strings Attached," *Saint Paul Pioneer Press,* April 6, 2002.

26. *In the Matter of Waste Management, Inc.,* SEC Administrative Proceeding File No. 3-10238, June 21, 2000.

27. David Grainger, "You Just Hired Him; Should You Have Known Better?" *Fortune,* October 29, 2001, p. 205.

28. "Al Dunlap's Disgrace," *Australian Financial Review,* July 21, 2001, p. 21.

29. "Al Dunlap's Disgrace," p. 21.

30. *In the Matter of Sunbeam Corporation,* Administrative Proceeding File No. 3-10481, Release No. 33-7976, 34-44305, May 15, 2001.

31. Patricia Sellers, "Exit for Chainsaw? Sunbeam's Investors Draw Their Knives," *Fortune,* June 8, 1998, p. 30.

32. Sellers, p. 30.

33. Jenny Andersen, "Al Gets the Chainsaw," *Institutional Investor,* October 1999, p. 224.

34. Barbara Demick and Daniel R. Biddle, "To Some, Rite Aid a Hard Pill to Swallow," *Chicago Tribune,* May 15, 1989, p. C3.

35. Rich Exner, "Bribery Charges Dismissed Against Rite Aid," *United Press International,* July 16, 1990.

36. "Rite Aid Vindicated, Returns to Business," *Chain Drug Review,* April 22, 1991, p. 47.

37. Vindu P. Goel, "Prescription for Growth," *Plain Dealer,* December 17, 1995, p. 1J.

38. *In the Matter of Rite Aid Corporation,* Administrative Proceeding File No. 3-10808, Exchange Act Release No. 46009, June 21, 2002, p. 8.

39. *In the Matter of Rite Aid Corporation,* p. 8.

40. Frank Ahrens, "History of Conflict for Rite Aid's Chief; Indictment Paints Picture of Grass as an Arrogant Bully," *Washington Post,* June 22, 2002, p. E01.

41. David Voreakos, "Rite Aid's Secret Fraud Tapes Broke No Rules, U.S. Says," *Bloomberg News,* October 16, 2002.

42. Thor Valdmanis, "Accounting Abracadabra: Cooking the Books Proves Common Trick of the Trade," *USA Today,* August 11, 1998, p. 1B.

43. Claire Makin, "Short-Changed," *Institutional Investor,* January 1993, p. 103.

44. Makin, p. 103.

45. *Dirks v. SEC,* 463 U.S. 646 (1983).

46. Carol J. Loomis, "Lies, Damned Lies, and Managed Earnings," *Fortune,* August 2, 1999, p. 74.

47. Carol J. Loomis, "Hard Time? Hardly," *Fortune,* March 18, 2002, p. 78.

48. Alan Murray, "Inflated Profits in Corporate Books Is Half the Story," *Wall Street Journal,* July 2, 2002, p. A4.

49. Valdmanis, p. 1B.

50. Kevin J. Murphy, "Executive Compensation," April 1998, p. 6 (available at www.ssrn.com).

51. Murphy, p. 90, Figure 15.

52. Murphy, p. 85, Figure 10.

53. The SEC confirmed this accounting treatment in 1992. "Executive Compensation Disclosure," Securities Act Release No. 6962, October 16, 1992.

54. Murphy, p. 6.

55. Jeremy J. Siegel, "Stocks Are Still an Oasis," *Wall Street Journal,* July 25, 2002.

56. Brian J. Hall and Kevin J. Murphy, "Stock Options for Undiversified Executives," *National Bureau of Economic Research,* Working Paper 8052, December 2000, p. 37, Table 1.

57. "The Art, Not Science, of Risk Management, Controlling Risk," *Risk,* June 1995, p. 2.

58. James Lacey, "The Consultants' Verdict: Still in Trouble," *Derivatives Strategy,* March 1996.

59. Linda Keslar, "The View from the Boardroom: Under Control," *Derivatives Strategy,* March 1996.

60. Keslar.

61. David Neustadt, "Morgan Stanley Touts Equity-Raising Vehicle," *American Banker*, September 15, 1988, p. 2.

62. Tom Pratt, "GM's PERCS Help It Avoid Dilutive Offer; May Not Be Using Structure As Well As Avon," *Investment Dealers' Digest*, May 20, 1991, p. 14.

63. Larry Light, "'PERCS' You May Be Better Off Without," *BusinessWeek,* April 20, 1992, p. 107; "Citicorp Raises $1 Billion in Capital but Dilutes Its Stock," *Bloomberg News,* October 15, 1992.

64. Tom Pratt, "Salomon Prices Huge Decs Deal for American Express," *Investment Dealers' Digest,* October 11, 1993, p. 16.

65. "Salomon's Debt Disguised as Equity Doesn't Impress Big Investors," *Bloomberg News,* August 1, 1993.

66. Tom Pratt, "Salomon and Amex Unveil New Exchangeable Debt," *Investment Dealers' Digest,* December 20, 1993, p. 16.

67. "Wall Street Profits May Drop after Record '93," *Bloomberg News,* March 30, 1994.

68. Malcolm Berko, "More than a Five-and-Dime," *Chicago Tribune,* July 15, 1994, p. N11.

69. Tom Pratt, "AMBAC 'Prides' Deal Sunk by SEC Accounting Ruling; Broad Impact on Exchangeables Is Feared," *Investment Dealers' Digest,* April 1, 1996, p. 10.

70. "MCN Financing Sells $115 Mln Preferred Securities Via Merrill," *Bloomberg News,* March 20, 1997.

71. Michael Bender, "The Latest from the Convertibles Desk at Merrill: FELINE PRIDES," *Investment Dealers' Digest,* April 7, 1997, p. 6.

Chapter 8: The Domino Effect

1. Robert J. McCartney, "'Skins Up By 10? You Make the Call: Punt or Put?" *Washington Post,* January 26, 1992, p. H1; "Swap Market: SocGen Mixes Super Bowl Hoopla and Trading Fever," *Bloomberg News,* January 28, 1993; Alan Gersten, "Another Superbowl Disaster," *Journal of Commerce,* February 2, 1993, p. 8A; Arthur M. Louis, "Derivatives Go to the Super Bowl," *San Francisco Chronicle,* January 19, 1995, p. D1.

2. McCartney, p. H1.

3. "Swap Market: SocGen Mixes Super Bowl Hoopla and Trading Fever."

4. Robert J. Shiller, *Macro Markets: Creating Institutions for Managing Society's Largest Economic Risks* (Clarendon Press 1994), p. 47.

5. "Of Votes and Volatility," *The Economist,* May 14, 1994, p. 86.

6. Norma Cohen and Alison Smith, "Heat Turned on Self-Regulation: Britain's Complex System of Financial Services Control Is under Attack," *Financial Times,* July 28, 1995, p. 17.

7. *Hazell v. Hammersmith & Fulham London Borough Council,* 2 QB (CA) 697 (1990), p. 801.

8. *Morgan Stanley UK Group v. Puglisi,* Commercial Court, January 29, 1998 (Longmore, J.); Helen Parry, "How Black Wednesday Broke Morgan Stanley's String of PERLS," London Guildhall University Working Paper, May 13, 1998; Helen Parry and Susan Scott Hunt, "Of Bears and Barings: Approaches to Enforcement in the US and UK," Swaps and Off-Exchange Derivatives Trading Law and Regulation (1996), p. 186.

9. Michael D. Mann and Joseph G. Mari, "Developments in International Securi-

ties Law Enforcement and Regulation," Practising Law Institute Order No. B4-7014, 788 PLI/Corp 7, October 5, 1992, pp. 21–22.

10. "Kidder Reportedly Woos Japanese Insurer with Accounting Arbitrage," *Derivatives Week, Volume 3,* October 31, 1994, pp. 1, 12.

11. "Lessons from the Hedging Scandals," *Derivatives Strategy,* February 20, 1994, p. 5.

12. Sharmila Rampeearee, "Japan's Finance Ministry Orders Transparency in Derivatives," *Bloomberg News,* November 29, 1994.

13. Chew Farn Chyi, "Derivatives: A Zero-Sum Game with Leverage?" *Business Times* (Singapore), January 13, 1995, p. 7.

14. Amy Balan, "Berjaya Industrial Denies Liability for Derivatives Loss," *Business Times* (Singapore), December 29, 1994, p. 1.

15. "Malaysia Executive to Sue Credit Suisse over Derivative," *Bloomberg News,* December 30, 1994, p. 1.

16. Alec D.B. McCabe and Robert B. Cox, "China's Minmetals Sues Lehman for $128 Mln in Damages," *Bloomberg News,* March 9, 1995, p. 1.

17. "Taiwan Punishes Overseas Chinese Bank for Derivatives Losses," *Bloomberg News,* January 19, 1995.

18. Laura Jereski and Ellen E. Schultz, "Glaxo Holdings Is Taking a Hit on Derivatives," *Wall Street Journal,* July 13, 1994, p. C1.

19. Steven Lipin, "Bankers Trust Woes Spread to Money Unit," *Wall Street Journal,* December 8, 1994, p. A3.

20. James G. Neuger, "Currency Trading May Boost Banks' Balsam Losses," *Bloomberg News,* June 10, 1994.

21. Jeffrey Taylor and Kenneth H. Bacon, "How the Nymex Cooled MG's Oil Crisis," *Wall Street Journal,* April 5, 1994, p. A1.

22. Their respective articles were published in the *Journal of Applied Corporate Finance* in 1994. Antonio S. Mello and John E. Parsons, "Maturity Structure of a Hedge Matters: Lessons from the Metallgesellschaft Debacle," *Journal of Applied Corporate Finance, Volume 8,* Spring 1995; Christopher L. Culp and Merton H. Miller, "Hedging in the Theory of Corporate Finance: A Reply to Our Critics," *Journal of Applied Corporate Finance, Volume 8,* Spring 1995.

23. Anatoli Kuprianov, "Derivatives Debacles: Case Studies of Large Losses in Derivatives Markets," *Federal Reserve Bank of Richmond Economic Quarterly, Volume 81,* September 22, 1995, p.1.

24. Jeremy Gray, "Bundesbank Watch: A Dilemma on Whether to Regulate Derivatives," *Bloomberg News,* March 9, 1995.

25. Raymond Frenken and Carine Cassuto, "Countries in Criminal Probe of Derivatives Brokers," *Bloomberg News,* November 29, 1994.

26. Thomas T. Vogel Jr., "Derivatives Darken Pall Over Mexico," *Wall Street Journal,* January 9, 1995, p. C1.

27. Richard Voorhees, "Double Duty," *Latin Finance,* June 1994, p. 63; Tom Pratt, "Merrill Brings Long-Rumored TelMex Prides to Private Mart," *Investment Dealers' Digest,* May 16, 1994, p. 13.

28. Frank Partnoy, *F.I.A.S.C.O.* (Penguin Books 1999), p. 194.

29. Hal Lux, "Levitt's Last Testimony," *Institutional Investor,* January 2001, p. 74.

30. "Mattel Says Mexican Currency Weakness to Hurt Results," *Bloomberg News,* January 4, 1995, p. 1.

31. Saul Hansell and Kevin Muehring, "Why Derivatives Rattle the Regulators," *Institutional Investor,* September 1992, p. 49.

32. "Message to the Congress on the Financial Crisis in Mexico," *Public Papers of the Presidents*, March 9, 1995.

33. David E. Sanger, "D'Amato Seeks to Limit Foreign Bailouts," *New York Times*, July 22, 1995, p. A34.

34. Russell Dean Covey, "Adventures in the Zone of Twilight: Separation of Powers and National Economic Security in the Mexican Bailout," *Yale Law Journal*, Volume 105 (1996), p. 1,311.

35. The Department of the Treasury, "December Monthly Report to Congress," *Summaries of the Treasury Secretary's Monthly Reports*, July–December 1996, p. 7.

36. David E. Sanger, "Mexico Repays Bailout by U.S. Ahead of Time," *New York Times*, January 16, 1997, p. A1.

37. "Frontline interview of Paul Krugman," *The Crash*, Spring 1999.

38. Partnoy, pp. 207–212.

39. Dominic Kennedy, "Man Who Broke the Bank in Singapore 'Is Just a Normal Bloke,'" *The Times* (London), February 28, 1995.

40. Nick Leeson, *Rogue Trader: How I Brought Down Barings Bank and Shook the Financial World* (Little Brown 1996).

41. "The Collapse of Barings: A Fallen Star," *The Economist*, March 4, 1995, p. 19.

42. Thomas B. Sanders, "Derivative Ruination in the 1990s: Les Apparences Sont Trompeuses," *Thunderbird International Business Review*, Volume 43(3), May–June 2001, p. 424.

43. Leeson, pp. 143–144.

44. Richard Morrissey, "Quantum Fund's Soros Bets Correctly on Japan," *Bloomberg News*, March 5, 1995.

45. John Gapper and Nicholas Denton, "Barings Reports Showed 'Nil' Risk," *Financial Times*, March 17, 1995, p. 19.

46. "Interview with David Frost," British Broadcasting Corporation, September 11, 1995.

47. "Risk Monitor Wasn't Chosen," *New York Times*, March 3, 1995, p. D15.

48. Catherine O'Mahony and Darrell Delamaide, "Barings Falls: German Police Seize Leeson in Frankfurt," *Bloomberg News*, March 2, 1995.

49. "Interview with Charlie Rose," PBS-TV, February 27, 1995.

50. "U.S. SEC Chief Says Barings a Supervision Problem," *Reuters*, March 2, 1995.

51. John Gapper, "NatWest Chiefs 'Failed to Spot' Deals Mispricing," *Financial Times*, March 8, 1997, p. 1.

52. Catherine O'Mahony, "Deutsche Bank Reveals DM22 Million Derivatives Loss," *Bloomberg News*, March 22, 1995, p. 1.

53. "What Really Happened at UBS?" *Derivatives Strategy*, October 1998, pp. 2–3.

54. "Daiwa's Iguchi Joins Gallery of Accused Rogue Traders," *Bloomberg News*, September 27, 1995.

55. Parry and Hunt, p. 183.

56. Edward J. Kane and Kimberly DeTrask, "Breakdown of Accounting Controls at Barings and Daiwa: Benefits of Using Opportunity-Cost Measures for Trading Activity," *Pacific-Basin Finance Journal*, Volume 7 (1999), p. 225.

57. "An Unusual Path to Big-Time Trading," *New York Times*, September 27, 1995, p. D6.

58. Abby Schultz, "Top JP Morgan Trader Is Asked to Step Down," *Investment Dealers' Digest*, March 9, 1992, p. 5.

59. Abby Schultz, "J. P. Morgan MBS Trader Turns Up Trading Same Product at Daiwa," *Investment Dealers' Digest,* June 8, 1992, p. 5.

60. Norihiko Shirouzu, "Ex-Daiwa Trader Alleges 'Double Cross,'" *Wall Street Journal,* January 8, 1997, p. A18.

61. Frank Partnoy, "Why Markets Crash and What Law Can Do about It," *University of Pittsburgh Law Review, Volume 61,* Spring 2000, pp. 813–815.

62. Kenneth Scott, "Corporate Governance and East Asia: Korea, Indonesia, Malaysia, Thailand," The First Annual World Bank Group–Brookings Institution Conference: Financial Markets and Development: Preventing Crises in Emerging Markets (1999), p. 12.

63. Raphael LaPorta, Florencio Lopez-de-Silanes, Andrei Shleifer, and Robert Vishny, "Law and Finance," *Journal of Political Economy, Volume 106* (1998), pp. 1,113, 1,149–1,151.

64. Stign Claessens et al., "Ultimate Controlling Owners of East Asian Corporations and Expropriation of Minority Shareholders," The First Annual World Bank Group–Brookings Institution Conference: Financial Markets and Development: Preventing Crises in Emerging Markets (1999), p. 18.

65. Stign Claessens et al., p. 18.

66. Charles Adams et al., *International Capital Markets* (International Monetary Fund 1998), p. 41.

67. Campbell R. Harvey and Andrew H. Roper, "The Asian Bet," The First Annual World Bank Group–Brookings Institution Conference: Financial Markets and Development: Preventing Crises in Emerging Markets (1999), pp. 1, 4, 42.

68. Charles P. Kindleberger, *Manias, Panics, and Crashes: A History of Financial Crises,* 3rd ed. (Basic Books 1996), pp. 23–34.

69. Frank Partnoy, "Why Markets Crash and What Law Can Do about It," pp. 808–809.

70. Charles Adams et al., p. 42.

71. As of late 2002, many of these disputes were still being litigated, and I had been retained as an expert witness in one such case, on behalf of a Korean life-insurance company.

72. Frank Partnoy, "Why Markets Crash and What Law Can Do about It," pp. 810–811.

73. Harvey D. Shapiro, "Old Dogs, Slightly New Tricks," *Institutional Investor,* June 1998, p. 81.

74. "Flaying the Fund," *The Economist,* January 23, 1999, p. 64.

75. Many of the details regarding Long-Term Capital Management are from "Hedge Funds, Leverage, and the Lessons of Long-Term Capital Management," Report of The President's Working Group on Financial Markets, April 1999. Other useful sources include, in chronological order: "Inside Long Term Capital," *Derivatives Strategy,* April 4, 1994; Kevin Muehring, "John Meriwether by the Numbers," *Institutional Investor,* November 1996, p. 69; Michael Lewis, "How the Eggheads Cracked," *New York Times Magazine,* January 24, 1998, p. 24; Michael Siconolfi, Anita Raghavan, and Mitchell Pacelle, "All Bets Are Off: How the Salesmanship and Brainpower Failed at Long-Term Capital," *Wall Street Journal,* November 16, 1998, p. A1; Joe Kolman, "LTCM Speaks," *Derivatives Strategy,* April 1999, p. 12; Nicholas Dunbar, *Inventing Money: The Story of Long-Term Capital Management and the Legends Behind It* (John Wiley & Sons 2001); Roger Lowenstein, *When Genius Failed: The Rise and Fall of Long-Term Capital Management* (Random House 2001); and Peter H. Huang, Kimberly D. Krawiec, and Frank Partnoy, "Derivatives on TV: A Tale of Two Derivatives Debacles in Prime-Time," *Green Bag 2nd, Volume 4,* Spring 2001, p. 257.

76. "Inside Long Term Capital," p. 9.

77. Siconolfi, Raghavan, and Pacelle, p. A1.

78. Siconolfi, Raghavan, and Pacelle, p. A1.

79. "Inside Long Term Capital," pp. 6–7.

80. Muehring, p. 69.

81. Muehring, p. 69.

82. "LTCM, Others Benefit from a Surge in Japanese Volatility," *Derivatives Week, Volume 4,* January 30, 1995, pp. 1, 11.

83. "Inside Long Term Capital," p. 8.

84. Muehring, p. 69.

85. Siconolfi, Raghavan, and Pacelle, p. A1.

86. Muehring, p. 69.

87. Siconolfi, Raghavan, and Pacelle, p. A1.

88. "Volatility Gives Greater Impetus to Hedge Funds," *Financial Times,* July 22, 1996, p. 29.

89. James Aley, "Wall Street's King Quant," *Fortune,* February 5, 1996, p. 108.

90. Partnoy, *F.I.A.S.C.O.,* pp. 259–260.

91. Aley, p. 108.

92. "Hedge Funds, Leverage, and the Lessons of Long-Term Capital Management," p. 30.

93. Kolman, p. 14.

94. Kolman, p. 15.

95. Siconolfi, Raghavan, and Pacelle, p. A1.

96. Mitchell Pacelle, "Three Hedge Funds, Hurt by Russia, Seek Protection of Bankruptcy Court," *Wall Street Journal,* August 28, 1998, p. C11.

97. Michael Pettis, "Latin America Needs a Bond Market," *Wall Street Journal,* September 4, 1998, p. A11.

98. "Emerging-Market Measles," *The Economist,* August 22, 1998, p. 56.

99. Kolman, p. 15.

100. Lewis, p. 24.

101. Kolman, p. 16.

102. Dunbar. The principals of LTCM easily avoided federal prosecution, but they had more trouble dodging the taxman. In 2003, the Internal Revenue Service brought an action against LTCM, seeking to recover $75 million of taxes LTCM had avoided through complex financial engineering. Government officials had expressed concerns about tax shelters, and LTCM was infamous for its "tax avoidance" deals. The Senate Finance Committee had estimated that such shelters cost the government at least $10 billion in lost tax revenue. At the LTCM trial during summer 2003, the Nobel laureate Myron Scholes was asked whether taking a $100 million tax deduction for something LTCM paid $1 million for was a tax shelter. His response was, "I prefer not to go into definitions like that. It was a mitigation of taxes." Ben White, "Long-Term Capital Case Puts Tax Shelters on Trial," *Washington Post,* July 23, 2003, p. E01.

103. "Hedge Funds, Leverage, and the Lessons of Long-Term Capital Management," p. 42.

104. "Hedge Funds, Leverage, and the Lessons of Long-Term Capital Management," p. 29.

105. "Hedge Funds, Leverage, and the Lessons of Long-Term Capital Management," p. B-9.

106. Tanya Styblo Beder, "Guidelines for a Brave New Pension World," *Derivatives Strategy,* November 1995, p. 59.

107. Joe Kolman, "Measuring Value at Risk," *Derivatives Strategy,* November 21, 1994, p. 4.

108. Capital Market Risk Advisors, "SEC Market Risk Disclosure Survey—Results" (1998), pp. 2–3; Capital Market Risk Advisors, "Outlook 2000" (2000), p. 3.

109. Peter Coy, "Taking the Angst out of Taking a Gamble," *BusinessWeek,* July 14, 1997, p. 52.

110. 17 C.F.R. § 229.305 (1999); Release Nos. 33-7386; 34-38223; IC-22487; FR-48, January 31, 1997, p. 37.

111. Hansell and Muehring, p. 49.

Chapter 9: The Last One to the Party

1. Susan Pulliam and Randall Smith, "Silicon Touch: For Frank Quattrone, With a Fief at CSFB, Tech Was a Gold Mine," *Wall Street Journal,* May 3, 2001, p. A1.

2. Randall Smith, "High-Tech Banker Scores Deals with Mule and 'Rocky Raccoon,'" *Wall Street Journal,* September 24, 1999, p. C1.

3. Pulliam and Smith, p. A1.

4. Smith, p. C1.

5. Hal Lux, "Valley of the Dollars," *Institutional Investor,* June 1998, p. 43.

6. Michael Siconolfi, "Under Pressure: At Morgan Stanley, Analysts Were Urged to Soften Harsh Views," *Wall Street Journal,* July 14, 1992, p. A1.

7. Lux, p. 43.

8. Anita Raghavan, "Credit Suisse Hires Frank Quattrone in Bid to Boost High-Tech Bank Effort," *Wall Street Journal,* July 1, 1998, p. B6.

9. Susan Pulliam, Randall Smith, Anita Raghavan, and Gregory Zuckerman, "Coming to Terms: CSFB Agrees to Pay $100 Million to Settle Twin IPO Investigations," *Wall Street Journal,* December 11, 2001, p. A1.

10. Lux, p. 43.

11. Smith, p. C1.

12. Joann S. Lublin, "As IPO Looms, Software CEO Cedes Her Post," *Wall Street Journal,* October 12, 1999, p. B1.

13. "Early Industry Reaction to F.I.A.S.C.O.: That #%@! Book," *Derivatives Strategy,* November 1997.

14. "That Was Then," *The Economist,* January 26, 2002.

15. John Maynard Keynes, *A General Theory of Employment, Interest, and Money* (1936; Prometheus Books 1997), p. 131; Donald C. Langevoort, "Taming the Animal Spirits of the Stock Markets: A Behavioral Approach to Securities Regulation," *Northwestern University Law Review,* forthcoming.

16. Joseph J. Mezrich and Lakshmi Seshadri, "It Started in Mexico," *Morgan Stanley U.S. Investment Perspectives,* March 6, 2002, p. 10.

17. Jeremy J. Siegel, *Stocks for the Long Run: The Definitive Guide to Financial Market Returns and Long-Term Investment Strategies* (McGraw-Hill Trade 2002).

18. Frank Easterbrook and Daniel Fischel, "Mandatory Disclosure and the Protection of Investors," *Virginia Law Review,* Volume 70 (1984), p. 669.

19. Andrei Shleifer, *Inefficient Markets: An Introduction to Behavioral Finance* (Oxford University Press 2000); Robert Shiller, "Do Stock Prices Move Too Much to be Justified by Subsequent Changes in Dividends?" *American Economic Review,* Volume 71 (1981), p. 421.

20. Andrei Shleifer and Robert Vishny, "The Limits of Arbitrage," *Journal of Finance,* Volume 52 (1997), p. 35.

21. John Maynard Keynes, *A Tract on Monetary Reform* (1924; Prometheus Books 2000), p. 88.

22. Saul Hansell and Kevin Muehring, "Why Derivatives Rattle the Regulators," *Institutional Investor,* September 1992, p. 49.

23. "Netscapades," *Institutional Investor,* January 1996, p. 64.

24. Inmoo Lee, Scott Lochhead, Jay Ritter, and Quanshui Zhao, "The Costs of Raising Capital," *Journal of Financial Research, Volume 19* (1996), p. 59.

25. Mark Hulbert, "The Fantasy and the Fact of New Stock Offerings," *New York Times,* January 2, 2000, Section 3, p. 8.

26. Frank Partnoy, "Strange New Math of Palm Inc.," *New York Times,* March 15, 2000, p. A29.

27. John Cassidy, "Striking It Rich; The Rise and Fall of Popular Capitalism," *The New Yorker,* January 14, 2002, p. 63.

28. "Affidavit in Support of Application for an Order Pursuant to General Business Law Section 354," *In the Matter of An Inquiry by Eliot Spitzer, Attorney General of the State of New York,* Supreme Court of the State of New York, County of New York, April 2002, p. 21.

29. Nelson D. Schwartz, "Inside the Market's Myth Machine," *Fortune,* October 2, 2000, p. 114.

30. "Affidavit in Support of Application for an Order Pursuant to General Business Law Section 354," p. 24.

31. Cassidy, p. 63.

32. Hulbert, Sec. 3, p. 8.

33. Charles Mackay, *Memoirs of Extraordinary Delusions and the Madness of Crowds* (1852; Metro Books 2002).

34. William G. Christie and Paul H. Schultz, "Why Do NASDAQ Market Makers Avoid Odd-Eighth Quotes?" *Journal of Finance, Volume 49* (1994), p. 1,813.

35. Frank Partnoy, *F.I.A.S.C.O.* (Penguin Books 1997), pp. 271–274.

36. Lux, p. 43.

37. *Securities and Exchange Commission v. Credit Suisse First Boston,* Complaint, U.S. District Court, District of Columbia, January 22, 2002, paragraph 47.

38. *Securities and Exchange Commission v. Credit Suisse First Boston,* paragraph 48.

39. *Securities and Exchange Commission v. Credit Suisse First Boston,* paragraph 50.

40. Pulliam and Smith, p. A1.

41. "That Was Then."

42. Susan Pulliam and Randall Smith, "CSFB Official Set Quota for Repayment of IPO Profits in Form of Commission," *Wall Street Journal,* August 10, 2001, p. C1.

43. *Securities and Exchange Commission v. Credit Suisse First Boston,* paragraphs 35, 38, 40, 41, and 43.

44. *Securities and Exchange Commission v. Credit Suisse First Boston,* paragraph 36.

45. Pulliam, Smith, Raghavan, and Zuckerman, p. A1.

46. Ian Kerr, "Barclays Capital Wins the Mind War," *Financial News,* March 5, 2001, p. 1.

47. Pulliam and Smith, "Silicon Touch: For Frank Quattrone, With a Fief at CSFB, Tech Was a Gold Mine," p. A1.

48. Randall Smith, *Frontline* interview, PBS, May 2001.

49. Administrative Complaint, *In the Matter of: Credit Suisse First Boston Corp.,* No. E-2002-41, October 21, 2002, pp. 5–6.

50. Pulliam and Smith, "CSFB Official Set Quota for Repayment of IPO Profits in Form of Commission," p. C1.

51. Randall Smith and Susan Pulliam, "CSFB Says It Has Fired 3 Brokers," *Wall Street Journal,* June 29, 2001, p. C1.

52. NASD Rule 2440.

53. Susan Pulliam and Randall Smith, "CSFB's Defense: We Didn't Break IPO Rules," *Wall Street Journal,* June 12, 2001, p. C1.

54. Tom Cahill, "CSFB's Mack Targets Goldman, Morgan Stanley: Mission Possible?" *Bloomberg News,* January 17, 2002.

55. Cahill.

56. Emily Thornton, "Can This Be a Wall Street Reformer?" *Business Week,* September 23, 2002, p. 90.

57. Patrick McGeehan, "His Rallying Cry at First Boston: Smaller, Cleaner, Fairer," *New York Times,* January 27, 2002, Sec. 3, p. 1.

58. Emily Thornton, "CSFB's Not-So-Painful Settlement," *Business Week,* December 31, 2001, p. 10.

59. David Wells, "C. E. Unterberg's John Gutfreund Comments on CSFB IPO Probe," *Bloomberg News,* December 11, 2001.

60. Pulliam, Smith, Raghavan, and Zuckerman, p. A1.

61. Siconolfi, p. A1.

62. Gretchen Morgenson, "Requiem for an Honorable Profession," *New York Times,* May 5, 2002, Sec. 3, p. 1.

63. Charles Gasparino, "Analysts' Contracts Link Pay to Deal Work," *Wall Street Journal,* May 6, 2002, p. C1.

64. Debbie Galant, "Financial Misstatements," *Institutional Investor,* July 1993, p. 171.

65. John C. Coffee Jr., "Guarding the Gatekeepers," *New York Times,* May 13, 2002, p. A19.

66. Debbie Galant, "Don't Ask, Don't Tell," *Institutional Investor,* September 1995, p. 159.

67. "Affidavit in Support of Application for an Order Pursuant to General Business Law Section 354," p. 21.

68. "Affidavit in Support of Application for an Order Pursuant to General Business Law Section 354," pp. 8–9.

69. "Affidavit in Support of Application for an Order Pursuant to General Business Law Section 354," p. 10.

70. "Affidavit in Support of Application for an Order Pursuant to General Business Law Section 354," p. 11.

71. "Affidavit in Support of Application for an Order Pursuant to General Business Law Section 354," p. 12.

72. "Affidavit in Support of Application for an Order Pursuant to General Business Law Section 354," p. 11.

73. "Affidavit in Support of Application for an Order Pursuant to General Business Law Section 354," p. 19.

74. "Affidavit in Support of Application for an Order Pursuant to General Business Law Section 354," p. 25.

75. "Affidavit in Support of Application for an Order Pursuant to General Business Law Section 354," p. 17.

76. Allan Sloan, "On Wall Street, Don't Cry for Henry Blodget," *Newsweek,* November 15, 2001.

77. *In the Matter of Microstrategy Inc.,* Securities Exchange Act Release No. 43724, Administrative Proceeding File No. 3-10388, December 14, 2000.

78. Charles Gasparino, Susanne Craig, and Randall Smith, "Salomon Faces Questions on IPO," *Wall Street Journal,* July 10, 2002, p. C1.

79. *Code of Federal Regulations, Volume 17,* Section 243.100 (2000); "Selective Disclosure and Insider Trading," Exchange Act Release No. 43,154 (August 20, 2000).

Chapter 10: The World's Greatest Company

1. Johnny Roberts and Evan Thomas, "Enron's Dirty Laundry," *Newsweek,* March 11, 2002, p. 22; Valentine Low, "Sex, Money and Power . . . The Fatal Mix that Spelt the End of Enron," *Evening Standard,* March 6, 2002, p. 19; Patricia Sellers, "Women, Sex & Power," *Fortune,* August 5, 1996, p. 42.

2. Bryan Gruley and Rebecca Smith, "Anatomy of a Fall," *Wall Street Journal,* April 26, 2002, p. A1.

3. Loren Steffy, "Enron's Original Sins: Lies Began Long before Current Crisis," *Bloomberg News,* March 20, 2002.

4. "Wordsmiths Play the Name Game," *United Press International,* July 6, 1986.

5. Steffy.

6. "U.S. Attorney Probing Alleged Illegal Trading by Former Enron Oil Executives," *Platt's Oilgram News,* June 15, 1988, p. 4.

7. Tricia Crisafulli, "Bulk Oil, Nichimen, Among Defendants in Enron Suit Charging Fraudulent Trading," *Platt's Oilgram News,* June 16, 1998, p. 4.

8. "Former Enron Oil Officials Charged with Fraud, Tax Violations by U.S. Attorney," *Platt's Oilgram News,* December 21, 1989, p. 3.

9. Crisafulli, p. 4.

10. Crisafulli, p. 4.

11. Mary Chung, Walid El-Gabry, John Labate, and Sheila McNulty, "Earlier Scandal Pointed to Need for Controls," *Financial Times,* January 16, 2002, p. 24.

12. Chung, El-Gabry, Labate, and McNulty, p. 24.

13. Russell Hubbard, "Enron Used Partnerships to Mask Debt, Holders Charge," *Bloomberg News,* November 6, 2001.

14. Loren Steffy, "Enron Ex-CFO Fastow Set Up Partnerships That Led to Failure," *Bloomberg News,* December 19, 2001.

15. Kurt Eichenwald, "Enron's Collapse; Audacious Climb to Success Ended in a Dizzying Plunge," *New York Times,* January 13, 2002, p. A1.

16. Jamie Dettmer, "Damaging Limitation," *Business A.M.,* January 25, 2002; Nick Cohen, "Influent, Affluent, Mostly Effluent; Hold on a Minute," *Observer,* September 6, 1998, p. 27.

17. Hubbard.

18. "In the City," *Private Eye,* February 21, 2002.

19. Ronald Fink, "Partnerships within Partnerships," *CFO Magazine,* January 1, 2002, p. 16.

20. "SEC No-Action Letter," April 26, 1994.

21. "Corporate Governance Failure at Enron," *Business Line,* March 4, 2002.

22. Dan Morgan and Kathleen Day, "For Gramms, Enron Is Hard to Escape," *Washington Post,* January 25, 2002, p. A18.

23. "Power Marketers Kick Off Campaigns to Become Household Word in Energy," *Energy Report,* January 20, 1997.

24. Enron 2000 Annual Report, p. 45.

25. Enron 2000 Annual Report, p. 44.

26. Charles Gasparino, Susanne Craig, and Randall Smith, "Salomon Faces Questions on IPO," *Wall Street Journal,* July 10, 2002, p. C1.

27. Steffy, "Enron Ex-CFO Fastow Set Up Partnerships That Led to Failure."

28. Steffy, "Enron Ex-CFO Fastow Set Up Partnerships That Led to Failure."

29. Since 1982, Financial Accounting Standard No. 57, entitled Related Party Disclosures, had required that companies disclose the nature of relationships they have with related parties, and describe transactions with them.

30. Report of Investigation by the Special Investigative Committee of the Board of Directors of Enron Corp., February 1, 2002, pp. 54–55.

31. Enron Form 8-K Filing, November 8, 2001, p. 9.

32. Enron Form 8-K Filing, November 8, 2001, p. 9.

33. April Witt and Peter Behr, "Losses, Conflicts Threaten Survival; CFO Fastow Ousted in Probe of Profits," *Washington Post,* July 31, 2002, p. A1; Michael A. Hiltzik and David Streitfeld, "Ex-Enron Employees Suggest Andersen Helped Veil Deals," *Los Angeles Times,* January 17, 2002, p. A1.

34. Tom Fowler, "Enron Hedging Web at Scandal's Core," *Houston Chronicle,* June 28, 2002, p. 2.

35. William Roberts and Jeff Bliss, "Merrill Executive Denies Firm Helped Enron Mask Its Liabilities," *Bloomberg News,* July 30, 2002; Otis Bilodeau, "In Eye of Enron Storm, A Partnership Is Rocked," *Delaware Law Weekly,* February 27, 2002, p. D4; Laurie Cohen and Flynn McRoberts, "Enron Scandals Crucial Recruit," *Chicago Tribune,* February 24, 2002, p. C1.

36. "Powers Report," p. 91.

37. "Powers Report," pp. 138–140.

38. Tom Fowler, "More Light May Be Shed on Enron," *Houston Chronicle,* June 29, 2002, p. 1.

39. Peter Spiegel, "The Architect of Enron's Downfall," *Financial Times,* May 20, 2002.

40. Loren Steffy, "What a Tangled Financial Web He Wove," *National Post,* December 20, 2001, p. FP9.

41. Jonathan Weil, "Enron's Auditors Debated Partnership Losses," *Wall Street Journal,* April 3, 2002, p. C1.

42. Enron 2000 Annual Report, p. 49, n.16.

43. Daniel Fisher, "Shell Game," *Forbes,* January 7, 2002, p. 52.

44. Enron 2000 Annual Report, p. 44, note 11.

45. "Powers Report," pp. 98–99.

46. David Barboza and Barnaby J. Feder, "Enron's Many Strands: The Transactions; Enron's Swap with Qwest Is Questioned," *New York Times,* March 29, 2002, p. C1.

47. David Barboza, "Former Officials Say Enron Hid Gains during Crisis in California," *New York Times,* June 23, 2002, p. A1.

48. Barboza, p. A21.

49. Barboza, p. A1.

50. Barboza, p. A21.

51. Jeff Manning, "Opportunism Part of Job, Former Enron Traders Say," *Oregonian,* May 15, 2002, p. C1.

52. David Barboza, "Enron Trader Had a Year to Boast of, Even If . . . ," *New York Times,* July 9, 2002, p. C1.

53. Burton Malkiel, "Watchdogs & Lapdogs," *Wall Street Journal,* January 16, 2002, p. A16.

54. Jerry Hirsch, "Andersen Fires Executive Who Oversaw Enron Audit," *Los Angeles Times,* January 16, 2002, p. A1.

55. Kurt Eichenwald, "Enron's Collapse; Audacious Climb to Success Ended in a Dizzying Plunge," *New York Times,* January 13, 2002, p. A1.

56. Loren Steffy and Russell Hubbard, "Enron Letter Shows Executives Knew of Partnership Accounting," *Bloomberg News,* January 17, 2002.

57. Enron 2000 Annual Report, p. 27.

58. Mark Pittman, "Enron's Fall Prompts Moody's to Focus on Triggers," *Bloomberg News,* December 7, 2001.

59. Paul Chivers, "Empowering Enron," *Project Finance,* June 1, 2000, p. 23.

60. Richard Oppel Jr., "Enron's Many Strands: The Hearings; Credit Raters to Explain Enron Role," *New York Times,* March 20, 2002, p. C1; Alex Berenson, "Enron's Collapse; The Rating Agencies," *New York Times,* November 29, 2001, p. C7.

61. James Higgins, "The Real Decade of Greed," *Weekly Standard,* July 15, 2002, p. 27.

62. Enron Form 8-K Filing, November 8, 2001, p. 9.

63. Stephen Fidler and Vincent Boland, "Debt Mountains Threaten Avalanche," *Financial Times,* May 31, 2002, p. 18.

64. Mark Lake and George Stein, "Dynegy Saved Enron Merger with Last Minute Pact," *Bloomberg News,* November 13, 2001.

65. William Roberts, "Citigroup, J. P. Morgan Chase Offered Enron Packages," *Bloomberg News,* July 23, 2002.

66. Roberts.

67. Roberts.

68. Richard A. Oppel Jr. and Kurt Eichenwald, "Citigroup Said to Mold Deal to Help Enron Skirt Rules," *New York Times,* July 23, 2002, p. A1.

69. Oppel Jr. and Eichenwald, p. C4.

70. Richard A. Oppel Jr., "U.S. Studying Merrill Lynch in Enron Deal," *New York Times,* July 27, 2002, p. C1.

71. Oppel Jr., "U.S. Studying Merrill Lynch in Enron Deal," p. C1.

72. Jathon Sapsford and Paul Beckett, "Enron Rival Used Complex Accounting to Burnish Its Profile," *Wall Street Journal,* April 3, 2002, p. A1.

73. Matt McGrath is not the trader's real name.

74. Jack Duffy, "Enron Collapse Destroyed Pensions, Prompts Calls for Change," *Bloomberg News,* December 7, 2001.

75. Enron Form 8-K Filing, November 8, 2001, p. 10.

76. Spiegel.

77. Loren Steffy, "Enron Insiders Sold More Than $1.2 Billion in Stock Since 1990," *Bloomberg News,* December 3, 2001.

78. "*BusinessWeek* Digitization Conference," Darden School of Business, December 16, 2001.

79. Richard W. Stevenson and Jeff Gerth, "Enron's Collapse: The System; Web of Safeguards Failed as Enron Fell," *New York Times,* January 19, 2002, p. A1.

80. Malkiel, p. A16.

81. Enron 2000 Annual Report, p. 30.

82. Enron 2000 Annual Report, pp. 32–33. Assets from "price risk management activities" were $2.2 billion in 1999 and $12 billion in 2000. Liabilities from "price risk management activities" were $1.8 billion in 1999 and $10.5 billion in 2000.

83. Ronald H. Coase, *The Firm, the Market, and the Law* (University of Chicago 1988), pp. 5–9.

84. Michael Jensen and William Meckling, "Theory of the Firm: Management

Behavior, Agency Costs and Ownership Structure," *Journal of Financial Economics,* Volume 3 (1976), p. 305.

Chapter 11: Hot Potato

1. Robert Lenzner, "Someone Knew," *Forbes,* March 4, 2002, p. 78.
2. John Cassidy, "Comment: High Hopes," *The New Yorker,* August 5, 2002, p. 21.
3. Simon Avery, "Global Crossing Head Shows Passion for Making Money, Bending Rules," *Associated Press,* March 5, 2002.
4. http://www.cwpost.liunet.edu/cwis/cwp/but11/2001/ps/1.html.
5. Julie Creswell, "The Emperor of Greed," *Fortune,* June 24, 2002, p. 106.
6. Edward J. Epstein, "Junk Bond King's Next Step," *San Francisco Chronicle,* October 9, 1987, p. C4.
7. Laurie P. Cohen, "U.S. Appears to Intensify Campaign Against Milken," *Wall Street Journal,* November 13, 1989, Sec. 2, p. 2.
8. "Business Briefs," *Sydney Morning Herald,* December 13, 1989; Kurt Eichenwald, "Prosecutors Said to Shorten Milken's Pre-Sentencing Case," *New York Times,* October 16, 1990, p. D1.
9. Anthony Bianco, "Little Drexels Are Popping Up All Over," *BusinessWeek,* October 6, 1986, p. 79.
10. "One Man's Junk," *Financial World,* March 10, 1987, p. 20.
11. Creswell, p. 106.
12. Creswell, p. 106.
13. Creswell, p. 106.
14. Geraldine Fabrikant and Saul Hansell, "At Global Crossing, Deals with Son of Executive Raise Questions," *New York Times,* February 18, 2002, p. C1.
15. Global Crossing Ltd. Form 10-K for the fiscal year ended December 31, 2000.
16. Creswell, p. 106.
17. Paul Chivers, "Empowering Enron," *Project Finance,* June 1, 2000, p. 23.
18. Simon Romero, "Memo Indicates Global Crossing Chief Knew of Troubles," *New York Times,* October 1, 2002, p. C6.
19. David Barboza and Simon Romero, "Enron Is Seen Having Link with Global," *New York Times,* May 20, 2002, p. C1.
20. Barboza and Romero, p. C5.
21. Barboza and Romero, p. C5.
22. Dennis K. Berman and Deborah Solomon, "Optical Illusion?: Accounting Questions Swirl around Pioneer in the Telecom World," *Wall Street Journal,* February 13, 2002, p. A12.
23. Karen Kaplan and Elizabeth Douglass, "Global's Exec with the Inside Knowledge," *Los Angeles Times,* February 20, 2002.
24. Berman and Solomon, p. A1.
25. Dennis K. Berman, "Global Crossing's Capacity Swaps Were of Little Value, Study Says," *Wall Street Journal,* February 19, 2002, p. B6.
26. Creswell, p. 106.
27. Berman and Solomon, p. A1.
28. Elizabeth Douglass and Tim Rutten, "Accounting Worried Global Crossing Exec.," *Los Angeles Times,* January 30, 2002, p. A1.
29. Laura Pearlman and Paul Braverman, "Unbillable Time," *American Lawyer,* May 2002.
30. Global Crossing Ltd. Form 10-Q for the quarter ended June 30, 2001.

31. Douglass and Rutten, p. A1.

32. Al Lewis, "Global Crossing's Revolving Door Pure Platinum," *Denver Post,* February 17, 2002, p. K-1.

33. Creswell, p. 106.

34. Specifically, Casey's employment agreement omitted October 11, 2001, as a vesting date. According to the terms of the agreement, 34 percent would vest in 2000, 22 percent in 2002, and 22 percent in 2003. The agreement should have included 22 percent vesting in 2001, but did not. I am grateful to Andrew Kimmel for spotting this mistake.

35. Elizabeth Douglass, "Global Eased Loan Terms," *Los Angeles Times,* February 7, 2002, Part 3, p. 1.

36. Rebecca Blumenstein, Deborah Solomon, and Kathy Chen, "As Global Crossing Crashed, Executives Got Loan Relief, Pension Payouts," *Wall Street Journal,* February 21, 2002, p. B1.

37. "Global Crossing Marine Unit Responds to Russian Submarine Rescue Effort," *Cambridge Telecom Report,* August 21, 2000.

38. Tim Cook, "Ebbers Recalled As Just One of the Guys," *Toronto Star,* June 30, 2002, p. C3.

39. Shane Holladay, "WorldCom Boss Recalled," *Edmonton Sun,* July 28, 2002, p. 6.

40. Scott Canon, "Telecommunications Mogul Is in a World All His Own," *Kansas City Star,* October 4, 1999, p. A1.

41. Holladay, p. 6.

42. Cook, p. C3.

43. Canon, p. A1.

44. Holladay, p. 6.

45. Gretchen Morgenson, "Despite Access, Star Analyst Missed WorldCom Trouble Signs," *New York Times,* July 9, 2002, p. C1.

46. Jack Grubman, Congressional Testimony, July 2002.

47. Charles Haddad, Dean Foust, and Steve Rosenbush, "WorldCom's Sorry Legacy," *BusinessWeek,* July 8, 2002, p. 38.

48. Haddad, Foust, and Rosenbush, p. 38.

49. Charles Gasparino, Susanne Craig, and Randall Smith, "Two Congressmen Want to Know If WorldCom Executives Received Hot Shares in Bid to Curry Favor," *Wall Street Journal,* July 10, 2002, p. C1.

50. WorldCom Revised Statement Pursuant to Section 21(a)(1) of the Securities Exchange Act of 1934, July 8, 2002, pp. 2–6.

51. WorldCom Revised Statement Pursuant to Section 21(a)(1) of the Securities Exchange Act of 1934, p. 6.

52. WorldCom Revised Statement Pursuant to Section 21(a)(1) of the Securities Exchange Act of 1934, p. 6.

53. WorldCom Revised Statement Pursuant to Section 21(a)(1) of the Securities Exchange Act of 1934, p. 2.

54. Michael E. Kanell and Russell Grantham, "WorldCom Scandal; CEO Had Great Run, Hard Fall," *Atlanta Journal-Constitution,* July 1, 2002, p. 1A.

55. WorldCom Revised Statement Pursuant to Section 21(a)(1) of the Securities Exchange Act of 1934, p. 2.

56. WorldCom Revised Statement Pursuant to Section 21(a)(1) of the Securities Exchange Act of 1934, p. 4.

57. WorldCom Revised Statement Pursuant to Section 21(a)(1) of the Securities Exchange Act of 1934, p. 5.

58. Morgenson, p. C1.

59. Creswell, p. 106; Melvyn Westlake, "Surviving the Credit Crisis," *The Banker*, May 1, 2002, p. 109.

60. Westlake, p. 109; Stephen Fidler and Vincent Boland, "Debt Mountains Threaten Avalanche," *Financial Times*, May 31, 2002, p. 18.

61. Lenzner, p. 78.

62. Nina Mehta, "Stress Test," *Institutional Investor*, February 2002, p. 73.

63. Mark Parsley, "Credit Derivatives: You Ain't Seen Nothing Yet," *Euromoney*, December 1997, p. 72.

64. Federal Reserve Supervisor Letter SR 97-18, Application of Market Risk Capital Requirements to Credit Derivatives, June 13, 1997.

65. Tom Kohn, "WorldCom Bankruptcy May Spark Payout on $10 Bln of Derivatives," *Bloomberg News*, July 22, 2002.

66. International Swaps and Derivatives Association, "Enron: Corporate Failure, Market Success," April 17, 2002, p. 12.

67. Shawn Tully, "Risky Business," *Fortune*, April 15, 2002, p. 116.

68. Ed Blount, "Can You Still 'Know Your Counterparty' in the Age of Enron?" *ABA Banking Journal*, April 2002, p. 41.

69. Phillip L. Zweig, "Dizzying New Ways to Dice Up Debt," *Business Week*, July 21, 1997, p. 102.

70. Grant Ringshaw, "Banks Pass the Bonds Buck," *Sunday Telegraph*, June 30, 2002, p. 8.

71. "Financial Fault-Lines," *Financial Times*, March 2, 2002, p. 14.

72. Westlake, p. 109.

73. "Financial Fault-Lines," p. 14.

74. Westlake, p. 109.

75. Greg Ip, "Credit Window: Alternative Lenders Buoy the Economy But Also Pose Risk," *Wall Street Journal*, June 10, 2002, p. A8.

76. Andy Serwer, "Dirty Rotten Numbers," *Fortune*, February 18, 2002, p. 74.

77. "The Jack and Jeff Show Loses Its Lustre," *The Economist*, May 4, 2002, p. 58.

78. "The Jack and Jeff Show Loses Its Lustre," p. 57.

79. Ip, p. A1.

80. General Electric Form 10-Q, July 23, 2001, Item 1.

81. Martin Mayer, "The Dangers of Derivatives," *Wall Street Journal*, May 20, 1999, p. A20.

82. "Global Financial Stability Report," International Monetary Fund, March 2002.

83. Stephen Fidler and Vincent Boland, "Debt Mountains Threaten Avalanche," *Financial Times*, May 31, 2002, p. 18.

84. Andrew Webb, "Four Questions Facing the Credit Derivatives Market," *Derivatives Strategy*, April 1999, p. 31.

85. John Ferry, "J. P. Morgan Refutes Credit Derivatives Wrongdoing," http://www.risknews.net, February 27, 2002. In October 2002, I was retained to testify on behalf of a Korean party to a dispute with J. P. Morgan Chase related to credit derivatives based on Argentina's debt.

86. Tully, p. 116.

87. Westlake.

88. Jenny Wiggins, "Growth of Structured Finance Sector Set to Slow," *Financial Times*, July 1, 2002, p. 26.

89. Rebecca Bream, "Moody's Expects Pressure on CDOs," *Financial Times*, July 10, 2002, p. 31.

90. Bream, p. 31.

91. Britt Tunick, "Williams' Boomerang: Should Merrill and Salomon Have Known before Pricing Convertible?" *Investment Dealers' Digest,* February 11, 2002.

92. David Barboza, "Complex El Paso Partnerships Puzzle Analysts," *New York Times,* July 23, 2002, p. C1.

93. Carol J. Loomis, "El Paso's Murky Magic," *Fortune,* July 22, 2002, p. 206.

94. David Barboza, "Ex-Executive Says Dynegy Asked His Help to Cook Books," *New York Times,* August 5, 2002, p. C1.

95. Dan Colarusso, "Derivatives Under Fire," *Investment Dealers' Digest,* May 20, 2002.

96. Heather Landy, "AOL Bonds Decline," *Bloomberg News,* July 8, 2002.

97. Wachtell, Lipton, Rosen & Katz, "Report to the Board of Directors of Allied Irish Banks P.L.C., et al.," March 12, 2002.

98. Deborah Solomon and Susan Pulliam, "Adelphia Off-Balance Sheet Debt Is Put Higher," *Wall Street Journal,* April 3, 2002, p. A10.

99. Gretchen Morgenson, "I.P.O. Plums for Titans of Telecom," *New York Times,* August 4, 2002, Sec. 3, p. 9.

100. Serwer, p. 74.

Epilogue

1. Stephen Labaton and Richard A. Oppel Jr., "Enthusiasm Ebbs for Tough Reform in Wake of Enron," *New York Times,* June 10, 2002, p. A16.

2. Sarbanes-Oxley Act of 2002.

3. Stuart Pfeifer, "O.C. to Restore Ties to Merrill," *Los Angeles Times,* June 4, 2002, Part 2, p. 1.

4. An excellent article discussing how the Securities and Exchange Commission might act to modernize its own rules—without the assistance of Congress—is James D. Cox, "The Future Content of the U.S. Securities Laws: Premises for Reforming the Regulation of Securities Offerings: An Essay," *Law & Contemporary Problems,* Volume 63 (2000), p. 11.

5. H. Stephen Labaton, "SEC's Embattled Chief Resigns in Wake of Latest Political Storm," *New York Times,* November 6, 2002, p. A1.

6. For a detailed description of how the SEC failed to fulfill the legislative mandate of Sarbanes-Oxley to improve off-balance sheet disclosure, see Frank Partnoy, "A Revisionist View of Enron and the Sudden Death of 'May,'" *Villanova Law Review,* 2003.

7. Harvey L. Pitt and David B. Hardison, "The Gibson Greetings Settlement: Sending an Unusual Greeting to End-Users of Derivatives," *Insights, Volume 10,* January 1996, pp. 8–12.

8. Frank Partnoy, "Financial Derivatives and the Costs of Regulatory Arbitrage," *Journal of Corporation Law, Volume 22* (1997), p. 211.

9. Frank Partnoy, "Adding Derivatives to the Corporate Law Mix," *Georgia Law Review, Volume 34* (2000), p. 599.

10. For an excellent article assessing the limits of the "rational actor" approach to thinking about the relationship between brokers and sophisticated customers, see Donald C. Langevoort, "Selling Hope, Selling Risk, Some Lessons for Law from Behavioral Economics About Stockbrokers and Sophisticated Customers," *California Law Review Volume 84,* May 1996, p. 627.

11. NASD Rule 2310.

12. James D. Cox, Robert W. Hillman, and Donald C. Langevoort, *Securities Regulation: Cases and Materials,* 3rd ed. (Aspen Publishers, Inc. 2001), pp. 1146–1148.

13. Frank Partnoy, "The Shifting Contours of Global Derivatives Regulation," *University of Pennsylvania Journal of International Economic Law, Volume 22* (2001), p. 421.

14. Jeff Madrick, "Enron: Seduction and Betrayal," *New York Review of Books,* March 14, 2002, pp. 21, 24.

15. International Swaps and Derivatives Association, "Enron: Corporate Failure," *Market Success,* April 17, 2002, p. 1.

16. www.opensecrets.com.

17. Michael Schroeder, "As Enron's Derivatives Trading Comes Into Focus, Gap in Oversight Is Spotlighted," *Wall Street Journal,* January 28, 2002, p. C1.

18. Enron's 2000 annual report stated, "In 2000, the value at risk model utilized for equity trading market risk was refined to more closely correlate with the valuation methodologies used for merchant activities." Enron 2000 Annual Report, p. 28.

19. Partnoy, "Financial Derivatives and the Costs of Regulatory Arbitrage," p. 211.

20. Floyd Norris, "Accounting Reform: A Bright Line Vanishes," *New York Times,* June 7, 2002, p. C1.

21. Robert E. Litan, "Accounting and Disclosure after Enron," Testimony before the Senate Committee on Banking, Housing, and Urban Affairs, March 2002, p. 17.

22. *United States v. Simon,* 425 F.2d 796 (2d Cir. 1969).

23. Floyd Norris, "An Old Case Is Returning to Haunt Auditors," *New York Times,* March 1, 2002, p. C1.

24. Frank Partnoy, "Barbarians at the Gatekeepers?: A Proposal for a Modified Strict Liability Regime," *Washington University Law Quarterly, Volume 79* (2001), p. 491.

25. Frank Partnoy, "The Siskel and Ebert of Financial Markets?: Two Thumbs Down for the Credit Rating Agencies," *Washington University Law Quarterly, Volume 77* (1999), p. 619.

26. Frank Partnoy, "The Wrong Way to Prosecute Fraud," *The San Diego Union-Tribune,* May 11, 2002, p. G-3.

27. Frank Partnoy, "Why Markets Crash and What Law Can Do about It," *University of Pittsburgh Law Review, Volume 61* (2000), p. 741.

28. Frank Partnoy, "Multinational Regulatory Competition and Single-Stock Futures," *Northwestern School of Law Journal of International Law & Business, Volume 21* (2001), p. 641.

29. *Dirks v. SEC,* 463 U.S. 646 (1983).

30. James Grant, "Bargains Everywhere but on Wall Street," *New York Times,* March 4, 2002, p. A27.

31. Bridget O'Brian, "Enron Backer Gets $2 Million for 2001," *Wall Street Journal,* April 3, 2002, p. C15.

32. Grant, p. A27.

ACKNOWLEDGMENTS

I could not have written this book, or even imagined it, without the encouragement and vision of John Sterling at Henry Holt. Thank you, John, for your wisdom in directing this project, for your trust in me as a writer, and for your brilliant last-minute counsel. I also am very grateful to David Sobel of Times Books. Thank you, David, for your insistence that this book be broad in scope, for your uncanny ability to focus my thinking, and for your keen insights into how a reader best understands technical material. It truly was an honor to work with both of you.

I am grateful to the staff at Times Books and Henry Holt, and especially Robin Dennis and Heather Rodino, for their skill in shepherding the manuscript through the editing process. I also want to thank Christine Ball and Elizabeth Shreve for their untiring efforts in making this book a success.

I especially want to thank my agent, Theresa Park. Thank you, Theresa, for taking me on as a client, for believing in my ability to pull off a "big picture" book, for being a hardnosed negotiator and lawyer, and for being a good friend and adviser. Yes, I am thinking about our next project.

I received invaluable comments on drafts from Laura Adams, Rex Adams, Laurence Claus, Anna Coppola, Michael Devitt, Michael Greenberger, Peter Huang, Henry Kaufman, Donald Langevoort, George Needham, Helen Parry, Shaun Martin, Michael Rieke, Gregg Shapiro,

John Tishler, Adam Winkler, and several others. Thanks to all of you for important insights, which greatly improved this book. Thanks to Andrew Franklin for helping me keep perspective. I owe special thanks to Dean Dan Rodriguez and the University of San Diego for their unwavering support.

In researching this book, I conducted more than 150 interviews of traders, regulators, corporate executives, and others, most of whom—understandably—wished to remain anonymous. I have honored those wishes, and I do not cite these individuals directly; I am grateful to each of you. I am especially indebted to Andy Krieger for agreeing to do interviews on the record. I also want to thank the many business reporters who agreed to share information with me about their various investigations.

Finally, thanks to Alan Greenspan for coining the phrase "infectious greed" in July 2002, just as I was abandoning hope of finding a pithy title that captured both the financial theme and viral metaphor of this book.

INDEX